EU External Relations Law

This major new textbook for students and practitioners in European law uses a text, cases and materials approach to explore the law, policy and practice of EU external relations, and navigates the complex questions at the interface of these areas. The book explores the core legal principles of EU external relations law, including EU competence, loyal cooperation and the effect of international law, and elaborates upon them in policy-specific chapters, ranging from common commercial policy and development policy over CFSP/CSDP and AFSJ to energy and enlargement policy. Specific attention is given to the relationship between European integration, the role of law and the EU as an effective international actor. Designed for easy navigation, the chapters include extracts, summaries and textboxes which frame key policy issues and guide the reader through the functioning of legal principles. The reader gains a detailed understanding of context and present functioning of EU external relations law in a highly politicized European and international environment.

Bart Van Vooren is Senior Associate in the EU Regulatory & Trade Practice Group at a Brussels-based law firm, and Honorary Associate Professor of EU Law at the University of Copenhagen. His practice focuses on general EU law and CJEU litigation as well as energy and trade law, external relations and neighbourhood policy. He advises governments, and private and public companies. He has published many books and articles on EU external relations, and most recent publications include *The Legal Dimension of Global Governance: What Role for the EU?* and *EU External Relations Law and the European Neighbourhood Policy.*

Ramses A. Wessel is Professor of International and European Law, and Co-Director of the Centre for European Studies, at the University of Twente, The Netherlands. He is also a member of the Governing Board of the Centre for the Law of EU External Relations. He has published widely on the constitutional and international law dimensions of EU external relations, as well as on international institutional law.

EU External Relations Law

TEXT, CASES AND MATERIALS

Bart Van Vooren and
Ramses A. Wessel

CAMBRIDGE
UNIVERSITY PRESS

CAMBRIDGE
UNIVERSITY PRESS

University Printing House, Cambridge CB2 8BS, United Kingdom

Cambridge University Press is part of the University of Cambridge.

It furthers the University's mission by disseminating knowledge in the pursuit of education, learning and research at the highest international levels of excellence.

www.cambridge.org
Information on this title: www.cambridge.org/9781107031128

© Bart Van Vooren and Ramses A. Wessel 2014

First published 2014
Reprinted 2014

Printed in the United Kingdom by Clays, St Ives plc

A catalogue record for this publication is available from the British Library

Library of Congress Cataloguing in Publication data
Van Vooren, Bart, author.
EU external relations law : text, cases and materials / Bart Van Vooren, Ramses Wessel.
    p.   cm.
ISBN 978-1-107-03112-8 (Hardback) – ISBN 978-1-107-68430-0 (Paperback)
1. International and municipal law–European Union countries.   2. European Union countries–Foreign relations–Law and legislation.   3. International cooperation–European Union countries. I. Wessel, Ramses A., author. II. Title. III. Title: European Union external relations law.
KJE5057.V3575 2014
341.242′2–dc23
2013039657

ISBN 978-1-107-03112-8 Hardback

ISBN 978-1-107-68430-0 Paperback

Contents

Table of cases

European Court of Justice: numerical order

European Court of Justice: alphabetical order

European Court of Justice: Opinions

European Court of Justice: rulings

European Court of Human Rights

National Courts

Table of instruments and legislation

Preface

THREE GUIDING PERSPECTIVES TO EU EXTERNAL RELATIONS LAW

The patchwork of EU external policies and instruments is the result of more than fifty years of European integration, and is in need of a strong sense of collective purpose in order to present a coherent response to challenges for Europe in the globalized world of the twenty-first century. Perhaps more than in any of its Member States, EU external relations law plays a crucial role in attaining that objective. In this introductory chapter, we wish to elaborate on what we consider the three 'guiding perspectives' crucial in studying this field of law.

- First, we must naturally study the *law*, its functioning, interpretation and application. In substantive terms, EU external relations law is a highly complex subject matter where questions of EU law (institutional, constitutional and substantive) meet questions of international law (public, institutional, trade, etc.). This is the self-evident core of this textbook, and its starting point.
- Second, while studying these rules, we must be fully aware that EU action in the world is then not neutral from the perspective of 'political union', e.g. the project of European integration. While at times the most effective option for the twenty-eight EU Member States would be to join forces and tackle international challenges through a single legal entity, that may raise questions relating to European integration itself: if the EU's voice is heard on the international scene, what does this mean for the Member States' individual voices? As a consequence, EU external relations law is often shaped by 'grand' debates on the future of European integration. Since international relations pertain to the core of state sovereignty, any legal rule organizing the EU as an international actor has the potential to raise questions as to the sort of political union the Member States desire. Furthermore, European integration itself is the consequence of developments in the global environment. Thus, developments in European and global politics will lead to shifting needs of the EU and its Member States in their global representation. This is often reflected through shaping the legal framework organizing any such action.
- The third aspect is that the body of EU external relations law is not purely the result of grand conceptions of European integration, but that the core purpose of law is to organize a societal reality towards a certain outcome. Concretely, this body of rules thus organizes the EU's and its Member States' endeavour to exert influence on a global stage, which is usually captured in the

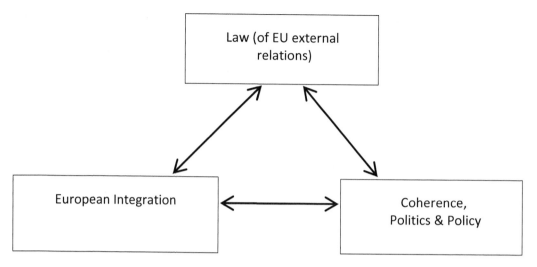

Figure 1   Three guiding perspectives

notion that the EU as an international actor must be *coherent and effective*. Thus, there is a clear *telos* to EU external relations law: pursuing 'European interests' in the world as coagulantly and effectively as possible. On the European continent, twenty-eight Member States have now agreed that their global interests are best served by conferring powers to a supranational entity, though only to a limited extent.

Figure 1 illustrates the three guiding perspectives that are adopted by this book when examining the rules concerning EU external relations.

Throughout this book, the reader will find that these guiding perspectives appear when analysing the legal questions that compose the body of EU external relations law. In doing so, these will provide the reader with an arch of coherence throughout the fifteen chapters. Each chapter then constitutes a building-block towards substantiating the broader picture of EU external relations law. It is for this reason that each chapter of this book ends with a subsection entitled 'broader picture', to draw together these three guiding perspectives. With this approach we invite the reader to look beyond the legal principles as existing in a vacuum. In this fashion, we hope to attain a fuller understanding of why the law developed as it did, and how it presently functions in a highly politicized environment of international politics and the past, present and future of European integration itself.

In sum, this book conceptualizes EU external relations law as a body of rules matured as a discipline against a historical and present-day political reality: on the one hand the grand project of European integration, and on the other hand the reality of international politics which requires a coherent and effective European response. Law is then the framework used to embed and express those realities in relation to EU external relations law's function of organizing the EU as an international actor (first perspective). These laws are then influenced by competing views on the state of European integration (second perspective), and by the need for a coherent and effective EU (in a political sense) international action against the background of European and global political developments in general (third perspective). As is visible in the schematic drawing, the interrelationship is a reciprocal one: law shapes the ability of the EU as an international actor to act effectively and coherently. European integration will have shaped the law such that effective international action becomes possible, or remains impossible; and so on.

These causal interrelationships are clarified further in the following three sections where we elaborate on the three guiding perspectives as summarily stated above. Note that we start by discussing coherence and policy/integration, to then point to the role of law therein.

FIRST PERSPECTIVE: COHERENCE OF THE EU AS AN INTERNATIONAL ACTOR

The challenge of coherence for external relations of the European Union is a perennial problem. In essence it means that in their relations with the Union, third parties must be able to rely on the fact that they have one counterpart only in a given policy area – and that the EU as an international actor does not 'blow hot and cold at the same time'.[1]

Communication from the Commission, *Europe in the World – Some Practical Proposals for Greater Coherence, Effectiveness and Visibility*, Brussels, 8 June 2006, COM(2006) 278 final, p. 6

As in national administrations, even when there is sufficient political will, the EU's impact falls short when there are unresolved tensions or a lack of coherence between different policies. There is a need for strong and permanent efforts to enhance the complementary interaction of various policy actions and to reconcile different objectives (for example in trade, agriculture, development, environment or migration). For the EU, there is the additional challenge in ensuring coherence between EU and national actions.

Unsatisfactory co-ordination between different actors and policies means that the EU loses potential leverage internationally, both politically and economically. Despite progress with improving co-ordination, there is considerable scope to bring together different instruments and assets, whether within the Commission, between the Council and Commission, or between the EU institutions and the Member States. Furthermore, the impact of EU's policy is weakened by a lack of focus and continuity in its external representation. Within the framework of the existing treaties the Community and intergovernmental methods need to be combined on the basis of what best achieves the desired outcome, rather than institutional theory or dogma.

In this excerpt the Commission refers to national administrations, and argues that there too the impact of any Member State will fall short if there is no coherence between its policies. This is certainly true: if a national justice ministry does not coordinate with the foreign ministry and/or the ministry of the interior in a treaty negotiation within their competence, problems in effectively attaining the goals of that state may arise. However, the legal and political diversity of the EU elevates this challenge of coherence beyond a managerial hurdle, and engrains it into the nature of the EU as an international actor itself – politically but also legally. The Commission Communication mentions several of the potential challenges to coherent external action, some of which are peculiar to the EU. Aside from the challenges of coordinating between different

---

[1] R. A. Wessel, 'The Inside Looking Out: Consistency and Delimitation in EU External Relations' (2000) 37 *Common Market Law Review* 1137.

actors and policies, and within different actors, it shows that above all, coordination between the EU and the Member States is particularly challenging. In the final sentence, it also argues that the choice between the 'Community' and 'intergovernmental' methods of carrying out EU external relations must be made by focusing on what is most effective, and not focusing on institutional dogma. This final sentence thus perfectly captures the interrelationship between law, coherence and European integration. This book will further explain that the choice between the Community method and intergovernmental methods is the consequence of competing views of the Member States on how far European integration should go in the sphere of conducting international relations: do we act through supranational institutions of a separate legal entity, or do we follow the more classical approach of international law based on inter-state relations? The compromise on these different methodologies of pursuing the European interest in the world has been laid down in EU primary law, and forms a core part of the internal dimension of EU external relations law.

The challenge of coherent EU external relations blends legal and policy considerations (the second and third guiding perspectives), and expresses itself in many different forms. We can distinguish at least the following iterations of coherence in its legal and policy aspects:

- First, one can distinguish *negative* from *positive coherence*, which covers the distinction between the absence of conflict and the pursuit of positive connections. For example, negative coherence could mean the absence of conflict between political statements made by the High Representative (HR) in the conduct of the EU's Common Foreign and Security Policy (CFSP) to Russia, and the German Foreign Minister in the context of its own relationship with Russia. On the side of positive connections, an example is the need for a positive substantive connection between the EU's Common Agricultural Policy (CAP) subsidizing EU farms, and EU development policy seeking to support the economic development of third countries (non-Member States).
- Second, one can distinguish between *material/substantive* and *institutional coherence* which concerns studying the coherence of policy substance, versus looking more closely at legal and institutional structures or procedures set up to work towards such coherence. Studying the fashion in which the European External Action Service (EEAS) communicates with the Member States' diplomatic services or with the European Commission is an example of institutional coherence. The previous example of the connection between the EU CAP and development policy is an instance of substantive coherence.
- Third, we can further distinguish between *vertical* and *horizontal coherence*. Vertical coherence concerns the interrelationship between the EU as a legal person, and its Member States, whereas horizontal coherence captures intra-EU (as a legal person) coherence either between the EU institutions (institutional coherence) or coherence between TEU and TFEU policy competences (material coherence).
- Fourth and finally, one can distinguish a *legal* and a *policy perspective to coherence*. The former focuses on relevant rules and their impact on policy coherence, and the latter focuses on policy and political action in the pursuit of the EU as a coherent international actor. Legal coherence can also have another meaning, namely the interrelationship between different rules themselves as part of a European – or international – 'legal order'.

As one of the guiding perspectives to EU external relations law, this book employs the word 'coherence'. However, scholars have pointed to the difficulty that exists due to the discrepancy between the English language versions of the Treaty which use 'consistency', whereas all other equally authentic versions use words that imply 'coherence':[2] Article 21(3) TEU refers to consistency in English, but to *la cohérence* in French, *la coerenza* in Italian, *die Kohärenz* in German, or *samenhang* in Dutch. Cremona states that coherence is defined as

> the 'action or fact of sticking together' or 'a harmonious connection to the several parts of a discourse, system etc. so that the whole hangs together'. Consistency, on the other hand, is 'the quality, state or fact of being consistent'. The former is therefore a more positive state while the latter is more neutral (it is possible to be consistently inconsistent).[3]

Hillion has argued that therefore both linguistically and functionally the notion of consistency in 'EU primary law and in particularly in the law of EU external relations suggest that it involves, beyond the assurance that the different policies do not legally contradict each other, a quest for synergy and added value in the different components of the EU policies'.[4]

SECOND PERSPECTIVE: POLITICS, POLICY AND EUROPEAN INTEGRATION

What is true for any field of law is perhaps even more the case for EU external relations law: the body of texts, rules, principles and judgments of which it is composed do not exist in a political vacuum. Rather, law is meant to organize society and (human) interaction within that society. In this instance, EU external relations law is the body of law that governs action of the EU in the world at all different stages: rules which govern EU institutions and Member States when devising what policy approaches are to be taken, and at which level; rules governing which instruments the Union may or may not adopt within its own legal order or the international legal order; principles concerning the legal effects of these instruments in the EU or international order, and so on. There are two predominant dimensions to the societal context shaping EU external relations law. On the one hand there is the European integration dimension to this body of law, and on the other hand there is the more general European and international socio-economic and geopolitical context.

First, the context of European integration itself: namely, the fact that the EU is an ongoing legal and political experiment of integrating twenty-eight Member States. In this experiment not all Member States necessarily agree on what should be the future direction of this project, and certain EU institutions may seek to favour a certain future course of European integration. Indeed, some Member States are quite content with the current state of integration, others may

---

[2] M. Cremona, 'Coherence in European Union Foreign Relations Law', in P. Koutrakos (ed.), *European Foreign Policy: Legal and Political Perspectives* (Cheltenham/Northampton: Edward Elgar, 2011); C. Tietje, 'The Concept of Coherence in the Treaty on European Union and the Common Foreign and Security Policy' (1997) 2 *European Foreign Affairs Review* 211–213; Wessel, 'The Inside Looking Out', 1150; C. Hillion, 'Tous pour un, un pour tous! Coherence in the External Relations of the European Union', in Cremona (ed.), *Developments in EU External Relations Law* (Oxford: Oxford University Press, 2008), p. 17; P. Gauttier, 'Horizontal Coherence and the External Competences of the European Union' (2004) 10 *European Law Journal* 25; Koutrakos, *Trade, Foreign Policy and Defence in EU Constitutional Law* (Oxford: Hart Publishing, 2001), pp. 39–44; Wessel, *The European Union's Foreign and Security Policy – A Legal Institutional Perspective* (The Hague: Kluwer Law International, 1999), p. 297.

[3] Cremona, 'Coherence in European Union Foreign Relations Law', in Koutrakos (ed.), *European Foreign Policy: Legal and Political Perspectives*, p. 18.

[4] Hillion, 'Tous pour un, un pour tous!' p. 23.

want 'more EU', whereas other governments may find that European integration and political union have already gone too far. Similarly, the European Parliament (EP) and the European Commission as the political, supranational institutions of the Union may favour a direction that favours advancing European integration – and with that their own role in the system. Against such considerations, it is then important to keep in mind that the conduct of international relations is generally considered to be at the hard core of a state's national interests and sovereignty.[5] The consequence is that debates on 'European Union' external relations policy and/or law will very often be coloured by these diverging opinions on the past, present and future of European integration. This influence has been tangible at the grand moments of European integration: Inter-Governmental Conferences (IGC) deciding on the future external competences of the EU in what became the Maastricht or Lisbon Treaties. More importantly however, its influence can also be felt in day-to-day policy- and law-making. Sometimes, then (or in fact, often), legal disputes before the Court of Justice concerning the correct interpretation or application of EU external relations law will actually have a political dispute over the state of European integration as their origin. There are many instances where this book will point to the fact that legal principles of EU external relations are imbued with this sense of impact on European integration – as well as a simultaneous impact on coherent and effective international action.

Second, EU external relations law has been shaped by socio-economic and geopolitical developments following World War II. The European Economic Community (EEC) itself was a product of a post-war need to stabilize the European continent. The fact that the EU today does not have a large standing army based on a proposed 'European Defence Community Treaty' of the mid 1950s is the consequence of global politics (the death of Stalin, end of the Korean war) and intra-Member State politics (French inter-party politics). Similarly, the break-up of the Soviet Union, German reunification and the Yugoslav War of the 1990s shaped EU CFSP. What we thus see time and again in the history of EU external relations, is that politics (within or outside the Union) shapes the legal framework in existence today.

Together, these elements form one of the 'guiding perspectives' to EU external relations law: namely the fact that the body of rules explained in this book emerged, was shaped by and evolved in a complex web of politics pertaining to European integration and international affairs in general. Whereas this textbook is indubitably a law book providing the relevant knowledge in this regard, nevertheless a good understanding of this broader and underlying context is indispensable to a good understanding of the nature and functioning of EU external relations law.

THIRD PERSPECTIVE: THE ROLE OF LAW VIS-À-VIS THE FIRST TWO PERSPECTIVES

The legal framework of EU external relations is shaped by the objective of a coherent and effective external policy, accompanied by competing views on European integration and the broader socio-economic and political context. This is certainly not a one-way street but rather a reciprocal process. In the short and long term, EU external relations law also shapes the

---

[5] J. S. Nye, 'Redefining the National Interest' (1999) 78 *Foreign Affairs* 22–35.

day-to-day process of external policy-making. The present state of the law as well as the role of legal actors therein (such as the Court of Justice) cast a long shadow on EU external relations. Similarly, in relation to coherence, legal rules can be a source of coherence by organizing the internal diversity of the Union so that it may function effectively and coherently in the world. They can also have a reverse impact by either not functioning well, or by being the result of political compromise which valued uniformity as less important than placing limits on where European integration is no longer politically desirable. In the latter case, it may indeed be that the drafters of the Treaty are well aware that a certain legal–organizational state of affairs is not ideal to achieve a coherent, single EU message in the world, but that they are unwilling to organize the Union in any other way. EU external relations law is then the thread which knits together the legal and political quilt that is EU external relations.

B. Van Vooren, *EU External Relations Law and the European Neighbourhood Policy: A Paradigm for Coherence* (Abingdon/New York: Routledge, 2012), p. 1

A bird's eye view of EU external relations appears as a Harlequin's costume of policies defined according to geography, initiatives delineated in a topical fashion, ad hoc coordination (or not) on major international events, commonly defined principles, and so on; all stitched together in pursuit of asserting an EU identity on the international scene. In that endeavour, the Union has famously suffered from the capability–expectations gap: the discrepancy between the increasing expectations vis-à-vis the EU within and outside the Union, and its ability to actually agree and engage its limited resources to certain common ends: the 'Union' interest in international relations. This perceived inability to meet these expectations can be partially attributed to the fragmented constitutional order underpinning EU external relations: the Member States' and EU's external policies in the TEU and TFEU which all need to interact in a coherent fashion to achieve 'EU' external action.

The subject of this book, EU external relations law, is then a body of law governing this *sui generis* international actor, and consists of an internal and an external dimension. In its internal dimension it consists of the set of rules which govern the constitutional and institutional legal organization of this legal entity in pursuit of its interests in the world: what are its powers to act, how wide are they, can the Member States still act, how does the EU exercise its powers, etc. In its external dimension, it includes the rules which govern its relationship to and interaction with other entities of the international (legal) order; notably through international agreements it can conclude with third countries and international organizations (IOs), or become a member of IOs itself. Both the internal and external dimension then come together in a complex web of legal and political considerations in concrete policy environments: trade, security, energy, development, and so on.

Acknowledgements

No book is the result of efforts by the authors alone, and we are indebted to many colleagues and friends for their contributions to this project. In Autumn 2012 the authors organized a 'book workshop', whereby they willingly subjected themselves to several hours of friendly grilling in order to improve the final manuscript. We are grateful that so many took the time to travel to Copenhagen for this session of live peer review, and that the University of Copenhagen was prepared to fund this event through its 'European Research in Copenhagen (EURECO)' initiative. In no particular order, we are grateful to the following for having made suggestions to our draft material: Adam Lazowski, Christophe Hillion, Joris Larik, Helle Krunke, Irene Blazquez, Joni Heliskoski, Lars Volck Madsen, Morten Broberg, Peter Van Elsuwege, Rass Holdgaard, Roberta Mungianu, Sinead Moloney, Steven Blockmans, Felix Schulyok, Claudio Matera and Luisa Marin. Beyond these names, we are equally indebted to our mentors and colleagues writing on EU external relations law over the years. Parts of our analyses were indubitably inspired by their guidance and writings, and although we decided to limit general references in the body of the text for pedagogic purposes, we have done our utmost to reference pertinent scholarship in the final sections of each chapter. Where this book has drawn on ideas and material which was co-authored with colleagues, we are indebted to Steven Blockmans, Christophe Hillion, Aurel Sari and Leonhard den Hertog. Finally, we are grateful to our invaluable assistants for support in collecting materials and proofreading the manuscript for its consistency: Laurens Klein Kranenburg, Nanna Louise Jensen, Nathalie Ivanoff and Stine Hellqvist Frey. Any omissions remain our own. The manuscript was closed on 1 July 2013.

Abbreviations

AA	Association Agreement
ACP	African, Caribbean, Pacific
AETR	European Road Transport Agreement
AFSJ	Area of Freedom, Security and Justice
AG	Advocate General
ARIO	Articles on the Responsibility of International Organizations
ASEAN	Association of South-East Asian Nations
ATAA	Air Transport Association of America
ATSA	US Aviation and Transportation Security Act
BIT	Bilateral Investment Treaty
BRICS	Brazil, Russian, India, China, South Africa
CAC	Codex Alimentarius Commission
CAP	Common Agricultural Policy
CBP	Bureau of Customs and Border Protection
CCP	Common Commercial Policy
CCT	Common Customs Tariff
CEECs	Central and Eastern European Countries
CEPOL	European Police College
CFI	Court of First Instance
CFSP	Common Foreign and Security Policy
CIVCOM	Committee for Civilian Aspects of Crisis Management
CJEU	Court of Justice of the European Union
CMEA	Council for Mutual Economic Assistance
CMPD	Crisis Management and Planning Directorate
COM	Communication
COMECON	Council for Mutual Economic Assistance
COMP	General Competition
COREPER	Committee of Permanent Representatives
COREU	Correspondance Européenne
CPCC	Civilian Planning and Conduct Capability
CRTA	Committee on Regional Trade Agreements
CSDP	Common Security and Defence Policy
CTC	Counter-Terrorism Coordinator
DARIO	Draft Articles on the International Responsibility of International Organizations
DCFTA	Deep and Comprehensive Free Trade Agreement

DG	Directorate General
DSB	Dispute Settlement Body
DSU	Understanding on Rules and Procedures Governing the Settlement of Disputes
EA	Europe Agreement
EAEC	European Atomic Energy Community
EASO	European Asylum Support Office
EBRD	European Bank for Reconstruction and Development
EC	European Community
ECHR	European Convention on Human Rights
ECJ	European Court of Justice
ECOSOC	UN Economic and Social Council
ECOWAS	Economic Community of West African States
ECR	European Court Reports
ECSC	European Coal and Steel Community
ECT	Energy Community Treaty
EDA	European Defence Agency
EDC	European Defence Community
EDF	European Development Fund
Eds.	Editors
EEA	European Economic Area
EEAS	European External Action Service
EEC	European Economic Community
EFTA	European Free Trade Agreement
EIB	European Investment Bank
EMU	Economic and Monetary Union
ENER	General Energy
ENP	European Neighbourhood Policy
ENPI	European Neighbourhood and Partnership Instrument
EP	European Parliament
EPA	Economic Partnership Agreement
EPC	European Political Cooperation
ERTA	European Road Transport Agreement
ESDP	European Security and Defence Policy
ESS	European Security Strategy
EU	European Union
EUCAP	European Union Capacity-Building Mission

EUCO European Council
EUMC European Union Military Committee
EUPM European Union Monitoring Mission
EUMS European Union Military Staff
EUNAVCO European Union Naval Coordination Cell
EUPOL European Union Police Mission
EURATOM Atomic Energy Community Treaty
Eurojust European Union Judicial Cooperation Unit
Europol European Police Office
EUTM European Union Training Mission
FAC Foreign Affairs Council
FAO Food and Agricultural Organization
FDI Foreign Direct Investment
FIAMM Fabbrica Italiana Accumulatori Motocarri Montecchio
FRONTEX European Agency for the Management of Operational Cooperation at the External Borders of the Member States of the European Union
FSB Financial Stability Board
FTA Free Trade Agreement
FYROM Former Yugoslav Republic of Macedonia
G–8/20 Group of 8/20
GAER General Affairs and External Relations
GATS General Agreement on Trade in Services
GATT General Agreement on Tariffs and Trade
GC General Court
GMO genetically modified organism
GNP Gross National Product
GSP Generalised System of Preferences
HOME Home Affairs
HoSG Heads of State and Government
HR High Representative
IATA International Air Transport Association
ICAO International Civil Aviation Organization
IEM Internal Energy Market
IGC Inter-Governmental Conference
IHL International Humanitarian Law
ILC International Law Commission
ILO International Labour Organization
IMF International Monetary Fund
IMO International Maritime Organization
IO International Organization
IOM International Organization for Migration
IP Intellectual Property
ISS Institute for Security Studies
ITLOS International Tribunal of the Law of the Sea
ITU International Telecommunications Union
JAIEX External JHA Issues
JCCM Judicial Cooperation in Criminal Matters
JHA Justice and Home Affairs
JUST Justice
LMO living modified organism
LNG Liquefied Natural Gas
MARPOL Marine Pollution – e.g. the International Convention for the Prevention of Pollution from Ships

MDGs Millennium Development Goals
MFF Multi-Annual Financial Framework
MFN Most-Favoured Nation
MLA Mutual Legal Assistance
MoU Memorandum of Understanding
MOX Mixed Oxide Fuel
MS Member States
n.y.r. not yet reported
NAFO Northwest Atlantic Fisheries Organization
NATO North Atlantic Treaty Organization
NIS Newly Independent States
NPT Non-Proliferation Treaty
OCTs overseas countries and territories
OECD Organisation for Economic Co-operation and Development
OIV International Organization for Vine and Wine
OJ Official Journal
OSCE Organization for Security and Cooperation in Europe
OTIF Organization on International Carriage by Rail
PCA Partnership and Cooperation Agreement
PCD Policy Coherence for Development
PFOS Perfluorooctoane Sulfonate
PHARE Pologne, Hongrie – Assistance á la Réstructuration des Economies
PIC Prior Informed Consent
PJCC Police and Judicial Cooperation in Criminal Matters
PNR Passenger Name Records
PSC Political and Security Committee
QMV Qualified Majority Voting
REIO Regional Economic Integration Organization
RELEX External Relations
REV Revision
RGA Remote Gambling Association
SAA Stabilisation and Association Agreement
SALW Small Arms and Light Weapons
SAP Stability and Association Process
SDGs Sustainable Development Goals
SEA Single European Act
SMEs Small and Medium Sized Enterprises
SOFAs Status of Forces Agreements
SOMAs Status of Missions Agreements
SP Stability Pact
SWIFT Society for Worldwide Interbank Financial Telecommunication
TAIEX Technical Assistance and Information Exchange Office
TBR Trade Barriers Regulation
TCA Trade and Cooperation Agreement
TEC Treaty establishing the European Community
TEU Treaty on European Union
TFEU Treaty on the Functioning of the Union
TREN Transport and Energy

TRIPS   Agreement on Trade Related Aspects of Intellectual Property Rights
TTIP   Transatlantic Trade and Investment Partnership
UMED   Union for the Mediterranean
UN   United Nations
UNC   United Nations Charter
UNCLOS   United Nations Convention on the Law of the Sea
UNCTAD   United Nations Conference on Trade and Development
UNESCO   UN Educational, Scientific and Cultural Organization
UNGA   United Nations General Assembly
UNHCR   UN High Commissioner for Refugees
UNODC   United Nations Office on Drugs and Crime
UNSC   United Nations Security Council
UNSCR   United Nations Security Council Resolution
USTR   United States Trade Representative
VCLT   Vienna Convention on the Law of Treaties 1969
VP   Vice President
WB   World Bank
WCO   World Customs Organization
WEU   Western European Union
WHO   World Health Organization
WIPO   World Intellectual Property Organization
WTO   World Trade Organization

1

The EU as a global legal actor

1 CENTRAL ISSUES

- This chapter points to the fact that the EU is an international actor. We define this notion as an entity which interacts with third countries and international organizations (and even its own Member States), in ways which are legally and politically distinguishable from its constitutive Member States. In the global context, this entity thus has a stand-alone identity composed of values, interests and policies which it seeks to define and promote internationally as its own.
- This chapter then indicates the importance of legal rules in organizing EU international action, and shows that EU external relations law consists of an internal and an external dimension. In its internal dimension it consists of the set of rules which govern the constitutional and institutional legal organization of this legal entity in pursuit of its interests in the world. The external dimension comprises the rules governing the relationship of the EU with the international legal order in which it is active.
- In order to study EU external relations law in all its complexity, this chapter provides an overview of the architecture of EU external relations. It outlines the existence of the EU as an international organization with legal personality, which exists legally distinct from its Member States. It also shows that the EU is based on the Treaty on European Union (TEU) and the Treaty on the Functioning of the Union (TFEU), which each contain crucial legal principles constituting the body of EU external relations law.
- Finally, in order to be an international *actor*, the EU needs *agents* to make the decisions and represent the EU on the global stage. These include the EU institutions, but also other key players in the law of EU external relations.

2 THE NATURE OF THE EU AS AN INTERNATIONAL ACTOR

(i) An international organization or something else?

A textbook on EU external relations law is founded on the premise that the EU can have legal relations with third states and other international organizations. Hence, it is an international actor, with a distinct legal existence just like EU Member States, or international organizations such as the United Nations. What does it mean to say that the EU is an international actor?

When the 1957 Rome Treaty founded the EEC, this new international organization was explicitly given competence to conduct international trade relations through its Common Commercial Policy (CCP), and to conclude international agreements through which it could associate itself with third countries. As European integration progressed, the EEC, later European Community (EC) and now European Union, acquired powers in other areas such as foreign security policy, environmental policy, energy policy and so on. So how does this amalgam of international policies render the EU an international actor? In political science literature there are a variety of definitions for the nature of the EU in the world, which commonly seek to categorize the 'kind' of power the Union exerts in its external relations: civilian power, soft power, normative power and so on.[1] These concepts often argue that there is something distinctive about EU action in the world, an 'EU-way' of conducting its international relations which is connected to the way post-World War II European integration itself has progressed: avoiding inter-state conflicts through integration on the basis of multilateral legally binding instruments. Other scholars do not seek to classify the EU normatively, and are content with the classification of the EU as quite simply an entity which stands in a category of its own, e.g. a *sui generis* international actor which cannot be defined with any pre-existing terminology.

C. Bretherton and J. Vogler, *The European Union as a Global Actor* (Abingdon/New York: Routledge, 2006), p. 2

The EU is not an intergovernmental organization as traditionally understood, nor is it a partially formed state. While it is clearly a regional organization, its degree of integration, and the range of policy competences and instruments it possesses, render comparison with other regional organizations such as the North American Free Trade Agreement (NAFTA) meaningless.

In this legal textbook we are primarily concerned with the rules and principles which govern the legal existence and functioning of this international actor. Consequently we define the EU as an international actor in abstract terms, as *an entity which interacts with third countries and international organizations (and even its own Member States), in ways which are legally and politically distinguishable from its constitutive Member States. In the global context, this entity thus has a stand-alone identity composed of values, interests and policies which it seeks to define and promote internationally as its own.*[2]

The term 'entity' may nevertheless not be too helpful in describing the nature of this 'animal', and the question emerges as to whether we can see the EU as an international organization. To lawyers, being an international actor at least means being an international *legal* actor. This, in turn, means that, although the EU is not a state, it is subject to the rules of international law when it wishes to participate on the global stage. International law, on the other hand, is still quite traditional. Created as 'inter-state' law it continues to struggle with the presence of

---

[1] Respectively: H. Bull, 'Civilian Power Europe: A Contradiction in Terms?' (1982) 21 *Journal of Common Market Studies*, 2, 149–164; J. Nye, *Soft Power: The Means to Success in World Politics* (New York: Public Affairs Press, 2005); I. Manners, 'Normative Power Europe: A Contradiction in Terms?' (2002) 40 *Journal of Common Market Studies*, 2, 235–258.

[2] This definition is inspired by Cremona's description of the different roles of the EU in the world. See M. Cremona, 'The Union as a Global Actor: Roles, Models and Identity' (2004) 42 *Common Market Law Review* 553–573.

non-state actors in the international order. Yet, international organizations obviously found their place as international legal actors, and other forums and networks are also increasingly recognized as legally relevant. It is a truism that the EU is not a regular international organization. From the outset Member States have been prepared to transfer competences to the Community and later the Union. The current Treaties again herald a new phase in which the Union's international 'actorness' in the global legal order will be further developed.

This is exactly why it is important to classify the EU under international law. Most international rules apply to states, some to international organizations and a limited set also to other internationally active entities (such as liberation movements or multinationals). Few would argue that the EU is a state; many would say that it is an international entity *sui generis*. International law, however, only works when it is applied across the board for certain categories of international actors. While it may be possible to create special rules for *sui generis* entities (compare the clauses on Regional Economic Integration Organisations (REIOs) in some multilateral agreements),[3] the rationale behind a legal system is that its rules should allow for a smooth cooperation between the different subjects.

The Treaties are still silent on this issue. Article 1 TEU merely refers to the fact that 'the High Contracting Parties establish among themselves a European Union' and that this Union 'shall replace and succeed the European Community'. Thus, it still does not give an answer to the classic question of whether the EU is an international organization or something else. This may also be the reason that textbooks are still uncertain about the legal nature of the Union and seem to have a preference for more political notions. Chalmers *et al.* refer to the EU as 'amongst other things, a legal system established to deal with a series of contemporary problems and realize a set of goals that individual states felt unable to manage alone'.[4] And, the 'nature of the Union's international presence' is related to its international legal personality only, whereas the nature of the entity as such is left open.[5] In its famous ruling on the Lisbon Treaty, the German Constitutional Court held that the Union was 'designed as an association of sovereign states (*Staatenverbund*) to which sovereign powers are transferred'. Yet, the further description by the Court comes close to generally accepted definitions of an international organization:

The concept of *Verbund* covers a close long-term association of states which remain sovereign, an association which exercises public authority on the basis of a treaty, whose fundamental order, however, is subject to the disposal of the Member States alone and in which the peoples of their Member States, ie the citizens of the states, remain the subjects of democratic legitimization.[6]

Indeed, the Union's nature is mostly defined on the basis of internal considerations. Not so much has been written on how it would be perceived by third states. A possible reason was presented by Tsagourias: 'By appropriating the instruments of its creation, the Union liberated

---

[3] See for example the 2004 Energy Charter Treaty (Article 3). See also E. Paasivirta and P. J. Kuijper, 'Does One Size Fit All? The European Community and the Responsibility of International Organisations' (2005) 36 *Netherlands Yearbook of International Law* 169–226 at 205; and Chapter 8 of this book.

[4] D. Chalmers, G. Davies and G. Monti, *European Union Law*, 2nd edn (Cambridge: Cambridge University Press, 2010), p. 3.

[5] *Ibid.*, p. 632.

[6] *Entscheidungen des Bundesverfassungsgericht*, 30 June 2009; available at www.bundesverfassungsgericht.de/entscheidungen. See also A. Steinbach, 'The Lisbon Judgment of the German Federal Constitutional Court – New Guidance on the Limits of European Integration' (2010) 11 *German Law Journal*, 4, 367.

itself from external – international – contingencies and also moved the source of its validation from the international legal order to the Union.'[7]

Yet, irrespective of the inward-looking basis for its creation and its 'liberation' from international contingencies, the current ambitions of the Union reveal the need to exist and be recognized as an international legal entity that somehow fits the fundamental starting points of the international legal order.

So, could the EU qualify as an international organization? Well, when it looks like a banana and smells like a banana, it may very well be a banana.[8] Indeed, many would agree with Curtin and Dekker that 'the legal system of the European Union is most accurately analysed in terms of the institutional legal concept of an international organization'.[9] But even this quote reveals how difficult it is to argue that the EU *is* an international organization (albeit a very special one).[10] Throughout their handbook on the law of international organizations, Schermers and Blokker nevertheless treat the EU as an international organization, while noting of course the 'far-reaching forms of cooperation' and the 'supranational features'.[11] The EU is indeed 'considered special not because of its identity problems but because of the high degree of "constitutional" development, supranational components and the rule of law features within this organization making it look almost like a federation of states', as argued by Bengoetxea in one of the few publications focusing on this question.[12]

As an international organization, the EU is subject to international law in its relations with third states and other international organizations. While international law can also be part of the internal set of rules (see Chapter 7), this chapter's focus is on the external dimension. There we would need to start from the presumption that the EU is bound by the international agreements to which it is a party as well as to the customary parts of international law. As more recent international law shows, it is capable of taking the differences between states and international organizations into account (see for instance the 1986 Vienna Convention on the Law of Treaties between States and International Organizations or between International Organizations; or the 2011 Articles on the Responsibility of International Organizations (ARIO)).[13] Yet, for third states

---

[7] N. Tsagourias, 'Conceptualizing the Autonomy of the European Union', in R. Collins and N. D. White (eds.), *International Organizations and the Idea of Autonomy: Institutional Independence in the International Legal Order* (London/New York: Routledge, 2011), pp. 339–352 at 340.

[8] As we will see in Chapter 10, the choice for 'banana' as a metaphor in a textbook on EU external relations law is less random than it seems.

[9] D. M. Curtin and I. F. Dekker, 'The European Union from Maastricht to Lisbon: Institutional and Legal Unity Out of the Shadow', in P. Craig and G. de Búrca (eds.), *The Evolution of EU Law* (Oxford: Oxford University Press, 2011), pp. 155–185 at 163.

[10] Compare the qualification as 'eine internationale Organisation eigener Art', by W. Schroeder, 'Die Europäische Union als Völkerrechtssubject' (2012) Beiheft 2 *Europarecht* 9–23 at 18. In general, the status of the EU as an 'international organization' seems to be accepted implicitly by many authors. Cf. P. Eeckhout, *EU External Relations Law*, 2nd edn (Oxford: Oxford University Press, 2011), who does not at all address the external legal nature of the EU, but merely refers to the fact that '[t]he EU is also a member of a number of *other* international organizations' (at 3, emphasis added).

[11] H. G. Schermers and N. M. Blokker, *International Institutional Law: Unity in Diversity* (Leiden/Boston: Martinus Nijhoff Publishers, 2011), pp. 55 and 57.

[12] J. Bengoetxea, 'The EU as (More Than) an International Organization', in J. Klabbers and Å. Wallendahl, *Research Handbook on the Law of International Organizations* (Cheltenham/Northampton: Edward Elgar Publishing, 2011), pp. 448–465 at 449. The author argues that it is above all the 'transitional' status of the EU (from international organization to federation) that justifies its 'specialness' (p. 450).

[13] Respectively to be found at http://untreaty.un.org/ilc/texts/instruments/english/conventions/1_2_1986.pdf; and http://untreaty.un.org/ilc/texts/instruments/english/draft%20articles/9_11_2011.pdf. Obviously, the extent to which these instruments successfully take the complex position of international organizations into account may be subject to debate.

the EU remains special. It may be an international organization, but the fact that it is exclusively competent to act in certain areas is unprecedented, as is the rule that EU Member States feel that, in the end, they should give priority to EU law in cases of a conflict with international law. Indeed, as underlined by case law, the *Gemeinschaftstreue* is believed to take precedence over international law obligations.[14] While for EU Member States (and most EU lawyers) these may be logical consequences of a dynamic division of competences, third states (and most public international lawyers) would remind us of the rule of *pacta tertiis nec nocent nec prosunt*; third states are in principal not bound by the EU Treaty as to them it is an agreement between others.[15] From a legal perspective they should not be bored with a complex division of competences that was part of a deal between the EU and its own Member States. Yet, these days one may expect a certain knowledge of the division of competences on the part of third states.

(ii) The EU and its Member States in the international legal order

Whereas the above discussion may seem like a purely semantic exercise, it points to the core difficulty of EU external relations: who represents the 'European interest' on the international scene – the EU or its Member States? How do these actions relate to each other – are they coherent, mutually supportive or perhaps contradictory? The following excerpt provides a good illustration of the diverse policy areas encompassed by the EU as an international actor. In this Communication, the European Commission provides a succinct summary of the diverse challenges facing the EU in the twenty-first century. Subsequently, it indicates the wide range of policies and instruments the EU has developed in the past sixty years in response, and how they could be improved.[16] Notice how the excerpt makes the distinction between 'Europe' and 'EU'. The latter is a reference to the international organization of which the Commission is an institution, the former is a reference to the EU and its Member States acting together across a vast range of subjects in a challenging global environment.

> **Communication from the Commission, *Europe in the World – Some Practical Proposals for Greater Coherence, Effectiveness and Visibility*, Brussels, 8 June 2006, COM(2006) 278 final, p. 2**
>
> Since the end of the Cold War, the world has changed very fast. Europe faces strong economic competition and new threats to its security. While Europe's mature economies have many strengths, they also suffer from sluggish growth and ageing populations. The economic balance of power has shifted. Countries such

---

[14] Examples include the *Open Skies* cases (e.g. Case C-469/98 *Commission* v. *Finland* [2002] ECR I-9627), *BITs* cases (Cases C-205/06 *Commission* v. *Austria* [2009] ECR I-1301; C-249/06 *Commission* v. *Sweden* [2009] ECR I-1335; C-118/07 *Commission* v. *Finland* [2009] ECR I-10889), or the *PFOS* case (Case 246/07 *Commission* v. *Sweden* [2010] ECR I-3317). From a more constitutional point of view, similar arguments that international law should be applied in a way that would not harm the constitutional principles of the EU legal order were made in the *Kadi* case (Joined Cases C-402/05 P and C-415/05 P *Yassin Abdullah Kadi and Al Barakaat International Foundation* v. *Council and Commission* [2008] ECR I-6351).

[15] This rule is laid down in Article 34 VCLT, adopted in Vienna, 22 May 1969 (hereinafter VLCT): 'A treaty does not create either obligations or rights for a third State without its consent.'

[16] The quoted Communication followed in the wake of the Dutch and French referenda rejecting the Draft Constitutional Treaty, and through this document the Commission sought to stimulate pragmatic advances in EU external relations without the need for changes to EU primary law.

as China and India are growing fast, and there is increasing competition for access to raw materials, energy resources and markets. Terrorism, the proliferation of weapons of mass destruction, regional conflicts, failed states and organised crime remain as pressing as ever.

Europe has the potential to rise to these challenges and to share in the new opportunities created by emerging markets and globalisation. It has an open society that can absorb people, ideas and new technologies. Successive enlargements over the last three and a half decades have demonstrated the EU's ability to promote stability and prosperity and the success of this model of regional integration. With a combined population of 470m and a quarter of the world's income, the EU now accounts for over a fifth of world trade. We provide more than half of development and humanitarian assistance worldwide. European countries make a central contribution to all the important global institutions. The EU model of co-operation and integration is a pole of attraction for countries in our neighbourhood and beyond.

Over the last fifty years the EU has developed a series of external policy instruments, political, economic, commercial and financial, which help us to protect and promote our interests and our values. More recently these instruments have been diversified in areas where member states felt they needed to work in common, and a High Representative for Common Foreign and Security Policy was appointed, to enhance the scope and effectiveness of the EU's external action. Military instruments have been created to reinforce civil instruments of crisis management.

Increasingly the EU's internal policies – for example the environment, energy, competition policy, agriculture and fisheries, transport, the fight against terrorism and illegal migration, dealing with global pandemics – impact on international relationships and play a vital part in the EU's external influence. Conversely, many of Europe's internal policy goals depend on the effective use of external policies.

This paper seeks to ... make pragmatic proposals to enable the Union to define a strong sense of collective purpose in our external action and to ensure that this is backed by the necessary policy instruments.

The first two paragraphs are a highly dense summary of the vast range of policies pursued by the EU as an international actor. To name but three of them: first, it starts out by referring to access to raw materials and markets in a global competitive environment, which is generally within the purview of the EU's CCP (Article 207 TFEU; see Chapter 9); second, the Communication mentions the challenge of terrorism and the proliferation of weapons of mass destruction, which falls within the scope of the EU's CFSP (Article 24 TEU; see Chapter 11), but certainly also within the scope of Member States' own foreign policies; third and finally, the excerpt refers to the fact that 'we' provide more than half of global development and humanitarian aid, by which the document refers to funds dispersed by the Union and its Member States within their respective development policies (Article 208 TFEU; see Chapter 10). In sum, the excerpt illustrates that the EU 'as an international actor' is an umbrella term for a set of external policies, instruments and actors across a vast range of substantive domains. It also illustrates the ambiguity as to who is acting: the EU alone, the EU Member States, or both simultaneously.

Article 47 TEU

The Union shall have legal personality.

Yet, from a legal perspective it makes sense to continue to distinguish between the EU as an international organization of which states can be members, and the (Member) States themselves. In that sense the EU is clearly something different from a collection of twenty-eight states. It has a distinct legal status, both in relation to its own members as well as towards third states. The EU as an international actor then refers to the entity which has express legal personality and capacity to act in the international legal order. What is then characteristic of this international actor, and what makes some define it a 'sui generis' international actor, is that the EU is neither a state with 'full international powers', nor is it a traditional international organization with limited powers to go against the will of its members. Yet, like any other international organization, the EU is based on the principle of conferred powers, e.g. it can only act where its Member States have given it the competence to do so. But, importantly, the Member States may no longer be allowed to act once competences have been transferred and have been placed 'exclusively' in the hands of the Union. As a consequence, depending on the legal existence, scope and nature of the EU's external powers (a synonym for competence, see Chapters 3 to 5), the Member States have to a lesser or greater degree a prominent role in the formation and execution of international action in the relevant area. Conversely, the role of the EU (as the legal person) and its supranational institutions will then shift depending on the policy area at issue. This is why it possesses significant legal competences and political clout which are distinct from those of its Member States. However, it is not a state, and its Member States remain equally significant on the international scene; the core of EU external relations law is based on this phenomenon.

3 THE ARCHITECTURE OF EU EXTERNAL RELATIONS IN THE TREATIES

The EU is a single legal person, but it is not based on a single constitutive document. In the following sections we explain the legal structure of the TEU and the TFEU, with specific emphasis on how external relations are organized in EU primary law. We have pointed to the notion of the EU as an international actor functioning as an umbrella term for a set of external policies, instruments and actors across a vast range of substantive domains pursued by a *sui generis* entity. Figure 2 schematically sets out the most important legal components of this entity to visualize its constitutive legal parts, both Member States and EU Treaties.[17]

Figure 2 illustrates that the EU is an international organization with legal personality (Article 47 TEU), which exists legally distinct from its Member States. It also shows that the EU is based on the TEU and the TFEU. These are not in a relationship of hierarchy, but have the same legal value, and together they constitute 'the Treaties' on which the Union is founded (Articles 1 TEU and 1 TFEU). Not included in the figure are the Charter of Fundamental Rights ('the Charter') and the Treaty establishing the Atomic Energy Community ('EURATOM'). The latter still exists as a separate legal instrument which has not been merged with the TEU and TFEU. Though it shares the EU's institutions, EURATOM exists as a distinct legal personality from the EU. In this book the focus is on the Union as based on the TEU and TFEU, and we only discuss EURATOM and the Charter in an ancillary fashion.

---

[17] In referring to the Treaties, this book will use the following acronyms: For the pre-Lisbon, post-Nice situation this text refers to 'TEC' for the EC Treaty, and 'EU' for the EU Treaty. For the post-Lisbon situation the text uses 'TFEU' for Treaty on the Functioning of the Union, and 'TEU' for the Treaty on European Union.

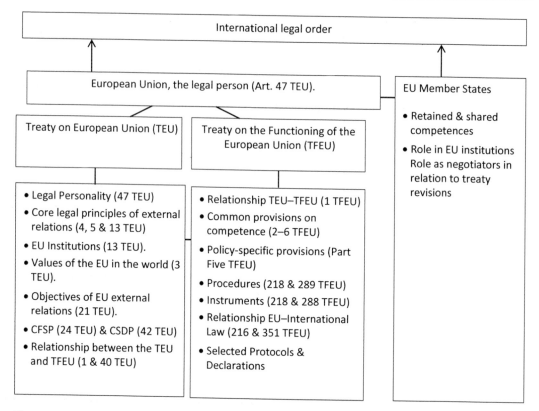

Figure 2   Treaty architecture of EU external relations

The TEU with its fifty-five articles is the shortest of the two, and is considered the framework treaty. Namely, the legal instrument which sets out the most fundamental legal properties of the EU: the aims and objectives for which it was set up, which of its organs has what role in making decisions binding the legal person, essential principles of conduct within the organization, how to leave or become a member of the Union, and how its constitutional rules can be changed. In the TEU the key provisions of EU external relations are those stating the core legal principles governing all EU action, including its international relations; the values and objectives of the EU in conducting its international relations; the EU institutions' roles in pursuing EU foreign policy; and the relationship between the TEU and the TFEU. For historical reasons (examined in Chapter 11), the TEU also contains the rules and procedures governing the EU's CFSP, the only substantive EU competence to be found in the TEU. Similarly, for reasons pertaining to the drafting of the Treaty of Lisbon following the failed Constitutional Treaty, the TEU contains an article on the European Neighbourhood Policy (ENP), examined in Chapter 15.

In comparison, the TFEU, as is clear from its name and with its 358 articles, 'fleshes out' the functioning of this international organization: in which areas the EU institutions can adopt measures in pursuit of the external objectives set out in the TEU, which procedures should its institutions adhere to and which (legally binding) instruments can they use. Furthermore, the TFEU contains crucial provisions governing the relationship between the EU and international law both as regards itself and its own international agreements, and the legal position of the

Member States and their international commitments. Finally, relevant to both the TEU and the TFEU are the legally binding Protocols attached to the TFEU, and the political Declarations, which serve to interpret or contextualize some of the provisions in the TEU and TFEU.

The following two sections provide a broad overview of these essential provisions, first of the TEU and then of the TFEU. This will provide the reader with an essential roadmap to understanding the remaining chapters of this book.

(i) The Treaty on European Union: a bird's-eye view

(a) Conferral, loyalty and institutional balance

While one should be aware that all principles of EU constitutional law remain pertinent for EU external relations, three in particular are the cement of the structure underpinning EU external relations: the principle of *conferral*, the obligation of *loyalty* and the principle of *institutional balance*.

First, the EU is established amongst the Member States as High Contracting Parties, and the Member States *confer competences* on the EU to attain *objectives they have in common* (Article 1 TEU). This means that while the EU has a fully fledged legal personality to act and contract in the world, it is legally permitted to act only where the Treaties give the EU powers to do so[18] (Articles 1; 4(1); 5(2) TEU).[19] It is thus a key defining feature of EU external relations that the Union shares external objectives with its Member States, but that it has limited legal capacity to pursue these objectives: the principle of conferral.

The second fundamental principle is the *loyalty obligation* of Article 4(3) TEU.[20] The loyalty obligation is crucial because it 'reflects a more general federal principle according to which each level and unit of government must always act to ensure the proper functioning of the system of governance as a whole'.[21] Looking at Figure 3 below, the loyalty obligation is thus the legal 'glue' which holds all composite parts together. The general provision of Article 4(3) TEU requires that Union and the Member States loyally and reciprocally cooperate in carrying out the tasks that flow from the Treaties. Article 13(2) imposes a similarly reciprocal obligation between the institutions, and Article 24(3) reiterates the same obligation in the field of CFSP.

The third principle which time and again rears its head in EU external relations is also stated in Article 13(2) TEU, the *principle of institutional balance*. In Article 13(1) TEU we find the list of seven institutions: the European Parliament, the European Council, the Council of Ministers, the European Commission, the Court of Justice of the European Union (CJEU), the European Central Bank and the Court of Auditors. The principle of institutional balance then does not mean that there is a 'balance of powers' whereby each of these seven institutions can be labelled as being part of the executive, legislative and judicial branch.[22] Rather, its meaning is more formal in nature and entails that each of these institutions has been given a 'specific function' and set of

---

[18] The words 'power' and 'competence' of the EU are synonymous and used interchangeably.

[19] Underlining its fundamental nature, the principle of conferral is repeated in different formulations dozens of times throughout the TEU and TFEU.

[20] With *lex specialis* provisions in Articles 13(2) (institutions) and 24(3) TEU (CFSP), as well as the specific iterations of the loyalty obligation in the articles on development policy, technical cooperation and humanitarian aid in Part V TFEU.

[21] G. de Baere, *Constitutional Principles of EU External Relations* (Oxford: Oxford University Press, 2008), p. 253.

[22] J.-P. Jacqué, 'The Principle of Institutional Balance' (2004) 41 *Common Market Law Review*, 2, 383.

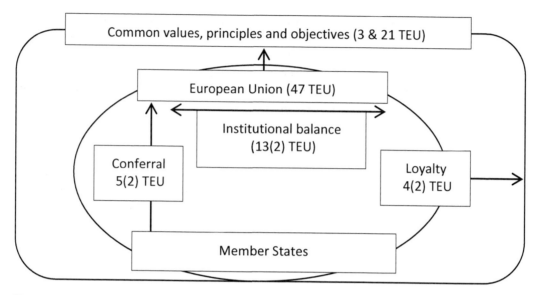

Figure 3   Conferral, institutional balance, loyalty and objectives

competences in the decision-making process of the Union (Articles 13–19 TEU). The principle of institutional balance simply means that this division of powers established by the Treaties is to be respected.

These three principles are deeply intertwined in the daily life of EU foreign policy-making. We have seen previously in this chapter that EU external relations are a quilt of different policies in areas ranging from international trade through migration to terrorism and global security. Within this policy quilt, the EU as a legal person has been *conferred* a limited set of competences by its Member States. Subsequently, in the exercise of these competences, the Treaties give specific roles to each of the EU institutions to exercise these competences in light of Treaty objectives. Finally, while exercising their respective competences, not only the institutions have to cooperate loyally between themselves, but also the EU and its Member States. Looking at these legal principles through the prism of coherence (see Preface), we can say that conferral is a principle relating to vertical coherence (assigning who does what in the EU–Member State relationship), institutional balance relates to horizontal coherence (who does what within the Union itself), and the duty of cooperation pertains to horizontal and vertical coherence at the same time (all have to be loyal to each other).

Figure 3 illustrates how the three main principles are positioned vertically and horizontally, and how they interact with each other. It adds an important element to the functioning of the three fundamental principles of EU external relations law: *values*, *principles* and *objectives*. While the EU has been given competences to act in certain fields, it cannot use those competences for any objective it pleases. Indeed, the EU has been set up for a specific purpose. The TEU sets out that purpose in Articles 2, 3 and 21 TEU, which list the set of values, interests, principles and objectives on which the Union is based, and in pursuit of which it has been conferred certain competences. Article 2 TEU defines the Union's self-perception – its identity, namely that it is based on a number of foundational values such as respect for human dignity, freedom, democracy, equality, the rule of law and so on. This provision is not specific to EU external relations, and for our purposes should be connected with Articles 3(5) and 21 TEU which do pertain specifically to EU external relations. As Figure 3 indicates, Articles 3(5) and 21 TEU have a 'unifying role' for EU external action, both in the legal and also policy sense by answering the following questions: the Member States may have conferred powers upon the Union, but for what purpose? The Member States and EU must cooperate loyally with each other, but to what end? The EU institutions each have been accorded a position within the EU decision-making process, but in order to decide what exactly? Articles 3(5) and 21 TEU provide answers to these questions by setting out the substantive objectives of EU international action. The three fundamental legal principles of the internal dimension to EU external relations law then 'function' in light of these objectives, and all EU external action should be geared towards pursuing them. Figure 3 above then illustrates this legal–political interaction: the EU and its Member States as well as the institutions are to cooperate loyally towards attaining TEU objectives; and the EU has been conferred powers which it should exercise through its institutions to allow it to attain these objectives.

(b) Values, objectives and coherence

The objectives of EU external relations deserve an in-depth look for two reasons. First, they govern the inner workings of the entire EU machinery: the principles of conferral, cooperation and institutional balance exist in light of them. Second, they shape the EU's relationship to the legal and political global reality in which it exists. The extract below on the EU's constitutional objectives gives a succinct overview and classification utilizing the concepts of possession goals and milieu goals. Possession goals are those which 'focus on the protection or strengthening of national possessions and resources, such as territory, trade advantages, and domestic sovereignty'.[23] Milieu goals on the other hand, are those which seek to shape and stabilize the surrounding and international environment. They 'emphasize the promotion of long-term security, stability, sustainability, cooperation and peaceful international relations'.[24] When reading Articles 3(5) and 21 TEU, the reader is invited to superimpose this conceptual distinction on the external objectives mentioned in these provisions, and think of the following questions: what kind of international actor is the EU? How does the EU relate to general international public law, and to other international organizations? How do these objectives relate to the three legal principles, and most notably conferral: is the legal capacity, and thus the EU's scope of action of the Union in the world very much limited by them, or rather the opposite?

Article 3(5) TEU

In its relations with the wider world, the Union shall uphold and promote its values and interests and contribute to the protection of its citizens. It shall contribute to peace, security, the sustainable development of the Earth, solidarity and mutual respect among peoples, free and fair trade, eradication of poverty and the protection of human rights, in particular the rights of the child, as well as to the strict observance and the development of international law, including respect for the principles of the United Nations Charter.

---

[23] G. De Búrca, 'EU International Relations: The Governance Mode of Foreign Policy', in B. Van Vooren *et al.*, *The Legal Dimension of Global Governance: What Role for the EU?* (Oxford: Oxford University Press, 2013).
[24] *Ibid.*

Article 21 TEU

1. The Union's action on the international scene shall be guided by the principles which have inspired its own creation, development and enlargement, and which it seeks to advance in the wider world: democracy, the rule of law, the universality and indivisibility of human rights and fundamental freedoms, respect for human dignity, the principles of equality and solidarity, and respect for the principles of the United Nations Charter and international law.

   The Union shall seek to develop relations and build partnerships with third countries, and international, regional or global organisations which share the principles referred to in the first subparagraph. It shall promote multilateral solutions to common problems, in particular in the framework of the United Nations.

2. The Union shall define and pursue common policies and actions, and shall work for a high degree of cooperation in all fields of international relations, in order to:
   (a) safeguard its values, fundamental interests, security, independence and integrity;
   (b) consolidate and support democracy, the rule of law, human rights and the principles of international law;
   (c) preserve peace, prevent conflicts and strengthen international security, in accordance with the purposes and principles of the United Nations Charter, with the principles of the Helsinki Final Act and with the aims of the Charter of Paris, including those relating to external borders;
   (d) foster the sustainable economic, social and environmental development of developing countries, with the primary aim of eradicating poverty;
   (e) encourage the integration of all countries into the world economy, including through the progressive abolition of restrictions on international trade;
   (f) help develop international measures to preserve and improve the quality of the environment and the sustainable management of global natural resources, in order to ensure sustainable development;
   (g) assist populations, countries and regions confronting natural or man-made disasters; and
   (h) promote an international system based on stronger multilateral cooperation and good global governance.

3. The Union shall respect the principles and pursue the objectives set out in paragraphs 1 and 2 in the development and implementation of the different areas of the Union's external action covered by this Title and by Part Five of the Treaty on the Functioning of the European Union, and of the external aspects of its other policies.

   The Union shall ensure consistency between the different areas of its external action and between these and its other policies. The Council and the Commission, assisted by the High Representative of the Union for Foreign Affairs and Security Policy, shall ensure that consistency and shall cooperate to that effect.

Articles 3(5) and 21 TEU give a double response to the questions of what kind of international actor is the EU, and how it relates to the international order. On the one hand, there is the substantive answer. As explained by the author in the extract below, these provisions in the TEU impose substantive requirements on EU international relations by stating that there are certain fundamental objectives which shall guide its internal and external policies. On the other hand, these provisions also impose a strong methodological imperative upon EU international action: it must pursue its action through a multilateral approach based on the rule of law. It is then also clear that the scope of objectives which EU action in the world must pursue, is extraordinarily broad. Aside from perhaps issuing a declaration of war, there is very little that does not fall within the purview of these objectives. In order to establish legally and conclusively what the EU can do in international relations, Chapters 3 to 5 of this book will examine the existence, nature and scope of EU external competence, in light of these objectives. Furthermore, in Chapter 7 we will examine the relationship between the EU and international law. On the basis of Articles 3(5) and 21 TEU, and as a creation of international law, we may assume that the Union legal order is open, supportive and receptive to international legal norms. This is partially true, but must be qualified in many respects.

J. Larik, 'Entrenching Global Governance: The EU's constitutional objectives caught between a sanguine world view and a daunting reality', in B. Van Vooren, S. Blockmans, J. Wouters, *The Legal Dimension of Global Governance, What Role for the EU?* (Oxford: Oxford University Press, 2013)

The Lisbon Treaty has both expanded and streamlined the Union's global objectives. The EU Treaties include now a set of general objectives of the Union, including their external dimension (Art. 3(5) TEU), an article containing general principles and goals of EU external action (Art. 21 TEU), and in some cases objectives specific to certain external policies (Arts. 206, 207, 208, 214 TFEU). . . .

While being careful to refer also to the pursuit of 'interests' (Arts. 3(5) TEU and 21(2)(a) TEU), thus keeping the door open for the pursuit of 'possession goals', the Treaties contain a wealth of substantive objectives that squarely fall into the category of milieu goals. These include contributions to 'peace, security, the sustainable development of the Earth, solidarity and mutual respect among peoples, free and fair trade, eradication of poverty and the protection of human rights, in particular the rights of the child' (Arts. 3(5) TEU and 21 TEU). The Treaties also make clear that this is largely an extrapolation of the Union's internal values to the outside world (Art. 21(1) TEU). Nevertheless, these goals are not all autonomously defined by the Union, but are indeed open to input from external sources by drawing on internationally defined concepts such as sustainable development, universal human rights or internationally agreed goals for development cooperation (Art. 208(2) TFEU).

In addition, we find a strong emphasis on law-based goals. The various references to human rights (Arts. 3(5); 21(1), first subpara; 21(2)(b) TEU), as *rights*, can also be seen as a matter of law. More straightforwardly, the Treaties oblige the Union to contribute 'to the strict observance and the development of international law' (Art. 3(5) TEU) and to spread and consolidate the rule of law in the world at large (Arts. 3(5) and 21(2)(b) TEU). They furthermore identify the United Nations as the forum of choice to 'promote multilateral solutions to common problems' (Arts. 21(1), second subpara TEU and 220(1) TFEU), which suggests abiding by and utilising the procedures and means provided under its Charter. Indeed, according to the Treaties 'stronger multilateral cooperation and good global governance' (Art. 21(2)(h) TEU) go hand in hand. . . .

In sum, we see that the EU Treaties codify a range of global objectives both in terms of substance but also specifically harnessing law. . . . Together, these elements coincide with the idea of the Union as a 'transformative power', changing not only fundamentally the relations among its members but also of the world around it.

One element not discussed in the above excerpt, though of crucial importance for EU external relations, is the fashion in which the third paragraph of Article 21 TEU establishes a legal connection between all these objectives. Indeed, it imposes a binding obligation of coherence in EU external relations, illustrating that coherence is not merely an academic notion but a tangible legal principle of EU primary law. Indeed, paragraph 3 of Article 21 TEU can be considered the *lex generalis* coherence obligation in EU external relations. There are then a number of *lex specialis* provisions in the TEU and TFEU imposing derived obligations in specific instances of vertical, horizontal or institutional coherence, etc. For example, in Chapter 10 we shall see that EU development policy cannot function without a strong emphasis on coherence in all its facets. In Figure 3, the role of this obligation in relation to EU external relations objectives is expressed through the large circle encompassing conferral, cooperation and the institutional balance. Thus, what this paragraph 21(3) TEU does is connect the list of policy objectives in Article 21(2) to each other, and to the functioning of pertinent legal principles, by imposing a legally binding obligation of coherence between all EU internal and external policies which must pursue them. Specifically through the case law of the Court of Justice, the obligation of loyalty has become directly connected to the objective of 'ensur[ing] the coherence and consistency of the action and its [the Union's] international representation'.[25]

The third paragraph of Article 21 specifically obliges the Commission, Council and HR to put coherence into effect, but the TEU contains four other provisions which pertain to coherence in its material and institutional dimensions. We name them at this juncture to point to the importance of coherence in EU external relations, but shall return to them throughout this book.

- Article 13(1) TEU imposes coherence as one of the overarching purposes for the activities of the EU institutions: 'The Union shall have an institutional framework which shall aim to promote its values, advance its objectives, serve its interests, those of its citizens and those of the Member States, and ensure the consistency, effectiveness and continuity of its policies and actions.' The explicit reference to the Member States can be read as meaning that it concerns not merely coherence between policies and action of the Union itself (horizontal), but also between that of the Union and its Member States (vertical).
- Article 16(6) TEU imposes on the General Affairs Council an obligation of substantive policy coherence between the work of the different Councils, and a specific obligation for the Foreign Affairs Council (FAC) since it 'shall elaborate the Union's external action on the basis of strategic guidelines laid down by the European Council and ensure that the Union's action is consistent'.
- Article 18(4) TEU imposes a specific coherence obligation on the EU HR with a strong institutional dimension, as it relates to the connection between the work of the HR and that of the Commission: 'The High Representative shall be one of the Vice-Presidents of the Commission. He shall ensure the consistency of the Union's external action. He shall be responsible within the Commission for responsibilities incumbent on it in external relations and for coordinating other aspects of the Union's external action.'
- Article 26(2) TEU contains an obligation of substantive policy coherence specifically for the EU's CFSP: 'The Council and the High Representative of the Union for Foreign Affairs and Security Policy shall ensure the unity, consistency and effectiveness of action by the Union.'

In the TFEU, we find coherence obligations that do not relate to the institutions as such, but are predominantly substantive in the nature of their requirement.

---

[25] Case C-266/03 *Commission* v. *Luxembourg* [2005] ECR I-4805, para 60 and Case C-476/98 *Commission v Germany* [2002] ECR I-9855, para 66.

- Article 7 TFEU is found in Title II of that Treaty, under the heading 'provisions having general application' and states that: 'The Union shall ensure consistency between its policies and activities, taking all of its objectives into account and in accordance with the principle of conferral of powers.' Because this article is of general application and not specific to EU external relations, it must be read as requiring substantive, positive coherence between EU internal policies and EU external policies. The importance of the principle of conferral as it relates to coherence and objectives as mentioned in this article, will be explained further in Chapter 3 of this book.

- Part V TFEU concerns 'external action by the Union'. Article 205 TFEU is the first and general provision of that Title and reads that 'the Union's action on the international scene, pursuant to this Part, shall be guided by the principles, pursue the objectives and be conducted in accordance with the general provisions laid down in Chapter 1 of Title V of the Treaty on European Union'. This article is a cross-reference to Articles 21 and 22 TEU and has a triple consequence: first, any of the external competences listed in Part V TFEU (CCP, development policy and so on) must be conducted in line with the coherence obligation of Article 21(3) TEU. Second, all of these competences must pursue the objectives listed in Article 21(2) TEU. Third, where Article 22(1) TEU states that 'the European Council shall identify the strategic interests and objectives of the Union', Article 205 TFEU is yet another confirmation that this EU institution is given the principal role in ensuring overarching coherence across all EU external policies.

In three competence-specific articles we also find obligations to maintain coherence. In Article 208(1) TFEU concerning development policy there is an obligation that it pursue 'the principles and objectives of the Union's external action' (e.g. an obligation of horizontal coherence with Articles 3(5) TEU and 21(2) TEU), and a vertical obligation of coherence stating that 'the Union's development cooperation policy and that of the Member States complement and reinforce each other'. In Article 212 TFEU concerning economic, financial and technical cooperation with third countries, we find similar obligations: one of horizontal coherence but this time with EU development policy, and one of vertical coherence with Member States' respective policies. Finally, Article 214 TFEU concerning humanitarian aid is formulated in similar terms: a general reference to the EU's principles and objectives in external relations, and the need for EU measures and those of Member States to 'complement and reinforce each other'. This is therefore a reciprocal obligation of substantive, positive policy coherence.

Across all of these articles, Article 21(3) TEU is the most prominent as it renders coherence into a general and legally binding obligation of EU external relations applicable to all external *and* internal policies of the EU. Notably, since the Lisbon Treaty, these obligations fall within the jurisdiction of the Court of Justice. This is not insignificant: the Lisbon Treaty has set up a carefully crafted legal regime governing EU external action, whereby vertically and horizontally operating legal principles interact towards a common purpose. In subsequent chapters of this book we point to the crucial importance of the Court in shaping the EU as an international actor, and this legal obligation of coherence only strengthens this role.

(c) The special nature of the CFSP and the TEU–TFEU relationship

Title V TEU has the rather unsavoury title, 'General provisions on the Union's external action and specific provisions on the Common Foreign and Security Policy'. It is composed of two chapters: the first chapter contains two articles – Article 21 TEU, which is applicable to *all* EU external relations (including the CFSP), and Article 22 which concerns the strategic policy-making role of the European Council on the basis of Article 21 TEU objectives; the second chapter contains the specific provisions on the CFSP. While the TEU is to be considered the 'framework treaty', setting out general principles, what institutions the EU has and what are the EU's values and objectives, CFSP is the only *substantive* conferral of competence upon the Union by the TEU. This anomaly in legal drafting is the result of the history of European integration. As is explained more elaborately in Chapter 11 of this book, the progression of integration between the Member States in the field of foreign policy has been particularly fraught with problems. Issues concerning the security of a state and global peace and stability are generally perceived to touch upon the core of state sovereignty – more so, wrongly or rightly, than for example international trade relations. As a consequence, whereas some Member States proactively sought to create a 'single voice' for EEC members also in matters pertaining to foreign and security policy (e.g. matters such as the Helsinki Final Act of 1975, imposition of martial law in Poland in 1982 by the USSR, the Gulf War of 1991, etc.), other Member States would under no circumstances permit the process of supranational integration to take place in this policy area. As a consequence, cooperation in this area of foreign and security policy developed legally distinct from the external trade relations based on the 1957 Treaty of Rome. The consequence is that to this day, the CFSP remains as a separate policy field in terms of decision-making rules and the role of the institutions. The Draft Constitutional Treaty would have eliminated this separate status of the CFSP and equated it to other external competences, but safeguarding the CFSP's distinctive position was one of the elements of 'de-constitutionalization' during the 2007 negotiations on the Lisbon Treaty which followed the referenda rejecting the Draft Constitution.

(ii) Treaty on the Functioning of the Union and external relations: a bird's-eye view

The TEU contains elements that belong to the general framework of EU external relations law: the fundamental legal principles, the institutions, the objectives and the CFSP's specificity. The TFEU then fleshes out the framework laid down by the TEU, and from the perspective of EU external relations we provide a brief overview of the common provisions on competence taken together with the policy-specific provisions on competence, as well as the Protocols and Declarations relevant to this field of law.

(a) Provisions pertaining to EU external competence
As regards competence, Chapters 3 to 5 of this book explain further that we must conceptually distinguish between the existence, nature and scope of EU competence. Existence pertains to the question of whether the EU has competence to act at all: has a competence been conferred upon the Union or not? The nature of this competence then pertains to its impact on the Member States' competence to act: have Member States lost their capacity to act, or not? Finally, scope pertains to the substantive width of that competence: which action does, or does not fall within the purview of a given conferred competence? Once we have established existence, nature and scope, we can then move to the question of exercise of EU competence: which institutions are responsible for bringing to fruition these competences, and through which instruments and procedures can or must they do so? The issue of competence is undoubtedly one of the most challenging aspects of EU external relations law, and the issue returns in most chapters of this book. At this juncture we thus limit ourselves to giving the

reader a brief roadmap to navigate the Treaty, without entering into further discussion of the underlying principles and their functioning.

The starting point is the *principle of conferral*, and all TFEU provisions on competence lead back to this essential principle stated in Article 5 TEU, that the limits of Union competences are governed by the principle of conferral, meaning that it shall act only within the limits of the competences conferred upon it by the Member States in the TEU and TFEU to attain the objectives set out therein. Any competences not conferred upon the EU in the Treaties remain with the Member States (Articles 5(1) and 5(2) TEU). The TFEU then fleshes out Article 5 TEU in its Articles 2–6 TFEU contained in Title I, Part I TFEU entitled 'categories and areas of Union competence'. In other words, these five TFEU provisions concern the *existence* and *nature* of EU competence to act. Unfortunately, these provisions are not at the zenith of clear legal drafting. Here we provide but a macroscopic overview, and we refer the reader to Chapters 3 to 5 of this book for an exhaustive study of EU external competence.

Article 2 TFEU describes the *nature* of EU competence, except for paragraphs 4 and 6. Article 2(1) TFEU explains what it means for the EU to possess an *exclusive* competence (Member States can no longer act), paragraph 2 describes what it means for the EU and the Member States to *share* competences (Member States can act under certain conditions), and paragraphs 3 and 5 describes what we call coordinative, supportive or supplementary competence. Paragraph 4 pertains to the CFSP, and upon careful reading actually concerns the *existence* of that competence ('The Union shall have competence …'), without saying anything on the nature of the CFSP competence (see Chapter 11). Paragraph 6 then functions as a sort of *chapeau* to this provision, by stating that the scope, procedures and instruments for exercising these competences 'shall be determined by the provisions of the Treaties relating to each area'. This final paragraph means that for every policy area – e.g. energy, environment, CFSP, trade – there is a *specific* competence-conferring provision in the TEU or TFEU to which we must look in order to examine how the EU may act externally in this area. This means that while Articles 3, 4, 5 and 6 state the areas in which the EU has competences of a given nature, these provisions are not considered themselves the 'competence-conferring' provision to the Union. For present purposes we must look in particular to Part V TEU entitled 'external action by the Union', though also to Part Three TFEU 'Union Policies and Internal Actions' since they very often have a significant external dimension.

Article 3 TFEU lists five areas in which the Union shall have exclusive competence: (a) customs union; (b) the establishment of the competition rules necessary for the functioning of the internal market; (c) monetary policy for the Member States whose currency is the euro; (d) the conservation of marine biological resources under the common fisheries policy; (e) CCP. Of these five policies, CCP is the only one which is purely external in nature, though the other four policies certainly have external aspects to them. Article 3(2) TFEU pertains purely to EU external relations, and concerns the existence and nature of implied external competence. It is very awkwardly drafted, and much of Chapters 3 and 4 of this textbook is devoted to presenting the rules of EU external competence it sought to codify.

Article 4 TFEU lists the competences which are shared between the Union and its Member States. Paragraph 2 of this provision concerns the shared pre-emptive competences, meaning that EU action in this area will exclude Member State action. This is true for the following areas: (a) internal market; (b) social policy, for the aspects defined in this Treaty; (c) economic, social and territorial cohesion; (d) agriculture and fisheries, excluding the conservation of marine biological resources; (e) the environment; (f) consumer protection; (g) transport; (h) trans-European networks; (i) energy; (j) areas of freedom, security and justice; and (k) common safety concerns in public health matters, for the aspects defined in the TFEU. Paragraphs 3 and 4 of Article 4 TFEU concern shared non-pre-emptive (in this book also referred to as 'complementary') competences not excluding Member State action in the same areas, which is true in the areas of research, technological development and space, as well as development cooperation and humanitarian aid.

Article 5 TFEU concerns the coordination of economic policies within the Union, and Article 6 TFEU lists competences of the Union where it can merely support, coordinate or supplement Member State action. This is true in the areas of (a) protection and improvement of human health; (b) industry; (c) culture; (d) tourism; (e) education, vocational training, youth and sport; (f) civil protection; and (g) administrative cooperation.

As is clear from paragraph 6 of Article 2 TFEU, each of these areas listed in Articles 2–6 TFEU has a specific competence-conferring provision dedicated to them (and sometimes more than one). For example, for the exclusive competence in the area of CCP stated in Article 3(1)(e) TFEU we must look to Article 207 TFEU (see Chapter 9). For the shared competence in the field of energy stated in Article 4(2)(i), we must look to Article 194 TFEU (see Chapter 13). For the CFSP stated in Article 2(4) TFEU we must look to Article 24 TEU (see Chapter 11); and so on. By looking at those competence-specific provisions, we can then establish which are the actors responsible in that area, and through which procedures and instruments they may act to *exercise* those competences conferred upon the EU.

(b) Protocols and Declarations

Attached to the TEU are thirty-seven legally binding Protocols, as well as sixty-five political Declarations. Many of them are of indirect relevance to EU external relations,[26] but of direct interest are the following Protocols: Protocol 2 on the application of the principles of subsidiarity and proportionality; Protocol 7 on the privileges and immunities of the EU; Protocol 8 relating to accession to the ECHR; Protocols 19, 21, 22 and 23 regarding the external dimension of the Area of Freedom, Security and Justice (AFSJ); and Protocol 25 on the exercise of shared competence. The most pertinent Declarations are 13 and 14 on the CFSP; Declaration 15 concerning establishment of the EEAS; Declaration 18 on the delimitation of competences; Declaration 24 on the legal personality of the Union; Declaration 36 on the negotiation and conclusion of international agreements by Member States relating to the AFSJ; Declaration 37 concerning the solidarity obligation in Article 222 TFEU; and finally Declaration 41 stating for which objectives of Article 3 TEU Article 352 TFEU can be used. We discuss them in further depth in the relevant chapters.

Protocols form an integral part of the Treaty structure on which the Union is based, and are as such legally binding equal to the TEU and the TFEU. Declarations are not legally binding, though have an important interpretative effect in relation to the TEU or TFEU provisions to which they refer.

---

[26] Or of direct relevance, but not discussed in this book: Protocol 31 concerning petroleum imports into the EU from the Netherlands Antilles and Protocol 34 on special arrangements for Greenland. See further, D. Kochenov (ed.), *EU Law of the Overseas: Outermost Regions, Associated Overseas Countries and Territories, Territories Sui Generis* (The Hague: Wolters Kluwer, 2011).

4 INTRODUCING THE KEY PLAYERS

(i) The European External Action Service and the High Representative

In examining the institutions, textbooks usually follow the order presented in Article 13 TEU, which lists the EU institutions starting with the European Council. However, in this section we focus first on the EEAS and the new role of the HR of the Union for Foreign Affairs and Security Policy established by the Lisbon Treaty, as the EEAS and the HR both play a pivotal role in EU external relations; readers can subsequently refer to this text when analysing the EU institutions. This will be followed by an analysis of the role of the traditional institutions (European Council, Council, Commission, EP and Court of Justice) in EU external relations.

Article 27 TEU

1. The High Representative of the Union for Foreign Affairs and Security Policy, who shall chair the Foreign Affairs Council, shall contribute through his proposals to the development of the common foreign and security policy and shall ensure implementation of the decisions adopted by the European Council and the Council.
2. The High Representative shall represent the Union for matters relating to the common foreign and security policy. He shall conduct political dialogue with third parties on the Union's behalf and shall express the Union's position in international organisations and at international conferences.
3. In fulfilling his mandate, the High Representative shall be assisted by a European External Action Service. This service shall work in cooperation with the diplomatic services of the Member States and shall comprise officials from relevant departments of the General Secretariat of the Council and of the Commission as well as staff seconded from national diplomatic services of the Member States. The organisation and functioning of the European External Action Service shall be established by a decision of the Council. The Council shall act on a proposal from the High Representative after consulting the European Parliament and after obtaining the consent of the Commission.

The EEAS, mentioned only in Article 27(3) TEU, was formally established by a Council Decision in 2010 and officially launched in January 2011.

Council Decision 2010/427/EU of 26 July 2010 establishing the organisation and functioning of the European External Action Service, OJ 2010 No. L201/30

Article 1 Nature and scope

1. This Decision establishes the organisation and functioning of the European External Action Service ('EEAS').
2. The EEAS, which has its headquarters in Brussels, shall be a functionally autonomous body of the European Union, separate from the General Secretariat of the Council and from the Commission with the legal capacity necessary to perform its tasks and attain its objectives.
3. The EEAS shall be placed under the authority of the High Representative of the Union for Foreign Affairs and Security Policy ('High Representative').
4. The EEAS shall be made up of a central administration and of the Union Delegations to third countries and to international organisations.

Article 2 Tasks

1. The EEAS shall support the High Representative in fulfilling his/her mandates as outlined, notably, in Articles 18 and 27 TEU:
   - in fulfilling his/her mandate to conduct the Common Foreign and Security Policy ('CFSP') of the European Union, including the Common Security and Defence Policy ('CSDP'), to contribute by his/her proposals to the development of that policy, which he/she shall carry out as mandated by the Council and to ensure the consistency of the Union's external action,
   - in his/her capacity as President of the Foreign Affairs Council, without prejudice to the normal tasks of the General Secretariat of the Council,
   - in his/her capacity as Vice-President of the Commission for fulfilling within the Commission the responsibilities incumbent on it in external relations, and in coordinating other aspects of the Union's external action, without prejudice to the normal tasks of the services of the Commission.
2. The EEAS shall assist the President of the European Council, the President of the Commission, and the Commission in the exercise of their respective functions in the area of external relations.

The way in which the position of the Union as an autonomous international actor developed was only partially by purposive design. By most standards, it is a piecemeal construction of political and legal developments pushed forward by geopolitical and socio-economic stimuli. As will be further elaborated in Chapter 11, the early years of European Political Cooperation (EPC) coincided with the process leading up to the Helsinki Final Act, as well as events in the Middle East. The birth of CFSP in the Maastricht Treaty is intimately connected to the collapse of the USSR and the Gulf War. The subsequent failure to formulate a common response to events in the former Yugoslavia gave impetus to CFSP reforms in the Amsterdam Treaty. This dynamic has continued in the twenty-first century. For example, the first ever European Security Strategy (ESS) was drawn up after deep disagreement among EU Member States over US action in Iraq. Each of these geopolitical realities prompted EU internal change to the legal and political machinery making up 'European Union' external action. The EEAS is, then, a continuation of that process: a new institutional structure set up against a decades-old struggle of the Union seeking to project a strong, coherent voice on the international scene, counterbalanced by the Member States' wish to retain control over various aspects of international relations. The EEAS was created to overcome this fragmentation. The idea is to bring together policy preparation and implementation on external relations into one new body, under the auspices of the HR for CFSP who is also Vice-President of the Commission and Chairperson of the FAC (Article 18 TEU). This is referred to as 'triple-hatting', and together with an EEAS is hoped to support attaining coherence in EU external relations (Article 21(3) TEU).

In terms of policy fields covered by the new EEAS, the current structure is a typical EU-type compromise. It is *not* an EU institution, which significantly constrains its power to influence EU external decision-making legally. Furthermore, the EEAS has no say whatsoever in the CCP ('the mother of all EU external policies'; see Chapter 9), where the Commission remains very firmly in the driver's seat. Development policy is more opaque, where both the EEAS and the Commission have been given a role in the policy-making process (see Chapter 10). Similarly, in the domain of EU external energy policy, the EEAS has 'some kind' of role to play, but disagreement persists as to its exact relationship with the European Commission (see Chapter 13).

Council Decision 2010/427/EU of 26 July 2010 establishing the organisation and functioning of the European External Action Service, OJ 2010 No. L201/30

Preamble

. . .

2. In accordance with the second subparagraph of Article 21(3) TEU, the Union will ensure consistency between the different areas of its external action and between those areas and its other policies. The Council and the Commission, assisted by the High Representative, will ensure that consistency and will cooperate to that effect.

The preamble of the Council Decision reaffirms that coherence remains the final objective of setting up the EEAS, and does this by copying and pasting the text of Article 21(3) second paragraph TEU. Article 2 of the EEAS Decision then describes the two tasks of the EEAS attaining that objective: first, Article 2(1) states that it 'shall support' the High Representative in fulfilling his mandates as outlined in Articles 18 and 27 TFEU. Three indents follow that statement, one for each of the HR's hats. The first indent requires the EEAS to support the HR while carrying out the CFSP and ensuring the consistency of the Union's external action. The second and third indents require the EEAS to support her in her mandate as President of the FAC and as Vice-President of the Commission, respectively. All of this is aimed at a coherent EU international policy, though each time qualified by stating that 'this is without prejudice to the normal tasks' of the General Secretariat of the Council, and the 'normal tasks' of the Commission services respectively. Article 2(2) adds that the EEAS also functions to assist the President of the European Council, the President of the Commission, as well as the Commission itself, 'in the exercise of their respective functions in the area of external relations'.

Article 1(2) of the EEAS Decision (see above) provides: 'The EEAS, which has its headquarters in Brussels, *shall be a functionally autonomous body* of the European Union, *separate* from the General Secretariat of the Council and from the Commission with the *legal capacity necessary* to perform its tasks and attain its objectives.'[27] Deep disagreement existed throughout the negotiation process on the EEAS' position in the EU institutional set-up. On the one hand, there was Member State agreement that 'the EEAS should be a service of a *sui generis* nature separate from the Commission and the Council Secretariat',[28] while the EP's opinion was that it should be connected to the Commission. The final result laid down in Article 1(2) reveals that Parliament lost out in the final compromise.

In Article 1 of the EEAS Decision we found that the EEAS is 'functionally autonomous' and 'separate' from the Council Secretariat and Commission. Given the negotiation history to the EEAS ('equidistance'), these notions should be interpreted as meaning that in supporting the HR, the EU diplomatic service does not take instructions from the Council or the Commission. Its instructions come from the *office of* the HR,[29] who is in her turn accountable to the EU institutions proper – notably also the Parliament. The EEAS is certainly part of a 'command structure' which

---

[27] Emphasis added.

[28] October 2009 Presidency Report, DOC 14930/09, 6.

[29] Heads of the EU delegations can also receive instructions from the Commission 'in areas where they exercise powers conferred upon it by the Treaties'. Otherwise the Delegations only receive instructions from the High Representative (Article 5(3) EEAS Decision).

runs vertically via the HR, then through to the Council and up to the European Council, with a strand of accountability connecting it to Parliament. However, the EEAS is horizontally not an institutional participant in the EU's institutional balance, or part of an institution itself.

B. Van Vooren, 'A Legal Institutional Perspective on the European External Action Service', (2011) 48 *Common Market Law Review* 475–502, at 500–501

The new diplomatic service is formally dissimilar from an EU institution or an EU regulatory agency, yet an EU institution for the purposes of budget and staff, with powers that formally resemble but substantively go beyond those of EU agencies. The diplomatic service does not have legal personality, but does possess functional legal capacity to assist the High Representative. The notion of assistance [in relation to the HR is] broadly defined. In combination with the EEAS' rather extensive policy discretion, the service was argued to be a significant actor in the EU external policy-making. Crucially however, the EEAS has not been delegated powers of the EU institutions, cannot take individually legally binding decisions, and has not been conferred any powers to shape EU external policy-making with legal effect. . . . [This] led us to characterize the EEAS as being functionally akin to Commission Directorates General, without the legal advantage of being part of an institution with decision-making powers proper, accountable to Parliament, while being placed under the HR's authority with a broad mandate of support within the chalk lines set by the Council and European Council.

Given the idea behind the establishment of the EEAS, does setting up such a complex new body do anything to resolve the decades-old tension of EU external relations? No inter-institutional reconfiguration is perfect, and the EEAS is clearly a compromise between the many different interests involved.

Council Decision 2010/427/EU of 26 July 2010 establishing the organisation and functioning of the European External Action Service, OJ 2010 No. L201/30

Article 3 Cooperation

1. The EEAS shall support, and work in cooperation with, the diplomatic services of the Member States, as well as with the General Secretariat of the Council and the services of the Commission, in order to ensure consistency between the different areas of the Union's external action and between those areas and its other policies.
2. The EEAS and the services of the Commission shall consult each other on all matters relating to the external action of the Union in the exercise of their respective functions, except on matters covered by the CSDP. The EEAS shall take part in the preparatory work and procedures relating to acts to be prepared by the Commission in this area.

    This paragraph shall be implemented in accordance with Chapter 1 of Title V of the TEU, and with Article 205 TFEU.
3. The EEAS may enter into service-level arrangements with relevant services of the General Secretariat of the Council, the Commission, or other offices or interinstitutional bodies of the Union.
4. The EEAS shall extend appropriate support and cooperation to the other institutions and bodies of the Union, in particular to the European Parliament. The EEAS may also benefit from the support and

cooperation of those institutions and bodies, including agencies, as appropriate. The EEAS internal auditor will cooperate with the internal auditor of the Commission to ensure a consistent audit policy, with particular reference to the Commission's responsibility for operational expenditure. In addition, the EEAS shall cooperate with the European Anti-Fraud Office ('OLAF') in accordance with Regulation (EC) No 1073/1999. It shall, in particular, adopt without delay the decision required by that Regulation on the terms and conditions for internal investigations. As provided in that Regulation, both Member States, in accordance with national provisions, and the institutions shall give the necessary support to enable OLAF's agents to fulfil their tasks.

Article 3 of the 2010 EEAS Decision on the duty of cooperation is exemplary of the carefully crafted new institutional balance in EU external relations: links have been established with national diplomatic services, though practice will show whether that is a reciprocally cooperative relationship. The legal obligations of cooperation are the strongest between the Commission and the EEAS, while relations with the Council and its 'normal tasks' are less clear. Accountability of the EEAS to Parliament is extensive, but will have to be given form and substance in practice. In many areas the new diplomatic service has merged elements that used to function separately, while past tendencies of delimitation remain. Undoubtedly, the EEAS has also created new schisms, and new 'institutional interests'. While the EEAS's role as an interlocutor provides good ground to work towards a single EU voice, the legal and institutional innovations are far from perfect and will require further legal and practical elaboration in the near future.

A key role is indeed played by the HR. Catherine Ashton was the first person appointed in the new system both as HR and as Vice-President of the Commission at the end of 2009. This combination of the functions of HR and Vice-President of the Commission is, without doubt, one of the key innovations of the Lisbon Treaty. Since the entry into force of that Treaty, the HR for the CFSP is named *High Representative of the Union for Foreign Affairs and Security Policy*. The name change reflects the fact that it has become clear that the HR indeed represents the Union and not the (collective) Member States. The HR's competences are clearly laid down in the EU Treaty and form part of the institutional framework. Although the term 'Foreign Minister', which was used in the Constitutional Treaty, has been abandoned, the new provisions make clear that the HR will indeed be the prime representative of the Union in international affairs. Even the President of the European Council (note: not the European *Union*) exercises that position's external competences 'without prejudice to the powers of the High Representative of the Union for Foreign Affairs and Security Policy' (Article 15(6)(d) TEU).

The HR is appointed by the European Council (with the agreement of the President of the Commission) by Qualified Majority Voting (QMV). This again underlines the HR's role as a person who can act on behalf of the Union and who is perhaps competent to act even in the absence of a full consensus among the Member States.

Article 18(2) TEU

The High Representative shall conduct the Union's common foreign and security policy. He shall contribute by his proposals to the development of that policy, which he shall carry out as mandated by the Council. The same shall apply to the common security and defence policy.

In addition, the HR's de facto membership of the European Council is codified in Article 15 TEU (although strictly speaking it is stated that the HR only 'takes part in the work' of the European Council). The HR is further to assist the Council and the Commission in ensuring consistency between the different areas of the Union's external action (Article 21 TEU), and together with the Council ensures compliance by the Member States with their CFSP obligations (Article 24(3) TEU). All in all, the position of HR has been upgraded to allow for stronger and more independent development and implementation of the Union's foreign, security and defence policy, which – potentially – allows for a more coherent and more effective role for the EU in the world.

(ii) The European Council

Article 22(1) TFEU

The European Council shall identify the strategic interests and objectives of the Union.

The European Council is one of the EU institutions, and can adopt 'Decisions' to that effect. However, most often this institution carries out this task through the adoption of 'Conclusions' at the end of its meetings. These can be considered an 'instrument' of EU external relations, but are not listed in Article 288 TFEU alongside the legal instruments. They are thus not considered to be legally binding instruments, as the European Council does not 'exercise legislative functions' (Article 15(1) TEU). Yet, what is certain is that they are 'politically important' for EU external relations. This is because the European Council is the top EU institution tasked with setting out the future policy direction of EU external action. Procedurally then, it is clear that we cannot neatly capture EU external policy-making through the ordinary legislative procedure for internal instruments, or the Article 218 TFEU procedure for international agreements (see below). Conclusions of the European Council may trigger action at all levels of governance within the EU as an international actor: within the Member States themselves, and within and between the EU institutions. It may lead the Commission to propose a new Regulation (e.g. autonomous internal legally binding instrument), or lead to the proposition by the Commission and/or EEAS of the negotiation of an international agreement (e.g. conventional external legally binding instrument). However, it may also lead to non-legal but important foreign policy activity: for example, the opening of a political dialogue with an important strategic partner (e.g. USA, Russia), or the adoption of a political demarche rejecting a certain international state of affairs (e.g. Iran's pursuit of nuclear weapons). Thus, different 'actors' will be implementing the strategic vision set out by the European Council in accordance with Article 22 TFEU. In order to implement European Council Conclusions adopted in carrying out Article 22 TEU, the HR, the EEAS or the President of the European Council may all have an important function.

Article 15(6) TEU

The President of the European Council shall, at his level and in that capacity, ensure the external representation of the Union on issues concerning its common foreign and security policy, without prejudice to the powers of the High Representative of the Union for Foreign Affairs and Security Policy.

The President of the European Council is thus one of the Union's representatives. Article 15(6) explicitly refers to the fact that the President ensures the representation *at his level*. The President would therefore be the contact person for heads of state of third countries, whereas the HR would generally act at the level of ministers.

(iii) The Council

Article 16(6) TEU

The Council shall meet in different configurations, the list of which shall be adopted in accordance with Article 236 of the Treaty on the Functioning of the European Union.

The General Affairs Council shall ensure consistency in the work of the different Council configurations. It shall prepare and ensure the follow-up to meetings of the European Council, in liaison with the President of the European Council and the Commission.

The Foreign Affairs Council shall elaborate the Union's external action on the basis of strategic guidelines laid down by the European Council and ensure that the Union's action is consistent.

In general and jointly with the EP, the Council of Ministers exercises legislative and budgetary functions, and also policy-making and coordinating functions (Article 16(1) TEU). This is not different in the area of external relations. Like the European Council, the Council also adopts 'Conclusions' which will reflect what has been discussed and decided during each meeting. Again these are not legally binding instruments of the Union, but they are crucial in driving forward the decision-making process that underpins EU external action. As will be illustrated in Chapter 15 on the EU and its neighbours, the ENP was originally crafted entirely on the basis of a succession of non-legally binding policy documents, with the Council firmly directing the heading of EU policy in this domain.

Article 16(6) TEU thus points to the FAC as the key configuration in the area of external action. In this configuration the Council is generally composed of the Ministers for Foreign Affairs, but it is up to the Member States to decide to send either their Minister for Foreign Affairs or, for instance, a Minister or Deputy Minister for European Affairs. The Council deals with the whole of the EU's external action, including CFSP, CSDP, foreign trade and development cooperation, which occasionally calls for other ministers (Development or Trade) to join in. Defence Ministers traditionally participate in FAC meetings twice a year, in addition to their informal meetings (also twice a year). In contrast to other Council configurations – which are presided over by the six-monthly Presidency held by the Member States representatives in the Council on the basis of equal rotation (Articles 16(9) TEU and 236 TFEU) – the FAC is chaired by the HR. Given the busy schedule of the HR (see below), (s)he may, where necessary, ask to be replaced by the member of the FAC holding the rotating Presidency (Article 2(5) of the Council's Rules of Procedure).

As indicated above, however, external relations do not only relate to CFSP, but can be considered a dimension of most other EU policies. This implies that other Council configurations also have an external dimension, and it would be a mistake only to take account of the FAC Council's work in analysing EU external relations. Thus, negotiations on EU enlargement are dealt with by the General Affairs Council, and issues concerning borders and visas may be on the agenda of the Justice and Home Affairs (JHA) Council (see Chapter 14). The same holds true for the other configurations (Economic and Financial Affairs; Transport, Telecommunications and Energy (see further Chapter 14); Agriculture and Fisheries; Environment; Education, Youth, Culture and Sport; Employment, Social Policy, Health and Consumer Affairs; and Competitiveness).

Preparation and implementation of Council decisions are in the hands of the Political and Security Committee (PSC).

Article 38 TEU

Without prejudice to Article 240 of the Treaty on the Functioning of the European Union, a Political and Security Committee shall monitor the international situation in the areas covered by the common foreign and security policy and contribute to the definition of policies by delivering opinions to the Council at the request of the Council or of the High Representative of the Union for Foreign Affairs and Security Policy or on its own initiative. It shall also monitor the implementation of agreed policies, without prejudice to the powers of the High Representative.

Within the scope of this Chapter, the Political and Security Committee shall exercise, under the responsibility of the Council and of the High Representative, the political control and strategic direction of the crisis management operations referred to in Article 43.

The Council may authorise the Committee, for the purpose and for the duration of a crisis management operation, as determined by the Council, to take the relevant decisions concerning the political control and strategic direction of the operation.

This turns the PSC into a key player in the area of CFSP and CSDP (see also Chapters 11 and 12). The reference to Article 240 TFEU indicates that the general role of the Committee of Permanent Representatives (COREPER) is maintained. A representative of the HR chairs the PSC, most of the other preparatory bodies of the Council dealing directly with the CFSP, and the geographical working parties, whereas the working parties are chaired by the rotating presidency. The EU Military Committee and its Working Group (see Chapter 12) continue to be chaired by an elected chairman.[30]

The role of the COREPER is similar in external relations issues as in other policy areas. There are two COREPER configurations, named COREPER I and COREPER II. COREPER II consists of EU Member State representatives at ambassadorial level, and deals with political, commercial, economic or institutional matters. COREPER I consists of representatives at deputy ambassadorial level, dealing with what are considered 'technical matters'.

(iv) The Commission

In terms of decision-making, external relations do not differ from internal policies in the sense that, generally, the Commission is in the lead and should initiate new decisions. With the introduction of the EEAS, the dedicated external relations Directorate General was removed

---

[30] See Council Decision 2009/908/EU of 1 December 2009 laying down measures for the implementation of the European Council Decision on the exercise of the Presidency of the Council, and on the chairmanship of preparatory bodies of the Council, OJ 2009 No. L322/28.

from the Commission to the EEAS. Yet, given the external dimension of most policy areas (energy, environment, financial system, etc.), the Commission has remained a key player also externally. Apart from its general role in negotiations with third states and other international organizations, some external relations domains were not transferred to the EEAS, but maintained in the Commission, including trade, energy and humanitarian aid.

Article 17(1) TEU

With the exception of the common foreign and security policy, and other cases provided for in the Treaties, it shall ensure the Union's external representation.

Apart from the general role of the Commission in the decision-making process, this provision allows the Commission to represent the Union externally. This is only the case with respect to non-CFSP issues and 'other cases provided for in the Treaties'. A clear example of such a case is formed by Article 218 TFEU. This provision addresses the specific cases of negotiation of international agreements and expression of the EU's position in international bodies in certain circumstances. It clearly indicates the many roles of different institutions: it is for the Council to authorize the opening of negotiations, to adopt negotiation Directives, and to authorize the signing of agreements and conclude them (with the consent or consultation of the EP). Yet, the negotiations themselves are conducted by the Commissioner, and in certain cases by the HR. Subsequently, the Council exercises a certain control of the negotiations by addressing Directives to the negotiator and designating a special committee which is to be consulted during the negotiations. Moreover, the EP should be immediately and fully informed at all stages (see below).

Most importantly, however, the Commission's competences are defined by the principle of conferral, which may limit the Commission's powers in international conferences and international organizations. Thus, the Commission represents the Union in the areas of exclusive Union competence listed in Article 3 TFEU (customs union, competition, monetary policy for Member States whose currency is the euro, the conservation of marine biological resources under the fisheries policy, the CCP); whereas in the areas of shared competence of the Union with the Member States listed in Article 4 TFEU, both the Commission and the Member States have powers of representation in respect of their respective competences (see also Chapters 2 and 7 on mixed agreements).

(v) The European Parliament

Despite its formally modest role in the area of external relations, the EP has maximized the use of its powers and proven to be a very active player. After the enforcement of the Lisbon Treaty, Parliament's role was supported by a number of innovations:

- For all international agreements, Parliament is required to give consent before the agreement can be concluded by the Council (Article 218(6)(a) TFEU).
- The TFEU foresees a Multiannual Financial Framework for at least a period of five years (Article 312 TFEU), which is adopted by the Council but following consent of the EP. The latter

now has a say, as has the Council, on expenses related to EU external relations, in particular concerning CFSP.

- A specific section of the EU budget (Section X) relates to the EEAS, which implies that the EP has to agree with this part of the budget. It also has competence to decide on the discharge of the EEAS, which provides a degree of political control on how the EEAS is organized. The EP Committee on budgetary control is particularly concerned in verifying how the EU budget is spent on external relations, in particular regarding CFSP.
- 'The President, the High Representative of the Union for Foreign Affairs and Security Policy and the other members of the Commission shall be subject as a body to a vote of consent by the European Parliament.' (Article 17(7) TEU)

In general, the EP is regularly consulted by the HR on the main aspects and basic choices of CFSP, and is informed of how those policies evolve (Article 36 TEU); it has a right to have its views 'duly taken into consideration' (Article 36(1) TEU); may ask questions of the Council or the High Representative and may make recommendations (Article 36(2) TEU); it holds a debate twice a year on progress in implementing the CFSP and the CSDP (Article 36(2) TEU); has a right to be immediately and fully informed on negotiations, suspension or positions on CFSP agreements (Article 218(10) TFEU); it has a right to be consulted before the Council adopts a decision establishing the specific procedures for guaranteeing rapid access to appropriations in the Union budget for urgent financing of initiatives in the framework of the CFSP (Article 41(3) TEU); it gives its consent or its advice prior to the conclusion of international agreements by the Council except where agreements 'relate exclusively' to the CFSP as laid down in Article 218(6) TFEU.

Throughout this book, there are many examples whereby the Parliament has proactively sought to defend and even expand its influence on EU external policy-making. For example, in Chapter 9 on CCP we illustrate that the Parliament does not hesitate to remind the Commission that its consent will be required for the Union to conclude a trade agreement with the United States (e.g. the Transatlantic Trade and Investment Partnership (TTIP)). In other policy fields the Parliament has shown that it will in fact utilize that veto power if its views are not taken into account. This, together with its budgetary powers, renders the Parliament a formidable power in EU external decision-making. Beyond these formal aspects, the EP has committees such as the AFET (foreign affairs) or DEVE (development) Committees, which are very proactive in commissioning studies, adopting non-binding Resolutions, organizing hearings, carrying out fact-finding missions and so on, to place a parliamentary stamp on EU external relations. In its view, this provides an important element of democratic input to EU external action.

(vi) The Court of Justice

Since, in particular in the early years, references to external relations in the Treaties were minimal, the role of the Court in this area simply cannot be overstated. Large parts of what we now consider to form part of the external relations legal doctrine find their basis in case law. Throughout this book we will come across many key examples: the doctrine of implied powers, the exclusive nature of CCP, the scope of development policy in relation to CFSP, the effect of international law (United Nations, WTO, law of the sea, etc.) in the EU legal order, and many other crucial elements of EU external relations law, are all based on judge-made law, parts of which were later codified in the Treaties.

The Court does not have jurisdiction with respect to the CFSP, except to monitor compliance with the dividing line between CFSP and non-CFSP matters laid down in Article 40 TEU, as well as to review the legality of the external restrictive measures laid down in Article 275(2) TFEU (Article 24(1) TEU) (see further Chapters 11 and 12).

A main task of the Court has been (and still is) to decide on the delimitation of external competences between the Union and its Member States. With the further intensification of the European integration process, more and more internal competences ended up in the hands of the European Institutions. This, in turn, led to an incremental transfer of external powers from the Member States to the Union. After all, once competences have become 'exclusive' internally, there is not much left for Member States to decide externally (see also Chapter 4).

P. Eeckhout, 'Exclusive External Competences: Constructing the EU as an International Actor', in A. Rosas, E. Levits and Y. Bot (eds.), *Court of Justice of the European Union – Cour de Justice de l'Union Européene, The Court of Justice and the Construction of Europe: Analyses and Perspectives on Sixty Years of Case-Law – La Cour de Justice et la Construction de l'Europe: Analyses et Perspectives de Soixante Ans de Jurisprudence* (The Hague: T.M.C. Asser Press, 2013), pp. 613–636

The concept of exclusive external competence, which the Court articulated in the absence of express guidance in the founding Treaties, has effectively constitutionalised the sphere of what is now called EU external action. Some might question whether such Court-led constitutionalisation was ever legitimate. Was not the original EEC Treaty sparsely worded as regards external relations, and did that not indicate that its framers did not seek a strong international role for the EEC?

However, a closer analysis of the case-law reveals that external and internal competences are closely linked. It is precisely the proper development and exercise of internal competences which led the Court to coin the concept of exclusivity.

In light of the strong link with the common/internal market, the common commercial policy has to be uniform, and this uniformity requires exclusive EU competence. AETR exclusive implied powers are no more than a particular form of pre-emption: it is to safeguard the effectiveness and uniformity of internal EU legislation, that the Member States are precluded from entering into international commitments which could affect such legislation or alter its scope.

Today the AETR doctrine produces effects throughout EU law territory, which has itself greatly expanded over the last couple of decades. Those effects are that, in areas where the EU has internal competences and has legislated, it is becoming next to impossible for the Member States to conclude international treaties and agreements without involving the EU. That does not mean that EU exclusive competence easily extends to the whole agreement – like the in that sense exceptional Lugano Convention case. More often than not the exclusive competence is limited to a particular part of a treaty or agreement, or even to some specific provisions – leading to mixed agreements. But the AETR requirement of EU participation is necessary to ensure that the relevant EU legislation is protected from external interference.

Without AETR, the EU would never have managed to participate in as many areas of international lawmaking as it does today. The AETR pre-emption criteria which the Court has developed over the decades are sophisticated, and not straightforward to apply. In practice, however, as soon as some AETR effect is established, EU participation is required, and therefore the sophistication of the case-law is rarely an issue. . . .

Overall, the case-law on exclusive external competences is a remarkable achievement, which has enabled the EU to become an international actor, in consonance with its internal competences, policies and objectives.

(vii) The Member States

While we will further elaborate on the different competences (exclusive, shared, etc.) in Chapter 4, the above excerpt underlines that, despite their membership of the EU, the Member States have not ceased to be international actors themselves. In fact, all Member States would argue that statehood – rather than EU membership – is still their primary identity. The principle of conferral leads to the fact that the EU is only competent to act once a competence exists (see further Chapter 3). In principle, this implies that in cases where the Union is not competent to act or where it shares its competences with the Member States, the latter can engage in legal relations with third states and other international organizations. As we will see throughout this book, it is this tension in particular (between being a state and being a Member State) that lies behind many of the rules in EU external relations law. The irony seems to be that Member States are generally happy with the internal market, but are not always equally happy with the consequences in terms of losing (external) powers.

5 THE BROADER PICTURE OF EU EXTERNAL RELATIONS LAW

This chapter provided the reader with a roadmap explaining the core reasons why EU external relations law is such a complex field, subsequently pointing to the essential features of the EU's architecture and the key institutional actors in this area. The starting point is the peculiar nature of the Union itself; neither state nor classic international organization, it is a unique species of international organization with legal existence distinct from that of its Member States, and with a stand-alone identity composed of values, interests and policies which it promotes internationally as its own. EU external relations law is then the body of law that governs action of the EU in the world both internally and externally. In its internal dimension it consists of the set of rules which govern the constitutional and institutional legal organization of this legal entity in pursuit of its interests in the world. In its external dimension, it includes the rules which govern its relationship to – and interaction with – other entities of the international (legal) order. What renders this field particularly complex is the fact that the functioning, interpretation and application of the rules it comprises are shaped by its specific *telos* as well as the context of political unification. Namely, the purpose of EU external relations law is to organize the EU and its Member States to exert their influence on the world stage in a coherent and effective fashion. This *telos* is then deeply intertwined with the project of European integration, and debates how far this process should continue. The consequence is that law, even constitutional law, plays a far more significant role in international relations of the Union than is common at national level. First of all, a large body of legal rules is required in order to ensure that this *sui generis* entity is sufficiently coagulant to ensure effective external action. Second of all, this internal law-based integration experience is then also translated into substantive external relations. Indeed, EU Treaty objectives also point to the Union as seeking to contribute 'to the strict observance and the development of international law' and to spread and consolidate the rule of law in the world at large.

Taking a step back, and looking at the broader picture of the material presented in this first chapter, we can now ask the following tantalizing question raised most prominently by Bruno de Witte: is there too much constitutional law in the EU's foreign relations?

B. de Witte, 'Too Much Constitutional Law in the European Union's Foreign Relations?', in M. Cremona and B. de Witte (eds.), *EU Foreign Relations Law: Constitutional Fundamentals* (Oxford: Hart Publishing, 2008)

The argument that there is 'too much constitutional law' in the EU is mainly based on the overabundance of primary law norms, which unduly constrains the normal democratic process. It is made worse by two other elements, namely the structural complexity of EU constitutional law which leads to a lack of 'legibility' for citizens, and the rigidity of the EU's rules of change. . . .

EU primary law tends to deal with many [issues of EU external relations] in a much more detailed way than national constitutions. In purely quantitative terms, a greater proportion of articles of the founding Treaties deal, entirely or in part, with foreign relations. This overabundant written text is complemented by an unusually abundant case law which has designed a fine pattern of rules on such foreign relations matters as the implied powers doctrine, the distinction between exclusive and shared competences, the duty of sincere cooperation in the context of mixed agreements, and the conditions under which international agreements have direct effect in the EC legal order. . . .

[T]here are too many 'un-fundamentals' in the foreign relations constitution of the EU. The formal constitutional law of the EU, which consists of the primary law of the Treaties as interpreted by the Court of Justice and supplemented by general principles, contains many norms that are not constitutional in their substance. They do not serve the useful purpose of constitutional rules, namely to limit and steer the activity of the institutions, but are merely obstructive. . . . [T]he drafters of the Treaties have not sufficiently reflected on the need for constitutional parsimony.

SOURCES AND FURTHER READING

Bengoetxea, J., 'The EU as (More Than) an International Organization', in J. Klabbers and Å. Wallendahl, *Research Handbook on the Law of International Organizations* (Cheltenham/Northampton: Edward Elgar Publishing, 2011), pp. 448–465.

Bretherton, C. and Vogler, J., *The European Union as a Global Actor* (Abingdon/New York: Routledge, 2006).

Bull, H., 'Civilian Power Europe: A Contradiction in Terms?' (1982) 21 *Journal of Common Market Studies*, 2, 149–164.

Cannizzaro, E., Palchetti, P. and Wessel, R. A. (eds.), *International Law as Law of the European Union* (Boston/Leiden: Martinus Nijhoff Publishers, 2011).

Chalmers, D., Davies, G. and Monti, G., *European Union Law*, 2nd edn (Cambridge: Cambridge University Press, 2011).

Cremona, M., 'The Draft Constitutional Treaty: External Relations and External Action' (2003) 40 *Common Market Law Review* 1347–1366.

Cremona, M., 'The Union as a Global Actor: Roles, Models and Identity' (2004) 42 *Common Market Law Review* 553–573.

Curtin, D. M. and Dekker, I. F., 'The European Union from Maastricht to Lisbon: Institutional and Legal Unity Out of the Shadow', in P. Craig and G. de Búrca (eds.), *The Evolution of EU Law* (Oxford: Oxford University Press, 2011), pp. 155–185.

De Baere, G., *Constitutional Principles of EU External Relations* (Oxford: Oxford University Press, 2008).

De Búrca, G., 'EU International Relations: The Governance Mode of Foreign Policy', in B. Van Vooren *et al.*, *The Legal Dimension of Global Governance: What Role for the EU?* (Oxford: Oxford University Press, 2012).

De Witte, B., 'Too Much Constitutional Law in the European Union's Foreign Relations?', in M. Cremona and B. de Witte (eds.), *EU Foreign Relations Law: Constitutional Fundamentals* (Oxford: Hart Publishing, 2008).

Eeckhout, P., *EU External Relations Law*, 2nd edn (Oxford: Oxford University Press, 2011).

Eeckhout, P., 'Exclusive External Competences: Constructing the EU as an International Actor', in A. Rosas, E. Levits and Y. Bot (eds.), *Court of Justice of the European Union – Cour de Justice de l'Union Européene, The Court of Justice and the Construction of Europe: Analyses and Perspectives on Sixty Years of Case-Law – La Cour de Justice et la Construction de l'Europe: Analyses et Perspectives de Soixante Ans de Jurisprudence* (The Hague: T.M.C. Asser Press, 2013), pp. 613–636.

Gosalbo Bono, R., 'The Organization of the External Relations of the European Union in the Treaty of Lisbon', in P. Koutrakos (ed.), *The European Union's External Relations a Year after Lisbon* (The Hague: CLEER Working Papers 2011/3), pp. 13–38.

Hillion, C., 'Tous pour un, un pour tous! Coherence in the External Relations of the European Union', in M. Cremona (ed.), *Developments in EU External Relations Law* (Oxford: Oxford University Press, 2008), pp. 10–36.

Jacqué, J. P., 'The Principle of Institutional Balance' (2004) 41 *Common Market Law Review*, 2, 383–391.

Kaddous, C., 'Role and Position of the High Representative of the Union for Foreign Affairs and Security Policy under the Lisbon Treaty', in S. Griller and J. Ziller (eds.), *The Lisbon Treaty: Constitutionalism without a Constitutional Treaty?* (Vienna: Springer, 2008), pp. 205–221.

Kochenov, D. (ed.), *EU Law of the Overseas: Outermost Regions, Associated Overseas Countries and Territories, Territories Sui Generis* (The Hague: Wolters Kluwer, 2011).

Kuijper, P. J., Wouters, J., Hoffmeister, F., de Baere, G. and Ramopoulos, T., *The Law of EU External Relations, Cases, Materials, and Commentary on the EU as an International Legal Actor* (Oxford: Oxford University Press, 2013).

Larik, J., 'Entrenching Global Governance: The EU's Constitutional Objectives Caught between a Sanguine World View and a Daunting Reality', in B. Van Vooren *et al.*, *The Legal Dimension of Global Governance, What Role for the EU?* (Oxford: Oxford University Press, 2012).

Manners, I., 'Normative Power Europe: A Contradiction in Terms?' (2002) 40 *Journal of Common Market Studies*, 2, 235–258.

Nye, J., *Soft Power: The Means to Success in World Politics* (New York: Public Affairs Press, 2005).

Paasivirta, E., 'The EU's External Representation after Lisbon: New Rules, a New Era?', in P. Koutrakos (ed.), *The European Union's External Relations a Year after Lisbon* (The Hague: CLEER Working Papers 2011/3), pp. 39–47.

Paasivirta, E. and Kuijper, P. J., 'Does One Size Fit All? The European Community and the Responsibility of International Organisations' (2005) 36 *Netherlands Yearbook of International Law* 169–226.

Passos, R., 'The European Union's External Relations a Year after Lisbon: A First Evaluation from the European Parliament', in P. Koutrakos (ed.), *The European Union's External Relations a Year after Lisbon* (The Hague: CLEER Working Papers 2011/3), pp. 49–56.

Paul, J., 'EU Foreign Policy after Lisbon: Will the New High Representative and the External Action Service Make a Difference?' (2008) 2 *Centre for Applied Policy Research (CAP) Policy Analysis*.

Schermers, H. G. and Blokker, N. M., *International Institutional Law: Unity in Diversity* (Leiden/Boston: Martinus Nijhoff Publishers, 2011).

Schroeder, W., 'Die Europäische Union als Völkerrechtssubject' (2012) Beiheft 2 *Europarecht* 9–23.

Steinbach, A., 'The Lisbon Judgment of the German Federal Constitutional Court – New Guidance on the Limits of European Integration' (2010) 11 *German Law Journal*, 4, 367–390.

Thym, D., 'Parliamentary Involvement in European International Relations', in M. Cremona and B. de Witte (eds.), *EU Foreign Relations Law: Constitutional Fundamentals* (Oxford: Hart Publishing, 2008), pp. 201–232.

Tsagourias, N., 'Conceptualizing the Autonomy of the European Union', in R. Collins and N. D. White (eds.), *International Organizations and the Idea of Autonomy: Institutional Independence in the International Legal Order* (London/New York: Routledge, 2011), pp. 339–352.

Van Vooren, B., 'A Legal Institutional Perspective on the European External Action Service' (2011) 48 *Common Market Law Review* 475–502.

Van Vooren, B., *EU External Relations Law and the European Neighbourhood Policy: A Paradigm for Coherence* (Abingdon/New York: Routledge, 2012).

Van Vooren, B., 'The Small Arms Judgment in an Age of Constitutional Turmoil' (2009) 14 *European Foreign Affairs Review*, 1, 231–248.

Van Vooren, B., Blockmans, S. and Wouters, J. (eds.), *The EU's Role in Global Governance: The Legal Dimension* (Oxford: Oxford University Press, 2013).

Wessel, R. A., 'The Inside Looking Out: Consistency and Delimitation in EU External Relations' (2000) 37 *Common Market Law Review* 1135–1171.

Wessel, R. A., 'The International Legal Status of the European Union' (1997) 2 *European Foreign Affairs Review* 109–129.

2

Instruments of EU external action

1 CENTRAL ISSUES

- In this chapter we analyse the instruments through which the EU conducts its external relations. We distinguish between instruments that are adopted within the EU legal order (internal) and those adopted by the Union in the international order (international). These may be instruments adopted by the EU alone (autonomous instruments) or the result of agreements between the Union and a counter-party (conventionally agreed instruments). These instruments can then be legally binding (hard law) or they may be committing in other more indirect or political ways (soft law).
- International agreements are the EU's legal external relations tools par excellence. They form the key legal instrument to allow the Union to play along in the global legal order and to establish legal relationships with third states and other international organizations. If the EU lacked the competence to conclude international agreements, its external relations would be the object of study of political scientists and international relations experts only, and not so much of lawyers. The main part of this chapter will therefore be devoted to the conclusion and variety of international agreements (including mixed agreements, association agreements (AAs) and agreements to accede or withdraw);

2 A TYPOLOGY OF INSTRUMENTS OF EU EXTERNAL ACTION

In the typology of instruments used to carry out EU external action, we distinguish between instruments that are adopted within the EU legal order (internal) and those adopted by the Union in the international order (international). These may be instruments adopted by the EU alone (autonomous) or the result of agreement between the Union and a counter-party (conventional). These instruments can then be legally binding (hard law) or they may be committing in other ways (soft law). Within the Union, the legally binding, autonomous instruments are those stated in Article 288 TFEU: Regulations, Directives and Decisions. The other instruments sometimes referred to as 'non-legally binding' autonomous instruments are recommendations and opinions listed in that article, but in practice there are many more 'soft law' instruments through which the EU projects its voice on the international scene. In their international dimension, the legally binding, conventional instruments are the international agreements concluded by the Union; in accordance with general international public law, the EU can also unilaterally adopt positions by which it will be legally bound. On the soft law side, the EU regularly adopts conventional instruments such as Joint Declarations or Memoranda of Understanding (MoU), or expresses its opinion through démarches which are diplomatic and political in nature. Despite the frequent reference to these instruments as 'non-legally binding', we treat these instruments as forming part of the EU legal order, given the fact that they may produce legal effects or may commit the EU and/or its Member States in other ways.

A typology such as this one is of course idealistic, as in practice the line between internal and external, autonomous or conventional, soft or hard law, will be hard to draw. In the day-to-day process of EU external relations policy-making, these three dimensions intertwine into a complex mix of law and politics to reach desirable external policy outcomes. It is then crucial to keep in mind that in EU external relations *law*, politics matters to a great extent. When an instrument has been adopted as soft law and is therefore non-legally binding on the parties, and may have limited legal enforcement possibilities, that does not mean that it is not important. For example: the ESS of December 2003 (see Chapter 11) is an autonomous instrument of the Union that cannot be categorized within Article 288 TFEU, yet it has been very influential in EU external policy-making over the past decade. Therefore, this chapter provides an overview of the toolbox of EU external relations law, utilizing the explanatory value of internal/international, binding/ non-binding, and conventional/autonomous. Since each external policy area possesses its own dynamic as to which of these instruments will be used more often and in which form, we refer the reader to the policy-specific chapters in this book.

3 EU INTERNAL INSTRUMENTS

(i) Hard law in EU external relations

Article 288 TFEU

To exercise the Union's competences, the institutions shall adopt regulations, directives, decisions, recommendations and opinions.

A regulation shall have general application. It shall be binding in its entirety and directly applicable in all Member States.

A directive shall be binding, as to the result to be achieved, upon each Member State to which it is addressed, but shall leave to the national authorities the choice of form and methods.

A decision shall be binding in its entirety. A decision which specifies those to whom it is addressed shall be binding only on them.

Recommendations and opinions shall have no binding force.

While this book is not the place for an exhaustive review of Union law-making, it should be clear that all instruments utilized by the Union to legislate internal policy matters can and are being used in the context of EU external relations. A good knowledge of EU legislative and non-legislative instruments and the procedures through which they are adopted (Article 289 TFEU, etc.) is therefore imperative, and for that we refer to relevant literature.[1]

---

[1] D. Chalmers, G. Davies and G. Monti, *European Union Law*, 2nd edn (Cambridge: Cambridge University Press, 2010), Chapter 3, Union Law-Making.

The first three instruments named in Article 288 TFEU are legally binding, and will only enjoy that status if they are duly adopted in accordance with the procedure set out in the relevant competence-conferring article. For example, Article 194 TFEU (energy) requires that the ordinary legislative procedure be used to adopt instruments in this domain (Article 289 TFEU), and only exceptionally the special legislative procedure. Regulations, Directives and Decisions all have their role to play in EU external relations.

Regulations can be relevant for external relations in at least two ways: they may regulate specifically a matter purely of external relevance; or where they organize an internal policy aspect they may also have a degree of external relevance. Examples of the first aspect include the Trade Barriers Regulation (TBR) and the many Regulations adopted in relation to anti-dumping and countervailing duties (see Chapter 9), Financing Regulations of EU development cooperation (see Chapter 10) or the Regulations organizing EU and Member State cooperation in certain policy areas, such as in the context of international civil aviation.[2] These Regulations are examples which legally organize an aspect purely of EU external relations, and by their nature have general application, are binding in their entirety and are directly applicable in all Member States. An example of the second aspect is the Rome I Regulation concerning contractual obligations. This instrument organizes an important aspect of the EU's *internal* AFSJ (see Chapter 14), but contains several clauses on the relationship with pertinent international conventions.[3]

Directives, by their nature focusing on the result to be achieved but giving Member States a choice of form and method, will most often display the second quality that Regulations may also exhibit. It is uncommon for a Directive to organize a purely external policy aspect, but where they regulate some aspect of the internal market they very often acquire an international dimension. For example, in Chapter 13 we analyse the Directive organizing the European gas market, including the way in which energy companies are structured. This Directive contains a politically highly sensitive article that requires companies in third countries to respect principles of EU market liberalization equally (the so-called 'Gazprom' clause).

Decisions mentioned in Article 288 TFEU may equally be relevant in external relations. Within the EU legal order, most Decisions are addressed to Member States, with fewer addressed to private parties and mostly in the area of competition law. In external relations, an example of such a general Decision will be further examined in Chapter 13, organizing cooperation between the EU and Member States in relation to Member State energy agreements with third countries. Among others, Decisions may also be found in anti-dumping and anti-subsidy proceedings.

These three legally binding instruments require that they be adopted in accordance with the procedures set out in the relevant competence-conferring provision. Most often, this will be the ordinary legislative procedure as set out in Article 289 TFEU.

(ii) Soft law in EU external relations

Article 288 states that recommendations and opinions shall have no binding force. Beyond these two non-binding instruments mentioned in the Treaties, there are many other measures which

---

[2] Regulation 847/2004/EC of the European Parliament and of the Council of 29 April 2004 on the negotiation and implementation of air service agreements between Member States and third countries, OJ 2004 No. L157/7.

[3] Regulation 593/2008/EC of the European Parliament and of the Council of 17 June 2008 on the law applicable to contractual obligations (Rome I), OJ 2008 No. L177/6.

are generically referred to as 'soft law'. These are defined as 'rules of conduct that are laid down in instruments which have not been attributed legally binding force as such, but nevertheless may have certain (indirect) legal effects, and that are aimed at and may produce practical effects'.[4] In the EU legal order, soft law reportedly accounts for 13 per cent of all EU law,[5] and in EU external relations law soft law equally occupies a prominent position. A non-exhaustive summary of soft law includes: European Council Conclusions, Council Conclusions, Commission Communications, Joint Communications, Green Papers, White Papers, Non-Papers, Joint Papers, Joint Letters, Resolutions, Strategies, Arrangements, Working Arrangements, Inter-Institutional Arrangements, Declarations, Resolutions, Action Plans, Reports, Interim Reports, Progress Reports, Programmes, Memoranda and so on.

Soft law instruments do not possess the legal effect of a Regulation or Directive. This because they have not been adopted through procedures laid down in the Treaties. However, they often will produce practical effects by setting in motion, or being part of, the external policy-making or legislative process. In that sense, soft law instruments will have to be 'adopted' by the relevant EU body within the scope of the role accorded to it by the Treaties. Soft law may not be utilized to avoid the principle of conferred powers (Article 5 TFEU) or institutional balance (Article 13 TFEU),[6] and the absence of legal binding force does not give an EU body the freedom to act as it pleases. In *France* v. *Commission*, that Member State sought annulment of the decision by which the Commission adopted non-legally binding 'Guidelines on Regulatory Cooperation and Transparency' between the Commission and the US Trade Representative (USTR). France argued that the prerogatives of the Council had been infringed under current Article 218 TFEU, insofar as it constituted a binding agreement which the Council should adopt. The Commission stated that the institutional balance could not be affected since the guidelines were to be applied on a voluntary basis, and lacked legal binding force.[7]

C-233/02 *France* v. *Commission* [2004] ECR I-2759

38. By its first plea, the French Government merely submits that the Guidelines should have been concluded by the Council rather than by the Commission, in accordance with Article 300 EC, since they constitute a legally binding agreement.

39. On the other hand, the French Government in no way claims that a measure exhibiting the characteristics of the Guidelines must, even if it has no binding force, come under the sole competence of the Council. There is therefore no need for the Court to extend the subject-matter of the action of which it is seized.

40. Nevertheless, this judgment cannot be construed as upholding the Commission's argument that the fact that a measure such as the Guidelines is not binding is sufficient to confer on that institution the competence to adopt it. Determining the conditions under which such a measure may be adopted requires that the division of powers and the institutional balance established by the Treaty in the field of the common commercial policy be duly taken into account, since in this case the measure seeks to reduce the risk of conflict related to the existence of technical barriers to trade in goods.

---

[4] The definition of soft law which we entertain is that of Linda Senden, *Soft Law in European Community Law* (Portland, Oregon: Hart Publishing, 2004), p. 112.

[5] Chalmers *et al.*, 'European Union Law', p. 101.

[6] C-233/02 *France* v. *Commission* [2004] ECR I-2759.

[7] C-233/02 *France* v. *Commission* [2004] ECR I-2759, para 33.

41. Moreover, both the Transatlantic Economic Partnership and the Action Plan were approved by the Council, as is made clear in the memorandum of 9 April 2002 sent by the Commission to the committee set up pursuant to Article 133(3) EC, and the committee was regularly informed of the progress of the negotiations relating to the drafting of the Guidelines by the Commission's services.

42. In the light of that clarification, the intention of the parties must in principle be the decisive criterion for the purpose of determining whether or not the Guidelines are binding, as the Commission rightly contends.

43. In the present case, that intention is clearly expressed, . . . in the text of the Guidelines itself, paragraph 7 of which specifies that the purpose of the document is to establish guidelines which regulators of the United States Federal Government and the services of the Commission 'intend to apply on a voluntary basis'. In those circumstances, and without its being necessary to consider the specific importance which the use of the terms 'should' or 'will' rather than 'shall' could assume in an international agreement concluded by the Community, it need only be stated that on the basis of that information, the parties had no intention of entering into legally binding commitments when they concluded the Guidelines.

44. As pointed out by the Commission, without contradiction by the French Government, the history of the negotiations confirms that the intention of the parties not to enter into binding commitments was expressly reiterated throughout the negotiations on the Guidelines.

45. It follows that the Guidelines do not constitute a binding agreement and therefore do not fall within the scope of Article 300 EC.

The Court thus ruled that even if a given instrument is non-binding, that this does not give an institution the power to adopt it. The application of the principles of conferral (Article 5 TEU) and institutional balance (Article 13 TEU) continue to apply and must be respected. While this case law concerned an international soft legal instrument, the principle evidently applies across all soft law utilized by the EU, internal or international. In paragraph 41, the Court then confirmed that the prerogatives of the Council had been duly respected by the Commission through approval of the overall Action Plan with the USA (another soft law instrument), and by regularly informing the Working Party responsible for CCP. Finally, notice that the final three paragraphs of the quotation are pertinent for the definition of international agreements discussed in section 4 below: the intention of the parties is essential in establishing whether or not a binding international agreement exists.

There are many actors in EU external relations that adopt a wide range of soft law instruments. In the following paragraphs we shall highlight 'Conclusions' adopted by the European Council and Council, and 'Communications' adopted by the Commission and possibly the HR. Of all soft law instruments, these form the bread and butter of EU external policy-making.

In the General Provisions on EU external action (Title V TEU), Article 22(1) TEU states that the European Council 'shall identify the strategic interests and objectives of the Union'. The European Council is one of the EU institutions, and is legally empowered to adopt Decisions to carry out its task. However, most often this institution carries out its mandate to steer the Union through the adoption of Conclusions at the end of its meetings. They are (meticulously) negotiated outcomes of meetings by the Heads of State and Government (HoSG), and are crucial soft law instruments because the Treaty endows the European Council with setting out the future direction of EU external action. Conclusions of the European Council will therefore trigger action at all levels of governance within the Union: within the Member States themselves, and within and between the EU institutions. European Council Conclusions may call on the Member States to refrain from certain action, may prompt the Council of Ministers to flesh out a new policy direction, may approve of the accession of a new Member State, or may decide the EU's position towards crucially important international events. Thus, different actors will be implementing the strategic vision set out by the European Council in accordance with Article 22 TEU.

European Council Conclusions, Brussels, 22 May 2013

6. It remains crucial to further intensify the diversification of Europe's energy supply and develop indigenous energy resources to ensure security of supply, reduce the EU's external energy dependency and stimulate economic growth. To that end:
   (a) the deployment of renewable energy sources will continue, while ensuring their cost effectiveness, further market integration and grid stability and building on the experience in some Member States which have heavily invested in renewable energy technologies;
   (b) the Commission intends to assess a more systematic recourse to on-shore and off-shore indigenous sources of energy with a view to their safe, sustainable and cost-effective exploitation while respecting Member States' choices of energy mix;
   (c) given the increasing interlinking of internal and external energy markets, Member States will enhance their cooperation in support of the external dimension of EU energy policy; before the end of 2013, the Council will follow up on its conclusions of November 2011 and review developments regarding EU external energy policy, including the need to ensure a level playing-field vis-à-vis third country energy producers as well as nuclear safety in the EU neighbourhood following up on the European Council conclusions of June 2012.

The above extract illustrates the constant interaction that takes place through the progressive adoption of Conclusions by the European Council and the Council. The European Council refers to preceding Council Conclusions in the energy sphere from November 2011, as well as its own conclusions on related matters of June 2012. Then the European Council looks to the future, and asks that the Council would formulate means by which the Member States could better cooperate in the external dimension of EU energy policy (see Chapter 13). It sets a deadline before the end of 2013, and gives a broad indication of what is expected in terms of content. The response to this request will be the adoption of Conclusions by the Council itself, with a greater level of depth and precision in accordance with its own position in the EU institutional balance. Namely, Article 16(6) prescribes that 'The Foreign Affairs Council shall elaborate the Union's external action on the basis of strategic guidelines laid down by the European Council and ensure that the Union's action is consistent'. This function for the Council applies across all policy domains, and not just its foreign affairs configuration. In short: in all policy areas of EU (external) action, a constant stream of Conclusions is adopted to follow up ongoing policy matters constantly, and push them forward in the desirable direction. The substance of these Conclusions will be prepared in the preparatory bodies of the Council (see Chapter 1), notably COREPER and the Working Groups. These bodies will receive much of their input not only from Member State representatives, but also from the Commission and the EEAS. The most effective instrument used is the Communication.

Communications are most often adopted by the Commission, sometimes jointly with the HR if it falls within the scope of her competence. The extract below explains the role of the Commission in formulating the ENP, and analyses the importance of soft legal Communications in doing so.

B. Van Vooren, 'A Case Study of "Soft Law" in EU External Relations: The European Neighbourhood Policy' (2009) 34 *European Law Review* 705

The first ENP Communication was published in March 2003, entitled 'Wider Europe–Neighbourhood: A New Framework for Relations with our Eastern and Southern Neighbours'. . . . In subsequent years, Commission Communications have at regular (yearly) intervals evaluated and redirected the course of this policy, and it is no exaggeration to state that these milestone Communications have formed the backbone of this policy. With the October 2003 European Council welcoming "progress made on the Commission's Wider Europe–New Neighbourhood Initiative", one may query whether those Communications may be considered informal steering soft (legal) acts? . . . The role of the Wider Europe Communication includes a definite steering function. Recall that steering instruments independently indicate the direction of future policy and the principles on which such action is based. The Wider Europe Communication is evidently not independent in that it exists in a policy vacuum, and is undoubtedly interrelated with [relevant European Council Conclusions, Council Conclusions,] the financing instruments of that time and the existing bilateral agreements with third countries. Nevertheless as the title of the instrument indicates, it seeks to lay down "[a] new framework for relations with the Eastern and Southern Neighbours" and can be considered steering both in terms of its substantive and methodological proposals. In terms of substance, this Communication famously stated that the neighbours should be offered the prospect of participation in the four freedoms and their "stake in the internal market". Evidently that Communication may be considered as only "preparatory" to the extent that this reflects previous political agreement [at Council level] or where the Council later rejects that assertion. . . . Subsequent Council Conclusions also did nothing to refute that position: the Council Conclusions of March 18, 2003 welcomed this Communication, and the ensuing debate focused on issues which were more contentious: the need to differentiate between third countries and the fact that the ENP is separate from the question of EU membership. The Communication is thus a steering instrument since it adds a distinct direction to a policy which is a priority for the Union as a whole [as decided at the level of the Council and European Council]. In terms of methodology, this Communication proposed "that the principles of differentiation and progressivity should be established by means of country and/or regional Action Plans". . . . the Commission is instrumental in shaping the substantial offer made to the neighbouring countries.

4 INTERNATIONAL AGREEMENTS

(i) The legal nature of international agreements

International agreements are not defined by the Treaties. Article 216 TFEU merely provides the following:

Article 216(1) TFEU

The Union may conclude an agreement with one or more third countries or international organisations where the Treaties so provide or where the conclusion of an agreement is necessary in order to achieve, within the framework of the Union's policies, one of the objectives referred to in the Treaties, or is provided for in a legally binding Union act or is likely to affect common rules or alter their scope.

Notwithstanding the absence of a definition (or perhaps exactly because of this), it is obvious that the term should be read in its international context, and thus the international law definitions apply. The difficulty lies in the fact that also the 1969 Vienna Convention on the Law of Treaties (VCLT) (Article 2(1)(a)) does not define international agreements. Instead, it defines the concept of 'treaty' as follows:

Article 2(1)(a) Vienna Convention on the Law of Treaties

'Treaty' means an international agreement concluded between States in written form and governed by international law, whether embodied in a single instrument or in two or more instruments and whatever its particular designation.

As we will see, the international agreements concluded by the EU can be said to follow this description and are therefore 'treaties' in the sense of the Vienna Convention. The same may hold true for international contractual obligations that have not been given the heading of 'international agreement', but bear labels such as 'Convention' or 'Memorandum of Understanding'. Agreements may also be concluded in the form of an exchange of letters. As long as parties agree that they enter into a legal commitment, the EU Treaty procedures apply (Article 218 TFEU). This has been confirmed by the Court when it described an international agreement as any undertaking entered into by entities subject to international law which has binding force, whatever its formal designation.[8] The fact that the 1969 Vienna Convention refers to states only is solved by the 1986 Vienna Convention on the Law of Treaties between States and International Organizations and between International Organizations, which contains a similar definition, taking into account the fact that international organizations may also conclude treaties. Although the concluding procedure is 'governed by EU law' (as the conclusion of treaties between states is usually regulated in domestic law), there is no doubt that the final agreement between the EU and a third state or international organization is governed by international law.

The use of the term 'international agreement' rather than 'treaty' therefore has no specific legal meaning, but at least prevents confusion as in EU law the term '(the) Treaties' is usually reserved for the TEU and the TFEU as well as for the accession Treaties. In other words, for primary EU law.

The internal binding nature of concluded international agreements is confirmed by Article 216(2) TFEU.

Article 216(2) TFEU

Agreements concluded by the Union are binding upon the institutions of the Union and on its Member States.

The first part of this sentence follows from the international law concept of *pacta sunt servanda*, which is codified in the Vienna Convention (Article 26). This principle holds that 'Every treaty in

---

[8] See Opinion 1/75 *Re Understanding on a Local Cost Standard* [1975] ECR 1355. See also Case C-327/91 *France* v. *Commission* [1994] ECR I-3641, para 27.

force is binding upon the parties to it and must be performed by them in good faith.' This also implies that the second part of Article 216(2) is in fact not a reflection of that principle, as the Member States are not (necessarily) parties to agreements concluded by the Union. Member States are therefore bound by EU international agreements on the basis of EU law, rather than on the basis of international law. In many cases the implementation of these agreements calls for Member State action. In a way, international agreements are similar to secondary legislation enacted by the EU and as an 'integral part' of the EU legal order they cannot be ignored by the Member States. Yet, as will be explained in Chapter 7, this does not automatically lead to supremacy and direct effect of all agreements concluded by the EU. While the status of international agreements within the EU legal order would perhaps lead to a de facto supremacy, the Court has not been willing to accept an automatic direct effect for all agreements.

(ii) Express and implied competences

As we have seen, Article 216(1) TFEU provides for a competence of the EU in various circumstances:

- where the Treaties so provide, or
- where the conclusion of an agreement is necessary in order to achieve, within the framework of the Union's policies, one of the objectives referred to in the Treaties, or
- is provided for in a legally binding Union act, or
- is likely to affect common rules or alter their scope.

The passages contained in this provision capture a rather simplified codification of highly complex case law on EU external competence. For a full understanding of this provision we refer to Chapters 3 and 4 on existence and nature of EU external competence. Here we briefly look at instances where the EU Treaties expressly mention that the EU may conclude international agreements.

Whereas the original Community Treaty did not include many express competences to conclude international agreements (in fact, these were limited to tariff agreements, trade agreements and AAs), the current Treaties list a number of areas in which the EU has an express competence to conclude international agreements: the readmission of illegal immigrants (Article 79(3) TFEU); cooperation in research and technological development (Article 186 TFEU); environmental policy (Article 191(4) TFEU); CCP (Article 207 TFEU); development cooperation (Article 209(2) TFEU); economic, financial and technical cooperation with third countries (Article 212(2) TFEU); humanitarian aid (Article 214(4) TFEU); AAs (Article 217 TFEU); the monetary union (Article 219(1) and (3) TFEU); and common foreign, security and defence policy (Article 37 TEU). In other provisions, the Treaty refers to the need for international cooperation in certain areas, without expressly mentioning international agreements. This is for instance the case in relation to education and sport (Article 165(3) TFEU); vocational training (Article 166(3) TFEU); culture (Article 167(3) TFEU) and public health (Article 168(3) TFEU), where it is provided that the Union and its Member States shall foster cooperation with third countries and international organizations. Similar references may be found elsewhere in the Treaties, such as in Article 220(1) TFEU: 'The Union shall establish all appropriate forms of cooperation with the organs of the United Nations and its specialised agencies, the Council of Europe, the Organisation for Security and Cooperation in Europe and the Organisation for Economic Co-operation and Development.'

The Agreement (below) between the EU and the US forms an example of a bilateral treaty to which the Member States as such are not a party. This means that their obligations would have to flow from EU law.

Agreement between the United States of America and the European Union on the use and transfer of passenger name records to the United States Department of Homeland Security, OJ 2012 No. L215/5

THE UNITED STATES OF AMERICA, hereinafter referred to also as 'the United States', and
  THE EUROPEAN UNION, hereinafter referred to also as 'the EU', together hereinafter referred to as 'the Parties' . . .
  HEREBY AGREE:
  CHAPTER I
  GENERAL PROVISIONS

Article 1 Purpose
1. The purpose of this Agreement is to ensure security and to protect the life and safety of the public.
2. For this purpose, this Agreement sets forth the responsibilities of the Parties with respect to the conditions under which PNR may be transferred, processed and used, and protected.

Article 2 Scope
1. PNR, as set forth in the Guidelines of the International Civil Aviation Organization, shall mean the record created by air carriers or their authorized agents for each journey booked by or on behalf of any passenger and contained in carriers' reservation systems, departure control systems, or equivalent systems providing similar functionality (collectively referred to in this Agreement as "reservation systems"). Specifically, as used in this Agreement, PNR consists of the data types set forth in the Annex to this Agreement ("Annex").
2. This Agreement shall apply to carriers operating passenger flights between the European Union and the United States.
3. This Agreement shall also apply to carriers incorporated or storing data in the European Union and operating passenger flights to or from the United States.

Article 3 Provision of PNR
The Parties agree that carriers shall provide PNR contained in their reservation systems to DHS as required by and in accordance with DHS standards and consistent with this agreement. Should PNR transferred by carriers include data beyond those listed in the Annex, DHS shall delete such data upon receipt.

Article 4 Use of PNR
1. The United States collects, uses and processes PNR for the purposes of preventing, detecting, investigating, and prosecuting:
(a) Terrorist offenses and related crimes, including
    (i) Conduct that –
        1. involves a violent act or an act dangerous to human life, property, or infrastructure; and
        2. appears to be intended to –
            a. intimidate or coerce a civilian population;
            b. influence the policy of a government by intimidation or coercion; or
            c. affect the conduct of a government by mass destruction, assassination, kidnapping, or hostage-taking.

(ii) Activities constituting an offense within the scope of and as defined in applicable international conventions and protocols relating to terrorism;

(iii) Providing or collecting funds, by any means, directly or indirectly, with the intention that they should be used or in the knowledge that they are to be used, in full or in part, in order to carry out any of the acts described in subparagraphs (i) or (ii);

(iv) Attempting to commit any of the acts described in subparagraphs (i), (ii), or (iii);

(v) Participating as an accomplice in the commission of any of the acts described in subparagraphs (i), (ii), or (iii);

(vi) Organizing or directing others to commit any of the acts described in subparagraphs (i), (ii), or (iii);

(vii) Contributing in any other way to the commission of any of the acts described in subparagraphs (i), (ii), or (iii);

(viii) Threatening to commit an act described in subparagraph (i) under circumstances which indicate that the threat is credible;

(b) Other crimes that are punishable by a sentence of imprisonment of three years or more and that are transnational in nature.

A crime is considered as transnational in nature in particular if:

(i) It is committed in more than one country;

(ii) It is committed in one country but a substantial part of its preparation, planning, direction or control takes place in another country;

(iii) It is committed in one country but involves an organized criminal group that engages in criminal activities in more than one country;

(iv) It is committed in one country but has substantial effects in another country; or

(v) It is committed in one country and the offender is in or intends to travel to another country.

2. PNR may be used and processed on a case-by-case basis where necessary in view of a serious threat and for the protection of vital interests of any individual or if ordered by a court.

3. PNR may be used and processed by DHS to identify persons who would be subject to closer questioning or examination upon arrival to or departure from the United States or who may require further examination.

4. Paragraphs 1, 2, and 3 shall be without prejudice to domestic law enforcement, judicial powers, or proceedings, where other violations of law or indications thereof are detected in the course of the use and processing of PNR. . . .

Article 27 Final provisions

1. This Agreement shall enter into force on the first day of the month after the date on which the Parties have exchanged notifications indicating that they have completed their internal procedures for this purpose.

2. This Agreement, as of the date of its entry into force, shall supersede the July 23 and 26, 2007 Agreement.

3. This Agreement will only apply to the territory of Denmark, the United Kingdom or Ireland, if the European Commission notifies the United States in writing that Denmark, the United Kingdom or Ireland has chosen to be bound by this Agreement.

4. If the European Commission notifies the United States before the entry into force of this Agreement that it will apply to the territory of Denmark, the United Kingdom or Ireland, this Agreement shall apply to the territory of the relevant State on the same day as for the other EU Member States bound by this Agreement.

5. If the European Commission notifies the United States after entry into force of this Agreement that it applies to the territory of Denmark, the United Kingdom or Ireland, this Agreement shall apply to the territory of the relevant State on the first day following receipt of the notification by the United States.

Done at Brussels this fourteenth day of December 2011, in two originals in the English language.

Pursuant to EU law, this Agreement shall also be drawn up by the EU in the Bulgarian, Czech, Danish, Dutch, Estonian, Finnish, French, German, Greek, Hungarian, Italian, Latvian, Lithuanian, Maltese, Polish, Portuguese, Romanian, Slovak, Slovenian, Spanish and Swedish languages.

For the European Union   For the United States

The EU is a party to well over 1,000 treaties.[9] With the increasing internal competences, the scope of the Union's legal dealings with third states was extended to almost all areas covered by the Treaties (see Chapter 3). The EU's Treaties Database thus lists international agreements in the areas of agriculture, coal and steel, commercial policy, competition, consumers, culture, customs, development, economic and monetary affairs, education, training, youth, energy, enlargement, enterprise, environment, external relations, fisheries, food safety, foreign and security policy, fraud, information society, internal market, justice, freedom and security, public health, research and innovation, taxation, trade and transport. Numbers range from 134 agreements in the trade area to one on culture.

(iii) Concluding international agreements

Whereas the Vienna Convention uses the term 'conclusion' for the entire treaty-making process, which encompasses, inter alia, the phases of negotiation, initialling and signing, the EU Treaties clearly differentiate between the different phases. While the procedures in principle apply to all Union areas, we will note that some special rules have been created for international agreements concluded in the area of CFSP (see also Chapter 11).

(a) Negotiating an international agreement

According to Article 218 TFEU, which lists the entire procedure, the process is very much in the hands of the Council, although in practice it is above all the Commission that is the central actor in both the preparation and the negotiations themselves.

Article 218(2) TFEU

The Council shall authorise the opening of negotiations, adopt negotiating directives, authorise the signing of agreements and conclude them.

Yet, it starts with a recommendation to the Council from the Commission or the HR:

Article 218(3) TFEU

The Commission, or the High Representative of the Union for Foreign Affairs and Security Policy where the agreement envisaged relates exclusively or principally to the common foreign and security policy, shall

---

[9] See the Treaties Office Database of the European External Action Service, at http://ec.europa.eu/world/agreements/default.home.do.

submit recommendations to the Council, which shall adopt a decision authorising the opening of negotiations and, depending on the subject of the agreement envisaged, nominating the Union negotiator or the head of the Union's negotiating team.

Thus, apart from the situation where an agreement 'relates exclusively or principally' to CFSP – in which case the HR is in charge of a recommendation – the Commission shall submit recommendations to the Council. History has shown that the question of whether an agreement 'relates exclusively or principally' to CFSP or CSDP may be difficult to answer (see the analysis of the *ECOWAS* case in Chapters 5 and 11). On the basis of the (unpublished) recommendation by either the Commission or the HR, the Council adopts a decision which in turn forms the basis for the negotiations. Depending on the subject matter of the agreement this is done by QMV or unanimity. The context of paragraph 3 suggests that the Commission will be appointed as the negotiator, unless it is a CFSP agreement, in which case the HR will be appointed negotiator. This would also be in line with the general role of the Commission in the union's external representation (compare Article 17 TEU). In case of a hybrid agreement which covers both CFSP and other matters, both the Commission and the HR may be part of the negotiating team. All of this reveals that the identification of the negotiator is largely settled by primary law.

The negotiator acts within the framework of special Directives issued by the Council:

Article 218(4) TFEU

The Council may address directives to the negotiator and designate a special committee in consultation with which the negotiations must be conducted.

The special committees are usually composed of national governmental experts, through which the Council will be able to control the process.

Article 218(1) refers to 'specific provisions laid down in Article 207'. This article deals with the Union's CCP (see Chapter 9), and its paragraph 3 lists the following:

Article 207(3) TFEU

The Commission shall make recommendations to the Council, which shall authorise it to open the necessary negotiations. The Council and the Commission shall be responsible for ensuring that the agreements negotiated are compatible with internal Union policies and rules.

The Commission shall conduct these negotiations in consultation with a special committee appointed by the Council to assist the Commission in this task and within the framework of such directives as the Council may issue to it. The Commission shall report regularly to the special committee and to the European Parliament on the progress of negotiations.

This provision ensures that the Commission is the only negotiator in the CCP. At the same time, the Commission is to report to the EP. While the latter institution is not mentioned explicitly in the regular negotiating procedure, on the basis of Article 218(10) TFEU the 'European Parliament shall be immediately and fully informed at all stages of the procedure'. This, arguably, includes the negotiating stage. Whenever consent of the Parliament in the end is needed, it can obviously use this as an instrument to claim to be heard during the earlier stages. In any case, the EP's involvement seems to be better guaranteed since the conclusion of the 2012 inter-institutional agreement, on the basis of which the Commission agreed to involve Parliament during the various stages of the process.[10]

In general, negotiations end by the initialling of the text. For the Union, this is done by the negotiator. This is what the Vienna Convention refers to as 'the adoption of the text' (Article 9) and implies that parties are ready to take the text back home for approval.

Council Decision 2012/471/EU of 13 December 2011 on the signing, on behalf of the Union, of the Agreement between the United States of America and the European Union on the use and transfer of Passenger Name Records to the United States Department of Homeland Security, OJ 2012 No. L215/1

THE COUNCIL OF THE EUROPEAN UNION,

Having regard to the Treaty on the Functioning of the European Union, and in particular Articles 82(1)(d) and 87(2)(a), in conjunction with Article 218(5) thereof,

Having regard to the proposal from the European Commission, ... HAS ADOPTED THIS DECISION:

Article 1

The signing of the Agreement between the United States of America and the European Union on the use and transfer of Passenger Name Records to the United States Department of Homeland Security is hereby authorised on behalf of the Union, subject to the conclusion of the said Agreement.

Article 2

The President of the Council is authorised to designate the person(s) empowered to sign the Agreement on behalf of the Union.

Article 3

The Declaration of the Union on the Agreement in respect of its obligations under Articles 17 and 23 thereof is hereby approved.

The text of the Declaration is annexed to this decision.

Article 4

This Decision shall enter into force on the day of its adoption.

Done at Brussels, 13 December 2011.

For the Council

The President

(b) Concluding an international agreement

The actual conclusion of an international agreement takes place in two stages on the basis of a decision by the Council: signature and conclusion. Article 218 therefore continues:

---

[10] Framework Agreement on Relations between the European Parliament and the European Commission, OJ 2010 No. L304/47.

Article 218(5) and (6) TFEU

5. The Council, on a proposal by the negotiator, shall adopt a decision authorising the signing of the agreement and, if necessary, its provisional application before entry into force.
6. The Council, on a proposal by the negotiator, shall adopt a decision concluding the agreement.

Although in practice it may not always be necessary to take these two steps, they follow the logic presented in the Vienna Conventions on the Law of Treaties. Even before a formal entry into force, signing the agreement already has legal consequences, in the sense that 'A State is obliged to refrain from acts which would defeat the object and purpose of a treaty' (Article 18 Vienna Convention). Indeed, on the basis of international treaty law, signature is one way for a state or international organization to express the necessary *consent to be bound*, albeit that failure to conclude/ratify the agreement formally (for instance because of domestic parliamentary objection) may form a reason for a state to 'un-sign' in order to get rid of its obligations under Article 18 Vienna Convention. Article 218(5) also refers to the possibility of provisional application (compare Article 25 Vienna Convention), which allows the parties to apply the treaty provision provisionally, pending the entry into force of the agreement. Considering the long period that is usually needed for the ratification of mixed agreements (see below), this may offer a way out.

Actual conclusion of the agreement has both an external and an internal dimension. *Externally*, it finalizes the expression of the consent to be bound and the Union becomes a party to the agreement (the entry into force of which is dependent on what the parties agreed on). This is usually done by notifying the other parties or the depositary by way of an instrument of ratification (a letter in which the ratification is expressed). Prior to that, *internally*, a decision has to be taken upon a proposal by the negotiator (Article 218(5)). This decision is comparable to other decisions taken by the Council and lists the considerations leading to the decision, the legal basis, as well as further procedural points.

Council Decision 2012/472/EU of 26 April 2012 on the conclusion of the Agreement between the United States of America and the European Union on the use and transfer of passenger name records to the United States Department of Homeland Security, OJ 2012 No. L215/4

THE COUNCIL OF THE EUROPEAN UNION,

Having regard to the Treaty on the Functioning of the European Union, and in particular Article 82(1)(d) and Article 87(2)(a), in conjunction with Article 218(6)(a) thereof,

Having regard to the proposal from the European Commission,

Having regard to the consent of the European Parliament ... HAS ADOPTED THIS DECISION:

Article 1

The Agreement between the United States of America and the European Union on the use and transfer of passenger name records to the United States Department of Homeland Security is hereby approved on behalf of the Union.

The text of the Agreement is attached to this Decision.

Article 2

The President of the Council shall designate the person(s) empowered to proceed, on behalf of the Union, to the exchange of the notifications provided for in Article 27 of the Agreement, in order to express the consent of the Union to be bound by the Agreement.

Article 3

This Decision shall enter into force on the day following that of its publication in the Official Journal of the European Union.

Done at Luxembourg, 26 April 2012.

For the Council

The President

Article 218(8) provides the voting rules.

Article 218(8) TFEU

The Council shall act by a qualified majority throughout the procedure.

However, it shall act unanimously when the agreement covers a field for which unanimity is required for the adoption of a Union act as well as for association agreements and the agreements referred to in Article 212 with the States which are candidates for accession. The Council shall also act unanimously for the agreement on accession of the Union to the European Convention for the Protection of Human Rights and Fundamental Freedoms; the decision concluding this agreement shall enter into force after it has been approved by the Member States in accordance with their respective constitutional requirements.

Hence, QMV is the rule, but unanimity shall be used in certain specific cases as well as in relation to subject matters that would internally also require unanimity. Examples include CFSP/CSDP matters, or indirect taxation (Article 113 TFEU). In addition, Article 207(4) refers to the need for unanimity in relation to certain trade agreements.

The above-mentioned decision to conclude the Agreement with the United States refers to the 'consent of the European Parliament'. Indeed, taking into account the fact that, once concluded, international agreements form an integral part of the Union's legal order and that their substance and procedural content may directly affect EU citizens and companies, it should not come as a surprise that the treaty legislator decided to extend the role the EP enjoys under the regular legislative procedure to the adoption of international agreements. Article 218(6) therefore calls for the consent of the EP in the following cases:

Article 218(6)(a) TFEU

...

(i) association agreements;

(ii) agreement on Union accession to the European Convention for the Protection of Human Rights and Fundamental Freedoms;

(iii) agreements establishing a specific institutional framework by organising cooperation procedures;

(iv) agreements with important budgetary implications for the Union;

(v) agreements covering fields to which either the ordinary legislative procedure applies, or the special legislative procedure where consent by the European Parliament is required.

The European Parliament and the Council may, in an urgent situation, agree upon a time-limit for consent.

In other cases the EP shall be 'consulted' only. The EP shall deliver its opinion within a time limit which the Council may set depending on the urgency of the matter. In the absence of an opinion within that time limit, the Council may act. The only exception is formed for cases 'where agreements relate exclusively to the common foreign and security policy'. However, based on the general rule in Article 218(10), 'The European Parliament shall be immediately and fully informed at all stages of the procedure', which implies that also in relation to CFSP/CSDP agreements the Parliament should at least be informed of the final result of the negotiations, at which stage it could deliver an opinion.

Although not explicitly referred to, this consultation may also be part of a special procedure that is foreseen in relation to agreements concluded in the framework of the monetary union.

Article 219(3) TFEU

Where agreements concerning monetary or foreign exchange regime matters need to be negotiated by the Union with one or more third States or international organisations, the Council, on a recommendation from the Commission and after consulting the European Central Bank, shall decide the arrangements for the negotiation and for the conclusion of such agreements. These arrangements shall ensure that the Union expresses a single position. The Commission shall be fully associated with the negotiations.

Article 218 is quite clear about the fact that international agreements to which the EU becomes a party are concluded by the Council. In the past, however, the Court agreed that under certain circumstances the Commission has a competence to conclude 'international administrative agreements'. In such cases the Commission would not act on behalf of the EU (and thus the EU itself would not be a party).[11]

At the same time, it is clear that the Council should respect the rules of the game. Since Article 218 provides for the Council (and the Council alone) to adopt the necessary decisions, the Commission raised the question of whether the decision to conclude a mixed agreement can also be taken by 'Council and of the Representatives of the Governments of the Member States of the European Union, meeting within the Council', as was the case with the Air Transport Agreement with the United States.

---

[11] Case C-327/91 *France* v. *Commission* [1994] ECR I-3641.

Action brought on 18 January 2012 – *European Commission* v. *Council of the European Union* (Case C-28/12)[12]

The applicant claims that the Court should:

annul the Decision of the Council and of the Representatives of the Governments of the Member States of the European Union, meeting within the Council of 16 June 2011 on the signing, on behalf of the Union, and provisional application of the Air Transport Agreement between the United States of America, of the first part, the European Union and its Member States, of the second part, Iceland, of the third part, and the Kingdom of Norway, of the fourth part; and on the signing, on behalf of the Union, and provisional application of the Ancillary Agreement between the European Union and its Member States, of the first part, Iceland, of the second part, and the Kingdom of Norway, of the third part, on the application of the Air Transport Agreement between the United States of America, of the first part, the European Union and its Member States, of the second part, Iceland, of the third part, and the Kingdom of Norway, of the fourth part (2011/708/EU);

order the effects of Decision 2011/708/EU to be maintained;

order the Council to pay the costs.

Pleas in law and main arguments

By way of the present application the Commission seeks the annulment of the "Decision of the Council and of the Representatives of the Governments of the Member States of the European Union, meeting within the Council" of 16 June 2011 (Decision 2011/708/EU) (hereinafter referred to as "the contested decision" or "the contested measure") which was adopted in the field of air transport. It concerns the signing and provisional application of the accession of Iceland and the Kingdom of Norway to the Air Transport Agreement between the United States, of the one part, and the EU and its Member States, of the other part, as well as the signing and provisional application of the Ancillary Agreement thereto.

The Application is founded on the following three pleas in law:

The Commission argues, first, that adopting the contested decision the Council has violated Article 13 (2) of the Treaty on European Union (TEU) in conjunction with Article 218 (2) and (5) of the Treaty on the Functioning of the European Union (TFEU), in so far as it transpires from Article 218 (2) and (5) TFEU that the Council is the institution designated to authorise the signing and provisional application of agreements. Therefore, the decision should have been solely taken by the Council and not also by the Member States, meeting within the Council.

With its second plea, the Commission argues that by adopting the contested decision, the Council violated the first subparagraph of Article 218 (8) TFEU in conjunction with Article 100 (2) TFEU pursuant to which the Council shall act by qualified majority. The decision of the Member States, meeting within the Council, is not a decision of the Council, but an act taken by the Member States collectively as members of their governments and not in their capacity as members of the Council. Due to its nature, such an act requires unanimity. As a result, taking both decisions as one and making it subject to unanimity divests the qualified majority rule set out in the first subparagraph of Article 218 (8) TFEU of its very nature.

Finally, the Council infringed the objectives set out in the Treaties and the principle of sincere cooperation laid down in Article 13 (2) TEU. The Council should have exercised its powers so as not to circumvent the institutional framework of the Union and the Union procedures set out in Article 218 TFEU and should have done so in conformity with the objectives set out in the Treaties.

---

[12] See also C-114/12, pending.

(c) Terminating or suspending an international agreement

Article 218(9) provides the following:

Article 218(9) TFEU

The Council, on a proposal from the Commission or the High Representative of the Union for Foreign Affairs and Security Policy, shall adopt a decision suspending application of an agreement and establishing the positions to be adopted on the Union's behalf in a body set up by an agreement, when that body is called upon to adopt acts having legal effects, with the exception of acts supplementing or amending the institutional framework of the agreement.

Obviously, this is an internal rule only and any suspension of an international agreement should be in accordance with international treaty law. This may also be the reason why these days suspension clauses are included in agreements with third states. Reasons for the EU to suspend an agreement may relate to human rights violations or war situations in third countries.[13]

Termination of international agreements should also be in line with international treaty law. The EU Treaties lack a specific procedure for the termination of treaties, but one could argue that for any modification or termination of an agreement the same procedure should be followed as for the conclusion of an agreement, unless the agreement itself settles the question in a different fashion.

A case concerning Article 218(9) TFEU was pending at the time this book went to press. Specifically, the question has been raised by Germany as to whether this provision can be used as a legal basis for the adoption of an EU position in an international organization of which it is not a member but the Member States are. Germany argues that this provision is the incorrect legal basis, and that in fact it sees no appropriate legal basis for a Decision such as the contested one. In all likelihood, the resolution of this case will not be in the interpretation of Article 218(9) TFEU, but rather in the application of the duty of cooperation (see Chapter 6). In that context the Court has previously stated that Member States should act as 'trustees' of the EU interest in international organizations of which the Union is not a member, and evidently the EU institutions should be able to lay the groundwork for such external representation.

Action brought on 28 August 2012 – *Bundesrepublik Deutschland* v. *Council of the European Union* (Case C-399/12)

Form of order sought
Annul the Council decision of 18 June 2012;
Order the Council of the European Union to bear the costs.

Pleas in law and main arguments
By its action, the Bundesrepublik Deutschland (Federal Republic of Germany) challenges the Council decision of 18 June 2012 'establishing the position to be adopted on behalf of the European Union with

---

[13] For a situation where a suspension clause was lacking, see Case C-162/96 *Racke GmbH & Co.* v. *Hauptzollamt Mainz* [1998] ECR I-3655.

regard to certain resolutions to be voted in the framework of the International Organisation for Vine and Wine (OIV)'.

According to the Federal Government, Article 218(9) TFEU was the incorrect legal basis for the adoption of the decision. Article 218(9) TFEU concerns in the first instance only the adoption of the positions of the Union in bodies, set up by international agreements, of which the Union is a member. Article 218(9) TFEU cannot however be applied in relation to the representation of the Member States in bodies of international organisations in which only the Member States participate by virtue of separate international treaties. Second, Article 218(9) TFEU covers only 'acts having legal effects', meaning acts binding under international law. OIV resolutions are however not acts in that sense.

Moreover no other legal basis for the adoption of the Council decision is apparent.

(iv) Soft legal international agreements

Apart from the international agreements concluded on the basis of Article 218 TFEU, the Union may enter into international soft legal commitments such as Codes of Conduct, Declarations or Joint Statements. Despite their formally 'non-legal' nature, such international soft legal agreements cannot be ignored in the EU legal order. They may form the interpretative context for legal agreements and may even commit the Union through the development of customary law or as unilateral Declarations. They are usually described as 'political commitments' rather than legal commitments. However, this may be confusing: soft and hard law instruments may both be politically important. Nevertheless, in international instruments, the EU often underlines their non-legal binding nature by reference to their 'political nature only'.

A key example of a political commitment is an MoU (see for example Chapter 13). MoUs reflect a political agreement between the Union and one or more third states or international organizations, with the express intention not to become bound in a legal sense. While legally speaking a legal basis is not necessary to establish a competence for the institutions to enact political commitments, the Treaties do seem to have been phrased in ways that leave room for the Union to be active in this area. Notably, Article 17(1) calls upon the Commission 'to ensure the Union's external representation', which leaves ample room for that institution to choose the means through which to do so. Hence, in practice the conclusion of political commitments does not differ too much from the conclusion of international agreements: the Commission (or in the case of CFSP MoUs, the HR) will negotiate and sign the agreement, where the actual conclusion lies in the hands of the Council (see above, *France* v. *Commission*).

Memorandum of Understanding between the Government of Iraq and the European Union on Strategic Partnership in Energy

The Government of the Republic of Iraq and the European Union,

Wishing to improve relations in the area of energy, as stipulated in the Energy Policy Action Plan 2007–2009 adopted by the European Council on 8–9 March 2007.

Taking into consideration ongoing developments in Iraq and the key role that energy plays in Iraq's economic development, as well as the opportunities offered by the EU energy market, as the largest integrated energy market in the world, for the development of Iraqi energy exports, in particular in the field of natural gas, . . .

Recalling, the shared common interests of the European Union, as an energy consumer, and Iraq, as a key oil and gas producer, in ensuring security of energy supply and demand and promoting sustainable development in their respective energy sectors, . . .

Both sides will endeavour to enhance their cooperation with a view to: . . .

(5) Given the importance of enhancing energy trade between Iraq and the European Union and developing the relevant exploration, production, processing and transportation infrastructure, both sides will endeavour to cooperate in the following areas:

a. assessing, where appropriate, the existing hydrocarbon transit and supply network, with a view to developing an infrastructure modernization plan.

b. enhancing the safety and reliability of Iraq's energy transit and export pipeline network, as well as LNG infrastructure where possible.

c. Identifying and putting into place additional sources and supply routes for gas from Iraq to the European Union, in particular in the context of the development of the Arab Gas Pipeline and other relevant projects. . . .

The present document records political intent alone and provides for no legal commitment. The present Memorandum of Understanding may be considered for possible future discussions between the two sides concerning further energy cooperation in the context of the implementation of the Partnership and Cooperation Agreement between Iraq and the EU.

The two sides intend cooperation under this Memorandum of Understanding to start on the date of its signature and intend it to continue until one of the two sides informs the other of its end.

Done in Baghdad on 18 January 2010, in two equal versions in the Arabic and English languages.

Any differences in understanding will be resolved amicably

For the European Union   For the Government of Iraq

European Commissioner for   Energy Minister of Oil

High Representative for Foreign Affairs and Security Policy

/Vice-President of the European Commission

Minister of Industry, Tourism and Trade

Presidency of the Council of the European Union

We may further also distinguish administrative and exploratory arrangements which are non-binding arrangements that are functional to the cooperation between the administration of the Union and the administration of third countries or international organizations. They may therefore be considered executive agreements which are necessary to allow (mainly) the Commission and the HR to fulfil the administrative and operational parts of their mandate. Examples include the Trust Funds and Co-Financing Framework Agreement between the Commission and the World Bank, or the Administrative Agreement concluded between the Central Commission for the Navigation of the Rhine and the European Commission on a systematic exchange of information and regular meetings to coordinate activities. Exploratory arrangements are the outcome of the exploratory talks that precede the negotiation of an international agreement. They are thus part of the negotiation process and are negotiated by the Commission or the HR (see above).

5 TYPES OF INTERNATIONAL AGREEMENTS

(i) Mixed agreements

As we have seen, international agreements may be concluded in all areas of Union activity. The reason is that, whenever the Union exercises more competences internally, there is simply no possibility of leaving the external relations in the hands of the Member States only. Chapter 3 will address the division of competences between the Union and its Member States. As we will see (also in Chapter 4) only in few instances are competences fully and exclusively in the hands of the EU. This is the source of the notion of 'mixity': in its external relations the Union will have to combine (mix) its competences with the competences that are still in the hands of the Member States to be able to cover the full spectrum of the external action at stake. In the case of the conclusion of international agreements, this implies that often both the Union and its Member States need to become parties to the agreement.

> **J. Heliskoski, *Mixed Agreements as a Technique for Organizing the External Relations of the European Community and its Member States* (The Hague: Kluwer Law International, 2001), pp. 6–7**[14]
>
> The fact that the Union's participation in international agreements is often coupled with that of the Member States is commonly supposed to find its rationale in the limited *scope* of the Union's competence. Whereas States have traditionally been regarded as possessing the totality of international rights and duties, the rights and duties of an entity such as the Union depend upon its functions and purposes. The Union is in other words based, not on any general but limited attribution of legal authority, specifically laid down by the EU Treaty. As it may however happen that a particular international agreement goes beyond the Union's competence, a practice has emerged whereby the Member States in their individual capacity assume the remainder of treaty commitments. This, according to standard theory, is the basic legal reason for having recourse to the mixed procedure. What is less frequently noticed is that the justification for the conclusion of an agreement as a mixed agreement may not always relate to the scope but rather to the *nature* of the Union's competence: ... the Court of Justice recognizes that Union competence, when it exists, does not necessarily exclude the competence of the Member States, and it may nevertheless be open to the latter to take part in the agreement alongside the Union. On both explanations, mixed agreements may be defined as agreements which include among their parties the Union and all or some of its Member States and which fall partly within the competence of the Union and partly within the competence of the Member States.

(a) Negotiation and conclusion of mixed agreements

As indicated above, the notion of mixity follows from the fact that in many cases both the EU and the Member States are competent to engage in external action, or that international agreements cover a variety of areas, all of which are subject to different divisions of competence. Only in very few cases would the EU be exclusively competent to conclude an agreement, which

---

[14] In the excerpt, 'Community' has been replaced by 'Union' in order to render it less dated.

implies that in most cases the Member States will have to become a party as well. While for political reasons this allows Member States to remain present and visible themselves on the international stage, the need to have a mixed agreement obviously complicates as well as prolongs the process of concluding international agreements. Mixed agreements can be both bilateral (between the EU/Member States and a third state or international organization) and multilateral (between the EU/Member States and a number of other states).

While for the EU the general procedure in Article 218 TFEU continues to apply, a number of issues render the conclusion of mixed agreements special. After all, at all stages of the process, account will have to be taken of the possibly different positions of the EU and its twenty-eight Member States. It is essential for the EU and its Member States to speak with one voice during the negotiations, and also not to allow the third party to abuse a possible difference of opinion. The European Union (read: European Commission) therefore has a strong preference to act as the sole negotiator, also on behalf of the Member States, but the sensitivity of the topic determines to what extent Member States will actually allow the Commission to act as their representative. In any case, it is important to agree on a common position, but as negotiations by definition require some flexibility on both sides, any negotiator would need a certain freedom to change its position.

The complexity is strengthened by the fact that it is virtually impossible to distinguish clearly between the areas falling under (exclusive) EU competence and areas in which the Member States still have a (perhaps large) role to play. Many agreements are a clear mix of issues, which calls for the need for acceptance both on the side of the EU and the Member States to accept a certain fuzziness. A strict division of competence would call for separate roles for the EU and the Member States during the process, but obviously this could seriously harm the negotiating position and would make it very unattractive for third states to enter into negotiations on mixed agreement. Indeed, one should bear in mind that for third states it is often far from clear where the competence lies; they rather deal with one (combined) party.

A clarification of the division of competences is nevertheless possible and may take the form of a 'Declaration of Competence', which lays down the respective competences of the EU and its Member States in the different fields addressed by the agreement.

A. Delgado Casteleiro, 'EU Declarations of Competence to Multilateral Agreements: A Useful Reference Base?' (2012) 17 *European Foreign Affairs Review*, 4, 491–510 at 509

In theory, declarations of competence are supposed to give legal certainty to non-EU parties to mixed agreements with regard to where responsibilities reside. By externalizing the internal division of competence, the declarations of competence give an a priori solution to the questions of implementation and compliance with mixed agreements. They also provide legal certainty to third parties that neither the EU nor its Member States will try to avoid their responsibility in case of a breach by hiding behind the other. This is even clearer in those agreements in which the REIO clause establishes the joint and several responsibility of the REIO and its Member State as a subsidiary mechanism to the declaration of competence. In such agreements, if neither the EU nor a Member State provides an answer as to who is responsible, both will have to answer for their silence on the issue.

Although in theory, declarations could provide an easy solution to the different responsibility scenarios which were identified in the introduction, a closer look suggests otherwise.

First, the internal division of competence is anything but simple. Competences do not only change over time, but also vary depending on the stage of the life-cycle of the agreement (e.g., negotiation, conclusion or implementation).

Second, it appears that declarations create more problems than they solve. In terms of content, they are vague and fail really to clarify when the EU is responsible under each specific mixed agreement. . . .

Moreover, they need to be constantly updated so as to keep up with the evolution of the EU's powers, but they are not. Consequently, after close examination, it is clear that declarations of competence do not answer the question of EU competence to implement mixed agreements but instead create more uncertainty. For instance, what are the legal effects of a declaration which carries outdated legislation? . . .

Having established that declarations of competence as they stand today do not provide legal certainty to third parties, one question arises: is there any other way that the EU and its Member States could provide legal certainty to the other parties to multilateral (mixed) agreements? First, the EU and its Member States should make a special effort during the negotiations of multilateral conventions to assure the other parties that the division of competence is an internal issue that does not affect their compliance with the multilateral convention. . . . Second, instead of trying to clarify the complexities surrounding the internal division of competence and its dynamic nature, the EU should stress in its declarations made to international agreements not the fact that it has competence over an issue, but that presented with a situation in which contracting parties may demand such clarification, the EU will promptly give an univocal response.

The problem with these Declarations is that the division of competences is dynamic: what can be a reasonable description for the division at the time of the conclusion of an agreement, may very well change over the years. And, although from an internal point of view the exact delimitation of competences is not required (as confirmed by the Court in Ruling 1/78),[15] third states may demand it, also to discover whom to address in cases of conflict on interpretation or implementation.

Because of the fact that they become full parties, Member States need to sign and conclude mixed agreements as well. This implies that a ratification procedure is necessary in each Member State. Although swift ratification is possible even in very complex cases (as the case of the WTO Agreement showed), the fact that each and every Member State may delay the process because of complex parliamentary or federal reasons usually creates a time-consuming process. While in certain cases provisional application may be possible (see above), practice reveals that the Council will await ratification by all Member States before concluding the agreement on behalf of the EU. In case the process takes too much time, the Council can propose an interim agreement, to which the Member States are not a party, but which would at least allow the Union and the third party to proceed with their cooperation in an area under control by the EU.

Obviously, once they become parties, Member States are bound to the agreement. Considering the rule that 'Agreements concluded by the Union are binding upon the institutions of the Union *and on its Member States*' (Article 216(2) TFEU) and the fact that mixed agreements are also to be considered an 'integral part of EU law',[16] the question may arise why we have mixed agreements

---

[15] Ruling 1/78 *Re Convention on the Physical Protection of Nuclear Materials, Facilities and Transports* [1978] ECR 2151. This judgment was delivered in the framework of the European Atomic Energy Community (EAEC).

[16] Case C-431/05 *Merck Genéricos-Produtos Farmacêuticos* v. *Merck* [2007] ECR I-7001.

at all. The answer lies in the fact that the Union is simply not competent to claim all areas of Union law exclusively; the Treaties foresee a division of competences which is also to be reflected in the external relations. Indeed, in both cases the Member States are bound by the agreements. The difference is that in the case of agreements concluded by the EU they are bound on the basis of EU law as they do not have a direct legal relationship with the third party; and in the case of mixed agreements Member States are bound on the basis of international treaty law, and at the same time will have to abide by the relevant rule of EU law (for instance in relation to the duty of cooperation; see below). In some cases not all Member States become party to a mixed agreement ('partial mixity'). When we follow the above rules, this would imply that those Member States that have not themselves become a party are not bound on the basis of international law, but they are still bound on the basis of EU law (Article 216(2)).

M. Gatti and P. Manzini, 'External Representation of the European Union in the Conclusion of International Agreements' (2012) 49 *Common Market Law Review* 1703–1734

In a legal perspective, mixity may be *compulsory* or facultative. Mixity is compulsory when an agreement contains matters falling within EU's exclusive competences, or already exercised shared competences, and aspects falling within Member States' sole competences. By contrast, mixity is often considered to be *facultative* when the agreement contains matters falling within EU's exclusive competences, or exercised shared competences, and aspects falling within shared competences not yet exercised; this form of mixity is seen as facultative by some authors, since the Council can decide to conclude an agreement in the EU-only form by exercising the shared competence. In practice, mixity might be determined by political reasons, when the entirety of an agreement is covered by Union competences (either exclusive or exercised shared competences), but the mixed form is chosen for reasons of *political* expediency. . . .

Although Member States may decide to entrust their representation to the Commission, they may prefer to be represented by the rotating Presidency, in order to preserve a purely "intergovernmental" method in their area of competence. In this case, however, the European position suffers from a duality of representation, since the Commission represents the Union, and the Presidency represents Member States. This duality implies three negative consequences. The EU may appear disunited; third subjects may even be puzzled about the identity of their counterparts and their respective obligations. Moreover, third subjects may foster conflicts between European negotiators by strategically selecting their European interlocutors according to political criteria, and not according to the distribution of competences.

Finally, the width of each negotiator's competences must be delimited, in order to prevent conflicts. The problems arising out of the division of representation between the Commission and the rotating Presidency must be tackled by relying on the "requirement of unity of international representation" identified by the Court of Justice. Although the scope of this principle is not completely manifest, the Court has clarified that it implies that, during the negotiation of a mixed agreement, EU institutions and Member States are under an obligation to cooperate, in order to facilitate the achievement of the EU's tasks and to ensure the coherence and consistency of its action.

(b) Mixed agreements and the duty of cooperation

The 'duty of cooperation' flows from the 'principle of sincere cooperation' as laid down in Article 4(3) TEU (see also Chapter 6):

Article 4(3) TEU

Pursuant to the principle of sincere cooperation, the Union and the Member States shall, in full mutual respect, assist each other in carrying out tasks which flow from the Treaties.

The Member States shall take any appropriate measure, general or particular, to ensure fulfilment of the obligations arising out of the Treaties or resulting from the acts of the institutions of the Union.

The Member States shall facilitate the achievement of the Union's tasks and refrain from any measure which could jeopardise the attainment of the Union's objectives.

Whereas the 'duty' is thus a general principle, applicable to all Union and Member State activity, it has a special importance in the area of external relations. Since the Treaties are often unclear about the exact division of competences, the Court has frequently used the duty of cooperation as a guideline to establish the Union's competences and/or the Member States' obligations in external relations law. In this context we examine the duty of cooperation specifically as regards mixed agreements, and in Chapter 6 we explore the legal obligations in all settings of EU and Member State external relations.

C. Hillion, 'Mixity and Coherence in EU External Relations: The Significance of the Duty of Cooperation', in C. Hillion and P. Koutrakos (eds.), *Mixed Agreements Revisited – The EU and its Member States in the World* (Oxford/Portland: Hart Publishing, 2010), pp. 87–115

On the basis of the general principle of loyal cooperation, the Court of Justice has articulated a specific duty of cooperation to foster harmony between the Union and the Member States when acting jointly on the international scene. In so doing, the Court is contributing towards enhancing the coherence and consistency of the external action and representation of the Union.

It has been argued that the duty of cooperation plays an increasingly significant role in the law of mixed agreements. Its greater significance stems from its progressive legalisation and the elaboration of its normative content by the Court. While it has mostly entailed an obligation of conduct, the normative strength of which may vary depending on the specific form of mixity of the agreement at hand, the duty of cooperation may also involve, albeit exceptionally, an obligation of result. Hence, Member States and EU judicial authorities may be called upon to ensure uniformity in the application of provisions of the agreement, where those have a procedural nature and are capable of applying at national and Union levels. The Court has also articulated enforceable procedural obligations (eg of consultation and information) that bind Member States and EU institutions, including where they exercise their powers. Such procedural obligations, which are still being elaborated, entail that while exercising their recognised powers, Member States and institutions should be aware and respectful of each other's undertakings, if not responsible for facilitating each other's tasks ultimately to promote the common good. The Court thus fosters an attitude of mutual support, rather than an instinctive territoriality reflex in the EU–Member States interactions. That apparent increasing jurisprudential emphasis on cooperation as a contribution to consistency and coherence in the organisation of the EU external relations counter-balances the traditional competence-distribution case law. It may signal lesser judicial apprehension, and perhaps more acceptance of the plurality that characterises the EU posture on the international stage. The Court's changing views on the function of the duty of cooperation attest to this. While often conceived of as a vehicle to achieve 'unity' – otherwise limited in view of the constitutional limitations to EU exclusive competence – the duty of cooperation is being reorientated to pursue consistency and coherence in the intrinsically multifarious action and international representation of the Union.

Ruling 1/78 (see above) is generally seen as the 'mother of all judgments on the duty of cooperation'. Indeed, in this judgment the Court used and further interpreted the duty of cooperation, which is phrased in Article 192 EURATOM in similar terms to that in Article 4(3) TEU. Like many subsequent cases, the situation related to (collective) Member State action, which negatively affected independent external action by the Community. Thus, the duty of cooperation proved to be a key principle in relation to shared external competences.

Recent case law, in very different areas (ranging from *Mox Plant* to *Kadi* (see Chapter 7)) made us aware of the implications of the stronger international presence of the EU, in particular in relation to the existing external competences of the Member States. In *PFOS*, the question was raised to what extent Member States are constrained in their actions under international law by the fact that they are not only states, but also (or perhaps above all) Member States of the EU. In this case, Sweden unilaterally nominated a substance (PFOS – perfluorooctane sulfonates) for a listing under the Stockholm Convention on Persistent Organic Pollutants (POPs), a mixed agreement. Obviously, this question was not new and lies at the heart of almost all struggles in EU external relations law, but in this case no inter-institutional agreement was concluded and no formal EU decisions were taken which would prima facie restrain Member States from exercising their own competences under international treaty law as we know from previous case law.[17] One could argue that by restricting the autonomous position of Sweden, the duty of cooperation was stretched a bit further (see Chapter 6). At the same time the case pointed clearly to the limits of 'procedural and substantive obligations of the Member States as loyal members of the Union when acting as contracting parties in their own right' when we do not want to undermine the very existence of separate competences of the Member States.[18] Mixity is the logical consequence of the existence of a shared competence, but cases such as *PFOS* underline that Member States cannot act on their own and have to take into account existing or planned Union action. In this case Sweden could not act unilaterally as that would dissociate it from a concerted common strategy within the Council and would deviate from a position submitted by the Commission.

In a way, the case built upon two other cases, in which the Commission claimed that Luxembourg and Germany violated the principle of sincere cooperation by continuing negotiations and even ratifications of bilateral agreements with a number of Central and Eastern European countries (CEECs) on transport by inland waterway, while the Commission had already been given a mandate to negotiate a multilateral agreement.[19] The outcome of the case was a

---

[17] Including Opinion 1/91 [1993] ECR I-6079; Opinion 1/94 [1994] ECR I-5267; Case C-53/96 *Hermès International* v. *FHT Marketing* [1998] ECR I-3603; Joined Cases C-300/98 & 392/98 *Parfums Christian Dior* v. *Tuk Consultancy* [2000] ECR I-11307; Case C-431/05 *Merck Genéricos-Produtos Farmacêuticos* v. *Merck* [2007] ECR I-7001; Case C-459/03 *Commission* v. *Ireland ('Mox Plant')* [2006] ECR I-4635; Case C-25/94 *Commission* v. *Council (FAO Fisheries Agreement)* [1996] ECR I-1469.

[18] M. Cremona, 'Case C-246/07, Commission v. Sweden (PFOS), Judgment of the Court of Justice (Grand Chamber) of 20 April 2010' (2011) 43 *Common Market Law Review* 1639–1665.

[19] Cases C-519/03 *Commission* v. *Luxembourg* [2005] ECR I-3067, and C-433/03 *Commission* v. *Germany* [2005] ECR I-6985.

clear statement, paraphrased by Eeckhout: 'unilateral treaty making action by a Member State coinciding with EU negotiation cannot be tolerated, unless that Member State consults and cooperates with the EU, and in particular with the Commission'.[20] As we see below, this reasoning may also have consequences for existing agreements concluded by the Member States.

These judgments did not come out of the blue and were in fact based on a line of argumentation that had gradually developed since Ruling 1/78. In Opinion 2/91 (ILO) the Court pointed to the need for the Union (then Community) and the Member States to cooperate. Whereas the topic matter partly falls within EU competence, the Union itself cannot become a party to the ILO Conventions. In this case, which concerned a shared competence that could not be exercised by the Union externally, Member States have to act on behalf of the Union. The Court also explicitly referred to the need for the Community and the Member States to act united in their external legal relations. Whereas in the case of the ILO we were dealing with a shared competence, but not with mixed agreements, Opinion 1/94 (WTO) drew attention to an actual mixed agreement (the WTO Agreement) and more particularly to the substantive trade agreements annexed to the WTO Agreement. It countered the Commission's worries that the Member States would probably not be able to resist taking individual positions which would harm the required unity. The duty of cooperation would also apply in this case and should also ensure that – for instance in dispute settlement situations – Member States would not take different positions (in fact, in practice the EU and its Member States do act in a unitary fashion in WTO dispute settlement). Finally, in *Commission* v. *Council*[21] the Court dealt with an unclear division of competence in relation to an agreement to promote compliance with international conservation and management measures by vessels on the high seas, which was to be concluded in the framework of the Food and Agricultural Organization (FAO – an organization of which both the EU and the Member States are a member). This case also revealed that the institutions themselves may take different positions. Here the Commission claimed an exclusive competence because of the topic area (fisheries); the Council (not surprisingly) supported the Member States' view that they would still have individuals rights and competences. The Court finally agreed that the main thrust of the agreement lay in the area of exclusive competence, but that the duty of cooperation was relevant for the areas of shared competence, which also reflected the institutional 'arrangement' that existed between the Commission and the Council. In fact, the duty of cooperation was reflected in that arrangement (section 2.3), and by allowing the Member States to act on their own, the Council had violated that principle.

One particular situation concerns the representation by the Commission even for parts of areas where the Union has no competence. The need for unity in representation calls for the Commission to act upon a mandate by the Member States. Obviously, in such cases the Commission's mandate cannot be derived from the Treaty or from a Council Decision. Hence, a special 'Decision of the representatives of the governments of the Member States, meeting within the Council' is adopted, through which the representatives of Member States 'authorize the Commission to negotiate, on behalf of Member States' for the elements of the agreement that fall within the competences of the Member States. The need for a separate document also flows from the fact that a Council decision is normally adopted by qualified majority, whereas that of Member States is taken by unanimity.

---

[20] P. Eeckhout, *EU External Relations Law*, 2nd edn (Oxford: Oxford University Press, 2011), p. 248.
[21] C-25/94 *Commission* v. *Council (FAO Fisheries Agreement)* [1996] ECR I-1469.

The developments in relation to 'mixity' will have consequences for the relationship between international law and EU law, as Member States' international competences may be further restrained on the basis of not only ongoing but also future EU action. One may regard this as a logical consequence of the (external) coming of age of the EU. Yet, new questions arise: first, internally – how far can the principle of sincere cooperation be stretched without turning existing shared competences into a mere theoretical notion? (see further Chapter 6); second, externally – to what extent is international law well enough developed to allow the EU to take over state-like functions (e.g. in relation to the law of treaties, diplomatic law and the law on international responsibility)?

(c) The question of international responsibility

It may be argued that the EU itself would be responsible for violations of international (treaty) law (see Chapter 7). In relation to mixed agreements, however, the question of responsibility is even more complex. After all, on the basis of international treaty law, third parties have a right to address both the EU and its Member States in cases of (perceived) violations. When a Declaration of Competence (see above) has been drafted, this may guide third parties to the most appropriate addressee, but in other cases a general joint responsibility is to be assumed.[22]

> **P. J. Kuijper, 'International Responsibility for EU Mixed Agreements', in C. Hillion and P. Koutrakos (eds.), *Mixed Agreements Revisited: The EU and its Member States in the World* (Oxford/Portland: Hart Publishing, 2010), pp. 208–227**
>
> What the cases tell us is that international tribunals, notably WTO Panels, are close to accepting the special character of the executive federalism of the European Union, and to not assuming that Member State acts in the framework of such federalism require attribution of these acts to the Member States instead of to the Union. The cases also show that tribunals are, without much ado, also ready to accept that certain matters within a mixed agreement, such as customs in the WTO Agreement, fall within exclusive Union competence and should be treated as such, in spite of assertions by other WTO Members that EU Member States as WTO Members are equally fully responsible for the performance of these obligations.
>
> The cases also tell us that the only international court that was really confronted with the doomsday scenario of the alleged abuse of an international organization in order to evade the international obligations of the Member States in the field of human rights, namely the European Court of Human Rights, in reality took a very non-dramatic approach to that phenomenon by inventing the theory of *de facto* equivalence of the protection of human rights observed by the Union and its institutions. This leads to the paradox that the same strain of cases gives the impression of being inspired, on the one hand, by an almost paranoiac fear that Member States may evade their obligations through an international organisation that is not, or rather cannot be, party to the same treaty as these Member States. On the other hand, perhaps as a kind of compensation, the cases seem to be inspired by an almost too lenient assumption that the organisation and its judicial organs will impose the same standards on itself and the Member States as the treaty in question.

---

[22] Cf. Case C-53/96 *Hermès International* v. *FHT Marketing* [1998] ECR I-3603 and Case C-316/91 *Parliament* v. *Council* [1994] ECR I-625.

Irrespective of the complex division of external competences in the Union, some international rules exist to decide on the responsibility of (either) the organization or its members. The ARIO place an emphasis on the attribution of conduct. Article 4 lists the conditions for an internationally wrongful act by an international organization that entails the international responsibility of that organization: 'There is an internationally wrongful act of an international organization when conduct consisting of an action or omission: (a) Is attributable to the international organization under international law . . . .' Irrespective of the presumption of a joint responsibility it could therefore be argued that third states will have to take the division of competence between the EU and its Member States into consideration. After all, it is simply less practical to address Member States in which the Union enjoys an exclusive competence. On the other hand – and this is the position we would take – third states cannot be expected to know and understand all the ins and outs of the internal EU division of competences. In fact, demanding this from third parties could seriously hamper negotiations. Where the division of competences as well as the attribution of conduct can and should play a role internally once possible international responsibility arises, both the EU and its Member States should at least be willing to act as a 'portal' for international claims (see further Chapter 7).

(ii) Association, accession and withdrawal agreements

Article 217 TFEU

The Union may conclude with one or more third countries or international organisations agreements establishing an association involving reciprocal rights and obligations, common action and special procedure.

Although the notion of 'association' is not defined by the treaties (apart from the fact that it would (obviously) involve 'reciprocal rights and obligations, common action and special procedure'), practice has revealed that AAs are indeed a special type of agreements, used to establish a far-reaching relationship with a third country. AAs are characterized by a number of specific features:

- The legal basis for their conclusion is Article 217 TFEU;
- There is an intention to establish close economic and political cooperation;
- Paritary bodies for the management of the cooperation are created, which are competent to take decisions that bind the contracting parties;
- A Most-Favoured Nation (MFN) treatment is included;
- A privileged relationship between the EU and its partner is provided for (in the words of the Court: 'a special, privileged link');[23]
- A clause on the respect of human rights and democratic principles is systematically included and constitutes an essential element of the agreement.

---

[23] Case 12/86 *Demirel* v. *Stadt Schwäbisch Gmünd* [1987] ECR 3719.

AAs (albeit not always under that name) currently exist with Turkey (1963), Iceland, Norway, and Liechtenstein (1993), Macedonia (2001), Croatia (2001), Albania (2006), Montenegro (2007), Bosnia and Herzegovina (2008), Tunisia (1995), Israel (1995), Morocco (1996), Palestinian authority (1997 Interim), Jordan (1997), Egypt (2001), Algeria (2002), Libya (2002), Chile (2002) and the African, Caribbean, Pacific (ACP) countries (2000/2005). Agreements with Syria and Serbia are under negotiation.

The different associations have led to a complex web of relations between the Union, its Member States and a number of third countries. As one observer held, the different forms of 'enhanced multilateralism and bilateralism' led to 'integration without membership' and an 'EU legal space'.

A. Lazowski, 'Enhanced Multilateralism and Enhanced Bilateralism: Integration without Membership in the European Union' (2008) 45 *Common Market Law Review* 1433–1458

The origins of enhanced multilateralism go back to the 1980s when EFTA countries and EEC Member States embarked on negotiations on the European Economic Space. The outcome of those was the emergence of the European Economic Area in 1994. As already argued, thus far it is the most advanced model of integration without membership in the European Union. In substantive terms it covers almost the entire internal market *acquis* as supplemented by numerous flanking policies (i.e. environmental protection). The sophisticated institutional arrangement serves as a guarantor of the homogeneity of the legal space. One has to admit that so far it has been very successful in this respect.

The first years of the XXIst century have seen further deepening of the relations between the EU/EC and the EEA–EFTA countries. It merits attention that this process has been arranged alongside the EEA, nevertheless is full of integration flavours. The prime example is the extension of the Schengen framework to Norway and Iceland (as well as the envisaged extension to Liechtenstein). . . .

A unique example of enhanced bilateralism is the relations between the EC/EU and Switzerland. In the course of the past decades, two sets of bilateral treaties have created a framework for a sectoral integration between the parties (so called Bilateral I and II). Trade-wise, one should also note the free trade agreement, dating back to early 1970s. The substantive scope of Bilateral I–II is very broad, starting with free movement of persons, through public procurement to association with the Schengen *acquis*. Several agreements falling under the umbrella of Bilateral I and II require the application of the *acquis communautaire* in bilateral relations between the EU and Switzerland, as well as incorporation of some of its parts into the Swiss legal order. Relevant lists of legislation are included in the annexes or even mentioned in the main body of the agreements. For example, under the EC/EU–Swiss Agreement on Schengen, Switzerland has an obligation to implement and apply the Schengen *acquis* listed in Annex 1 to the Agreement. This includes, inter alia, the Schengen Agreement as well as parts of the Schengen Implementing Convention.

Associations agreements were often used as a first step towards accession and, indeed, many of the current members first enjoyed an association status. In other cases, they are the follow-ups of so-called cooperation agreements, which may be concluded on the basis of Article 212 TFEU. Associations are far-reaching and may extend key internal market principles to third countries, as was also recognized by the Court (see below).

Nevertheless, AAs differ, also procedurally, from accession agreements. On the basis of Article 49 TEU, 'The conditions of admission and the adjustments to the Treaties on which the Union is founded, which such admission entails, shall be the subject of an agreement.' But, although the EU (and in particular the Commission) is the key negotiator, the final agreements is concluded 'between the Member States and the applicant State' and '[it] shall be submitted for ratification by all the contracting States in accordance with their respective constitutional requirements'. Accession agreements are thus not concluded by the Union.

A similar situation would occur in the event of a withdrawal of a Member State. Article 50 TEU calls upon the Union to negotiate and conclude 'an agreement with that State, setting out the arrangements for its withdrawal, taking account of the framework for its future relationship with the Union'. Yet, in this case a reference is made to Article 218(3) TFEU for the negation stage, and the agreement 'shall be concluded on behalf of the Union by the Council, acting by a qualified majority, after obtaining the consent of the European Parliament'. It is interesting to note that to join the Union a legal relationship with the current Member States needs to be established, but to leave the Union a Member State will have to settle the issue with the organization of which it has become a member.

A. Lazowski, 'Withdrawal from the European Union and Alternatives to Membership' (2012) 37 *European Law Review* 523–540

This analysis demonstrates that a departure is politically and legally possible; at the same time it will be an extremely complex and controversial exercise. Article 50 TEU provides only a general legal framework for withdrawal and a lot of additional decisions would be required in order to develop this into a fully fledged withdrawal *acquis*. Although theoretically one can come to the conclusion that art. 50 TEU allows for a unilateral withdrawal, the analysis above shows that this is rather illusory. It is argued that to facilitate an exit the European Union will have to negotiate an agreement with the departing State which will not only outline the terms of departure but also regulate future relations between the two sides. Such an agreement would be concluded in accordance with art. 218 TFEU, and therefore would fall fully under the jurisdiction of the Court of Justice. Furthermore, lacunae left by the legislator will have to be filled by the decision-makers when the departure of a particular Member State from the European Union becomes a reality. . . .

The best arrangement for future relations between a divorcee and the European Union remains uncertain. The two existing models of integration without membership may be tempting for those whose understanding of the idiosyncrasies of the European Economic Area and the Swiss model is limited. But as soon as the basic issues in these models are explored, however, it becomes clear that neither would now be acceptable for a former Member State of the European Union (or the European Union itself). Furthermore, one should also remember that if a country decides to leave the European Union, art. 50(5) TEU must be taken into account. In order to return to the European Union such a country would have to go through the entire accession process from scratch. In the case of a country like the United Kingdom, the renegotiation of existing opt-outs and budgetary rebate would be politically very difficult, if not impossible. One has to remember that any new entrant is obliged to accept participation in the Economic and Monetary Union and the Schengen Conventions.

In conclusion, a divorce from the European Union should not be the triumph of the imagination over intelligence or hope over experience, but a decision based on a very thorough political, economic and legal analysis – as the consequences in all possible respects will be profound.

(iii) Accession to international organizations

As will be discussed in Chapter 8, the Union may be become a member of other international organizations once a competence on the side of the EU can be established and the other organization is (statutorily as well as politically) willing to welcome the EU as a member. Membership of international organizations typically implies joining the constituent treaty of the organization which may include the need to become party to an accession treaty.

In relation to the question as to whether an agreement 'establishing a European laying-up fund for inland waterway vessels' is compatible with the provisions of the Treaty, the Court argued the following:

Opinion 1/76 [1977] ECR 741

[T]he Community is ... not only entitled to enter into contractual relations with a third country in this connexion but also has the power, while observing the provisions of the Treaty, to cooperate with that country in setting up an appropriate organism such as the public international institution which it is proposed to establish under the name of the 'European laying-up fund for inland waterway vessels'.[24]

In subsequent situations, such as the establishment and joining of the EU (at the time the EC) of the WTO,[25] the Court underlined this view. The Treaties do not provide for a specific procedure for agreements to establish or join international organizations, which implies that the general rules of Article 28 TFEU apply.

(iv) (The future of) international agreements concluded by the Member States only

(a) Member States' treaty-making capacity

Obviously, the competence of the EU to conclude international agreements and the possibility to conclude mixed agreements did not deprive the Member States of their individual competence to conclude treaties. Over the years, however, the extensions of the competences of the EU and its external activities called for a careful assessment of the extent to which the agreements concluded by the Member States would be conflicting with EU law.

As far as international agreements concluded prior to the establishment of the EEC are concerned, the matter is regulated by Article 351 TFEU:

Article 351 TFEU

The rights and obligations arising from agreements concluded before 1 January 1958 or, for acceding States, before the date of their accession, between one or more Member States on the one hand, and one or more third countries on the other, shall not be affected by the provisions of the Treaties.

---

[24] Opinion 1/76 *Re draft Agreement establishing a European laying-up fund for inland waterway vessels* [1977] ECR 741, para 5.

[25] Opinion 1/94 *Re WTO Agreement* [1994] ECR I-5267.

To the extent that such agreements are not compatible with the Treaties, the Member State or States concerned shall take all appropriate steps to eliminate the incompatibilities established. Member States shall, where necessary, assist each other to this end and shall, where appropriate, adopt a common attitude.

In applying the agreements referred to in the first paragraph, Member States shall take into account the fact that the advantages accorded under the Treaties by each Member State form an integral part of the establishment of the Union and are thereby inseparably linked with the creation of common institutions, the conferring of powers upon them and the granting of the same advantages by all the other Member States.

In other words: these agreements shall not be affected, but incompatibilities with EU law should be removed. This again reveals an uneasy relationship between international treaty law and the supremacy of EU law. After all, in the case of conflicts between provisions in an international agreement and EU law, Member States may be obliged to give priority to EU law based on the general rules on supremacy, but whenever these arguments are not accepted by a third party (which is not bound on the basis of the *pacta tertiis nec nocent nec prosunt* rule – see above), they have every right to ask for a correct implementation of the agreement. From the EU side, the pressure on Member States at least to find interpretation which would allow for EU law to work properly may be hard. In its case law, the Court held that international agreements 'may in no circumstances permit any challenge to the principles that form part of the very foundations of the [EU] legal order',[26] and indeed, Article 351 is generally believed not to form an unlimited reason for Member States to evade EU law.

F. Casolari, 'The Principle of Loyal Co-operation: A 'Master Key' for EU External Representation?', in S. Blockmans and R. A. Wessel (eds.), *Principles and Practices of EU External Representation* (CLEER Working Papers, No. 5, 2012)

In this respect, the case-law made it clear that the purpose of that provision is to clarify, 'in accordance with the principles of international law, that application of EC Treaty does not affect the duty of the Member States concerned to respect the rights of non-member countries under an earlier agreement and to perform its obligations thereunder'. Whilst criticized on its approach to the law of treaties, this Court's position was clearly put forward in order to ensure the fulfillment of the Member States' obligations vis-à-vis the third contracting parties: it thus expressed a friendly attitude towards international law.

A second line of case-law developed since 2000 suggests a new approach by the Court as far as Article 351 TFEU is concerned. In particular, the new line of reasoning of the Court seems to be based on the necessity to establish a more 'EU-oriented' balance between the foreign-policy interests of the Member States, which are incorporated in the first paragraph of Article 351, and the EU interest to ensure the effectiveness of internal law, enshrined in the second paragraph of that Article.

The BITs judgments are a clear example of this judicial evolution: here, indeed, the Court offers a very narrow interpretation of the obligations stemming from the second paragraph of the Article, according to

---

[26] Joined Cases C-402/05 P and C-415/05 P *Kadi and Al Barakaat International Foundation* v. *Council & Commission* [2008] ECR I-6351.

which Member States are requested to take immediately all appropriate steps to eliminate incompatibilities between the pre-existing agreements (in casu, some bilateral investment agreements concluded with third States) and EU law (namely the law of free movement of capital), even if such incompatibilities may never arise in concreto. . . .

The recourse to the specific obligation of loyal cooperation enshrined in the second paragraph of Article 351 TFEU thus imposes a new reading of the content of this provision and determines a revised balance between the Member States' international commitments and EU law, which seems to ensure in any event the primacy of the latter. At the same time, as in the recent case-law on mixity, the specific loyalty clause introduces substantive duties of result since the obligation to take all appropriate steps to eliminate incompatibilities (including renegotiation and denunciation of the pre-existing agreements) cannot be considered as a best efforts obligation.

Apart from pre-existing agreements with third states, also agreements among the Member States (so-called agreements *inter se*) potentially challenge the principles and foundation of the EU legal order. After all, they run the risk of allowing Member States to bypass EU law. These agreements are not covered by Article 351.[27] Yet, ever since the European Road Transport Agreement (ERTA; see Chapter 3) it is clear that Member States cannot freely choose either the international or the EU route whenever the subject is covered by EU law, which implies that agreements *inter se* should be limited to topics that are not (at all) covered by the EU Treaties.

Considering the extensive legal relations Member States maintain with third states, the potential for conflict is real. How to prevent conflicts with EU law? Several options have been developed in practice.

1. *Ex ante*: for new agreements the best solution seems to be to prevent Member States from negotiating and concluding agreements in areas which fall under EU competence. In the case of an exclusive competence it is clear that the Member States are simply no longer allowed to conclude the agreement; in the case of a shared or a parallel competence the case law indicates that it would be strongly recommended to cooperate with the Commission in order to prevent conflicts with (planned) EU activities. Already in *Kramer*[28] the Court held that Member States are 'not to enter into any commitment within the framework of these [fisheries] conventions which could hinder the Community in carrying out the tasks entrusted to it'.

2. *Ex post*: the principle of supremacy implies that agreements concluded by the Member States are seen as national legislation. In contrast to agreements concluded by the EU, they do not rank above secondary law, but below it. This means that they will simply have to be implemented in accordance with EU law and that Member States have an obligation to renegotiate possible conflicting provisions with the respective third parties.

That this may have serious consequences for a large number of existing international agreements is exemplified by the so-called *BITs* (Bilateral Investment Treaties) cases.[29] The EU's presence in the field of foreign investment not only forms an example of new international ambitions, but

---

[27] Case C-812/79 *Attorney General* v. *Juan C. Burgoa* [1980] ECR 2787.
[28] Joined Cases C-3/76, C-4/76 and C-6/76 *Cornelis Kramer and Others* [1976] ECR I-1279.
[29] Case C-205/06 *Commission* v. *Austria* [2009] ECR I-1301; Case C-249/06 *Commission* v. *Sweden* [2009] ECR I-1335; Case C-118/07 *Commission* v. *Finland* [2009] ECR I-10889.

ironically also triggered the traditional reflex: an acceptance of the authority of international law, but at the same time a preservation of the autonomy of EU law. Although the cases differ from the above-mentioned *PFOS* case, they seem to reflect a similar trend: exclusivity by stealth. The outcome of the *BITs* cases is that all (over 1,000) BITs will have to be renegotiated in order to prevent incompatibilities with EU law. As indicated by Dimopoulos, the long-term objective of the EU is to replace Member State BITs with EU investment agreements. In the meantime an authorization system should combine the validity of the BITs that were concluded on the basis of international treaty law with the primacy of EU law.[30]

It is indeed the need for primacy of EU law that undermines existing competences Member States enjoy, both under EU law and under international law. Where, traditionally, Member States are not a priori pre-empted from rule-making in an area of shared competence, the BITs cases reveal a number of Member States' obligations even when the EU itself has not legislated, the reason being the 'hypothetical incompatibility' of existing international agreements with EU law.[31] The Court argued that even a perceived – but not yet materialized – conflict between the international agreements and EU law would lead to a violation of the capital movement provisions in Article 351 TFEU (then Article 307 EC). The incompatibilities could jeopardize the future exercise of EU competences. In that sense, the judgments indeed continue 'the trend set by the ECJ in its *Mox Plant* and *Kadi* judgments by first decoupling the international law obligations from the EU law obligations and subsequently subordinating the former from the latter'.[32] As in earlier case law, in the BITs cases the Court does not simply deny the relevance of international law, but it claims that it cannot be used in this case. Indeed,

[the fact that the EU has powers] on a matter which is identical to or connected with that covered by an earlier agreement concluded between a Member State and a third country, reveals the incompatibility with that agreement where, first the agreement does not contain a provision allowing the member State concerned to exercise its rights and to fulfil its obligations as a member of the [EU] and, second, there is also no international law mechanism which makes that possible.[33]

This is indeed the complex conflict we face. By arguing that international law itself does not offer solutions, the Court has no choice but to preserve the autonomy of EU law by limiting Member States' traditional treaty-making competences under international law, and by doing so it also hinders the exercise of shared competences and thus also reinterprets primary EU law. Yet, it has been argued that a narrow reading of the judgments would render the outcome of the cases more comprehensible.[34] In that interpretation Member States' international agreements are incompatible with EU law only when they preclude the future exercise of EU competence, so that *any* measure taken by the EU under a relevant power-conferring provision is conflicting with the Member States' obligations. While there are certainly reasons to opt for this interpretation, the language used by the Court is more worrisome and could also be read as a hostile

---

[30] A. Dimopoulos, 'The BITs Cases and their Practical and Doctrinal Implications', in J. Díez-Hochleitner *et al.* (eds.), *Recent Trends in the Case Law of the Court of Justice of the European Union (2008–2011)* (Madrid: La Ley, 2012), pp. 737–758.

[31] N. Lavranos, 'Case Note, Cases C-205/06 and C-249/06' (2009) 103 *American Journal of International Law* 716–722.

[32] *Ibid.*

[33] Case C-205/06 *Commission* v. *Austria* [2009] ECR I-1301, paras. 37 and 31.

[34] Dimopoulos, 'The BITs Cases'.

takeover by the EU of both Member States' competences and international (treaty) law. After all, it is not at all clear that the BITs would in fact be incompatible with EU law, as long as EU competences have not been exercised. In these cases the Member States argue that an incompatibility could only exist after the EU had actually adopted the measures. Moreover, in case of an actual conflict, international treaty law offers mechanisms to deal with this situation (such as suspension, renegotiation or ultimately denouncement of the agreements, in line with the *rebus sic stantibus* doctrine). The question indeed is whether a hypothetical conflict could be seen as an incompatibility, in particular taking into account the consequences Member States enjoy in an area of shared competence.

(b) Member States' agreements in areas of exclusive competence

A particularly ironic situation occurs in areas when the EU enjoys an exclusive competence, but lacks the possibility of using it. For several reasons Member States may participate in international agreements falling (at least partly) within exclusive Union competence. Case law of the CJEU illustrates the possibly complex situation. *Intertanko* was about a request for a preliminary ruling on the compatibility between a Directive on ship-source pollution and the MARPOL Convention. The CJEU argued that the Convention fell outside its jurisdiction as there was no transfer of powers:

It is true that all the Member States are parties to Marpol 73/78. Nevertheless, in the absence of a full transfer of the powers previously exercised by the Member States to the Community, the latter cannot, simply because all those states are parties to Marpol 73/78, be bound by the rules set out therein, which it has not itself approved.[35]

The content of such agreements can become part of EU law through secondary legislation. Through 'good faith' and the principles of sincere cooperation conventions such as MARPOL achieve an interpretative function within EU law.

The *Open Skies* cases deal with a situation where the Union becomes exclusively competent, but a large number of bilateral treaties exist. The solution offered by the Court was to try to remove inconsistencies, and accept a transition period until the EU can fully take over. Given the nature of the competence, Member State authorization is required for amendments or renewal.[36]

These situations illustrate the need for the Union to occasionally accept a role by the Member States in areas of exclusive competence.

M. Cremona, 'Member States Agreements as Union Law', in E. Cannizzaro, P. Palcheti and R. A. Wessel (eds.), *International Law as Law of the European Union* (Leiden/Boston: Martinus Nijhoff Publishers, 2011), pp. 291–324

While not common, the participation of the Member States in international agreements falling within exclusive Union competence is not as unusual as we might imagine, and it gives rise to a number of

---

[35] C-308/06 *Intertanko and Others* [2008] ECR I-4057.

[36] Open Skies Cases: C-467/98 *Commission v. Denmark (Open Skies)* [2002] ECR I-9519; C-468/98 *Commission v. Sweden (Open Skies)* [2002] ECR I-9575; C-469/98 *Commission v. Finland (Open Skies)* [2002] ECR I-9627; C-472/98 *Commission v. Luxembourg (Open Skies)* [2002] ECR I-9741; C-475/98 *Commission v. Austria (Open Skies)* [2002] ECR I-9797; C-476/98 *Commission v. Germany (Open Skies)* [2002] ECR I-9855.

interesting legal questions as to the status of the agreement, if any, in Union law and the Member States' obligations under Union law arising as a consequence. Such a situation may occur for several reasons:

1. It is decided that it is in the Union interest, for political or other reasons, that the Member States rather than the Union should participate in an agreement. The classic example of this is the European Road Transport Agreement (ERTA or AETR). . . .

2. In some cases, an individual Member State may be given authorisation to enter into an agreement that falls within exclusive Union competence. Here a distinction needs to be made between those cases where the Member State acts *on behalf of* the Union and those where it acts on its own account, albeit under Union authorisation. In the first case, the Member State acts in the Union interest, and the position will be similar to the previous scenario. In the second case, the authorization is given on the ground that it is not contrary to the Union interest for the Member State to conclude the agreement. . . .

3. It may be the case that only States, and not regional economic integration organisations (REIOs) such as the EC or EU, are entitled to participate in the agreement. This is the case for agreements concluded under the aegis of many UN agencies such as the ILO and the IMO.

6 THE BROADER PICTURE OF EU EXTERNAL RELATIONS LAW

In legal terms, international agreements are essential tools for the EU to be able to play its role as a global actor. In the current Treaties, the conclusion of international agreements is laid down in detailed terms. Over the years, the EU has made full and dynamic use of its treaty-making competences and '[t]oday few parts of the world remain unconnected to the EU by some form of bilateral or regional trade-related agreement'.[37]

While tariffs and trade formed the subject of many early agreements, the EU has clearly expanded the scope of its external legal relations to its other policy areas. Subsequent chapters will reveal the need for the EU to enter into international agreements following developments in the internal market, or other areas (such as the AFSJ or the CSDP). Yet, the need for mixity remains apparent and reveals that the EU's powers are far from exclusive in most areas. Indeed, Member States have not at all ceased to conclude treaties themselves and have in fact also expanded their territory.[38]

International agreements are the key legal instruments in EU legal relations, and their conclusion reflects the tension between the EU's own (sometimes exclusive) competences and the wish of Member States to stay connected once elements in the agreements fall under their competences. For third states the division of competences remains a complex element in international negotiations, in particular since this division is not fixed but may change on the basis of treaty modifications or new case law. In that sense, the so-called Declarations of Competence which are sometimes annexed to an international agreement are of limited value only.

---

[37] M. Mendez, *The Legal Effects of EU Agreements: Maximalist Treaty Enforcement and Judicial Avoidance Techniques* (Oxford: Oxford University Press, 2013), p. xvii.

[38] *Ibid.*, at xv. Mendez points to the fact that since the 1990s France, for instance, has been negotiating roughly 200 bilateral treaties a year, which is equivalent to 2.5 times the annual number of treaties negotiated during the 1950s. In 2005, France was bound by over 7,400 treaties.

Beyond international agreements, we must keep in mind that all instruments used by the EU to regulate or legislate internal policy matters can and are also being used in the context of EU external relations. In this chapter we have pointed specifically to the importance of soft law, utilized both within the EU legal order, and in the international legal order. Soft law instruments all have in common that as such they do not possess legal effect because they have not been adopted through procedures laid down in the Treaties. However, they often will produce practical effects by setting in motion, or being part of, the external policy-making or legislative process. A good understanding of, and even sensitivity to, the relationship between these 'hard' law and 'soft' law instruments is crucial for a good comprehension of EU external relations law.

SOURCES AND FURTHER READING

Casolari, F., 'The Principle of Loyal Co-operation: A 'Master Key' for EU External Representation?', in S. Blockmans and R. A. Wessel (eds.), *Principles and Practices of EU External Representation* (CLEER Working Papers, No. 5, 2012).

Chalmers, D., Davies, G. and Monti, G., *European Union Law*, 2nd edn (Cambridge: Cambridge University Press, 2011).

Cremona, M., 'Case C-246/07, Commission v. Sweden (PFOS), Judgment of the Court of Justice (Grand Chamber) of 20 April 2010' (2011) 43 *Common Market Law Review* 1639–1665.

Cremona, M., 'Defending the Community Interest: The Duties of Cooperation and Compliance', in M. Cremona and B. de Witte (eds.), *EU Foreign Relations Law: Constitutional Fundamentals* (Oxford: Hart Publishing, 2008), pp. 125–170.

Cremona, M., 'Member States Agreements as Union Law', in E. Cannizzaro, P. Palcheti and R. A. Wessel (eds.), *International Law as Law of the European Union* (Leiden/Boston: Martinus Nijhoff Publishers, 2011), pp. 291–324.

Czuczai, J., 'Mixity in Practice: Some Problems and their (Real or Possible) Solution', in C. Hillion and P. Koutrakos (eds.), *Mixed Agreements Revisited – The EU and its Member States in the World* (Oxford: Hart Publishing, 2010), pp. 231–248.

Delgado Casteleiro, A., 'EU Declarations of Competence to Multilateral Agreements: A Useful Reference Base?' (2012) 17 *European Foreign Affairs Review*, 4, 491–510.

Dimopoulos, A., 'The BITs Cases and their Practical and Doctrinal Implications', in J. Díez-Hochleitner *et al.* (eds.), *Recent Trends in the Case Law of the Court of Justice of the European Union (2008–2011)* (Madrid: La Ley, 2012), pp. 737–758.

Eeckhout, P., *EU External Relations Law*, 2nd edn (Oxford: Oxford University Press, 2011).

Gaja, G., 'The European Community's Rights and Obligations under Mixed Agreements', in D. O'Keefe and H. G. Schermers (eds.), *Mixed Agreements* (The Hague: Kluwer, 1983).

Gatti, M. and Manzini, P., 'External Representation of the European Union in the Conclusion of International Agreements' (2012) 49 *Common Market Law Review* 1703–1734.

Heliskoski, J., *Mixed Agreements as a Technique for Organizing the External Relations of the European Community and its Member States* (The Hague: Kluwer Law International, 2001).

Hillion, C., 'Mixity and Coherence in EU External Relations: The Significance of the Duty of Cooperation', in C. Hillion and P. Koutrakos (eds.), *Mixed Agreements Revisited – The EU and its Member States in the World* (Oxford: Hart Publishing, 2010), pp. 87–115.

Hoffmeister, F., 'Curse or Blessing? Mixed Agreements in the Recent Practice of the European Union and its Member States', in C. Hillion and P. Koutrakos (eds.), *Mixed Agreements Revisited – The EU and its Member States in the World* (Oxford: Hart Publishing, 2010), pp. 249–268.

Klabbers, J., *The Concept of Treaty in International Law* (The Hague: Kluwer Law International, 1996).

Klabbers, J., *Treaty Conflict and the European Union* (Cambridge: Cambridge University Press, 2009).

Kuijper, P. J., 'International Responsibility for EU Mixed Agreements', in C. Hillion and P. Koutrakos (eds.), *Mixed Agreements Revisited – The EU and its Member States in the World* (Oxford: Hart Publishing, 2010), pp. 208–227.

Lavranos, N., 'Case Note, Cases C-205/06 and C-249/06' (2009) 103 *American Journal of International Law* 716–722.

Lazowski, A., 'Enhanced Multilateralism and Enhanced Bilateralism: Integration without Membership in the European Union' (2008) 45 *Common Market Law Review* 1433–1458.

Lazowski, A., 'Withdrawal from the European Union and Alternatives to Membership' (2012) 37 *European Law Review* 523–540.

Maresceau, M., 'A Typology of Mixed Bilateral Agreements', in C. Hillion and P. Koutrakos (eds.), *Mixed Agreements Revisited – The EU and its Member States in the World* (Oxford: Hart Publishing, 2010), pp. 11–29.

Mendez, M., *The Legal Effects of EU Agreements: Maximalist Treaty Enforcement and Judicial Avoidance Techniques* (Oxford: Oxford University Press, 2013).

Rosas, A., 'The European Union and Mixed Agreements', in A. Dashwood and C. Hillion (eds.), *The General Law of EC External Relations* (Cambridge/London: Sweet & Maxwell, 2000).

Senden, L., *Soft Law in European Community Law* (Portland, Oregon: Hart Publishing, 2004).

Van Vooren, B., 'A Case Study of "Soft Law" in EU External Relations: The European Neighbourhood Policy' (2009) 34 *European Law Review* 696–719.

3

Existence of EU external competence

1 CENTRAL ISSUES

- The EU possesses legal personality and capacity to act as a legal subject in international relations. However, the EU cannot undertake whatever international action it wishes. Its capacity is governed by the principle of conferral laid down in Article 5 TFEU, which states that the Union shall act within the powers conferred on it by the Member States. As regards external competence of the Union, we distinguish between the existence, nature and scope of that power.
- In this chapter we examine the conditions under which competence to act externally will *exist* for the Union. First, this is the case when the Treaty expressly confers such external competence on the Union. Second, such competence may also be implied when, pursuant to the *ERTA* principle, the EU has adopted internal rules on the basis of expressly conferred internal powers; or when, pursuant to the complementarity principle, in the absence of internal rules, it is necessary to attain an EU Treaty objective for which the Treaty confers upon the Union an internal power. Third, when none of the above-mentioned sources are available, recourse to Article 352 TFEU is possible if this is necessary to attain objectives set for the Union in the EU Treaties.
- Political battles between the institutions and Member States over international presence and representation have regularly translated into litigation concerning the question of whether the EU actually has competence at all. In resolving these conflicts, the CJEU has shown itself sensitive to the legal–political context of European integration in which the legal proceedings took place. At times borderline activist, at other times protective of Member States' sovereignty, the role of the CJEU in this area of law, and consequently in the development of the EU as an international actor, cannot be understated.

2 THE PRINCIPLE OF CONFERRAL

In Chapter 1 we have addressed the EU's development as an international actor towards its distinct legal and political existence separate from that of its Member States. As noted there, this distinct legal existence of the Union is now explicitly recognized in Article 47 TEU:

> ### Article 47 TEU
>
> The Union shall have legal personality.

While the Union may exist legally distinct from its Member States, the Union does not possess legal capacity equivalent to that of the Member States: legal personality is the quality through which the entity can participate in legal life and be subject to rights and responsibilities. Legal capacity denotes the scope of its power to engage in such legal relationships. As regards the latter, the Union is different from the Member States because its capacity to act is governed by the principle of conferral. This principle is laid down in Article 5 TEU.

> ### Article 5 TEU
>
> 1. The limits of Union competences are governed by the principle of conferral. The use of Union competences is governed by the principles of subsidiarity and proportionality.
> 2. Under the principle of conferral, the Union shall act only within the limits of the competences conferred upon it by the Member States in the Treaties to attain the objectives set out therein. Competences not conferred upon the Union in the Treaties remain with the Member States.

The principle of conferred (synonym: attributed) powers (synonym: competences) implies that the Union does not have general law-making capacity and that it is incapable of extending its own competences beyond those conferred by the constitution-making authority.[1] In Opinion 2/94, the Court formulated the principle of conferral as follows:

> ### Opinion 2/94, *Accession by the Community to the European Convention for the Protection of Human Rights and Fundamental Freedoms* [1996] ECR I–1759
>
> 23. It follows from Article [5 TFEU], which states that the Community is to act within the limits of the powers conferred upon it by the Treaty and of the objectives assigned to it therein, that it has only those powers which have been conferred upon it.
> 24. That principle of conferred powers must be respected in both the internal action and the international action of the Community.
> 25. The Community acts ordinarily on the basis of specific powers which, as the Court has held, are not necessarily the express consequence of specific provisions of the Treaty but may also be implied from them.

The Court thereby authoritatively restated the implications of the principle of conferral, namely that internal and international action of the Union is constrained by the fact that the Member States decided to confer only a *limited* catalogue of powers upon the Union (Articles 3 to 6 TFEU). The Court mentions that such powers can be expressly found in specific provisions of the

[1] A. Dashwood, 'The Attribution of External Relations Competence', in A. Dashwood and C. Hillion (eds.), *The General Law of EC External Relations* (London: Sweet and Maxwell, 2000), p. 116.

Treaty, but also implied from them. This is called the question of existence of EU external powers. For a good understanding of EU external competence, it is then important to draw the conceptual distinction between the *existence* of competence of the EU, and the *nature* of that competence.

A. Dashwood, 'The Attribution of External Relations Competence', in A. Dashwood and C. Hillion (eds.), *The General Law of EC External Relations* **(London: Sweet and Maxwell, 2000), p. 115**

[B]oth the case law and the academic literature on the external relations competence of the European Community have been dominated by two great questions of principle, which were designated "the existence question" and "the exclusivity question". The logically prior of those, "the existence question" ... may be formulated ... as follows: how do the powers of the Community come to extend to relationships arising from international law, and hence involve the need in the sphere in question for agreements with the third countries concerned? The exclusivity question becomes relevant only once it is clear that the Community enjoys external relations competence in a certain matter.

This distinction between the *existence* and *nature* of EU external competence is often difficult to make in legal and policy practice, yet it is conceptually fundamental. Existence refers to two instances where the Union has competence to act internationally, as stated by the Court in Opinion 2/94: first, express attribution of competence, meaning that the Treaty states explicitly that the Union can act externally. For example, Article 207 TFEU explicitly confers upon the Union a power to conduct a common commercial policy. Second, implied attribution of competence, meaning that the Union's capacity to act can be implied from the conferral of an 'internal' competence in EU primary law. For example, Article 194 TFEU confers upon the Union competence in the sphere of energy, but makes no express reference to the possibility of concluding international agreements. Such power may then be implied, provided certain conditions are fulfilled (see below). The nature of that express or implied competence then refers to whether the Union can act alone in a certain field to the exclusion of the Member States or whether the EU should act alongside the Member States (see Chapter 4). It is impossible to understate the importance of legally and conceptually distinguishing the existence and nature of EU external competence; this because first, forty years of case law has generated an avalanche of formulations and competing interpretations, rendering the question of competence one of the most complex areas of EU external relations law; second, it is important to understand thoroughly how these principles legally function in distinct ways, so as to comprehend how they influence the political decision-making process of EU external relations. In the remainder of this chapter we focus solely on the existence of EU external competence, namely the expressed or implied existence of external powers. Chapter 4 will examine their nature as exclusive to the Union or shared with the Member States.

3 EXPRESS EXISTENCE OF EXTERNAL COMPETENCE

In the original Treaty of Rome, the EEC was only conferred two substantive competences in the external field, namely its competence to implement progressively a common commercial policy (Article 113 EC-Rome) and the competence to conclude AAs with one or more states or international organizations (Article 238 EC-Rome).[2] The EEC Treaty also provided for the establishment and maintenance of appropriate relations with the UN, the Council of Europe and the OECD (respectively Articles 302, 303 and 304 EC-Rome). In keeping with the progressive development of the Union as an international actor, successive treaty changes have added to the catalogue of internal and external competences of the Union. The Single European Act (SEA) added competences to conclude international agreements in the sphere of research and technology as well as the environment. The Treaty of Maastricht transformed EPC into CFSP while adding development policy to the EU's range of competences, as well as treaty-making powers in the monetary field. Since the Lisbon Treaty, Part I TFEU ('Principles') contains a catalogue of competences conferred upon the Union. In Title I on 'Categories and Areas of Union Competence', Article 1 TFEU states the following:

Article 1 TFEU

This Treaty organises the functioning of the Union and determines the areas of, delimitation of, and arrangements for exercising its competences.

In Article 2 TFEU we then find the definition of the exclusive, shared or coordinative (though not complementary)[3] nature of different EU competences. In Articles 3 to 6 of the TFEU we find a catalogue of areas in which competences are conferred upon the Union, divided according to their nature.

Article 3 TFEU

1. The Union shall have exclusive competence in the following areas:
   (a) customs union;
   (b) the establishing of the competition rules necessary for the functioning of the internal market;
   (c) monetary policy for the Member States whose currency is the euro;
   (d) the conservation of marine biological resources under the common fisheries policy;
   (e) common commercial policy.
2. The Union shall also have exclusive competence for the conclusion of an international agreement when its conclusion is provided for in a legislative act of the Union or is necessary to enable the Union to exercise its internal competence, or in so far as its conclusion may affect common rules or alter their scope.

Article 4 TFEU

1. The Union shall share competence with the Member States where the Treaties confer on it a competence which does not relate to the areas referred to in Articles 3 and 6.
2. Shared competence between the Union and the Member States applies in the following principal areas:
   (a) internal market;
   (b) social policy, for the aspects defined in this Treaty;

---

[2] R. Holdgaard, *External Relations Law of the European Community: Legal Reasoning and Legal Discourses* (Alphen aan den Rijn: Kluwer Law International, 2008), p. 22.
[3] See Article 4(4) TFEU which defines the nature of development policy, and see further Chapter 5 on nature of competence and Chapter 12 on development policy in this book.

(c) economic, social and territorial cohesion;

(d) agriculture and fisheries, excluding the conservation of marine biological resources;

(e) environment;

(f) consumer protection;

(g) transport;

(h) trans-European networks;

(i) energy;

(j) area of freedom, security and justice;

(k) common safety concerns in public health matters, for the aspects defined in this Treaty.

3. In the areas of research, technological development and space, the Union shall have competence to carry out activities, in particular to define and implement programmes; however, the exercise of that competence shall not result in Member States being prevented from exercising theirs.

4. In the areas of development cooperation and humanitarian aid, the Union shall have competence to carry out activities and conduct a common policy; however, the exercise of that competence shall not result in Member States being prevented from exercising theirs.

Article 6 TFEU

The Union shall have competence to carry out actions to support, coordinate or supplement the actions of the Member States. The areas of such action shall, at European level, be:

(a) protection and improvement of human health;

(b) industry;

(c) culture;

(d) tourism;

(e) education, vocational training, youth and sport;

(f) civil protection;

(g) administrative cooperation.

A number of elements are noteworthy in these three Treaty articles. First, only three of the more than two dozen policy fields explicitly concern external policy areas: Article 3(1)(e) TFEU on CCP, and Article 4(4) TFEU on development cooperation and humanitarian aid. Second, Articles 3 to 6 TFEU are no more than a *catalogue* of different areas in which the Union has competence, and they themselves do not actually confer competence upon the Union. For example, in the area of CCP, Article 207 TFEU is the competence-conferring article. They do however give us an important indication of the nature of EU competences as exclusive, shared, coordinative or complementary, without actually defining what that entails. Third, where this catalogue of competences mentions policy fields such as environment, energy, or the AFSJ, it states nothing on the possibility of the Union acting outside the EU legal order in these areas. For example, Article 4(2)(e) TFEU lists 'environment' as a shared competence, and Article 191(4) TFEU explicitly mentions the possibility of the Union to conclude agreements in the sphere of the environment. Article 4(2)(i) lists 'energy' as a shared competence, though the specific competence-conferring Article 194 TFEU is entirely silent on the possibility of acting externally. As a consequence not all conferred competences listed in these articles have an expressly stated external dimension. These articles therefore do not provide information on whether external competence will be expressly conferred, or may have to be implied from the article conferring the competence to act within the EU legal order. Fourth, the catalogue is not exhaustive and is incomplete. Notably, in the Draft Constitutional Treaty this catalogue of exclusive, shared and complementary competences also included a reference to the CFSP as one of the competences conferred upon the Union.[4] With the entry into force of the Lisbon Treaty, we no longer find the CFSP listed in that catalogue, and in the TFEU we now only find this policy mentioned in Article 2(4) TFEU. While this Article 2 TFEU is meant to define the *nature* of EU competences and will be discussed in the following Chapter 4, its fourth paragraph is nonetheless a purely competence-conferring article (existence) making no statement on the nature of the CFSP.

Article 2(4) TFEU

The Union shall have competence, in accordance with the provisions of the Treaty on European Union, to define and implement a common foreign and security policy, including the progressive framing of a common defence policy.

This change between the Draft Constitution and the Lisbon Treaty is however not without significance, as it is one example of a continuation of the foreign policy–community dichotomy we uncovered in Chapter 1. Not stating the CFSP as a distinct competence in the TFEU was meant to underline the 'distinctive' nature of the CFSP from the 'communitarized' EU competences in the TFEU. From a legal perspective this change is not necessarily merely cosmetic, as it may be queried whether this change allows deeper inferences on the nature of the CFSP as not actually being a competence which has been 'conferred' upon the Union. The answer to that question has commensurate effects on the application of legal principles such as direct effect and primacy, and the nature of the EU legal order itself. Such questions are examined further in Chapter 11 on the CFSP.

Fifth and finally, aside from omitting the CFSP, the competence catalogue of Articles 3 to 6 equally does not include a reference to a number of other expressly stated external competences in the Treaties, or competences which have an express external dimension. As regards the first category, these provisions exclude reference to four notably substantive competences:

- the competence to accede to the European Convention on Human Rights (ECHR) (Article 6(2) TEU);[5]
- the competence to establish special relations with the neighbourhood, including through concluding international agreements (Article 8 TEU);
- the competence to adopt restrictive measures (Article 215 TFEU);
- the competence to conclude AAs (Article 217 TFEU).

---

[4] M. Cremona, 'The Draft Constitutional Treaty: External Relations and External Action' (2003) 40 *Common Market Law Review* 1347–1366.

[5] See also Opinion 2/94 discussed further in this chapter: Opinion 2/94 *Accession of the Community to the ECHR* [1996] ECR I-1759.

The following areas mentioned in Articles 3 to 6 also include an explicit external dimension in their relevant competence-conferring articles: the conclusion of agreements on the readmission of illegal immigrants (Article 79(3) TFEU); 'fostering cooperation' with third countries in the field of education (165(3) TFEU), vocational training (166(3) TFEU), culture (167(3) TFEU), public health (168(3) TFEU); cooperating with third countries on Trans-European networks (171(3) TFEU); the conclusion of international agreements in the fields of research and technological development (186 TFEU); the conclusion of international agreements in the field of the environment (191(4) TFEU); the conclusion of agreements on economic, financial and technical cooperation with third countries (212(2) TFEU); the conclusion of agreements in the sphere of monetary Union (219(4) TFEU); and establishing appropriate relations with the UN, Council of Europe, OECD and other international organizations (Article 220(1) TFEU).

In all these areas, primary law explicitly confers upon the Union competence to act externally, or internal powers have an express external dimension. The difference between an article concerning an external policy in its entirety, such as the CCP, or an article providing only for a specific external dimension, is not without its significance.[6] The more limited articles such as Article 191(4) TFEU which expressly confer powers 'to negotiate and conclude international agreements' for the 'arrangement of international cooperation' are to be construed restrictively. This implies that international agreements which also introduce specific substantive rules cannot be based on such limited provisions alone, and require recourse to the implied powers doctrine and the general competence-conferring article.[7] As we shall see further in this chapter as well as Chapter 4, this need for recourse to the implied powers doctrine has significant implications for the possibility of Member States' capacity to act in these instances.

4   IMPLIED EXISTENCE OF EXTERNAL COMPETENCE

The legal personality of the Union is matched by a capacity to act internationally within the confines of the principle of conferred powers (Article 5 TEU). In case no express external competence has been conferred, the subsequent question we must pose is this: does the fact that an EU competence (such as the energy competence in Article 194 TFEU) not expressly state an external dimension, exclude the possibility of any international action by the Union? In abstract terms, when the Union has been expressly conferred an *internal* power, can a competence to act *externally* be implied from that provision? The EURATOM agreement, from its entry into force in 1957, contained a separate, general chapter on external relations, and provided an explicit answer to that question. In that chapter, Article 101 European Atomic Energy Treaty (EUROTOM) established a *general parallelism* between the internal powers of the EAEC and its power to be bound internationally.

Article 101 EURATOM

The Community may, within the limits of its powers and jurisdiction, enter into obligations by concluding agreements or contracts with a third State, an international organization or a national of a third State.

---

[6] See P. Koutrakos, *EU International Relations Law* (Oxford: Hart Publishing, 2006), p. 10.

[7] *Ibid.*, and see further M. Klamert, *New Conferral or Old Confusion? – The Perils of Making Implied Competences Explicit and the Example of the External Competence for Environmental Policy* (The Hague: CLEER Working Paper, 2011/6).

The Treaty of Rome did not contain such a general external power in parallel to its internal powers. The drafters made that omission on purpose, given the much broader transfer of powers from the Member States to the EEC. A similar article establishing general parallel external powers would have too significant an impact on the Member States' external powers.[8] Where the Treaties were silent on the external dimension of certain powers conferred upon the EU, the CJEU has filled that lacuna by setting out a doctrine of implied powers. However, it has not established full parallelism such as is with EURATOM. The Lisbon Treaty has now codified this doctrine, but has done so in a rather convoluted fashion in Articles 216(1) TFEU and 3(2) TFEU. Most notably, the distinction between the existence and nature of EU external competence has not been clearly maintained in these articles. Because a thorough understanding of the relevant case law is necessary in order to comprehend these Treaty provisions, they are not discussed at this point of this textbook. Instead they are reproduced in Chapter 4 on the nature of EU external competence, where they are followed by a brief analysis of their drafting history, and the impact of judge-made law on the existence and nature of EU external competence.

(i) The *ERTA* doctrine: *effet utile* and implied powers

(a) The existence of implied external competence

The landmark judgment of 1970 which lent its name to the most important strand of the doctrine of implied powers (the '*ERTA* doctrine') is the first ever case where the Commission initiated annulment proceedings against the Council.[9] It concerned a dispute between these institutions on the negotiation and conclusion of an Agreement concerning the work of crews of vehicles engaged in international road transport (*ERTA*).[10] This topic was sensitive for the Member States, as since 1939 attempts had been made to regulate this matter at international level, to no avail. The ERTA itself had been previously signed by the Member States in 1962, but did not reach sufficient ratifications to enter into force.[11] In 1967 negotiations for the revision of the said agreement were resumed, while from 1966 onwards a draft Regulation was being prepared on this topic within the Community.[12] In March 1969 Work at EC level resulted in Council Regulation No. 543/69.[13] This Regulation stated that it would apply to carriage by vehicles registered in a Member State with effect from 1 October 1969 and in the case of vehicles registered in a third country from 1 October 1970.[14] In March 1970 the Council then decided that the Member States would conduct and conclude the new European Agreement, in spite of protests from the Commission which argued that because the Council Regulation had been adopted, the Community was now competent to conclude the agreement.

---

[8] P. Eeckhout, *EU External Relations Law*, 2nd edn (Oxford: Oxford University Press, 2011), p. 71.

[9] J. Temple Lang, 'The ERTA Judgment and the Court's Case-Law on Competence and Conflict' (1986) 6 *Yearbook of European Law* 183–218.

[10] Case 22/70 *Commission* v. *Council (European Road Transport Agreement)*, [1971] ECR 263.

[11] Eeckhout, *EU External Relations Law*, p. 72.

[12] Opinion of AG Dutheillet de Lamothe, delivered on 10 March 1971, Case 22/70 *Commission* v. *Council (European Road Transport Agreement)* [1971] ECR 263.

[13] Council Regulation 543/69/EEC of 25 March 1969 on the harmonization of certain social legislation relating to road transport, OJ 1969 No. L77/49.

[14] Opinion of AG Dutheillet de Lamothe, Case 22/70 [1971] ECR 263.

We start our examination of this case by reproducing the relevant passages of the Council proceedings targeted by the Commission's annulment action. These proceedings, laying out the planned international negotiations, provide important insight into the connection between policy and legal argument in the development of the EU as an international actor, and provide important context to gauge the legal and political impact of the implied powers doctrine. The *ERTA* story shows us a number of important elements on implied external competence, and EU external relations law more generally:

- It sets the stage for two of the most important principles of EU external relations law: the *implied* existence of EU external competence, and the possibility of such competence *excluding* power of the Member States to act.
- It thereby also illustrates how diametrically opposed views of the Member States (Council) and Commission on external representation translate into legal arguments before the Court, while simultaneously reflecting more fundamental questions on European integration in relation to the EU speaking with the proverbial single voice.
- It shows us how diverse interpretative methods employed by the Court of Justice, while legally certainly justifiable, will tip the scale in favour of the Council or the Commission. As a consequence, the role of the Court in the development of the EU as an international actor through law cannot be understated.

Minutes of the Council Meeting, 20 March 1970[15]

The Council agrees that in accordance with the course of action decided during its meeting of 18 and 19 July 1968, negotiations with third countries shall be carried on and concluded by the six Member States – which are to become the contracting parties to the ERTA. Throughout the negotiations and at the conclusion of the agreement the Member States shall take common action, coordinating their position in accordance with the usual procedures, in close association with the Community institutions, the delegation of the Member State currently occupying the presidency of the Council acting as spokesman. In confirming its reservations as to this procedure, the Commission declares that it considers that the attitude adopted by the Council does not conform to the Treaty ... With regard to the modification of the regulation to take account of the provisions of the ERTA, the Council finds that in order that the Member States may fulfil their obligations arising from the latter, Community Regulation No 543/69 should be amended in sufficient time before 1 October 1970, in order to allow the two bodies of rules to exist concurrently. Having regard to this requirement and with the object of furthering implementation of social legislation over the whole of Europe, the Council ... requests the Commission to submit to it in sufficient time its proposals for the necessary amendments to [the Regulation] in relation to the ERTA.

The Commission disagreed with this reasoning of the Council, and therefore lodged an application for annulment of these Council proceedings.[16] When reading the above excerpt, one should pay particular attention to the fashion in which the six Member States constructed

---

[15] Reproduced in Opinion of AG Dutheillet de Lamothe, *supra*, 285–286.
[16] Case 22/70, *supra*, paras 35–55.

the relationship between the Regulation and their international action. In spite of the common rules at EC level, the Member States were of the opinion that they remained competent to conclude international agreements in the same matter. There was no parallel external power conferred by the Treaty, and the Member States opined that at most a legal obligation stemming from EC law existed to avoid discrepancies between the Regulation by which they were bound, and their international commitment on the same subject matter. The Commission thus had to initiate the necessary legislative action so that the 'Member States meeting as the Council' could ensure the coexistence of the EC rules and their international commitment.

The competing visions on EC–Member State coexistence of the Commission and the Council translate into diametrically opposing legal arguments before the Court. In the following excerpt, pay particular attention to the following two questions: what is each party's construction of the principle of conferral as it relates to implied external powers compared to express internal competences, and which interpretative methods of primary law are the Commission and Council employing to justify their views legally?

Case 22/70 *ERTA* [1971] ECR 263

6. The Commission takes the view that Article 75 [now Article 91 TFEU], which conferred on the Community powers defined in wide terms with a view to implementing the common transport policy, must apply to external relations just as much as to domestic measures in the sphere envisaged.

7. It believes that the full effect of this provision would be jeopardized if the powers which it confers, particularly that of laying down "any appropriate provisions"... did not extend to the conclusion of agreements with third countries.

8. Even if, it is argued, this power did not originally embrace the whole sphere of transport, it would tend to become general and exclusive as where the common policy in this field came to be implemented.

9. The Council, on the other hand, contends that since the Community only has such powers as have been conferred on it, authority to enter into agreements with third countries cannot be assumed in the absence of an express provision in the Treaty.

10. More particularly, Article 75 [now Article 91 TFEU] relates only to measures internal to the Community, and cannot be interpreted as authorizing the conclusion of international agreements.

11. Even if it were otherwise, such authority could not be general and exclusive, but at the most concurrent with that of the Member States.

The political and constitutional importance of this judgment is underlined by the wholly opposing views of the Commission and Member States. They raise a number of further questions pertaining to the doctrine of implied powers: to which extent are the existence and nature of external competences being separated by the Court? Which of the competing interpretations of the principle of conferral does the Court uphold, and how does it legally justify its assertion? What are the legal criteria for EU external powers to exist through implication? Do any of the parties argue for parallelism such as that embedded in the EURATOM? How do the respective arguments relate to the connection between law, policy and European integration, as explained in the Preface to this book?

Case 22/70 *ERTA* [1971] ECR 263

12. In the absence of specific provisions of the Treaty relating to the negotiation and conclusion of international agreements in the sphere of transport policy – a category into which, essentially, the AETR falls – one must turn to the general system of Community law in the sphere of relations with third countries.

13. Article 210 [now Article 47 TEU] provides that 'The Community shall have legal personality'.

14. This provision, placed at the head of Part Six of the Treaty, devoted to 'General and Final Provisions', means that in its external relations the Community enjoys the capacity to establish contractual links with third countries over the whole field of objectives defined in Part One of the Treaty, which Part Six supplements.

15. To determine in a particular case the Community's authority to enter into international agreements, regard must be had to the whole scheme of the Treaty no less than to its substantive provisions.

16. Such authority arises not only from an express conferment by the Treaty – as is the case with Articles 113 and 114 for tariff and trade agreements and with Article 238 for association agreements – but may equally flow from other provisions of the Treaty and from measures adopted, within the framework of those provisions, by the Community institutions.

17. In particular, each time the Community, with a view to implementing a common policy envisaged by the Treaty, adopts provisions laying down common rules, whatever form these may take, the Member States no longer have the right, acting individually or even collectively, to undertake obligations with third countries which affect those rules.

18. As and when such common rules come into being, the Community alone is in a position to assume and carry out contractual obligations towards third countries affecting the whole sphere of application of the Community legal system.

19. With regard to the implementation of the provisions of the Treaty the system of internal Community measures may not therefore be separated from that of external relations. . . .

23. According to Article 74 [now 90 TFEU], the objectives of the Treaty in matters of transport are to be pursued within the framework of a common policy.

24. With this in view, Article 75 (1) [now 91 TFEU] directs the Council to lay down common rules and, in addition, 'any other appropriate provisions'.

25. By the terms of subparagraph (a) of the same provision, those common rules are applicable 'to international transport to or from the territory of a Member State or passing across the territory of one or more Member States'.

26. This provision is equally concerned with transport from or to third countries, as regards that part of the journey which takes place on Community territory.

27. It thus assumes that the powers of the Community extend to relationships arising from international law, and hence involve the need in the sphere in question for agreements with the third countries concerned.

In distilling the implied powers or *ERTA* doctrine from this judgment, we must commence by distinguishing between the existence and nature of external competence: paragraphs 14 to 16 concern the *existence* of implied EC powers (Is the EC competent at all?), whereas paragraphs 17 to 19 deal with the *nature* of that power (Is this competence exclusively in the hands of the EU?). In paragraphs 16 and 17 the CJEU lays down the basic rules of the *ERTA* doctrine:

- on the *existence* of implied external competence: authority to enter into international commitments may flow from Treaty articles which confer on the EU powers to take measures within the EU legal order, but only when the EU institutions have adopted such measures.
- on the *nature* of that competence: when the EU adopts common rules of whatever form, the Member States can no longer undertake international commitments which would affect those rules. Paragraphs 17 to 19 have been termed the '*ERTA*' effect, or *ERTA* pre-emption. The legal criteria under which such pre-emption takes place receives thorough investigation in Chapter 4.

Quite evidently, this ruling of the Court is very different from the Member States' opinion observed in the Council proceedings quoted above. The Council argued that conferral requires that the Treaties *expressly* state that the EU can act externally, and that even if this is not the case, that such powers would not exclude the Member States. The Court of Justice decided differently on both points. Focusing on the existence of implied powers, the core question is how to reconcile the implied existence of external powers with the principle of conferral. The argument of the Council left no doubt that conferral is to be interpreted restrictively, and no EC competence to enter into agreements with third countries can be assumed in the absence of an express Treaty provision to that effect. The Commission on the other hand championed a teleological approach to conferral, by arguing that EC powers in the sphere of transport would be devoid of their *effet utile* if they did not extend to the conclusion of international agreements. In the eyes of the Commission, a conferral of powers applies equally to domestic and international measures. Stated differently, there is a parallelism between the internal and the external powers of the EC.

The Court of Justice was certainly not very explicit in its legal justification for the implied powers doctrine, and it can only be uncovered through a very thorough examination of the judgment. The starting point lies in paragraphs 13 to 15, where the Court recounts key elements of the EU, or any national Member State's legal system. To reconcile conferral with implied competences, the European Court of Justice (ECJ) starts from the legal personality of the EC (current Article 47 TEU). From that starting point it distinguishes between on the one hand *capacity* to act – which the Court infers must logically exist because the EU has legal personality – and *authority* to act, which is here synonymous with EU competence. By this reasoning, competence is thus the narrower concept giving substantive meaning to the broader concept of legal capacity.[17] Therefore, the legal personality of the Union provides no independent, fully fledged capacity to enter into international commitments. By thus distinguishing capacity from authority, the Court accepts the initial portion of the Council's argument that the Community only has such powers as have been conferred on it,[18] and positions the doctrine of implied powers within the scope of the principle of conferral.[19] However, this does not in itself legally justify the existence of implied powers for the Community. The key is in paragraph 15. Here the CJEU states that 'the whole scheme of the Treaty as well as its individual substantive provisions require examination' in order to establish whether external competence exists. With that statement, the Court rejects the narrow interpretation of the principle of conferral offered by the Council and makes room for the teleological interpretation of the Commission. However, the

---

[17] Dashwood and J. Heliskoski, 'The Classic Authorities Revisited', in Dashwood and Hillion (eds.), *The General Law of EC External Relations*, p. 6.

[18] Case 22/70 (*ERTA*), *supra*, paras 12–14.

[19] Dashwood and Heliskoski, 'The Classic Authorities Revisited', p. 7.

CJEU does not go on to spell out this teleological approach in any more detail, and what follows in paragraph 16 is a simple statement of legal axiom: powers to enter into an international agreement may 'equally flow from other provisions of the Treaty and from measures adopted'.[20] That axiomatic statement is problematic because absent is any justification for the source of the existence of the EC's implied competence. Is it the implied competence conferred in primary law, or is it the measure adopted which confers the competence on the Community?[21] The CJEU gives no clear answer to that question, though in the application of its statement of principle in the later paragraphs we do find that the Court says that: 'This grant of power is moreover expressly recognized by Article 3 of the said Regulation which prescribes that: "The Community shall enter into any negotiations with third countries which may prove necessary for the purpose of implementing this regulation".' Hence, the secondary legislative instrument 'recognizes' primary law as the source of the implied competence, which exists so as to ensure effectiveness of that article. This is supported by the Court's treatment of Article 91 TFEU in paragraphs 23 to 27, whereby the Court explains that the language of that article itself implies the existence of external competence. In the words of Dashwood and Heliskoski:

A. Dashwood and J. Heliskoski, 'The Classic Authorities Revisited', in A. Dashwood and C. Hillion (eds.), *The General Law of EC External Relations* (London: Sweet and Maxwell, 2000), p. 8

The logic underlying the inference is that, in order to be effective, provisions of the kind contemplated by the Article may have to have an international, as well as a purely internal, aspect. If the objective is to regulate the parts of journeys taking place in third countries, then the Community must be authorised to enter into international agreements, as and when it may be useful to do so.

In this quotation the authors are right to infer from paragraph 27 of the *ERTA* judgment that the Court recognizes an implied external power when it may be useful to attain objectives of the Treaty. Hence, the Court does not agree with the assertion of the Commission that any internal power in the Treaty has an unconditional, parallel external dimension. Instead, effectiveness of the competences conferred upon the Union in order to achieve its Treaty objectives, is the core rationale for the existence of implied, external powers. In the *Kramer* judgment five years after *ERTA*, the CJEU was more explicit about this *effet utile* rationale:

Joined Cases 3/76, 4/76 and 6/76 *Cornelis Kramer and Others* [1976] ECR 1279, 30–33

It follows from these provisions taken as a whole that the Community has at its disposal, on the internal level, the power to take any measures for the conservation of the biological resources of the sea ... The only way to ensure the conservation of the biological resources of the sea both effectively and equitably is through a system of rules binding on all the States concerned, including non-member countries. In these

---

[20] Case 22/70 (*ERTA*), *supra*, para 16.
[21] For an extensive and comprehensive comment on the *ERTA* judgment see: Koutrakos, *EU International Relations Law*, pp. 77–88, and Dashwood and Heliskoski, 'The Classic Authorities Revisited', pp. 5–9.

circumstances it follows from the very duties and powers which Community law has established and assigned to the institutions of the Community on the internal level that the Community has authority to enter into international commitments for the conservation of the resources of the sea.

(b) Legal–political context to the *ERTA* doctrine

In the *ERTA* judgment the Court thus established the principle whereby an EU external competence exists when it has exercised its internal competence, and when this is deemed to contribute to achieving objectives of the EU Treaty. This teleological approach to powers conferred upon the Union was controversial, and therefore the *ERTA* judgment is an excellent example of the relationship between European integration, law, adjudication and policy. The Advocate General (AG) admitted that he was highly sympathetic to 'the view that authority in external matters can be transferred to the Community through the adoption of a Community regulation'.[22] However, he continued that it is 'with some regret that upon reflection' he suggested to the Court that this view should not be accepted. He was of the opinion that this 'would involve the Court in a discretionary construction of the law, or, in other words, a judicial interpretation far exceeding the bounds which the Court has hitherto set regarding its power to interpret the treaty'.[23] Eeckhout is of the opposite opinion: 'the Court was not guilty of creating, through judicial interpretation, a significant expansion of the Community's competences'.[24] This prompts reflection on the role of the Court, law and this judgment in the process of EU constitutionalization – some would say judicial activism – as it also applies to EU external relations law. Recall that the Member States were of the opinion that at most, they had a legal obligation stemming from EC law to avoid discrepancies between the EC Regulation and their own international commitments. They themselves would organize coordination so that their individual international action would reflect the common, EC interest. The Court went in the opposite direction. Where it rendered a judgment on the existence of implied powers to the exclusion of Member States if EU internal rules are affected, this case is organically linked to the constitutionalization process through ongoing landmark judgments at that time:[25] only a few years before the *ERTA* judgment, the ECJ had introduced supremacy in *Costa* v. *Enel*[26] and direct effect in *Van Gend en Loos*.[27] In *ERTA*, the Court essentially applies the principle of supremacy by introducing the exclusion (pre-emption) of Member States in instances where internal competence is exercised by the Community. The empowerment of Community structures through legal principles introduced by the Court is therefore clearly perceptible in this judgment.[28] What is however notable, is the contrast between principle and pragmatism in this judgment, a common theme in case law on EU external

---

[22] Opinion of AG Dutheillet de Lamothe, *supra*, 290.

[23] Opinion of AG Dutheillet de Lamothe, *supra*, 289.

[24] Eeckhout, *EU External Relations Law*, p. 75.

[25] Koutrakos, *EU International Relations Law*, p. 85; G. de Baere, *Constitutional Principles of EU External Relations* (Oxford: Oxford University Press, 2008), pp. 34–38.

[26] Case 6/64 *Costa* v. *ENEL* [1964] ECR 585.

[27] Case 26/62 *Van Gend en Loos* v. *Nederlandse Administratie der Belastingen* [1963] ECR 1.

[28] Koutrakos, *EU International Relations Law*, pp. 85 and 88: 'The system of external relations of the Community is not immune to the constitutionalising process of the Community legal order. Instead it is intertwined with the establishment of the internal market and stems from its regulation.'

relations.[29] Indeed, after making this all-important statement, the Court dismissed the action of the Commission. The Court argued that a significant part of the negotiations had been previously undertaken by the Member States, and that in the 1970 proceedings they had sought to act in the common interest of the Community. The AG had pointed to the sensitive and difficult negotiations in this field, with attempts to negotiate relevant international instruments first having been taken in 1939.[30] The Court's dismissal of the action was therefore imbued with pragmatist sensitivity to the policy context of the judgment:[31] 'At that stage of the negotiations, to have suggested to the third countries concerned that there was now a new distribution of powers within the Community might well have jeopardized the successful outcome of the negotiations, as was indeed recognized by the Commission's representative in the course of the Council's deliberations.'

In subsequent case law the Court has often restated the principle of implied powers. Because the principle of *existence* of *ERTA* implied that external powers have remained consistent throughout those cases, we shall not examine them at this juncture. Much more controversial have been the criteria for that competence to pre-empt Member State action, and we refer to Chapter 4 for the examination of the relevant jurisprudence. That same clarity of principle did not characterize the second strand of implied competences, those in existence in the absence of the exercise of internal EU competences.

(ii) Implication without prior internal legislation: 'Necessity'

In *ERTA* the Court had stated that competences could implicitly exist 'in particular'[32] when the Community had adopted common rules. Opinion 1/76 is then the authoritative statement that competence can also be implied in the absence of internal legislation. This case affirms what had been hinted at in the *ERTA* and *Kramer* judgments.[33] Opinion 1/76 concerned the Commission's request for compatibility with the EC Treaty of the conclusion of a draft agreement establishing a European fund to provide financial means of compensation for the temporary laying-up of inland waterway vessels, as a measure to deal with transportation overcapacity. The first few paragraphs of this opinion concerned competence of the EC to conclude this agreement.

> **Opinion 1/76, *Draft Agreement establishing a European laying-up fund for inland waterway vessels* [1977] ECR 741**
>
> 1. The object of the system laid down by the draft Agreement and expressed in the Statute annexed thereto is to rationalize the economic situation of the inland waterway transport industry in a

---

[29] T. Tridimas and Eeckhout, 'The External Competence of the Community and the Case-Law of the Court of Justice: Principle versus Pragmatism' (1994) 14 *Yearbook of European Law* 143–177.

[30] Opinion of AG Dutheillet de Lamothe, *supra*, 284.

[31] Case 22/70 (*ERTA*), *supra*, para 86.

[32] Case 22/70 (*ERTA*), *supra*, para 17.

[33] Joined Cases 3/76, 4/76 & 6/76 *Kramer and Others* [1976] ECR 1279. This case concerned preliminary references on the 1959 North East Atlantic Fisheries Convention. One of the questions referred concerned competence of the Community to enter alone into commitments undertaken by all but two of its Member States. In this judgment, the Court added to *ERTA* by stating that competence could be implied from EC primary law along with the Act of Accession of the UK, Ireland and Denmark. See *Kramer*, paras 19–20.

geographical region in which transport by inland waterway is of special importance within the whole network of international transport. Such a system is doubtless an important factor in the common transport policy, the establishment of which is included in the activities of the Community laid down in Article 3 of the EEC Treaty. In order to implement this policy, Article 75 of the Treaty instructs the Council to lay down according to the prescribed procedure common rules applicable to international transport to or from the territory of one or more Member States. This article also supplies, as regards the Community, the necessary legal basis to establish the system concerned.

2. In this case however, it is impossible fully to attain the objective pursued by means of the establishment of common rules pursuant to Article 75 of the Treaty, because of the traditional participation of vessels from a third State, Switzerland, in navigation by the principal waterways in question, which are subject to the system of freedom of navigation established by international agreements of long standing. It has thus been necessary to bring Switzerland into the scheme in question by means of an international agreement with this third State.

3. The power of the Community to conclude such an agreement is not expressly laid down in the Treaty. However, the Court has already had occasion to state, most recently in its [*Kramer* judgment], that authority to enter into international commitments may not only arise from an express attribution by the Treaty, but equally may flow implicitly from its provisions. The Court has concluded inter alia that whenever Community law has created for the institutions of the Community powers within its internal system for the purpose of attaining a specific objective, the Community has authority to enter into the international commitments necessary for the attainment of that objective even in the absence of an express provision in that connexion.

4. This is particularly so in all cases in which internal power has already been used in order to adopt measures which come within the attainment of common policies. It is, however, not limited to that eventuality. Although the internal Community measures are only adopted when the international agreement is concluded and made enforceable, as is envisaged in the present case by the proposal for a regulation to be submitted to the Council by the Commission, the power to bind the Community vis-à-vis third countries nevertheless flows by implication from the provisions of the Treaty creating the internal power and in so far as the participation of the Community in the international agreement is, as here, necessary for the attainment of one of the objectives of the Community.

In relation to the existence of competence and the principle of conferral, this Opinion raises a number of issues: first, is it possible for an external power to exist in the sphere of transport without first having adopted internal legislation? Second, if this is indeed so because it is necessary to achieve EU objectives, how do we define the 'necessity' criterion? Third and finally, does this case make any pronunciation on the nature of this implied external competence?

In this excerpt the Court states that the existence of implied powers is not limited to the instance of the EU already having used its internal power to adopt measures within the Union. In the case of Opinion 1/76 there is indeed no pre-existing legislation. In fact, it is in the nature of the policy initiative on the Rhine Basin that only by including Switzerland can the necessary policy action be effectively undertaken. Therefore purely EU-internal legislation is excluded, and an international agreement is factually unavoidable. In response, the Court states that a power to conclude that agreement is implied from the Treaty when it is necessary for the attainment of EU policy objectives. Conceptually this means that the competence to conclude the agreement is implied ('comes into existence') at the exact moment the international instrument is being concluded, and that unlike the case in *ERTA*, it is not necessary that the EU first adopt internal common rules. This does not mean that the EU is given carte blanche external powers whenever deemed useful, or that it could undertake substantive policy measures which it could not undertake internally. Indeed, only where it is 'necessary' will the relevant powers be implied even in the absence of internal legislation, and this only to pursue objectives stated in the Treaties. This is why Dashwood and Heliskoski have termed it the *principle of complementarity*, which indicates that the external competence complements the express internal competence.[34] In Opinion 2/91 concerning competence to conclude an ILO Convention concerning chemicals at work, the CJEU had the opportunity to clarify the necessity criterion. In the words of the two aforementioned authors:[35]

> **A. Dashwood and J. Heliskoski, 'The Classic Authorities Revisited', in A. Dashwood and C. Hillion (eds.), *The General Law of EC External Relations* (London: Sweet and Maxwell, 2000), pp. 11–14**
>
> The Court, it seems, does not understand 'necessary' as indispensable to attain the objective for which competence to legislate internally has been granted. Health and safety standards such as those prescribed by Convention No 170 could just as well have been introduced through autonomous Community measures ... The test applied in practice by the Court may, we suggest, be formulated thus: does the Community need treaty-making power to ensure the optimal use, over time, of its expressly conferred internal competence?

When that criterion is fulfilled, then EU external competence to act externally will exist without prior internal legislation. It should be pointed out that the Opinion 1/76 strand of implied competence has been consistently upheld throughout the decades of case law on implied powers, but that in fact the *ERTA* doctrine is of most practical importance. Since Opinion 1/76, there have not actually been instances where the Court of Justice has accepted its criteria to be fulfilled.[36]

A brief word on the nature of this strand of implied external competence is necessary. Throughout the development of the case law on implied competences, there has been much discussion on whether Opinion 1/76 implies the existence of a competence *exclusive* to the Union, or shared with the Member States. In the case concerning competence to conclude the WTO Opinion, the Commission had argued to that effect, and the unguarded language of the Court tacitly appeared to accept the premise that Opinion 1/76 implies the immediate existence of *exclusive* external competence for the Community.[37] After years of discussion, in Opinion 1/03 of 2006 the Court clearly stated that both *ERTA* and Opinion 1/76 implied that competences can be either shared or exclusive.

---

[34] Dashwood and Heliskoski, 'The Classic Authorities Revisited', p. 13.

[35] *Ibid.*, 16.

[36] See for example its rejection in the *Open Skies* cases: Case C-467/98 *Commission* v. *Denmark* [2002] ECR I-9519, paras 54–64.

[37] Opinion 1/94, *Re World Trade Organization Agreement* [1994] ECR I-5267, paras 72–73.

(iii) Review: express and implied existence of external competence

In Opinion 1/03 concerning EU competence to conclude the Lugano Convention, the Court of Justice summarized the rules concerning the existence of (1) express and (2) implied EU external competence as follows. In the excerpt below, the references (a) and (b) indicate the two distinct strands of implied competence. The first sentence of the next paragraph has been included to underline that the Court clearly viewed the existence of express or implied EU external competence as separate from the question of their nature as shared or exclusive.

Opinion 1/03, *Competence to conclude the Lugano II Convention* [2006] ECR I-1145

114. The competence of the Community to conclude international agreements may arise not only from an **(1) express conferment** by the Treaty but may equally **(2) flow implicitly** from other provisions of the Treaty and **(a) from measures adopted**, within the framework of those provisions, by the Community institutions (see *ERTA*, paragraph 16). The Court has also held that whenever Community law created for those institutions powers within its internal system for the purpose of attaining a specific objective, the Community had authority to undertake **(b) international commitments necessary** for the attainment of that objective even in the **absence** of an express provision to that effect (Opinion 1/76, paragraph 3, and Opinion 2/91, paragraph 7).
115. **That competence of the Community may be exclusive or shared** with the Member States.[38]

---

5 RESIDUAL IMPLIED EXTERNAL COMPETENCE: ARTICLE 352 TFEU

Article 352 TFEU

1. If action by the Union should prove necessary, within the framework of the policies defined in the Treaties, to attain one of the objectives set out in the Treaties, and the Treaties have not provided the necessary powers, the Council, acting unanimously on a proposal from the Commission and after obtaining the consent of the European Parliament, shall adopt the appropriate measures. Where the measures in question are adopted by the Council in accordance with a special legislative procedure, it shall also act unanimously on a proposal from the Commission and after obtaining the consent of the European Parliament.

We have seen that historically the Treaty of Rome conferred very few express external competences on the Community. While treaty changes from the SEA to the Lisbon Treaty have led to more express external competence, implied competence remains a crucial source for the existence of external competence. However, there may be instances where a certain kind of international action is deemed necessary on the part of the Union, but where no express or implied competences

---

[38] Emphasis and numbering added.

may exist. In that case the question arises of whether Article 352 TFEU can provide a legal basis for such external action. This was at issue in Opinion 2/94 concerning accession to the ECHR.

With the entry into force of the Lisbon Treaty, Article 6(2) TEU states that the Union shall accede to the ECHR, and that 'Such accession shall not affect the Union's competences as defined in the Treaties.' Prior to Lisbon such a competence to accede to the ECHR did not exist in the Treaties, and during the mid 1990s the Council requested the CJEU to rule on the compatibility of accession to the ECHR. The Council recognized that the Community was not conferred specific powers in the field of human rights, and in the absence of such an express conferral it was submitted that the Community might accede on the basis of current Article 352 TFEU.[39] The Council further asked whether submission to judicial machinery such as that in existence in Strasbourg would be compatible with the EU legal order. However, the Court did not respond to that question and solely focused on the competence of the Community to accede to the Convention. Therefore, regardless of explicit post-Lisbon competence to accede, Opinion 2/94 remains important today for the Court's treatment of Article 352 TFEU as a legal basis for the existence of an EU external competence. What is more, from the perspective of constitutionalization in EU external relations law, it is important to contrast the findings in this Opinion with those in *ERTA*. In the latter we saw what could be termed an activist Court handing down 'the single most important judgment … in the field of EC external relations law' of which 'it is difficult to overestimate its significance'.[40] In Opinion 2/94 we saw a Court which preserved Member States' powers by limiting the so-called 'competence creep' by reference to the principle of conferral.[41] In other words, in *ERTA*, the principle of conferral was no obstacle to recognizing the implied powers doctrine opposed by both the Council and the AG, whereas in Opinion 2/94 conferral exactly limited the reach of EC residual powers.

The Court first reiterated that the Community is to act within the limits of the powers conferred upon it, and that those powers can be expressly stated or implied from Treaty provisions.

Opinion 2/94, *Accession by the Community to the European Convention for the Protection of Human Rights and Fundamental Freedoms* [1996] ECR I-1759

27. No Treaty provision confers on the Community institutions any general power to enact rules on human rights or to conclude international conventions in this field.
28. In the absence of express or implied powers for this purpose, it is necessary to consider whether Article [352 TFEU] may constitute a legal basis for accession.
29. Article [352 TFEU] is designed to fill the gap where no specific provisions of the Treaty confer on the Community institutions express or implied powers to act, if such powers appear none the less to be necessary to enable the Community to carry out its functions with a view to attaining one of the objectives laid down by the Treaty.
30. That provision, being an integral part of an institutional system based on the principle of conferred powers, cannot serve as a basis for widening the scope of Community powers beyond the general framework

---

[39] Opinion 2/94, *Accession by the Community to the European Convention for the Protection of Human Rights and Fundamental Freedoms* [1996] ECR I-1759, para 8.

[40] Eeckhout, 'Bold Constitutionalism and Beyond', in M. Poiares Maduro and L. Azoulai (eds.), *The Past and Future of EU Law* (Oxford: Hart Publishing, 2010), p. 218.

[41] Hillion, 'ERTA, ECHR and Open Skies: Laying the Grounds of the EU System of External Relations', in Poiares Maduro and Azoulai (eds.), *The Past and Future of EU Law*, p. 226.

created by the provisions of the Treaty as a whole and, in particular, by those that define the tasks and the activities of the Community. On any view, Article [352 TFEU] cannot be used as a basis for the adoption of provisions whose effect would, in substance, be to amend the Treaty without following the procedure which it provides for that purpose. ....

35. Such a modification of the system for the protection of human rights in the Community, with equally fundamental institutional implications for the Community and for the Member States, would be of constitutional significance and would therefore be such as to go beyond the scope of Article [352 TFEU]. It could be brought about only by way of Treaty amendment.

From this judgment we can discern three distinct criteria for the EU to act externally on the basis of this Article:

1. It follows from this Opinion that the position of Article 352 TFEU to provide the EU with powers to enter into an international agreement is clearly of a subsidiary nature. Only if there exists no express or implied EU external power to achieve certain Treaty objectives can this article be considered as a possible legal basis for external relations action.

2. A second condition is subsequently to be fulfilled: existence of EU external competence on the basis of Article 352 TFEU requires that a necessity criterion reminiscent of Opinion 1/76 be fulfilled: only when it is necessary to attain Treaty objectives is recourse to this stopgap article possible. Is the substantive meaning of the 'necessity' criterion identical to that defined in Opinion 1/76? Namely, are they both defined not as 'aiding to ensure' that EU Treaty objectives are achieved? In his case note of Opinion 2/94 Gaja has argued in the affirmative:

If only by providing an additional remedy against Community acts, accession to the European Convention would enhance protection of human rights under the same Convention. The requirement of 'necessity' for the use of Article 352 TFEU in order to conclude an international agreement would also be met because, as was said in Opinions 1/94 and 2/92, the same objective 'cannot be attained by the adoption of autonomous rules'.[42]

In this sense, in both cases the necessity criterion aims to reconcile the implied (Opinion 1/76) or subsidiary (Article 352 TFEU) existence of EU external powers with the principle of conferral, while still interpreting the Treaties in such a way as to give effect to them (*effet utile*).

3. The third criterion is then that Article 352 TFEU cannot serve as a basis for widening the scope of Union powers beyond the general framework created by the provisions of the Treaty as a whole and, in particular, by those that define the tasks and activities of the Union.[43] It is on this basis that the Court found that the Community could not accede to the ECHR. Because the Community had no *general* power to enact rules on human rights,[44] Article 352 TFEU could not serve as a basis to conclude an international instrument which would have such a fundamental impact on

---

[42] G. Gaja, 'Annotation: Opinion 2/94 (EC Accession to the ECHR)' (1996) 33 *Common Market Law Review* 984–985 (where he refers to paragraph 85 of Opinion 1/94).

[43] Opinion 2/94, para. 30.

[44] Opinion 2/94, para. 27.

the EU legal order and its institutional set-up. This example underlines that the external competences of the EU do have their limits. Note however that the consequences of this reasoning should be read restrictively. It does not mean that the EU cannot include human rights conditionality or other means of protecting human rights in its external relations instruments.[45] (See further Chapter 10 on the specific external policies in this book.)

Examples of where the Union in the past has used the residual powers for external relations include international environmental agreements prior to the SEA conferring an environmental competence on the Community, as well as in the field of development prior to the Treaty of Maastricht. One concrete example is the financing for development of Asia and Latin America on the basis of the ALA (Asian and Latin American Countries) Regulation of February 1992.[46] This instrument was adopted before the Maastricht Treaty expressly conferred competence on the Community in the sphere of development, and its sole legal basis was the current Article 352 TFEU.

6 CFSP: A *SUI GENERIS* COMPETENCE

CFSP is often referred to as a '*sui generis*' competence, meaning that its legal and institutional characteristics are intrinsic to this policy field. As indicated in Chapter 1, this peculiarity is underscored by the fact that it is the sole substantive policy area which is to be found in the TEU, rather than the TFEU. Article 24 TEU is the key provision on the CFSP, and it is a rather 'thick' article which indicates the many ways in which the CFSP is peculiar. Specifically, it tells us something on the existence of competence, its nature, the decision-making procedures, the limitation of judicial review, and finally, on the CFSP-specific duty of cooperation. As regards nature, we opt for the term 'parallel competence' for the CFSP.

Article 24 TEU

1. The Union's competence in matters of common foreign and security policy shall cover all areas of foreign policy and all questions relating to the Union's security, including the progressive framing of a common defence policy that might lead to a common defence.

   The common foreign and security policy is subject to specific rules and procedures. It shall be defined and implemented by the European Council and the Council acting unanimously, except where the Treaties provide otherwise. The adoption of legislative acts shall be excluded. The common foreign and security policy shall be put into effect by the High Representative of the Union for Foreign Affairs and Security Policy and by Member States, in accordance with the Treaties. The specific role of the European Parliament and of the Commission in this area is defined by the Treaties. The Court of Justice of the European Union shall not have jurisdiction with respect to these provisions, with the exception of its jurisdiction to monitor compliance with Article 40 of this Treaty and to review the legality of certain decisions as provided for by the second paragraph of Article 275 of the Treaty on the Functioning of the European Union.

---

[45] Arguing in that sense: J. H. H. Weiler and S. Fries, 'A Human Rights Policy for the European Community and Union: The Question of Competences', in P. Alston (ed.), *The EU and Human Rights* (Oxford: Oxford University Press, 1999).

[46] Council Regulation 443/92/EEC of 25 February 1992 on financial and technical assistance to, and economic cooperation with, the developing countries in Asia and Latin America, OJ 1992 No. L052/1.

2. Within the framework of the principles and objectives of its external action, the Union shall conduct, define and implement a common foreign and security policy, based on the development of mutual political solidarity among Member States, the identification of questions of general interest and the achievement of an ever-increasing degree of convergence of Member States' actions.

3. The Member States shall support the Union's external and security policy actively and unreservedly in a spirit of loyalty and mutual solidarity and shall comply with the Union's action in this area.

   The Member States shall work together to enhance and develop their mutual political solidarity. They shall refrain from any action which is contrary to the interests of the Union or likely to impair its effectiveness as a cohesive force in international relations.

   The Council and the High Representative shall ensure compliance with these principles.

Chapter 11 examines in depth the legal specificity of the CFSP, but we can already highlight six specific elements which render this policy field 'the odd one out' of EU external competences:

- First, the scope of the CFSP is very widely defined by simply stating that it shall 'cover all areas of foreign policy and all questions relating to the Union's security'. As we shall see further in Chapters 5 (choice of competence), 10 (development) and 11 (CFSP), these open-ended objectives make it sometimes difficult to conclude whether action falls within or outside this policy area. It is however important to establish this, given that the institutional balance, financing rules, etc. are very different from other policy areas.

- Second, in the past it could be queried whether CFSP was truly a distinct 'own competence' of the Union. In paragraph 2 of Article 24 TEU we can see this tension: on the one hand it is the Union who shall conduct, define and implement a CFSP, yet on the other hand it is based on an ever-increasing degree of convergence of Member States' actions. There is thus a progressive process-like development aspect to CFSP, which is different from other 'common policies' of the Union.

- Third, the nature of this competence certainly deserves the *sui generis* label. Article 24 foresees implementation by the HR *and* the Member States. While the competence is certainly not exclusive or shared pre-emptive, its peculiarity can also not be seen as another shared non-pre-emptive (complementary) policy such as in development, but rather as a parallel competence.

- Fourth, Article 24 refers to specific rules and procedures. Indeed, CFSP is very different from former Community policies in that it gives a distinct role to the European Council and Council in this policy field, with reduced powers for the Commission and in particular the EP. Furthermore, the EEAS is adopted on the basis of a CFSP primary law provision (Article 27(3) TEU), raising questions as to the nature of the EU diplomatic service in relation to the *sui generis* nature of CFSP and other EU external policies.

- Fifth, and quite crucially, the jurisdiction of the Court of Justice is severely constrained to an enforcement position in relation to Article 40 TEU (the non-affectation clause) as well as in relation to sanctions adopted by the Union on the basis of Article 275 TFEU.

- Sixth and finally, the CFSP contains a specific duty of cooperation (see also Article 34 TEU). Specific to this policy area is that, unlike the duty of cooperation more generally applicable across the Union (4(3) TFEU) and its other external policies, in CFSP this duty is not enforceable before the Court of Justice.

In Chapter 11 dedicated to CFSP, we further flesh out these elements which render CFSP truly an external policy '*sui generis*'.

7 THE BROADER PICTURE OF EU EXTERNAL RELATIONS LAW

The developments examined in this chapter are deeply reflective of the three key dynamics of EU external relations law we identified in the Preface to this book. In *ERTA*, the Council and Commission were arguing in legal terms a dispute which was deeply rooted in – and would have a deep impact on – their respective roles in international negotiations. The Council argued for a restrictive interpretation of the principle of conferral, whereas the Commission argued for a teleological interpretation. Leading up to the *ERTA* judgment, we saw that the Member States argued that they had an obligation in EU law to ensure that the common EU interest be properly maintained. That obligation, in their view, took on the form of an obligation of coordination under the leadership of whichever Member State held the Presidency. The Court chose the teleological track, and with that caused what can only be termed a constitutional revolution in EU external relations law. In deciding on the existence and nature of EU external competence, from that moment onwards and under certain conditions, Member States were excluded from acting internationally in areas where the Community/Union had legislated internally. That this would thoroughly change the relationship between the institutions was already clear from the Opinion of the AG writing in 1971: 'The unusual and exceptional nature of this dispute indicates the fundamental good relationship which obtains between a couple [Commission and Council] whose fertility is evinced by some seven thousand Community regulations and the several thousand decisions or directives which they together have engendered.'[47] Through the implied powers doctrine these thousands of instruments now led to the existence of a possibly exclusive external power of the Community. Thus, the *ERTA* judgment is a key example of the Court of Justice empowering the Union in its growth as an international actor, even if it had been counterbalanced by its pragmatic decision to allow the Member States to negotiate and conclude the ERTA. Similar facts preceded Opinion 2/94, with the Court however turning in a different direction: the Member States were heavily divided over whether or not the Community should accede to the ECHR. At first the UK had scuttled an initiative to that effect as early as 1980,[48] and it was not until 1990 that the Commission made another attempt with a Communication. This lasted until 1994 when the Belgian Presidency took the initiative to ask for an Opinion of the Court, with the Court finally calling a halt to ECHR accession by requiring Treaty amendment. The reason for the Court's more restrictive approach to EU competence and the principle of conferral has been argued to lie in the broader legal and political context: the German *Bundes-verfassungsgericht* was adamant about the importance of the principle of limited conferred powers,[49] and the ratification of the Maastricht Treaty was marred with problems. In this legal–political context, quite different from that of the early 1970s, the Court was not inclined to take the road it had gone down in *ERTA* (see further Chapter 4).

In sum, political battles between the institutions and Member States over what it means for the Union to speak with a single voice have regularly translated into litigation before the Court. In resolving these conflicts, the Court has shown itself sensitive to the legal–political context of

---

[47] Opinion of AG Dutheillet de Lamothe, *supra*, 284.

[48] Gaja, 'Annotation: Opinion 2/94', 975–991.

[49] *Brunner* v. *European Union Treaty* [1994] 1 CLMR 57, para 6 ('The requirement for sufficiently determined regulation of the sovereign powers granted to the European organs means at the same time, that later significant changes in the programme of integration set out in the Treaty and the authorisations to act will no longer be covered by the law ratifying the Treaty.').

European integration in which the legal proceedings took place. At times borderline activist, at other times protective of Member States' sovereignty, the role of the CJEU in the development of the EU as an international actor cannot be understated. This dynamic will be equally visible in the next chapter of this book, which examines the impact of EU external powers on the possibility for the Member States to act internationally. In the words of Post and Weiler:

> **R. Post, 'Constructing the European Polity: ERTA and the Open Skies Judgments', in M. Poiares Maduro and L. Azoulai (eds.), _The Past and Future of EU Law_ (Oxford: Hart Publishing, 2010), p. 234**
>
> Whatever unification Europe is destined to achieve will owe a great debt to the statesman-like decisions of the European Court of Justice. Consistently sidestepping 'the presumptive rule of interpretation typical in international law, that treaties must be interpreted in a manner that minimizes encroachment on state sovereignty', the ECJ has 'favoured a teleological, purposive rule drawn from the book of constitutional interpretation.'[50] The Court has forcefully promoted the emergence of a distinctive transnational entity endowed with forms of authority that are both significant and unique.

SOURCES AND FURTHER READING

Collinson, D. S., 'The Foreign Relations Powers of the European Communities: A Comment on Commission v. Council' (1971) 23 _Stanford Law Review_ 956–972.

Cremona, M., 'Defining Competence in EU External Relations: Lessons from the Treaty Reform Process', in A. Dashwood and M. Maresceau (eds.), _Law and Practice of EU External Relations – Salient Features of a Changing Landscape_ (Cambridge: Cambridge University Press, 2008).

Cremona, M., 'External Relations and External Competence: The Emergence of an Integrated Policy', in P. Craig and G. de Búrca (eds.), _The Evolution of EU Law_, 2nd edn (Oxford: Oxford University Press, 2011).

Cremona, M., 'The Draft Constitutional Treaty: External Relations and External Action' (2003) 40 _Common Market Law Review_ 1347–1366.

Dashwood, A., 'The Attribution of External Relations Competence', in A. Dashwood and C. Hillion (eds.), _The General Law of EC External Relations_ (London: Sweet and Maxwell, 2000).

Dashwood, A., 'The Limits of European Community Powers' (1996) 21 _European Law Review_ 113–128.

Dashwood, A. and Heliskoski, J., 'The Classic Authorities Revisited', in A. Dashwood and C. Hillion (eds.), _The General Law of EC External Relations_ (London: Sweet and Maxwell, 2000).

De Baere, G., _Constitutional Principles of EU External Relations_ (Oxford: Oxford University Press, 2008).

Eeckhout, P., 'Bold Constitutionalism and Beyond', in M. Poiares Maduro and L. Azoulai (eds.), _The Past and Future of EU Law_ (Oxford: Hart Publishing, 2010).

Eeckhout, P., _EU External Relations Law_, 2nd edn (Oxford: Oxford University Press, 2011).

Gaja, G., 'Annotation: Opinion 2/94 (EC Accession to the ECHR)' (1996) 33 _Common Market Law Review_ 975–991.

Ganshof Van der Meersch, W. J., 'Les Relations Extérieures de la CEE dans le Domaine des Politiques Communes et l'Arrêt de la Cour de Justice du 31 mars 1971' (1972) _Cahiers de Droit Européen_ 127–158.

---

[50] Post is here quoting Weiler, 'The Transformation of Europe' (1991) 100 _Yale Law Journal_ 2416.

Hillion, C., 'ERTA, ECHR and Open Skies: Laying the Grounds of the EU System of External Relations', in M. Poiares Maduro and L. Azoulai (eds.), *The Past and Future of EU Law* (Oxford: Hart Publishing, 2010).

Holdgaard, R., *External Relations Law of the European Community: Legal Reasoning and Legal Discourses* (Alphen aan den Rijn: Kluwer Law International, 2008).

Klamert, M., *New Conferral or Old Confusion? – The Perils of Making Implied Competences Explicit and the Example of the External Competence for Environmental Policy* (The Hague: CLEER Working Paper, 2011/6).

Koutrakos, P., *EU International Relations Law* (Oxford: Hart Publishing, 2006).

Kuijper, P. J., *De Eerste Zaak ooit tussen de Commissie en de Raad. Het Recht van de Europese Unie in 50 Klassieke Arresten* (The Hague: Boom Juridische Uitgevers, 2010).

Post, R., 'Constructing the European Polity: ERTA and the Open Skies Judgments', in M. Poiares Maduro and L. Azoulai (eds.), *The Past and Future of EU Law* (Oxford: Hart Publishing, 2010).

Temple Lang, J., 'The ERTA Judgment and the Court's Case-Law on Competence and Conflict' (1986) 6 *Yearbook of European Law* 183–218.

Tridimas, T. and Eeckhout, P., 'The External Competence of the Community and the Case-Law of the Court of Justice: Principle versus Pragmatism' (1994) 14 *Yearbook of European Law* 143–177.

Van Vooren, B., *EU External Relations Law and the European Neighbourhood Policy: A Paradigm for Coherence* (Abingdon/New York: Routledge, 2012).

Waelbroeck, M., 'L'Arrêt AETR et les Compétences Externes de la Communauté Économique Européenne' (1971) *Integration* 79–89.

Weiler, J. H. H., 'The Transformation of Europe' (1991) 100 *Yale Law Journal* 2403–2483.

Weiler, J. H. H. and Fries, S., 'A Human Rights Policy for the European Community and Union: The Question of Competences', in P. Alston (ed.), *The EU and Human Rights* (Oxford: Oxford University Press, 1999).

Wessel, R. A., 'Revisiting the International Legal Status of the EU' (2000) 5 *European Foreign Affairs Review* 507–537.

Winter, J. A., 'Casenote Case C-22/70' (1971) 8 *Common Market Law Review* 550–556.

4

Nature of EU external competence

1 CENTRAL ISSUES

- Once it is established that competence for the Union to act exists, we must examine the impact this will have for the Member States' ability to act internationally. This is the question of the 'nature' of EU competence, and is subdivided into two main categories according to how they impact the Member States' powers: exclusive EU competence, or shared with the Member States.
- In the category of exclusive competences, we distinguish between a priori exclusivity, conditional exclusivity and exclusivity through necessity. In the first instance, EU primary law expressly states that a given competence is to be exercised by the EU alone. In the case of conditional exclusivity, Member States are pre-empted from acting when their international action may affect common rules adopted by the EU. The third is a minor sub-category of conditional exclusivity.
- In the category of shared competences we distinguish between: shared pre-emptive competences, shared non-pre-emptive (complementary) powers, supplementary powers and parallel powers. In each category the scope for the EU and the Member States to act alone or alongside each other differs, depending on the fulfilment of certain conditions. Much of this chapter is focused on the first category, namely the conditions under which the exercise of a shared competence will pre-empt Member State international action, and the legal justification given by the CJEU.

2 INTRODUCTION: SCOPE OF EU LAW VERSUS SCOPE OF EU POWERS

In the previous chapter we distinguished between the *existence* and *nature* of EU external competence. Existence refers to the express or implied attribution of external powers to the Union. The nature of that competence concerns the impact on the Member States' external relations authority. In principle Member States have inherent powers to act internationally, but this is subject to restrictions imposed by EU law. To understand better the kinds of legal restrictions for the Member States which the *nature* of EU external competence entails, we must distinguish between the scope of EU law and the scope of EU competence.[1] In either case the EU

---

[1] A. Dashwood, 'The Limits of European Community Powers' (1996) 21 *European Law Review* 113.

Member States have a duty of loyalty towards the EU (Article 4(3) TEU). This implies certain legal obligations, namely that 'The Member States shall facilitate the achievement of the Union's tasks and refrain from any measure which could jeopardise the attainment of the Union's objectives.' This broad legal principle then expresses itself through different kinds of legal obligations imposed on the Member, depending on whether these legal obligations are derived from the scope of EU law, or derived from the scope of EU competence. First, as regards the scope of *EU law*, this is the broader category. Legal obligations for the Member States within this category are connected to the long list of objectives which the TEU states the Union must pursue. Specifically in EU external relations, we have seen in Chapter 1 that Article 21 TEU lists many external objectives: from preserving international peace and security to sustainable management of global environmental resources. It is then clear that these policy objectives pursued by the EU are by no means *unique* to the EU, and evidently shared with the Member States. Conversely, the scope of *EU powers* is the more limited category, and relates to the fact that the Union has been attributed limited competences, specifically to pursue those objectives (see Chapter 5 on how to establish the scope of EU powers). Legally, the consequence is then this: both in relation to the scope of EU law, and in relation to the scope of EU powers, the Member States have a duty of loyalty to the EU (Article 4(3) TEU). However, the specific legal obligations and consequences flowing from that duty of loyalty are different depending on whether the Union and the Member States share common policy objectives (scope of EU law); or whether the EU specifically possesses a limited catalogue of powers (scope of EU powers). When the scope of EU law is at stake, the Member States are subject to a duty of cooperation in external relations (see Chapter 6). When the scope of EU powers is at stake, the Member States *may* be excluded from acting at all. This is the more restrictive category of obligations imposed on the Member States' ability to act, and concerns the nature of EU competence discussed in this chapter.

In sum, when we speak of the nature of EU external competence, we are examining the legal obligations imposed on the Member States where the EU has express or implied external competence in a certain policy area (scope of EU powers).

3 CATEGORIES OF EXCLUSIVE AND SHARED COMPETENCES

(i) Two categories

The nature of external competences can be divided into two main categories according to how they impact the Member States' powers: *exclusive* competences or *shared* competences. In the case of an exclusive competence, Member States in principle lack the power to enter into international commitments; in the case of shared competence, both the EU and the Member States are in principle competent to act.

(ii) Exclusive external competences

The first category of the nature of EU external powers is that of exclusive powers, and we find its definition and effects described in Article 2(1) TFEU:

> ### Article 2(1) TFEU
>
> 1. When the Treaties confer on the Union exclusive competence in a specific area, only the Union may legislate and adopt legally binding acts, the Member States being able to do so themselves only if so empowered by the Union or for the implementation of Union acts.

There are three distinct instances or sub-categories where the Union possesses such exclusive powers:

- First, exclusivity based directly on the interpretation of the provisions in the EU Treaty. This is called **a priori exclusivity** or **policy area exclusivity**, because EU primary law itself states that certain policy areas are to be exercised exclusively by the Union (Article 3(1) TFEU);
- Second, exclusivity that follows from the adoption of internal Union measures, the Member States being excluded from adopting rules which affect EU measures. This is called **conditional exclusivity** or **pre-emption**,[2] because the Treaties and CJEU case law lay out a number of conditions for the Member States to lose their competence to act (Article 3(2) TFEU);
- Third, exclusive powers can occur when absolutely indispensable to achieve EU Treaty objectives, without there being internal EU measures. This is a small sub-category of conditional exclusivity called **exclusivity through necessity** (Article 3(2) TFEU).

The first category of a priori exclusive powers is found in Article 3(1) TFEU. As seen, the Treaty of Rome only expressly attributed powers to the EEC in the sphere of CCP and the conclusion of AAs. These articles were entirely silent on how they affected Member States' foreign relations authority, and therefore the Court was soon called upon to clarify the *nature* of EC external competence. This first occurred from the early 1970s onwards in the sphere of international trade and fisheries. Through interpretation by the Court of former Article 113 TEEC, the CCP became the prototype EU external relations power which a priori excludes powers of the Member States. The Lisbon Treaty has now included in Article 3(1) TFEU a list of subject matter areas where the EU has exclusive competence.

> ### Article 3 TFEU
>
> 1. The Union shall have exclusive competence in the following areas:
>   (a) customs union;
>   (b) the establishing of the competition rules necessary for the functioning of the internal market;
>   (c) monetary policy for the Member States whose currency is the euro;
>   (d) the conservation of marine biological resources under the common fisheries policy;
>   (e) common commercial policy.

Some of these areas concern EU internal matters, but all of them have significant external dimensions. This kind of a priori exclusivity on the basis of interpretation of a Treaty provision is

---

[2] The term 'conditional exclusivity' comes from P. Craig and G. de Búrca (eds.), *The Evolution of EU Law*, 2nd edn (Oxford: Oxford University Press, 2011), p. 79.

the subject of section 4 below. The second and third categories of exclusivity have been briefly discussed when examining the judicial emergence of the implied powers doctrine. Indeed, in the *ERTA* judgment the Court found that when the Union adopts common rules, the Member States may no longer undertake international commitments which would 'affect' those rules. The EU's internal legislative action thereby pre-empts individual Member State external action, meaning that the EU has an exclusive external power to the extent that its internal legislation would be affected by such national action. As explained below, this kind of exclusive external power is in fact nothing but the conceptual counterpart of shared pre-emptive competences.

(iii) Shared external competences

The second main category in the nature of EU external powers is that of shared competences. This term covers a number of situations where both the EU and its Member States may both act internationally in the same policy area. The terminology of 'sharing powers' can be confusing because the EU institutions, the Court and authors have oftentimes used this concept in diverse and incongruent ways. Conceptual clarity and consistency are crucial, and we distinguish the following four sub-categories of shared competence:

- *Shared pre-emptive competences*, where Member State action is only excluded if the competence is exercised by the Union. In the literature these are sometimes referred to as 'concurrent' competences.[3] For example, in the area of civil aviation, Member States are only excluded from concluding agreements with third countries insofar as the EU has adopted rules pertaining to the EU's internal aviation market, or concluded its own agreements with third countries, and insofar as Member State action would affect those rules (Articles 2(2) TFEU *iuncto* 3(2) TFEU and 216(1) TFEU). This category is the conceptual twin of conditional exclusivity mentioned above.
- *Shared non-pre-emptive competences*:[4] this is a sub-category of shared competences where the EU can fully deploy a policy, but exercising its competence does not exclude Member State action in the same field. Within this category we can further subdivide between the *complementary* EU competences (Article 4(3 and 4) TFEU) and *supportive or supplementary* EU competences (Article 6 TFEU). The most important external competence of the EU that is complementary, is development cooperation (see Chapter 10). In this area, the EU and its Member States may both deploy full-blown policies in third countries, without one restricting the other (Article 4(4) TFEU). An example of a supplementary policy is education (Article 6(e) TFEU). In its external dimension this supportive characteristic implies that while the EU pursues initiatives such as the Erasmus Mundus programme complementary to EU Member State action, this is not a full-blown 'EU education policy' as is the case for development.
- Shared competences in case of *minimum Union standards*, where Member States can adopt more stringent measures. This we can observe in areas where the EU has adopted minimum harmonization such as in the case of social policy.

---

[3] A. Rosas, 'The European Union and Mixed Agreements', in Dashwood and C. Hillion (eds.), *The General Law of EC External Relations* (Cambridge/London: Sweet & Maxwell, 2000), p. 203.

[4] Sometimes referred to as parallel competences: Rosas, 'The European Union and Mixed Agreements', p. 203.

- Shared competence in the area of foreign and security policy is termed a *parallel* EU external competence. The EU's CFSP is subject to specific rules and procedures not found in the TFEU, but in the TEU. Its nature is highly specific since it is 'based on the development of mutual political solidarity among Member States' (Article 24(2) TFEU). Due to its *sui generis* nature, we shall not discuss this competence further in this chapter, and refer entirely to Chapter 11. At present, the reader should solely keep in mind that much of what is contained in this chapter does not apply to the CFSP.

The category of **shared pre-emptive competences** is defined in Article 2(2) TFEU.

Article 2(2) TFEU

When the Treaties confer on the Union a competence shared with the Member States in a specific area, the Union and the Member States may legislate and adopt legally binding acts in that area. The Member States shall exercise their competence to the extent that the Union has not exercised its competence. The Member States shall again exercise their competence to the extent that the Union has decided to cease exercising its competence.

As indicated, the category of shared pre-emptive competences overlaps with exclusivity through pre-emption in the category of exclusive powers. The difference is a conceptual one, but nonetheless important to keep in mind: when looking from the perspective of 'pre-emptive exclusivity', the EU has *exercised* the relevant competence, thus excluding Member State action. Conversely, 'shared pre-emptive competence' takes the Member States' perspective in the absence of EU action: namely, when the Union has expressly or impliedly been conferred a shared pre-emptive external competence, though has not yet exercised that competence, the Member States can still exercise this competence for as long as the Union has not exercised its competence. This notion of 'exercising' a competence is absolutely crucial, and much of section 5 below revolves around its interpretation and effects.

This first type of shared pre-emptive competences is the most common. Article 4(2) TFEU lists eleven policy areas, stating that shared competence applies 'in the following principal areas'. In a combined reading with Article 4(1) TFEU it is then clear that shared, pre-emptive competence is the 'default nature' of competences conferred on the Union: Article 4(1) TFEU states that the Union shares competences with the Member States, unless otherwise stated in Article 3 TFEU (exclusive competence) or Article 6 TFEU (supplementary competence). Nevertheless, for external relations, the most important *expressly* conferred external competences do not fall within this category of shared, pre-emptive competences. CCP is *a priori exclusive*, development policy and humanitarian aid are *complementary* competences, and the CFSP is a parallel competence. When the Union does have *express* shared pre-emptive external competences, they are very narrow in substantive scope:[5] the

---

[5] Other expressly conferred external competences are either exclusive: the conclusion of agreements in the sphere of monetary union (Article 219(4) TFEU); complementary: the conclusion of agreements on economic, financial and technical cooperation with third countries (Article 212(2) TFEU), establishing relations with other international organizations (Article 220 TFEU); or supportive: 'fostering cooperation' with third countries in the field of education (Article 165(3) TFEU), vocational training (Article 166(3) TFEU), culture (Article 167(3) TFEU), public health (Article 168(3) TFEU) and the conclusion of international agreements in the fields of research and technological development (Article 186 TFEU).

conclusion of agreements on the readmission of illegal immigrants (Article 4(2) TFEU *iuncto* Article 79(3) TFEU); cooperating with third countries on Trans-European networks (Article 4(2) TFEU *iuncto* Article 171(3) TFEU) and the conclusion of international agreements on establishing cooperation with third countries and international organizations in the field of environment (Article 4(2) TFEU *iuncto* Article 191(4) TFEU). In those few areas of express shared external competence, such as readmission policy, the conclusion of an EU-level readmission agreement with a certain third country will exclude Member States' competence to conclude an agreement with that country on that topic.

This means that, if we look beyond EU external action in the areas of CCP, CFSP or development, EU action in many external domains such as energy, environment or civil aviation actually takes place on the basis of *implied* external competences. EU external competence in those areas exists because there are internal rules which form the basis for implying external competence (see Chapter 3). As a consequence we often find that the nature of EU external competence is that of conditional exclusivity or pre-emption. Therefore, much of this chapter will focus further on how the adoption of internal rules excludes Member State external action in line with Article 2(2) TFEU and the case law of the Court of Justice. This also shows that despite our conceptual distinction between the *existence* (Chapter 3) and *nature* (this chapter) of EU competence, it is thus clear that the two dimensions are deeply intertwined. In fact, because implied powers and EU external relations are so intimately connected, conditional exclusivity through the exercise of an internal competence is in external relations often referred to by the name of the landmark judgment that originally established it: *ERTA* pre-emption or 'the *ERTA* effect'.

The second sub-category is that of **shared non-pre-emptive** competences, further subdivided into complementary competences and supplementary competences. The latter are not explicitly defined in Article 6 TFEU, which merely states that the Union 'shall have competence to carry out actions to support, coordinate or supplement the actions of the Member States'. This is for example the case for vocational training and education, and any international action on the part of the Union therefore can only have the same supportive nature as the internal competence. The complementary competences are defined in Articles 4(3) TFEU (research, technological development and space) and 4(4) TFEU (development and humanitarian aid). That last article defines the nature of EU competence in development policy and humanitarian aid as one 'to carry out activities and conduct a common policy; however, the exercise of that competence shall not result in Member States being prevented from exercising theirs'. The difference between Articles 4(3) and 4(4) TFEU is that Article 4(3) TFEU mentions the EU's competence 'to carry out activities', whereas Article 4(4) TFEU states that the EU has competence 'to carry out activities and implement a common policy'. The latter indicates a more mature and integrated policy on the part of the Union. In either case, the effect of this kind of shared non-pre-emptive competence is that the EU's external actions do not exclude those of the Member States. Instead, the policies of both levels should be complementary, implying a strong legal obligation of cooperation and coordination between them (see Chapter 10).

The third sub-category of shared competences is that of Member State competence in case of the Union having undertaken only *minimum standards* of protection through the international instrument. In this case the Member States can undertake commitments which provide more stringent protection than that of the Union (see below, Opinion 2/91).

Two further remarks on shared competences are appropriate. First, across these three instances of shared competence, even when Member States are not excluded from acting, they are not entirely free to do as they please. Indeed, in the exercise of their own competences Member States are still subject to obligations stemming from EU law, most notably the duty of loyalty (Article 4 (3) TEU). This principle is examined further in Chapter 6 of this book. Second, it is important to avoid terminological confusion stemming from the different uses of 'shared competence' by different actors in the EU. For example, a situation which may lead to confusion is the following: if the Union only partially exercises a competence in a certain field, the Member States remain competent for that portion in which the Union has not exercised its powers. Part of a given policy area has therefore become exclusive through pre-emption, yet we may still speak of shared competences because the field effectively falls within the shared responsibility of the Union and its Member States.[6] Furthermore, because the EU and the Member States are both active in the field of development, there too one sometimes finds that they 'share' competences in this field. However, it is crucial to keep in mind the legal differences depending on the subject matter at issue.

A final category of competence which nature-wise is *sui generis* is the CFSP mentioned in Article 2(4) TFEU. This category is termed a *parallel* external competence of the Union.

Article 2(4) TFEU

The Union shall have competence, in accordance with the provisions of the Treaty on European Union, to define and implement a common foreign and security policy, including the progressive framing of a common defence policy.

Although the previous paragraphs of Article 2 TFEU define the exclusive and shared nature of EU external competence, as regards the CFSP that article only contains a statement of existence of that competence for the Union ('the Union shall have competence'). From this brief statement we cannot make any inferences on its nature, and we must look to Article 24(2) TEU for further clarification.

Article 24(2) TFEU

Within the framework of the principles and objectives of its external action, the Union shall conduct, define and implement a common foreign and security policy, based on the development of mutual political solidarity among Member States, the identification of questions of general interest and the achievement of an ever-increasing degree of convergence of Member States' actions.

Due to the historically distinct development of foreign and security policy, CFSP is now the sole remaining external policy found in the TEU. It is because of that same historical diversity that this policy can also not be captured by the shared exclusive categorization of other (former Community) external competences. Since CFSP is truly the odd one out, we will examine its nature separately in Chapter 11 of this book.

---

[6] Rosas refers to this category of shared competences as 'co-existing' competences: Rosas, 'The European Union and Mixed Agreements', p. 204. Neuwahl discusses this situation as 'joint competences' specifically in relation to Opinion 2/91: N. Neuwahl, 'Annotation: Opinion 2/91 (ILO Convention No 170)' (1993) 30 *Common Market Law Review* 1193.

(iv) The nature of external competences as codified by the Lisbon Treaty

In the following sections we investigate the exclusive and shared categories of the nature of EU external competences in more depth, with particular focus on the large body of case law. With the Treaty of Lisbon, these judgments have been codified in the following two Treaty provisions. This codification is particularly confusing for the first-time reader, because these provisions make no proper distinction between the existence and nature of EU external competence. In this section we briefly point to some of the core difficulties with these Treaty articles, and the key message is that deep knowledge of the case law is crucial for a good understanding of the nature of EU external competence.

Article 3(2) TFEU

The Union (1) shall also have exclusive competence for the conclusion of (2) an international agreement when its conclusion is provided for in a legislative act of the Union or (3) is necessary to enable the Union to exercise its internal competence, or (4) in so far as its conclusion may affect common rules or alter their scope.[7]

Article 216(1) TFEU

The Union may conclude an agreement with one or more third countries or international organisations where the Treaties so provide or where the conclusion of an agreement is necessary in order to achieve, within the framework of the Union's policies, one of the objectives referred to in the Treaties, or is provided for in a legally binding Union act or is likely to affect common rules or alter their scope.

As stated, the first problem with these articles is the lack of distinction between existence and nature of EU external competence: Article 3(2) TFEU states that the EU 'shall have' EU external competence (number 1 in the excerpt), and this thus concerns the existence of competence. However, the next portion (number 2 in the excerpt) then continues 'when its conclusion is provided for in a legislative act'. This is a criterion drawing on case law which concerned not the existence of external competence, but its exclusivity and thus nature of competence. Namely, in Opinion 1/94 and *Open Skies* discussed below, it was argued that Member States were pre-empted to act (1) when the policy sphere covered by internal legislative acts includes provisions relating to the treatment of nationals of non-member countries, (2) when they expressly confer on the EU institutions powers to negotiate with non-member countries, and (3) when the EU has achieved complete harmonization. However, the Court of Justice has made clear in Opinion 1/03 – a ruling which precedes the Lisbon Treaty – that those are 'only examples' of instances where common rules can be affected and pre-emptive exclusivity arises. Thus, Article 3(2) TFEU is poorly drafted because it improperly blends existence and nature of EU external competence, and cherry-picks different elements from the case law. The passages marked with numbers 3 and 4 illustrate this further: the excerpt marked number 3 refers to the criterion for the existence of

---

[7] Numbering added.

implied competence through necessity (Opinion 1/76), whereas number 4 names the crucial criterion for implied competence to become exclusive, thus pre-empting Member State action. This poor quality codification is not without its impact, as EU primary law adopted after forty years of case law supersedes those judgments in the hierarchy of sources of EU law. However, much academic debate exists as to whether these two provisions actually do change the case law, and if so, to what extent.

In the case of Article 3(2) TFEU one could argue that the impact is largely negligible, but Article 216(1) TFEU is potentially problematic by blending conditions for the existence and exclusivity of EU external powers. It thus more starkly illustrates the possible legal effect of this poor drafting. Commenting on the passages marked 1 and 2 in Article 3(2) TFEU, Schütze observed the following.

R. Schütze, 'Lisbon and the Federal Order of Competences: A Prospective Analysis' (2008) 33 *European Law Review* 713

The first situation presents a restrictive codification of the "WTO Principle". According to this doctrine, exclusive external competences may be created: "Whenever the Community has concluded *in its internal legislative acts* provisions relating to the treatment of nationals of non-member countries or expressly conferred on the institutions powers to negotiate with non-member countries." This principle undermines the idea of competence typologies as a *constitutionalised* division of power. The European Union can empower itself with an exclusive competence and, thereby, circumvent the principle of subsidiarity in the area of international agreements. Moreover, if we assume that the inclusion *in a legislative act* of a provision granting the European Union the power to conclude an international agreement automatically excludes the Member States, could the same reasoning not apply a fortiori to Treaty provisions? Such a broadly understood "WTO doctrine" would transform all express external competences of the European Union into *exclusive* external competences . . .

The second situation mentioned in Art.3, 2 TFEU grants the European Union an exclusive external competence where an international agreement "is necessary to enable the Union to exercise its internal competence". This appears to codify the "Opinion 1/76 Principle", albeit with a decisive difference: it omits the restrictive formulation that the doctrine has received in recent jurisprudence. There, the Court had made its application dependent on the impossibility of achieving an internal objective through internal legislation and the internal objective being "inextricably linked" with the external sphere. Instead of codifying this restrictive version of the *Opinion 1/76* doctrine, Art.3, 2 borrows, ironically, the wording of the European Union's general "residual" competence. Will this give the European Union a "residual" exclusive external power? Moreover, the "almost identical wording" of Art.216 TFEU – defining the scope of the European Union's implied external powers, as M. Cremona has pointed out, suggests that "implied *shared* competence would disappear". Yet, this would be "a wholly undesirable departure from the case law" if it means that the "*Union must have either no competence at all or exclusive competence*".[8]

Overall, the Convention was not very successful in their attempt to draft a Treaty provision that would reflect the ECJ's jurisprudence on implied competences.[9] Schütze argued that this could

---

[8] Schütze is here referring to: M. Cremona, *A Constitutional Basis for Effective External Action? An Assessment of the Provisions on EU External Action in the Constitutional Treaty* (EUI Working Paper, 2006/30), pp. 10–11 (emphasis added).

[9] CONV 458/02, Final Report of Working Group VII on External Action, Brussels, 16 December 2002, p. 18.

represent a 'textual revolution' in EU external relations law: 'Within the textual corset of Article 3(2) TFEU, it might well be difficult after the Lisbon amendments to imagine a sphere of shared external powers. Were the Member States aware of the potentially suicidal consequences of these amendments for their future existence on the international scene?'[10] It will be for the Court of Justice to interpret these articles as a continuation of, or departure from, previously established principles. In what follows we outline the case law as it has evolved since the 1970s, and the law of EU external relations as it stands, pointing to the potential impact of these post-Lisbon Treaty provisions where relevant.

4 A PRIORI EXCLUSIVE COMPETENCE: POLICY AREA EXCLUSIVITY

Aside from customs, competition and monetary policy for Eurozone countries, Article 3 TFEU states that the EU has exclusive competence in the field of CCP and the conservation of biological resources in the context of the common fisheries policy. The latter two are particularly relevant for external relations, and the Treaty of Rome was silent on the question of exclusivity. It is the Court of Justice that pronounced itself on the nature of these domains. In Opinion 1/75, the CJEU argued that the Member States had set up a Common Market, and the CCP was conceived to defend the common external interests of the Community in its operation. If the Member States could continue to act alongside the Community to defend their own interests, the essence of pooling interests at the supranational level would be impinged.

Opinion 1/75, *Local Cost Standard* [1975] ECR 1355 at 1364

[The CCP] is conceived in 113 TEC [current Article 207 TFEU] in the context of the operation of the common market, for the defence of the common interests of the Community, within which the particular interests of the Member States must endeavour to adapt to each other.

Quite clearly, however, this conception is incompatible with the freedom to which the Member States could lay claim by invoking a concurrent power, so as to ensure that their own interests were separately satisfied in external relations, at the risk of compromising the effective defence of the common interests of the Community.

In fact any unilateral action on the part of the Member States would lead to disparities in the conditions for the grant of export credits, calculated to distort competition between undertakings of the various Member States in external markets. Such distortion can be eliminated only by means of a strict uniformity of credit conditions in the Community, whatever their nationality.

It cannot therefore be accepted that, in a field such as that governed by the understanding in question, which is covered by export policy and more generally by the Common Commercial Policy, the Member States should exercise a power concurrent to that of the Community, in the Community sphere, and in the international sphere. The provisions of articles 113 and 114 concerning the conditions under which, according to the treaty, agreements on commercial policy must be concluded show clearly that the exercise of concurrent powers by the Member States and the Community in this matter is impossible.

---

[10] R. Schütze, 'Lisbon and the Federal Order of Competences: A Prospective Analysis' (2008) 33 *European Law Review* 714.

> To accept that the contrary were true would amount to recognizing that, in relations with third countries, member States may adopt positions which differ from those which the Community intends to adopt, and would thereby distort the institutional framework, call into question the mutual trust within the Community and prevent the latter from fulfilling its task in the defence of the common interest.

In a judgment concerning the conservation of fisheries, the Court ruled on the basis of Article 102 of the Act of Accession of the UK, Ireland and Denmark, that after the expiry of a transitional period on 1 January 1979, 'the Community was exclusively competent to adopt, as part of the common fisheries policy, measures relating to the conservation of the resources of the sea'.[11] The principal consequence of the existence of exclusive competence which is based on an express Treaty article (Article 3 TFEU) is that the Member States may not act in these areas. Importantly, this inability to act remains whether or not the competence has been exercised by the Union. Hence, there is no room for the Member States to act even if it is perceived that the EU should undertake action, and it fails to do so.[12]

5 SHARED PRE-EMPTIVE COMPETENCE: CONDITIONAL EXCLUSIVITY

(i) Express and implied shared competences in the TFEU

Article 2(2) TFEU defines shared pre-emptive EU competence. It does so without regard as to whether it concerns an internal or external EU power. Notice the crucial difference with a priori policy area exclusivity.

Article 2(2) TFEU

When the Treaties confer on the Union a competence shared with the Member States in a specific area, the Union and the Member States may legislate and adopt legally binding acts in that area. The Member States shall exercise their competence to the extent that the Union has not exercised its competence. The Member States shall again exercise their competence to the extent that the Union has decided to cease exercising its competence.

This article defines shared competences and says that while both may act in a given area, the Member States are pre-empted to exercise their competence when the Union has exercised its competence. We have already pointed out that Article 4(2) TFEU enumerates the principal policy areas in which it applies, and that shared competence is the 'default' nature for EU external competence. All EU competences are shared, unless expressly stated otherwise by the EU Treaties. In external relations, many of the expressly conferred external competences of the EU do not fall within this general category: CCP is a priori exclusive, development policy and humanitarian aid are complementary competences, and the common foreign and security policy is a parallel

---

[11] Case 804/79 *Commission* v. *United Kingdom* [1981] ECR 1045 at para 17.
[12] Case 804/79 *Commission* v. *United Kingdom* [1981] ECR 1045 at para 22.

competence. The Union possesses few *expressly* conferred external competences that fall within the general category of shared competences, and most external competences will exist through the implied powers doctrine. As a consequence we will often find that conditional exclusivity or pre-emption in the external sphere occurs through the adoption of EU internal rules: these internal rules are the basis for implying external competence (existence), and exclude Member State action in line with Article 2(2) TFEU and the case law set out below. In sum, shared pre-emptive competence is possible for express and implied competences, but in the external sphere, most shared pre-emptive competences will exist through implication.

Opinion 1/03, *Lugano Convention* [2006] ECR I-1145[13]

114. The competence of the Community to conclude international agreements may arise not only from an **express conferment** by the Treaty but may equally **flow implicitly** from other provisions of the Treaty and from measures adopted, within the framework of those provisions, by the Community institutions (see *ERTA*, paragraph 16). The Court has also held that whenever Community law created for those institutions powers within its internal system for the purpose of attaining a specific objective, the Community had authority to undertake international commitments necessary for the attainment of that objective even in the absence of an express provision to that effect (Opinion 1/76, paragraph 3, and Opinion 2/91, paragraph 7).

115. **That competence** of the Community **may be exclusive or shared** with the Member States.

Article 2(2) TFEU generally defines shared competences, but it is silent on conditions under which this pre-emptive exclusivity arises. These conditions are to be found elsewhere, namely in the four decades of case law accompanied by volumes of academic debate, now codified rather unsatisfactorily in the Treaty of Lisbon. The latter sought to codify the case law on exclusive external competence in Articles 3(2) and 216(1) TFEU, but these provisions fail to capture properly the complexity of the case law. As a consequence, a good understanding of the case law is prerequisite to understanding the individual phrases of these articles.[14] Article 3(1) TFEU states that the Union shall have exclusive competences in such areas as the CCP, and its second paragraph lists the conditions under which the Union shall 'also' have exclusive competences. However, '[n]ot only does this provision fail to distinguish between a priori exclusivity and pre-emptive exclusivity (or pre-emption), it also conflates the two separate questions of the existence of implied external competence and the exclusivity of that competence'.[15] Article 216 suffers from the same problem: the article starts by stating that the Union 'may conclude' agreements, thereby indicating that it concerns the existence of EU external competence. However, thereafter it restates the three criteria already stated in Article 3(2) TFEU, i.e. those concerning exclusivity of EU external competence. The following paragraphs will flesh out the conditions for pre-

---

[13] Emphasis added.

[14] Cremona, 'The Draft Constitutional Treaty: External Relations and External Action' (2003) 40 *Common Market Law Review* 1353.

[15] Cremona, 'Defining Competence in EU External Relations: Lessons from the Treaty Reform Process', in Dashwood and M. Maresceau (eds.), *Law and Practice of EU External Relations – Salient Features of a Changing Landscape* (Cambridge: Cambridge University Press, 2008), p. 62.

emptive exclusivity as it emerged from four decades of case law, which is crucial for understanding the intricacies of Articles 3(2) and 216(1) TFEU.

(ii) Two types of conditional exclusive powers

There are two kinds of conditional exclusive powers: the first is *ERTA* exclusivity, where an implied or express shared EU external competence becomes exclusive to the extent that the Union has adopted common rules. The second is a small category where implication of powers and their exclusivity coincide, because certain policy objectives can only be achieved through external action.

The first category is by far the most prominent, where the Member States are excluded from adopting rules which could affect measures adopted by the Union. This is called conditional, pre-emptive exclusivity. To this day, the CJEU consistently refers to the landmark *ERTA* judgment of the early 1970s which lent this principle its name:

Opinion 1/03, *Lugano Convention* [2006] ECR I-1145

116. In paragraph 17 of the ERTA judgment, the Court established the principle that, where common rules have been adopted, the Member States no longer have the right, acting individually or even collectively, to undertake obligations with non-member countries which affect those rules. In such a case, the Community also has exclusive competence to conclude international agreements.

The second instance of EU exclusive powers is that in which excluding Member State action is 'necessary' to attain EU Treaty objectives, and this without the adoption of internal rules.

Opinion 1/03, *Lugano Convention* [2006] ECR I-1145

115. As regards exclusive competence, the Court has held that the situation envisaged in Opinion 1/76 is that in which internal competence may be effectively exercised only at the same time as external competence (see Opinion 1/76, paragraphs 4 and 7, and Opinion 1/94, paragraph 85), the conclusion of the international agreement being thus necessary in order to attain objectives of the Treaty that cannot be attained by establishing autonomous rules (see, in particular, Commission v Denmark, paragraph 57).

Sections (iii) and (iv) below explain further the conditions for these two types of conditional exclusivity to arise.

(iii) First type of conditional exclusivity: *ERTA* pre-emption

(a) The 'common rules' criterion: a broad interpretation

In the *ERTA* judgment, the CJEU ruled that when the EU exercises its internal competence by adopting *common rules*, Member States can no longer act externally – individually or even collectively – in a way which would *affect* those internal EU rules.[16] Therefore, the following

---

[16] Case 22/70 *Commission* v. *Council (ERTA)* [1971] ECR 263, paras 17–18.

conditions have to be fulfilled for *ERTA* pre-emption to occur: (1) common rules have been adopted by the Union, and (2) Member State action would affect those common rules.

Case 22/70 *Commission* v. *Council (ERTA)* [1971] ECR 263

17. In particular, each time the Community, with a view to implementing a common policy envisaged by the Treaty, adopts provisions laying down common rules, whatever form these may take, the Member States no longer have the right, acting individually or even collectively, to undertake obligations with third countries which affect those rules.

18. As and when such common rules come into being, the Community alone is in a position to assume and carry out contractual obligations towards third countries affecting the whole sphere of application of the Community legal system. . . .

31. These Community powers exclude the possibility of concurrent powers on the part of Member States, since any steps taken outside the framework of the Community institutions would be incompatible with the unity of the Common Market and the uniform application of Community law.

The justification of the Court for implied exclusive competences to pre-empt Member State action is very similar to that given in Opinion 1/75 in relation to the CCP. If the Member States could continue to act alongside the Community to defend their own interests, the essence of pooling interests at the supranational level would be impinged on. This judgment does not clearly define the meaning of 'common rules', though the notion is evidently wide given that it states that they may take whichever form. This raised the question as to whether the *ERTA* principle would only apply where the Treaty explicitly attributes competence to implement a '*common policy*', such as for example the CAP, or common transport policy?[17] In Opinion 2/91 the CJEU responded that this was not the case:

Opinion 2/91, *Convention No 170 ILO on Safety in the Use of Chemicals at Work* [1993] ECR I-1061

10. In all the areas corresponding to the objectives of the Treaty, Article 5 EEC Treaty requires Member States to facilitate the achievement of the Community's tasks and to abstain from any measure which could jeopardize the attainment of the objectives of the Treaty.

11. The Community's tasks and the objectives of the Treaty would also be compromised if Member States were able to enter into international commitments containing rules capable of affecting rules already adopted in areas falling outside common policies or of altering their scope.

The Court thus argued that the scope of common rules extends beyond merely the 'common policies' in the Treaties and to all other policy areas as well. Its reasoning is straightforward, since the rationale for pre-empting Member States from acting internationally is not limited to those policies: in other fields the tasks of the Community could equally be jeopardized if Member

---

[17] *Ibid.*, paras 23–24.

States were allowed to act.[18] In the more recent Opinion 1/03, the CJEU confirmed this explicitly:[19]

Opinion 1/03, *Lugano Convention* [2006] ECR I-1145

118. In paragraph 11 of Opinion 2/91, the Court stated that that principle also applies where rules have been adopted in areas falling outside common policies and, in particular, in areas where there are harmonising measures.

We can therefore readily state that any legally binding instrument adopted by the Union within any policy area can potentially exclude Member State international action where such would affect the EU common rules (*ERTA* pre-emption). Evidently, that statement is strongly qualified by the interpretation of the 'affect' criterion. Indeed, the ECJ will thoroughly look at the nature and content of the common rules to establish whether and when they would be affected by Member State action.

(b) The 'affect' test: a two-step methodology

When common rules have been adopted by the Union, it must be investigated whether Member State action 'affects' those common rules. The Court states that a rigorous 'affect' test is called for, due to the principle of conferred powers. According to the CJEU, 'especially' in the case of implied competences pre-empting the Member States, establishing exclusivity must be the result of an in-depth analysis of the relationship between the common rules and the international instrument at issue.

Opinion 1/03, *Lugano Convention* [2006] ECR I-1145

120. ... the Community enjoys only conferred powers and that, accordingly, any competence, especially where it is exclusive and not expressly conferred by the Treaty, must have its basis in conclusions drawn from a specific analysis of the relationship between the agreement envisaged and the Community law in force and from which it is clear that the conclusion of such an agreement is capable of affecting the Community rules.

In Opinion 1/03, the Court summarized its method as shown below. Notice that this passage confirms that there is a separate analysis as to whether external EU competence exists, and whether it is exclusive. At this point we must again emphasize the distinction between the existence and nature of EU external competences: the adoption of internal common rules can give rise to the existence of external EU competence (see Chapter 3), but that test is different from the one discussed here, i.e. as to whether these common rules could be affected so that Member State action is excluded.

---

[18] R. Holdgaard, *External Relations Law of the European Community: Legal Reasoning and Legal Discourses* (Alphen aan den Rijn: Kluwer Law International, 2008), p. 105.

[19] Opinion 1/03, *supra*, 118.

Opinion 1/03, *Lugano Convention* [2006] ECR I–1145

133. ... a comprehensive and detailed analysis must be carried out to determine whether the Community has the competence to conclude an international agreement and whether that competence is exclusive. In doing so, account must be taken not only of the area covered by the Community rules and by the provisions of the agreement envisaged, insofar as the latter are known, but also of the nature and content of those rules and those provisions, to ensure that the agreement is not capable of undermining the uniform and consistent application of the Community rules and the proper functioning of the system which they establish.

The legal method through which the CJEU establishes whether common rules are affected by Member State action has grown organically from decades of case law. In a simplified fashion, the process described in paragraph 133 quoted above can be explained as follows: on the one hand there are the EU common rules, for example a regulation organizing a certain aspect of the internal market. On the other hand, there is Member State international action, for example a treaty it wishes to conclude with a third country in the policy area where the regulation applies. The Court must establish what would be the effect of the Member State international agreement on the EU Regulation.

We can identify two steps in this method:

- The first step consists in matching the rules according to their material overlap in scope. If no overlap in substance can be found, there is no pre-emption. If overlap can be established then the Member States may be pre-empted from acting (*rule pre-emption*).
- The second step should be taken if the first step shows that material overlap of rules is only partial, and then the question must arise as to whether the policy field to which those rules belong is 'largely covered' by Union law (*field pre-emption*). If the second step shows that the policy field is not largely covered, then there is simple rule pre-emption where the material overlap exists. The method of examining whether or not the field is largely covered by EU common rules consists of (a) looking at the scope of the common rules, and (b) examining the nature and content of these common rules. In essence, the CJEU queries whether 'the nature and content' of the rules is such that the effectiveness in application of the common EU rules would be hampered by Member State action? If so, then pre-emption is not just limited to the areas of material overlap, but applies to the area of common rules as a whole (field pre-emption). Whether uniformity in application of common rules is obstructed is then not decided by a formalistic matching of rules, but by a finding of obstruction of effectiveness in the application of EU law.

We shall now explain these consecutive steps to the 'affect' test.

(c) First step: the formal approach

The first step consists in matching the rules according to their material overlap in scope. If no overlap in substance can be found, there is no pre-emption. If overlap can be established then the Member States may be pre-empted from acting. The 'effect' occurs when the same areas are materially legislated, and can therefore be referred to as 'rule pre-emption'.[20] The Court stated as

[20] Schütze, 'Supremacy without Pre-Emption? The Very Slowly Emergent Doctrine of Community Pre-Emption' (2006) 43 *Common Market Law Review* 1023.

much in Opinion 1/03, referring to a number of earlier cases in which it had applied this initial step of the method, and concluded that this was sufficient to establish or deny conditional exclusive EU powers:

Opinion 1/03, *Lugano Convention* [2006] ECR I-1145

125. In certain cases, analysis and comparison of the areas covered both by the Community rules and by the agreement envisaged suffice to rule out any effect on the former (see Opinion 1/94, paragraph 103; Opinion 2/92, paragraph 34, and Opinion 2/00, paragraph 46).

The *Open Skies* judgments are a good example of applying this first step of the methodology. In these cases, the Commission initiated proceedings against eight Member States for their conclusion of 'open skies' agreements in the field of civil aviation with the Member States.[21] During the early 1990s, the United States undertook an open skies policy whereby it wished to liberalize air traffic between themselves and the European continent through the conclusion of bilateral agreements, amending earlier post-World War II aviation agreements. At the same time, between 1987 and 1992 the Community had adopted three packages of measures designed to ensure freedom to provide services in the air transport sector.[22] As a consequence the Commission argued that because a comprehensive system of rules designed to establish an internal aviation market had been established, the Member States no longer had the competence to conclude these bilateral open skies agreements with the USA since they would affect those EU common rules on aviation.[23] In order to answer this question, the Court undertook a meticulous examination of the Regulations constituting the internal aviation market, which the Commission submitted would be 'affected' by the Member State international commitments to the USA.[24] The Court first examined individual articles of the Regulation on access to intra-Community air routes, and stated that it does not govern traffic rights on intra-Community routes to non-Community carriers.[25] Because of this mismatch in substantive content, there was no overlap with the international instrument:

C-472/98 *Commission* v. *Luxembourg* (*Open Skies*) [2002] ECR I-9741

105. Since the international commitments in issue do not fall within an area already covered by Regulations Nos 2407/92 and 2408/92, they cannot be regarded as affecting those regulations for the reason put forward by the Commission.

---

[21] *Open Skies* Cases C-466/98 *Commission* v. *United Kingdom* [2002] ECR I-9427; Case C-467/98 *Commission* v. *Denmark* [2002] ECR I-9519; Case C-468/98 *Commission* v. *Sweden* [2002] ECR I-9575; Case C-469/98 *Commission* v. *Finland* [2002] ECR I-9627; Case C-471/98 *Commission* v. *Belgium* [2002] ECR I-9681; Case C-472/98 *Commission* v. *Luxembourg* [2002] ECR I-9741; Case C-475/98 *Commission* v. *Austria* [2002] ECR I-9797; Case C-476/98 *Commission* v. *Germany* [2002] ECR I-9855.

[22] Case C-471/98 *Commission* v. *Belgium* [2002] ECR I-9681, para 4.

[23] *Ibid.*, para 33.

[24] *Ibid.*, para 100.

[25] *Ibid.*, paras 103–104.

106. Moreover, the very fact that those two regulations do not govern the situation of air carriers from non-member countries which operate within the Community shows that, contrary to what the Commission maintains, the 'third package' of legislation is not complete in character.

This excerpt thus clarifies that the *Open Skies* agreements are being targeted as illegal in the infringement proceedings. Therefore the Member State agreements with the USA did not 'affect' the EU common rules. Using the same method of meticulously examining the relevant civil aviation Regulations, the Court did find that the Union had 'acquired exclusive competence' in relation to air fare pricing[26] and computer reservation systems,[27] though not on slot allocation at European airports[28] insofar as it concerns non-Member State air carriers. One example from this judgment suffices to illustrate the in-depth nature of the Court's investigation:

C-472/98 *Commission* v. *Luxembourg* (*Open Skies*) [2002] ECR I-9741

110. In that regard, it should be noted, first, that, according to Article 1(2)(a) of Regulation No 2409/92, that regulation does not apply to fares and rates charged by air carriers other than Community air carriers, that restriction however being stated to be 'without prejudice to paragraph 3' of the same article. Under Article 1(3) of Regulation No 2409/92, only Community air carriers are entitled to introduce new products or fares lower than the ones existing for identical products.
111. It follows from those provisions, taken together, that Regulation No 2409/92 has, indirectly but definitely, prohibited air carriers of non-member countries which operate in the Community from introducing new products or fares lower than the ones existing for identical products. By proceeding in that way, the Community legislature has limited the freedom of those carriers to set fares and rates, where they operate on intra-Community routes by virtue of the fifth-freedom rights which they enjoy. Accordingly, to the extent indicated in Article 1(3) of Regulation No 2409/92, the Community has acquired exclusive competence to enter into commitments with non-member countries relating to that limitation on the freedom of non-Community carriers to set fares and rates.

While the first step of the method entails a thorough investigation of the common rules at issue, notice that in paragraph 105 of the *Open Skies* judgment the Court also states that the Member States' international commitments 'do not fall within an area already covered' by EU common rules. The Court thus concluded that the internal aviation market was not completely legislated for by the Union, and that the Member States' international commitments substance does not completely match with the internal common rules adopted by the EU. Therefore, no field pre-emption of the Member States' competence to act in aviation altogether could take place, only the more specific rule pre-emption. The consequence of the *Open Skies* judgments was that the Member States and EU would both have to become contracting parties to the international civil aviation agreements at issue. This thus shows the connection with the second step of the affect

---

[26] *Ibid.*, para 113.
[27] *Ibid.*, para 116.
[28] *Ibid.*, paras 120 and 123.

test: the extent to which a field is covered by EU rules has a crucial bearing on excluding Member State international action. Before examining that second portion of the affect test, a final word is necessary on what it means for there to be 'overlap' between the EU common rules and the international instrument under investigation.

When a given policy area is covered by EU rules, and Member State international action 'overlaps' with the same field, it is not necessary for there to be substantive contradiction between the relevant rules in order to exclude such Member State action. As stated by AG Tizzano in the *Open Skies* judgments: 'even if the texts of the agreements reproduce the common rules verbatim or incorporate them by reference' and they therefore do not contradict the meaning or effect of EU common rules, it still implies that these rules are 'affected' in the *ERTA* meaning of the word. This is because on the one hand there is no guarantee that they are uniformly applied by the Member States,[29] and on the other hand the inclusion in the Member States' agreements might have the 'effect of distorting the nature and legal regime of the common rules'.[30] As a consequence, the affect criterion is a formal one, requiring a simple examination of overlap of subject matter between the internal common rules and the international instrument. It was later confirmed in the *IMO* judgment that this implies that the Member States lose competence to adopt any measures once the field has been 'occupied' by the Union, regardless of actual content. In *IMO*, Member State international action concerned a mere proposal by Greece to the International Maritime Organization (IMO) Maritime Safety Committee, which through processes in that international organization could over time lead to new rules.[31] Therefore, even if the Member State has not committed to a legally binding measure, and even if those Member State international measures might be viewed as actually supportive of EU Treaty objectives,[32] they would still affect EU common rules.

This formal approach then has as its consequence that economic arguments on the affect criterion are not accepted by the Court. In *Open Skies*, the Commission argued that the agreements of the Member States with the USA distorted the flow of services in the internal market.[33] The Court does not accept such arguments as part of the affect criterion, since pre-empting Member State international action is a measure of last resort when other means to ensure the common interest are available. This was confirmed by the Court in Opinion 1/03.

Opinion 1/03, *Lugano Convention* [2006] ECR I-1145, para 123

. . . Similarly, the Court did not recognise the need for exclusive Community competence where there was a chance that bilateral agreements would lead to distortions in the flow of services in the internal market, noting that there was nothing in the Treaty to prevent the institutions from arranging, in the common rules laid down by them, concerted action in relation to non-member countries or from prescribing the approach to be taken by the Member States in their external dealings (Opinion 1/94, paragraphs 78 and 79, and Commission v Denmark, paragraphs 85 and 86).

---

[29] Case 22/70 *Commission* v. *Council (ERTA)* [1971] ECR 263, para 31.
[30] Opinion of AG Tizzano delivered on 31 January 2002, Case C-466/98 *Commission* v. United Kingdom [2002] ECR I-9427, para 72.
[31] Case C-45/07 *Commission* v. *Greece (International Maritime Organization)* [2009] ECR I-701, para 21.
[32] *Ibid.*, para 25.
[33] Case C-471/98 *Commission* v. *Belgium* [2002] ECR I-9681, paras 98–99.

(d) Second step: scope, nature and content of the common rules

Scope – is the field largely covered?

The second step of the affect criterion applies when the following question poses itself: when the international action or instrument of the Member State falls within the policy 'field' where the EU has adopted common rules, can pre-emption take place if there is only partial substantive overlap? The question is here not one of rule-specific pre-emption, but one of 'broader' *field* pre-emption. The criterion under examination is whether a given field has been largely covered by EU common rules, and is deduced by first looking at the *scope* of the common rules adopted by the Union, and subsequently at their *nature* and *content*.

This was for the first time at issue in a judgment concerning the area of social policy. The Court found that when a policy field is constituted by a number of instruments adopted progressively over time, and even though there is no exact match between all elements of the EU common and international rules, that pre-emption may still occur when the policy area is 'largely covered' by Union rules. This criterion emerged from Opinion 2/91 concerning the International Labour Organization (ILO) Convention No. 170 on safety in the use of chemicals on the workplace.[34] Since 1967 the Community had progressively adopted twelve Directives 'broadly' though not always exactly covering the subject matter dealt with in this ILO Convention. Already before the start of negotiations on this instrument, the Commission argued that the Community was competent to negotiate and conclude this international instrument. In August 1991 the Commission requested an Opinion of the Court to clarify the existence and the nature of the competence to conclude Convention No. 170. When reading the extract of the judgment below, notice that social policy is an area where the EU has a competence to adopt minimum rules. Thus, while in the final paragraphs the Court is discussing the 'largely covered' criterion (first half of the second step), the ECJ simultaneously examines the 'nature and content' of the common rules adopted in social policy as an element to decide on the exclusive nature of the EU's external competence to adopt the ILO Convention. The second half of the second step, nature and content, here concerns the question as to whether rules that lay down minimum harmonization can pre-empt Member State international action. This illustrates our earlier point that conceptually the two portions of the second step can be distinguished, but that the Court has often employed them simultaneously in its legal reasoning. Nevertheless, examining the scope, nature and content of the common rules are individually distinct elements of the affect criterion towards establishing field pre-emption.

Opinion 2/91, *Convention No 170 ILO on Safety in the Use of Chemicals at Work* [1993] ECR I–1061

15. The field covered by Convention No 170 falls within the social provisions of the EEC Treaty which constitute Chapter 1 of Title III on social policy.

16. Under Article 118a of the Treaty, Member States are required to pay particular attention to encouraging improvements, especially in the working environment, as regards the health and safety of workers, and to set as their objective the harmonization of conditions in this area, while maintaining the improvements made. In order to help achieve this objective, the Council has the power to adopt minimum requirements

---

[34] Opinion 2/91, *Convention No. 170 ILO on Safety in the Use of Chemicals at Work* [1993] ECR I-1061.

by means of directives. It follows from Article 118a(3) that the provisions adopted pursuant to that article are not to prevent any Member State from maintaining or introducing more stringent measures for the protection of working conditions compatible with the Treaty.

17. The Community thus enjoys an internal legislative competence in the area of social policy. Consequently, Convention No 170, whose subject-matter coincides, moreover, with that of several directives adopted under Article 118a, falls within the Community's area of competence.

18. For the purpose of determining whether this competence is exclusive in nature, it should be pointed out that the provisions of Convention No 170 are not of such a kind as to affect rules adopted pursuant to Article 118a. If, on the one hand, the Community decides to adopt rules which are less stringent than those set out in an ILO convention, Member States may, in accordance with Article 118a(3), adopt more stringent measures for the protection of working conditions or apply for that purpose the provisions of the relevant ILO convention. If, on the other hand, the Community decides to adopt more stringent measures than those provided for under an ILO convention, there is nothing to prevent the full application of Community law by the Member States under Article 19(8) of the ILO Constitution, which allows Members to adopt more stringent measures than those provided for in conventions or recommendations adopted by that organization.

19. The Commission notes, however, that it is sometimes difficult to determine whether a specific measure is more favourable to workers than another. Thus, in order to avoid being in breach of the provisions of an ILO convention, Member States may be tempted not to adopt provisions better suited to the social and technological conditions which are specific to the Community. The Commission therefore takes the view that, in so far as this attitude risks impairing the development of Community law, the Community itself ought to have exclusive competence to conclude Convention No 170.

20. That argument cannot be accepted. Difficulties, such as those referred to by the Commission, which might arise for the legislative function of the Community cannot constitute the basis for exclusive Community competence. . . .

22. A number of directives adopted in the areas covered by Part III of Convention No 170 do, however, contain rules, which are more than minimum requirements. This is the case, for instance, with regard to Council Directive . . . on the approximation of laws, regulations and administrative practices relating to the classification, packaging and labelling of dangerous substances . . .

23. Those directives contain provisions which in certain respects constitute measures conferring on workers, in their conditions of work, more extensive protection than that accorded under the provisions contained in Part III of Convention No 170. . . .

24. The scope of Convention No 170, however, is wider than that of the directives mentioned. . . .

25. While there is no contradiction between these provisions of the Convention and those of the directives mentioned, it must nevertheless be accepted that Part III of Convention No 170 is concerned with an area which is already covered to a large extent by Community rules progressively adopted since 1967 with a view to achieving an ever greater degree of harmonization and designed, on the one hand, to remove barriers to trade resulting from differences in legislation from one Member State to another and, on the other hand, to provide, at the same time, protection for human health and the environment.

26. In those circumstances, it must be considered that the commitments arising from Part III of Convention No 170, falling within the area covered by the directives cited above in paragraph 22, are of such a kind as to affect the Community rules laid down in those directives and that consequently Member States cannot undertake such commitments outside the framework of the Community institutions.

Paragraph 16 starts from the finding that the Community enjoys internal legislative competence in the field of social policy, where it can adopt minimum requirements by means of Directives.[35] The following paragraph 17 then confirms that 'consequently' the matter falls within the EC's area of external competences, because of several Directives adopted within the Community.[36] With the existence question settled, the Court moves to the nature of these competences. Since it is clear that common rules have been adopted by the Union, the focus lies on the affect criterion. In the examination of the nature of EU competence, we then need to separate paragraphs 17–20 and 22–26, because here we can observe the two different kinds of shared competence as outlined in the introduction to this chapter: shared competence in the case of minimum standards and shared pre-emptive competences.

Paragraph 18 concerns the situation where both EU law and international law allow the adoption of more stringent measures than set out either in the Directive or in the international instrument. As a consequence there is no possibility for a conflict, and Union powers are not exclusive: if the Member States are obliged by EU law to implement more stringent measures than stated in the international instrument, this is not a conflict with the international instrument. Likewise, if the international instrument requires stricter measures of the Member States than the Directive, then this is not problematic in light of the EU instrument. As stated in paragraph 16, the Council only has the power to adopt minimum requirements through Directives on the basis of current Article 153(2)(b) TFEU. This translates into an external competence which by nature does not pre-empt the Member States. Note that this example of the 'nature and content'-prong of the affect test is the consequence of the Court's acute awareness of the sweeping nature of exclusivity from a constitutional perspective: the Commission argued that in practice it may be difficult to distinguish when a national measure is more stringent or not, and that such difficulties can justify exclusive powers. However, the Court rightly does not accept that argument: practical difficulties in the *exercise* of a certain competence cannot inform arguments on their existence or nature. As the Court will later reaffirm in Opinion 1/94, establishing the existence and nature of EU external competence is a logical prerequisite to exercising that competence.

Paragraphs 22–26 of the Opinion concern the more common situation of shared pre-emptive competences, where the EU internal rules are more than mere minimum requirements.[37] These paragraphs confirm the criteria we have set out for the application of *ERTA* pre-emption. First, it concretizes the point that pre-emption is also possible beyond the sphere of the *common transport policy*, i.e. in social policy. Second, in paragraph 25, the Court also states what we have already indicated in relation to the first step. The first sentence of that paragraph clarifies that the affect criterion does not require the presence of contradiction between the international instrument at issue and the EU internal rules. Third, as regards the 'largely covered' criterion, notice that the Court in matching the content of the international instrument and EU rules does not require that the EU has 'completely covered' the field of health in the workplace.[38] It is sufficient that the Union has 'already covered to a large extent' this area by Union rules, for the

---

[35] *Ibid.*, para 16.
[36] *Ibid.*, para 17.
[37] Not all of the twelve Directives were adopted on the legal basis allowing only for minimum requirements Article 118, a(3) EEC, but some also were adopted on the basis of Articles 100 and 100A EEC.
[38] Opinion 2/91, *supra*, para 26.

Member States to be pre-empted. The Court argued that even though the scope of Convention No. 170 is wider than that of the common rules (and there is thus no exact material match), and even though there is no contradiction between the common rules and the ILO Convention, that international instrument does fall within an area which is already covered to a large extent by Union rules. EU common rules are therefore affected. However, stating that an area is largely covered, or covered to a large extent, is of no help whatsoever, and a further inquiry is necessary.

What is the nature and content of the common rules?

From the first part of the second step we can conclude that even if we do not find that the material overlap of the first step is entirely fulfilled, the largely covered criterion may still lead to exclusive EU external powers. The vagueness of that criterion is problematic, and in its submissions to the Court in Opinion 1/03, the UK government had argued that the largely covered criterion is 'neither clear nor precise, which gives rise to uncertainty and is unacceptable when it comes to limiting competences of the Member States'.[39] Thus, for reasons of respect for the principle of conferral and internal consistency of the *ERTA* case law, the UK requested that the Court clarify this criterion.[40] The Court responded by employing Opinion 2/91 to elevate an investigation of the 'nature and content' of the common rules to an integral part of the second step of the *ERTA* affect test, to attain a conclusion on when a field is largely covered.

Opinion 1/03, *Lugano Convention* [2006] ECR I-1145

120. Giving its opinion on Part III of Convention No 170 of the International Labour Organisation concerning safety in the use of chemicals at work, which is an area already largely covered by Community rules, the Court took account of the fact that those rules had been progressively adopted for more than 25 years with a view to achieving an ever greater degree of harmonisation designed, on the one hand, to remove barriers to trade resulting from differences in legislation from one Member State to another and, on the other hand, to provide, at the same time, protection for human health and the environment. It concluded that that part of that Convention was such as to affect those Community rules and that consequently Member States could not undertake such commitments outside the framework of the Community (Opinion 2/91, paragraphs 25 and 26).

The ECJ assesses its methodology in Opinion 2/91, and draws from it a more general conclusion for the affect test.

Opinion 1/03, *Lugano Convention* [2006] ECR I-1145

126. However, it is not necessary for the areas covered by the international agreement and the Community legislation to coincide fully. Where the test of 'an area which is already covered to a large extent by Community rules' (Opinion 2/91, paragraphs 25 and 26) is to be applied, the assessment must be based not only on the scope of the rules in question but also on their nature and content. It is also necessary to take into account not only the current state of Community law in the area in question but also its future

---

[39] Opinion 1/03 *Lugano Convention* [2006] ECR I-1145, para 47.
[40] *Ibid.*, para 46.

development, insofar as that is foreseeable at the time of that analysis (see, to that effect, Opinion 2/91, paragraph 25).

127. That that assessment must include not only the extent of the area covered but also the nature and content of the Community rules is also clear from the Court's case-law referred to in paragraph 123 of the present opinion, stating that the fact that both the Community rules and the international agreement lay down minimum standards may justify the conclusion that the Community rules are not affected, even if the Community rules and the provisions of the agreement cover the same area.

Thus, when the common rules at EU level do not materially and substantively overlap with the international instrument under investigation, we must look at the scope, nature and content of the common rules to establish whether they can be affected by an international instrument (field pre-emption). At present, the two-step methodology is firmly established in the case law: first, the formal step of matching content, and second, examining the scope and subsequently nature and content of the EU common rules.

Defining the meaning of 'nature and content' of common rules
What does it mean to take into account the nature and content of common rules? The Court justifies its assertion with reference to Opinion 2/91, whereby it took into account that the rules laid down minimum harmonization excluding *ERTA* pre-emption, and constituted a progressively developing body of law over several decades. However, entirely new, and quite contentious, is the CJEU's addition that it is also necessary to consider the 'future state' of EU rules, which may be affected in their nature or content. This suggests that it is possible that Member States are pre-empted from acting because the Union might act in the future. To better understand the scope, nature and content aspect of the affect test as it emerged from Opinion 1/03, we must examine the specific factual situation that gave rise to that ruling.

Opinion 1/03 concerned competence of the Community to conclude the Lugano II Convention.[41] The Brussels Convention regulated the rules on the jurisdiction of courts and the rules on the recognition and enforcement of judgments in civil and commercial matters.[42] These rules were 'communautarized' in Regulation 44/2001 ('Brussels I'),[43] and as a consequence the amended rules were to be extended to a group of non-EC and non-European Economic Area (EEA) members as had previously been done with the Brussels Convention through the first Lugano Convention.[44] Disagreement ensued between the Council/Member States and Commission/European Parliament as to whether this new Lugano Convention should be concluded by the EC alone or by the EC and its Member States as a mixed agreement.

In the initial few paragraphs of the Opinion, the Court applies the common rules criterion. Here the ECJ emphasizes that indeed common rules have been adopted by the EU, and it accepts it as self-evident that Member States' international agreements will also regulate the jurisdiction of their own courts, thereby *materially* overlapping with the Brussels I

---

[41] Opinion 1/03 *Lugano Convention* [2006] ECR I-1145.

[42] Convention of 27 September 1968, OJ 1998 No. C27, pp. 1 and 28.

[43] Council Regulation 44/2001/EC of 22 December 2000 on jurisdiction and the recognition and enforcement of judgments in civil and commercial matters, OJ 2001 No. L012/1.

[44] First Lugano Convention, OJ 1988 No. L319/9; Second Lugano Convention, OJ 2007 No. L339/1.

Regulation.[45] Thus, the first step of the affect criterion – the formal approach – was affirmative, though not necessarily complete: on the basis of Article 4(1) of Regulation 44/2001 the Council and some Member State governments had argued that the *scope* of the Regulation was limited, in that the Member States remained competent to determine the jurisdiction of their courts as regards defendants domiciled outside the Union.[46] Hence, the coverage of the field was not complete, which should imply that the Lugano Convention be concluded as a mixed agreement. In abstract terms, they thus argued purely from a rule-pre-emption perspective: certain areas had been covered by EU common rules, but not all areas – the scope of the common rules could be clearly delineated. Consequently the EU could not be said to be exclusively competent for the whole area because it was not 'largely covered' by EU rules. This is then where the nature and content of the affect criterion enters the stage: because the Brussels I Regulation contains an intricate set of rules which seek among others to avoid lacunae in determining the jurisdiction of courts, the nature and content of the rules is such that it amounts to a 'unified and coherent system'.[47] The Court thus argued that taken altogether, the scope, nature and content of the rules justified that the EU be exclusively competent to conclude the Convention as a whole, since uniformity was absolutely essential to the proper functioning of the system.[48]

To sum up, the 'largely covered' portion of the affect test is an investigation of the scope, nature and content of the common rules as they relate to the international instrument, and it implies that the Court of Justice will put greater focus on factual interaction between international and Union common rules.[49] Opinion 1/03 contains one further example of how this portion of the affect test may lead to a finding on exclusive EU powers, namely disconnection clauses. These are common clauses in international agreements concluded by the EU which provide that the agreement does not affect the application by the Member States of EU law between themselves in respect of the matter covered by the international agreement. The Member States had argued that the presence of such a clause would preclude that EU common rules are affected, because EU law could operate as it normally would between the Member States.[50] The Court was rather of the opposite opinion, stating that the presence of such a clause is actually an indication that EU common rules could be affected. Hence, the content of the international rules informed the Court that EU common rules might be affected. Furthermore, actual contradiction – as is the nature of a disconnection clause – is not necessary to establish fulfilment of the affect criterion.

(e) Are there instances where the affect criterion is always fulfilled?

A final question in relation to the affect portion of the *ERTA* pre-emption test is whether there are certain criteria by which we straightforwardly know that all aspects of the affect criterion are fulfilled. From Opinion 1/94 and *Open Skies* one could get that impression:

---

[45] Opinion 1/03 *Lugano Convention* [2006] ECR I-1145, paras 134 and 142.
[46] *Ibid.*, in particular paras 45–53; 105–106.
[47] *Ibid.*, para 148.
[48] *Ibid.*, para 141.
[49] P. J. Kuijper, 'International Responsibility for EU Mixed Agreements', in Hillion and P. Koutrakos (eds.), *Mixed Agreements Revisited – The EU and its Member States in the World* (Oxford: Hart Publishing, 2010), p. 209.
[50] Opinion 1/03 *Lugano Convention* [2006] ECR I-1145, paras 130 and 154.

Opinion 1/94, *Re World Trade Organization Agreement* [1994] ECR I-5267

95. Whenever the Community has included in its internal legislative acts provisions relating to the treatment of nationals of non-member countries or expressly conferred on its institutions powers to negotiate with non-member countries, it acquires exclusive external competence in the spheres covered by those acts.

96. The same applies in any event, even in the absence of any express provision authorizing its institutions to negotiate with non-member countries, where the Community has achieved complete harmonization of the rules governing access to a self-employed activity, because the common rules thus adopted could be affected within the meaning of the AETR judgment if the Member States retained freedom to negotiate with non-member countries.

In the more recent Opinion 1/03, the ECJ stated that these are not distinct criteria of the *ERTA* pre-emption doctrine; rather, they are concrete examples of where the affect criterion was fulfilled:

Opinion 1/03, *Lugano Convention* [2006] ECR I-1145

121. In Opinion 1/94, and in the Open Skies judgments, the Court set out three situations in which it recognised exclusive Community competence. Those three situations, which have been the subject of much debate in the course of the present request for an opinion ... are, however, only examples, formulated in the light of the particular contexts with which the Court was concerned.

(f) A brief look back at Articles 3(2) and 216(1) TFEU

Recall now that Article 3(2) provides several instances of when the EU has an exclusive competence to conclude an international agreement.

Article 3(2) TFEU

The Union (1) shall also have exclusive competence for the conclusion of (2) an international agreement when its conclusion is provided for in a legislative act of the Union or (3) is necessary to enable the Union to exercise its internal competence, or (4) in so far as its conclusion may affect common rules or alter their scope.[51]

In light of the case law we have discussed, the problems with the drafting of this provision are now much clearer. The fashion in which Article 3(2) TFEU is written seems to indicate that the proposed EU international agreement may affect common EU rules, and thus gives rise to exclusivity for the Union. Evidently it is the Member States' international action that is pre-empted if it would affect common rules or alter their scope. Furthermore, exclusivity

---

[51] Numbering added.

in the case of the conclusion of an international agreement is foreseen in EU legislation, and is but one of the examples for *ERTA* pre-emption to take place, as confirmed in Opinion 1/03.

Article 216(1) TFEU

The Union may conclude an agreement with one or more third countries or international organisations where the Treaties so provide or where the conclusion of an agreement is necessary in order to achieve, within the framework of the Union's policies, one of the objectives referred to in the Treaties, or is provided for in a legally binding Union act or is likely to affect common rules or alter their scope.

Similarly problematic is Article 216(1) TFEU which concerns existence of EU competence by reference to 'the EU may conclude'. However, it mentions the affect test at the end of this paragraph, which would mean that EU external competence exists whenever Member State international action could affect EU common rules. As stated in section 3 above, it is however unlikely that the drafters of the Treaties would have wanted all implied external EU competence to be instantaneously exclusive. Finally, notice that the final passages of Articles 3(2) and 216(2) speak of 'affect common rules or alter their scope'. In the original pronouncement in *ERTA* the CJEU indeed articulated the affect criterion also by reference to scope. However, the Court has never used altering the scope as a distinct criterion, but the notion of 'altering scope' of common rules is entirely in line with the method of rule pre-emption. In Opinion 1/03 this notion of scope has been fully integrated into the investigation of the 'scope, nature and content' of common rules. Whereas Articles 3(2) and 216(1) TFEU do refer to it, it does not actually change anything in the methodology set out above.

(g) Review: existence and nature of implied competence

Table 4.1 connects Chapters 3 and this chapter on the implied existence of EU external competence and the nature of that competence as shared or exclusive.

Table 4.1 – Existence and nature of implied external competence

	In the **absence of express** conferral, the existence of external competence can be **implied** . . .	This competence can be **exclusive** . . .
Principle of complementarity	. . . in the **absence** of prior internal legislation, when necessary to achieve EU objectives. This 'necessity' is one of 'aiding to ensure optimal exercise' of the expressly conferred internal competence	. . . in the **absence** of internal legislation, when there is an inextricable link between EU objectives and external action, i.e. necessity is interpreted as **'indispensable'** for achieving EU objectives
ERTA **doctrine**	. . . or when an internal competence has been **exercised** internally through common rules.	. . . to the extent to which Member States' external action would **'affect'** EU common rules.

(iv) Second type of conditional exclusivity: necessity

In our discussion of Opinion 1/76 in Chapter 3 we saw that this Opinion established the principle that an EU external power could be implied without first having adopted internal legislation (existence). In the facts of that Opinion it was in the nature of the policy initiative on the Rhine Basin that only by including Switzerland could the necessary policy action be effectively undertaken. Therefore, purely EU internal legislation was inherently excluded, and an international agreement factually unavoidable to attain EU objectives. The Court thus established the principle of complementarity, whereby EU external powers will be implied even in the absence of internal legislation, when it is 'necessary' to attain objectives in the EU Treaty for which the Union has been expressly conferred internal powers. We then pointed to the literature which argued that this necessity criterion does not mean 'indispensable', but merely whether the Union needs that external power 'to ensure the optimal use, over time, of its expressly conferred internal competence'. The subsequent question concerns the nature of this kind of implied competence. Indeed, there has been quite a bit of debate as to whether this strand of implied competences is inherently exclusive, or whether it can be shared as well. The difference is important given the different impact of a priori exclusive or shared pre-emptive competences on Member States' powers to act. The source of this disagreement lay in the peculiar factual reality of Opinion 1/76, as well as the Commission's argumentation and the CJEU's pronouncement in Opinion 1/94.

As regards the first point, in Opinion 1/76 there was the peculiar problem that the international agreement provided for the participation of the Member States as individual contracting parties, and this alongside the Community and Switzerland. The reason for this was the following: the Member States were parties to earlier conventions relating to the European river environment, and in the proposed international instrument before the Court, there was a provision which required amendment of those earlier conventions by the Member States.[52] It is for that reason that the Court stated:

Opinion 1/76, *Draft Agreement establishing a European laying-up fund for inland waterway vessels* [1977] ECR 741

7. This particular undertaking ... explains and justifies the participation in the Agreement, together with the Community, of the six abovementioned States. ... The participation of these States in the Agreement must be considered as being solely for this purpose and not as necessary for the attainment of other features of the system. In fact, under Article 4 of the Agreement, the enforceability of this measure and of the Statute extends to the territories of all the Member States including those who are not party to the agreement; it may therefore be said that, except for the special undertaking mentioned above, the legal effects of the agreement with regard to the Member States result, in accordance with Article 228(2) of the Treaty, exclusively from the conclusion of the latter by the Community. In these circumstances, the participation of the six Member States as contracting parties to the Agreement is not such as to encroach on the external power of the Community.

---

[52] Opinion 1/76, *supra*, para 6.

It is this reasoning of the Court which seemed to suggest that participation of the Member States would normally have been excluded, but that the Court merely sanctioned it because of that specific factual situation. However, there is no explicit reference in this paragraph to the nature of the implied competence as exclusive.[53] Nonetheless, the Court was of the opinion that specific justification was necessary for the participation of the Member States. It is on that basis that the Commission in Opinion 1/94 argued that Opinion 1/76 concerned the existence of an *exclusive* implied external competence. The Commission argued as follows:

Opinion 1/94, *Re World Trade Organization Agreement* [1994] ECR I–5267

82. Referring to Opinion 1/76 (paragraphs 3 and 4), the Commission submits, second, that the Community's exclusive external competence is not confined to cases in which use has already been made of internal powers to adopt measures for the attainment of common policies. Whenever Community law has conferred on the institutions internal powers for the purposes of attaining specific objectives, the international competence of the Community implicitly flows, according to the Commission, from those provisions. It is enough that the Community's participation in the international agreement is necessary for the attainment of one of objectives of the Community.

83. The Commission puts forward here both internal and external reasons to justify participation by the Community, and by the Community alone, in the conclusion of GATS and TRIPs. At internal level, the Commission maintains that, without such participation, the coherence of the internal market would be impaired. At external level, the European Community cannot allow itself to remain inactive on the international stage: the need for the conclusion of the WTO Agreement and its annexes, reflecting a global approach to international trade (embracing goods, services and intellectual property), is not in dispute.

84. That application of Opinion 1/76 to GATS cannot be accepted.

85. Opinion 1/76 related to an issue different from that arising from GATS. It concerned rationalization of the economic situation in the inland waterways sector in the Rhine and Moselle basins, and throughout all the Netherlands inland waterways and the German inland waterways linked to the Rhine basin, by elimination of short-term overcapacity. It was not possible to achieve that objective by the establishment of autonomous common rules, because of the traditional participation of vessels from Switzerland in navigation on the waterways in question. It was necessary, therefore, to bring Switzerland into the scheme envisaged by means of an international agreement … It is understandable, therefore, that external powers may be exercised, and thus become exclusive, without any internal legislation having first been adopted.

86. That is not the situation in the sphere of services: attainment of freedom of establishment and freedom to provide services for nationals of the Member States is not inextricably linked to the treatment to be afforded in the Community to nationals of non-member countries or in non-member countries to nationals of Member States of the Community.

The Court rejected the arguments of the Commission by finding that 'necessity' was not as strictly present in the case of concluding the General Agreement on Trade in Services (GATS) and Agreement on Trade Related Aspects of Intellectual Property Rights (TRIPS), compared to the factual situation in Opinion 1/76. The Court thereby established a clear link between the exercise

---

[53] Koutrakos, *EU International Relations Law* (Oxford: Hart Publishing, 2006), p. 94; P. Eeckhout, *EU External Relations Law*, 2nd edn (Oxford: Oxford University Press, 2011), p. 80.

of the competence, its existence without internal common rules, and attaining objectives laid down in the Treaties. Nevertheless, the Court did add to misunderstandings on this strand of implied competences, because in the final sentence of paragraph 85 the Court did not make the conceptual distinction between existence and nature of competence. It thereby seemed to recognize the Commission's assertion that Opinion 1/76 did not concern the existence of a shared implied external competence, but a shared exclusive external competence. Existence and nature thereby seemed entirely connected. Additionally, paragraph 86 then utilizes the expression 'inextricably linked', which subsequent to this judgment became the common expression to capture Opinion 1/76 necessity. The Court thus had seemed to state that if there is an inextricable link between the internal power and the external action, there exists an exclusive external competence for the Union.

Alan Dashwood submitted that the necessity criterion should be read in a dual sense:[54] when the international action is indispensable to achieve TEU objectives, that competence will be exclusive; but when that international action only 'facilitates' those EU objectives, the implied competence will be shared. Opinion 1/03 has now confirmed the reading offered by Dashwood.[55] Therefore we can now state that the nature of implied competence through necessity is as follows: when necessity is to be interpreted as an inextricable link between the external competence to act and the EU treaty objectives, an *exclusive* external competence emerges. When it is rather a question of facilitation of those internal TEU objectives, a *non-exclusive* external competence is implied. Note then, that in the latter case the Member States could still not conclude international rules which would affect those EU common rules, in the case of Opinion 1/76, an international agreement. Indeed, the criteria of *ERTA*-type conditional exclusivity apply – as with any other express or implied shared competence.

(v) Constitutional justification and effect of *ERTA* pre-emption

We have now established the two types of conditional exclusivity, whereby the Member States 'no longer have the right, acting individually or even collectively, to undertake obligations with third countries'.[56] However, Member States retain capacity both under national and international law, and in accordance with Article 2(2) TFEU, Member States shall again exercise their competence to the extent that the Union has decided to cease exercising its competence. Nonetheless, the effects of pre-emption are indubitably clear: Member States cannot adopt any international instrument in an area where the EU has adopted common rules, or even undertake any international action that might lead to international rules which would affect those common rules. It is not necessary that there is a contradiction between international action of the Member States for it to be excluded, and the simple fact of overlap suffices. Having discussed the conditions under which the EU can acquire exclusive external competences, and effects for the Member States, we must now examine the more fundamental question underlying *ERTA* pre-emption: why do Union powers have exclusivity which thoroughly impacts the sovereignty of its

---

[54] Dashwood, 'The Attribution of External Relations Competence', in Dashwood and Hillion (eds.), *The General Law of EC External Relations*, pp. 132–134.

[55] M. Klamert and N. Maydell, 'Lost in Exclusivity: Implied Non-Exclusive External Competences in Community Law' (2008) 13 *European Foreign Affairs Review*, 493–513 at 503.

[56] Case 22/70, *Commission* v. *Council (ERTA)* [1971] ECR 263, para 17.

Member States? What legal foundation is there for EU law to restrict the Member States from acting internationally?

In *ERTA*, the Court gave the following response to this question:

Case 22/70 *Commission* v. *Council (ERTA)* [1971] ECR 263

20. Under Article 3 (e), the adoption of a common policy in the sphere of transport is specially mentioned amongst the objectives of the Community.

21. Under Article 5, the Member States are required on the one hand to take all appropriate measures to ensure fulfilment of the obligations arising out of the Treaty or resulting from action taken by the institutions and, on the other hand, to abstain from any measure which might jeopardize the attainment of the objectives of the Treaty.

22. If these two provisions are read in conjunction, it follows that to the extent to which Community rules are promulgated for the attainment of the objectives of the Treaty, the Member States cannot, outside the framework of the Community institutions, assume obligations which might affect those rules or alter their scope. . . .

30. Since the subject-matter of the AETR falls within the scope of Regulation No 543/69, the Community has been empowered to negotiate and conclude the agreement in question since the entry into force of the said regulation.

31. These Community powers exclude the possibility of concurrent powers on the part of Member States, since any steps taken outside the framework of the Community institutions would be incompatible with the unity of the Common Market and the uniform application of Community law.

The final paragraph shows that legal justification for pre-emption given by the Court is the negative impact of individual or collective action by the Member States on the unity of the internal market and the uniform application of EU law.[57] To contextualize the Court's argument in this respect, recall the Council proceedings subject to this annulment procedure, reproduced in Chapter 3 of this book. In these Council minutes the Member States recognized that their external action might negatively impact the Regulation adopted within the Community. This is why they stated that 'the Member States shall take common action, coordinating their position in accordance with the usual procedures, in close association with the Community institutions',[58] and this to ensure that the Member States externally represent what is perceived as the common EU interest. However, the Court viewed this as an insufficient safeguard for the uniform application of EU law and therefore as incompatible with the unity of the Common Market. Member State action thus had to be excluded and not simply coordinated, acting individually or even collectively.[59] The legal foundation for a principle with such sweeping consequences is to be found in current Article 4(3) TEU (Article 5 EEC, Article 10 TEC).[60] As the Court noted again in Opinion 1/03:

---

[57] *ERTA, supra,* para 31.
[58] Opinion of AG Dutheillet de Lamothe, *supra,* 285–286.
[59] *ERTA, supra,* para 17.
[60] *ERTA, supra,* para 21.

Opinion 1/03, *Lugano Convention* [2006] ECR I-1145

119. ... in all the areas corresponding to the objectives of the Treaty, [current Article 4(3) TFEU] requires Member States to facilitate the achievement of the Community's tasks and to abstain from any measure which could jeopardise the attainment of the objectives of the Treaty (Opinion 2/91, paragraph 10).

Former Article 10 TEC, now Article 4(3) TEU reads as follows:

Article 4(3) TEU

Pursuant to the principle of sincere cooperation, the Union and the Member States shall, in full mutual respect, assist each other in carrying out tasks which flow from the Treaties.

The Member States shall take any appropriate measure, general or particular, to ensure fulfilment of the obligations arising out of the Treaties or resulting from the acts of the institutions of the Union.

The Member States shall facilitate the achievement of the Union's tasks and refrain from any measure which could jeopardize the attainment of the Union's objectives.

This Treaty article with its obligation of abstention has provided the legal foundation for primacy within the EU legal order, and also provides the justification for *ERTA* pre-emption as regards EU external competence. In *Costa* v. *ENEL*,[61] the Court famously made the following statement:

Case 6/64, *Costa* v. *ENEL* [1964] ECR 585, no paragraph numbering

The integration into the laws of each Member State of provisions which derive from the Community, and more generally the terms and the spirit of the Treaty, make it impossible for the States, as a corollary, to accord precedence to a unilateral and subsequent measure over a legal system accepted by them on a basis of reciprocity. Such a measure cannot therefore be inconsistent with that legal system. The executive force of Community law cannot vary from one state to another in deference to subsequent domestic laws, without jeopardizing the attainment of the objectives of the Treaty set out in [current Article 4(3) TFEU].

By comparing *Costa* v. *ENEL* on the legal justification for primacy, and *ERTA* on the legal justification for pre-emption, their common legal provenance is very clear. There is an indubitable parallel reasoning between primacy aimed at avoiding legal inconsistency within the EU legal order, and pre-emption seeking to ensure the effectiveness of EU internal rules which would be 'affected' if Member States could undertake international obligations. More concretely, as pointed out by the AG, in the *ERTA* case there was at least one instance where the international agreement explicitly diverged from the Council Regulation.[62] It was for that reason that the

---

[61] Case 6/64, *Falminio Costa* v. *ENEL* [1964] ECR 585.

[62] Opinion of AG Dutheillet de Lamothe, *supra*, 291. Namely the date of entry into force of the provisions concerning the maximum daily driving time differed in the *ERTA* from those in the Council Regulation.

Member States stated in the Council Proceedings that the Regulation needed to be adapted to conform with the international agreement the Member States were about to sign. The Court was however strongly concerned about the dangers of attaining the objectives of the Treaties, and did not wish to accept such a state of affairs:

Opinion 1/03, *Lugano Convention* [2006] ECR I-1145

128. In short, it is essential to ensure a uniform and consistent application of the Community rules and the proper functioning of the system which they establish in order to preserve the full effectiveness of Community law.

The response of the Court was therefore sweeping in pronouncing the effects of pre-emption: as and when EU internal rules come into being, Member States are no longer competent to undertake international obligations which may affect those rules. The effects of pre-emption are therefore *not* identical. In *Simmenthal* the Court stated that primacy meant the inapplicability of conflicting provisions of national law.[63] However, with pre-emption the Court preferred to *prevent* any conflicts between Union law and Member State action such as seen in the *ERTA* dispute, rather than resolve them when they occur as with primacy.[64] The effect of pre-emption goes further:

Case 22/70, *Commission* v. *Council (ERTA)* [1971] ECR 263, para 17

Each time the [Union], with a view to implementing a common policy envisaged by the Treaty, adopts provisions laying down common rules, whatever form these may take, the Member States no longer have the right, acting individually or even collectively, to undertake obligations with third countries which affect those rules.

---

6 SHARED NON-PRE-EMPTIVE (COMPLEMENTARY) POWERS: DEVELOPMENT POLICY AND HUMANITARIAN AID

We have seen that the non-pre-emptive, complementary EU competencies are generally defined in Articles 4(3) TFEU (research, technological development and space) and in 4(4) TFEU (development and humanitarian aid, see Chapter 10). The difference between these provisions is that the latter indicates that the EU can develop a 'common policy and carry out activities', whereas Article 4(3) TFEU merely points to carrying out activities. In both cases, these paragraphs indicate that 'the exercise of that competence shall not result in Member States being prevented from exercising theirs'. Articles 208(1) and 214(1) TFEU in the sphere of development policy and humanitarian aid respectively, define this coexistence in a more positive, constructive fashion.

---

[63] Case 106/77, *Amministrazione delle Finanze dello Stato* v. *Simmenthal SpA* [1978] ECR 629, para 17.
[64] Eeckhout, *EU External Relations Law*, p. 76. See also Holdgaard, *External Relations Law of the European Community*, pp. 99–100.

Article 208(1) TFEU – Development

Union policy in the field of development cooperation shall be conducted within the framework of the principles and objectives of the Union's external action. The Union's development cooperation policy and that of the Member States complement and reinforce each other.

Article 214(1) TFEU – Humanitarian Aid

1. The Union's operations in the field of humanitarian aid shall be conducted within the framework of the principles and objectives of the external action of the Union. Such operations shall be intended to provide ad hoc assistance and relief and protection for people in third countries who are victims of natural or man-made disasters, in order to meet the humanitarian needs resulting from these different situations. The Union's measures and those of the Member States shall complement and reinforce each other.

The purpose of defining these policy areas in this fashion is that there is a 'bias towards action', or even an approach of 'the more the better' in these fields. The consequence of this peculiar nature of EU external competence is that the EU–Member State coexistence takes on a form rather different from that in pre-emptive shared competences. In essence, the Member States remain free to organize their own development policies as they see fit, alongside a full-blown EU development policy, without the latter pre-empting the former. We refer the reader to Chapter 10 for a full discussion on the impact of the complementary nature of development competence on pertinent legal principles, actors and instruments in this policy field.

7 THE BROADER PICTURE OF EU EXTERNAL RELATIONS LAW

The principles and criteria flowing from the *ERTA* case law set out in this and the previous chapter have come about in an evolutionary and piecemeal fashion. More often than not, the cases we discussed originated from power struggles between the Commission and the Member States on competence and representation on the international plane. In Chapter 3 we saw that the *ERTA* judgment was the first ever case where the Commission initiated annulment proceedings against the Council,[65] and this over diametrically opposed views on whether the EEC had competence to conclude the road transport agreement simply because the EU had adopted an EU internal Regulation on the matter. The same was true for cases discussed in this chapter. To illustrate this 'broader picture' of EU external relations law, we shall utilize Opinion 1/94 as an

---

[65] Kuijper, *De Eerste Zaak ooit tussen de Commissie en de Raad. Het Recht van de Europese Unie in 50 Klassieke Arresten* (Den Haag: Boom Juridische Uitgevers, 2010), pp. 44–51; J. Temple Lang, 'The ERTA Judgment and the Court's Case-Law on Competence and Conflict' (1986) 6 *Yearbook of European Law* 183; J. A. Winter, 'Casenote Case C-22/70' (1971) 8 *Common Market Law Review* 550–556; D. S. Collinson, 'The Foreign Relations Powers of the European Communities: A Comment on Commission v. Council' (1971) 23 *Stanford Law Review* 956–972; M. Waelbroeck, 'L'Arrêt AETR et les Compétences Externes de la Communauté Économique Européenne' (1971) *Integration* 79–89; W. J. Ganshof Van der Meersch, 'Les Relations Extérieures de la CEE dans le Domaine des Politiques Communes et l'Arrêt de la Cour de Justice du 31 Mars 1971' (1972) *Cahiers de Droit Européen* 127–158.

example of the interaction between competence case law and its relationship to the broader political and legal context from which it originates.

Opinion 1/94 examined the scope and nature of Community powers to conclude the Multilateral Agreements on Trade in Goods insofar as it concerned EURATOM and European Coal and Steel Community (ECSC) products, the GATS and TRIPS.[66] The latter two were at the heart of the dispute, and were to be concluded as part of the results from the Uruguay Round whereby the General Agreement on Tariffs and Trade (GATT) was replaced by the World Trade Organization (WTO). During the Uruguay Round which ran from 1986 up to 15 December 1993, the Commission had been assigned the role of sole negotiator on behalf of the Community and its Member States. However, the question of competence to conclude the agreements was left open throughout the negotiations: the Commission opined that the Community alone could become a member of the WTO, but at least eight Member States asserted that it was to be concluded by the Community and Member States jointly (e.g. a mixed agreement).[67]

The Commission's primary argument on the conclusion of TRIPS and GATS was that these agreements fell within the ambit of the CCP. In case that argument was to be rejected by the Court, the Commission's subsidiary argument was that such competence could be implied from the relevant internal powers. The Court responded that the Community had exclusive competence to conclude the Multilateral Agreements on Trade in Goods, and this pursuant to Article 207 TFEU (see Chapter 9).[68] However, thereafter it rebutted the Commission's arguments and said that GATS and TRIPS largely fell outside the scope of the CCP.[69] As a consequence, the Court had to rule on the question of whether the Community had implied powers to conclude these agreements. The Commission deployed three distinct arguments which run entirely parallel to the three sources of competence discussed in Chapter 3 of this book: first, the Commission argued that there is a parallelism between the powers conferred upon the Union institutions by the Treaty at internal level (*ERTA*); second, the Commission submitted that there was a real 'necessity' to conclude the agreement in order to achieve a Treaty objective which meant that such competence could be implied (Opinion 1/76); and third, competence could be implied from a combined reading of Articles 114 and 352 TFEU (residual external competence).[70] The Court very firmly rejected all these arguments. In the words of Eeckhout:

that argument had little if any basis in the Court's previous case law, and the Commission's lawyers must have been aware of this. The Court did not accept the argument, and the result . . . is an Opinion which, in an attempt to defuse arguments which were difficult to understand, does not contribute much to clarifying the law on implied powers.[71]

We concur with that sentiment. What the Opinion lacks in legal clarity, it makes up for in providing a wonderful example of the blend of legal and political interests conjoined in EU external relations law – this because the legal dispute remained unresolved throughout the years

---

[66] Opinion 1/94 Re World Trade Organization Agreement [1994] ECR I-5267.
[67] Kuijper, 'International Responsibility for EU Mixed Agreements', in Hillion and Koutrakos (eds.), *Mixed Agreements Revisited*, p. 223.
[68] Opinion 1/94, *supra*, para 34.
[69] Opinion 1/94, *supra*, para 47 (GATS) and 71 (TRIPS).
[70] Opinion 1/94, *supra*, para 73.
[71] Eeckhout, *EU External Relations Law*, p. 88.

of negotiations in the Uruguay Round, right up until the signing ceremony of the WTO Agreement at Marrakesh on 15 April 1994. At the time, the *Financial Times* wrote: 'This week's ministerial conference of the GATT has not so far been a glorious showcase for the European Union's post-Maastricht solidarity. Indeed, many member governments have seemed determined to cling to sovereign prerogatives with a tenacity which would warm the heart of diehard Eurosceptics in Britain.'[72] The request for the Opinion was itself submitted by the Commission only a week before the signing ceremony and consequently, the Court had to give its ruling extremely quickly, because the WTO Agreement was to enter into force on 1 January 1995.

M. Hilf, 'The ECJ's Opinion 1/94 on the WTO – No Surprise, but Wise?' (1995) 6 *European Journal of International Law* 245, 248

Even the final and successful conclusion of the Round and the experience of a common negotiating power had not changed the mind of most Member States who definitely did not want to cede their chairs at the table of the WTO. Their international presence and appearance as individual sovereign States was after all too important to consent to the concept of 'an exclusive competence of the EC' in all matters covered under the WTO. . . . States are sensitive when it comes to limitations of their foreign relations powers which are still considered to be the hard core of the ageing concept of national sovereignty. If it has already been difficult for them to accept constitutional restraints, it seems even more difficult for them to consent to being bound institutionally in relation to the process of European integration or international cooperation. . . . The advisory Opinion given by the Court has to be seen in the light of the present atmosphere within various Member States as to the future development of the European Union.

Thus, three distinct elements defined the legal and political context in which the Court of Justice was asked to give its ruling in Opinion 1/94: first, the political backdrop of years of disagreement between the Commission and Member States as to the final competence and institutional configuration in which the Community would participate in the WTO. Second, disagreement between the more intergovernmental and pro-integration Member States at the Maastricht IGC, as well as the difficult ratification process of that Treaty thereafter. Overall, the political context was one where European integration was politically a hotly debated issue, and notably controversial was the accusation of 'competence creep'. Third and an important explanatory factor for the Court strongly rejecting the arguments of the Commission favouring exclusive EC competence, was the German *Bundesverfassungsgericht* which had just a year earlier rendered its judgment on the ratification of the Maastricht Treaty. It had sent a clear signal to the European institutions and the Court that the principle of conferral was to be taken seriously:

German Constitutional Court, Judgement of 12 October 1993, *Brunner* v. *European Union Treaty* [1994] 1 CLMR 57

The Treaty, however, defines the tasks of the European Union and the communities belonging to it in a sufficiently foreseeable manner. The Treaty follows the principle of limited individual authorisation, and so

---

[72] 'EU countries lose sight of solidarity – Marrakesh Diary', *Financial Times*, 14 April 1994.

> allows activity by the Union exclusively on the basis of an express treaty authorisation. . . . The requirement for sufficiently determined regulation of the sovereign powers granted to the European organs means at the same time, that later significant changes in the programme of integration set out in the Treaty and the authorisations to act will no longer be covered by the law ratifying the Treaty. If European institutions or organs were to implement and extend the Treaty in such a way that it was not covered by the Treaty, as it underlies the German ratification law, then the legal acts flowing from it would not be binding in the German field of sovereignty.

The German Constitutional Court used the open-ended formulation of 'later significant changes' to the principle of conferral as no longer being covered by the German ratification of the Maastricht Treaty. Since the term 'European institutions' encompasses both the political institutions and the judiciary, treaty interpretation by the CJEU on the principle of attributed powers was indubitably captured by the national Court's warning. It is for this reason, as well as aforementioned political factors, that the Court's restrained approach to the scope of the CCP (see Chapter 5) and the doctrine of implied competences came as 'no surprise'.[73]

Given that the *Open Skies* judgments or Opinion 2/91 equally originated from similar power struggles to that in Opinion 1/94, the key point is this: the legal criteria on the existence and nature of EU external competence are very much alive *in political discussions on EU external action*. Indeed, many of the principles and criteria discussed in this chapter, will very much come alive in the policy-specific chapters of this book. Indeed, competence debates are alive and well in Brussels:

> **A. Dashwood, 'The Attribution of External Relations Competence', in A. Dashwood and C. Hillion (eds.), *The General Law of EC External Relations* (London: Sweet and Maxwell 2000), p. 136**
>
> At all events, it is treated as axiomatic in the day-to-day practice of [EU] external relations that the adoption of a piece of internal legislation has among its automatic consequences (and aside from any issue of complementarity) the acquisition by the [Union] of competence to undertake international commitments in all the matters covered by the measure, including ones in respect of which such competence had previously been lacking. . . . Nobody with experience of Council practice in the conclusion of international agreements could be in the slightest doubt that the [ERTA] principle is alive and well, in both of its aspects [existence and nature].

SOURCES AND FURTHER READING

Bourgeois, J., 'The EC in the WTO and Advisory Opinion 1/94: An Echternach Procession' (1995) 32 *Common Market Law Review* 763–787.

Collinson, D. S., 'The Foreign Relations Powers of the European Communities: A Comment on Commission v. Council' (1971) 23 *Stanford Law Review* 956–972.

---

[73] M. Hilf, 'The ECJ's Opinion 1/94 on the WTO – No Surprise, but Wise?' (1995) 6 *European Journal of International Law* 245–259.

Craig, P. and de Búrca, G. (eds.), *The Evolution of EU Law*, 2nd edn (Oxford: Oxford University Press, 2011).

Cremona, M., *A Constitutional Basis for Effective External Action? An Assessment of the Provisions on EU External Action in the Constitutional Treaty* (EUI Working Paper, 2006/30).

Cremona, M., 'Defining Competence in EU External Relations: Lessons from the Treaty Reform Process', in A. Dashwood and M. Maresceau (eds.), *Law and Practice of EU External Relations – Salient Features of a Changing Landscape* (Cambridge: Cambridge University Press, 2008).

Cremona, M., 'The Draft Constitutional Treaty: External Relations and External Action' (2003) 40 *Common Market Law Review* 1347–1366.

Dashwood, A., 'The Attribution of External Relations Competence', in A. Dashwood and C. Hillion (eds.), *The General Law of EC External Relations* (London: Sweet and Maxwell 2000).

Dashwood, A., 'The Limits of European Community Powers' (1996) 21 *European Law Review* 113–128.

Eeckhout, P., *EU External Relations Law*, 2nd edn (Oxford: Oxford University Press, 2011).

Emiliou, N., 'Towards a Clearer Demarcation Line? The Division of External Relations Power between the Community and Member States' (1996) 21 *European Law Review* 76–86.

Ganshof Van der Meersch, W. J., 'Les Relations Extérieures de la CEE dans le Domaine des Politiques Communes et l'Arrêt de la Cour de Justice du 31 Mars 1971' (1972) *Cahiers de Droit Européen* 127–158.

Hilf, M., 'The ECJ's Opinion 1/94 on the WTO – No Surprise, but Wise?' (1995) 6 *European Journal of International Law* 245–259.

Hillion, C., 'ERTA, ECHR and Open Skies: Laying the Grounds of the EU System of External Relations', in M. Poiares Maduro and L. Azoulai (eds.), *The Past and Future of EU Law* (Oxford: Hart Publishing, 2010).

Holdgaard, R., *External Relations Law of the European Community: Legal Reasoning and Legal Discourses* (Alphen aan den Rijn: Kluwer Law International, 2008).

Holdgaard, R., 'The European Community's Implied External Competence after the Open Skies Cases' (2003) 8 *European Foreign Affairs Review* 365–394.

Klamert, M. and Maydell, N., 'Lost in Exclusivity: Implied Non-Exclusive External Competences in Community Law' (2008) 13 *European Foreign Affairs Review* 493–513.

Koutrakos, P., *EU International Relations Law* (Oxford: Hart Publishing, 2006).

Kuijper, P. J., *De Eerste Zaak ooit tussen de Commissie en de Raad. Het Recht van de Europese Unie in 50 Klassieke Arresten* (The Hague: Boom Juridische Uitgevers, 2010).

Kuijper, P. J., 'International Responsibility for EU Mixed Agreements', in C. Hillion and P. Koutrakos (eds.), *Mixed Agreements Revisited – The EU and its Member States in the World* (Oxford: Hart Publishing, 2010), pp. 208–227.

MacLeod, I., Hendry, I. D. and Hyett, S., *The External Relations of the European Communities* (Oxford: Clarendon Press, 1996).

Neuwahl, N., 'Annotation: Opinion 2/91 (ILO Convention No 170)' (1993) 30 *Common Market Law Review* 1185–1195.

O'Keeffe, D., 'Exclusive, Concurrent and Shared Competence', in A. Dashwood and C. Hillion (eds.), *The General Law of EC External Relations* (London: Sweet and Maxwell, 2000).

Pescatore, P., 'External Relations in the Case-Law of the Court of Justice of the European Communities' (1979) 16 *Common Market Law Review* 615–645.

Rosas, A., 'The European Union and Mixed Agreements', in A. Dashwood and C. Hillion (eds.), *The General Law of EC External Relations* (London: Sweet & Maxwell, 2000).

Schütze, R., *From Dual to Cooperative Federalism: The Changing Structure of European Law* (Oxford: Oxford University Press, 2009).

Schütze, R., 'Lisbon and the Federal Order of Competences: A Prospective Analysis' (2008) 33 *European Law Review* 709–722.

Schütze, R., 'Supremacy without Pre-Emption? The Very Slowly Emergent Doctrine of Community Pre-Emption' (2006) 43 *Common Market Law Review* 1023–1048.

Temple Lang, J., 'The ERTA Judgment and the Court's Case-Law on Competence and Conflict' (1986) 6 *Yearbook of European Law* 183–218.

Van Vooren, B., 'The Principle of Pre-Emption after Opinion 1/2003 and Coherence in EU Readmission Policy', in M. Cremona, J. Monar and S. Poli (eds.), *The External Dimension of the Area of Freedom, Security and Justice* (College of Europe Studies No. 13, 2011), pp. 163–190.

Von Bogdandy, A. and Bast, J., 'The European Union's Vertical Order of Competences: The Current Law and Proposals for its Reform' (2002) 39 *Common Market Law Review* 227–268.

Waelbroeck, M., 'L'Arrêt AETR et les Compétences Externes de la Communauté Économique Européenne' (1971) *Integration* 79–89.

Winter, J. A., 'Casenote Case C-22/70' (1971) 8 *Common Market Law Review* 550–556.

5

Scope and choice of EU external competence

- Once we have established that the EU has a competence to act (existence of competence), and know the impact of this competence on the Member States' capacity to act in the same field (nature of competence), we must also examine the scope (width, or ambit) of the competence which exists, and we may need to make a choice between different legal bases if EU international action may be based on more than one Treaty article.
- Establishing the appropriate legal basis entails an assessment of the exact scope of EU powers, and classification of the measure as falling within that scope. Given the different procedures tied to competence-conferring provisions, and the different nature as shared or exclusive, the choice of legal basis is a highly politicized and sometimes controversial process.
- In scope and choice of EU competence, we can distinguish between a vertical situation between the Member States and the Union, and a horizontal intra-EU situation. From a vertical perspective, the question is, can a given external measure be undertaken *at all* by the Union on the basis of the powers which have been established to exist? The horizontal situation concerns the question, if a measure does indeed fall within the powers of the Union, and if a number of candidate legal bases exist, which is the correct legal basis?
- The legal methods to establish the scope of Treaty provisions and choose the correct legal basis provide a central role to the Court in arbitrating competing intra-EU power relations. To avoid subjective views deciding the choice of competence, the Court developed an 'objective' legal method to ensure legal certainty for the institutions and Member States: the appropriate legal basis, or centre-of-gravity test.

2 APPROPRIATE LEGAL BASIS: CONFERRAL AND INTRA-EU POLITICS

(i) Introduction: scope and choice of legal basis

In Chapter 3 we looked at the conditions under which the EU *has* competence to act, e.g. existence of competence. In order to establish conclusively which measures the Union can take within a certain policy sphere, we must also examine the *scope*, *width* or *ambit* of the competence which expressly or impliedly exists. An example to illustrate the question of scope of competence in EU external relations: assume that the EU only has an express competence in the area of international trade (Article 207 TFEU), and assume for this example that the EU has no competence whatsoever in the field of environment. The EU wants to accede to an international agreement which subjects international trade in hazardous chemicals and pesticides to strict procedures to curtail risks to the environment posed by such trade. Does this fall within the EU's common commercial policy, or not? This concerns the *scope* of EU competence: which kind of measures can or cannot be taken on the basis of a given competence. Deciding the scope of EU competence is usually made in the context of a decision on the choice of the correct legal basis for EU external action. To continue the above example: the Union wishes to accede to the same instrument, but as is the case under the Treaties today, the EU has competence both in the fields of international trade (Article 207 TFEU) and the environment (Article 191(4) TFEU).[1] Does the EU adopt its Decision to approve the agreement on the trade legal basis, or the environment legal basis, or both simultaneously, and through which legal method do we make this choice? The answer to that question will require an examination of the respective scope of both Treaty provisions, and subsequently will require an objective legal method to decide the choice between two provisions. Together, both aspects form two essential steps of the 'correct legal basis test'.

(ii) Constitutional importance of correct legal basis: conferral and institutional balance

The Court of Justice has on several occasions emphasized the constitutional importance of indicating the proper legal basis for all EU (external) action.[2]

Opinion 1/08, *Amendments to EU Schedules of Commitments under GATS* [2009] ECR I-11129

110. ... [T]he choice of the appropriate legal basis has constitutional significance. Since the Community has conferred powers only, it must tie the [agreement to be concluded] to a Treaty provision which empowers it to approve such a measure. To proceed on an incorrect legal basis is therefore liable to invalidate the act concluding the agreement and so vitiate the Community's consent to be bound by the agreement it has signed. That is so in particular where the Treaty does not confer on the Community sufficient competence to ratify the agreement in its entirety, a situation which entails examining the allocation as between the Community and the Member States of the powers to conclude the agreement that is envisaged with non-member countries, or where the appropriate legal basis for the measure concluding the agreement lays down a legislative procedure different from that which has in fact been followed by the Community institutions.

From this excerpt we may infer two situations with respect to choosing the appropriate legal basis:

---

[1] See Chapter 3, 'express existence of competence' on the narrow interpretation of this provision, and the need for implied external competence as the case may be.

[2] Opinion 2/00, *Cartagena Protocol on biosafety and the transboundary movements of living modified organisms resulting from biotechnology* [2001] ECR I-9713, para 5; and exactly the same text is reproduced in Opinion 1/08 *Amendments to EU Schedules of Commitments under GATS* [2009] ECR I-11129, para 110.

1. A *vertical situation* which concerns allocation of powers between the Union and the Member States: does the Treaty in fact confer on the *Union the necessary competence* at all, to adopt the act or conclude the agreement? Here the assumption is that existence of EU competence has been established as seen in Chapter 3. However, in order to know whether the EU is competent in its entirety for a given measure, or only partially, we must establish the scope of the existing EU competence.

2. A *horizontal situation* where it is accepted that the EU has competence, but the debate focuses largely on which of the competence-conferring articles in the Treaties is the appropriate one for the specific instrument to be adopted.

In the first situation, the Court will mostly focus on establishing the scope of the EU legal basis to render its decision. In the second situation, the Court may have to establish the scope of the respective competence-conferring articles as well, and then utilize its centre-of-gravity method to decide which of the articles is the correct one.

The constitutional importance of a correct legal basis for EU action stems from the principle of conferral, according to which the EU shall act only within the limits of the competences attributed to it by the Member States, to attain the objectives set out in the Treaties (Article 5(2) TEU). The legal importance of choice of legal basis is both formal and substantive.

Formally, the choice of legal basis for an EU act should be made explicit as part of the broader obligation to state reasons for which an act has been adopted (Article 296 TFEU). This is necessary to make a review by the Court possible, and so that EU nationals may have knowledge of the conditions under which the Union institutions have applied the Treaties.[3]

Substantively, each conferred competence may entail a different procedure through which to adopt legally binding instruments, and thus the institutional balance linked to various conferred powers may be different. In the *GSP* case, the Court stated that using QMV (CCP legal basis) or unanimity (flexibility) in Council is not just a formality. Indeed, the choice of legal basis through its diverse procedural aspect may influence the content of the contested measure.[4]

Opinion of AG Maduro in Case C–133/06 *Parliament* v. *Council* [2008] ECR I–3189, para 32

[It] is because it affects the institutional balance that the Court attaches so much importance to the choice of legal basis. It is the choice of legal basis that determines the applicable decision-making procedure. The competent Community institution, the voting rules to which the adoption of the measure by the Council is subject and the extent of the Parliament's participation in the adoption of the act are therefore dependent on that choice. In addition, any dispute as regards the choice of the appropriate legal basis does not have only purely formal significance. Where the legal basis propounded by an applicant provides for a decision-making procedure which is different from that required under the legal basis chosen by the author of the act, the choice of legal basis has ramifications for the determination of the content of the act. Consequently, that choice cannot be at the discretion of an institution, but must be based on objective factors which are amenable to judicial review, such as the aim and content of the measure.

---

[3] Case 158/80 *Rewe* v. *Hauptzollamt Kiel* [1981] ECR 1805 para 25.
[4] Case 45/86 *Commission* v. *Council (Generalized System of Preferences)* [1987] ECR 1493, para 12; also Case 62/88 *Greece* v. *Council (Chernobyl)* [1990] ECR I-1527, paras 10–12.

Due to its impact on inter-institutional or EU–Member State power relations, establishing the scope of EU competence and choosing the correct legal basis is often politically charged. The choice of legal basis will therefore often be subject to political compromise during the legislative process or during the negotiation of an international agreement. This is why, when no compromise can be attained, litigation on the 'correct' legal basis usually has a power struggle underlying it: the EP wishing to be co-legislator rather than being merely consulted;[5] or a Member State arguing for a legal basis requiring unanimity because it will not accept being outvoted through QMV;[6] or the Commission seeking to utilize a competence where it has a stronger position than the Member States under a different competence.[7] The CJEU has ruled that the impact of the choice of legal basis on the prerogatives of one of the institutions cannot decide *in itself* the outcome of the centre-of-gravity test. It may however be relevant in a case of dual legal basis and procedural incompatibility (see below, the fifth dimension).

Case C-130/10 *European Parliament* v. *Council of the European Union*, 19 July 2012, n.y.r.

79. While it is true that choosing between Articles 75 TFEU and 215 TFEU as the legal basis for the contested regulation has consequences for the Parliament's prerogatives, inasmuch as the former provides for recourse to the ordinary legislative procedure whereas, under the latter, the Parliament is merely informed, that fact cannot, however, determine the choice of legal basis.

80. As the Council argues, it is not procedures that define the legal basis of a measure but the legal basis of a measure that determines the procedures to be followed in adopting that measure.

81. Admittedly, participation by the Parliament in the legislative process is the reflection, at Union level, of the fundamental democratic principle that the people should participate in the exercise of power through the intermediary of a representative assembly (see, to that effect, Case 138/79 *Roquette Frères* v *Council* [1980] ECR 3333, paragraph 33, and *Titanium dioxide*, paragraph 20).

82 Nevertheless, the difference between Article 75 TFEU and Article 215 TFEU, so far as the Parliament's involvement is concerned, is the result of the choice made by the framers of the Treaty of Lisbon conferring a more limited role on the Parliament with regard to the Union's action under the CFSP.

Competence conflicts are not merely pertinent to EU external relations law. For example, the EU actions which could be undertaken on the basis of Articles 114 (internal market) and 352 (flexibility clause) TFEU have never ceased to be controversial.[8] However, specific to EU external relations is that the choice of legal basis will significantly impact the international presence of the Member States in particular, and whether the EU replaces them: who negotiates the international agreement, who becomes a party to the agreement, which prominent politician addresses an international conference, and should officials of EU institutions or Member States travel to exotic venues? Such struggles are then connected to procedure and institutional

---

[5] Case 62/88 *Greece* v. *Council (Chernobyl)* [1990] ECR I–1527, para 11.

[6] Case 45/86 *Commission* v. *Council (Generalized System of Preferences)* [1987] ECR 1493.

[7] C-91/05 *Commission* v. *Council (Small Arms/ECOWAS)* [2008] ECR I-3651.

[8] See further D. Chalmers, G. Davies and G. Monti, *European Union Law*, 2nd edn (Cambridge: Cambridge University Press, 2011), pp. 211–219 (214); P. Craig and G. de Búrca, *EU Law: Text, Cases and Materials* (Oxford: Oxford University Press, 2011), pp. 89–93; and further on Article 114 TFEU: D. Wyatt, 'Community Competence to Regulate the Internal Market', in M. Dougan and S. Currie (eds.), *50 Years of the European Treaties, Looking Back and Thinking Forward* (Oxford: Hart Publishing, 2009), Chapter 5.

balance, but also to the nature of EU external competence. For example, if a CCP legal basis is used rather than environment, this entails a priori EU exclusive competence rather than a shared competence. The consequences for the Member States' capacity to act are different: if the international agreement falls under CCP, the Member States could not act even if the Union decides not to conclude that agreement; if it falls within the environmental competence, the Member States are only pre-empted in accordance with the rules discussed in Chapter 4.

The Court of Justice has had to navigate this complex legal and political situation, with high legal and political stakes: conferral, institutional balance, as well as the proverbial EU single voice in the world. Behind the legal arguments in the case law discussed thus lay numerous competing legal and political interests, with the Court of Justice fulfilling a crucial and not uncontested role.[9] While some critique may be valid, the Court has gone to great lengths to deploy a judicial methodology which is based on 'objective factors amenable to judicial review' rather than the subjective considerations of the actors involved.

3 THE TWO-PRONGED 'APPROPRIATE LEGAL BASIS' TEST: SCOPE AND CENTRE OF GRAVITY

In its legal basis case law, the CJEU has steered clear from subjective reasons of the actors involved, and aims at judicial review detached from the power struggles which underlie them.

Case 45/86 *Commission* v. *Council* (Generalized System of Preferences) [1987] ECR 1493

11. It must be observed that in the context of the organization of the powers of the Community, the choice of the legal basis for a measure may not depend simply on an institution's choice of the legal basis, for a measure may not depend simply on an institution's conviction as to the objective pursued, but must be based on objective factors amenable to judicial review.

Through decades of case law the Court has developed what amounts to an 'appropriate legal basis' test which encompasses both the vertical and horizontal situation identified above. The test is composed of two distinct elements.

- In the **first step**, the Court establishes the scope of the competence-conferring article(s) at issue in the dispute. Concretely it means that the Court will seek to define the substantive *width of the conferral* to the Union. It deploys a number of interpretative methods to assess the objectives of competence-conferring provisions, in order to conclude which kinds of EU acts the CCP, development policy, etc. provides the legal basis for. In vertical situations this is where the emphasis of the judicial reasoning will lie, although establishing the respective scope of competing legal bases is equally important in horizontal situations.

---

[9] R. Barents, 'The Internal Market Unlimited: Some Observations on the Legal Basis of Community Legislation' (1993) 30 *Common Market Law Review* 85–109 at 89; H. Cullen and A. Charlesworth, 'Diplomacy by Other Means: The Use of Legal Basis Litigation as a Political Strategy by the European Parliament and Member States' (1999) 36 *Common Market Law Review* 1243–1270; R. H. Van Ooik, *De Keuze der Rechtsgrondslag voor Besluiten in de Europese Unie* (Deventer: Kluwer, 1999), p. 57.

- In the second step, the Court examines the instrument itself, to conclude whether its aim and content fall within the scope of one or the other, or none, of the competence-conferring provisions which are prima facie possible. In other words, the Court has to find the centre of gravity of an EU act in relation to the objectives and scope of a competence-conferring provision. This step will occur in vertical and horizontal situations, but is most significant in the latter instance.

P. Koutrakos, 'Legal Basis and Delimitation of Competence in EU External Relations', in M. Cremona and B. de Witte (eds.), *EU Foreign Relations Law: Constitutional Fundamentals* (Oxford: Hart Publishing, 2008), pp. 183–184

The lack of clarity in the Court's case law on the relationship between trade and environmental policy, the politically charged nature of the choice of the appropriate legal basis and its constitutional function, the wide, flexible, albeit not unlimited, and pragmatic interpretation of Article [207 TFEU], all suggest that the standard formulation that 'the choice of the legal basis . . . must rest on objective factors' is only partly accurate: whilst the choice of legal base is not dependent upon 'an institution's conviction as to the objective pursued', it becomes apparent from the Court's case law that this may not be determined on the basis of specific and easily identifiable criteria either.

---

4 THE FIRST STEP: SCOPE OF EU EXTERNAL COMPETENCE

(i) Trade legal basis case law pre-Maastricht

(a) The wide scope of CCP: teleology and dynamic approach

Since the CCP was the principal external competence conferred upon the Union with the Treaty of Rome, this is where the Court first pronounced itself on the issue of scope of EU external competence. In the early cases of the 1970s and 1980s we see two modes of interpretation being deployed:[10]

- First, a formal approach which plants the first seeds for the centre-of-gravity reasoning, examined further in section 5 of this chapter.
- Second, a teleological approach which aims to give effect to the purpose and spirit of the competence-conferring provision. The Court does this by making the analogy between the EU's competence in international trade, and the equivalent commercial policies of (Member) States.

The result is a dynamic and wide interpretation of the CCP's scope.

Opinion 1/75, *Re Understanding on a Local Costs Standard* [1975] ECR 1355, no paragraph numbering

The Court was asked to rule on whether the CCP's scope encompassed measures concerning credits for the financing of local costs linked to export operations. Within the OECD, a soft legal 'understanding' had been

---

[10] Opinion 1/75 *Re Understanding on a Local Costs Standard* [1975] ECR 1355.

drawn up on this topic, and the Commission had participated in the negotiations alongside Member States. The former argued that the EEC was exclusively competent to conclude it, while the latter thought the EEC not competent at all, or that it had to be concluded a mixed instrument. Upon conclusion of negotiations at the OECD, it was stated by the Chairman of the Group on Export Credits and Credit Guarantees that whereas 'all delegations had given their approval to the draft understanding', the form of the participation in the EEC needed to be clarified.[11] Using the procedure in [Article 218(11) TFEU][12] the Commission asked the Court whether the Community had the power to conclude the Understanding, and if so, whether that power was exclusive.

Articles 112 and 113 of the [EEC Treaty] must be borne in mind in formulating a reply to this question. The first of these provisions provides that: '... Member States shall, before the end of the transitional period, progressively harmonize the systems whereby they grant aid for exports to third countries, to the extent necessary to ensure that competition between undertakings of the Community is not distorted'.

Since there is no doubt that the grant of export credits falls within the system of aids granted by Member States for exports, it is already clear from Article 112 that the subject-matter of the standard laid down in the Understanding in question relates to a field in which the provisions of the Treaty recognize a Community power. Furthermore, Article 113 of the Treaty lays down, in paragraphs (1) and (2), that: '... the Common Commercial Policy shall be based on uniform principles, particularly in regard to ... export policy ...'

The field of the Common Commercial Policy, and more particularly that of export policy, necessarily covers systems of aid for exports and more particularly measures concerning credits for the financing of local costs linked to export operations. In fact such measures constitute an important element of commercial policy, that concept having the same content whether it is applied in the context of the international action of a State or to that of the Community.

The first portion of the Court's reasoning matches the content of the 'Understanding on a local cost standard' with the objectives of the CCP. For the CJEU, 'there is no doubt' export credit 'falls within' the systems of aid mentioned in the Treaty. As we shall see further in this chapter, this approach and language are a typical centre-of-gravity reasoning of linking an instrument to the objectives of the competence-conferring provision. The second important element is the Court's state-analogy in establishing the flexible and evolving scope of Article 113 TEC (now 207 TFEU). The teleological and evolutive approach means that the competence conferred upon the Community is not as it stood in 1957. For the Court, states are not inherently limited in what they can do to pursue their trade interests. As international trade relations evolve, so do commercial policies of states. According to the Court then, what is true for states is also true for the commercial policy of the Community.[13]

---

[11] H. H. Maas, 'The External Powers of the EEC with Regard to Commercial Policy: Comment on Opinion 1/75' (1976) 13 *Common Market Law Review* 380.

[12] It was controversial whether the Court could be asked to give a ruling where the sole submissions concerned matters of competence. The Court affirmed that its jurisdiction extended 'to all rules of the Treaty' which could lead to complications as regards the compatibility with the Treaty of international agreements binding upon the Community.

[13] P. Pescatore, 'External Relations in the Case-Law of the Court of Justice of the European Communities' (1979) 16 *Common Market Law Review* 615–645 at 621; J. Steenbergen, 'The Common Commercial Policy' (1980) 17 *Common Market Law Review* 229–249 at 230–231.

In Opinion 1/78, the Court further explained what this state-like and dynamically evolving interpretation meant. Changing trends in international relations are crucial to understand the Court's ruling. In Chapter 9, we will see that the Treaty of Rome had a strong affinity with the GATT, and hence the importance of trade liberalization as an objective also in the Community's CCP. As colonies began to regain their independence, the nature of international trade relations changed. This led inter alia to the establishment in 1964 of the UN Conference on Trade and Development (UNCTAD) devoted to tackling concerns of developing countries on their place in the global trade system. Subsequently, a number of commodity agreements were concluded on wheat, cocoa, coffee and tin, which were all concluded jointly by the Member States and the EEC on the basis of Article 113 EEC.[14] They thus incorporated development concerns, but equally crucial from the perspective of the scope of the CCP is that these agreements meant to organize (rather than liberalize) world markets of commodities of economic importance to developing countries. So too the natural rubber agreement, the subject of Opinion 1/78, which would regulate prices so that producers could receive 'just remuneration' and developing nations receive stable export earnings.[15] Because the internal market and the CCP were being put into place in a progressive fashion, by the time of the rubber agreement the Commission was of the opinion that the agreement fell entirely within the scope of the CCP. Member States argued that the development goals of the instrument rendered it outside the scope of the CCP,[16] and that a mixed agreement was the only option. The Court sided with the Commission, utilizing the state-analogy to interpret the list of objectives in current Article 207 TFEU in a non-exhaustive way. The Court further affirmed the need for the scope of CCP to evolve over time to ensure that it remains a policy capable of fulfilling its purpose.

Opinion 1/78, *International Agreement on Natural Rubber* [1979] ECR 2871

43. The link between the various agreements on commodities ... must also be taken into account. As an increasing number of products which are particularly important from the economic point of view are concerned, it is clear that a coherent Commercial Policy would no longer be practicable if the Community were not in a position to exercise its powers also in connection with a category of agreements which are becoming, alongside traditional commercial agreements, one of the major factors in the regulation of international trade.

44. Following the impulse given by UNCTAD to the development of this type of control, it seems that it would no longer be possible to carry on any worthwhile Common Commercial Policy if the Community were not in a position to avail itself also of more elaborate means devised with a view to furthering the development of international trade. It is therefore not possible to lay down, for Article 113 of the EEC Treaty, an interpretation the effect of which would be to restrict the Common Commercial Policy to the use of instruments intended to have an effect only on the traditional aspects of external trade to the exclusion of more highly developed mechanisms such as appear in the agreement envisaged. A "Commercial Policy" understood in that sense would be destined to become nugatory in the course of time. Although it may be thought that at the time when the Treaty was drafted liberalization of trade was the dominant idea, the Treaty nevertheless does not form a barrier to the possibility of the Community's developing a

---

[14] Opinion 1/78 *International Agreement on Natural Rubber* [1979] ECR 2871, para 3.
[15] *Ibid.*, para 8.
[16] See further below on these arguments 'step two, centre of gravity in a vertical situation'.

Commercial Policy aiming at a regulation of the world market for certain products rather than at a mere liberalization of trade.

45. Article 113 empowers the Community to formulate a Commercial "Policy", based on "uniform principles" thus showing that the question of external trade must be governed from a wide point of view, and not only having regard to the administration of precise systems such as customs and quantitative restrictions. The same conclusion may be deduced from the fact that the enumeration in Article 113 of the subjects covered by Commercial Policy (changes in tariff rates, the conclusion of tariff and trade agreements, the achievement of uniformity in measures of liberalization, export policy and measures to protect trade) is conceived as a non-exhaustive enumeration which must not, as such, close the door to the application in a Community context of any other process intended to regulate external trade. A restrictive interpretation of the concept of Common Commercial Policy would risk causing disturbances in intra-Community trade by reason of the disparities which would then exist in certain sectors of economic relations with non-member countries.

The approach taken by the Court of Justice to the scope of the CCP is clearly one of teleology utilizing both EU internal and EU external arguments. From an *internal perspective*, the function of the CCP is to serve the internal market. So as to support its function, the list of Article 207 TFEU must be seen as non-exhaustive, because if disparities exist in non-listed fields, EU companies could still come to face distortion of competition in their operations in third-country markets. From an *external perspective* the Court equally seeks to ensure effectiveness of EU action in international trade. It contrasts the 'traditional aspects' of CCP with its focus on reducing tariff barriers with the evolution of international trade relations. In the new post-colonial environment, the CCP would soon become devoid of purpose if it did not evolve with the new dominant idea which is not purely about liberalization, but about trade regulation.

(b) Early case law in context: intra-EU power-play and the role of the court
The 1985 judgment in *Commission* v. *Council (Generalized System of Preferences (GSP))*[17] is the closing milestone for the pre-Maastricht Treaty construction of the CCP's scope. The Court again confirmed the state-like analogy of the CCP as well as the evolutive interpretation of its scope.[18] The dispute illustrates well the connection between EU external relations law, institutional conflict and effective external policy-making. Since 1971 the Commission had always proposed a CCP legal basis for the Generalised System of Preferences (GSP),[19] but the Council consistently added the flexibility clause (Article 352 TFEU) as an additional legal basis.[20] This meant that decisions on the GSP Regulation were taken by unanimity, rather than by QMV. The rationale for the Commission to bring the case after fifteen years of acquiescing to the Council's modus operandi was succinctly captured in the 1985 Communication proposing to revise the GSP. The Commission used the international relations argument to buttress the alleged sole need for Article 207 TFEU, and stated that it can no longer accept pragmatism over principle because unanimity is less effective than QMV. With the GSP case, the Commission thus had not wished to

---

[17] Case 45/86 *Commission* v. *Council (Generalized System of Preferences)* [1987] ECR 1493.
[18] *Ibid.*, paras 16 and 19.
[19] A. Arnull, 'Legal Principles and Practical Politics' (1987) 12 *European Law Review* 448–451.
[20] Case 45/86 *Commission* v. *Council (Generalized System of Preferences)* [1987] ECR 1493, para 7.

establish the scope of the CCP firmly in line with the expansive reading of Opinion 1/78, but it also explicitly stated a wish to reinforce the 'Community method' in decision-making in EU external relations.

Communication from the Commission, *Review of the European Community's Generalized Tariff Preferences Scheme*, Brussels, 6 May 1985, COM(1985) 203 final, p. 8[21]

Despite its legally autonomous nature, the GSP has to be seen as part of a well-established international framework for trade and has thus to be considered as an integral part of the Community's overall commercial policy. Each year since the first inauguration of the EC's GSP scheme in 1971 the Commission has presented its formal legislative proposals for the implementing regulations on the basis of Article [207 TFEU]. Although convinced that the GSP should be viewed as operating within the context of the EC's Common Commercial Policy, the Commission has not hitherto sought to override the objections of certain Member States who have insisted on substituting an unspecified reference to the Treaty. Now, however, not merely principle but the practical necessities of decision-making following the latest Enlargement of the EC require that the GSP be grounded on Article [207 TFEU]. The annual examination of the Commission's proposals has become increasingly difficult and time-consuming and if the whole procedure is not to risk grinding to a halt, the adoption of majority voting must now be accepted.

(ii) Post-Maastricht: towards a general balance of competences

(a) Introduction: balancing a multitude of competences

A. Dashwood, 'The Limits of European Community Powers' (1996) 21 *European Law Review* 113

There is a school of thought that no opportunity should be missed of moving the Community caravan forward, if necessary by night marches. I do not belong to that school. To vary the metaphor: I believe it is neither wise nor right to treat the Community like a tender plant that must be left alone in the dark to achieve its natural growth.

It is certainly not *wise*, because there are too many people who suspect the Community of being a Triffid, quietly gaining strength in order to gobble up everything that gives substance to our sense of having separate national identities. That is not a peculiarly British phobia. It surfaced in several countries during the campaign for the ratification of the Maastricht Treaty; and it received judicial articulation in the *Brunner* opinion of Germany's Constitutional Court. In rejecting a challenge directed against German parliamentary assent to the Treaty, and against certain consequential amendments to the constitution, the Court stressed the limited scope of the democratic authorisation for investing additional powers in the Community. A courteous but clear warning was given that, if the provisions of the Treaty were interpreted in such a way as effectively to enlarge the Community's powers, the exercise of those powers would not produce consequences binding within the German legal order.

---

[21] Emphasis in original.

The role and impact of the Court of Justice through this early line of cases discussed above cannot be understated. The judgments are contemporaries of the *ERTA* judgment examined in Chapters 3 and 4. In relation to *ERTA*, Post spoke of the CJEU as forcefully promoting 'the emergence of a distinctive transnational entity endowed with forms of authority that are both significant and unique'.[22] This observation is equally valid for case law on the scope of the CCP and subsequent rulings. Through its purposive and dynamic interpretation the Court strengthened the Community as an international actor with its wide CCP, which excluded Member State action in the field. However, the extract from Dashwood reflects the discussion during the early 1990s with regard to the existence and nature of competence discussed in Chapters 3 and 4. Similarly, the scope of the CCP could not expand indefinitely. In search of a balance between different EU competences, the Court would change tack following the Maastricht Treaty.

The notion of 'balance of competences' was coined by Koutrakos who criticizes the Court's legal basis case law for lacking predictability, and for not always consistently weighing different competence-conferring provisions against each other. The Court can certainly not be accused of not having attempted to attain such balance, but whether it has achieved it is another matter. From the mid 1980s primary law of the EEC was changing rapidly through successive Treaty amendments explicitly conferring new competences upon the E(E)C. With the SEA, the EEC was conferred a competence in the sphere of environmental policy, alongside the inclusion of EPC (later CFSP) into primary law. The Maastricht Treaty explicitly conferred a development competence upon the Community and created the CFSP (second) pillar and the third (JHA) pillar of the Union (see Chapters 11 and 14). The Amsterdam Treaty incorporated part of that third pillar into the Community, and introduced a treaty-making competence into the CFSP, whereas the Nice Treaty introduced current Article 212 TFEU on technical cooperation with third countries. Parallel to these new competences, much was happening on the international scene in which the EU found itself: the creation of the WTO, the collapse of the USSR, globalization and greater attention to global environmental challenges. These events provided ample opportunity for the EU to become a fully fledged international actor post-Maastricht, but led to numerous legal queries on the scope of – and relationship between – the CCP, development, CFSP and other EU external competences.

P. Koutrakos, 'Legal Basis and Delimitation of Competence in EU External Relations', in M. Cremona and B. de Witte (eds.), *EU Foreign Relations Law: Constitutional Fundamentals* **(Oxford: Hart Publishing, 2008), p. 198**

In the multilayered system of EU external relations, it is necessary that the notion of the balance of competence should become central in the choice of the appropriate legal basis and the delimitation of competence. Attention should be paid to drawing the outer limits of not only the CCP but also the other external relations legal basis in a way which would ensure that the conditions for their application do not become irrelevant. ... All external relations legal bases are part of a system of external powers and the conditions for their application and their implications for the EU institutions should be taken seriously.

---

[22] R. Post, 'Constructing the European Polity: ERTA and the Open Skies Judgments', in M. Poiares Maduro and L. Azoulai (eds.), *The Past and Future of EU Law* (Oxford: Hart Publishing, 2010), p. 234.

(b) The evolving scope of the CCP

The scope of CCP in relation to security policies of the Member States

In *Werner*, German authorities refused an export licence for equipment to Libya on the basis of German federal legislation. Similarly, *Leifer* concerned criminal proceedings for having delivered dual-use goods to Iraq without the necessary export licenses. Both cases concerned essentially the same question: whether the CCP solely covers measures which pursue commercial objectives, or whether it also covers commercial measures having foreign policy objectives. In *Werner* the Court found:[23]

Case C-70/94 *Werner* [1995] ECR I-3189

9. Implementation of such a common commercial policy requires a non-restrictive interpretation of that concept, so as to avoid disturbances in intra-Community trade by the reason of the disparities which would then exist in certain sectors of economic relations with non member countries.

10. So, a measure such as that described in the national court's question, whose effect is to prevent or restrict the export of certain products, cannot be treated as falling outside the scope of the common commercial policy on the ground that it has foreign policy and security objectives.

In other words, EU instruments adopted on the basis of the CCP do not necessarily have to promote or regulate trade to fall within its scope: they may also restrict it.[24] In *Centro-Com* the Court formulated a more general principle as regards the relationship between CCP and foreign security policies of the Member States.

Case C-124/95 *Centro-Com* [1997] ECR I-81

27. ... while it is for Member States to adopt measures of foreign and security policy in the exercise of their national competence, those measures must nevertheless respect the provisions adopted by the Community in the field of the CCP.

These three judgments confirm that the Court keeps to the wide interpretation of the CCP but that it becomes more attuned to interests beyond an 'effective CCP'. In *Werner*, *Leifer* and *Centro-Com*, the Community had already adopted pertinent Regulations which captured the facts at issue in the cases. As such, the Court was not so much expanding the scope of the CCP. Rather, it was guaranteeing the effectiveness of Community instruments which had been previously adopted on its basis, by keeping exceptions of public security within the scope of the CCP and its implementing instruments. The general trend from the early 1990s onwards is indeed that the Court is less inclined to allow the wide scope of the CCP to be stretched to the fullest, and that it takes account of competing legal and political interests at issue.

---

[23] Case C-70/94 *Werner* [1995] ECR I-3189, para 10; Case C-83/94 *Leifer* [1995] ECR I-3231, para 10; and Case C-124/95 *Centro-Com* [1997] ECR I-81, para 26; Case C-94/03 *Rotterdam Convention* [2006] ECR I-1, para 49.

[24] Similarly in Case C-83/94 *Leifer* [1995] ECR I-3231, para 10.

The post-Maastricht trend: taking into account EU and Member State interests

In Chapter 4 we have seen that in the wake of the difficult ratification of the Maastricht Treaty and the emphasis on the limits of conferral from the German *Bundesverfassungsgericht* the CJEU operated in a changed legal and political environment on the future of European integration. In Opinion 1/94 the Commission had submitted that the scope of CCP encompassed the entire WTO Agreement and all its annexes, including the GATS and TRIPS.[25] On GATS, the Commission's arguments were entirely in line with the CJEU's dynamic and wide construction of the CCP:

Opinion 1/94, *Re World Trade Organization Agreement* [1994] ECR I-5267

40. ... in certain developed countries the services sector has become the dominant sector of the economy and ... the global economy has been undergoing fundamental structural changes. The trend is for basic industry to be transferred to developing countries, whilst the developed economies have tended to become, in the main, exporters of services and of goods with a high value-added content. The Court notes that this trend is borne out by the WTO Agreement and its annexes, which were the subject of a single process of negotiation covering both goods and services.

The Court stated that the combination of these shifting trends in international trade and 'the open nature of the common commercial policy'[26] entailed that services were not necessarily excluded from its scope.[27] The wide and dynamic interpretation of the CCP did not disappear, but the Court began to temper its implications by reference to the principle of conferral. Indeed, the Court looked less at the scope of Article 207 TFEU as a stand-alone competence in isolation from other competence-conferring provisions. Gone is the 'state-analogy' and gone is the reference to CCP becoming 'nugatory over time'.[28] Instead, the CJEU limits the scope of the CCP by reference to other provisions of the Treaties: in the case of services, transport services and movement of persons as encompassed by three modes of services defined in GATS fall within the scope of relevant provisions of the Treaties. Finally, the method by which the Court concludes whether GATS falls within the scope of CCP is a centre-of-gravity reasoning 'light'. The Court looks at the *content* of GATS, e.g. the four modes of services which it covers. It then inquires whether these can be brought under the scope of the CCP as it stood in Article 113 TEC by looking to analogies between the fashion in which trade in goods is conducted, and trade in services.

Opinion 1/94, *Re World Trade Organization Agreement* [1994] ECR I-5267

43. Under Article I(2) of GATS, trade in services is defined, for the purposes of that agreement, as comprising four modes of supply of services: (1) cross-frontier supplies not involving any movement of persons; ... (4) the presence of natural persons from a WTO member country, enabling a supplier from one member country to supply services within the territory of any other member country.

---

[25] Opinion 1/94 *Re World Trade Organization Agreement* [1994] ECR I-5267, para 35.
[26] As previously already recognized in Case 45/86, *supra*, para 19.
[27] Opinion 1/91 *Re European Economic Area* [1991] ECR I-6079, para 41.
[28] Opinion 1/94 *Re World Trade Organization Agreement* [1994] ECR I-5267, para 41.

44. As regards cross-frontier supplies, the service is rendered by a supplier established in one country to a consumer residing in another. The supplier does not move to the consumer's country; nor, conversely, does the consumer move to the supplier's country. That situation is, therefore, not unlike trade in goods, which is unquestionably covered by the common commercial policy within the meaning of the Treaty. ...

45. The same cannot be said of the other three modes of supply of services covered by GATS, namely, consumption abroad, commercial presence and the presence of natural persons.

46. As regards natural persons, it is clear from Article 3 of the Treaty, which distinguishes between 'a common commercial policy' in paragraph (b) and 'measures concerning the entry and movement of persons' in paragraph (d), that the treatment of nationals of non-member countries on crossing the external frontiers of Member States cannot be regarded as falling within the common commercial policy. More generally, the existence in the Treaty of specific chapters on the free movement of natural and legal persons shows that those matters do not fall within the common commercial policy. ...

48. Turning next to the particular services comprised in transport, these are the subject of a specific [Part III – Title VI TFEU], distinct from [Part V – Title II TFEU] on the common commercial policy. It was precisely in relation to transport policy that the Court held for the first time that the competence of the Community to conclude international agreements 'arises not only from an express conferment by the Treaty – as is the case with [Article 207 TFEU] for tariff and trade agreements and with [Article 217 TFEU] for association agreements – but may equally flow from other provisions of the Treaty and from measures adopted, within the framework of those provisions, by the Community institutions' (Case 22/70 ERTA). The idea underlying that decision is that international agreements in transport matters are not covered by [Article 207 TFEU].

The scope of the CCP is constrained by the fact that the Union is conferred other competences on free movement of persons and in transport policy. As regards the TRIPS, the Court rejected the Commission's arguments on a similar basis: it was recognized that the TRIPS would entail EU-wide harmonization where previously no such measures existed yet. The Court found that it was not possible to do through an external instrument with CCP legal basis, what should be done through an internal instrument based on the internal market legal basis together with the flexibility clause (Articles 114 and 351 TFEU).[29] Allowing that would not be in line with the principle of conferral. Illustrative of the subtlety (though not necessarily consistency) by which the Court aims to balance different competences, is the fact that a similar argument on the Agreement on Agriculture was rejected. The Council had argued that the legal basis for that agreement should have been Article 38 TFEU (CAP). It argued that these agreements concern not just the commercial measures applicable to international trade in agricultural products but also, and above all, the internal rules on the organization of agricultural markets.

Opinion 1/94, *Re World Trade Organization Agreement* [1994] ECR I–5267

29. The objective of the Agreement on Agriculture is to establish, on a worldwide basis, 'a fair and market-oriented agricultural trading system' (see the preamble to that Agreement). The fact that the commitments entered into under that Agreement require internal measures to be adopted on the basis of Article 43 of

---

[29] Opinion 1/94, paras 58–60.

the Treaty does not prevent the international commitments themselves from being entered into pursuant to Article 113 alone.

In Opinion 1/08 the Court was again confronted with questions essentially the same as in Opinion 1/94. The case concerned the negotiation and conclusion of amendments to the Schedules of Commitments of the EC and its Member States under GATS. The Court gave its ruling one day before the Lisbon Treaty entered into force, and it concerned the complex treaty provisions of CCP as they stood under Nice. Nevertheless, the continued relevance of the Opinion lies in the Court's willingness to engage the competing EU and Member State interests subtly in the scope of the CCP: the requirement of unity in external representation of the Union as balanced against Member States' interests in certain sensitive service sectors pertaining to culture, health and education.

M. Cremona, 'Balancing Union and Member State interests: Opinion 1/2008, Choice of Legal Base and the Common Commercial Policy under the Treaty of Lisbon' (2010) 35 *European Law Review* 678–694

As is often the case, the starting point of the Court's reasoning on this issue is telling. It starts by making three observations which serve to emphasise that we are here dealing not simply with a choice of legal basis for Community competence, but with the limits of that competence and with the allocation of competence between Community and Member States. First, it reiterates its position in Opinion 1/94 that any practical difficulties associated with joint participation cannot affect the allocation of competence. Second, it denies that the nature of the modifications contained in the agreements (whether increasing or decreasing the commitments of the Member States) can affect the determination of competence. Third, it reminds us that the Community only has conferred powers. From this perspective, it explains the rationale of [Article 133(6) subpara. 2 TEC] as regards the sensitive sectors. The provision "reflects a concern" that trade in such services should not be governed by agreements concluded by the Community alone, providing instead for common action so as to reflect the interests of both Community and Member States:

"The second subparagraph of art. 133(6) TEC allows the interest of the Community in establishing a comprehensive, coherent and efficient external commercial policy to be pursued whilst at the same time allowing the special interests which the Member States might wish to defend in the sensitive areas identified by that provision to be taken into account."[30]

The directness with which the Court recognizes the different interests involved is striking: the collective interest of the Community in an effective common commercial policy and the special sectoral-based interests of individual Member States. But although those interests may compete, neither Community nor Member States may act alone. The requirement of unity in the international representation of the Community calls for common action and close cooperation. It is from this perspective that the Court concludes that any agreement which concerns services in these sectors must be concluded also by the Member States. . . .

How might this state of play be affected by the Lisbon Treaty amendments to art. 207 TFEU? The provision for shared competence and joint participation has disappeared; the whole of the CCP now falls

---

[30] Opinion 1/08 *Amendments to EU Schedules of Commitments under GATS* [2009] ECR I-11129, para 136.

within exclusive Union competence, even, strikingly, those services sectors (health, culture, education) where the European Union has only supporting competence to act internally. Instead, there is provision for unanimous voting (in certain circumstances) in relation to agreements on sensitive services sectors.

(c) Beyond CCP: taking into account objectives from a different competence

The area which pushed the Court to rethink its approach to the scope of the CCP was in its relationship to EU environmental competence and the Treaty obligation of ensuring a high standard of environmental protection in all its policies.[31] In the 1990 *Chernobyl* case, Greece challenged the legal basis of a Regulation imposing conditions on the imports of agricultural products originating in third countries following the nuclear accident in Ukraine.[32] The Court looked at aim and content of the measure and found that the Regulation had rightly been adopted on the basis of the CCP alone. The fact that the Regulation contained environmental measures did not mean that it fell outside the scope of CCP.

Case 62/88 *Greece* v. *Council (Chernobyl)* [1990] ECR I–1527

18. The fact that maximum permitted levels of radioactive contamination are fixed in response to a concern to protect public health and that the protection of public health is also one of the objectives of Community action in environmental matters, in accordance with the Article 130r(l), likewise cannot remove Regulation No 3955/87 from the sphere of the common commercial policy.

19. Articles 130r and 130s are intended to confer powers on the Community to undertake specific action on environmental matters. However, those articles leave intact the powers held by the Community under other provisions of the Treaty, even if the measures to be taken under the latter provisions pursue at the same time any of the objectives of environmental protection.

20. Moreover, that interpretation is confirmed by the second sentence of Article 130r(2), pursuant to which 'environmental protection requirements shall be a component of the Community's other policies'. That provision, which reflects the principle whereby all Community measures must satisfy the requirements of environmental protection, implies that a Community measure cannot be part of Community action on environmental matters merely because it takes account of those requirements.

The same approach of 'keeping competencies intact' has also been reproduced in other fields such as agricultural policy and environmental protection,[33] transport policy and environmental protection,[34] or development policy and human rights. The latter arose in the 1994 *Portugal* v. *Council* case,[35] where that Member State requested the annulment of the Decision

---

[31] Case 240/83 *ADBHU* [1985] ECR 531, para 13, Case 302/86 *Commission* v. *Denmark* [1988] ECR 4607, para 8, Case C-213/96 *Outokumpu* [1998] ECR I-1777, para 32; Case C-176/03 *Commission* v. *Council (Environmental Crimes)* [2005] ECR I-7879, paras 41–42.

[32] Case 62/88 *Greece* v. *Council (Chernobyl)* [1990] ECR I–1527.

[33] C-336/00 *Huber* [2002] ECR I-7699, paras 30–36.

[34] C-176/03 *Commission* v. *Council (Environmental Crimes)* [2005] ECR I-7879, para 41 and C-440/05 *Commission* v. *Council (Ship-Source Pollution)* [2007] ECR I-9097, para 60.

[35] C-268/94 *Portugal* v. *Council* [1996] ECR I-6177.

concluding the 'Cooperation agreement between the EC and India on Partnership and Development'. The Decision had been founded on trade and development legal bases (Articles 207 TFEU and 208), but Portugal argued that the inclusion of human rights in the agreement entailed that Article 352 TFEU should have been added. The contested provision was a so-called 'essential elements clause' which usually reads that: 'Respect for human rights and democratic principles is the basis for the cooperation between the Contracting Parties and for the provisions of this Agreement, and it constitutes an essential element of the Agreement.'

The debate between Portugal and the Council essentially revolved around human rights as central or ancillary to the agreement, notably in light of the wording 'essential'. Portugal considered that respect for human rights could at most be a general objective if based on the development competence, and that it could not lead to any means of action such as suspending the agreement for human rights violations. That, it argued, would require recourse to the flexibility clause. The Council argued that action could be taken without recourse to that provision, and the Danish government argued that Article 352 TFEU would constitute the proper legal basis were the Community to conclude a specific agreement which would have as its sole purpose to safeguard human rights (see further third dimension). The Court sided with the Council. The fact that respect for human rights in development has to be 'taken into account' (ex Article 177 TEC, current Article 208(1) TFEU) entails that it is possible for the EU to give substantive policy meaning to that provision, without needing recourse to the flexibility clause. Again the Court is seeking to guarantee the *effet utile* of the competence conferred upon the EU: it would not make sense for the drafters of the Treaties to refer to human rights in the competence-conferring provision, if no real-world action could be taken on their basis (see also Chapter 10). Notice then that the Court uses language similar to that of early case law on the CCP: the scope of development policy must be defined in a broad fashion, so as to not render it devoid of substance.

C-268/94 *Portugal* v. *Council* [1996] ECR I-6177

23. By declaring that 'Community policy . . . shall contribute to the general objective of developing and consolidating democracy and the rule of law, and to that of respecting human rights and fundamental freedoms', [current Article 21 TEU] requires the Community to take account of the objective of respect for human rights when it adopts measures in the field of development cooperation.

24. The mere fact that Article 1(1) of the Agreement provides that respect for human rights and democratic principles 'constitutes an essential element' of the Agreement does not justify the conclusion that that provision goes beyond the objective stated in [Article 208 TFEU]. The very wording of the latter provision demonstrates the importance to be attached to respect for human rights and democratic principles, so that, amongst other things, development cooperation policy must be adapted to the requirement of respect for those rights and principles. . . .

38. That being so, to require a development cooperation agreement concluded between the Community and a non-member country to be based on another provision as well as on [Article 210 TFEU] and, possibly, also to be concluded by the Member States whenever it touches on a specific matter would in practice amount to rendering devoid of substance the competence and procedure prescribed in [Article 210 TFEU].

The wide scope of EU development policy has been affirmed in later case law on a border management project in the Philippines[36] and in the case concerning EU support to the Economic Community of West African States (ECOWAS) to combat the illegal dissemination of small arms and weapons.[37] In both cases, the Court defined the EU's development competence in broad terms stating that security concerns could be encompassed by EU development policy.[38] For an examination of the scope of EU development policy in relation to the EU's CFSP, we refer to Chapters 10 and 11.

It is important that the obligation to take into account objectives from a different competence 'end somewhere'. Namely, there must be a point at which an instrument does more than take into account an objective, but actually predominantly pursues that objective and thus requires a separate legal basis. Teasing out when that is so, is the domain of the centre-of-gravity test explained in section 5, and specifically in the third dimension of the content test.[39] However, before moving to the second step of the 'appropriate legal basis' test, we must examine how the Lisbon Treaty has impacted the scope, objectives and choice of legal basis in EU external relations, and how future case law is likely to evolve.

(d) Joining legal principle with policy coherence post-Lisbon

The scope of the CCP evolved in lock-step with progressive treaty changes, balancing this competence against newly conferred powers of the Union. While a legal methodology to choose between different provisions with their own objectives and procedural requirements became imperative, EU external policy-making in practice does not always permit neat divisions between measures on trade or environment, environment or development, development or security, trade or security, and so on. The Treaties and the Court certainly took account of this tension between law and policy, a tension between needs for a coherent and effective EU external policy, and requirements imposed by key legal principles such as conferral and institutional balance.

- At Treaty level, this occurs through provisions which require that action undertaken under one provision (for example, trade) take into account objectives from other competence-conferring provisions (for example, environment). These kinds of connections have been significantly strengthened with the Lisbon Treaty.
- The Court takes account of this tension in two ways. First, by balancing the respective scopes of competence-conferring provisions against each other. Second, in the centre-of-gravity test, by stating that when content which is far from the central aim of a measure (for example, fiscal provisions in a trade agreement) does not necessarily lead to a different legal basis under certain conditions (see section 5 – third dimension). As a result of the Lisbon Treaty, this element is likely to become key in future legal basis case law.

As said, the Lisbon Treaty intensified the obligation to ensure policy connections across different EU competences. Key provisions are Articles 21 TEU, 7 TFEU and 205 TFEU. These articles are partially overlapping and essentially lay down a web of legal connections between different policy competences. Article 7 TFEU is the *lex generalis* applicable across all EU policies. It applies

---

[36] C-403/05 *Parliament* v. *Commission (Philippine Border Mission)* [2007] ECR I-9045.
[37] C-91/05 *Commission* v. *Council (Small Arms/ECOWAS)* [2008] ECR I-3651.
[38] C-91/05, *supra*, para 66 which is an exact copy of para 57 of CaseC-403/05, *supra*, para 57.
[39] See also that section for a brief discussion of the pending action Case C-377/12 n.y.r.

to all internal and external competences and perfectly captures the tension between the interconnectedness of policy and the inherently separating nature of choice of legal bases.

Article 7 TFEU

The Union shall ensure consistency between its policies and activities, taking all of its objectives into account and in accordance with the principle of conferral of powers.

The *lex specialis* for EU external relations are Articles 21 TEU and 205 TFEU. As seen in Chapter 1, Article 21 TEU establishes an obligation for all EU external policies to respect the principles and objectives listed in paragraphs 1 and 2 of that article. Further, it states that the Union must respect these principles and objectives in the exercise of its external competences conferred in Part V TFEU (which contains the CCP, development policy, etc.) as well as in the 'external dimensions' of internal policies.[40]

Article 21(3) TEU

The Union shall respect the principles and pursue the objectives set out in paragraphs 1 and 2 in the development and implementation of the different areas of the Union's external action covered by this Title and by Part Five of the Treaty on the Functioning of the European Union, and of the external aspects of its other policies.

Article 205 TFEU

The Union's action on the international scene, pursuant to this Part, shall be guided by the principles, pursue the objectives and be conducted in accordance with the general provisions laid down in Chapter 1 of Title V of the Treaty on European Union.

There are further provisions which contain a similar obligation for specific policy areas. Some are applicable across internal or external policies, while other provisions are specific to EU external relations only: Articles 8 and 10 TFEU concerning elimination of any form of discrimination (sex, race, etc.) in all EU policies;[41] Article 11 TFEU concerning environmental protection requirements in all EU policies; Articles 208(1) and 209(2) TFEU concerning the link between development policy and Article 21 TEU; Article 212(1) TFEU concerning the link between economic, financial and technical cooperation with third countries and development policy (208 TFEU); Article 214(4) concerning the link between EU humanitarian aid and Article 21 TEU.

These are important provisions from the perspective of policy coherence and the scope of EU competence. Where the Treaty mandates that objectives from one competence be 'taken into

---

[40] Article 22 TEU as well, which concerns the central role of the European Council and the HR/VP.
[41] De Búrca, 'The EU in the Negotiation of the UN Disability Convention' (2010) 35 *European Law Review*, 2, 174–196.

account' in EU action undertaken under another competence, this is an expression of the Treaty drafters' recognition that international relations cannot be captured in a neat taxonomy of legal bases. Articles 21 TEU, 205 TFEU *et al.* reflect a desire to ensure that pertinent legal requirements do not obstruct effective and coherent EU external policy. However, Article 7 TFEU reminds us that this does not negate the importance of the principle of conferral, institutional balance and thus the choice of correct legal basis. As a consequence, it will be necessary to establish where the 'threshold' lies: does a measure merely take into account objectives for coherence sake – as mandated by the Treaties (for example, environmental objectives in trade agreement), or does it actually pursue those objectives to the extent that it falls within the scope of the relevant legal basis (the instrument is really an environmental treaty)?

In *Parliament* v. *Council* of July 2012, the EP asked the CJEU to annul a Council Regulation imposing certain restrictive measures against persons associated with Al-Qaeda. The contested Regulation was adopted by the Council on 22 December 2009. It was based on Article 215(2) TFEU, the legal basis for restrictive measures in Part V TFEU on external action by the Union. Importantly, its procedure only requires that the Parliament 'be informed'. That institution argued that Article 75 TFEU is the correct legal basis. This provision allows for measures to combat terrorism in the context of the AFSJ, and here the ordinary legislative procedure applies. The Court was asked to establish the scope of Article 215 TFEU, and specifically whether restrictive measures which pursued the objective of combating terrorism fell within its ambit.

C-130/10 *Parliament* v. *Council*, n.y.r.

The ambit of Article 215 TFEU

55. It is necessary to examine the wording of Article 215 TFEU, the context of which that provision forms part and the objectives it pursues, in relation to those pursued by Article 75 TFEU, before determining, in the light of the purpose and content of the contested regulation, whether Article 215(2) TFEU constitutes the correct legal basis for the regulation.

56. Article 215 TFEU appears in Title IV, entitled 'Restrictive measures', of Part Five of the TFEU on external action by the Union.

57. Article 215(1) concerns the adoption of measures necessary for the interruption or reduction, in part or completely, of economic and financial relations with one or more third countries. In this context, Article 215(2) concerns the adoption by the Council of 'restrictive measures . . . against natural or legal persons and groups or non-State entities', without specifically referring to the combating of terrorism and without limiting those measures to those measures alone that concern capital movements and payments.

58. Moreover, Article 215(2) TFEU, unlike Article 75 TFEU, provides . . . that it may not be used until a decision under the CFSP has provided for the adoption of restrictive measures against natural or legal persons, groups or non-State entities. For its part, Article 75 TFEU states that it may be used where necessary to achieve the objectives set out in Article 67 TFEU, that is to say, in connection with creating an area of freedom, security and justice. . . .

61. While admittedly the combating of terrorism and its financing may well be among the objectives of the area of freedom, security and justice, as they appear in Article 3(2) TEU, the objective of combating international terrorism and its financing in order to preserve international peace and security corresponds, nevertheless, to the objectives of the Treaty provisions on external action by the Union.

62. Article 21(2)(c) TEU, which forms part of Chapter 1 laying down general provisions on the Union's external action in Title V of the EU Treaty, provides: 'The Union shall define and pursue common policies and actions, and shall work for a high degree of cooperation in all fields of international relations, in order to ... preserve peace, prevent conflicts and strengthen international security, in accordance with the purposes and principles of the United Nations Charter'. With more specific regard to the CFSP, it is to be noted that, according to the first subparagraph of Article 24(1) TEU, '[t]he Union's competence in matters of [the CFSP] shall cover all areas of foreign policy and all questions relating to the Union's security, including the progressive framing of a common defence policy that might lead to a common defence'.

63. Given that terrorism constitutes a threat to peace and international security, the object of actions undertaken by the Union in the sphere of the CFSP, and the measures taken in order to give effect to that policy in the Union's external actions, in particular, restrictive measures for the purpose of Article 215(2) TFEU, can be to combat terrorism.

64. That assertion is borne out by, in particular, the tenor of Article 43(1) TEU, which makes it clear that all the tasks covered by the common security and defence policy 'may contribute to the fight against terrorism, including by supporting third countries in combating terrorism in their territories'.

65. It follows from the foregoing that Article 215(2) TFEU may constitute the legal basis of restrictive measures, including those designed to combat terrorism, taken against natural or legal persons, groups or non-State entities by the Union when the decision to adopt those measures is part of the Union's action in the sphere of the CFSP.

66. As the Advocate General observed in point 69 of his Opinion, in so far as Articles 75 TFEU and 215 TFEU relate to different European Union policies that pursue objectives which, although complementary, do not have the same scope, it would not seem possible to regard Article 75 TFEU as a more specific legal basis than Article 215(2) TFEU.

From this extract we can observe the continuing need to balance competences against each other after the Lisbon Treaty also. Articles 75 and 215 TFEU both relate to combating terrorism, but the first provision is more internally focused on the AFSJ, while the second is more externally focused on preserving international peace and security. However, given that Article 75 could give rise to implied external competence, the Court is careful in making that internal versus external distinction in defining the scope of these two Treaty provisions. Rather, it utilizes Article 21 TEU as a bridge to establish a connection between CFSP and CSDP with their external security orientation and Article 215 TFEU, while no such connection exists with Article 75 TFEU. It then adds that Article 75 TFEU cannot be considered the *lex specialis* provision of Article 215 TFEU. Rather, they each have a distinct scope connected to AFSJ and CFSP respectively.

5 THE SECOND STEP: CENTRE-OF-GRAVITY TEST

(i) Overview of key components of the test

In order to find the correct legal basis, the first step whereby the scope of the competence is established may suffice. In vertical situations between the EU and the Member States this is often the case. For example, if the scope of the CCP only partially covers the proposed international agreement, and no other EU competences are viable, the Member States will conclude the instrument together with the EU because the legal basis is appropriate, but not sufficient. In horizontal situations, as in the 2012 *Parliament* v. *Council* case above, the Court will have to take a second step: not only establish the scope of the provisions under scrutiny, but also adjudicate which of the two Treaty articles is the 'correct' legal basis on which to adopt the measure. The centre-of-gravity test has been developed to find the appropriate legal basis. The 2008 judgment on an EU guarantee to the European Investment Bank (EIB) is exemplary for the Court's effort to provide us with a structured test through which to 'find' the appropriate legal basis.

In the *EIB* judgment, Parliament sought the annulment of a Decision providing a Union guarantee to the EIB for projects outside the Union. The council had adopted the Decision on the basis of Article 212 TFEU (economic, financial and technical cooperation with third countries), and Parliament sought to add Article 209 TFEU (development) as a legal basis. Pre-Lisbon, there was only a consultation requirement of Parliament in the former legal basis, with co-decision applicable in the latter case. The case is yet another example of the continuing inter-institutional tug-of-war for involvement in EU external relations.

C-155/07 *Parliament* v. *Council (EIB Guarantees)* [2008] ECR I-8103

34. According to settled case law, the choice of the legal basis for a Community measure must rest on objective factors amenable to judicial review, which include the aim and content of that measure, and not on the legal basis used for the adoption of other Community measures which might, in certain cases, display similar characteristics. In addition, where the Treaty contains a more specific provision that is capable of constituting the legal basis for the measure in question, the measure must be founded on that provision.

35. If examination of a measure reveals that it pursues two aims or that it has two components and if one of those aims or components is identifiable as the main one, whereas the other is merely incidental, the measure must be founded on a single legal basis, namely that required by the main or predominant aim or component.

36. With regard to a measure that simultaneously pursues a number of objectives, or that has several components, which are inseparably linked without one being incidental to the other, the Court has held that, where various provisions of the Treaty are therefore applicable, such a measure will have to be founded, exceptionally, on the various corresponding legal bases.

37. None the less ... recourse to a dual legal basis is not possible where the procedures laid down for each legal basis are incompatible with each other.

The reference to 'objective factors amenable to judicial review' in the Court's case law implies that the legal basis for a measure taken by the Union depends entirely 'on the specific characteristics of the measure and on whether those characteristics meet the objective criteria determining the applicability of that legal basis'.[42] The key to the centre-of-gravity reasoning is to examine the aim and content of the measure in order to match it to the correct legal basis. The *content of a measure* is the action undertaken by the Union: providing financial support to an international organization, setting itself as guarantor for EIB loans, agreeing new cooperation procedures with third countries, and so on. The *aim* is the EU's reason for undertaking such

---

[42] C-176/03 *Commission* v. *Council (Environmental Crimes)* [2005] ECR I-7879, para 53.

action; what the EU hopes to achieve with the action at issue: liberalize trade, improve the environment, aid a developing country, support global peace and security, and so on.

The judicially constructed centre-of-gravity reasoning is a woefully complex set of steps of which the outcome can be difficult to predict. Although the test has over time become very streamlined through the many cases where it was repeated, its actual application has been far from consistent, which does not aid legal certainty. For example, the Court has never explicitly distinguished between autonomous instruments and international agreements in its application of the test.[43] However, we will see in our investigation that certain 'dimensions' of the test are more or less applicable only to autonomous EU instruments, or international agreements.

(ii) Aim of the instrument: a textual examination

Most legal basis judgments start with a statement on the aim of the instrument, followed by an examination of its content in light of that initial statement. In comparison to the assessment of an instrument's content, the examination of the 'aim' is normally the shortest and least substantive part of the reasoning. Sometimes, it may even come across as 'an initial sentiment' on where the centre of gravity may lie, which would then be refuted or confirmed by looking at the content of the measure. Overall, the aim of the centre-of-gravity test should be viewed as a mere preview on the final outcome of the case: the actual judicial reasoning is in the content, and this is where legal basis cases are decided. The examination of an instrument's aim can take on the following configurations:

- The Court may state that *one* aim clearly emerges from the instrument,[44] and either (1) keep it at that (not look at content at all),[45] (2) immediately support it with relevant content,[46] or (3) continue to look at content separately to support its initial statement on aim. The latter option is the most common in recent case law.
- The Court may also state that *one* aim clearly emerges from the instrument, but that by looking at the content another aim also emerges.[47] The investigation of content may then show that the additional aim may be pursued equally, or merely incidentally, leading to a dual legal basis decision, or not. Importantly, there are no cases where the content of the instrument has ever led the Court to refute or reverse that initial reading of aim, thus leading to a different legal basis. At most, the investigation of content has 'added' an aim to the initial statement on aim.
- The Court may also begin by stating that *two* aims are being pursued by the instrument,[48] without initially according more weight to one over the other.[49] It will then look at the content of

---

[43] M. Cremona, 'Balancing Union and Member State Interests: Opinion 1/2008, Choice of Legal Base and the Common Commercial Policy under the Treaty of Lisbon' (2010) 35 *European Law Review* 687.

[44] Case C-211/01 *Commission v. Council (Transport Agreements with Bulgaria and Hungary)* [2003] ECR I-8913; Opinion 2/00 *Cartagena Protocol on biosafety and the transboundary movements of living modified organisms resulting from biotechnology* [2001] ECR I-9713; Case C-36/98 *Spain v. Council (Sustainable use of the river Danube)* [2001] ECR I-779, para 60.

[45] Opinion 1/75 *Re Understanding on a Local Costs Standard* [1975] ECR 1355, Case 45/86 *Commission v. Council (Generalized System of Preferences)* [1987] ECR 1493.

[46] C-94/03 *Commission v. Council (Rotterdam Convention)* [2006] ECR I-1, paras 38–41.

[47] *Ibid.*, paras 42–48.

[48] Case C-281/01 *Commission v. Council (Energy Star)* [2002] ECR I-12049, paras 37–39.

[49] Case C-300/89 *Commission v. Council (Titanium Dioxide)* [1991] ECR I-2867; Case C-281/01 *Commission v. Council (Energy Star)* [2002] ECR I-12049; Case C-155/07 *Parliament v. Council (EIB Guarantees)* [2008] ECR I-8103.

the measure either to find that one is predominant over the other,[50] or that both are being pursued equally and are indissociably linked.[51]

In any of the above options, establishing the aim of the instrument is an entirely textual and formal exercise. Across decades of case law and to this day, the CJEU has consistently used expressions such as 'there is no doubt that',[52] it 'is plainly (or unequivocally) clear'[53] and 'it is common ground'[54] that an EU instrument pursues a given aim. While in earlier CCP case law the Court would leave it at that, the more recent judgments support this statement by reference to title, preamble and initial provisions on objectives in the operative part of instruments.

The *Waste Shipments* case concerned the legal basis of a Regulation on supervision and control of shipments within, and in and out of the Union.[55] It replaced a preceding Regulation which was based solely on Article 192 TFEU, which was meant to implement obligations under the Basel Convention. The new Regulation intended to integrate content of a new Decision taken at the OECD, and the Commission submitted that the Regulation ought to be based on a dual legal basis, Articles 207 and 194 TFEU, rather than solely the latter provision.[56]

C-411/06 *Commission* v. *Parliament and Council (Waste Shipments)* [2009] ECR I-7585

51. First, as regards the objective of the contested regulation, recital 1 in the preamble thereto states that '[t]he main and predominant objective and component of this Regulation is the protection of the environment'. Although disputed by the Commission, that statement is reiterated in recital 42 in the preamble to that regulation, which was contained in the Commission's proposal for that same regulation and which states that the objective of the contested regulation is 'to ensure protection of the environment when waste is subject to shipment'.

52. The other recitals in the preamble to the contested regulation confirm the environmental purpose thereof. As stated by the Advocate General in point 18 of his Opinion, apart from recitals 16 and 19, which refer to the proper functioning of the internal market, all of the recitals, albeit some more directly than others, bespeak environmental concerns.

53. By way of example, recital 33 in the preamble to the contested regulation states that necessary steps should be taken to ensure that waste shipped within the Community and waste imported into the Community is managed ... 'without endangering human health and without using processes or methods which could harm the environment' and that, as regards exports from the Community, 'efforts should be made to ensure that the waste is managed in an environmentally sound manner throughout the period of shipment and including recovery or disposal in the third country of destination'.

54. By contrast, and as observed by the Parliament and the Council, the preamble to the contested regulation does not make any reference to the pursuit of objectives falling within the common commercial policy.

---

[50] Case C-281/01 *Commission* v. *Council (Energy Star)* [2002] ECR I-12049.

[51] Case C-155/07 *Parliament* v. *Council (EIB Guarantees)* [2008] ECR I-8103.

[52] Opinion 1/75 *Re Understanding on a Local Costs Standard* [1975] ECR 1355.

[53] Case C-402/05 P & C-415/05 *P Kadi and Al Barakaat International Foundation* v. *Council* [2008] ECR I-6351, para 186; similarly Case C-336/00 *Huber* [2002] ECR I-7699, para 35; C-36/98 *Spain* v. *Council (Sustainable use of the river Danube)* [2001] ECR I-779, para 60.

[54] Case 45/86 *Commission* v. *Council (Generalized System of Preferences)* [1987] ECR 1493, para 15.

[55] C-411/06 *Commission* v. *Parliament and Council (Waste Shipments)* [2009] ECR I-7585.

[56] *Ibid.*, para 30.

The CJEU's approach is the same across EU autonomous instruments or international agreements, as was visible in Opinion 2/00 concerning the conclusion of the Cartagena Protocol to the Biodiversity convention.[57] In this Opinion, the Court also held the title of the Cartagena Protocol as indicative of its aim, although the Court later ignored an argument to that effect in the *Rotterdam Convention* case.[58]

Overall, Klamert argues that there is a clear over-reliance of the Court in determining the predominant aim of a Union measure. The objective approach of the Court implies that it will have to 'refut[e] the right of the lawmaker to freely choose the competence norm and prevent an institution from participating in passing a certain measure whenever it wishes to do so'.[59] The Court's tendency to take an instrument's statements on their aim at face value is then problematic, since this reintroduces subjectivity into supposedly objective legal basis case law.

N. Emiliou, 'Opening Pandora's Box: The Legal Basis of Community Measures before the Court of Justice' (1994) 19 *European Law Review* 488, 499

In practice, it will almost always be possible to formulate the objectives of the measure in different ways. In defending the measure, the Commission and/or the Council will argue for a formulation which justifies their preferred legal basis. One can even expect that the preamble and wording of the measure will be drafted so as to facilitate this. In such a situation, everything will depend on the Court. It will decide whether the measure falls within an area in which the [Union] has competence, it will formulate the objectives of the measure, and it will decide whether the legal basis of the latter corresponds to its objectives. All these questions involve so many imponderables that it will almost always be possible for the Court, if it wishes, to find grounds for upholding the measure.

At the end of Section 4 on the scope of EU external competence, we have seen that the Treaty of Lisbon has established a large web of interconnections between different competence-conferring provisions. As such, it has become a legal requirement that EU instruments take into account a whole array of objectives alongside its 'central aim'. The consequence is that establishing the aim of an instrument has become all but superfluous as a distinct element of the centre-of-gravity test: the Union is legally obliged to pursue more than one aim at the same time (Articles 21 TEU and 205 TFEU). Therefore, post-Lisbon, the investigation of content has become the most important element in matching the instrument to its correct legal basis.

(iii) Content of the instrument: strong, direct and immediate effect on aim

(a) Overview of the five dimensions to the Court's reasoning

Whereas 'aim and content' together form the objective factors on which the centre-of-gravity test is based, the bite of legal reasoning lies in the CJEU's assessment of the actual content of the instrument. This second part of the centre-of-gravity test consists of establishing *a strong, direct*

---

[57] Opinion 2/00 *(Cartagena Protocol)* [2001] ECR I-9713, paras 29–30.

[58] C-94/03, *Rotterdam Convention*, paras 23 and 37.

[59] M. Klamert, 'Conflicts of Legal Basis: No Legality and No Basis but a Bright Future under the Lisbon Treaty?' (2010) 35 *European Law Review* 501.

and immediate effect or link between content of the instrument and its aim. The underlying reasoning is the following: the initial statement of aim matches the objectives of a competence-conferring provision. If and when the content of a measure is also strongly connected to the aim of the measure, and therefore equally to the objectives for which the EU has been conferred competence, then that Treaty article is the correct legal basis.

The method through which the Court assesses content of an instrument is highly complex, and composed of what we term different 'dimensions'. We utilize this term to indicate that the different modes of reasoning do not exist as stand-alone, separate approaches. Rather, they are interlocking dimensions of the same centre-of-gravity test to form an overall assessment of the content of a measure. These different dimensions will be used to a lesser or greater extent depending on the instrument at issue: some are more appropriate for EU autonomous instruments, others more for international agreements; and some depend on the nature of the content itself. A brief summary of the dimensions is fleshed out further below:

- The *first dimension* is an approach whereby the Court appreciates the substantive, temporal and immediate connection of the content, in order to establish whether one aim or which of two or more aims is predominantly pursued. This *qualitative approach* entails that the Court reasons through the *actual impact* of content on policy outcomes. Across legal basis case law, this is the dominant approach to content, and any legal basis case – whether it concerns autonomous EU, or international instruments – can be decided on the basis of such a mode of reasoning alone. For example, when a measure would immediately change the commercial behaviour of companies, and much less indirectly the environmentally friendly behaviour of consumers, the legal basis could be qualitatively established as being the CCP over environment. No other dimensions are needed.

- The second dimension is what we call a *quantitative approach*, and most commonly appears alongside the qualitative dimension. It implies that the predominant aim of the instrument is established by enumerating all the portions of content which 'inherently' support the central aim, and that the enumeration shows there is a predominant quantity of content of that kind. This approach is only possible when the international agreement or EU instrument consists of 'objective-laden content'. For example, through pointing to a wide array of content elements which are 'typical' to environmental policy, it may be possible to rebut an argument that an instrument has a trade objective. It is highly exceptional that simple enumeration of 'objective-laden content' would support the final conclusion. A quantitative reasoning will not stand on its own and will be flanked by some form of qualitative reasoning of the first dimension.

- The *third dimension* appears when an instrument has content which clearly falls outside the scope of the predominant aim, but without changing the assessment that that predominant aim is the centre of gravity. The Court has established that it is possible when the 'far-off' content is very closely connected to the central aim, where Treaty articles require to 'take into account certain objectives', or when the instrument under examination can be defined as a framework instrument; for example, labour or fiscal provisions in a development or trade agreement.

- The *fourth dimension* is the extent to which the 'context' (and not just aim and content) of an instrument impacts the assessment on centre of gravity alongside aim and content. For example, in an assessment of a protocol to an international agreement, the predominant aim of that international agreement will influence the centre-of-gravity assessment of the Protocol, and thus the legal basis on which the EU can conclude it.

- The *fifth* and final dimension is the extent to which the Court takes account of 'similar' internal or external EU instruments and their legal basis, and whether this influences the final decision. In general all legal bases of instruments have to be judged on their own merits, but there are exceptions.

(b) The first dimension: qualitative assessment of 'strong, immediate effect'

Initial outlines: instrumentalist vs voluntarist perspective

The origins of having to establish a strong, direct and immediate effect of the content of an instrument on its central aim can be traced back to early legal basis case law on the CCP. Once the wide scope of the EU's 'state-like' trade competence was established, the Court had to decide when an instrument fell within the scope of the CCP.

In Opinion 1/78, the Court considered the different components of an international rubber agreement, and was asked to adjudicate on whether it could be concluded solely on the CCP legal basis.[60] Literature at that time points to the institutions' competing interpretations on how to assess whether an international agreement fell within the purview of the CCP:

- The Commission argued for an instrumental test which would lead to the widest possible number of instruments falling within the scope of the CCP:[61] any measure which *influences* the volume or pattern of international trade was to fall within the scope of the CCP.
- The Council argued for a more *voluntarist* (and consequently: restrictive) interpretation, namely that measures only fall within the scope of CCP when it is *their objective to alter* the volume or pattern of trade.[62]

In Opinion 1/78, the Court did not make a final choice on either interpretation 'anxious to preserve flexibility for a case-by-case determination'.[63] Instead, the approach was a nascent 'strong and immediate effect test' of content on aim.

Opinion 1/78, *International Agreement on Natural Rubber* [1979] ECR 2871

42. The Nairobi Resolution, which is the basis of the negotiations in progress on natural rubber, shows that commodity agreements have *complex objectives*. Whilst stressing the needs of the developing countries, the Resolution includes many references to mechanisms of a commercial nature and does not overlook the needs of the industrialized countries. As regards, more particularly, the interests of the developing countries, it is true that commodity agreements may involve the granting of advantages which are characteristic of development aid; it must however be acknowledged also that for those countries such agreements respond *more fundamentally* to the preoccupation of bringing about an improvement in the "terms of trade" and thus of *increasing their export earnings*. This characteristic is particularly brought out

---

[60] The formulation in para 52 is perhaps ill-chosen when it states 'a negation of the community's exclusive competence'. The Court does not mean to say that the CCP would be a shared competence, but rather that the natural rubber agreement would have to be agreed jointly by the Union and its Member States.

[61] E. Stein, 'External Relations of the European Community: Structure and Process', in A. Clapham (ed.), *Collected Courses of the Academy of European Law* (Oxford: Oxford University Press, 1990/1), p. 149.

[62] Steenbergen, 'The Common Commercial Policy' (1980) 17 *Common Market Law Review* 231. The debate continued in the GSP case; see Steenbergen, 'Casenote of C-45/86 Commission v. Council' (1987) 24 *Common Market Law Review* 731–737 at 735.

[63] Stein, 'External Relations of the European Community', p. 149.

in the agreement in question, which seeks to establish a fair balance between the interests of the producer countries and those of the consumer countries.[64]

In this paragraph the Court does not yet use the 'objective factors' terminology, but the methodology is clearly there. As to aim, it refers to the Nairobi Resolution and the complex objectives of the negotiations on natural rubber. In light of the preceding paragraphs of the judgment this is the Court's way of saying that the agreement pursues both trade and development objectives simultaneously. What follows is then an assessment of the content of the natural rubber agreement to see which of those aims dominates: The conclusion is that it predominantly pursues a trade objective because its content is essentially preoccupied with improving the terms of international trade (voluntarist Council viewpoint); but also more generally because it positively impacts export earnings (instrumental Commission viewpoint). The Court does not indicate a specific preference for the Commission's or the Council's viewpoint, but it does establish for the first time the more general test of establishing an effect of the content of the instrument on the aim(s) in ruling on which aim dominates in the instrument.

Fine-tuning the test through the relationship between trade and other legal bases
The SEA and the Maastricht Treaty saw the conferral of competences with important external dimensions, most notably environment and development policy. As a consequence, the Court was soon asked to rule whether certain measures pursued a trade aim, or rather an environmental or development aim. The response of the Court was in lock-step with the evolution described above in section 4. The fact that other competence-conferring provisions were now present in the Treaties required a balance between them, and thus a judicial methodology capable of making an objective choice between them. That, together with the decreased interpretative generosity to the CCP, led to the following standard phrasing:[65]

A Union act falls within competence in the field of the common commercial policy only if it *relates specifically* to international trade in that it is *essentially intended to promote, facilitate or govern* trade and has *direct and immediate effects* on trade.

In Opinion 1/94, the Court examined whether the EU was in its entirety competent to conclude the TRIPS agreement. It stated that indeed intellectual property (IP) has 'an effect' on international trade but it found that this was not sufficient to bring it within the scope of the CCP because it also affected internal trade. In more general terms, it thus found that the connection between IP and international trade in goods was insufficiently strong and immediate.

---

[64] Emphasis added.
[65] Opinion 1/94 [1994] ECR I-5267, para 57, Opinion 2/00 [2001] ECR I-9713, para 40, and Case C-281/01 *Commission* v. *Council* [2002] ECR I-12049, paras 40 and 41; Case C-347/03 *Regione autonoma Friuli-Venezia Giulia and ERSA* [2005] ECR I-3785, para 75, CJ Joint Cases C-402/05 and C-415/05 *P Yassin Abdullah Kadi and Al Barakaat International Foundation* v. *Council and Commission* [2008] ECR I-6351, para 183 (emphasis added).

Opinion 1/94, *Re World Trade Organization Agreement* [1994] ECR I-5267

57. Admittedly, there is a connection between intellectual property and trade in goods. Intellectual property rights enable those holding them to prevent third parties from carrying out certain acts. The power to prohibit the use of a trade mark, the manufacture of a product, the copying of a design or the reproduction of a book, a disc or a videocassette inevitably has effects on trade. Intellectual property rights are moreover specifically designed to produce such effects. That is not enough to bring them within the scope of Article 113. Intellectual property rights do not relate specifically to international trade; they affect internal trade just as much as, if not more than, international trade.[66]

On the basis of this excerpt, we may ask whether the Court seemed to accept the instrumental or voluntarist approach. Would a measure be considered a trade measure if it purely influences international trade only, without explicitly having the objective to do so (Commission argument)? Or should it explicitly have that objective as well (Council)? The Court responded affirmatively to the latter question in a number of cases concerning EU environmental policy which had an effect on international trade. The 'strong and immediate effect' test was thus fine-tuned by the Court's having to make a choice between Article 207 TFEU (trade) and Article 195 TFEU (environment).

The 2002 *Energy Star* Agreement case revolved around the trade or environmental legal basis for an EU–US agreement on energy efficiency labels for office equipment. The CJEU first stated that the instrument at the same time pursued a commercial policy and an environmental protection aim,[67] and the Court should establish which of the goals was predominant. It did so by reading a *temporal dimension* into the 'immediate effect' test. It found that the Energy Star Agreement predominantly pursued a trade aim because the environmental aim would not be instantly realized by the labelling programme it contained. Rather, it would more instantaneously positively affect (facilitate) trade due to uniform labelling requirements between EU and US markets. The environmental impact was more remote since it depended on shifting consumer behaviour which was less immediately affected and lay further into the future.

C-281/01 *Commission* v. *Council (Energy Star)* [2002] ECR I-12049

40. It is clear from the terms in which the Energy Star Agreement is couched, in particular from Articles I and V, that the Energy Star labelling program is essentially intended to enable manufacturers to use, in accordance with a procedure for the mutual recognition of registrations, a common logo to identify for consumers certain products complying with a common set of energy efficiency specifications which they intend to sell on the American and Community markets. An instrument having a direct impact on trade in office equipment is therefore involved.

41. It is true that in the long term, depending on how manufacturers and consumers in fact behave, the programme should have a positive environmental effect as a result of the reduction in energy consumption which it should achieve. However, that is merely an indirect and distant effect, in contrast to the effect on trade in office equipment which is direct and immediate.[68]

---

[66] Opinion 1/94 *Re World Trade Organization Agreement* [1994] ECR I-5267, para 57.
[67] C-281/01 *Commission* v. *Council (Energy Star)* [2002] ECR I-12049, paras 37–39.
[68] *Ibid.*, paras 40–41.

In further case law, the Court further explained its response to the question as to whether a 'large impact on international trade' is sufficient in itself, even if the instrument did not necessarily *intend* to capture predominantly commercial activities within its ambit. In Opinion 2/00 the Court examined the legal basis for the conclusion of the Cartagena Protocol to the Biodiversity Convention. This Protocol concerned the transboundary movement of living modified organisms (LMOs) that may have an adverse effect on the conservation and sustainable use of biological diversity. At the core of the Protocol lay a procedure for advance informed agreement on cross-border movements of LMOs. The Court found that this Protocol pursued an environmental aim, and through a quantitative approach (see below) much of the content and context of the international agreement supported its initial statement. However, where the Cartagena Protocol focused on 'transboundary movements' of LMOs, the Commission argued that de facto the large majority of movements captured by the instrument were of a commercial nature. The Court accepted that the content of the Cartagena Protocol in practice applies most frequently to movement of a commercial nature, but argued that this does not detract from the aim and content of the instrument which is to promote an environmental objective.

Opinion 2/00, *Cartagena Protocol on biosafety and the transboundary movements of living modified organisms resulting from biotechnology* [2001] ECR I-9713

37. ... even if, as the Commission maintains, the control procedures set up by the Protocol are applied most frequently, or at least in terms of market value preponderantly, to trade in LMOs, the fact remains that, as is shown by the examination carried out in paragraphs 26 to 33 of this Opinion, the Protocol is, in the light of its context, its aim and its content, an instrument intended essentially to improve biosafety and not to promote, facilitate or govern trade.[69]

In a subsequent judgment on the environmental or trade legal basis for the Rotterdam Convention on the Prior Informed Consent ('PIC') Procedure for certain hazardous chemicals and pesticides in international trade (*Rotterdam Convention* case), the Court made clear that the key in Opinion 2/00 had been the fact that it encompassed all *movement* of LMOs, and not just *trade* in LMOs. In the *Rotterdam Convention* case the Commission sought the annulment of the Council Decision, because it had approved the Convention on an environmental legal basis only. The subject of the agreement was to set up a procedure which is intended to ensure that no party to the Convention is confronted with imports of hazardous chemicals without first having had an opportunity to take the requisite precautions to protect human health and the environment.[70] The Court had stated that its aim was environmental, supporting that claim by reference to the PIC Procedure which is a 'typical instrument' of environmental policy.[71] However, without having previously mentioned trade as a potential aim as well (as in *Energy Star*), the CJEU took a further look at the content of the Convention, and stated that *the application* of this

---

[69] Opinion 2/00 *Cartagena Protocol on biosafety and the transboundary movements of living modified organisms resulting from biotechnology* [2001] ECR I-9713, para 37.

[70] Case C-94/03 *Commission* v. *Council (Rotterdam Convention)* [2006] ECR I-1, para 38.

[71] See below 'the second dimension, quantitative approach to content supporting or adding aim'.

typical environmental instrument was purely conditional upon its being a trade activity in hazardous chemicals. For that reason it concluded that a CCP legal basis was required alongside the environmental legal basis as the impact (control) on trade was considered sufficiently direct.[72]

Taking together the previous cases, a strong, direct and immediate effect on trade is to be read in rather strict terms: international trade means *trade* only, with noticeable *intent* to impact commercial activity, and the *impact* of the instrument on trade needs to be discernible *within a reasonable time span* upon the instrument being applied in practice. The intention to impact trade is not limited to liberalization but encompasses *promoting, facilitating or governing* trade. The intent to govern the movement of certain goods for purposes other than trade, may then be sufficient to render the centre of gravity outside the scope of CCP.

The following case is pending at the time this book went to press, and concerns the question of whether an international agreement on services must be based on the CCP legal basis (Article 207 TFEU), or rather the internal market legal basis (Article 114 TFEU). The source of the conflict lies in the nature of EU competence: a priori exclusive versus shared pre-emptive. The resolution of this case is sure to depend on two elements: an assessment of the scope of the CCP in relation to the internal market competence, and an assessment of the impact of the instrument in light of internal market versus international trade objectives.

C-137/12 *European Commission* v. *Council*, pending

Form of order sought
Annul Council decision 2011/853/EU of 29 November 2011 on the signing, on behalf of the Union, of the European Convention on the legal protection of services based on, or consisting of, conditional access.
   Order the Council of the European Union to pay the costs.

Pleas in law and main arguments
By its first plea, the Commission claims that Article 114 TFEU is not an appropriate legal basis for the adoption of the contested decision. According to the applicant, the decision should have been based on Article 207(4) TFEU which authorises the Council to conclude international agreements in the field of the common commercial policy, as defined in Article 207(1) TFEU. The present convention does not aim to 'improve the functioning of the internal market', its principal objective being to 'facilitate' or 'promote' the provision of services based on conditional access between the European Union and other European countries. It would have a direct and immediate effect on the provision of services based on conditional access and on the trade in illicit devices and on the services relating to those devices. Consequently, the convention falls within the scope of the common commercial policy.

   By its second plea, the applicant claims that the European Union's exclusive external competence (Articles 2(1) and 3(1) and (2) TFEU) has been infringed because the Council considered that the conclusion of the convention did not fall within the European Union's exclusive competence whereas the convention falls within the common commercial policy or, in any case, that the conclusion of the convention is capable of affecting common rules or of altering their scope.

---

[72] Case C-94/03, *supra*, para 45.

The 'strong effect test' beyond trade cases

Due to the piecemeal conferral of competences in progressive Treaty amendments, a large number of case law directly or indirectly relates to the CCP. However, this does not mean that the 'strong effect test' is applied solely to assess 'the effect on trade', and it indubitably applies to *any* choice of correct legal basis, such as for example cultural policy vs industrial policy,[73] environment vs agriculture,[74] and so on. The environmental competence was conferred in the SEA, and with the Maastricht Treaty the CFSP and development competences followed. Thus, soon the Court was seized to balance these new competences against EU trade competence, and also between each other.[75]

The 2007 judgment on the EIB contains one of the most meticulous assessments to date of the effect of the content of a measure on its central aim. The case concerned an EU guarantee to the EIB for loans it provides in third countries in the context of EU technical cooperation projects. The Council had adopted the Decision on the basis of Article 212 TFEU (economic, financial and technical cooperation with third countries), and the Parliament sought the annulment of the Decision as it should also have been concluded on the basis of Article 209 TFEU (development policy). Parliament had two main arguments: first, the contested Decision contained a list of third countries eligible for EIB financing which included both developing and non-developing nations, and the inclusion of developing countries should inform the choice of correct legal basis.[76] Second, if all technical cooperation with third countries required an Article 212 TFEU legal basis, the EU's development competence would be rendered largely redundant.[77] The Council argued that 'the *indirect nature* of the relationship between the Community guarantee and the developing country' was the decisive reason why the decision should not also be based on Article 209 TFEU.[78] In other words, for the Council there was no strong, immediate connection to development, because the sole purpose of the decision was to establish a financial cooperation measure with third countries without distinguishing between them.[79] The Council argued that any positive effect on development objectives is incidental and insufficient to justify its adoption on the basis of Article 209 TFEU too. Any such effect was merely an expression of the obligation in Article 212(1) TFEU that any action under this provision be 'consistent with development policy' (see below, the third dimension).

In order to establish the centre of gravity of the Council Decision, the Court moved to examine *the effect* of the EU guarantee to the EIB to contribute to external action objectives. It meticulously traced how the EU guarantee was not simply an instrument setting up a financing structure for technical cooperation – possibly with a development aim at a later stage. Rather, the EU guarantee has a clear link to pursuing EU external objectives in the most effective fashion. As in the previous case law, the Court looks at *qualitative impact* of content on the EU's objectives in development policy, *intent* to attain that impact through the measure at issue,

---

[73] C-42/97 *Parliament v. Council (Linguistic Diversity in the Information Society)* [1999] ECR I-869, para 63.

[74] C-336/00 *Huber* [2002] ECR I-7699.

[75] A case which concerned purely environmental competence: C-36/98 *Spain v. Council (Sustainable use of the river Danube)* [2001] ECR I-779.

[76] C-155/07 *Parliament v. Council (EIB Guarantees)* [2008] ECR I-8103, para 23.

[77] *Ibid.*, para 22.

[78] *Ibid.*, para 29.

[79] *Ibid.*, para 27.

and explicitly examines the *temporal and substantive* nature of how the content will resort its effect in a reasonably immediate fashion.

C-155/07 *Parliament* v. *Council (EIB Guarantees)* [2008] ECR I-8103

59. ... It follows from that decision that the grant of the Community guarantee pursues objectives going beyond a measure which is directed merely incidentally at development cooperation. Thus, it is apparent in particular from recital 3 that the contested decision seeks to support EU external action without affecting the EIB's credit rating. Moreover, under Article 1 of that decision, the Community guarantee is granted only where, inter alia, the financing operations in question have been decided upon 'in support of the relevant external policy objectives of the European Union'.

60. As the Parliament stated at the hearing, it is possible that, in the absence of such a guarantee, the EIB may be unable to undertake financing operations in the countries concerned. In view of the heightened risks connected with the grant of financing in certain third countries, the EIB's credit rating might be affected by carrying out such operations in those countries, with the result that, in order to prevent damage to its credit rating, the EIB would be deterred from going ahead with those operations or at least be obliged to impose in their respect appreciably less favourable terms for borrowers. Thus, EIB investment in third countries is fostered or made possible as a result of the Community guarantee, through its favourable effect on the EIB's credit rating. Accordingly, maintaining that credit rating is necessary in order to fulfil the fundamental objective of the contested decision, which is to contribute to the external policy of the Community.

61. Moreover, assuming, as the Council and the Parliament have maintained, that, in respect of third countries concerned by the contested decision, the Community guarantee produces only indirect effects, by enabling the EIB to grant finance for those countries subject to more favourable terms, this circumstance does not preclude that measure from forming part of Community policy in the development cooperation field.

62. Furthermore, contrary to the view put forward by the Commission, the contested decision cannot be considered essentially to be an internal Community measure. Admittedly, at first, the Community guarantee produces its effects primarily within the Community, namely in the relationship between the EIB and the Community budget. None the less, as is clear from paragraph 59 above, the guarantee does not constitute the objective of the contested decision, but the means chosen in order to attain that objective, which consists of supporting the external policy of the Community by facilitating and strengthening financial cooperation with third countries, through the EIB. ...

65. ... Thus, it is apparent from recital 12 of the decision, cited by the Parliament at the hearing, that in Asia and Latin America – regions in which the 'EIB should endeavour to progressively expand its activities across a larger number of countries ... including in the less prosperous countries' – EIB financing should focus on environmental sustainability and energy security projects, as well as the continued support of the EU's presence in those regions through foreign direct investment and the transfer of technology and know-how. Furthermore, it is apparent from recitals 13 and 14 respectively of the contested decision that the EIB should focus in Central Asia on major energy supply and energy transport projects with cross-border implications and in South Africa on infrastructure projects of public interest and private sector support, including small and medium-sized enterprises.

66. It follows that the financial cooperation which the contested decision implements through the Community guarantee granted to the EIB also pursues, in so far as developing countries are concerned, the socio-economic objectives referred to in [Article 208 TFEU], particularly the sustainable economic and social development of such countries.

(c) The second dimension: quantitative approach to content supporting or adding aim

Alongside the qualitative assessment of an instrument's content, the reasoning of the CJEU may also consist of a quantitative approach. The reasoning will not be an explanation on how the instrument's content impacts the main objective in time and space, but instead consists of mentioning as much as possible of the content in support of a given aim, to show that it is the centre of gravity. There is one precondition to that approach, namely it is only possible when content of the instrument largely consists of content with an *inherent aim* ('objective-laden content'). For example, the Court did not follow this approach in the EIB judgment because it concerned an EU guarantee, and acting as a financial guarantor can serve all kinds of purposes and thus does not have an inherent aim. Conversely, an example of content with an inherent aim is the PIC Procedure of international environmental law, which the Court in two judgments described as a 'typical instrument of environmental policy'.[80] Finding such a procedure is for the Court a strong hint that the instrument predominantly pursues an environmental aim, illustrative of the quantitative approach, though with some caveats.

The starting point is Opinion 2/00, where the Court argued that the PIC, alongside other typically environmental measures contained in the Cartagena Protocol, supported its final assessment on the environmental legal basis (Article 195 TFEU). In this judgment we can clearly see the approach of enumerating a large quantity of content of the instrument with a certain objective, in support of the initial statement on aim. The following is but a small extract of a lengthy enumeration.

Opinion 2/00, *Cartagena Protocol on biosafety and the transboundary movements of living modified organisms resulting from biotechnology* [2001] ECR I-9713

31. Finally, as to the Protocol's content, there is a clear reflection of the Protocol's environmental aim in the fundamental obligation imposed on the parties by Article 2(2) thereof to prevent or reduce the risks to biological diversity . . .

33. [I]n order to enable the parties to fulfil their fundamental obligation, laid down in Article 2(2), the Protocol sets up various control procedures (see Articles 7 to 13), including the advance informed agreement procedure which is a typical instrument of environmental policy . . .

The Protocol also deals with the assessment and management of risks associated with the use, handling and transboundary movement of LMOs (Articles 15 and 16), unintentional transboundary movements and emergency measures (Article 17) and the handling, transport, packaging and identification of LMOs (Article 18). Finally, Articles 19 to 28 of the Protocol, whose subject-matter has been outlined in the background to the request for an Opinion, apply to any kind of transboundary movement and are also essentially intended to enable the parties to comply with their fundamental obligation laid down in Article 2(2) of the Protocol.

While in this Opinion and in the later *Waste Shipments* judgment[81] the Court accepted that the PIC procedure supported environment as the centre of gravity, the finding of such content with

---

[80] C-411/06 *Commission v. Parliament and Council (Waste Shipments)* [2009] ECR I-7585, para 59, and Opinion 2/00 *Cartagena Protocol on biosafety and the transboundary movements of living modified organisms resulting from biotechnology* [2001] ECR I-9713, paras 31–33.

[81] C-411/06 *Commission v. Parliament and Council (Waste Shipments)* [2009] ECR I-7585, para 59.

an inherent objective was not in itself conclusive. This was shown in the *Rotterdam Convention* judgment which also set up a PIC Procedure. That case followed Opinion 2/00, and the Council argued that this was a clear indicator of its environmental aim and commensurate legal basis.[82] The Court accepted that the PIC procedure rendered environment an important aim of the Convention, but rejected that this was sufficient to exclude a trade aim because the typically environmental PIC procedure applied only to certain hazardous chemicals and pesticides when they were traded internationally.[83] The fact that the application of the PIC (e.g. inherently environmental content) was conditional upon it being a trade activity was finally decisive.[84] This is an illustration of the first, qualitative dimension, functioning together with this second, qualitative dimension of the test. A similar approach was followed in a case concerning sustainable use of the river Danube.[85] Here the Court found that the application of water management measures contained in the Convention were conditional upon them having a transboundary impact on the ecology.[86] In Opinion 2/00 the court explicitly stated that such a strong connection between the trade and environmental content was not present in the Cartagena Protocol.

C-94/03 *Commission* v. *Council (Rotterdam Convention)* [2006] ECR I-1

42. ... A reading of the provisions of the Convention and, more particularly, of its articles concerning the [Prior Informed Consent] procedure, prompts the conclusion that the Convention also contains rules governing trade in hazardous chemicals and having direct and immediate effects on such trade. ...

44. [A]lthough ... the informed consent procedure is in fact a typical instrument of environmental policy, its implementation under the Convention is governed by provisions which directly regulate the trade in the products that it covers. It is clear from the very title of the Convention and from Article 5(6) thereof – read in conjunction with Annex II(c)(iv) to the Convention – that the Convention applies only to certain hazardous chemicals and pesticides which are traded internationally, that in turn being an essential precondition for the listing of such products in Annex III to the Convention and, therefore, for their being subject to the PIC procedure. Such an explicit link between trade and the environment was lacking in the Cartagena Protocol examined by the Court in Opinion 2/00.

In conclusion, the quantitative dimension of the centre-of-gravity test does not have an independent value. Where the quantitative approach figures in the case law, it is never as a purely stand-alone argument in favour of the centre of gravity and it generally appears alongside a qualitative assessment of aim and content. Importantly then, there are no cases where the quantitative enumeration of content leads to negating the initial statement of aim. At most, it would lead to the Court finding that an additional aim is pursued as well, and that dual legal bases could be necessary if both aims are found to be pursued equally strongly. While it is at present not possible to distil a general rule as to when a qualitative assessment would overturn the quantitative approach, from Opinion 2/00 and the river Danube judgment we can infer that

---

[82] C-94/03 *Commission* v. *Council (Rotterdam Convention)* [2006] ECR I-1, para 29.
[83] *Ibid.,* para 44.
[84] *Ibid.,* paras 42–44.
[85] Concerning Article 191 or 191(2)(b) TFEU as legal basis, the latter requiring unanimity in the Council.
[86] C-36/98 *Spain* v. *Council (Sustainable use of the river Danube)* [2001] ECR I-779, paras 64–65.

this occurs when application of the 'content with an inherent aim' is entirely conditional upon being clearly applied towards a different aim. This is in line with the Court's approach to *ancillary content*, discussed in the following section.

(d) The third dimension: ancillary content distant from the central aim

In some cases, the instrument under examination has content which by nature has a certain aim, but which straightforwardly falls outside the central aim as established through the initial assessment on aim, the qualitative and quantitative approach. The Court has on several occasions ruled that this does not necessarily lead to the instrument falling outside the scope of EU competence (vertical situation), or requiring an additional legal basis (horizontal situation). This is the case when the content is in fact very closely connected to the central aim, or when the instrument under examination can be defined as a framework instrument. Here the methodology of approaching content is entirely in line with the Court's approach to the scope of competences at issue, and notably the issue of 'taking into account objectives' linked to a different competence. In section 4 we have seen that the obligation to take into account environmental objectives (Article 11 TFEU) has the consequence that trade measures will less quickly 'fall outside' the scope of CCP.[87] This is essentially a different way of stating that the (environmental, etc.) aim of an instrument will be considered non-central (ancillary) to the instrument's central objective. The goal of the judicial method here is to find the threshold as to when a goal is pursued merely to support the central aim, and when something amounts to a central aim as well. There are two key factors: first, the Court accepts that the threshold will not be crossed when the approach of integrating such ancillary content with a different aim accords to the general practice of international relations in that policy sphere. Second, it looks at the nature of the measure as a framework instrument. This approach is valid both for EU autonomous measures as well as international agreements.

The starting point is once again Opinion 1/78. After having established that the natural rubber agreement pursued a trade objective, the Court dealt with the argument that certain provisions on labour aspects of rubber production, as well as open-ended provisions on tax cooperation, could make it fall outside the scope of Article 207 TFEU. For the Court, such content of the instrument did not alter its initial finding on trade as the central aim, because these individual terms of the agreement existed merely to attain that essential objective. From the case law three criteria emerge as to when ancillary content with an inherent aim does not change the initial finding on the centre of gravity: first, the individual terms are merely *required to attain the overarching objective* of the EU instrument or international agreement. The provisions *do not have stand-alone value*, and the Union would not adopt the measure with merely those specific terms.[88] Second, *a qualitative assessment* must show that a strong, direct link exists between the ancillary clauses and the central aim of the instrument.[89] Third, the nature of the individual provisions and even the instrument as a whole, is of a *framework*. The three conditions apply both for EU autonomous instruments and international agreements.

---

[87] In Chapter 10, we further analyse the EU competence in development policy, and the obligation to take account of trade, environmental, etc. objectives in that context.

[88] Opinion 1/78 *International Agreement on Natural Rubber* [1979] ECR 2871, paras 52–56.

[89] *Ibid.*, para 56.

In Opinion 1/94, the Commission argued that the CCP's scope encompassed IP, and in support it cited provisions on the protection of IP in certain agreements which were concluded solely on the CCP legal basis.[90]

Opinion 1/94, *Re World Trade Organization Agreement* [1994] ECR I-5267

67. It should be noted that those provisions are extremely limited in scope. The agreement between the EEC and China on trade in textile products, ... merely provides for a consultation procedure in relation to the protection of trademarks or designs in respect of textile products. Moreover, the three interim agreements concluded between the Community and [four Newly Independent States] all contain identically worded clauses calling upon those countries to improve the protection of intellectual property in order to provide, within a given time, 'a level of protection similar to that provided in the Community' by Community acts. ...

68. ... the Community and its institutions are entitled to incorporate within external agreements otherwise falling within the ambit of Article 113 ancillary provisions for the organization of purely consultative procedures or clauses calling on the other party to raise the level of protection of intellectual property.

Thus, the nature of the clauses at issue is such that they do not contain substantive commitments on the part of the Union.[91] Similarly, in a 2003 judgment concerning fiscal provisions in two road transport agreements with Bulgaria and Hungary,[92] the Court found that 'the aspect of the agreements which concerns the harmonization of fiscal laws is, in the light of their aim and their content, only secondary and indirect in nature compared with the transport policy objective which they pursue'.[93] It reached that conclusion because the Agreement itself defined these provisions as 'supporting measures', and through a mixed qualitative/quantitative reasoning the Court found that the various fiscal exemptions were 'closely linked' to the central aim of simplification of transit through Bulgaria and Hungary.[94]

In *Portugal* v. *Council* concerning the EC–India development and cooperation agreement the Court engrafted this line of reasoning onto the principle of conferral. In the area of development policy (see further also Chapter 10), the Court argued that when the instrument has the nature of a 'cooperation framework', individual clauses will not detract from the centre of gravity. The nature of specific provisions on human rights, energy and tourism is such that they do not impose such extensive obligations concerning specific matters, so that those obligations in fact constitute objectives distinct from the central aim. Due to their open-ended nature they do not predetermine the allocation of competences between the EU or its Member States for their implementation.

---

[90] Opinion 1/94 *Re World Trade Organization Agreement* [1994] ECR I-5267, para 66.

[91] Opinion 1/94 also contained a similar reasoning on the suspension of transport services as ancillary to import/export embargoes adopted on the basis of the CCP. See Opinion 1/94, *supra*, para 51.

[92] C-211/01 *Commission* v. *Council (Transport Agreements with Bulgaria and Hungary)* [2003] ECR I-8913.

[93] *Ibid.*, para 48.

[94] *Ibid.*, para 49.

C-268/94 *Portugal* v. *Council* [1996] ECR I-6177

39. It must therefore be held that the fact that a development cooperation agreement contains clauses concerning various specific matters cannot alter the characterization of the agreement, which must be determined having regard to its essential object and not in terms of individual clauses, provided that those clauses do not impose such extensive obligations concerning the specific matters referred to that those obligations in fact constitute objectives distinct from those of development cooperation. . . .

45. As regards more particularly the provisions of the Agreement which relate to specific matters, those provisions establish the framework of cooperation between the contracting parties. Taken as a whole, they are limited to determining the areas for cooperation and to specifying certain of its aspects and various actions to which special importance is attached. By contrast, those provisions contain nothing that prescribes in concrete terms the manner in which cooperation in each specific area envisaged is to be implemented. . . .

47. The mere inclusion of provisions for cooperation in a specific field does not therefore necessarily imply a general power such as to lay down the basis of a competence to undertake any kind of cooperation action in that field. It does not, therefore, predetermine the allocation of spheres of competence between the Community and the Member States or the legal basis of Community acts for implementing cooperation in such a field.

It is not necessary that the instrument under examination is an international agreement. In the *ECOWAS* judgment concerning the legal basis for a measure to combat the illegal spread of small arms and light weapons, the Court reasoned similarly as regards a CFSP Joint Action (post-Lisbon: Decision). This instrument laid down a general framework for support to third countries in this area, and the Court stated that this CFSP instrument clearly allowed for tasks to be divided between CFSP and development policies on a case-by-case basis.[95] The Court thus found that Article 40 TEU (former Article 47 TEU) was not violated because of the framework nature of the clauses in the Joint Action. The Court added a novel element to its reasoning why so-called 'framework instruments' do not require an additional legal basis: the need for consistency in EU external relations. This should be read as an implicit statement by the Court that legal basis litigation and its underlying power struggles may detract from the essence of effective EU external policy-making.

C-91/05 *Commission* v. *Council (Small Arms/ECOWAS)* [2008] ECR I-3651

87. Indeed, Article 7 of the contested joint action points out that it is for the Council to decide on the allocation of the financial and technical assistance referred to in Article 6 of the joint action, but explains, in Article 7(2), that the Council is to decide 'without prejudice to . . . operation of the Community', on a case-by-case basis, on the principle, arrangements and financing of the projects implementing the joint action. The fact that the contested joint action can be implemented both by the Community and the Union is confirmed in Article 8 thereof, in which the Council notes that the Commission intends to direct its action towards achieving the objectives and the priorities of the joint action, where appropriate by

---

[95] C-91/05 *Commission* v. *Council (Small Arms/ECOWAS)* [2008] ECR I-3651, paras 86–87.

pertinent Community measures, and in Article 9 of the joint action, which places in the hands of the Council and the Commission the responsibility for ensuring the consistency of the Union's activities in the field of small arms, 'in particular with regard to its development policies', and for ensuring implementation of their respective action, each in accordance with its powers. The need for consistency of the Union's activities in the field of small arms and light weapons is also stated, with an identical reference to 'development policies [of the Union]' in Article 4(2) of the contested decision.

In the following case which is pending at the time this book went to press, the Court is asked to rule on the legal basis of a mixed agreement between the EU, Member States and the Philippines. The Commission argues that the development legal basis is sufficient, whereas the Commission added the legal bases for transport, readmission and environment as well. The Court has several avenues through which it can resolve this case: it could focus on the scope of EU competence, and argue quite simply that the scope of EU development competence in Article 209 TFEU does, or does not support the adoption of this instrument solely on that legal basis. In making that assessment, it then will indubitably look at the aim, nature and content of the instrument before it, and it may decide that the agreement under scrutiny does, or does not, rise to the level of a framework agreement. This action illustrates that depending on the facts of the case, the first and second steps of the appropriate legal basis test will form an organic whole.

Action brought on 6 August 2012 – *European Commission* v. *Council of the European Union* (Case C–377/12)

The applicant claims that the Court should:

annul the Decision of the Council of 14 May 2012 on the signing, on behalf of the Union, of the Framework Agreement on Partnership and Cooperation between the European Union and its Member States, of the one part, and the Republic of the Philippines, of the other part (2012/272/EU) insofar as the Council has added the legal bases relating to transport (Articles 91 and 100 TFEU), readmission (Article 79(3) TFEU) and environment (Article 191(4) TFEU);

maintain the effects of the contested decision;

order Council of the European Union to pay the costs.

Pleas in law and main arguments

By way of the present application the Commission seeks the annulment of the Decision of the Council on the signing, on behalf of the Union, of the Framework Agreement on Partnership and Cooperation between the European Union and its Member States, of the one part, and the Republic of the Philippines, of the other part of 14 May 2012 (2012/272/EU) (hereinafter referred to as "the contested decision"), insofar as the Council has added the legal bases relating to transport (Articles 91 and 100 TFEU), readmission (Article 79(3) TFEU) and environment (Article 191(4) TFEU).

This application is based on a single plea of law, namely that the Council has violated the rules of the Treaties and the case-law of the Court in relation to the choice of the legal basis for the adoption of a Union measure, including a decision on the signature of an international agreement.

The Commission takes the view that the addition of the above mentioned legal bases was unnecessary and illegal. Indeed, the provisions of the PCA which have triggered the addition of these legal bases by the

Council relate to cooperation on specific policy matters which form an integral part of the development cooperation policy of the EU and do not impose extensive obligations distinct from those of development cooperation. Therefore, all these provisions of the PCA are covered by Article 209 TFEU.

(e) The fourth dimension: assessing context to aim and content of the instrument

Aside from aim and content, the Court has recently explicitly stated that it is willing to uphold context as an additional objective factor amenable to judicial review, though so far only in cases on international agreements. This openness to context in these situations was already present in early case law on CCP. Specifically in Opinion 1/78, the natural rubber agreement was interpreted in light of the complex trade and development objectives of the Nairobi Resolution which formed the basis for the negotiations in natural rubber. In a number of cases that followed, context did not receive a prominent position, and it was not until Opinion 2/00 that the Court explicitly stated context to be pertinent to the centre-of-gravity test.[96] In Opinion 2/00 on the Cartagena Protocol, the Court teased out the context element with reference to Article 31 VCLT on treaty interpretation. From that article, the Court found that the 1992 UNCED Conference and the resulting Biodiversity Convention form an important element of the context in light of which the Protocol to that Convention had to be interpreted.

Opinion 2/00, *Cartagena Protocol on biosafety and the transboundary movements of living modified organisms resulting from biotechnology* [2001] ECR I-9713

24. Since interpretation of an international agreement is at issue, it should also be recalled that, under Article 31 VCLT, a treaty shall be interpreted in good faith in accordance with the ordinary meaning to be given to the terms of the treaty in their context and in the light of its object and purpose. ...

27. [The Convention] results from the United Nations Conference on Environment and Development (UNCED), held in Rio de Janeiro in June 1992. Article 1 of the Convention states, in particular, that its objectives are the conservation of biological diversity, the sustainable use of its components and the fair and equitable sharing of the benefits arising out of the utilisation of genetic resources.

28. In accordance with Article 31 VCLT, it is by reference to that context relating to the Convention on Biological Diversity that it is necessary to identify the purpose and define the subject-matter of the Protocol, in whose preamble the second and third recitals refer to certain provisions of the Convention.

In the *Rotterdam Convention* case, the Court first had elaborated a number of arguments confirming the environmental aim of the international agreement. Thereafter it added that the international context affirms that previous reading of the preamble and text of the instrument itself.[97] From these three cases, we can infer that context functions as a supplementary factor in support of the main qualitative and quantitative assessment of the instrument's content. This

---

[96] For example, in the case concerning the Implementing Regulation of the Rotterdam Convention, impact on intra-EU trade (or not) was not held as pertinent to the assessment of whether the CCP was a correct legal basis for that regulation. C-178/03 *Commission* v. *Parliament and Council (Regulation implementing the Rotterdam Convention)* [2006] ECR I-107, para 53.

[97] C-94/03 *Commission* v. *Council (Rotterdam Convention)* [2006] ECR I-1, para 41.

functions through 'imbuing' the instrument's content with a certain aim through the context from which it emerged.

(f) The fifth dimension: legal bases of instruments with similar characteristics

Each instrument has to be judged on its own merits, and the choice of the legal basis does not rest on the legal basis used for the adoption of other measures which might display similar characteristics.[98] Furthermore, previous practice of the institutions in a particular field cannot derogate from primary rules laid down in the Treaties, and such practice does not create a precedent with regard to the future determination of correct legal bases.[99] The Court is very strict in applying these criteria, and this equally to autonomous instruments or international agreements.

In the *ECOWAS* judgment, the Court had defined the Joint Action on combating the spread of small arms and light weapons as a framework instrument, where specific decisions would thus be used to implement them. The legal basis assessment showed the Joint Action and the Decisions had no rapport with each other, and either instrument could be based on a development or CFSP legal basis depending on the aim and content assessment.[100] What is more, the implementing Decisions of the same joint action were each to be judged on their own merits.[101] Concretely, this means that a legal instrument combating the illegal spread of small arms in Western Africa could be based on a development legal basis; but a Decision based on the same Joint Action to combat the presence of small arms in Ukraine or Cambodia could be based on a CFSP legal basis.[102]

The general principle is therefore that the legal basis for an act must be determined having regard to its own aim and content and not to the legal basis used for the adoption of other Union measures.[103] This is true whether it concerns internal or external measures, as the powers conferred upon the Union constitute a coherent whole.[104] In further case law, the Court emphasizes this point by confirming that an independent assessment is required for the legal bases of Decisions approving international agreements and Regulations which implement EU obligations from that international agreement.[105] Of course, this does not exclude that when the aim and content assessment of two related instruments uncover the same centre of gravity, they will require identical legal bases. If the implementing instrument and the international agreement have clear rapport in terms of pursuing the same aim and content, then the same legal bases will be inevitable.

---

[98] C-155/07 *Parliament* v. *Council (EIB Guarantees)* [2008] ECR I-8103, para 34.

[99] Case 131/86 *United Kingdom* v. *Council* [1988] ECR 905, para 29.; C-411/06 *Commission* v. *Parliament and Council (Waste Shipments)* [2009] ECR I-7585, para 77.

[100] C-91/05 *Commission* v. *Council (Small Arms/ECOWAS)* [2008] ECR I-3651, paras 79–99 (on the joint action) versus 99–109 (on the decision).

[101] *Ibid.*, para 106.

[102] Council Decision 2004/792/CFSP of 22 November 2004 extending and amending Decision 1999/730/CFSP implementing Joint Action 1999/34 with a view to a European Union contribution to combating the destabilising accumulation and spread of small arms and light weapons in Cambodia, OJ 2004 No. L348/47, and Council Decision 2005/852/CFSP of 29 November 2005 for the destruction of small arms and light weapons (SALW) and their ammunition in Ukraine, OJ 2005 No. L315/27.

[103] Opinion 1/94 *Re World Trade Organization Agreement* [1994] ECR I-5267, para 29; Case C-187/93 *Parliament* v. *Council* [1994] ECR I-2857, para 28. Even if the Court has not always been perfectly consistent in this: see C-178/03 *Commission* v. *Parliament and Council (Regulation implementing the Rotterdam Convention)* [2006] ECR I-107 and see P. Koutrakos, 'Legal Basis and Delimitation of Competence in EU External Relations', in Cremona and B. de Witte (eds.), *EU Foreign Relations Law: Constitutional Fundamentals* (Oxford: Hart Publishing, 2008), pp. 171–198.

[104] C-29/99 *Commission* v. *Council (Convention on Nuclear Safety)* [2002] ECR I-11221, para 79.

[105] C-281/01 *Commission* v. *Council (Energy Star)* [2002] ECR I-12049, para 46; C-178/03 *Commission* v. *Parliament and Council (Regulation implementing the Rotterdam Convention)* [2006] ECR I-107, para 46.

> **C-178/03 *Commission* v. *Parliament and Council (Regulation implementing the Rotterdam Convention)* [2006] ECR I-107**
>
> 47. In this case, however, use of the same legal bases both for the decision approving the Convention on behalf of the Community and for the contested regulation, which implements the Convention at Community level, is necessary in any event, in view of the clear convergence of the provisions of those two measures, reflecting both the concern to regulate trade in hazardous chemicals and the concern to ensure sound management of those products and/or to protect human health and the environment against the harmful effects of trade in such products.

The Commission subsequently relied on that argument in the later *Waste Shipments* judgment concerning the CCP or environmental legal basis of the Regulation implementing EU obligations under the Basel Convention. However, here the Court rejected that argument because rapport between the internal instrument and international agreement was not sufficiently complete:[106] the Regulation before it did not have a sufficiently strong commercial policy component that justified recourse to dual legal basis as in the *Rotterdam Convention* case.

(iv) Outcome of the centre-of-gravity test: possible complications

(a) Two indissociably linked objectives

The purpose of the centre-of-gravity test is to reveal its predominant aim, and thus conclude that it matches the objectives of a certain EU competence in the Treaties. When the Court identifies the main objective of the instrument, with all others being incidental, that will result in the correct legal basis. However, we have already seen that at times the measure pursues different objectives at the same time: the *Energy Star* and *Rotterdam Convention* cases found these instruments to pursue both environmental and commercial aims, whereas the EU guarantee to the EIB concerned both technical cooperation as well as EU development objectives. In *Small Arms* too, the Court found that security and development objectives were pursued equally. In such cases the finding that two aims are pursued by the measure is insufficient to lead to a conclusion that a dual legal basis is required.[107] Thus, further reasons must justify whether one aim dominates (single legal basis), or whether they are pursued equally and are indissociably linked (dual legal basis). In *Energy Star*, the Court found that the trade aim was predominant for the agreement had the most direct impact on commercial behaviour. However, in *Titanium Dioxide*, *Rotterdam*, *EIB* and *Small Arms* the Court found that the measures simultaneously pursued several aims, and that they were inseparable and *indissociably linked*.[108] In all cases where the Court found inseparably linked objectives, the reasons for the conclusion were effectively concerns of policy coherence.[109] In the *Rotterdam Convention* case, it stated that:

---

[106] C-411/06 *Commission* v. *Parliament and Council (Waste Shipments)* [2009] ECR I-7585, para 76.

[107] C-155/07 *Parliament* v. *Council (EIB Guarantees)* [2008] ECR I-8103, para 68.

[108] Though legal basis may be impossible for procedural reasons (*Titanium Dioxide*) or constitutional reasons (*Small Arms/ECOWAS*).

[109] C-94/03 *Commission* v. *Council (Rotterdam Convention)* [2006] ECR I-1, para 51; C-155/07 *Parliament* v. *Council (EIB Guarantees)* [2008] ECR I-8103, para 71; C-91/05 *Commission* v. *Council (Small Arms/ECOWAS)* [2008]

> ### C-94/03 *Commission v. Council (Rotterdam Convention)* [2006] ECR I-1
>
> 51. ... as is also clear from the express terms of the eighth recital in the preamble to the Convention, according to which the commercial and environmental policies of the parties to the Convention should be mutually supportive with a view to achieving sustainable development, it must therefore be concluded that the Convention includes, both as regards the aims pursued and its contents, two indissociably linked components, neither of which can be regarded as secondary or indirect as compared with the other.

Similarly, in the *EIB* case the Court argued that it would be problematic for the well-functioning of the instrument before it.

> ### C-155/07 *Parliament v. Council (EIB Guarantees)* [2008] ECR I-8103
>
> 71. The contested decision seeks to strengthen financial cooperation both with developing countries and with other third countries by means of the Community guarantee granted to the EIB. That decision thus concerns actions of a similar nature, distinguished only in relation to the regions and countries concerned. ... it would be hazardous, even arbitrary, to try to identify a predominant geographical component in the decision. That is particularly true in view of the evolving nature of the category of developing countries within the meaning of Title XX of the Treaty and of the possibility, provided for in Article 2(2) of that decision, for the Council to decide, on a case by case basis, on the eligibility of countries which are not even mentioned in Annex I to the decision to receive EIB financing coupled with a Community guarantee.

A final, though more contestable, reason for dual legal bases for the EU approval of the *Rotterdam Convention* was the fact that it indicates EU competence to other parties to the Convention at the moment of conclusion, as well as later during the implementation of the Convention.[110]

(b) Dual legal basis, *lex specialis* and procedural compatibility

Each competence conferred upon the Union has a distinct procedure for exercising it which the Treaty drafters viewed as best fitting that policy area. A dual legal basis will be utilized for an instrument if there is no procedural incompatibility. While post-Lisbon many provisions share identical procedures, there are instances where dual legal bases are impossible due to procedural incompatibility.

ECR I-3651, paras 86 and 108 (in this judgment coherence also underpinned the reasoning on both aims being pursued equally, but the Court found that the development legal basis was the correct one due to its interpretation of former Article 47 TEU (Article 40 TEU).

[110] C-94/03 *Commission v. Council (Rotterdam Convention)* [2006] ECR I-1, though the Court has previously maintained the opposite: see e.g. Ruling 1/78 *re Convention on the Physical Protection of Nuclear Materials, Facilities and Transports* [1978] ECR 2151, para 35.

M. Klamert, 'Conflicts of Legal Basis: No Legality and No Basis but a Bright Future under the Lisbon Treaty?' (2010) 35 *European Law Review* 497–515

The Lisbon Treaty, however, still does not apply the ordinary legislative procedure to all policy areas. This lack of uniformity may either concern the rights of participation of the Parliament which is curtailed in areas where it may only consult but not co-decide. On the other hand, it may affect the voting procedure in the Council when it requires unanimity instead of qualified majority voting. The CFSP, above all, continues to be governed by specific rules and procedures also under the Lisbon Treaty and provides for little participation of the Parliament and mostly unanimity voting. Also, a number of special procedures originally set forth in the Nice Treaty, such as those concerning agreements on trade in certain sensitive services, have been kept in place by the Lisbon Treaty. Finally, despite the "depillarisation" of the former third pillar by fully integrating the whole field of Justice and Home Affairs (JHA) into the TFEU, this does in many instances not go as far as providing for the ordinary legislative procedure in this area.

The standard judgment on procedural incompatibility concerns the environment internal market legal basis for a Directive concerning waste from the titanium dioxide industry. The Court found that the Directive ought to be based on both legal bases at the same time. However, former Article 100a TEC (Article 114 TFEU) required the cooperation procedure thus involving Parliament and the Council voting under QMV, whereas former Article 130s TEC (Article 192 TFEU) required unanimity in Council after merely consulting Parliament. The Court found that 'use of both provisions as a joint legal basis would divest the cooperation procedure of its very substance'.[111] It did not automatically prefer 'the more democratic' legal basis, though it did state that participation of Parliament 'reflects a fundamental democratic principle that the peoples should take part in the exercise of power through the intermediary of a representative assembly'.[112] Instead, the Court 're-opened' the assessment of centre of gravity. Utilizing the provisions in the Treaty which require that EU policies incorporate environmental protection requirements (current Articles 11 and 114(3) TFEU), it found that the internal market legal basis prevailed.[113] Similarly, in a case concerning a Directive relating to the system of financing the European Agricultural Guidance and Guarantee Fund, the Court was confronted with procedural incompatibility between Articles 114 and 115 TFEU. At the outset of the judgment, immediately after its recollection of the 'objective factors', the Court excluded dual legal bases as a possible outcome of the judgment.[114] The issue of procedural incompatibility was then again a priori avoided by the finding that the content of the measure indeed supported that one provision sufficed as the correct legal basis. Importantly, where Article 115 TFEU is the *lex specialis* to Article 114 TFEU, the Court ruled that 'if a more specific provision is capable of constituting the legal basis for the measure in question, that measure must be founded on such provision'.[115]

In the *Rotterdam Convention* judgment where the Court did find that dual legal bases are required because of aim and content, it did not at the outset mention the issue of procedural

[111] C-300/89 *Commission* v. *Council (Titanium Dioxide)* [1991] ECR I-2867, para 18.
[112] *Ibid.*, para 20.
[113] C-338/01 *Commission* v. *Council* [2004] ECR I-4829.
[114] *Ibid.*, para 57.
[115] *Ibid.*, para 60 and C-533/03 *Commission* v. *Council* [2006] ECR I-1025, para 45.

incompatibility. After reasoning through the centre-of-gravity test, it found that CCP and environmental legal bases are not procedurally incompatible.[116]

C-94/03 *Commission* v. *Council (Rotterdam Convention)* [2006] ECR I-1

53. First, the Convention does not fall within the category of agreements which, under Article 133(5) EC, require unanimity within the Council, so that additional recourse to Article 133 EC could not in this case have any impact on the voting rules applicable within the Council, since the latter provision provides in principle, in the same way as Article 175(1) EC, for recourse to qualified majority voting.

54. Second, recourse to Article 133 EC jointly with Article 175(1) EC is likewise not liable to undermine the Parliament's rights because, although the first-mentioned article, read in conjunction with the first subparagraph of Article 300(3) EC, does not provide for consultation of that institution prior to the conclusion of an agreement in the area of commercial policy, the second article, on the other hand, does lead to such a result. In contrast to the situation at issue in the abovementioned *Titanium dioxide* case, the use of a combination of legal bases does not therefore in this case involve any encroachment upon the Parliament's rights.

In her Opinion on the *Rotterdam Convention* case, AG Kokott had entertained another element which could have led to procedural incompatibility in her opinion.

Opinion of Advocate General Kokott delivered on 26 May 2005, Case C-94/03 *Commission* v. *Council (Rotterdam Convention)*

56. Nor are there any specific indications that the absence of Article 133 EC as an additional legal basis weakened the *Commission's role as negotiator*.[117] For the common commercial policy (Article 133 EC) the Community indeed has exclusive competence, whereas in environmental policy (Article 175 EC) it shares its competence in principle with the Member States; so only in the latter case do the Member States sit at the negotiating table alongside the Commission, while in the former case it is for the Commission alone to carry on the negotiations. Additional recourse to Article 133 EC as a legal basis can thus strengthen the Commission's position as a matter of procedural law.

In sum, the accumulation of two legal bases is possible where they are compatible procedures.[118] Since the Lisbon Treaty, the likelihood of procedural incompatibility has decreased further through changes such as the increased mainstreaming of the ordinary legislative procedure and the 'depillarization' of the Union. This is important in light of the strengthened post-Lisbon obligation to 'take into

---

[116] C-94/03 *Commission* v. *Council (Rotterdam Convention)* [2006] ECR I-1, paras 53–54. With regard to the implementing Regulation of the Rotterdam Convention the Court stated identical arguments to rule on the compatibility of these legal basis. See C-178/03, *supra*, paras 57–59. However, AG Kokott had argued that in this case the co-decision procedure applicable to former Article 175(1) TEC could not be reconciled with the absence of any formal right to participate for the Parliament in the CCP (former Article 133(4) TEC); it argued that Parliament's most important right of participation, an important contribution to the democratic legitimacy of Community legislation, cannot be dispensed with. See Opinion of AG Kokott delivered on 26 May 2005 in Case C-178/03 *Implementing Regulation Rotterdam Convention*, paras 59–60.

[117] Emphasis in original.

[118] See also Joined Cases C-184/02 and C-223/02 *Spain and Finland* v. *European Parliament and Council* [2004] ECR I-7789, paras 42 to 44.

account objectives' from different policies in exercising a given competence (see Chapter 10 on development and CFSP dual legal basis). The Union is legally mandated to adopt provisions which pursue complex objectives, and in light of conferral and institutional balance this should lead to increased use of dual or multiple legal bases. From the perspective of 'objective factors' amenable to judicial review, the Court is likely to place greater emphasis on the assessment of content of an instrument and be more open to dual legal bases as it has been in the past. One example of post-Lisbon novelty is the EU's accession to the Treaty of Amity and Cooperation in Southeast Asia (see extract in Chapter 10). The Council Decision was based on Articles 37 TEU (CFSP), 209 TFEU (development) and 212 TFEU (technical cooperation), whereas prior to the Lisbon Treaty a CFSP–Development legal basis was unthinkable. Procedural compatibility was guaranteed through unanimity in Council under Articles 37 TEU and 212 TEU, with consent of Parliament under Article 218(6) TFEU.[119]

A remaining source of procedural incompatibility is between the CFSP and other areas of external action. In a 2012 judgment, the EP had challenged a Council Regulation imposing certain specific restrictive measures directed against certain persons and entities associated with Usama bin Laden. The Court confirmed the following:

Case C–130/10 *European Parliament* v. *Council of the European Union*, 19 July 2012, n.y.r.

45. None the less, the Court has held also, in particular in paragraphs 17 to 21 of Case C-300/89 Commission v Council [1991] ECR I-2867 ('Titanium dioxide'), that recourse to a dual legal basis is not possible where the procedures laid down for each legal basis are incompatible with each other (see, in particular, Parliament v Council, paragraph 37 and case-law cited).

46. If it was in the context of the cooperation procedure that the Court found, in Titanium dioxide, an incompatibility between that procedure, provided for by one of the two legal bases concerned in that judgment, and the Council's acting unanimously after merely consulting the European Parliament, provided for by the other, the Court has, nevertheless, in its subsequent decisions adopted a similar approach in connection with the procedure under Article 251 EC, known as 'the co-decision procedure' (see, to this effect, Case C-178/03 Commission v Parliament and Council [2006] ECR I-107, paragraphs 58 and 59, and Parliament v Council, paragraphs 76 to 79). Such an approach is still valid, after the entry into force of the Treaty of Lisbon, in the context of the ordinary legislative procedure.

47. In this instance, while Article 75 TFEU provides for application of the ordinary legislative procedure, which entails qualified majority voting in the Council and the Parliament's full participation in the procedure, Article 215(2) TFEU, for its part, entails merely informing the Parliament. In addition, recourse to Article 215(2) TFEU, unlike recourse to Article 75 TFEU, requires a previous decision in the sphere of the CFSP, namely, a decision adopted in accordance with Chapter 2 of Title V of the EU Treaty, providing for the adoption of restrictive measures such as those referred to in that provision. As a general rule, adoption of such a decision calls for unanimous voting in the Council acting alone.

48. Differences of that kind are such as to render those procedures incompatible.

(v) Annulment for incorrect legal basis: legal and political effects

When the Court finds that an act has been based on an incorrect legal basis, this will not necessarily lead to annulment of the instrument if the error is purely formal in nature. One

---

[119] See Council Decision on the accession of the European Union to the Treaty of Amity and Cooperation in Southeast Asia, Brussels. 20 March 2012, DOC 7434/12.

example is *Swedish Match* where the act was incorrectly based on a dual instead of a single legal basis. The CJEU found that:

> ### C-210/03 *R* v. *Secretary of State for Health, ex parte Swedish Match* [2004] ECR I-11893
>
> 25. Such an error in the citations of a Community act is no more than a purely formal defect, unless it gave rise to irregularity in the procedure applicable to the adoption of that act.

Such irregularity is more than purely formal when the incorrect legal basis has a tangibly negative impact either on the principle of conferral or the institutional balance. This was the case in the judgment on the road transport agreements with Hungary and Bulgaria:[120]

> ### C-211/01 *Commission* v. *Council (Transport Agreements with Bulgaria and Hungary)* [2003] ECR I-8913
>
> 52. In principle, the incorrect use of a Treaty article as a legal basis which results in the substitution of unanimity for qualified majority voting in the Council cannot be considered a purely formal defect since a change in voting method may affect the content of the act adopted.

The annulment of a decision for such reasons may have far-reaching real-world effects since the EU internal instruments and international agreement cease to have legal effect in the legal order in which they exist. In the case concerning the implementing Regulation for the *Rotterdam Convention*, the Court described its impact as follows.

> ### C-94/03 *Commission* v. *Council (Rotterdam Convention)* [2006] ECR I-1
>
> 64. Since 7 March 2003, exports and imports of hazardous chemicals have thus been governed by that regulation and the Commission has been prompted to adopt, in implementation of it, a number of Community import decisions concerning certain chemical products and substances.

For that reason the Court regularly limits the effects of the annulment for reasons of legal certainty (Article 264 TFEU).[121] It will thus maintain the effects of the contested instrument until the legal basis defect can be rectified within a reasonable period of time. The Court does not always give an explicit time limit, though at times it does explicitly state what is reasonable: twelve months in the *EIB* judgment.[122] However, in the case of international agreements there is the added complication that under Article 46 VCLT[123] – which is applicable to the Union in the

---

[120] C-211/01 *Commission* v. *Council (Transport Agreements with Bulgaria and Hungary)* [2003] ECR I-8913.

[121] C-178/03 *Commission* v. *Parliament and Council (Regulation implementing the Rotterdam Convention)* [2006] ECR I-107, para 65; C-155/07 *Parliament* v. *Council (EIB Guarantees)* [2008] ECR I-8103, para 89.

[122] In case C-94/03 on the Rotterdam Convention itself, the Court did not maintain the effects of the Decision approving the agreement.

[123] The text reads: 'A State may not invoke the fact that its consent to be bound by a treaty has been expressed in violation of a provision of its internal law regarding competence to conclude treaties as invalidating its consent unless that violation was manifest and concerned a rule of its internal law of fundamental importance.'

form of international customary law – the Union cannot invoke the absence of an internal incompetence to invalidate its earlier consent vis-à-vis external parties. Namely, an incorrect choice of legal basis cannot invalidate the Treaty between the EU and its external treaty partner. This need not be a problem: in the *Rotterdam Convention* case the Union could simply adopt a new Decision approving the agreement on a correct legal basis. However, at times it requires denunciation of the agreement and renegotiation with the third party. The judgment concerning the EU–US agreement on Passenger Name Records (PNR) in civil aviation is a prominent example. Through an extremely short reasoning of four paragraphs, the Court implied that the PNR agreement had a predominantly security aim. It could thus not have been adopted on the basis of Article 114 TFEU, but should have been adopted on the second and third pillar legal bases.[124] In light of the deeply different procedural requirements, the EU was forced to denounce the agreement with the US and could not simply adopt a new decision. Soon after the CJEU's annulment decision the Council terminated the PNR agreement,[125] and gave the Commission a mandate to negotiate a novel agreement on the basis of the second and third pillar legal basis (former Articles 24 and 38 TEU). This is evidently not conducive to the credibility of the EU as an international actor.

G. Gilmore and J. Rijpma, 'Case Law [Joined Cases C-317/04 and C-318/04]' (2007) 44 *Common Market Law Review* 1097–1098

The need to negotiate a new agreement and the urgency to do so in order not to disrupt air traffic from and to the US, will have undoubtedly weakened the Commission's negotiating position. Indeed it has been argued that the US has exacted changes in the operation of the agreement, in particular through Undertakings of the CBP attached to the Agreement, which state that the CBP will process data in accordance with US law.

In order to avoid such consequences, the parties may ask that if Court rules that the legal basis used was improper, it would maintain the effects of the agreement until a new Decision ratifying the international agreement has been adopted. The following action where the Parliament made such a request, was still pending at the time this book went to press.[126]

Action brought on 3 April 2012 – *European Commission* v. *Council of the European Union* (Case C-165/12)

Form of order sought

  Annul Council Decision 2012/19/EU of 16 December 2011 on the approval, on behalf of the European Union, of the Declaration on the granting of fishing opportunities in EU waters to fishing vessels flying the flag of the Bolivarian Republic of Venezuela in the exclusive economic zone off the coast of

---

[124] C-317/04 and C-318/04 *Parliament* v. *Commission (European Network and Information Security Agency)* [2006] ECR I-3771, paras 67–70.
[125] Council Notice concerning the denunciation of the Agreement OJ 2006, C 219/1.
[126] A similar case was filed two months earlier, and is equally still pending: C-103/12.

French Guiana, inasmuch as it is based on Article 218(6)(b) TFEU in conjunction with Article 43(3) TFEU;

Maintain the effects of the annulled decision until the entry into force of a new decision adopted, within a reasonable period, on an appropriate legal basis, namely Article 218(6)(a) TFEU in conjunction with Article 43(2) TFEU, or, in the event of a refusal by the Parliament to give its approval, until expiry of a reasonable short period after the Parliament's decision refusing approval, and order the Council of the European Union to pay the costs.

Pleas in law and main arguments

The Commission seeks the annulment, with maintenance of its effects until adoption of a new measure, of Council Decision 2012/19/EU, inasmuch as the choice of legal basis departs fundamentally from that proposed by the Commission, namely Article 218(6)(a) TFEU (in conjunction with Article 43(2) TFEU), with the approval of the Parliament.

The Commission submits that, by so acting, the Council has erred and that, in accordance with the Commission's proposal, it should seek the approval of the Parliament before adopting the measure in question.

In support of its action, the Commission puts forward three pleas in law: the first plea in law, split into three parts, alleging, firstly, infringement of Article 218(6)(a) TFEU and Article 43(2) TFEU in that the Council has used Article 218(6)(b) TFEU and Article 43(3) TFEU as the legal basis for the contested measure and, secondly, infringement of the second paragraph of Article 296 TFEU in that the Council has given contradictory reasons for its choice of legal basis.

The second plea in law, following from the first, also alleges infringement of Article 218(6)(a) TFEU in that the Council has disregarded the institutional prerogatives of the European Parliament by failing to obtain its approval despite the fact that that approval is required by the article in question.

The third plea in law alleges infringement of Articles 17 TEU and 218(6) TFEU in that the Council has distorted the Commission's proposal.

6 THE BROADER PICTURE OF EU EXTERNAL RELATIONS LAW

The three dynamics underpinning EU external relations law (see Preface) clearly emerged from teasing out the law on the scope of EU external competence and choice of legal bases.

First, the question of effectiveness and coherence of EU international action has implicitly or explicitly figured in the case law. On the one hand, the Court has rejected arguments that practical difficulties flowing from joint EU–Member State participation in an international context should influence the choice of legal basis. Instead, the appropriate legal basis is of constitutional importance and it is therefore a logical prior to any issue pertaining to the exercise of these conferred competences. On the other hand, the legal basis case law has progressively become more attuned to taking into account the issue of coherence. Notably, in its reasoning on taking into account multiple objectives and accepting that framework instruments have a single legal basis, the Court recognized the arbitrariness (*EIB*) or need for complementarity (*Rotterdam*) militating against separating an instrument where such does not reflect policy reality. Overall, the Treaties and case law increasingly had – and still have – to come to grips with the reality that international relations cannot be captured by delimited legal bases, whereas the principle of conferral continues to impose requirements of constitutional importance.

Second, the importance of law playing an important role in attaining effective and coherent EU external action is indubitable. Whereas the authors of this book have worked towards streamlining legal basis litigation in a coherent structure, the case law certainly does not excel in terms of methodological consistency or providing legal certainty. Numerous questions remain: is the over-reliance on the preamble on statement of aim not a strong element of subjectivity? How far will the context-criterion develop in addition to aim and content? To what extent do the qualitative and/or quantitative approaches provide sufficient legal certainty for legal services of EU institutions and Member States? The problem with lack of clarity in competence case law is that it does not diminish appetite for litigation, where energy is better spent on policy questions rather than competence battles.

Third, the interaction between policy realities and competing visions on European integration as shaping EU external relations law was most present in the Court's approach to the scope of EU competence. The open-ended nature of Treaty provisions led to inter-institutional and EU–Member State disputes over the scope of competences conferred upon the Union. This placed the Court in the position of independent arbitrator, while fully aware of the significant impact of its rulings on policy-making and the future development of the EU as an international actor. The state-analogy in CCP combined with the evolutive interpretation form the prime example, but the teleological approach and the wish to ensure that no competence would become 'devoid of substance or nugatory over time' has equally influenced case law on development or foreign and security policy. In navigating the difficult terrain of competing visions on the future of EU external relations, and taking the principle of conferral seriously by balancing competing competencies, the role of the Court could not be overstated in developing the EU as a mature international actor.

A. Dashwood, 'The Limits of European Community Powers' (1996) 21 *European Law Review* 128

. . . it must be apparent what a vital role the Court of Justice has played, and will be called upon again to play in the future, in maintaining the balance intended by the Treaty between the Community's powers and those of the Member States. The point is so obvious that I should have been embarrassed to make it with force, if there had not been recent attacks on the Court's intellectual integrity, suggesting that it is a Court with a federalising mission. The cases I have cited this evening should be sufficient to refute that: a missionary Court would certainly have grasped the opportunity offered in [Titanium Dioxide case *et al.*], for example, of establishing that any measure affecting the internal market, however remotely, falls to be adopted under Article [114 TFEU]; or the opportunity offered by the dispute over the conclusion of the WTO Agreements to assimilate the whole field of external economic relations to the common commercial policy. I reject any suggestion that the Court's decisions may be skewed by doctrinal or idiosyncratic policy considerations. If the Court has a policy, it is the one and only policy a professional court should have, which is to follow the argument where it leads. Of course, the terms of the argument are unique, because they relate to that unique construct, the constitutional order of States created by the Treaties. I try never to play the game of activism v. strict constructionism; but, if it is true that a certain shift towards the latter may be evident in the recent jurisprudence, I do not believe that has anything to do with nervousness about offending political sensitivities: it is because Maastricht altered the terms of the argument, and the Court is loyally giving effect to the Treaties as they must now be interpreted.

SOURCES AND FURTHER READING

Arnull, A., 'Legal Principles and Practical Politics' (1987) 12 *European Law Review* 448–451.

Barents, R., 'The Internal Market Unlimited: Some Observations on the Legal Basis of Community Legislation' (1993) 30 *Common Market Law Review* 85–109.

Chalmers, D., Davies, G. and Monti, G., *European Union Law*, 2nd edn (Cambridge: Cambridge University Press, 2011).

Craig, P. and de Búrca, G., *EU Law: Text, Cases and Materials* (Oxford: Oxford University Press, 2011).

Cremona, M., 'Balancing Union and Member State Interests: Opinion 1/2008, Choice of Legal Base and the Common Commercial Policy under the Treaty of Lisbon' (2010) 35 *European Law Review* 678–694.

Cullen, H. and Charlesworth, A., 'Diplomacy by Other Means: The Use of Legal Basis Litigation as a Political Strategy by the European Parliament and Member States' (1999) 36 *Common Market Law Review* 1243–1270.

Dashwood, A., 'The Limits of European Community Powers' (1996) 21 *European Law Review* 113–128.

De Búrca, G., 'The EU in the Negotiation of the UN Disability Convention' (2010) 35 *European Law Review*, 2, 174–196.

Emiliou, N., 'Opening Pandora's Box: The Legal Basis of Community Measures before the Court of Justice' (1994) 19 *European Law Review* 488–507.

Gilmore, G. and Rijpma, J., 'Case Law [Joined Cases C-317/04 and C-318/04]' (2007) 44 *Common Market Law Review* 1081–1099.

Hilf, M., 'The ECJ's Opinion 1/94 on the WTO – No Surprise, but Wise?' (1995) 6 *European Journal of International Law* 245–259.

Klamert, M., 'Conflicts of Legal Basis: No Legality and No Basis but a Bright Future under the Lisbon Treaty?' (2010) 35 *European Law Review* 497–515.

Koutrakos, P., 'Casenote of Cases C-94/03 and C-178/03' (2007) 44 *Common Market Law Review* 171–194.

Koutrakos, P., 'Legal Basis and Delimitation of Competence in EU External Relations', in M. Cremona and B. de Witte (eds.), *EU Foreign Relations Law: Constitutional Fundamentals* (Oxford: Hart Publishing, 2008), pp. 171–198.

Maas, H. H., 'The External Powers of the EEC with Regard to Commercial Policy: Comment on Opinion 1/75' (1976) 13 *Common Market Law Review* 379–387.

Pescatore, P., 'External Relations in the Case-Law of the Court of Justice of the European Communities' (1979) 16 *Common Market Law Review* 615–645.

Post, R., 'Constructing the European Polity: ERTA and the Open Skies Judgments', in M. Poiares Maduro and L. Azoulai (eds.), *The Past and Future of EU Law* (Oxford: Hart Publishing, 2010).

Steenbergen, J., 'Casenote of C-45/86 Commission v. Council' (1987) 24 *Common Market Law Review* 731–737.

Steenbergen, J., 'La Notion de Politique Commerciale Commune après l'avis 1/78 de la Cour de Justice' (1980) *Cahiers de Droit Europeén* 54–74.

Steenbergen, J., 'The Common Commercial Policy' (1980) 17 *Common Market Law Review* 229–249.

Stein, E., 'External Relations of the European Community: Structure and Process', in A. Clapham (ed.), *Collected Courses of the Academy of European Law* (Oxford: Oxford University Press,1990/1), pp. 115–188.

Tridimas, T. and Eeckhout, P., 'The External Competence of the Community and the Case-Law of the Court of Justice: Principle versus Pragmatism' (1994) 14 *Yearbook of European Law* 143–177.

Van Ooik, R. H., *De Keuze der Rechtsgrondslag voor Besluiten in de Europese Unie* (Deventer: Kluwer, 1999).

Van Vooren, B., *EU External Relations Law and the European Neighbourhood Policy: A Paradigm for Coherence* (Abingdon/New York: Routledge, 2012), Chapters 3 and 4.

Wyatt, D., 'Community Competence to Regulate the Internal Market', in M. Dougan and S. Currie (eds.), *50 Years of the European Treaties, Looking Back and Thinking Forward* (Oxford: Hart Publishing, 2009), Chapter 5.

6

The duty of cooperation

1 CENTRAL ISSUES

- As a consequence of the complex raft of rules pertaining to EU exclusive, shared pre-emptive, shared non-pre-emptive, parallel and retained Member State competences, there are many scenarios where the EU and the Member States will conduct external relations in a 'mixed' configuration.
- This chapter revolves around Article 4(3) TEU, which contains the generally applicable duty of loyalty in EU law. Derived from that principle is the duty of cooperation, which is of paramount importance in the relationship between the EU and Member States in their external relations. It is a legal duty which applies across the scope of the EU Treaty, and which legally requires certain forms of behaviour of the EU and Member States in international contexts.
- Tracing the evolution in CJEU case law, this chapter shows that the Court has judicially constructed a duty of cooperation which has evolved from merely requiring duties of best effort, to now requiring duties of result. In this chapter we conceptualize the duty of cooperation in the form of a policy timeline which is subdivided into two phases: the strategy and preparation phase; and the execution and implementation phase. This conceptual framework will explain that the duty of cooperation imposes different obligations of action or inaction on the EU and Member States, depending on which phase of the policy timeline they are currently in, and on the 'intensity' of collaboration and state of affairs within each phase.

2 LEGAL FOUNDATION OF THE DUTY OF COOPERATION: DISTINCT FROM PRE-EMPTION

Article 4(3) TFEU

Pursuant to the principle of sincere cooperation, the Union and the Member States shall, in full mutual respect, assist each other in carrying out tasks which flow from the Treaties.

The Member States shall take any appropriate measure, general or particular, to ensure fulfilment of the obligations arising out of the Treaties or resulting from the acts of the institutions of the Union.

The Member States shall facilitate the achievement of the Union's tasks and refrain from any measure which could jeopardise the attainment of the Union's objectives.

Article 4(3) TFEU contains the 'duty of loyalty' applicable in the EU legal order: the Member States shall take any action in order to ensure the effective attainment of the Treaty's objectives. Since the Treaty of Lisbon, this former Article 10 TEC has been amended, with the first sentence containing an explicit reciprocal duty of cooperation. In order to understand the legal obligations stemming from this duty, and their scope of application, we must look back at the relationship between the scope of EU competence and the scope of EU law, a distinction which was similarly pertinent in Chapter 4 on the nature of EU competence.

A. Dashwood, 'The Limits of European Community Powers' (1996) 21 *European Law Review* 114

'Community powers' are the authorisations the Treaty has given the institutions to do things. Discovering the limits of those authorisations is not the same as discovering the limits of the Treaty's scope of application. That is because the objectives of the Treaty are not exclusively pursued through actions of the Community institutions: the Member States, too, have a part to play through the observance of rules that require them sometimes to take action, but more often to refrain from exercising, or from exercising fully, powers that would normally be available to them as incidents of sovereignty. To put the point in Hohfeldian terms, duties or disabilities for the Member States do not imply correlative powers for the Community.

The distinction between the scope of Union powers and Union law is a crucial one in relation to the functioning of the duty of cooperation. In Chapter 4 we have seen that in *ERTA* the Court stated that because the Member States are required to take appropriate measures in line with Article 4(3) TEU, when the EU has exercised its competence in the sphere of transport, the Member States are excluded from assuming international obligations 'affecting' those EU rules. The Court thus derived *ERTA*-type pre-emptive exclusivity from Article 4(3) TEU,[1] and pre-emption thus shares its legal foundation with the duty of cooperation. However, the rationales for pre-emption and the duty of cooperation are entirely different: in Opinion 1/03, the CJEU stated the following rationale for pre-empting Member State action.

Opinion 1/03, *Competence of the Community to conclude the new Lugano Convention on jurisdiction and the recognition and enforcement of judgments in civil and commercial matters* [2006] ECR I-1145, para 128

... it is essential to ensure a uniform and consistent application of the Community rules and the proper functioning of the system which they establish in order to preserve the full effectiveness of Community law.

Applying the distinction between the scope of EU powers and the scope of the EU Treaty, the application of the pre-emption principle is connected to the *scope of powers* conferred upon the

---

[1] Case 22/70 *Commission* v. *Council (ERTA)* [1971] ECR 263, paras 21–22 and Opinion 1/03 *Lugano Convention* [2006] ECR I-1145, para 119.

Union. It is not connected to the scope of application of the Treaties as a whole: not all objectives the EU must pursue according to the TEU and TFEU exclude Member State action in pursuit of those same objectives ('international peace', 'sustainable development', etc.). The purpose of excluding the Member States from acting is solely to ensure effective application of EU rules through uniformity where the EU has exercised its shared powers conferred upon it, or where it possesses an a priori exclusive power. The scope of application of the duty of cooperation is connected to *the scope of the Treaties as a whole*, which is also reflected in a different rationale. Compare the Court's explanation of the duty of cooperation in *Commission* v. *Germany*, with the above extract from Opinion 1/03.

> ### Case C-433/03 *Commission* v. *Germany* [2005] ECR I-6985, para 60
>
> ... to facilitate the achievement of the [Union] tasks and to ensure the coherence and consistency of the action and its international representation.

The differences between the two extracts are important: pre-emption 'ensures' application of EU rules through 'uniformity', whereas the duty of cooperation seeks to 'facilitate' effectively attaining EU tasks and 'coherent' EU international action. Therefore, the legal contexts which activate these principles are very different since their finality is not the same: pre-emption is connected to protecting the principle of *conferral* from encroachment, whereas cooperation exists to ensure that the *objectives* laid down in Union law are attained. As pointed out by Dashwood, the objectives pursued by the EU are by no means unique to that organization and may require Member State action, whereas the former captures that the means conferred to pursue those objectives are necessarily limited.[2]

As we shall explain in this chapter, the procedural and substantive legal obligations stemming from pre-emption and cooperation are then commensurately different: when EU *competences* could be affected, the Member States are excluded from acting at all: *an obligation of result*. Member States are not permitted to act *at all*, even if they perceive it to be for the benefit of the EU Treaty objectives.[3] Conversely, when *EU treaty objectives* are at stake, this triggers reciprocal obligations for the Member States and Union institutions to cooperate loyally: an obligation of *best efforts*. However, in practice, the line between them may be blurred.

> ### E. Neframi, 'The Duty of Loyalty: Rethinking its Scope through its Application in the Field of EU External Relations' (2010) 47 *Common Market Law Review* 323–359, at 359
>
> The duty of loyalty is a general principle inherent in membership of the EU. [Its] transcription in Article 4(3) TEU and its specification through the duty of loyal cooperation allows the CJEU to determine its scope and impact and to restrict the Member States' autonomy through the recognition of duties contributing to the constitutionalization of the European Union. The duties stemming from Article 4(3) TEU may cover

---

[2] A. Dashwood, 'The Limits of European Community Powers' (1996) 21 *European Law Review* 113.

[3] Opinion of AG Tizzano delivered on 31 January 2002 Case C-466/98 [2002] ECR I-9427, para 73.

effectiveness in the context of implementation of common rules, or other aspects in the interest of the Union, such as the respect for the *effet utile* of EU law, the contribution to the effective exercise of Union competence, or the fulfilment of the requirement of unity with a view to asserting the identity of the EU on the international scene. The effectiveness of EU law can thus be considered as the tangible facet of the duty of loyalty, specified through obligations of loyal cooperation incumbent on the national authorities, including the national courts. The duty of loyalty is thus the legal basis for both procedural duties and substantive principles, while the specific obligations stemming from it interfere and converge in the pursuit of the interest of the Union.

In the field of external relations, the duty of loyalty may constrain the exercise of the Member States' competence, both at legislative and implementation levels, following principles developed internally and by means of a procedural or substantive duty of cooperation. Such a constraint has a particular meaning in the external relations field, as the duty of loyalty impacts on the EU relations with non-member countries and on the international status of the Member States, while the parallel to the internal field confirms the general character of the duty. Giving rise to a best-endeavours obligation, without excluding an obligation of result – namely when common rules are at stake –, the constraints of loyalty are reconciled with the autonomy of Member States, the latter being of particular importance when Member States act as subjects of international law.

3 SCOPE OF APPLICATION OF THE DUTY OF COOPERATION

(i) A policy timeline with two phases

By its nature, Court case law provides us only with snapshots of specific situations, in which EU–Member States' side-by-side presence on the international scene did not function to the point where relevant actors thought litigation before the Court was the sole solution. At present, there are two distinct lines in the duty of cooperation case law:

- First, there are a number of cases that pertain to mixed situations in international organizations or under multilateral international agreements, where either the Member States alone are parties, or are party to the multilateral Treaty alongside the Union, and where the internal competence configuration requires close cooperation (see Chapter 2).
- Second, there are a number of cases which pertain to the negotiation of bilateral agreements with third countries by the EU, raising questions as to the Member States' legal obligations in relation to these obligations.

In the most recent *PFOS* judgment discussed below, the Court of Justice has begun to merge these lines of jurisprudence into a more organic whole in terms of the kinds of obligations or effort and result the duty of cooperation requires in EU external relations. However, this evolution towards a coherent set of obligations is as of yet incomplete, and not without its imperfections.

In this chapter we conceptualize the duty of cooperation as a single legal principle to which different procedural and substantive obligations are attached, and this depending on (1) the bilateral and multilateral international context in which the principle is applied, and (2) distinct phases of 'timeline' of the policy process ongoing in that context. This timeline applies to multilateral and bilateral settings with a mixed Member State and EU presence, and functions as a framework to concretize the legal obligations in material instances. This time-line consists of two distinct phases:

1. *Strategy and preparation phase*: this first phase begins with the EU and its Member States, even remotely contemplating any international initiative (negotiate a new treaty, or propose action in a multilateral organization or setting), be that through the EU or not, without having pinpointed who will exercise which competence. This may concern discussions in the relevant EU structures (working groups, task forces, COREPER, and upwards) in Brussels, but also discussions between Member State delegations and the EU delegation at international organizations such as the FAO, International Civil Aviation Organization (ICAO), UN and so on. As time progresses, the 'intensity' of this phase may increase, as EU actors are beginning to prepare the actual substance of the common initiative or strategy. At some point, this may then lead to an agreement on whether and what kind of common initiatives will be pursued at EU level; or that it will be pursued by the Member States individually or collectively outside the Union. This phase includes setting the stage for EU action and decisions on the division of competences between EU and Member States, though there have been cases of 'agreeing to disagree'.

2. *Execution and implementation phase*: the second phase is the execution of the previously agreed upon common initiative or strategy within the international context. This could concern negotiations for a new international instrument, where the Commission, and/or EEAS, possibly together with the Member States depending on the subject at issue, negotiates a new instrument with a third party. In a multilateral or plurilateral context, it could concern the proposal of new action in the Association Council of an AA, speaking at – or making proposals at – a conference of the parties in a multilateral environmental agreement, and so on.

From a practical perspective it is certainly difficult to draw the line between phases in such fashion. Moreover, especially in long-standing multilateral contexts such as the UN, ICAO, etc., there is an ongoing feedback loop of EU and Member State preparation and external representation. However, what we wish to indicate through this policy timeline is that *the duty of cooperation will impose different obligations of action or inaction on the EU and Member States, depending on which phase they find themselves in, and depending on the 'intensity' of collaboration and state of affairs within each phase.* These obligations must reflect the need to 'facilitate the achievement of the [Union] tasks and to ensure the coherence and consistency of the action and its international representation',[4] depending on the legal-policy context in which the EU Treaty objectives are pursued. Concretely, this means that we must reply to the following questions in relation to the duty of cooperation:

- What kind of substantive obligations are expected of the EU institutions in the Member States? A duty to inform each other, a duty to consult each other, a duty to refrain from action until having consulted/informed the other, a duty to refrain from action until a given process has run its course? To what extent does the nature of competence influence the response to these questions?
- At which point in the policy timeline are these duties triggered through what sort of policy-related occurrences, and at which intensity (inform, consult or abstain)? For example,

---

[4] C-433/03 *Commission* v. *Germany* [2005] ECR I-6985, para 60.

is a given actor excluded from acting at all as soon as discussions in relevant auxiliary EU bodies (working groups, etc.) have started, or merely required to inform its counterparts that it is exercising its competence?

In the literature it has been argued that the Court has taken a strong turn on the nature of obligations stemming from duty of cooperation as they apply across these phases. Indeed, the Court has *temporally extended* the reach of these obligations along the policy timeline, as well as *substantively deepened* obligations connected to them.

(ii) Earliest case law: an open-ended best efforts obligation

Early case law on the duty of cooperation between the EU and its Member States focused specifically on mixed international settings, and conceived the duty of cooperation as one requiring an obligation of best efforts. This means that the Court stated that close coordination and cooperation are necessary, but it did not provide substantive guidance on how the institutions or the Member States should fulfil their loyalty obligation in concrete instances. In Opinion 2/91 on the ILO Convention concerning safety in the use of chemicals at work, Member States were members of that organization and the Union was to be represented by them in areas falling within its competence. As to when the duty of cooperation is *triggered*, the Court stated that this is so 'when it appears that the subject matter of an agreement or contract falls in part within the competence of the Community and in part within that of the Member States'.[5] The Court further found that the duty of cooperation results from the requirement of unity in the international representation of the Community, but gave only limited guidance on the substantive obligations imposed on the EU and Member States.

Opinion 2/91, *Convention No 170 ILO on Safety in the Use of Chemicals at Work* [1993] ECR I-1061

36. ... in Ruling 1/78 the Court pointed out that when it appears that the subject-matter of an agreement or contract falls in part within the competence of the Community and in part within that of the Member States, it is important to ensure that there is a close association between the institutions of the Community and the Member States both in the process of negotiation and conclusion and in the fulfilment of the obligations entered into. This duty of cooperation ... results from the requirement of unity in the international representation of the Community. ...

38. It is therefore for the Community institutions and the Member States to take all the measures necessary so as best to ensure such cooperation both in the procedure of submission to the competent authority and ratification of Convention No 170 and in the implementation of commitments resulting from that Convention.

This obligation of best effort was repeated word-for-word by the Court in Opinion 1/94 and the *FAO* judgments of 1996.[6]

---

[5] Opinion 2/91, *Convention No 170 ILO on Safety in the Use of Chemicals at Work* [1993] ECR I-1061, para 36.

[6] Opinion 1/94, *Competence of the Community to conclude international agreements concerning services and the protection of intellectual property*, [1994] ECR I-5267, para 108; Case C-25/94 *Commission v. Council (FAO)* [1996] ECR I-1469, para 48.

In Opinion 1/94 concerning competence to conclude the WTO Agreement, the Commission warned that grave problems would arise with the administration of the agreements, if the Community and the Member States were recognized as sharing competence to participate in the conclusion of the GATS and TRIPS agreements. According to the Commission:

Opinion 1/94, *Re World Trade Organization Agreement* [1994] ECR I-5267, para 106

... the Member States will, in the context of the WTO, undoubtedly seek to express their views individually on matters falling within their competence whenever no consensus has been found. Furthermore, interminable discussions will ensue to determine whether a given matter falls within the competence of the Community, so that the Community mechanisms laid down by the relevant provisions of the Treaty will apply, or whether it is within the competence of the Member States, in which case the consensus rule will operate. The Community's unity of action vis-à-vis the rest of the world will thus be undermined and its negotiating power greatly weakened.

The Court of Justice responded that this concern is quite legitimate, but did not accept that it could have legal consequences.

Opinion 1/94, *Re World Trade Organization Agreement* [1994] ECR I-5267, para 107

[A]ny problems which may arise ... as regards the coordination necessary to ensure unity of action where the Community and the Member States participate jointly cannot modify the answer to the question of competence, that being a prior issue [however] the allocation of competence cannot depend on problems which may possibly arise in administration of the agreements.

There was no willingness of the Court to engage more substantively in EU–Member State cooperation in a mixed context. It thereby did follow the Commission's argument that in order to prevent chaos, more competences should be allocated to the EU. It also emphasized that due to the nature of the WTO with its annexed agreements and the connection between them, the duty of cooperation is 'all the more imperative'.

Opinion 1/94, *Re World Trade Organization Agreement* [1994] ECR I-5267

108. Next, where it is apparent that the subject-matter of an agreement or convention falls in part within the competence of the Community and in part within that of the Member States, it is essential to ensure close cooperation between the Member States and the Community institutions, both in the process of negotiation and conclusion and in the fulfilment of the commitments entered into. That obligation to cooperate flows from the requirement of unity in the international representation of the Community.

109. The duty to cooperate is all the more imperative in the case of agreements such as those annexed to the WTO Agreement, which are inextricably interlinked, and in view of the cross-retaliation measures established by the Dispute Settlement Understanding. Thus, in the absence of close cooperation, where

a Member State, duly authorized within its sphere of competence to take cross-retaliation measures, considered that they would be ineffective if taken in the fields covered by GATS or TRIPs, it would not, under Community law, be empowered to retaliate in the area of trade in goods, since that is an area which on any view falls within the exclusive competence of the Community under Article 113 of the Treaty. Conversely, if the Community were given the right to retaliate in the sector of goods but found itself incapable of exercising that right, it would, in the absence of close cooperation, find itself unable, in law, to retaliate in the areas covered by GATS or TRIPs, those being within the competence of the Member States.

In the *FAO* judgment, the Court confirmed that the EU institutions and Member States could embed their reciprocal duty of cooperation, and that such a document could have legal effect. Concretely, the case concerned a written 'arrangement' between the Commission and Council on the distribution of speaking and voting rights in that international organization. The Court stated that this arrangement 'represents fulfilment of that duty of cooperation'.

Case C-25/94 *Commission* v. *Council (FAO Fisheries Agreement)* [1996] ECR I-1469, para 49

49. ... the Arrangement between the Council and the Commission represents fulfilment of that duty of cooperation between the Community and its Member States within the FAO. It is clear, moreover, from the terms of the Arrangement, that the two institutions intended to enter into a binding commitment towards each other.

The most recent case where the Court of Justice held on to the duty of cooperation as an obligation of best efforts is the *Mox Plant* litigation. In that case, Ireland had instituted proceedings against the UK before the International Tribunal of the Law of the Sea (ITLOS). The Commission services had beforehand sent a letter to the Irish authorities that the dispute was a matter falling within the exclusive jurisdiction of the Court of Justice, but Ireland proceeded regardless.

Case C-459/03 *Commission* v. *Ireland (Mox Plant Case)* [2006] ECR I-4635

178. Moreover, in their letter of 8 October 2001, the Commission's services had already contended that the dispute relating to the MOX plant, as referred by Ireland to the arbitral tribunal constituted pursuant to the Convention for the Protection of the Marine Environment of the North-East Atlantic, was a matter falling within the exclusive jurisdiction of the Court.

179. In those circumstances, the obligation of close cooperation within the framework of a mixed agreement involved, on the part of Ireland, a duty to inform and consult the competent Community institutions prior to instituting dispute-settlement proceedings concerning the MOX plant within the framework of the Convention.

180. The same duty of prior information and consultation was also imposed on Ireland by virtue of the EAEC Treaty in so far as that Member State contemplated invoking provisions of that Treaty and measures

adopted pursuant to it within the framework of the proceedings which it was proposing to bring before the Arbitral Tribunal.

181. It is common ground that, at the date on which those proceedings were brought, Ireland had not complied with that duty of prior information and consultation.

By not informing and consulting with the Commission after it sent the letter to the Irish authorities, Ireland violated its duty of active information and consultation. Of course, at that point one could already query whether information and consultation would have changed the outcome of the case. It seems unlikely that the Commission would not have pursued this case concerning the exclusive jurisdiction of the Court of Justice itself.

In sum, the Court constructed a duty of cooperation as an obligation of best efforts applying both to the institutions and the Member States. Those obligations crystallize in the form of obligations of information and consultation along a 'policy timeline' which in Opinion 2/91 was vaguely defined as starting from the negotiation instrument in the mixed international context, and continuing through to the implementation of commitments resulting from the concluded (mixed) instrument, e.g. during the lifetime of the mixed agreement. In the following subsection, it becomes clear that with the *Inland Waterway* cases of 2005, the *IMO* case of 2009 and the *PFOS* case of 2010, the Court has taken a significant turn in the interpretation of – and legal consequences connected to – the duty of cooperation.

(iii) First signs of a turn to an obligation of result

The first two judgments under consideration were rendered in June and July 2005 against Germany and Luxemburg. These two Member States had concluded bilateral agreements on inland waterway navigation, while Community negotiations were underway towards a multilateral convention on the same topic. This case thus did not arise from a mixed international setting, but from negotiations with third partners which were pursued simultaneously by the Member States and the European Union on the same subject. Rejecting the claim of *ERTA* pre-emption in both judgments, the Court turned to the claim that the Member States had failed to cooperate loyally with the EU institutions. In both cases the Commission argued that the Member States had violated their obligations under EU law in two ways: first, 'Community negotiations and its subsequent conclusion by the Council are inevitably made more difficult by interference from a Member State's own initiatives'.[7] Second, the Community's 'position is weakened because the Community and its Member States appear fragmented'. In both judgments the Court confirmed that the duty of cooperation aims to 'facilitate the achievement of the Community tasks and to ensure the coherence and consistency of the action and its international representation'.[8] The cases are important because they marked the moment where the duty of cooperation was triggered:

---

[7] C-266/03 *Commission* v. *Luxembourg* [2005] ECR I-4805, para 53.
[8] *Ibid.*, para 60.

> ### Case C-433/03 *Commission* v. *Germany* [2005] ECR I-6985, para 66, and see also Case C-266/03 *Commission* v. *Luxembourg* [2005] ECR I-4805, para 59
>
> 66. The adoption of a decision authorising the Commission to negotiate a multilateral agreement on behalf of the Community marks the start of a concerted Community action at international level and requires for that purpose, if not a duty of abstention on the part of the Member States, at the very least a duty of close cooperation between the latter and the Community institutions in order to facilitate the achievement of the Community tasks and to ensure the coherence and consistency of the action and its international representation.

The Court of Justice argued that the policy timeline started from the moment 'concerted EU action' can be established, and that a Council Decision adopting negotiation guidelines provides a marker for close cooperation, though not abstention. This notion of 'close' cooperation as different from mere cooperation but not all that far from 'a duty of abstention', is then an important 'strengthening' of the best efforts obligation from previous case law. Additionally, the Court said that that duty is of 'general application', and does not depend on whether the EU competence is exclusive or whether the Member States have retained their external competences.[9]

Against the claim that it had violated the duty of cooperation, Luxembourg offered little resistance since no consultations had taken place between it and the Commission.[10] Germany had more to offer:[11] the AG and CJEU acknowledged that consultations with the Commission had taken place during negotiation and signature of the agreement, and Germany pointed to the fact that during such consultations it had agreed to denounce the agreement, and had negotiated a decreased period for denunciation of six months.[12] It is then no surprise that Luxembourg was found to have failed its duties under Article 4(3) TEU, but the case against Germany illustrates that the addition of 'close' cooperation is not without meaning as to the intensity of the obligations stemming from the duty. In the German case, the Court acknowledged the cooperative efforts of Germany during negotiation and signature of its own agreements, but brushed these aside because after the negotiation mandate had been adopted within the EU context, German had still ratified the bilateral agreement without consulting with the Commission.[13] The Court also did not accept that the German promise to denounce the bilateral agreement would lead to compliance with the duty of cooperation, since that would not facilitate the Commission's multilateral negotiations.[14] Thus consultation during initial negotiations and substantive changes to content of the bilateral agreements concluded by Germany were insufficient to ensure compliance with the duty of cooperation.

In these two cases, the Court construes a strong duty of cooperation between the EU and its Member States in cases where the latter were not pre-empted because the Community had already acted. However, the legal consequences, in particular in the case of Germany, are far-reaching. It had consulted within the Community context during the preparation of the

---

[9] *Ibid.*, para 58.
[10] *Ibid.*, paras 63–65.
[11] C-433/03 *Commission* v. *Germany* [2005] ECR I-6985, paras 55–57.
[12] *Ibid.*, para 58.
[13] *Ibid.*, para 68.
[14] *Ibid.*, para 72.

bilateral agreement, arguably in step with its best efforts obligation elaborated in earlier case law. The argument of the CJEU that Germany should also have consulted at the point of ratification poses broader questions: in what form would such consultation have been sufficient to comply with the duty of cooperation? If Germany had indeed consulted, would agreement from the Commission have been necessary by stating that it should not go ahead with ratification due to the state of negotiations at Union level? Would this not have constituted a de facto request for permission by Germany to ratify its agreement? It is not unlikely that at that stage of negotiations the Court might have envisaged that the duty of cooperation requires a duty to abstain from going ahead with the ratification of a bilateral agreement. This is borne out by the *PFOS* judgment discussed further in this chapter, and such a duty to abstain would therefore constitute a de facto pre-emption effect. However in this case, given the advanced stage of ongoing EU-level negotiations, the Court's requirement is not unreasonable when placed in the perspective of the policy timeline: Germany had agreed to EU-level negotiations in the Council, and it should not have circumvented that process as consultation with the EU institutions is indeed kept to a minimum. However, the greater problem arises when the requirement of consultation and consent from the Commission (with the possible effect of quasi-pre-emption) is moved to the beginning of the policy timeline, namely at the moment where discussions exist on whether or not a shared competence will be exercised through the Union, or by the Member States individually. We shall return to this hypothesis below when discussing the most recent *PFOS* decision of the Court. Before discussing that judgment, we will look at the *IMO* judgment which concerned the exercise of exclusive EU competences by the Member States in a mixed international context where the EU itself is not a member. As stated before, not only should the phase in which the policy process finds itself influence the legal consequences of the duty of cooperation, but the nature of the EU competence is also an important factor in establishing legal consequences of cooperation.

(iv) *IMO* judgment: true reciprocity in the duty of cooperation?

In *Commission* v. *Greece* of 2009, that Member State had submitted to the IMO Maritime Safety Committee a proposal which could potentially lead to new international rules on international safety at sea. However, such rules had already been incorporated in the Community legal order through a Regulation, and hence the Commission argued that the EC was exclusively competent in this area.[15] The Court accepted that argument and stated that Greece assumed obligations which might 'affect' the Regulation in the *ERTA* definition of the word, violating its obligations under Articles 10 EC, 71 EC and 80(2) EC.[16] Greece's duty of abstention before the IMO thus flows from the pre-emption doctrine, but this points us to an important distinction: duties stemming from the principles pertaining to EU powers, and principles stemming from the scope of EU law; but both stemming from the general application from Article 4(3) across all areas of EU competence regardless of their nature.[17]

Whereas Greece had violated its duty of abstention stemming from the pre-emption doctrine, that Member State argued that the Commission had itself failed in its duty to cooperate loyally

---

[15] Case C-45/07 *Commission* v. *Greece (International Maritime Organization)* [2009] ECR I-701 p. 25, para 14.
[16] *Ibid.*, paras 19 and 23.
[17] J. Heliskoski, 'Adoption of Positions under Mixed Agreements', in C. Hillion and P. Koutrakos (eds.), *Mixed Agreements Revisited – The EU and its Member States in the World* (Oxford: Hart Publishing, 2010), p. 158.

with the Member States by not allowing discussion of Greece's proposal in the Marsec committee, a preparatory body within the Union.[18] It thus invoked the failure of the Commission to fulfil its legal obligation with regard to the scope of Union law, as defence against its own failure with regard to Union competence. The Court's reply is by no means surprising:[19] a breach by the Commission of the duty of cooperation does not entitle a Member State to undertake actions which affect rules adopted at Union level. Nonetheless, the Court did take the opportunity to emphasize the reciprocal nature of the duty of cooperation. When the Union has an exclusive power, it too has to cooperate loyally with its Member States:

Case C–45/07 *Commission v. Greece (International Maritime Organization)* [2009] ECR I–701, paras 24–25

It is true that, in order to fulfil its duty of genuine cooperation under Article 10 EC, the Commission could have endeavoured to submit that proposal to the Maritime Safety Committee and allowed a debate on the subject. As is apparent from Article 2(2)(b) of the Standard rules of procedure, such a committee is also a forum enabling exchanges of views between the Commission and the Member States. The Commission, in chairing that committee, may not prevent such an exchange of views on the sole ground that a proposal is of a national nature.[20]

In terms of our policy timeline, this is an important statement: during the first phase considering what international action could be taken and by whom, the Commission too is under an obligation to enable a full and open exchange of views. Assuming that the Commission had indeed wilfully excluded discussion on Greece's proposal, that paragraph can be read as a reprimand of its failure to do exactly that, and this is a confirmation that the duty of cooperation ought to work as a two-way street. However, this reciprocity is partially illusory because the Member States are dealt a worse hand in terms of enforcement. If Greece feels the Commission has not met its obligations under Article 4(3) TEU, what recourse to enforcement does that Member State have? Given that there is no Commission act to be challenged, and given that the duty of cooperation is an insufficient ground in itself, that Member State would have to utilize Article 265 TFEU (failure to act). However, the wide discretion of the Commission, the fact that the Commission must be called upon to act, combined with the two-month time limit, makes this option unlikely for any practical purposes. As a consequence, the duty of cooperation is slightly lopsided: reciprocal between Member States and EU Institutions in theory, but largely applicable and enforceable towards the Member States in practice.

(v) The latest iteration: stretching the timeline and a duty to remain silent

In the *Inland Waterway* case against Germany, the Court stated that the adoption of a decision authorizing the Commission to negotiate a multilateral agreement marks the start of a concerted EU action triggering the duty of cooperation. However, in a much earlier case of the 1980s the

---

[18] Case C-45/07 *IMO judgment* [2009] ECR I-701, para 26.
[19] *Ibid.*, para 26.
[20] *Ibid.*, paras 24–25.

Court had already said that 'special duties of action and abstention [are imposed on Member States] from the moment the Commission has submitted to the Council a proposal, even if that has not yet been adopted by the Council, since it represents the point of departure for concerted Community action'.[21] In the 2010 judgment in *Commission* v. *Sweden* of April 2010, the court builds on that élan to trigger the duty of cooperation at an earlier stage. However, the exact beginning of the policy timeline becomes more difficult to establish.

The case concerns the exercise of shared environmental competences in the context of a mixed multilateral environmental Convention and its Protocol. Sweden had submitted a hazardous POP, with the case itself named after perfluorooctane sulfonates (*PFOS*) to the international conference for addition to the Convention. The Commission argued that Sweden was precluded from acting given that an EU regulatory framework existed on the matter, although the specific substance submitted by the Member State was not included in the relevant EU legislation.[22] AG Maduro quickly accepted that the EU did not possess exclusive competences, thus accepting that in principle Sweden could indeed propose to add harmful substances to the international convention. However, he elaborated meticulously on the fashion in which Sweden should have exercised its shared competence.

Opinion of AG Maduro delivered on 1 October 2009 on Case C–246/07 *Commission* v. *Sweden (PFOS)* [2010] ECR I-3317

46. The implications of the duty of loyal cooperation do not end with the analysis of whether it was possible for Sweden to exercise its competence; the manner in which it did so is equally, if not more, important. . . .

49. The implications of the duty of loyal cooperation are therefore twofold: first, that Member States cooperate with the Community decision-making process; and, second, that they refrain from taking individual action, at least for a reasonable period of time, until a conclusion to that process has been reached.

50. Sweden seems to have successfully discharged the first part of that duty: it sought to achieve a common proposal on adding PFOs to the Convention. However, Sweden's later threats to act individually could be perceived as intended to disproportionately influence the Community decision-making process and therefore to interfere with the integrity of the Community's political process.

51. Furthermore, Sweden failed to discharge the second part of that duty in its entirety. If a Community decision had been reached not to add PFOs to the Convention, it would have been free to act individually. However, a careful examination of the Community decision-making process reveals that no conclusion had been reached by the time Sweden acted. Therefore, Sweden should have refrained from acting.

52. At the time of Sweden's proposal, an agreement had been reached in the Council's 'international environment group' that a common proposal would be made to add substances to the Convention. Although an agreement was still to be reached on whether those substances would include PFOs, previous Council conclusions had established a preference for substances already included in the Protocol.

53. Not only had Sweden already proposed that PFOs be added to the Protocol, but there was also an agreement in the Council's 'international environment group' to submit such a proposal under the Protocol

---

[21] Case 804/79 *Commission* v. *United Kingdom* [1981] ECR I-1045, para 28.

[22] Opinion of AG Maduro delivered on 1 October 2009 on case C-246/07 *Commission* v. *Sweden (PFOS)* [2010] ECR I-3317, paras 25–26.

(which indeed later resulted in a Council decision). With the addition of PFOs to the Protocol imminent, Sweden cannot assert in good faith that a decision not to propose PFOs to the Convention had been taken.

54. The fact that the Council decision which followed Sweden's proposal did not include PFOs is irrelevant. Sweden's proposal made a Community proposal superfluous. In any event, Sweden should have forborne from acting individually precisely until a decision of that sort was taken, so as to respect the integrity of the Community decision-making process and not to interfere with its internal balance of power.

55. Sweden argues that, had it not acted promptly, it would not have been possible to submit the proposal for the addition of PFOs to the Convention to an impending conference of the parties, which would have delayed matters for at least one more year. However, abiding by the duty of loyal cooperation may involve the sacrifice of a Member State's interests.

56. The Community decision-making process is slow, and Member States must acknowledge that results will not be achieved as promptly as when they act individually. If, however, they were allowed to bypass this process whenever it suited them, Community decision-making would serve no purpose. Furthermore, I am of the opinion that a degree of prudence should be exercised with regard to Member States using their external competences to interfere with the internal balance of power of the Community decision-making process.

Regardless of the reading of the facts in this case, the arguments set out by the AG have important implications. The case concerns an area of shared competence, which specifically with regard to the aforementioned POP had not yet been exercised by the Union. Therefore: if indeed a Member State is to await the slow EU decision-making process, does this not severely constrain the exercise of a Member State's retained competence? Not only does this blur the separation between shared and exclusive competences, but it also significantly changes the nature of the obligations imposed during the initial phase of the policy timeline because it comes dangerously close to an obligation of total abstention, an obligation of result rather than best efforts. A Member State would not be entitled to exercise its retained shared competence until there is a clear decision *not* to act on a common basis through the Union. Furthermore, the final sentence of the extract in the AG's opinion utilizes the duty of cooperation in such a fashion that it blurs the dividing line between existence of competence, and its exercise.

Before the Court, the Commission argued that the Council Working Party on International Environmental Issues had on 6 July 2005 reached agreement on a common position to wait for the inclusion of PFOS, until it had gone ahead to include it in the relevant internal legislation.[23] In other words, a formal decision is no longer required for the duty of cooperation to be triggered, e.g. to establish the beginning of the policy timeline of cooperation. Sweden and the intervening Member States argued that no such common position existed. They argued that at a meeting of that same Working Party on 8 September 2004, Sweden had indeed proposed that PFOS be included in the Convention, and explicitly raised the possibility that it would unilaterally present a proposal to that effect. Given that eleven months passed after that initial discussion, Sweden finally submitted its proposal to the Stockholm Convention. The Netherlands pointed out that the 'Commission could [not] legitimately expect Sweden, despite its repeated efforts, to wait for an

[23] C-246/07 *Commission* v. *Sweden (PFOS)* [2010] ECR I-3317, paras 51 and 52.

indefinite period for internal action on the part of the EC'.[24] Denmark and the UK emphasized that if such were the case, the duty of cooperation would be rendered into a principle relating to the allocation of competence, resulting in a de facto exclusive external competence.[25]

The decision of the Court starts by recalling the essential principles of the duty of cooperation: its general application across exclusive or shared competences,[26] and the relevant passages from Opinions 2/91 and 1/94 referred to earlier in this chapter. The reasoning of the Court then continues by recalling the fact that a decision authorizing the negotiation of an EU agreement by the Commission 'marks the start of a concerted Community action at international level and requires for that purpose, if not a duty of abstention on the part of the Member States, at the very least a duty of close cooperation between the latter and the Community institutions in order to facilitate the achievement of the Community tasks'.[27] From a legal technical perspective, the Court does the following two things in a subsequent paragraph: first, it transfers that statement made in relation to the negotiation of international agreements on inland waterways[28] to the context of EU–Member State cooperation in a mixed international setting. Second, it transforms the formal criterion – or marker if you will – of when the 'EU policy timeline' begins into a more substantive criterion:

C-246/07 *Commission* v. *Sweden (PFOS)* [2010] ECR I-3317

76. In the present case, it is settled ground that, at the time when the Kingdom of Sweden submitted the proposal for the listing of PFOS in Annex A to the Stockholm Convention on 14 July 2005, the Council had not adopted any formal decision as regards a proposal to list substances in that annex. However, the Court must examine whether, as the Commission maintains, there was at the time a Community strategy in that regard which was not to propose the listing of PFOS immediately in the context of that convention, inter alia for economic reasons.

77. In that regard, it does not appear to be indispensable that a common position take a specific form for it to exist and to be taken into consideration in an action for failure to fulfil the obligation of cooperation in good faith, provided that the content of that position can be established to the requisite legal standard (see, to that effect, *Commission* v *Council*, paragraph 49).[29]

Hence, the *Inland Waterway* cases had confirmed that the duty of cooperation was triggered from the moment the Council took a decision to open negotiations, a slightly formal yet easily discernible marker as to when the duty of cooperation is triggered. However, the Court now opts for a more open-ended criterion of a 'common strategy' which should be established to the requisite legal standard.[30] The problem with that criterion is that this new notion of common strategy is rather vague, as is the threshold to be established to the 'requisite legal standard'. This

---

[24] *Ibid.*, para 62.

[25] *Ibid.*, para 65

[26] *Ibid.*, para 71.

[27] *Ibid.*, para 75.

[28] C-266/03 *Commission* v. *Luxembourg* [2005] ECR I-4805, para 60 and C-433/03 *Commission* v. *Germany* [2005] ECR I-6985, para 66.

[29] This reference to FAO arguably does not support that point, as this paragraph describes the arrangement between the Commission and Council on the duty of cooperation.

[30] C-246/07 *Commission* v. *Sweden (PFOS)* [2010] ECR I-3317, para 77.

new approach of the Court is in itself not necessarily problematic, as it could simply mean that the duty of cooperation requires information and consultation when it seems that a common strategy is emerging. It is in line with EU membership that the Member States loyally engage in the decision-making process to which they signed up.[31] However, the problem arises from the subsequent paragraphs in the *PFOS* judgment where Sweden's exercise of its competence *tout court* violated the duty of cooperation, in spite of preceding discussions in Council preparatory bodies. We flesh out both elements in the following paragraphs.

From the *PFOS* judgment onwards, the duty of cooperation is activated at the moment when it is possible to establish 'concerted EU action to a requisite legal standard'.[32] From a practitioner's perspective, it would be highly useful were the Court to provide more guidance on when the criterion of 'concerted EU action' is fulfilled, and the *PFOS* judgment provides little in this regard. From the summary of the arguments it is clear that all intervening Member States argued that no point of concerted EU action had been reached. However, the Court maintains that the Council Working Party did reach a point of concerted EU action, even though this had not been recorded in the minutes. Namely, the CJEU argued that the Working Party had decided to postpone the inclusion of PFOS in the Convention because of its financial repercussions,[33] and because of the need to prioritize other harmful substances. The Court argues that a meeting held on 6 July 2005 is the turning point: 'although [the minutes of the Working Party meeting] do not expressly mention the economic considerations which were discussed, that fact is not disputed by the Kingdom of Sweden and is admitted inter alia by the Kingdom of the Netherlands'. In that paragraph it then refers to its earlier statement of facts in the judgment where it outlines the content of those minutes in greater detail. Notably, the CJEU states that 'the Presidency drew the attention of that group to the economic consequences of a proposal to include PFOS in the Stockholm convention . . . since that might result in a call for additional financial aid on the part of developing countries'.[34] In our submission, it is problematic that a discussion during a Council Working Party, which has not even been noted in the minutes of that meeting, constitutes 'the requisite legal standard' on the basis of which to establish a common position at Community level. Arguably it is rather the reverse: a discussion occurred at Community level, and no agreement could yet be attained on a common position to be adopted. As Cremona rightly points out, if a common position had indeed materialized, it should have been adopted in accordance with Article 218(9) TFEU, with commensurate duties of abstention for the Member States. In our policy timeline, these are legal effects associated with the end of the second phase, not the first. With Sweden having previously made its intention clear during a similar meeting during September 2004, its submission of PFOS to the Stockholm Convention should not constitute a violation of the duty of cooperation because the best efforts obligation seems to have been fulfilled. The *PFOS* judgment reverses the logic which distinguishes shared from exclusive competences, and Sweden could only have avoided a violation of Article 4(3) TEU if there was an indubitably clear decision within the Union institutions that there would not be concerted Union action. The AG said as much in his opinion: 'If a Community decision had been

---

[31] E. Neframi, 'The Duty of Loyalty: Rethinking its Scope through its Application in the Field of EU External Relations' (2010) 47 *Common Market Law Review* 323–359 at 323 (on the transformation of sovereign states to 'EU Member States').

[32] C-233/03 *Linea GIG* v. *Commission* [2003] ECR I-7911.

[33] C-246/07 *Commission* v. *Sweden (PFOS)* [2010] ECR I-3317, para 81.

[34] *Ibid.*, para 29.

reached not to add *PFOS* to the Convention, it would have been free to act individually.'[35] This is perilously close to the language of exclusive competences. The Court concluded that 'in unilaterally proposing the addition of PFOS ... Sweden dissociated itself from a concerted common strategy within the Council'.[36] This then constitutes de facto pre-emption, since permission at EU level is required to exercise a shared competence, by way of an absence of a common strategy established to a requisite legal standard.

What is the impact of this legal standard on the policy process in a mixed international context? The eight months before the unilateral submission of PFOS by Sweden constituted a political process preceding the formulation of a common strategy, the first phase of our policy timeline. The AG considered at this stage that 'threats to act individually could be perceived as intended to disproportionately influence the Community decision-making process and therefore to interfere with the integrity of the Community's political process'.[37] However, this 'threat' – though one should arguably not call it that – of a Member State using its retained competence is an inherent Member State tool for influencing the EU political decision-making and negotiation process. Certainly, the Member States are to exercise their competences in line with EU law, but disallowing Member States to ('threaten to') exercise their competence indeed amounts to a 'duty to remain silent',[38] rather than a *reciprocal* duty of loyal cooperation. In practice, the open-ended 'common strategy' criterion, combined with the duty to remain silent, creates a situation of de facto pre-emption.

4 THE BROADER PICTURE OF EU EXTERNAL RELATIONS LAW

With the *PFOS* case, the Court has transferred its case law on the duty of cooperation from the context of parallel negotiations by the EU and Member States on the same subject to that of cooperation in international mixed contexts. Given the specific situation at issue in PFOs, the case law of the Court of Justice at present will require further elaboration to be better attuned to the different phases of the policy timeline encompassing EU–Member State cooperation in a mixed international setting. While the CJEU constructs a strong duty of cooperation to ensure EU external policy coherence, its jurisprudence on this principle is still evolving: in Opinion 1/94 it refused to take into account difficulties associated with mixed contexts, and refused to engage the day-to-day practice of EU–Member State cooperation at the WTO, while recent case law uncovers a new willingness to do exactly that. Having taken that road, any future cases must now seek to work towards a more coherent framework of legal obligations stemming from the duty of cooperation, and should thus further recognize the complexity raised by mixed situations and be sensitive to specific contexts across the policy timeline. Often a clear line cannot be drawn between considering policy options and actual agreement on concerted action, and the duty of cooperation ought to retain its conceptualization as an enforceable obligation of best efforts which progressively strengthens as the policy process progresses. Only exceptionally, in

---

[35] Opinion of AG Maduro delivered on 1 October 2009 on case C-246/07 *Commission* v. *Sweden (PFOS)* [2010] ECR I-3317, para 52.

[36] *Ibid.*, para 91.

[37] Opinion of AG Maduro delivered on 1 October 2009 on case C-246/07 *Commission* v. *Sweden (PFOS)* [2010] ECR I-3317, para 50.

[38] J. Larik and A. Delgado Casteleiro, 'The Duty to Remain Silent: Limitless Loyalty in EU External Relations' (2011) 36 *European Law Review* 524–541.

the later, more mature phases of the policy timeline, should it imply abstention or silence on the part of the Member States. If not, and if such a vague term as 'concerted action with a due legal standard' remains connected to a duty to remain silent, then the net effect on effective and coherent EU external relations will be negative rather than positive. This is because the present legal state of affairs has the potential of extending the 'shadow of exclusivity through pre-emption' to 'the shadow of abstention through the duty of cooperation'. Where at times Member States wish to avoid the *ERTA* pre-emptive effect through occupying the field, the recent interpretative turn in the duty of cooperation may now be detrimental for the cooperative spirit in mixed settings. Indeed, the vague criterion on a common EU strategy combined with the de facto obligation of abstention may have the unwanted consequence that any hint of cooperation at EU level might now lead to de facto prohibiting the Member States from acting internationally, even in the absence of exclusive EU competence. Legal certainty requires that such a consequence should only flow from an explicit decision of the Council or collective decision of the Member States and the Commission, and not from a common strategy not even noted in the minutes of a Working Party meeting.

Joris Larik and Andres Delgado Casteleiro, 'The Duty to Remain Silent: Limitless Loyalty in EU External Relations' (2011) 36 *European Law Review* 524–541 at 540

... we conclude that contrary to earlier ambivalence, [the CJEU] now has revealed the wideness of the scope of the duty of co-operation in three directions. First, on the intra-EU level, whereas previously the duty seemed to be triggered from the moment a concerted Union position had been launched by a positive legal act (giving the Commission a mandate or at least an official Commission proposal), now, after these cases, it has become unclear until which point Member States would still be free to act. They must now be silent even before the Union has made up its own mind about whether and when it is going to speak. The concept of a Union position has been broadened by the Court so as to include situations in which the EU institutions have not reached a decision or choose not to discuss an issue like in *IMO*. One might even say that, according to the ECJ, indecisiveness constitutes a valid Union position or strategy.

Secondly, on the international level, merely submitting for consideration a non-legal proposal to a technical committee already constitutes setting in motion a procedure that compromises both the division of competences and the unity of international representation of the European Union. Even if the Member State's proposal pursues and respects Union interests (or admittedly what Member States consider to be the Union's interest), the fact that the Member State acted independently breaches the duty of co-operation, regardless of whether it has informed and consulted with the Union and regardless of whether the Union had a clear substantive position on the issue at the time of the proposal. Reticence on the international plane therefore seems to be inherent in the task of being a good "trustee of the Union interest".

Thirdly, the scope of the "duty to remain silent" seems to make the distinction between exclusive and shared competence virtually irrelevant. Simply because a Member State still is competent about a matter, it does not mean that it can speak up about it outside the European Union. As the recent case law shows, it seems that Member States need a kind of EU authorisation in order to exercise "their share" of shared competence. ...

Hence the duty of sincere co-operation in external relations manifests itself indeed rather often as a duty for the Member States to keep silent, unless told to speak by the EU institutions.

SOURCES AND FURTHER READING

Cremona, M., 'Defending the Community Interest: The Duties of Cooperation and Compliance', in M. Cremona and B. de Witte (eds.), *EU Foreign Relations Law: Constitutional Fundamentals* (Oxford: Hart Publishing, 2008), pp. 125–170.

Cremona, M., *Member States as Trustees of the Community Interest: Participating in International Agreements on Behalf of the European Community* (EUI Working Paper 2009/17).

Dashwood, A., 'The Limits of European Community Powers' (1996) 21 *European Law Review* 113–128.

Heliskoski, J., 'Adoption of Positions under Mixed Agreements', in C. Hillion and P. Koutrakos (eds.), *Mixed Agreements Revisited – The EU and its Member States in the World* (Oxford: Hart Publishing, 2010).

Hillion, C., 'Mixity and Coherence in EU External Relations: The Significance of the Duty of Cooperation', in C. Hillion and P. Koutrakos (eds.), *Mixed Agreements Revisited – The EU and its Member States in the World* (Oxford: Hart Publishing, 2010), pp. 87–115.

Hyett, S., 'The Duty of Co-operation: A Flexible Concept', in A. Dashwood and C. Hillion (eds.), *The General Law of EC External Relations* (London: Sweet and Maxwell, 2000).

Kuijper, P. J., 'Re-Reading External Relations Cases in the Field of Transport: The Function of Community Loyalty', in M. Bulterman *et al.* (eds.), *Views of European Law from the Mountain* (Alphen aan den Rijn: Wolters Kluwer Law & Business, 2009).

Larik, J. and Delgado Casteleiro, A., 'The Duty to Remain Silent: Limitless Loyalty in EU External Relations' (2011) 36 *European Law Review* 524–541.

Neframi, E., 'The Duty of Loyalty: Rethinking its Scope through its Application in the Field of EU External Relations' (2010) 47 *Common Market Law Review* 323–359.

Rosas, A., 'Mixed Union – Mixed Agreements', in M. Koskenniemi (ed.), *International Law Aspects of the European Union* (The Hague: Kluwer Law International, 1998), pp. 125–148.

Timmermans, C., 'Organising Joint Participation of E.C. and Member States', in A. Dashwood and C. Hillion (eds.), *The General Law of EC External Relations* (London: Sweet and Maxwell, 2000).

Van Vooren, B., *EU External Relations Law and the European Neighbourhood Policy: A Paradigm for Coherence* (Abingdon/New York: Routledge, 2012), pp. 116–125.

7

EU law and international law

1 CENTRAL ISSUES

- The EU is usually considered a special, or *sui generis*, organization (see Chapter 1). This special status does not only flow from the relationship with its Member States (which indeed differentiates it from other international organizations), but also from its position towards international law. In the early days in particular, the CJEU tended to underline this special position by referring to the 'autonomous' legal order that was created in which the relationship between the Member States was no longer primarily regulated by international law, but by EU law. Indeed, the states were first and foremost *Member* States.

- Yet, without international law, the EU would not exist. It is based on a treaty concluded within the framework of international treaty law. At the same time, and keeping in mind the rule of *pacta tertiis nec nocent nec prosunt*, third states are in principal not bound by the EU Treaty since to them it is an agreement between others.[1] This implies that in its external legal relations the EU will have to act under international law and will also have to respect its basic rules. Within the EU legal order, however, this may lead to conflicting norms, and over the years the Court has had quite a task in finding solutions for these conflicts.

- This leads to a number of questions that will be addressed in this chapter: what is the hierarchical position of international law within the EU legal order? What are the effects of international law (both written and unwritten) in the EU legal order? How did the ECJ solve conflicts between EU law and international law?

- The Union is not the sole international actor in Europe. Despite their EU membership, the Member States did not cease to be states. They continue to conclude international agreements, not only with third states, but also between themselves ('*inter se*'). The dynamic shift of external competences (see Chapter 3) frequently results in Member States facing diverging EU and international law obligations, which raises specific questions such as, what if a legitimate Member State has been competent to conclude investment treaties with third states up to a given date, and subsequently the competence in that area shifts from the Member States to the EU, either because of an EU Treaty modification or on the basis of a sudden exercise by the EU of

---

[1] This rule is laid down in Article 34 VCLT, adopted in Vienna, 22 May 1969: 'A treaty does not create either obligations or rights for a third State without its consent.'

an already existing competence? Obviously, third states are less interested in complex competence divisions within the EU, but Member States are confronted with a new situation. The question of the division of international competences and obligations therefore also returns in this chapter.

2 THE RELATIONSHIP BETWEEN EU LAW AND INTERNATIONAL LAW

(i) An autonomous EU legal order . . .?

(a) . . . or international law as an integral part of the EU legal order?

A striking tension underlies the many judicial cases on the effects of international law in the EU legal order: the EU's struggle to find solutions between autonomy and dependence. To make certain key principles of EU law work (including primacy and direct effect), the EU needs to stress its autonomous relation vis-à-vis international law. At the same time, as an international actor, there is a need for the EU to live up to the rules that make up the international legal order and that are binding on it.

Both the ECJ and the General Court (GC) felt obliged to stress the EU's autonomous legal order in the *Kadi* cases on the question of whether the EU would be bound by UN Security Council Resolutions: 'the institutions . . . had no *autonomous* discretion [in relation to UNSC Resolutions]' (Case T-315/01) and 'the validity of any Community measure . . . must be considered to be the expression . . . of a constitutional guarantee stemming from the EC Treaty as an *autonomous* legal system' (Case C-402/05P). The notion of 'autonomy' was even a central element in the discussion between the CJEU and the GC in the *Kadi* saga when the latter argued: 'the Court of Justice thus seems to have regarded the constitutional framework created by the EC Treaty as a wholly *autonomous* legal order, not subject to the higher rules of international law' (Case T-85/09).[2]

'*A wholly autonomous legal order, not subject to the higher rules of international law.*' Phrases like these meant to indicate that the EU as such is not automatically bound by international law. They seem to suggest the dualism that many Member States are familiar with: international law can only be part of a domestic legal order once it has been transformed to or incorporated into that legal order. Yet, the legal order of the Union is widely identified as 'monist' in its relation to public international law (see below). Indeed, in practice the EU does not seem to have a problem with allowing binding international norms to become part of its legal order. One observer even noted the Union's 'good international citizenship'.[3]

Article 216(2) TFEU

Agreements concluded by the Union are binding upon the institutions of the Union and on its Member States.

From the outset the novel and special nature of the EU (then EEC) was stressed by the Court. In *Van Gend & Loos* the Court argued that 'the Community constitutes *a new legal order of*

---

[2] Emphasis added in all sentences.
[3] T. Dunne, 'Good Citizen Europe' (2008) 84 *International Affairs* 13.

international law for the benefit of which the states have limited their sovereign rights'.[4] In *Costa v. ENEL* the Court further stressed the 'special' nature of the EU: 'By contrast with *ordinary* international treaties, the EEC Treaty has created its own legal system.'[5] It can now been concluded that the phrase 'a new legal order *of international law*' is not without importance:

B. de Witte, 'Direct Effect, Primacy and the Nature of the Legal Order', in P. Craig and G. de Búrca (eds.), *The Evolution of EU Law*, 2nd edition (Oxford: Oxford University Press, 2011), pp. 323–362

The invention in the 1960s, by the European Court of Justice, of the principles of direct effect and primacy was accompanied by sweeping statements about the special nature of the European Community treaties as compared with other international agreements. Some of those arguments may have been overstated, and were needed more to convince the national judicial interlocutors of the Court than to justify the formulation of the principles themselves. But the sweeping discourse used by the European Court in those judgments of the 1960s has left its mark on doctrinal writing and, indeed, on the way national courts have come to view EU law.

The argument linking primacy/direct effect and the nature of EU law has gradually acquired an element of circularity. At first, primacy and direct effect were to be recognized *because* the EC Treaty was unlike other international treaties, a theory which proved to be particularly successful in those countries where the domestic status of (other) international treaties was modest, like Italy, Germany, the UK and Ireland, and the Scandinavian countries. But now that these principles have been accepted everywhere, at least for most practical purposes, the direction of the argument is often reversed: EU law is now often presented as being unique because it is endowed with direct effect and primacy.

In the early case law the need to distinguish EU law from international law was above all triggered by the existence and development of the two notions that are so characteristic for EU law (and generally absent in international law): primacy and direct effect. Although over time the EU adopted a more relaxed attitude towards international law (see below), also in more recent case law the Court frequently used the term 'autonomy' to indicate the need for the Union to live up to its own rules (and perhaps to preserve its own prerogatives). Thus, the 'preservation of the autonomy of the Community legal order' formed a crucial element in Opinion 1/00 on the possible establishment of a European Common Aviation Area. Similar references could already be found in Opinion 1/76 (on the possible establishment of a European laying-up fund for inland waterway vessels) and Opinion 1/91 (on the creation of the EEA). The safeguarding of the EU's judicial system was at stake when in *Mox Plant* (Case C-459/03) the Court held that 'an international agreement cannot affect . . . the autonomy of the Community legal system'.

Indeed, after an initial period in which the Court's emphasis was laid on a strengthening of the autonomous nature of the Community, beginning in the early 1970s, the Court indicated that this does not imply that international treaties are not to be considered a part of EU law.

---

[4] Case 26/62 *Van Gend en Loos* v. *Nederlandse Administratie der Belastingen* [1963] ECR 1. Emphasis added.
[5] Case 6/64 *Costa* v. *ENEL* [1964] ECR 585. Emphasis added.

> ### Case 181/73 *Haegeman* v. *Belgian State* [1974] ECR 449
>
> 3. The Athens Agreement was concluded by the Council under Articles 228 and 238 of the Treaty as appears from the terms of the Decision dated 25 September 1961.
> 4. This Agreement is therefore, in so far as concerns the Community, an Act of one of the Institutions of the Community within the meaning of subparagraph (b) of the first paragraph of Article 177.
> 5. The provisions of the Agreement, from the coming into force thereof, form an integral part of Community law.
> 6. Within the framework of this law, the Court accordingly has jurisdiction to give preliminary rulings concerning the interpretation of this Agreement.

Indeed: international agreements concluded by the EU form 'an integral part of Union law'. As we will see below, this status of international law is not restricted to international agreements (including mixed agreements), but also holds true for customary law,[6] and secondary international law deriving from international agreements such as Association Council decisions.[7]

Accepting that international law forms part of the EU legal order raises the question of where to place it in the EU's hierarchy of norms. The Court frequently dealt with this question and concluded that international law ranks between primary and secondary law.[8] This leads to the following hierarchy:

1. The EU Treaties
2. International law binding upon the EU
3. Decisions adopted by the EU.

Obviously, this hierarchy could work internally, but it raises problems in relation to obligations both the Member States and the EU may have vis-à-vis third states. In the *Kadi* case the CJEU was challenged to reconcile UN Security Council obligations with the protection of fundamental rights as part of the general principles of law to be ensured by the Court. In this case the Court held that the obligations imposed by an international agreement (in this case the UN Charter) could not have the effect of prejudicing the constitutional principles of the EU Treaty. Thus it followed the hierarchy scheme presented above.

(b) The *Kadi* case: hierarchy settled?

On 3 September 2008 the CJEU delivered its first judgment in the so-called *Kadi* case.[9] This judgment may be seen as having an impact on the traditional monist approach of the EC towards international law and hence on the way we look at hierarchy in the international legal order. With regard to the question of whether or not UN Security Council Resolutions should enjoy immunity from jurisdiction as to their lawfulness in the Community legal order, the Court held the following.

---

[6] Case C-162/96 *Racke GmbH & Co.* v. *Hauptzollamt Mainz* [1998] ECR I-3655, *supra* note 19, para 45; CFI, Case T-115/94 *Opel Austria GmbH* v. *Council* [1997] ECR II-39; as well as Case C-84/95 *Bosphorus Hava Yollari Turizm ve Ticaret AS* v. *Minister for Transport, Energy and Communications and Others* [1996] ECR I-3953.

[7] See for instance: ECJ, Case C-192/89 *Sevince* v. *Staatssecretaris van Justitie* [1990] ECR I-3461.

[8] See for instance: ECJ, Case C-179/97 *Spain* v. *Commission* [1999] ECR I-1251; ECJ, Case C-162/96 *Racke GmbH & Co.* v. *Hauptzollamt Mainz* [1998] ECR I-3655, para 45.

[9] A second ECJ judgment is expected in Autumn 2013.

Case T-306/01 *Yusuf and Al Barakaat International Foundation* v. *Council and Commission* [2005] ECR II-3533 (see also Case T-315/01 *Kadi* v. *Council and Commission* [2005] ECR II-3649), 21 September 2005

327. ... that the Community judicature must ... ensure the review, in principle the full review, of the lawfulness of all Community acts in the light of the fundamental rights forming an integral part of the general principles of Community law, including review of Community measures which, like the contested regulation, are designed to give effect to the resolutions adopted by the Security Council under Chapter VII of the Charter of the United Nations.

In this case the acts of the EU and the EC[10] were to be seen as a direct implementation of Security Council Resolution 1267 (1999).[11] Mr Kadi was one of the persons on the UN list of individuals and entities associated with Usama bin Laden or the Al-Qaeda network and hence appeared on the list of the EU as well.

In 2001 Yassin Abdullah Kadi, together with Ahmed Yusuf and the Al Barakaat Foundation filed an action with the GC (then the Court of First Instance of the European Communities (CFI)), claiming that the Court should annul the implementing EC and EU acts which brought them within the scope of the sanctions.[12] In these cases Yusuf (and in similar wordings as Kadi) had argued the following:

Case T-306/01 *Yusuf and Al Barakaat International Foundation* v. *Council and Commission* [2005] ECR II-3533 (see also Case T-315/01 *Kadi* v. *Council and Commission* [2005] ECR II-3649), 21 September 2005

190. The applicants, referring both to Article 6(2) of the Treaty on European Union and to the Court's case-law (Case 11/70 Internationale Handelsgesellschaft and Case 4/73 Nold v Commission, paragraph 13), maintain that the contested regulation infringes their fundamental rights, in particular their right to the use of their property and the right to a fair hearing, as guaranteed by Article 6 of the European Convention for the Protection of Human Rights and Fundamental Freedoms (ECHR), inasmuch as that regulation imposes on them heavy sanctions, both civil and criminal, although they had not first been heard or given the opportunity to defend themselves, nor had that act been subjected to any judicial review whatsoever.

[10] Respectively EU Common Position 2002/402/CFSP concerning restrictive measures against Usama bin Laden, members of the Al-Qaeda organization and the Taliban and other individuals, groups, undertakings and entities associated with them, OJ 2002 No. L139/4; and Regulation 881/2002/EC imposing certain specific restrictive measurements directed against certain persons and entities associated with Usama bin Laden, the Al-Qaeda network and the Taliban, OJ 2002 No. L139/9.

[11] Security Council Resolution 1267 (1999) provides that all the states must, in particular, 'freeze funds and other financial resources, including funds derived or generated from property owned or controlled directly or indirectly by the Taliban, or by any undertaking owned or controlled by the Taliban, as designated by the Committee established by paragraph 6 below, and ensure that neither they nor any other funds or financial resources so designated are made available, by their nationals or by any persons within their territory, to or for the benefit of the Taliban or any undertaking owned or controlled, directly or indirectly, by the Taliban, except as may be authorised by the Committee on a case-by-case basis on the grounds of humanitarian need' (para 4b).

[12] CFI, Cases T-306/01 *Yusuf and Al Barakaat International Foundation* v. *Council and Commission* [2005] ECR II-3533 and T-315/01, *Kadi* v. *Council and Commission* [2005] ECR II-3649.

191. With more particular regard to the alleged breach of the right to a fair hearing, the applicants stress that they were not told why the sanctions were imposed on them, that the evidence and facts relied on against them were not communicated to them and that they had no opportunity to explain themselves. The only reason for their names being entered in the list in Annex I to the contested regulation is the fact that they were entered in the list drawn up by the Sanctions Committee on the basis of information provided by the States and international or regional organisations. Neither the Council nor the Commission examined the reasons for which that committee included the applicants in that list. The source of the information received by that committee is especially obscure and the reasons why certain individuals have been included in the list, without first being heard, are not mentioned. The entire procedure leading to the addition of the applicants to the list in Annex I to the contested regulation is thus stamped with the seal of secrecy. Such infringements of their rights cannot be remedied after the event.

While the GC in its judgment in 2005 agreed with the applicants that in the current anti-terrorism cases there is 'no judicial remedy available',[13] it concluded the following:

Case T–306/01 *Yusuf and Al Barakaat International Foundation* v. *Council and Commission* [2005] ECR II-3533

276. It must therefore be considered that the resolutions of the Security Council at issue fall, in principle, outside the ambit of the Court's judicial review and that the Court has no authority to call in question, even indirectly, their lawfulness in the light of Community law. On the contrary, the Court is bound, so far as possible, to interpret and apply that law in a manner compatible with the obligations of the Member States under the Charter of the United Nations.

277. None the less, the Court is empowered to check, indirectly, the lawfulness of the resolutions of the Security Council in question with regard to jus cogens, understood as a body of higher rules of public international law binding on all subjects of international law, including the bodies of the United Nations, and from which no derogation is possible.

278. In this connection, it must be noted that the Vienna Convention on the Law of Treaties, which consolidates the customary international law and Article 5 of which provides that it is to apply 'to any treaty which is the constituent instrument of an international organisation and to any treaty adopted within an international organisation', provides in Article 53 for a treaty to be void if it conflicts with a peremptory norm of general international law (jus cogens), defined as 'a norm accepted and recognised by the international community of States as a whole as a norm from which no derogation is permitted and which can be modified only by a subsequent norm of general international law having the same character'. Similarly, Article 64 of the Vienna Convention provides that: 'If a new peremptory norm of general international law emerges, any existing treaty which is in conflict with that norm becomes void and terminates.'

279. Furthermore, the Charter of the United Nations itself presupposes the existence of mandatory principles of international law, in particular, the protection of the fundamental rights of the human person. In the preamble to the Charter, the peoples of the United Nations declared themselves determined to 'reaffirm

---

[13] Case T-306/01 *Yusuf and Al Barakaat International Foundation* v. *Council and Commission* [2005] ECR II-3533 (see also Case T-315/01, *Kadi* v. *Council and Commission* [2005] ECR II-3649), 21 September 2005, para 340.

faith in fundamental human rights, in the dignity and worth of the human person'. In addition, it is apparent from Chapter I of the Charter, headed 'Purposes and Principles', that one of the purposes of the United Nations is to encourage respect for human rights and for fundamental freedoms.

280. Those principles are binding on the Members of the United Nations as well as on its bodies. Thus, under Article 24(2) of the Charter of the United Nations, the Security Council, in discharging its duties under its primary responsibility for the maintenance of international peace and security, is to act 'in accordance with the Purposes and Principles of the United Nations'. The Security Council's powers of sanction in the exercise of that responsibility must therefore be wielded in compliance with international law, particularly with the purposes and principles of the United Nations.

281. International law thus permits the inference that there exists one limit to the principle that resolutions of the Security Council have binding effect: namely, that they must observe the fundamental peremptory provisions of jus cogens. If they fail to do so, however improbable that may be, they would bind neither the Member States of the United Nations nor, in consequence, the Community.

282. The indirect judicial review carried out by the Court in connection with an action for annulment of a Community act adopted, where no discretion whatsoever may be exercised, with a view to putting into effect a resolution of the Security Council may therefore, in some circumstances, extend to determining whether the superior rules of international law falling within the ambit of jus cogens have been observed, in particular, the mandatory provisions concerning the universal protection of human rights, from which neither the Member States nor the bodies of the United Nations may derogate because they constitute 'intransgressible principles of international customary law' (Advisory Opinion of the International Court of Justice of 8 July 1996, The Legality of the Threat or Use of Nuclear Weapons, Reports 1996, p. 226, paragraph 79; see also, to that effect, Advocate General Jacobs's Opinion in Bosphorus, paragraph 239 above, paragraph 65).

While many lawyers pointed to a 'legal protection deficit' which thus became apparent (when neither the EU Courts nor the domestic courts would be able to review the UN measures, where could plaintiffs go?), others were more worried about the part of the judgment in which the Court claimed to be competent to check the lawfulness of the Resolutions of the Security Council with regard to *jus cogens*. Although the Court came to the conclusion that none of the allegedly infringed rights formed part of *jus cogens*, the very idea of a regional Court checking the validity of UN Security Council Resolutions – while potentially widening the scope of *jus cogens* obligations – proved to be a source for heated academic debates.

In that respect, the appeals judgment before the Court of Justice in the *Kadi* case[14] could be seen as another step in this debate as it essentially reversed several findings of the GC. Most importantly, the ECJ found that the GC (then the CFI) had erred in law when it held that a regulation designed to give effect to UN Security Council Resolutions must enjoy immunity from jurisdiction as to its internal lawfulness save with regard to its compatibility with the norms of *jus cogens*. This case has become essential to understanding the relationship between EU law and international law. The Court argued as follows:

[14] Joined Cases C-402/05 P & C-415/05 P *Kadi and Al Barakaat International Foundation* v. *Council* [2008] ECR I-6351. The cases have received abundant attention in academic literature. See for instance G. de Búrca, 'The European Court of Justice and the International Legal Order after *Kadi*' (2010) 51 *Harvard International Law Journal* 1–49. Cf. also the special 'Forum' on the *Kadi* judgment, (2008) *International Organizations Law Review*.

Joined cases C-402/05 P & C-415/05 *P Kadi and Al Barakaat International Foundation* v. *Council* [2008] ECR I-6351

283. In addition, according to settled case-law, fundamental rights form an integral part of the general principles of law whose observance the Court ensures. For that purpose, the Court draws inspiration from the constitutional traditions common to the Member States and from the guidelines supplied by international instruments for the protection of human rights on which the Member States have collaborated or to which they are signatories. In that regard, the ECHR has special significance (see, inter alia, Case C-305/05 Ordre des barreaux francophones et germanophone and Others, paragraph 29 and case-law cited).

284. It is also clear from the case-law that respect for human rights is a condition of the lawfulness of Community acts (Opinion 2/94, paragraph 34) and that measures incompatible with respect for human rights are not acceptable in the Community (Case C-112/00 Schmidberger, paragraph 73).

285. It follows from all those considerations that the obligations imposed by an international agreement cannot have the effect of prejudicing the constitutional principles of the EC Treaty, which include the principle that all Community acts must respect fundamental rights, that respect constituting a condition of their lawfulness which it is for the Court to review in the framework of the complete system of legal remedies established by the Treaty.

286. In this regard it must be emphasised that, in circumstances such as those of these cases, the review of lawfulness thus to be ensured by the Community judicature applies to the Community act intended to give effect to the international agreement at issue, and not to the latter as such.

To arrive at this conclusion without having to challenge the validity of norms flowing from UN Security Council Resolutions, the Court pointed to the fact that the UN Charter leaves the members 'the free choice among the various possible models for transposition of those resolutions into their domestic legal order'.[15] This would allow for judicial review of the 'internal lawfulness' of the EU and EC acts, keeping in mind that fundamental rights form an integral part of the general principles of law, the observance of which is to be ensured by the Court.

Although the Court's focus is on the *implementation* of the Security Council Resolutions by the Union and the Community, rather than on the validity of the international norms as such, the consequence of this exercise could very well be that any implementation of a Security Council Resolution could entail the violation of fundamental EU rights. In this concrete case the Court annulled the contested acts (while maintaining the legal effects for three months).[16] Rather than taking the formal hierarchical relationship between UN law and EU law as the basis for establishing the immunity from jurisdiction of Security Council Resolutions (as was done by

---

[15] C-402/05 P & C-415/05 *P Kadi and Al Barakaat International Foundation* v. *Council* [2008] ECR I-6351, para 298.

[16] See para 375: 'Having regard to those considerations, the effects of the contested regulation, insofar as it includes the names of the appellants in the list forming Annex I thereto, must, by virtue of Article 231 EC, be maintained for a brief period to be fixed in such a way as to allow the Council to remedy the infringements found, but which also takes due account of the considerable impact of the restrictive measures concerned on the appellants' rights and freedoms.' The only action taken was not by the Council itself, but by the Commission, which on 28 November 2008 (five days before the deadline) adopted Regulation 1190/2008/EC (OJ 2008 No. L322/25, published 2 December 2008, one day before the deadline). In this decision the Commission claims that it has communicated the narrative summaries of reasons provided by the UN Al-Qaida and Taliban Sanctions Committee, to Mr Kadi and to Al Barakaat International Foundation, and given them the opportunity to comment on these grounds. The comments received from Mr Kadi and Al Barakaat formed a reason for the Commission to conclude on a justified listing.

the CFI), the Court chose to look at this hierarchy in more substantive terms. Security Council Resolutions remain 'untouchable', but the acts by which the EU implements the Resolutions are not, and are subject to the fundamental rights and principles that form the basis of the Union legal order. This certainly offered the Court a smart way out of the dilemma, but in the virtual absence of judicial remedies at the UN level, the consequence can (and perhaps should) be that the EU may not be able to fully implement Security Council Resolutions that are in conflict with fundamental human rights obligations flowing not only from the EU legal order and the European Convention for the Protection of Human Rights and Fundamental Freedoms, but also from the UN Charter itself.

G. de Búrca, *The European Court of Justice and the International Legal Order after Kadi* (Jean Monnet Working Paper 01/09)

Late in 2008 the European Court of Justice delivered what is arguably its most important judgment to date on the subject of the relationship between the European Community and the international legal order. The case was a high-profile one involving a challenge by an individual to the EC's implementation of a UN Security Council Resolution which had identified him as being involved with terrorism and had mandated that his assets be frozen. The Court of Justice delivered a powerful judgment annulling the relevant implementing measures, and declaring that they violated fundamental rights protected by the EC legal order. The judgment has been hailed by human rights activists, it has delighted many of those concerned about Security Council accountability, and it has reassured EU scholars and actors interested in strengthening the autonomy of the EU legal order. This article argues however that despite the welcome it has received on these grounds, the nature and reasoning of the judgment should give serious pause for thought on other grounds. In particular, the judgment represents a significant departure from the conventional presentation and widespread understanding of the EU as an actor which maintains a distinctive commitment to international law and institutions.

In adopting a sharply dualist tone in its approach to the international legal order, and to the relationship between EC law and international law, the ECJ identifies itself in certain striking ways with the reasoning and approach of the US Supreme Court in recent cases such as *Medellin* [*Medellin* v. *Texas* 552 U.S. (2008)], which assert the separateness of international law from the domestic constitutional order and the absence of any domestic judicial role in shaping the relationship between the two.

And although the two cases are quite different in many respects, it is precisely the similarity of the ECJ's approach in *Kadi* to the larger question of the relationship between international law and the 'domestic' legal order to that of the Supreme Court in *Medellin* and the way the ECJ's expression of that relationship abandons the reasoning and tone of some of its leading earlier judgments on the position of international law, which is its most striking feature. Despite the praise which *Kadi* has drawn from various quarters, it sits uncomfortably with the traditional self-presentation of the EU as a virtuous international actor in contradistinction to the exceptionalism of the US, as well as with the broader political ambition of the EU to carve out a distinctive international role for itself as a 'normative power' committed to effective multilateralism under international law. Finally the fact that a major judgment about the role, relationship and authority of international law which chooses to express important parts of its reasoning in rather chauvinist and parochial tones was delivered not by a powerful nation-state but by an international organization which is itself a creature of international law, renders it all the more remarkable to the outside world.

The *Kadi* case is just one of a series of recent instances involving UN-authorized activity which caused significant harm to individuals and led them to bring human rights-based challenges before Europe's main regional courts. The legal and jurisprudential, not to mention the human, dilemmas which the cases reveal are merely instances of a more general phenomenon, namely the increasing complexity and density of the international political and legal environment, and the growing multiplicity of governance regimes with the capacity to affect human welfare in significant ways. At one level, therefore, the *Kadi* case is simply another instance of an increasingly common occurrence, namely a specific conflict between the norms of different regimes or sub-systems within the global legal arena. But in reality it is a particularly compelling instance in so far as the conflict involves some of the most fundamental norms of the modern international law system, namely Article 103 of the UN Charter, peremptory or jus cogens norms, and Chapter VII Resolutions of the Security Council. The range of traditional international law rules which aim at systemic coherence such as the lex specialis rule or the later-in-time rule provided no easy answers in this case. Instead the case presented a direct confrontation between the UN system of international security and peace with its aspirations to general applicability and universal normative force, and the EU system situated somewhere between an international organization and a constitutional polity, in the context of an individual's claim that a significant violation of his rights had been committed in the interplay between the two. The broader picture of this article therefore concerns the upward drift of international authority and its decoupling from national or regional mechanisms of accountability and control.

But its specific focus is the response of Europe's main regional courts, and in particular that of the European Court of Justice, to the question of the relationship between the EC legal order and the international legal order. Some may view the *Kadi* judgment mainly as a reaction to the particular context of the case, namely the widespread concern about the UN Security Council's regime of targeted sanctions and about the strong influence exercised by the United States in the process of listing and de-listing suspects. A close scrutiny of the judgment however suggests that its significance goes well beyond the context of UN smart sanctions. On the contrary, the broad language, carefully-chosen reasoning, and uncompromising approach of this eagerly awaited judgment by the plenary Court suggests that the ECJ seized this high-profile moment to send out a strong and clear message about the relationship of EC law to international law, and about the autonomy of the European legal order. . . .

Much of the political and legal discourse of the EU sets out to distinguish the EU and its international activity from the kind of self-interested selectivity and ad hoc exceptionalism of which the United States is generally accused. Instead . . . the EU has generally asserted an approach to international relations – in political terms a multilateralist approach and in juridical terms a constitutionalist approach – which emphasizes Europe's distinctive fidelity to international law and institutions. The approach of the ECJ in *Kadi* however sits uncomfortably with this conventional understanding and with official discourse, and departs from a previously dominant stream of the Court's case law on the EC's relationship with international law. This line of case-law had emphasized the EC's respect for international law and the 'integral' place of international agreements as part of the EC legal order. The *Kadi* judgment however takes its place instead within a different strand of the Court's jurisprudence on the legal effect of the GATT/World Trade Organization agreements. This strand of case law had previously been considered as an outlier – as an exceptional line of case law and, for many, a problematic line – which was explicable by reference to the specific political and economic circumstances of the multilateral trade agreements. Situating *Kadi* alongside this case-law on the legal effect of WTO agreements, however, reveals a court which increasingly adopts . . . a robustly pluralist approach to international law and governance, emphasizing the separateness, autonomy, and constitutional priority of the EC legal order over international law.

(ii) A monist or dualist relationship?

(a) Terminology

The terms 'monism' and 'dualism' are generally used to characterize the relationship between domestic legal orders and international law. Although in their extreme form neither notion can be found in practice, a monist system views international law as being part of the national legal order, whereas in a dualist system international rules need to be 'translated' to national law before being able to be recognized as valid law. Although labelling the relationship between international and European law in terms of 'monism' may be helpful to indicate that international law forms part of the EU legal order from the moment an international norm is (lawfully) concluded, it has been pointed out that it may raise questions as well. The above findings – and the *Kadi* case in particular – reveal the tension between the principles of 'autonomy' and 'reception' that together form the cornerstones of the relation between European and international law. At the same time the analysis points to the limited explanatory power offered by an application of the notions of monism and dualism. If we wish to understand what it means for international law to form an integral part of Union law – in terms of validity, direct effect and supremacy (see below) – we may need more sophisticated theoretical tools. In times where the relationship between international law and Union law seems to be under construction, it is worthwhile to know where we stand.

A number of issues must be addressed in this respect.

First, the complexity of the Union's legal order is related to the role of the Member States in this order. When the fact that international agreements are an 'integral part' of Community law is linked to the notion of primacy, the effects of international agreements reach the internal law of (both monist and dualist) Member States and would lead to their supremacy over this national law. This has led one observer to point to European law as a 'door opener' for international law, '[i]n that event, the traditional approaches of the Member States for explaining the relationship between municipal law and public international law do not matter anymore'.[17] At the same time the status as an 'integral part' of Union law does not settle the hierarchical position of international law in relation to other sources of Union law.

Second, 'monism' and 'dualism' are often used to describe the relationship between legal orders in far too general terms. Claims based on monism often confuse the 'validity' of norms with their 'direct applicability', 'direct effect' or even their 'supremacy'. At least at a theoretical level, it may still be helpful to differentiate between the different notions. Monism and dualism would relate formally only to the status of international norms within the European or domestic legal orders. In that sense, monism/dualism relates to the 'validity' (or existence) of international norms in those orders. In monist systems, international norms enjoy automatic validity, whereas in dualist systems, they need to be transferred into domestic law in order to become valid. The fact that international agreements are an 'integral part' of EU law seems to relate to this idea. Hence, the existence of international norms should not be equated with the question of whether they can be invoked by individuals before a court of law, let alone with the question of whether they would be of a hierarchically higher order in case of a conflict with a domestic or European norm.

---

[17] F. C. Mayer, 'European Law as a Door Opener for Public International Law?', in J. M. Thouvenin and C. Tomuschat (eds.), *Droit International et Diversité des Cultures Juridiques – International Law and Diversity of Legal Cultures* (Paris: Pédone, 2008), pp. 241–255 at 253.

Article 216(2) TFEU provides that international agreements are 'binding', but it does not offer a priority rule to solve a conflict with other binding (Union) norms. In fact, the Court held that 'the primacy of international agreements concluded by the Community over provisions of secondary Community legislation means that such provisions must, *so far as possible*, be interpreted in an manner that is consistent with those arguments'.[18] This shows that the validity (existence within the EU legal order) of international norms does not automatically lead to the supremacy of those norms.

Third, as will also be addressed below, this validity does not imply a direct effect, in the sense that the international norms (as part of the EU legal order) may be invoked to challenge existing, conflicting Union law. The classic example is formed by WTO law, in which area the Court denied direct effect as a possibility of individuals to refer to WTO law, both before national courts and the court of the EU (see also below and Chapter 9 on CCP).

The well-analysed cases of *Yusuf* and *Kadi* may have given some answers, but at the same time, they left many fundamental theoretical questions unanswered. In addition, the judgments even raised new questions in relation to the monist nature of the Union legal order. The effects of international agreements and international decisions were all quite clearly confirmed by the GC when it argued that 'the Court is bound, so far as possible, to interpret and apply [Community] law in a manner compatible with the obligations of the Member States under the Charter of the United Nations'.[19] The notion of the monism (or perhaps even unity) of EU and international law was even more strengthened by the claim of the GC that it was 'empowered to check, indirectly, the lawfulness of the resolutions of the Security Council in question with regard to *jus cogens*, understood as a body of higher rules of public international law binding on all subjects of international law, including the bodies of the United Nations, and from which no derogation is possible'.[20] The idea must have been that monism works both ways.

As we have seen, the CJEU came to a different view in its appeal judgment. The intention was to give priority to Union law and to limit the effect of binding international norms. In his Opinion, AG Poiares Maduro already started to highlight the good old (dualist?) notion of the autonomous EU legal order, by arguing that the relationship between international law and EC law 'is governed by the Community legal order itself, and international law can permeate that legal order only under the conditions set by the constitutional principles of the Community'.[21] In turn, the ECJ held that 'the obligations imposed by an international agreement cannot have the effect of prejudicing the constitutional principles of the EC Treaty, which include the principle that all Community acts must respect fundamental rights' (paragraph 285). Again, the Court did not clearly deny the legal nature (validity) of 'an international agreement' (e.g. the UN Charter).[22] To arrive at this conclusion without having to challenge the validity of norms flowing from UN Security Council Resolutions, the Court pointed to the fact that the UN Charter leaves the members 'the free choice among the various possible models for transposition of those resolutions into their domestic legal order' (paragraph 298). This would allow for a judicial

---

[18] Case C-61/94 *Commission* v. *Germany* [1996] ECR I-3989, para 52.
[19] See para 276 in Case T-306/01 *Yusuf and Al Barakaat International Foundation* v. *Council and Commission* [2005] ECR II-3533 and Case T-315/01 *Kadi* v. *Council and Commission* [2005] ECR II-3649.
[20] *Ibid.*, para 277.
[21] Opinion of AG Poiares Maduro in Joined Cases C-402/05 P & C-415/05 P *Kadi and Al Barakaat International Foundation* v. *Council* [2008] ECR I-6351, para 21.
[22] But note the somewhat ambiguous reasoning in *ibid.*, paras 305–308.

review of the 'internal lawfulness' of the EU acts, keeping in mind that fundamental rights form an integral part of the general principles of law, the observance of which is also to be ensured by the Court.

As a fourth problematic area in relation to monism/dualism, we point to the division between the TEU and the TFEU. While the merging of the Community and the Union legal order reached an all-time high after the entry into force of the Lisbon Treaty, the status of international law in relation to the Union's CFSP as well as the CSDP may still differ from what has been established on the basis of the classic authorities in the case law on the policy fields that are now to be found in the TFEU (see Chapters 11 and 12). The potential impact of the loyalty principle on the freedom of the Member States under for instance the Union's CFSP should not be underestimated. On the basis of the limited availability of case law related to CFSP no final conclusions can be drawn on the primacy, direct effect and justiciability of CFSP decisions and agreements. While there are good reasons to argue that CFSP agreements are also to be regarded as forming 'an integral part of Union law' (a statement that is less controversial now that new Article 216 TFEU does not discriminate between CFSP and other EU agreements), there are still different parts of 'Union law', and the monism/dualism approach may even be less helpful for understanding the internal effects of international agreements concluded by the EU because of the less developed nature of certain parts of the Union's legal order.

The above findings reveal that the Court's case law is not always very precise on the different elements of the relationship between international law and EU law. In what follows we will revisit the relationship between international and EU law with respect to its three main dimensions: validity, direct effect and supremacy. From a pragmatic perspective, this is what we need to know when confronted with conflicts between international and European law. From a more theoretical point of view, this may give us some more insight into the toolbox that is often implicitly used to decide on the role of international norms in the Union's legal order.

A legal theoretical approach has frequently been used to study and understand the relationship between European and national law. Less often, a similar exercise has been made with regard to the relation between international and European law.

(b) Validity

Validity refers to the *existence* of a norm in a particular legal order. It is difficult to leave the question of supremacy aside for a moment, but not impossible. Comparable to the position of national constitutional lawyers, who would perhaps opt for the model in which Union law is derived from national law and defines the relationship on the basis of constitutional choices (monism or dualism), many traditional EU lawyers would have a natural tendency to stress the autonomy of EU law and would only accept international law as valid once the Union itself decided that it is. From their point of view, Union law and the domestic law of Member States form an 'integrated' legal order (compare *Costa–ENEL*); at the same time, the 'autonomy' of the EU legal order makes it difficult to accept the same integration in relation to international law. Nevertheless the notion of integrated legal orders seems to be at the basis of the recent judgments of the Court. Both in *Intertanko* and in *Kadi* – but also in the standing case law on the effects of WTO norms in the Community legal order – the Court faced a conflict of norms. From a theoretical perspective, it would be very difficult to accept a conflict without accepting the validity of both norms. Therefore, the notion that relevant (written and unwritten) international law forms an 'integral part' of Union law seems to be upheld by the recent cases, albeit that these cases equally make clear that it is EU law itself that sets the conditions for the validity of international norms within its legal order. Thus – as *Intertanko* for instance revealed in relation to the MARPOL Treaty to which the EU is not a party – not *all* international norms can be an 'integral' part of the EU legal order.[23] Whereas the EU defines the status of its norms in the legal orders of its Member States, a similar system does not exist in the international legal order.

(c) Direct effect

It is quite easy to combine validity with direct effect, understood as the possibility to invoke provisions of a legal act before a court. Article 93 of the Constitution of The Netherlands, for instance, even links the two notions explicitly: 'Provisions of treaties and of resolutions by international institutions which may be binding on all persons by virtue of their contents shall become binding after they have been published.' Although one may still argue that 'binding on all persons' does not by definition imply a right of these persons actually to invoke international provisions, practice did reveal the close link between the two aspects. The *Intertanko* judgment in particular comes quite close to this idea by bringing in the argument that the international agreement 'does not establish rules intended to apply directly and immediately to individuals and to confer upon them rights or freedoms capable of being relied upon against States' (paragraph 64). However, in both cases (the Dutch and the European legal order), it would be difficult to argue on this basis that the absence of direct effect denies the 'binding force' of international agreements in the international legal order. This would imply that state and Union institutions would have a duty under international law to live up to their obligations, irrespective of the status of the agreements in their own legal order. The question of hierarchy may thus also emerge in the absence of direct effect.

(d) Supremacy

The supremacy rule is nothing more (or less) than a rule to establish which norm precedes in case of a collision. With regard to a possible conflict between European law and international law, this rule is not articulated in the Treaties. Article 216(2) TFEU does indeed refer to the fact that international agreements concluded by the EU are binding in the EU legal order, but remains silent on the hierarchy in relation to all other 'binding' norms within that order. One may argue that a hierarchy between legal orders can only be established once one legal order forms a part of the other. The hierarchy then implies that all norms in the higher (overarching) legal order precede over all norms in the lower (or sub) legal order. Exceptions to this rule can only be made through norms in the higher legal order.

The question of the subordination of the EU legal order to the international legal order has been raised ever since the Court held that the Community was to be seen as 'a new legal order of international law'.[24] In this new legal order, international legal norms may collide with other norms. One way to solve this collision may be by denying the direct effect of the international norms (as has traditionally been the approach with regard to WTO norms). The problem the Court faced in *Kadi* was that the norms set by the UN Security Council clearly had an effect on individuals. This left the Court with a conflict of norms. The Court seemed to conclude (although indeed not quite clearly) that international agreements (such as the UN Charter) form an 'integral

---

[23] This was in fact the main point of this case.
[24] Case 6/64 *Costa* v. *ENEL* [1964] ECR 585.

part' of EU law, but also noted that 'fundamental rights form *an integral part* of the general principles of law whose observance the Court ensures'.[25] The fact that both norms were part of the EU legal order allowed the Court to solve the supremacy question in an 'internal' setting, in which it gave priority to the constitutional principles related to the protection of fundamental rights.[26]

This underlines the complexity of the relationship between international and European law and the difficulty of analysing this relationship in terms of monism and dualism. In the end neither notion is very useful for understanding the (absence of) hierarchy between international and European law. In various legal analyses in reaction to the *Kadi* judgment, some of the arguments that are traditionally used by the 'communautarists' (or 'neocoms') to stress the supremacy of EU law in relation to national law are now used to point to the need to accept the supremacy of international law over Union law. So, where EU law enjoys primacy over national law because without a uniform application it would lose its relevance, at least with respect to the nature and function of the Charter of the United Nations, it is argued that without the supremacy of the Charter and the decisions based on it (cf. Article 103 of the Charter), the United Nations system of collective security would not be able to function. So far, the controversy between the 'internationalists' (stressing the values of a coherent legal world order) and the 'European constitutionalists' (pointing to higher ranking constitutional values) could not be overcome on the basis of legal theoretical arguments. This seems to have triggered new approaches to make sense of the relationship between the different legal orders.[27]

E. Cannizzaro, 'The Neo-Monism of the European Legal Order', in E. Cannizzaro, P. Palchetti and R. A. Wessel (eds.), *International law as Law of the European Union* (Boston/Leiden: Martinus Nijhoff Publishers, 2011), pp. 35–58

Assessed against the background of the classical approach, the ECJ's case law conveys a sense of disconcert. It appears to deviate significantly from the founding Treaties, which were inspired by a sense of openness towards international law. The weight of consideration of judicial policy appears considerable and its logical coherence is precarious. Not surprisingly, this case law has been received with ample criticism by legal scholarship.

However, comprehensively considered, the attitude adopted by the ECJ towards international law seems to highlight the insufficiency of the traditional conceptualization of the relations between international rules and the EU legal order. The classical conception tends to consider international rules within domestic legal orders as a de-structured set of rules, uprooted from their international legal environment and transplanted in another one, where they are administered and enforced through a different set of remedies. By contrast, the approach emerging from the ECJ's case law tends to look at

---

[25] C-402/05 P & C-415/05 P *Kadi and Al Barakaat International Foundation* v. *Council* [2008] ECR I-6351, para 283.

[26] More in general, the 'internalization' of international law has been referred to as a 'Europeanisation' of international law: 'To the extent that it is binding upon the EU institutions, international law becomes part of the EU legal order and is therefore "europeanised".' J. Wouters, A. Nollkaemper and E. de Wet, 'Introduction: The "Europeanisation" of International Law', in Wouters, Nollkaemper and de Wet (eds.), *The Europeanisation of International Law: The Status of International Law in the EU and its Member States* (The Hague: T.M.C. Asser Press, 2008), pp. 1–13 at 3.

[27] Rather than 'monism 'or 'dualism', 'pluralism' seems to receive abundant attention. As an example of this pluralist turn see: N. Krisch, *Beyond Constitutionalism: The Pluralist Structure of Postnational Law* (Oxford: Oxford University Press, 2010).

international law as a *structured* set of rules or even a full-fledged and fully effective normative system, with its own set of remedies.

The theoretical value of this new approach thus seems to reside primarily in the consideration of international law not so much in terms of its abstract legal value or as a set of isolated substantive rules, but rather as the final product of a complex process of law-making and law-determining. It is this final product, and not so much the legal provisions considered as abstract sources of law, which must be implemented and enforced through internal remedies.

In this light, there seems to be a common thread in the various cases decided by the ECJ, which consists of the tendency to consider international rules not in isolation but rather as part of a more complex legal *system*. Ultimately, it is this legal system with its idiosyncratic dynamics – and not a series of isolated substantive rules, de-contextualized from their own legal order of origin – that becomes part of the European 'domestic' law. Since this approach seems inspired by the need to respect the comprehensiveness and consistency of international law in the process of domestic implementation, it seems appropriate to characterise it as 'neo-monism'. . . .

Respect and promotion of international law is one of the principles inspiring the external action of the EU, as expressly stated in Articles 5 and 21, paras. 1 and 2, of the Treaty on European Union. Arguably, the principle of respect and strict observance of international law also constitutes an inspiring principle for the EU's domestic legal order. Indeed, the European legal order is among the *völkerrechtsfreundlischsten* contemporary legal orders. As seen above, international law is an integral part of EU law and, if compatible with the founding Treaties, it prevails over inconsistent legislation.

The founding Treaties thus seem to enshrine an idealistic view of international law, conceived of as the realm of universal values and legality. This is, *hélas*, only a part of the reality. A more realistic view tends to regard international law as the arena where states vie to affirm their selfish interests. Understandably, the judicial wisdom of the ECJ is equally inspired by these two competing visions. While upholding the *Völkerrechtsfreundlischkeit* emerging from the founding Treaties, therefore, the ECJ has also tended to leave the door open for a more realistic conception of international law and to secure a certain margin of discretion to political institutions in their international intercourse.

It is in this complex frame that the case law of the ECJ should be explained. In other words, the adoption in the founding Treaties of a monist model can explain, in a systemic assessment, the tendency of the ECJ case law to use tools and instruments designed to mitigate the apparent excesses produced by the concomitance of direct effect and primacy of international law. Paradoxically, therefore, neo-monism was conceived of and prospered as a reaction against the systemic effect of classical monist theories.

However, by doing so, the ECJ has also radically transformed the methodology adopted by the Treaties in order to deal with conflicts between international and domestic law. Whereas the Treaties adopted a formal hierarchical method of settling conflicts based on the primacy of international law, the judicial management of conflict is based on a more flexible and nuanced approach in which considerations of policy play a great role. Not surprisingly, recent legal analysis tends to consider the ECJ as the gatekeeper of the domestic legal order, and as being entitled to determine the outcome of the conflict on a case-by-case basis.

In turn, the judicial policy of the ECJ has gradually evolved into something very akin to a full-fledged legal doctrine which, for the sake of brevity, was referred to in this paper by the term neo-monism. In the particular legal order of the Union, neo-monism seems to have found appropriate soil on which to take root and flourish. Its underlying idea – that the process of implementation must not consider international rules in isolation but rather as part of a comprehensive legal system – seems to be particularly apt to cure some of the unbalances of a monist system and to offer a more flexible frame of reference for the relations between international law and EU law.

However, the reasons of political expediency prompted a further development, which raises the risk of upsetting the philosophy of the relations between international law and domestic EU law and ultimately of asserting the right of the EU to violate international law at will in order to pursue its own interests in the international arena.

By injecting a dose of realism into the idealistic view embedded in the Treaties, the ECJ deserves credit for starting a process of theoretical revision of the old schemes. Hopefully, this will lead to a development of more adequate models for the relations between international law and domestic law. Over-realistic misconceptions about political interests asserting themselves in the international arena may endanger the entire theoretical edifice and may pervert the wise aspiration of the EU to present itself as a promoter of international law around the globe.

3 THE EFFECTS OF INTERNATIONAL LAW WITHIN THE EU LEGAL ORDER

(i) Internal effects of international law and external effects of EU law

So far we have established that international law may be binding on the EU. The current section looks at the consequences of this assertion, in particular within the EU legal order. In other words, we look at the internal effects of international law. As an introduction to this theme we look at a 2012 judgment in which the Court not only nicely summarized some of the relevant issues, but also addressed the question of whether non-EU states can be bound by EU legislation.

In December 2010 the CJEU ruled in a case concerning the applicability of rules of written and unwritten international law in relation to a Directive to include aviation activities in the scheme for greenhouse gas emission allowance trading within the Union.[28] This Directive affects not only EU Member States, but in fact all aircraft operators when their flight schedule departs or arrives in the territory of one of the Member States and, more specifically, at an airport situated there. Obviously, third states are not too eager to pay for greenhouse gas emission for those miles they do not fly in EU airspace. On 16 December 2009, the American Air Transport Association and others brought judicial review proceedings asking the referring court to quash the measures implementing the Directive in the United Kingdom.[29] In support of their action, they pleaded that that Directive was unlawful in the light of international treaty law and customary international law. In this ruling the Court neatly summarized the main principles related to the effect of international law in the EU legal order, to which we will return below.

---

[28] Directive 2008/101/EC to include aviation activities in the scheme for greenhouse gas emission allowance trading within the Community, OJ 2009 No. L8/3.

[29] Case C-366/10 *Air Transport Association of America and Others*, n.y.r.

Case C–366/10 *Air Transport Association of America and Others*, n.y.r.

[On the criteria to assess the effects of international agreements]

52. First, the European Union must be bound by those rules (see Joined Cases 21/72 to 24/72 International Fruit Company, paragraph 7, and Intertanko, paragraph 44).

53. Second, the Court can examine the validity of an act of European Union law in the light of an international treaty only where the nature and the broad logic of the latter do not preclude this (see Joined Cases C–120/06 P and C–121/06 P FIAMM and Others v Council and Commission, paragraph 110).

54. Finally, where the nature and the broad logic of the treaty in question permit the validity of the act of European Union law to be reviewed in the light of the provisions of that treaty, it is also necessary that the provisions of that treaty which are relied upon for the purpose of examining the validity of the act of European Union law appear, as regards their content, to be unconditional and sufficiently precise (see IATA and ELFAA, paragraph 39, and Intertanko and Others, paragraph 45). . . .

[On the question of whether the EU is bound by an international agreement to which it is not a party: the Chicago Convention]

63. Indeed, in order for the European Union to be capable of being bound, it must have assumed, and thus had transferred to it, all the powers previously exercised by the Member States that fall within the convention in question (see, to this effect, Intertanko and Others, paragraph 49, and Bogiatzi, paragraph 33). Therefore, the fact that one or more acts of European Union law may have the object or effect of incorporating into European Union law certain provisions that are set out in an international agreement which the European Union has not itself approved is not sufficient for it to be incumbent upon the Court to review the legality of the act or acts of European Union law in the light of that agreement (see, to this effect, Intertanko and Others, paragraph 50). . . .

69. Nevertheless, whilst it is true that the European Union has in addition acquired certain exclusive powers to agree with third States' commitments falling within the field of application of the European Union legislation on international air transport and, consequently, of the Chicago Convention (see, to this effect, Case C–476/98 Commission v Germany, paragraph 124), that does not mean that it has exclusive competence in the entire field of international civil aviation as covered by that convention. . . .

71. Consequently, it must be concluded that, since the powers previously exercised by the Member States in the field of application of the Chicago Convention have not to date been assumed in their entirety by the European Union, the latter is not bound by that convention.

72. It follows that in the context of the present reference for a preliminary ruling the Court cannot examine the validity of Directive 2008/101 in the light of the Chicago Convention as such.

[On the question of whether the EU is bound by an international agreement to which it is a party: the Kyoto Protocol]

73. It is apparent from Decisions 94/69 and 2002/358 that the European Union has approved the Kyoto Protocol. Consequently, its provisions form an integral part of the legal order of the European Union as from its entry into force (see Case 181/73 Haegeman, paragraph 5). . . .

76. It is thus clear that, even though the Kyoto Protocol imposes quantified greenhouse gas reduction commitments with regard to the commitment period corresponding to the years 2008 to 2012, the parties to the protocol may comply with their obligations in the manner and at the speed upon which they agree.

77. In particular, Article 2(2) of the Kyoto Protocol, mentioned by the referring court, provides that the parties thereto are to pursue limitation or reduction of emissions of certain greenhouse gases from aviation

bunker fuels, working through the ICAO. Thus, that provision, as regards its content, cannot in any event be considered to be unconditional and sufficiently precise so as to confer on individuals the right to rely on it in legal proceedings in order to contest the validity of Directive 2008/101.

[On the question of whether the EU is bound by an international agreement to which it is a party: the Open Skies Agreement]

79. The Open Skies Agreement has been approved on behalf of the European Union by Decisions 2007/339 and 2010/465. Consequently, its provisions form an integral part of the legal order of the European Union as from its entry into force (see Haegeman, paragraph 5). . . .

84. Since the Open Skies Agreement establishes certain rules designed to apply directly and immediately to airlines and thereby to confer upon them rights and freedoms which are capable of being relied upon against the parties to that agreement, and the nature and the broad logic of the agreement do not so preclude, the conclusion can be drawn that the Court may assess the validity of an act of European Union law, such as Directive 2008/101, in the light of the provisions of the agreement.

[On the question of whether the EU is bound by customary international law]

101. Under Article 3(5) TEU, the European Union is to contribute to the strict observance and the development of international law. Consequently, when it adopts an act, it is bound to observe international law in its entirety, including customary international law, which is binding upon the institutions of the European Union (see, to this effect, Case C-86/90 Poulsen and Diva Navigation [1992] ECR I-6019, paragraphs 9 and 10, and Case C-162/96 Racke [1998] ECR I-3655, paragraphs 45 and 46).

102. Thus, it should be examined first whether the principles to which the referring court makes reference are recognised as forming part of customary international law. If they are, it should, secondly, then be determined whether and to what extent they may be relied upon by individuals to call into question the validity of an act of the European Union, such as Directive 2008/101, in a situation such as that in the main proceedings. . . .

108. In the main proceedings, those principles of customary international law are relied upon, in essence, in order for the Court to determine whether the European Union had competence, in the light thereof, to adopt Directive 2008/101 in that it extends the application of Directive 2003/87 to aircraft operators of third States whose flights which arrive at and depart from an aerodrome situated in the territory of a Member State of the European Union are carried out in part over the high seas and over the third States' territory.

109. Therefore, even though the principles at issue appear only to have the effect of creating obligations between States, it is nevertheless possible, in circumstances such as those of the case which has been brought before the referring court, in which Directive 2008/101 is liable to create obligations under European Union law as regards the claimants in the main proceedings, that the latter may rely on those principles and that the Court may thus examine the validity of Directive 2008/101 in the light of such principles.

110. However, since a principle of customary international law does not have the same degree of precision as a provision of an international agreement, judicial review must necessarily be limited to the question whether, in adopting the act in question, the institutions of the European Union made manifest errors of assessment concerning the conditions for applying those principles (see, to this effect, Racke, paragraph 52).

[On the question of whether the EU is competent to adopt rules binding on third parties in the light of international law]

123. The European Union must respect international law in the exercise of its powers, and therefore Directive 2008/101 must be interpreted, and its scope delimited, in the light of the relevant rules of the international law of the sea and international law of the air (see, to this effect, Poulsen and Diva Navigation, paragraph 9).
124. On the other hand, European Union legislation may be applied to an aircraft operator when its aircraft is in the territory of one of the Member States and, more specifically, on an aerodrome situated in such territory, since, in such a case, that aircraft is subject to the unlimited jurisdiction of that Member State and the European Union (see, by analogy, Poulsen and Diva Navigation, paragraph 28). ...
127. It is only if the operator of such an aircraft has chosen to operate a commercial air route arriving at or departing from an aerodrome situated in the territory of a Member State that the operator, because its aircraft is in the territory of that Member State, will be subject to the allowance trading scheme. ...
130. It follows that the European Union had competence, in the light of the principles of customary international law capable of being relied upon in the context of the main proceedings, to adopt Directive 2008/101, in so far as the latter extends the allowance trading scheme laid down by Directive 2003/87 to all flights which arrive at or depart from an aerodrome situated in the territory of a Member State.

First, the Court confirmed that the EU is in principle bound by international law. This has indeed been standard case law ever since the *International Fruit Company* case in 1972.[30] Second, the Court can examine the validity of an act of EU law in the light of an international treaty only where the nature and the broad logic of the latter do not preclude this.[31] Finally, where the nature and the broad logic of the treaty in question permit the validity of the act of EU law to be reviewed in the light of the provisions of that treaty, it is also necessary that the provisions of that treaty which are relied upon for the purpose of examining the validity of the act of EU law appear, as regards their content, to be unconditional and sufficiently precise.[32]

Yet, the question is of course different when the EU is not a party to a particular international agreement. In that case, in order for the EU to be capable of being bound, it must have assumed, and thus had transferred to it, all the powers previously exercised by the Member States that fall within the international agreement in question. In this case, however, the question related to the Chicago Convention, and the Court held that as in that particular case the powers previously exercised by the Member States had not been assumed in their entirety by the EU, the latter is not bound by that convention. In other words: the EU was not bound because it was not itself a party to the agreement and it had not replaced the Member States. This led to the conclusion that the provisions of the Chicago Convention cannot be said to form part of the EU legal order.

But what if the EU *is* a party to an international agreement? In the same *ATAA* case the Court answered this question as follows. Here it concerned the Kyoto Protocol, an international agreement on CO_2 emissions. Since the EU is a party, the provisions of the Kyoto Protocol form an integral part of the legal order of the EU as from its entry into force.[33] A similar reasoning

---

[30] Joined Cases 21/72 – 24/72 *International Fruit Company and Others* v. *Produktschap voor Groenten en Fruit* [1972] ECR 1226.

[31] See also Joined Cases C-120/06 & C-121/06 *FIAMM and Others* v. *Council and Commission* [2008] ECR I-6513, para 110.

[32] Case C-344/04 *R, ex parte IATA* v. *Department for Transport* [2006] ECR I-403, para 39, and Case C-308/06 *Intertanko and Others* [2008] ECR I-4057, para 45.

[33] See also Case 181/73 *Haegemann* v. *Belgian State* [1974] ECR 449, para 5.

was followed in relation to the *Open Skies* Agreement, to which the EU is also a party. And, since the agreement

establishes certain rules designed to apply directly and immediately to airlines and thereby to confer upon them rights and freedoms which are capable of being relied upon against the parties to that agreement, and the nature and the broad logic of the agreement do not so preclude, the conclusion can be drawn that the Court may assess the validity of an act of European Union law . . . in the light of the provisions of the agreement. (paragraph 84)

Hence, in order to know whether international agreements can play a role within the EU (primarily to set aside internal EU legislation), the Union will have to be bound by the agreement, and the agreement must allow for it to be directly applicable to individuals or companies. We will come back to this in the next subsection, but at this point it is important to underline that international law is not only seen as an integral part of the Union's legal order, but that it can also set aside internal EU legislation.

But what about unwritten international law, usually referred to as 'customary law'? The Court referred to Article 3(5) TEU (see Chapter 1), on the basis of which the EU is to contribute to the strict observance and the development of international law. The Court argued that this implies that the Union is bound to observe international law in its entirety, including customary international law, which is binding upon the institutions of the EU.[34] However, since a principle of customary international law does not have the same degree of precision as a provision of an international agreement, judicial review is necessarily limited to the question of whether, in adopting internal legislation, the institutions of the EU made manifest errors of assessment concerning the conditions for applying those principles. In other words: because customary law is often less precise, it is more difficult to apply it in detail.

The main question which the American airline companies were interested in, however, was whether they could be subjected to rules based on treaties (the EU Treaties) to which they were not a party. The Court held that EU legislation applies in the territory of the EU Member States and may thus be applied to an aircraft operator when its aircraft is in the territory of one of the Member States and, more specifically, on an airport situated in such territory, since, in such a case, that aircraft is subject to the unlimited jurisdiction of that Member State and the EU. It follows that the EU has competence to apply its internal rules to external parties once they enter 'EU territory' and, since the emission rules in the Kyoto Protocol concern complete flights, the EU Directive could be applied to all flights which arrive at or depart from an airport situated in the territory of a Member State, even when for the most part they would not fly over EU territory. International law is thus not only applicable in the EU: international actors may also be subject to EU law.

In the remaining part of this chapter, we will focus more closely on the effects of written and unwritten international law in the EU legal order.

(ii) Direct applicability of international agreements

As far as international agreements are concerned, we have seen that the *Haegeman* doctrine that international law forms an integral part of EU law implies what is now laid down in Article 216(2)

---

[34] See, to this effect, Case C-286/90 *Poulsen and Diva Navigation* [1992] ECR I-6019, paras 9 and 10; and Case C-162/96 *Racke GmbH & Co.* v. *Hauptzollamt Mainz* [1998] ECR I-3655, paras 45 and 46.

TFEU, which reads that 'agreements concluded by the Union are binding upon the institutions of the Union and on its Member States'. This means that there is no specific need to transpose international agreements to Union law or to the domestic law of the Member States (for instance by means of a special Regulation). Indeed, at first sight this would reflect a perfect monist situation. In practice, however, the CJEU's case law is not that uniform and reveals a need to take the nature of the agreement into consideration whenever the question of its 'direct effect' comes up.

(a) Direct effect of international agreements

Where 'direct applicability' refers to the validity of international norms without having to be transposed into European law, 'direct effect' relates to the question of whether these norms can actually be invoked by individuals before a domestic or EU court (see also above). As we have seen, the basic rule is that this is the case. In the case of *Bresciani*,[35] the Court of Justice established that Community [now: Union] AAs could be used in national courts to challenge national law. In the seminal *Kupferberg* case,[36] it confirmed the direct effect of an 'ordinary' bilateral trade agreement. This was an important difference, as from Bresciani it was possible to infer that an AA was given direct effect only because of their special status and because it prepares a third country for accession (see Chapter 15). Indeed, all international agreements concluded by the EU can resort to direct effect if the conditions are fulfilled.

Case 104/81 *Hauptzollamt Mainz* v. *Kupferberg* [1982] ECR 3641

9. in the first place the Bundesfinanzhof wishes to know whether the German importer may rely on the said Article 21 before the German Court in the proceedings which it has brought against the decision of the tax authorities. ....

13. In ensuring respect for commitments arising from an agreement concluded by the Community institutions the Member States fulfil an obligation not only in relation to the non-member country concerned but also and above all in relation to the Community which has assumed responsibility for the due performance of the agreement. That is why the provisions of such an agreement, as the Court has already stated in its judgment of 30 April 1974 in Case 181/73 *Haegeman* form an integral part of the Community legal system.

14. It follows from the Community nature of such provisions that their effect in the Community may not be allowed to vary according to whether their application is in practice the responsibility of the Community institutions or of the Member States and, in the latter case, according to the effects in the internal legal order of each Member State which the law of that state assigns to international agreements concluded by it. Therefore it is for the Court, within the framework of its jurisdiction in interpreting the provisions of agreements, to ensure their uniform application throughout the Community. ....

17. It is true that the effects within the Community of provisions of an agreement concluded by the Community with a non-member country may not be determined without taking account of the

---

[35] Case 87/75 *Conceria Daniele Bresciani* v. *Amministrazione delle finanze dello Stato* [1976] ECR 129; see also: Case C-18/90 *Office national de l'emploi* v. *Kziber* [1991] ECR I-199 (Association Agreement between the Community and Morocco) and ECJ, Case C-268/99 *Jany and Others* v. *Staatssecretaris van Justitie* [2001] ECR I-8615 (Provisions of the Association Agreement between the Community and Poland and the Community and Czech Republic have direct effect notwithstanding the fact that the authorities of those states remain competent to apply to those nationals their own national laws and regulations regarding entry, stay and establishment).

[36] Case 104/81 *Hauptzollamt Mainz* v. *Kupferberg & Cie.* [1982] ECR 3641.

international origin of the provisions in question. In conformity with the principles of public international law Community institutions which have power to negotiate and conclude an agreement with a non-member country are free to agree with that country what effect the provisions of the agreement are to have in the internal legal order of the contracting parties. Only if that question has not been settled by the agreement does it fall for decision by the courts having jurisdiction in the matter, and in particular by the court of justice within the framework of its jurisdiction under the treaty, in the same manner as any question of interpretation relating to the application of the agreement in the Community.

18. According to the general rules of international law there must be bona fide performance of every agreement. Although each contracting party is responsible for executing fully the commitments which it has undertaken it is nevertheless free to determine the legal means appropriate for attaining that end in its legal system unless the agreement, interpreted in the light of its subject-matter and purpose, itself specifies those means. Subject to that reservation the fact that the courts of one of the parties consider that certain of the stipulations in the agreement are of direct application whereas the courts of the other party do not recognize such direct application is not in itself such as to constitute a lack of reciprocity in the implementation of the agreement. . . .

22. It follows from all the foregoing considerations that neither the nature nor the structure of the agreement concluded with Portugal may prevent a trader from relying on the provisions of the said agreement before a court in the Community.

23. Nevertheless the question whether such a stipulation is unconditional and sufficiently precise to have direct effect must be considered in the context of the agreement of which it forms part. In order to reply to the question on the direct effect of the first paragraph of article 21 of the agreement between the Community and Portugal it is necessary to analyse the provision in the light of both the object and purpose of the agreement and of its context.

In *Sevince*, the Court found that decisions adopted by an Association Council and created by an AA were capable of having direct effect, provided they fulfil the same criteria that determine whether an international agreement has direct effect.[37] Similarly, it was confirmed that third-country nationals could rely on the provisions of agreements concluded with the EU. Thus, the Russian football player Igor Simutenkov, at the time employed by the Spanish club Deportivo Tenerife, could invoke relevant provisions of the Partnership and Cooperation Agreement (PCA) with Russia. Article 23(1) of that PCA provided the following:

Subject to the laws, conditions and procedures applicable in each Member State, the Community and its Member States shall ensure that the treatment accorded to Russian nationals, legally employed in the territory of a Member State shall be free from any discrimination based on nationality, as regards working conditions, remuneration or dismissal, as compared to its own nationals.

In examining this provision, the Court of Justice found that it laid down 'in clear, precise and unconditional terms, a prohibition precluding any Member State from discriminating on grounds of nationality, against Russian workers vis-à-vis their own nationals'.[38] This judgment further

---

[37] Case C-192/89 *Sevince* v. *Staatssecretaris van Justitie* [1990] ECR I-3461.

[38] Case C-265/03 *Igor Simutenkov* v. *Ministerio de Educación y Cultura, Real Federación Española de Fútbol* [2005] ECR I-2579.

affirmed that even PCAs which do not establish the 'special relationship' that AAs do (Article 217 TFEU), can resort to direct effect.

(b) Limits to direct effect

Ten years after *Haegeman*, the Court was less clear in applying its doctrine. In *Kupferberg* (see above) the Court not only confirmed the possible direct effect of international agreements, but at the same time placed the pure monist starting point into perspective, when it argued that 'the effects within the Community of provisions of an agreement concluded by the Community with a non-member country may not be determined without taking account of the international origin of the provisions in question'. This idea was elaborated in further case law, starting with *Demirel*.

Case 12/86 *Demirel* v. *Stadt Schwäbisch Gmünd* [1987] ECR 3719

14. A provision in an Agreement concluded by the Community with non-member countries must be regarded as being directly applicable when, regard being had to its wording and the purpose and nature of the Agreement itself, the provision contains a clear and precise obligation which is not subject, in its implementation or effects, to the adoption of any subsequent measure.

Indeed, this implies that the original monistic starting points (international law as an integral part of EU law) do not automatically entail direct applicability of all international agreements concluded by the Union. Reasons for the Court to limit the domestic effects of international agreements vary. A classic argument is *reciprocity*: third states also limit the direct effect of the same agreement. This argument was leading in for instance *Kupferberg*, and returned in *Van Parys*.[39]

Case C-377/02 *Van Parys* v. *BIRB* [2005] ECR I-1465

53. To accept that the Community Courts have the direct responsibility for ensuring that Community law complies with the WTO rules would deprive the Community's legislative or executive bodies of the discretion which the equivalent bodies of the Community's commercial partners enjoy. It is not in dispute that some of the contracting parties, which are amongst the most important commercial partners of the Community, have concluded from the subject-matter and purpose of the WTO agreements that they are not among the rules applicable by their courts when reviewing the legality of their rules of domestic law. Such lack of reciprocity, if admitted, would risk introducing an anomaly in the application of the WTO rules.

More generally, the Court held that 'having regard to their nature and structure, the WTO Agreements are not in principle among the rules in the light of which the Court is to review the legality of measures adopted by the Community institutions'.[40] The nature of WTO law

---

[39] Later confirmed in Joined Cases C-120/06 & C-121/06 *FIAMM and Others* v. *Council and Commission* [2008] ECR I-6513.

[40] Case C-377/02 *Van Parys* v. *BIRB* [2005] ECR I-1465, para 39, but established case law ever since Case 21/72–24/72 *International Fruit Company and Others* v. *Produktschap voor Groenten en Fruit* [1972] ECR 1226.

thus prevents the Court from giving effect to these norms within the EU legal order. This may be referred to as a dualist exception in a mostly monist system, but is it really? There is perhaps no doubt that the norms of WTO Agreements are valid within the EU legal order; the problem lies more in the possibilities of *applying* them in case of a conflict (see further Chapter 9).

While WTO law had long been the odd one out, more recently the Court seems to have extended the idea in relation to the United Nations Convention on the Law of the Sea (UNCLOS). Here, however, it was not so much reciprocity that triggered the Court to be careful with the domestic application of an international agreement, but rather the *effects on individual rights*.

Case C-308/06 *Intertanko and Others* [2008] ECR I-4057

64. In those circumstances, it must be found that UNCLOS does not establish rules intended to apply directly and immediately to individuals and to confer upon them rights or freedoms capable of being relied upon against States, irrespective of the attitude of the ship's flag State.

65. It follows that the nature and the broad logic of UNCLOS prevent the Court from being able to assess the validity of a Community measure in the light of that Convention.

Earlier the Court had established that 'when an agreement established cooperation between the parties, some of the provisions of that agreement may ... directly govern the legal position of individuals'.[41] Now, in *Intertanko*, the absence of individual rights and obligations, together with 'the nature and broad logic of UNCLOS' prevents the Court from being able to assess the validity of a Community measure in the light of that Convention. It seems that the absence of direct effect causes the problem; the Court does not deny the legal status of the Convention within the EU legal order. The question may rightfully be posed whether the criterion of 'the governance of the legal position of individuals' – which seems to be relevant for the acceptance of direct effect[42] – would not virtually rule out the legal effects of most international law within the EU legal order and hence de facto limit the much applauded monist attitude of the Union.[43]

A third argument used by the Court to limit the internal effects of international agreements relates to the possible existence of a dispute settlement mechanism in the agreement. However, the argument is not used in a consistent manner. It played a role in a number of classic cases[44] (see further Chapter 9) before finally in *Portugal* v. *Council* the Court held the following:

---

[41] Case C-265/03 *Simutenkov* v. *Ministerio de Educacion y Cultura and Others* [2005] ECR I-2579.

[42] Cf. Case T-174/00 *Biret International SA* v. *Council* [2002] ECR II-17; CFI, Case T-210/00 *Etablissements Biret et Cie SA* v. *Council* [2002] ECR II-47; ECJ, Case C-93/02 P *Biret International SA* v. *Council* [2003] ECR I-10497; ECJ, Case C-94/02 P *Établissements Biret et Cie SA* v. *Council* [2003] ECR I-10565; ECJ, Case C-265/03 *Simutenkov* [2005] ECR I-2579 *supra* note 30; ECJ, C-344/04 *The Queen, on the Application of International Air Transport Association (IATA) and European Low Fares Airline Association (ELFAA)* v. *Department for Transport* [2006] ECR I-403. See more extensively and eloquently E. Cannizzaro, P. Palchetti and R. A. Wessel (eds.), *International Law as Law of the European Union* (Boston/Leiden: Martinus Nijhoff Publishers, 2011).

[43] *Ibid.*

[44] Including Case C-469/93 *Chiquita* [1995] ECR I-4533; Case 270/80 *Polydor* [1982] ECR 329; and Case 21/72–24/72 *International Fruit Company and Others* v. *Produktschap voor Groenten en Fruit* [1972] ECR 1226.

Case C-149/96 *Portugal* v. *Council* [1999] ECR I-8395

40. To require [domestic] courts to refrain from applying rules of domestic law which are inconsistent with the WTO agreements would have the consequence of depriving the legislative or executive organs of the contracting parties of the possibility afforded by Article 22 of that memorandum of reaching a negotiated settlement, even on a temporary basis.

The idea was that the existence of a dispute settlement system in the WTO Agreement was the proper forum for the Member States to settle conflicts related to the agreement.[45] Again, however, one could argue that this does not affect the status of international agreements in the EU legal order. Yet, these exceptions seriously limit the effects of international law in concrete situations:

Opinion of AG Poiares Maduro of 20 February 2008, in Joined cases C-120/06 & C-121/06 *FIAMM and Others* v. *Council and Commission* [2008] ECR I-6513

... the fact that WTO law cannot be relied upon before a court does not mean that it does not form part of the Community legal system. From this point of view, the formulation used by the Court in *Portugal v. Council* is undoubtedly unfortunate. It nurtures a belief that an international agreement does not form part of the body of Community legality, whereas it is merely a question of the provision's enforceability, of the jurisdiction of the courts to take cognisance of it.

International law does not regulate its own status in the domestic legal orders of states or the legal orders of international organizations. Nevertheless, one may argue that the international principle of *pacta sunt servanda* (see also Chapter 8) may call for internal measures to allow the state or international organization to live up to its international obligations. Whether this is done by accepting the international norms as valid norms in the domestic legal order or by transferring international norms into domestic law (or even by accepting a conflict between national and international obligations), is at the discretion of the state or international organization.

(iii) International customary law and EU law

So far we have mainly focused on the status and effect of international agreements binding upon the EU. Yet, we have seen that the GC in the *Kadi* case referred to *jus cogens*, and generally the Court does take unwritten international law into account as well. The Treaties are silent on the status of international customary law in the EU legal order, but in general terms Article 3(5) TEU hints at the idea that the EU considers itself bound by international law. This was confirmed by the Court in the *ATAA* judgment discussed at the outset of section 3 of this chapter.

---

[45] See also Case C-27/00 *R* v. *Secretary of State for the Environment, Transport and the Regions, ex parte Omega Air Limited* [2002] ECR I-2569.

Article 3(5) TEU

In its relations with the wider world, the Union ... shall contribute to ... the strict observance and development of international law including respect for the principles of the United Nations Charter.

The last part is repeated in the General Provisions on the Union's External Action in the TEU, where Article 21(1) refers to 'respect for the principles of the United Nations Charter and international law'. As we will see, over the years, the Court accepted the fact that the Community (and now the Union) was bound by international customary law. Yet, the hierarchical position of customary law (see section 2 above) is less clear.

In the landmark case *Racke*, the Court for the first time shed some light on the effects of international customary law in the EU legal order and the possibilities for individuals to invoke customary law to challenge an EU Regulation. This case was about the rule of *rebus sic stantibus* (a fundamental change in circumstances as a legitimate reason to suspend an international agreement) which is laid down in Article 62 VCLT. As the EC was not a party to that Convention, the Court had to rely on the customary nature of that rule.

Case C-162/96 *Racke GmbH & Co.* v. *Hauptzollamt Mainz* [1998] ECR I-3655

41. As far as the Community is concerned, an agreement concluded by the Council with a non-member country in accordance with the provisions of the EC Treaty is an act of a Community institution, and the provisions of such an agreement form an integral part of Community law (see *Demirel*, paragraph 7).

42. If, therefore, the disputed regulation had to be declared invalid, the trade concessions granted by the Cooperation Agreement would remain applicable in Community law until the Community brought that Agreement to an end in accordance with the relevant rules of international law.

43. It follows that a declaration of the invalidity of the disputed regulation by reason of its being contrary to rules of customary international law would allow individuals to rely directly on the rights to preferential treatment granted to them by the Cooperation Agreement.

44. For its part, the Commission doubts whether, in the absence of an express clause in the EC Treaty, the international law rules referred to in the order for reference may be regarded as forming part of the Community legal order. Thus, in order to challenge the validity of a regulation, an individual might rely on grounds based on the relationship between him and the Community, but does not, the Commission argues, have the right to rely on grounds deriving from the legal relationship between the Community and a non-member country, which fall within the scope of international law.

45. It should be noted in that respect that, as is demonstrated by the Court's judgment in Case C-286/90 Poulsen and Diva Navigation, paragraph 9, the European Community must respect international law in the exercise of its powers. It is therefore required to comply with the rules of customary international law when adopting a regulation suspending the trade concessions granted by, or by virtue of, an agreement which it has concluded with a non-member country.

46. It follows that the rules of customary international law concerning the termination and the suspension of treaty relations by reason of a fundamental change of circumstances are binding upon the Community institutions and form part of the Community legal order.

Although in this particular case the Court held that there was no manifest violation of the law of treaties, it did not hesitate to state that 'it is required to comply with the rules of customary international law'. In fact the last sentence of paragraph 46 strongly resembles the legal status of international agreements laid down in current Article 216(2). As one observer holds: 'Based on these observations, one can proceed on the assumption that it is unlikely that the EU system should adopt a very different approach in its relationship with international agreements and custom.'[46] A similar reason can be found in *Opel Austria*.

Case T-115/94 *Opel Austria* v. *Council* [1997] ECR II-39

84. The Council does not take issue with the applicant's statement that Article 18 of the First Vienna Convention and Article 18 of the Second Vienna Convention codify rules of customary international law which are binding on the Community. ...

90. The Court holds in this connection, first, that the principle of good faith is a rule of customary international law whose existence is recognized by the International Court of Justice (see the judgment of 25 May 1926, German interests in Polish Upper Silesia, CPJI, Series A, No 7, pp. 30 and 39) and is therefore binding on the Community.

Obviously, the obligation to respect international customary law holds in particular with regard to relations with third states (compare also Article 3(5) TEU referred to above). Unless we are dealing with *jus cogens* norms, the EU – in both primary and secondary law – may deviate from international law to regulate the relationship with and between its Member States.[47] This was the case, for example, with regard to the rule *inadimplenti non est adimplendum* ('One has no need to respect his obligation if the counter-party has not respected his own.'),[48] or to the freedom left by international law to states in choosing the criteria upon which to bestow and maintain their citizenship[49] or to grant their nationality to ships.[50]

Recent case law on the one hand confirms the idea laid down in *Racke* that 'the rules of customary international law ... form part of the Union legal order', but at the same time it is not completely consistent. The unambiguous statements in Articles 3(5) and 21 TEU indicating that the Union shall contribute to the strict observance and development of international law, lead to the presumption that in its relations with other international actors the EU is bound by international law, be it written or unwritten. The question, however, is how this can be squared with the statement in *Kadi* that in the end priority should be granted to the constitutional principles of the EU itself. One answer is that at the time of *Kadi*, Articles 3 and 21 TEU did not

---

[46] A. Gianelli, 'Customary International Law in the European Union', in Cannizzaro, Palchetti and Wessel (eds.), *International Law as Law of the European Union*, pp. 93–110 at 99.

[47] *Ibid.*

[48] ECJ, Joined Cases 90–91/63 *Commission* v. *Luxembourg and Belgium* [1964] ECR-625; ECJ, Case 52/75 *Commission* v. *Italy* [1976] ECR 277; ECJ, Case 325/82 *Commission* v. *Germany* [1984] ECR-777; ECJ, Case C-5/94 *The Queen* v. *Ministry of Agriculture, Fisheries and Food, ex parte Hedley Lomas (Ireland) Ltd* [1996] ECR I-2553; Opinion by AG Jacobs in ECJ, Case C-228/00 *Commission* v. *Germany* [2003] ECR I-1439.

[49] Case 41/74 *Yvonne Van Duyn* v. *Home Office* [1974] ECR 1337; Case C-369/90 *Micheletti* v. *Delegación del Gobierno Cantabria* [1992] ECR I-4239, para 10; Case C-192/99 *The Queen* v. *Secretary of State for the Home Department ex parte Kaur* [2001] ECR I-1237, para 19; Case C-200/02 *Zhu and Chen* v. *Secretary of State for the Home Department* [2004] ECR I-9925, para. 37; Case C-135/08 *Janko Rottmann* v. *Freistaat Bayern* [2010] ECR I-1449.

[50] Case C-221/89 *R* v. *Sectretary of State for Transport (ex parte Factortame)* [1991] ECR I-3905, paras 15–17.

yet exist. A post-Lisbon *Kadi* case may have to use a slightly different reasoning while the outcome may be the same: the duty to respect international law today amounts to a constitutional principle of the EU.[51] Obviously, the Court would still have a task to balance this constitutional principle against other constitutional principles (including the protection of fundamental rights).

A special type of customary law is formed by *jus cogens*. While deviation from regular customary law is allowed between parties, this is not the case in relation to *jus cogens*, referred to by the GC in the first *Yusuf* and *Kadi* cases.

Case T-306/01 *Yusuf and Al Barakaat International Foundation* v. *Council and Commission* [2005] ECR II-3533 (see also Case T-315/01 *Kadi* v. *Council and Commission* [2005] ECR II-3649), 21 September 2005

276. It must therefore be considered that the resolutions of the Security Council at issue fall, in principle, outside the ambit of the Court's judicial review and that the Court has no authority to call in question, even indirectly, their lawfulness in the light of Community law. On the contrary, the Court is bound, so far as possible, to interpret and apply that law in a manner compatible with the obligations of the Member States under the Charter of the United Nations.

277. None the less, the Court is empowered to check, indirectly, the lawfulness of the resolutions of the Security Council in question with regard to jus cogens, understood as a body of higher rules of public international law binding on all subjects of international law, including the bodies of the United Nations, and from which no derogation is possible.

The words 'in principle', however, formed a reason for many commentators to start raising their eyebrows. Linguistically one could argue that the Court purported to point to a principle precluding a role for itself in the judicial review of Security Council Resolutions. In fact, the subsequent sentence seems to support this view as the Court provides that it has 'no authority to call in question, not even indirectly' the lawfulness of Security Council Resolutions. However, a few lines later the principle proves to be less firm than presented as the Court chooses not to have its own competences completely blocked by it. Upon its own initiative, it decided that it is 'empowered to check, indirectly, the lawfulness of the resolutions of the Security Council in question with regard to jus cogens'. And, in fact, this is exactly what the Court did. In assessing whether the freezing of funds provided for by the contested regulation, and, indirectly, by the Resolutions of the Security Council, infringes the applicants' fundamental rights, the Court considered that such is not the case, measured by the standard of universal protection of the fundamental rights of the human person covered by *jus cogens*. It is only an arbitrary deprivation of the right to property that might, in any case, be regarded as contrary to *jus cogens*. Irrespective of the fact that the Court left some room in relation to the content of *jus cogens* ('in so far as respect for the right to property must be regarded as forming part of the mandatory rules of general international law'), it showed no hesitation in judging the lawfulness of the relevant Security Council Resolutions. In similar terms, the argumentation was used in relation to the right to be heard.

---

[51] Gianelli, 'Customary International Law in the European Union', p. 105.

What would have happened if the Court had established that the Security Council had, indeed, violated *jus cogens*? Would the relevant Resolution be void (cf. Article 53 of the Vienna Convention)? Would the Court have had no alternative but to annul the relevant Regulation or declare it inapplicable? How would this have related to the obligation of the EU member states to carry out the decisions of the Security Council? Could parts of the Regulation (i.e. the part of the Annex listing Yusuf and Kadi) be set aside? And, if so, could other (regional or national) courts or tribunals do the same? We can rest assured that the members of the Security Council would take *their* turn in raising eyebrows. In the appeal cases, the ECJ agreed with the CFI that the Union would not be bound to give effect to norms violating *jus cogens*.

Joined cases C–402/05 P & C–415/05 *P Kadi and Al Barakaat International Foundation* v. *Council* [2008] ECR I-6351

230. International law thus permits the inference that there exists one limit to the principle that resolutions of the Security Council have binding effect: namely, that they must observe the fundamental peremptory provisions of jus cogens. If they fail to do so, however improbable that may be, they would bind neither the Member States of the United Nations nor, in consequence, the Community.

231. The indirect judicial review carried out by the Court in connection with an action for annulment of a Community act adopted, where no discretion whatsoever may be exercised, with a view to putting into effect a resolution of the Security Council may therefore, highly exceptionally, extend to determining whether the superior rules of international law falling within the ambit of jus cogens have been observed, in particular, the mandatory provisions concerning the universal protection of human rights, from which neither the Member States nor the bodies of the United Nations may derogate because they constitute "intransgressible principles of international customary law" (Advisory Opinion of the International Court of Justice of 8 July 1996, The Legality of the Threat or Use of Nuclear Weapons, Reports 1996, p. 226, paragraph 79; see also, to that effect, Advocate General Jacobs's Opinion in Case C-84/95 Bosphorus [1996] ECR I-3953, paragraph 65). . . .

287. With more particular regard to a Community act which, like the contested regulation, is intended to give effect to a resolution adopted by the Security Council under Chapter VII of the Charter of the United Nations, it is not, therefore, for the Community judicature, under the exclusive jurisdiction provided for by Article 220 EC, to review the lawfulness of such a resolution adopted by an international body, even if that review were to be limited to examination of the compatibility of that resolution with jus cogens.

288. However, any judgment given by the Community judicature deciding that a Community measure intended to give effect to such a resolution is contrary to a higher rule of law in the Community legal order would not entail any challenge to the primacy of that resolution in international law.

Yet, as we have seen above, the ECJ argued that – apart from judging the compatibility with norms of *jus cogens*, it remains competent to assess the internal lawfulness of a Regulation designed to give effect to UN Security Council Resolutions: 'the obligations imposed by an international agreement cannot have the effect of prejudicing the constitutional principles of the EC Treaty, which include the principle that all Community acts must respect fundamental rights' (paragraph 285). This way, the Court did not have to check the lawfulness of the Security Council Resolutions against norms of *jus cogens*, it simply relied on the constitutional principles of the EU itself.

(iv) The doctrine of consistent interpretation

The above analyses reveal the possibility of a direct effect of international law in the EU legal order. At the same time the case law of the Court introduced another possibility: *indirect* effect of international law. This mode of application is usually referred to as the doctrine of consistent interpretation.

Case C-61/94 *Commission* v. *Germany* [1996] ECR I-3989

52. When the wording of secondary Community legislation is open to more than one interpretation, preference should be given as far as possible to the interpretation which renders the provision consistent with the Treaty. Likewise, an implementing regulation must, if possible, be given an interpretation consistent with the basic regulation (see Case C-90/92 Dr Tretter v Hauptzollamt Stuttgart-Ost, paragraph 11). Similarly, the primacy of international agreements concluded by the Community over provisions of secondary Community legislation means that such provisions must, so far as is possible, be interpreted in a manner that is consistent with those agreements.

Given the notion that agreements concluded by the EU form an integral part of the EU legal order, the principle of consistent interpretation did not appear out of the blue.[52] It is an elegant way of solving (potential) conflict between EU law and international obligations when international agreements lack direct effect (as is the case with the WTO Agreements and, as we have seen, UNCLOS). The duty to interpret EU law in conformity with binding international law stems from the superior hierarchical status of international law within the EU legal order as discussed above. The WTO Agreements in particular have been a source of inspiration. The principle of consistent interpretation has been said to be relevant for the Anti-Dumping Agreement, the Anti-Subsidy Agreements and for the TRIPS.[53] In the *Werner* and *Leifer* judgments the Court argued that Article XI GATT was relevant for the interpretation of a Community Regulation establishing common rules for exports (Cases C-70/94 and C-83/94).

While these cases, just like *Commission* v. *Germany*, were about the lack of direct effect of the 1947 GATT and thus concerned the need to assess the indirect effect of provisions of an international agreement, in *Poulsen* the Court confirmed that this also holds true for international customary law.

Case C-286/90 *Poulsen and Diva Navigation* [1992] ECR I-6019

9. As a preliminary point, it must be observed, first, that the European Community must respect international law in the exercise of its powers and that, consequently, Article 6 [of Regulation 3094/86 on certain technical measures for the conservation of fishery resources] must be interpreted, and its scope limited, in the light of the relevant rules of the international law of the sea.

---

[52] In fact, a more implicit reference could already be found in Case 92/71 *Interfood GmbH* v. *Hauptzollamt Hamburg-Ericus* [1972] ECR 231: 'Since agreements regarding the Common Custom Tariff were reached between the Community and its partners in GATT the principles underlying those agreements *may be of assistance* in interpreting the rules of classification applicable to it' (para 6, emphasis added).

[53] Cases C-61/94 *Commission* v. *Germany* [1996] ECR I-3989, para 52; C-286/02 *Bellio F.lli Srl* v. *Prefettura di Treviso* [2004] ECR I-3465, para 33; and C-49/02 *Heidelberger Bauchemie GmbH* [2004] ECR I-6129, para 20.

It is important to note that the principle of consistent interpretation not only applies in relation to the international agreements themselves, but equally to decisions flowing from those agreements. In general terms this was made clear by the Court in *Sevince* (Case C-192/89): 'in order to be recognized as having direct effect, the provisions of a decision of the council of association must satisfy the same conditions as those applicable to the provisions of the Agreement itself'.[54] EU law should be interpreted in the light of the provisions in international decisions that are binding upon the EU. The main area concerns WTO decisions. Interpretation and application of WTO law is regularly influenced by the reports of the WTO Appellate Body and the Dispute Settlement Body (DSB). Although no case law is available as of yet, it would make sense if not only the provisions of the WTO Agreements themselves would form a source for interpretation of EU law, but also the authoritative application of them by the WTO bodies.[55] However, so far the Court has been hesitant to interpret EU secondary legislation in the light of WTO dispute decisions.[56] Yet, in general, decisions by international organizations have an impact on the EU legal order and may be of interpretative assistance.

The duty of consistent interpretation may also be applicable in the domestic legal order of the Member States in the case of an agreement to which the Member States are a party. In *Commune de Mesquer* (Case C-188/07) the Court pointed to the possible necessity for Member States to interpret EU law in the light of international obligations to allow EU law to function well. Similarly, in *Intertanko* (see above) it became clear that there is a role for the Court to prevent a clash between Member States' international agreements and EU obligations by way of a consistent interpretation. The rationale behind the doctrine of consistent interpretation therefore seems the need to assure the principle of respect for international law.

Finally, it is important to note that the conclusion of the above analysis cannot be used the other way around: that provisions in international agreements should always be interpreted in exactly the same manner as under EU law. Even if the provisions are identical (which may be the case in, for instance, trade agreements which have as their main goal to extend certain internal market rules to external parties), there remains a difference between international law and EU law. A classic case in this regard is *Polydor*,[57] in which the question was raised whether the internal market interpretation of the exhaustion of IP rights could also be applied to trade with Portugal on the basis of the Free Trade Agreement (FTA) with that country, which contained identical provisions. The Court noted the differences between Community law and international law, and concluded that different interpretations were justified. A similar conclusion was drawn in the *Kupferberg* case, referred to above.

Case 270/80 *Polydor* v. *Harlequin Record Shop* [1982] ECR 329

14. The provisions of the agreement on the elimination of restrictions on trade between the Community and Portugal are expressed in terms which in several respects are similar to those of the EEC Treaty on the abolition of restrictions on intra-Community trade. Harlequin and Simons pointed out in particular the

---

[54] See also Case 30/88 *Greece* v. *Commission* [1989] ECR 3711.
[55] G. Gattinara, 'Consistent Interpretation of WTO Rulings in the EU Legal Order?', in Cannizzaro, Palchetti and Wessel (eds.), *International Law as Law of the European Union*, pp. 269–287.
[56] See for instance Case C-351/04 *Ikea Wholesale* v. *Commissioners of Customs & Excise* [2007] ECR I-7723.
[57] Case 270/80 *Polydor* v. *Harlequin Record Shop* [1982] ECR 329.

similarity between the terms of Articles 14 (2) and 23 of the agreement on the one hand and those of Articles 30 and 36 of the EEC Treaty on the other.

15. However, such similarity of terms is not a sufficient reason for transposing to the provisions of the agreement the above-mentioned case-law, which determines in the context of the Community the relationship between the protection of industrial and commercial property rights and the rules on the free movement of goods.

16. The scope of that case-law must indeed be determined in the light of the Community's objectives and activities as defined by articles 2 and 3 of the EEC Treaty. As the Court has had occasion to emphasize in various contexts, the Treaty, by establishing a common market and progressively approximating the economic policies of the Member States, seeks to unite national markets into a single market having the characteristics of a domestic market.

4 INTERNATIONAL RESPONSIBILITY

In Chapter 1 we addressed the international legal personality of the EU. We argued that, as an international legal person, the EU occupies a separate position in the international legal order. As we have seen, this position as an international actor implies that in its relations with third states and other international organizations the EU must adhere to the norms that make up that international legal order. This leads to the question of whether and to what extent the EU may be held responsible by its international partners in case of a violation of international law. This question may occur in relation to all international obligations of the union, but is particularly salient in the context of the EU's foreign, security and defence policy (see Chapters 11 and 12).

Since the entry into force of the Lisbon Treaty we are left with one international legal entity: the EU (Article 1 TFEU). It is difficult not to regard this entity as an international organization and hence within the scope of the Draft Articles on the International Responsibility of International Organizations (DARIO) as adopted by the International Law Commission (ILC) of the UN in August 2011 and endorsed by the UN General Assembly in December 2011 (thus dropping the draft status, and therefore more recently referred to as the ARIO).[58] These ARIO are the latest stage in a development that started in 2002 when the ILC took up this project. While these articles are not to be seen as a formal agreement between states on the issue of the international responsibility of international organizations, they are regarded as the most authoritative source of interpretation at the moment.

Indeed, by now it has become widely accepted that the EU as such may bear international responsibility for an internationally wrongful act. It indeed seems to fit the definition of an international organization used in the ARIO: 'For the purposes of the present draft articles, the term "international organization" refers to an organization established by a treaty or other

---

[58] ILC, 'Draft Arts. on the responsibility of international organisations, with commentaries 2011', adopted by the ILC at its sixty-third session, in 2011, and submitted to the General Assembly as part of the Commission's report covering the work of that session (A/66/10) (2011) *Yearbook of the International Law Commission*, vol. II, Part Two, 5, see in particular pt. 6 where the Commentary refers to Article 57 of the Articles on Responsibility of States for internationally wrongful acts.

instrument governed by international law and possessing its own legal personality. International organizations may include as members, in addition to States, other entities.'

On the basis of Article 1, the articles 'apply to the international responsibility of an international organisation for an internationally wrongful act', as well as 'to the international responsibility of a State for an internationally wrongful act in connection with the conduct of an international organisation'. Not being dealt with in the Articles on the Responsibility of States for Internationally Wrongful Acts, the latter paragraph is meant inter alia to incorporate those cases of state responsibility for internationally wrongful acts by an international organization where a state is a member of that organization, such as the Member States of the Union.[59]

The ARIO suggest in Article 3 that as a point of departure the EU is responsible for its own internationally wrongful acts. Article 4 lists the conditions for an internationally wrongful act by an international organization that entails the international responsibility of that organization.

> ### Article 3 ARIO
>
> Every internationally wrongful act of an international organization entails the international responsibility of that organization.

> ### Article 4 ARIO
>
> There is an internationally wrongful act of an international organization when conduct consisting of an action or omission: (a) is attributable to the international organization under international law; and (b) constitutes a breach of an international obligation of that organization.

The next question is what conduct can be attributed to the Union.

> ### Article 6(1) ARIO
>
> The conduct of an organ or agent of an international organization in the performance of functions of that organ or agent shall be considered an act of that organization under international law, whatever position the organ or agent holds in respect of the organization.

This somewhat obvious rule indicates that conduct by organs and agents can establish the international responsibility of the Union. According to Article 6(2) ARIO, the 'rules of the organisation' shall be applied when determining the 'organs and agents'. In view of the Union rules on 'internal' responsibility, there are good reasons to interpret the term 'organs and agents' as 'institutions, bodies, offices and agencies and their servants' as is used in the TFEU.[60] In any

---

[59] See in particular pt. 6 of the ARIO Commentaries where the Commentary refers to Article 57 of the Articles on Responsibility of States for Internationally Wrongful Acts.

[60] Cf. Hoffmeister, 'Litigating against the European Union and its Member States – Who Responds under the ILC's Draft Articles on International Responsibility of International Organizations?' (2010) 21 *European Journal of International Law* 723–747, p. 740, who refers to Articles 340(2) and 263 TFEU as well as to Article 51(1) of the EU Charter of

case, as is suggested by the broad definitions of 'organs and agents' in Articles 2(c) and (d) ARIO, the articles do not envisage the attribution of conduct to 'depend on the use of particular terminology in the internal law' of the Union.[61]

Yet, the EU is not a normal international organization and the division of external competences is both complex and dynamic (see Chapters 1, 3 and 4). One of the key questions is therefore how to divide the responsibility between the EU and its Member States. The responsibility of the Union in relation to the role of the Member States is dealt with in Article 17. What, for instance, happens if the Union adopts a decision which would force (or authorize) the Member States to commit an internationally wrongful act? The rules suggest that the EU *itself* could incur international responsibility both in the case of binding decisions addressed to the Member States, and when the latter act because of an authorization by the Union. It is important to realize that this article applies to 'circumvention' *by the Union* and that hence the conduct of the 'implementing' Member State itself need not necessarily be unlawful; it is the binding or 'authorising act' of the Union that, if it were to implement that itself, should qualify as unlawful.[62] At the same time, Member States may be responsible once they hide behind an international organization (Article 61 ARIO).

Irrespective of the notion that the EU itself can be responsible under international law for internationally wrongful acts, it is worth keeping in mind that it is quite difficult to enforce the rules. The immunity of international organizations in general makes proceeding before domestic courts extremely difficult. At the same time, the International Court of Justice may only rule in conflicts between states. This means that the role of the ARIO in establishing an international responsibility of the Union may be limited to an argumentative function.

Frank Hoffmeister, 'Litigating against the European Union and its Member States' (2010) 21 *European Journal of International Law* 723–747

When one compares the results of the analysis of international case law and of the special rules of the European Union, there is considerable overlap. Both international case law and European Union rules attach significance to the actor, but are also aware of the situation that a Member State may not act on his own behalf, but merely as an agent of the Union. International practice also takes account of the fact that the Union is exclusively competent or has exercised its shared competence in a certain policy field, with the consequence that the Union is considered to have the power to bring an end to the alleged breach, provided that it has assumed an international obligation in the field. That leads inevitably to the rules of the European Union on external competences and their differentiation between exclusive, shared, and parallel competences. Such rules are hence of primordial importance for both the third state or applicant in question and the Union and its Member States alike.

In view of this remarkable overlap, it is suggested that one should always examine and evaluate three criteria in order to determine whether action can be attributed to the Union or its Member States under international law:

Fundamental Rights. Article 10(2) confirms that also 'the breach of any international obligation that may arise for an international organisation towards its members under the rules of the organisation' is included in the ARIO.

[61] Draft Articles with commentaries, above, 17. The commentary invokes also some case law on the point such as the ICJ Advisory Opinion, *Reparation for injuries suffered in the service of the United Nations*, ICJ Reports 1949, 177, where the Court held that an agent is 'any person through whom it [the international organisation] acts'.

[62] Draft Articles with commentaries, above, 40–42.

(a) Who is the factual actor of the alleged breach?

(b) Who has the legal power to bring an end to the alleged breach?

(c) Who bears the international obligation invoked concerning the alleged breach? ...

Certainly, the exact application of the three criteria may be subject to debate and controversy. But codifying and progressively developing international law is a tremendous task in any event. Having finished its first reading on responsibility of international organizations, the ILC has so far decided not to propose a special rule for the attribution of Member States' conduct to the European Union in particular circumstances. But it opened the door to accepting such a rule as *lex specialis* under Draft Article 63 provided that it can be firmly rooted in international law, including the rules of the organization applicable between the international organization and its members.

5 THE BROADER PICTURE OF EU EXTERNAL RELATIONS LAW

This chapter revealed the tension that may exist between EU law and international law. This tension flows from the original idea to create an entity which would have a certain autonomous relation vis-à-vis international law, and the need for that entity to live up to the international rules in order to be able to play along. Over the years, the Court had an important role in balancing interests in the relationship between EU and international law and taking account of the sensitive links between law and policy/politics in EU external relations law.

The *Kadi* cases serve as prime examples of that tension and the Court found itself in a difficult position, attempting to square some of the foundations of EU law with the obligations flowing from UN law. But, also in the WTO cases, it became clear that legal analysis was largely influenced by political arguments. Given the fact that the Treaties are virtually silent on the relationship between the EU and international law, the Court's role in this area cannot be underestimated.

The effect of external policy objectives on legal assessment can also be felt when you look at international agreements, their interpretation, and their objective; for example, *Polydor* on the interpretation of the Portugal agreement on its own objectives.

As far as the relationship between EU and international law is concerned, the Court made clear that there is a certain hierarchy, that international law in most cases has an internal effect in the EU legal order and that it can even set aside the application of EU rules.

This chapter also highlighted the interconnectedness between the internal division of competences and external responsibilities. The complex combination of roles of the EU and its Member States make it difficult to apply; for instance, the general rules on the international responsibility of international organizations.

SOURCES AND FURTHER READING

Blokker, N. M., 'Abuse of the Members: Questions Concerning Draft Art. 16 of the Draft Arts. on Responsibility of International Organizations' (2010) 7 *International Organizations Law Review* 35–48.

Cannizzaro, E., 'The Neo-Monism of the European Legal Order', in E. Cannizzaro, P. Palchetti and R. A. Wessel (eds.), *International Law as Law of the European Union* (Boston/Leiden: Martinus Nijhoff Publishers, 2011), pp. 35–58.

Cannizzaro, E., Palchetti, P. and Wessel, R. A. (eds.), *International Law as Law of the European Union* (Boston/Leiden: Martinus Nijhoff Publishers, 2011).

Casolari, F., 'Giving Indirect Effect to International Law', in E. Cannizzaro, P. Palchetti and R. A. Wessel (eds.), *International Law as Law of the European Union* (Boston/Leiden: Martinus Nijhoff Publishers, 2011), pp. 395–415.

d'Aspremont, J., 'Abuse of the Legal Personality of International Organizations and the Responsibility of Member States' (2007) 4 *International Organizations Law Review* 91–119.

De Búrca, G. 'The European Court of Justice and the International Legal Order after *Kadi*' (2010) 51 *Harvard International Law Journal* 1–49.

De Búrca, G., *The European Court of Justice and the International Legal Order after Kadi* (Jean Monnet Working Paper 01/09).

De Witte, B., 'Direct Effect, Primacy and the Nature of the Legal Order', in P. Craig and G. de Búrca (eds.), *The Evolution of EU Law*, 2nd edition (Oxford: Oxford University Press, 2011), pp. 323–362.

Dunne, T., 'Good Citizen Europe' (2008) 84 *International Affairs* 13–28.

Eckes, C., 'International Law as Law of the EU: The Role of the Court of Justice', in E. Cannizzaro, P. Palchetti and R. A. Wessel (eds.), *International Law as Law of the European Union* (Boston/Leiden: Martinus Nijhoff Publishers, 2011), pp. 351–377.

Gattinara, G., 'Consistent Interpretation of WTO Rulings in the EU Legal Order?', in E. Cannizzaro, P. Palchetti and R. A. Wessel (eds.), *International Law as Law of the European Union* (Boston/Leiden: Martinus Nijhoff Publishers, 2011), pp. 269–287.

Gattini, A., 'Effects of Decisions of the UN Security Council in the EU Legal Order', in E. Cannizzaro, P. Palchetti and R. A. Wessel (eds.), *International Law as Law of the European Union* (Boston/Leiden: Martinus Nijhoff Publishers, 2011), pp. 213–227.

Gianelli, A., 'Customary International Law in the European Union', in E. Cannizzaro, P. Palchetti and R. A. Wessel (eds.), *International Law as Law of the European Union* (Boston/Leiden: Martinus Nijhoff Publishers, 2011), pp. 93–110.

Griller, S., 'International Law, Human Rights and the European Community's Autonomous Legal Order: Notes on the European Court of Justice Decision in *Kadi*' (2008) 4 *European Constitutional Law Review*, 3, 528–553.

Hillion, C. and Wessel, R. A., 'Restraining External Competences of EU Member States under CFSP', in M. Cremona and B. de Witte (eds.), *EU Foreign Relations Law: Constitutional Fundamentals* (Oxford: Hart Publishing, 2008), pp. 79–121.

Hoffmeister, F., 'Litigating against the European Union and its Member States – Who Responds under the ILC's Draft Articles on International Responsibility of International Organizations?' (2010) 21 *European Journal of International Law* 723–747.

Jacobs, F. G., 'Direct Effect and Interpretation of International Agreements in the Recent Case Law of the European Court of Justice', in A. Dashwood and M. Maresceau (eds.), *Law and Practice of EU External Relations: Salient Features of a Changing Landscape* (Cambridge: Cambridge University Press, 2008), pp. 13–33.

Klabbers, J., 'International Law in Community Law: The Law and Politics of Direct Effect' (2001) 21 *Yearbook of European Law* 263–298.

Koutrakos, P., 'International Agreements in the Area of the EU's Common Security and Defence Policy', in E. Cannizzaro, P. Palchetti and R. A. Wessel (eds.), *International Law as Law of the European Union* (Boston/Leiden: Martinus Nijhoff Publishers, 2011), pp. 157–187.

Krisch, N., *Beyond Constitutionalism: The Pluralist Structure of Postnational Law* (Oxford: Oxford University Press, 2010).

Kuijper, P. J., 'Customary International Law, Decisions of International Organisations and Other Techniques for Ensuring Respect for International Legal Rules in European Community Law', in J. Wouters, A. Nollkaemper and E. de Wet (eds.), *The Europeanisation of International Law: The Status of International Law in the EU and its Member States* (The Hague: T.M.C. Asser Press, 2008), pp. 87–106.

Mayer, F. C., 'European Law as a Door Opener for Public International Law?', in J. M. Thouvenin and C. Tomuschat (eds.), *Droit International et Diversité des Cultures Juridiques – International Law and Diversity of Legal Cultures* (Paris: Pédone, 2008), pp. 241–255.

Naert, F., 'The Application of International Humanitarian Law and Human Rights Law in CSDP Operations' in E. Cannizzaro, P. Palchetti and R. A. Wessel (eds.), *International Law as Law of the European Union* (Boston/Leiden: Martinus Nijhoff Publishers, 2011), pp. 189–212.

Palchetti, P., 'Judicial Review of the International Validity of UN Security Council Resolutions by the European Court of Justice', in E. Cannizzaro, P. Palchetti and R. A. Wessel (eds.), *International Law as Law of the European Union* (Boston/Leiden: Martinus Nijhoff Publishers, 2011), pp. 379–393.

Pescatore, P., 'Die Rechtsprechung des Europäischen Gerichtshofs zur gemeinschaftlichen Wirkung völkerrechtlicher Abkommen', in Festschrift für H. Mosler, *Völkerrecht als Rechtsordnung, Internationale Gerichtsbarkeit Menschenrechte* (Berlin: Springer, 1983).

Pescatore, P., *Le Droit de l'Intégration. Emergence d'un Phénomène Nouveau dans les Relations Internationales selon l'Expérience des Communautés Européennes* (Dordrecht: Martinus Nijhoff, 1972).

Schermers, H., 'Community Law and International Law' (1975) 12 *Common Market Law Review* 77–90.

Timmermans, C., 'The EU and International Public Law' (1999) 4 *European Foreign Affairs Review* 181–194.

Tizzano, A., 'Quelques Réflexions sur la doctrine du Droit de l'Union Européenne: les 'Communautaristes' et les Autres' (2008) *Il Diritto dell'Unione Europea* 225–235.

Van Rossem, J. W., 'Interaction between EU Law and International Law in the Light of *Intertanko* and *Kadi*: The Dilemma of Norms Binding the Member States but not the Community' (2009) 40 *Netherlands Yearbook of International Law* 183–227.

Van Rossem, J. W., 'The EU at Crossroads: A Constitutional Inquiry into the Way International Law Is Received within the EU Legal Order', in E. Cannizzaro, P. Palchetti and R. A. Wessel (eds.), *International Law as Law of the European Union* (Boston/Leiden: Martinus Nijhoff Publishers, 2011), pp. 59–89.

Wessel, R. A. and Blockmans, S. (eds.), *Between Autonomy and Dependence: The EU Legal Order under the Influence of International Organisations* (The Hague: T.M.C. Asser Press/Springer, 2013).

Wouters, J. and Van Eeckhoute, D., 'Giving Effect to Customary International Law through European Community law', in J. N. Prinssen and A. Schrauwen (eds.), *Direct Effect* (Groningen: European Law Publishing, 2004), pp. 183–234.

Wouters, J., Nollkaemper, A. and de Wet, E. (eds.), *The Europeanisation of International Law: The Status of International Law in the EU and its Member States* (The Hague: T.M.C. Asser Press, 2008).

8

The EU and international institutions

1 CENTRAL ISSUES

- This chapter explores to what extent the EU Treaties, secondary legislation and case law regulate the position of the EU in international institutions, understood as both formal international organizations and the less formal treaty-regimes. As highlighted by the position of the EU in the WTO in particular, the division of competences between the EU and its Member States forms an important part of this legal framework.
- The Treaties list a number of general and specific competences related to the participation of the EU in international institutions. This chapter will list and analyse those provisions in order to assess the legal possibilities in this area.
- The EU participates in many international organizations and other international forums. In which international institutions does the EU have a formal position, and which different forms of representation can be discovered?
- Two examples deserve special attention: the WTO and the UN. On the basis of the participation of the EU in these two major organizations, we will further analyse the complexities related to this international role of the EU.
- Finally, the active participation of the EU in international institutions leads to a number of normative effects of these organizations on the EU. What is the influence of international institutions on the EU?

2 INTRODUCTION

As explained in Chapter 1, with the entry into force of the Lisbon Treaty, the EU has entered a new phase. No longer is the world confronted with both the EC and the EU as actors on the international stage; since 1 December 2009 the EU acts as the legal successor to the EC (Article 1 TEU), while maintaining one of its original policy fields: the foreign, security and defence policy (see Chapters 11 and 12). The EU has thus also replaced the Community in international institutions. In addition, the Lisbon Treaty increased the number of references to the role of the Union in the world and to its relationship with the United Nations (Article 21 TEU).

We use the term 'international institutions' to refer to both formal international organizations and other 'institutionalised treaty-regimes'.[1] Apart from its participation in a number of actual international organizations, the institutionalization of the role of the EU in the world is reflected in its position in international regimes in various policy fields. The question of whether the EU itself is an international organization is still open to debate, but as explained in Chapter 1, legally there are not too many reasons to deny the Union this status. The position of the EU in international institutions is part and parcel of EU external relations law, and it is at these forums that a *structural* role of the EU in global governance becomes most visible. Moreover, it is this role that has become more interesting now that it becomes clear that many EU (and national) rules find their origin in decision-making processes in other international organizations.

Over the years the EU has obtained a formal position in some international institutions, either as a full member or as an observer. It is generally held that the participation in a formal international organization relates to the participation in its organs; i.e. the right to attend the meetings, being elected for functions in the organ, and exercising voting and speaking rights. In that sense the term 'position' is related to a formal influence on the output of the international organization (UN, ICAO, etc.): decisions (often recommendations, in some occasions binding decisions) and conventions (international agreements prepared and adopted by an organ of an international organization). In addition the EU participates in less formal international institutions (or regimes) such as the G-20 for example. The Treaties herald an increase of the engagement of the EU in other international institutions, including the future membership of additional international organizations such as the Council of Europe (Article 6 TEU).

3 TREATY COMPETENCES RELATED TO THE PARTICIPATION OF THE EU IN INTERNATIONAL INSTITUTIONS

(i) Implied and express competences

In Chapter 3 we analysed the need for competence to exist so that the EU is able to act externally. The TEU and the TFEU deal with the position of the EU in other international institutions in various ways. Generally, the possibility or need for the EU to occupy a separate position in an international organization or international treaty-regime depends on two factors: first, the division of competences between the EU and its Member States in the particular issue area; and, second, the statute of the international institution. As only few international institutions allow for other international organizations to become a full member, one would assume the second factor in particular to stand in the way of an extension of the Union's role based on the further development of its external relations. At the same time, however, internal struggles between Member States or between Member States and EU institutions may form an obstacle to the accession of the EU to an international organization. Thus, even in areas where the EU has extensive competences, the EU may be barred from full participation in the global decision-making process (cf. the IMO, the ICAO, the River Rhine Commissions, the International

---

[1] Schermers and Blokker define international organizations as: 'forms of cooperation (1) founded on an international agreement; (2) having at least one organ with a will of its own; and (3) established under international law'. H. G. Schermers and N. M. Blokker, *International Institutional Law: Unity in Diversity* (Leiden/Boston: Martinus Nijhoff Publishers, 2011), p. 37.

Energy Agency, the executive board of the UN High Commissioner for Refugees (UNHCR) or in bodies under UNCLOS.

The general preference of Member States to remain present and visible in international institutions is perhaps even clearer in relation to international regimes that cannot be considered formal international organizations. Due to its (perhaps even exclusive) competences in a particular area, the EU nevertheless may need to participate in such international regimes. In many cases, the participation of the EU as such is based not on formal negotiating procedures, but rather on the need to make sure that both legal and political arrangements that are the result of cooperation within a regime conform to the Union's political agenda and respect its competences. In these cases the legal EU decision-making machinery is limited to providing the content of the EU position (for instance, in relation to the EU's participation in the G-20). This implies that large parts of the EU's multilateral activities are not directly regulated by the Treaties, but find their basis in numerous Decisions and Declarations which aim to present a unified EU position. By way of example we have included an excerpt of a Joint Letter of the European Council President and Commission President to the Member States, meant to coordinate the 'European' stance in an upcoming G-20 Summit.

Joint Letter of President Van Rompuy and President Barroso on the G20 Summit in Seoul, Brussels, 29 October 2010, PCE 250/10.

Looking ahead to the European Council tomorrow, we would like to share with you our views on the key issues coming up for discussion at the G20 Summit in Seoul . . . We hope this letter could serve as the basis of a constructive discussion at the dinner of the European Council.

The G20 Summit in Seoul comes at a critical time. It will be a real test of whether the G20 can continue to deliver in its role as the premier global forum for international economic cooperation. We believe it can, and we are convinced that the EU can play a key role in making Seoul a success. The G20 at Leaders level resulted from a European initiative, and it has played a pivotal role in tackling the economic and financial crisis, demonstrating that the world can act together in the face of adversity.

With the world economy slowly recovering despite very large uncertainties, the G20 is now at a turning point. Its focus has shifted from immediate crisis response to longer-term global economic coordination. Sustaining the recovery and laying the foundations for strong and more balanced growth remains a significant policy challenge. As we move into a new phase of economic challenges, there is a risk that the momentum of collective and cooperative action might weaken. It will be important to show in Seoul that leading global economies are ready to make the G20 the central global forum to work on both governance – crisis response as well as prevention – and medium term cooperation.

A strong EU position drawing on its experience in political and economic integration and its track record of support to global economic governance, can play a key role in making Seoul a success.

For participation in such informal regimes, EU Treaty framework then only sets the outer boundaries of the Union's actions, in that they may not conflict with EU or international law. However, when regimes do find their basis in an international agreement, the EU's formal participation depends on its legal competences to join a particular treaty-regime. The need for a formal role of the EU in international institutions is obvious whenever the EU has a competence related to the objectives and functions of the other international institution. This holds true in particular for areas in which the EU enjoys an exclusive competence (CCP), but seems equally valid when the competence is shared with the Member States (aviation, environment, etc.). However, despite an active role of the EU in international institutions in practice, one will look in vain for an express legal competence in the Treaties. The absence of a clear and explicit competence means that the participation in (and the membership of) international institutions is predominantly based on implied powers, which find their source in the general competences the Union enjoys in the different policy fields. Thus, the Union's membership of the FAO is based on Articles 43 TFEU (agriculture and fisheries), 207 TFEU (commercial policy) and 209 TFEU (development cooperation). However, we do refer to section (ii) below with regard to specific policy areas where *cooperation* with international organizations is expressly incorporated into the TFEU.

Nonetheless, what comes closest to a general competence-conferring provision is Article 211 TEU.

Article 211 TFEU

Within their respective spheres of competence, the Union and the Member States shall cooperate with third countries and with the competent international organisations.

That this 'cooperation' may also lead to the establishment of legal relationships can be derived from the provisions creating a competence for the Union to conclude international agreements.

Article 216(1) TFEU

The Union may conclude an agreement with one or more third countries or international organisations where the Treaties so provide or where the conclusion of an agreement is necessary in order to achieve, within the framework of the Union's policies, one of the objectives referred to in the Treaties, or is provided for in a legally binding Union act or is likely to affect common rules or alter their scope.

Article 217 TFEU

The Union may conclude with one or more third countries or international organisations agreements establishing an association involving reciprocal rights and obligations, common action and special procedure.

The procedures to conclude these international agreements are to be found in Articles 218 and 219(3) TFEU) (see Chapter 2). So-called 'constitutive agreements' by which new international organizations are created, or accession agreements to acquire membership of an international organization, are not excluded. In fact, the ECJ has established that the EU's competences in the field of external relations included the power to create new international organizations.

> **Opinion 1/76, *Draft Agreement establishing a European laying-up fund for inland waterway vessels* [1977] ECR 741**
>
> 5. In order to attain the common transport policy, the contents of which are defined in Articles 74 and 75 of the treaty, the council is empowered to lay down 'any other appropriate provisions', as expressly provided in Article 75(1)(c). The Community is therefore not only entitled to enter into contractual relations with a third country in this connexion but also has the power, while observing the provisions of the treaty, to cooperate with that country in setting up an appropriate organism such as the public international institution which it is proposed to establish under the name of the 'European laying-up fund for inland waterway vessels'. The Community may also, in this connexion, cooperate with a third country for the purpose of giving the organs of such an institution appropriate powers of decision and for the purpose of defining, in a manner appropriate to the objectives pursued, the nature, elaboration, implementation and effects of the provisions to be adopted within such a framework.

Both the EEA and the 'associations' created by AAs (see Chapters 7 and 15) serve as examples of international organizations created by (at that time) the EC (now Article 217 TFEU). At the same time, in Opinion 1/94 the Court implicitly accepted a role of the EU as one of the founding members of the WTO. Although not explicitly regulated, this also seems to imply a competence of the EU to fully participate in so-called 'treaty-regimes', on the basis of a formal accession to a treaty (e.g. the UN Framework Convention on Climate Change and the Kyoto Protocol, which were formally ratified by the EU in 1993 and 2002 respectively). As in formal international organizations, participation of the EU is either based on decisions by the participating states to grant the EU observer or full participant status, or on the inclusion of a REIO clause in international conventions. For example, Article II of the FAO Constitution was specifically modified to allow for the accession of 'regional economic organizations'. A REIO is commonly defined in UN protocols and conventions as 'an organization constituted by sovereign states of a given region to which its Member States have transferred competence in respect of matters governed by … convention or its protocols and [which] has been duly authorised, in accordance with its internal procedures, to sign, ratify, accept, approve or accede to it [the instruments concerned]'.[2] In the new United Nations Convention on the Rights of Persons with Disabilities, the REIO clause seems to have evolved to a RIO (Regional Integration Organization) clause, which does justice to the large scope of activities of the EU these days. In Article 44 of that Convention, a '"Regional integration organization" shall mean an organization constituted by sovereign States of a given region, to which its member States have transferred competence in respect of matters governed by this Convention'. Since Member States usually have retained certain competences, 'mixed agreements' are the appropriate instrument for the EU and its Member States to engage in international institutions in which both participate fully (Chapters 2, 3 and 4).

Express competences are not always needed for the EU to conclude an international agreement. As we have seen in Chapter 3, ever since the 1971 *ERTA* case, the CJEU also acknowledged the treaty-making capacity of the Union in cases where this was not explicitly provided for by the Treaty. This means that international agreements, including the ones whereby the EU becomes a member of another international organization or participates in a treaty-regime (Opinion 1/94

---

[2] See for instance Articles 4.1, 4.2, 4.3 and 4.5, 21 and 22 of the Kyoto Protocol.

WTO), may also be based on the external dimension of an internal competence. This is also confirmed by Article 216(1) TFEU, which – as we have seen – explicitly refers to international organizations: 'The Union may conclude an agreement with one or more third countries or international organisations.' At least to establish membership of the EU in international organizations, this provision seems to give a broad mandate to the EU to conclude international agreements in order to become a member of an international organization or to join a treaty-regime.

(ii) Specific areas indicated in the Treaties and the role of Member States

Irrespective of these more *general* indications of a competence to engage in international institutions, the Treaties explicitly refer to a number of *specific* policy terrains or international organizations (see also Chapter 3). Thus, Article 37 TEU allows for international agreements to be concluded 'with one or more states or international organizations' in the area of the CFSP. Similar provisions may be found in relation to environmental policy (Article 191(4) TFEU), development cooperation (Article 209(2) TFEU), economic, financial and technical cooperation (Article 212(3) TFEU) and humanitarian aid (Article 214(4) TFEU). In the environmental sphere, the Treaty reads that 'Within their respective spheres of competence, the Union and the Member States shall cooperate with third countries and with the competent international organisations'. In the field of humanitarian aid, the Treaty refers to 'international organizations and bodies, in particular those forming part of the United Nations system' to coordinate operations with (Article 214(7) TFEU). The UN (and its Charter) is also mentioned in relation to a number of other policy areas of the Union (Articles 3(5) TEU, 21(1–2) TEU, 34(2) TEU, 42(1 and 7) TEU, 208(2) TFEU, 214 (7) TFEU and 220(1) TFEU) (see also below). In relation to development cooperation, a number of provisions have been included to strengthen explicitly commitments of both the Union and its Member States in that area. Thus, Article 208(2) TFEU provides the following:

Article 208(2) TFEU

The Union and the Member States shall comply with the commitments and take account of the objectives they have approved in the context of the United Nations and other competent international organisations.

Article 210(1) TFEU adds to that an obligation of coordination, which, as we shall see in Chapter 10 on development, means concretely that the EU and Member States must take account of the Millennium Development Goals (MDGs), and their planned post-2015 follow-up ('Sustainable Development Goals' or SDGs), drawn up in the context of the UN.

Article 210(1) TFEU

In order to promote the complementarity and efficiency of their action, the Union and the Member States shall coordinate their policies on development cooperation and shall consult each other on their aid programmes, including in international organisations and during international conferences. They may undertake joint action. Member States shall contribute if necessary to the implementation of Union aid programmes.

In addition one may come across some references in relation to the European Central Bank and the EIB (see Protocols 4 and 5 to the Treaty). A somewhat more general provision, and the first one in a specific Treaty title on 'The Union's Relations with International Organisations and Third Countries and Union Delegations' is the following:

Article 220(1) TFEU

The Union shall establish all appropriate forms of cooperation with the organs of the United Nations and its specialised agencies, the Council of Europe, the Organisation for Security and Cooperation in Europe and the Organisation for Economic Co-operation and Development.

The Union shall also maintain such relations as are appropriate with other international organisations.

K. E. Jørgensen and K. V. Laatikainen, 'Introduction', in K. E. Jørgensen and K. V. Laatikainen (eds.), *Routledge Handbook on the European Union and International Institutions: Performance, Policy, Power* (London/New York: Routledge, 2013)

While the European Union's prolonged effort to address the debt crisis within Europe captured headlines through 2012, a broader perspective of the international institutional landscape revealed an EU very much at the centre of the twenty-first century multilateralism. Europeans congratulated themselves in May 2011 for successfully obtaining enhanced observer status in the UN General Assembly so that, in accordance with the Lisbon Treaty, the European Union delegation could represent the EU when there is a common position. While the modalities of this observer status are still being defined (e.g. when the EU can speak among the major groups in the General Assembly meetings), the resolution conferring this status was passed only after an extensive diplomatic campaign that encountered resistance among other regional groups and small states within the UN. Yet it is not only the UN General Assembly that has seen EU attention. The EU has been centrally involved in efforts to resolve the Iran nuclear issue since 2004, first as the EU-3+1 (the UK, France and Germany as well as the EU HR), then through the P5+1 through the UN Security Council. As diplomatic efforts have been stymied, the EU and EU member states were central in pushing for tightened economic sanctions through a half-dozen or so UN Security Council resolutions since 2004. In March 2012, the global banking communications network SWIFT (Society for World-wide Interbank Financial Telecommunication), based in Belgium, took the unprecedented step of expelling dozens of Iranian financial institutions as well as its Central Bank in order to comply with EU sanctions against Iran. . . .

[D]uring the same period that the EU has championed 'effective multilateralism' and experienced a dramatic internal reform process to improve its performance in external relations, broader multilateral processes have also undergone dramatic change, partly through negotiated reform processes and partly in ad-hoc response to broader global crises. This book therefore attempts to capture how scholars have wrestled with two moving targets – the evolving role of Europe in international institutions, and the transformations in international institutions themselves.

These two dynamics are playing out in a global environment of new emerging powers and a great deal of uncertainty. Europe and the post-Lisbon European Union contribute to this shifting terrain of global governance. While the Lisbon Treaty introduces reforms to enhance EU foreign policy, it has not clarified the long-standing question of whether the EU is a participant in or partner to other international institutions. Critical appraisals of the notion of 'effective multilateralism' have also cast a spotlight on how the EU interacts with a variety of international institutions: does 'effectiveness' require working through and empowering existing institutions, working against existing international institutions because they are ineffective, or working outside existing institutions and thereby consigning them to an indifferent fate. These questions lie at the heart of a growing body of scholarship that the present volume aims to review and summarise existing research, while also pointing to new avenues of inquiry.

This short overview reveals that the competences of the EU in relation to international institutions are fragmented and scattered across the Treaties. Apart from these competences of the EU itself, many of the provisions relate to 'cooperation' or to the role of Member States. Thus, the idea of fostering cooperation with third countries and competent international organizations returns in fields of education and sport (Article 165(3) TFEU), vocational training (Article 166(3) TFEU), culture (Article 167(3) TFEU) and public health (Article 168(3) TFEU). A similar promotion of cooperation with other international organizations is mentioned in relation to social policy (Article 156 TFEU) and cooperation in Union research, technological development and demonstration (Article 180(b) TFEU). In addition, the Union's foreign and security policy includes a number of rules on the way in which the EU wishes to present itself in international organizations.

4 INTERNATIONAL INSTITUTIONS IN WHICH THE EU HAS A LEGAL POSITION

(i) Membership

The EU can have a legal position in another international organization or body either through full membership or through an observer status with a variety of legal rights and duties. Full membership is mainly found in areas where the EU has extensive competences (such as trade, fisheries and largely harmonized dimensions of the internal market).

The EU is a *full member* of a limited number of international organizations only, including the FAO, the WTO, the European Bank for Reconstruction and Development (EBRD), Eurocontrol, the Energy Commission, the Codex Alimentarius Commission (CAC) and the Hague Conference on Private International Law. In addition it is a de facto member of the World Customs Organization (WCO), and also its participation in the Organisation for Economic Co-operation and Development (OECD) comes quite close to full membership. In this case it is made known that 'this participation goes well beyond that of a mere observer, and in fact gives the Commission quasi-Member status', despite the more modest formal arrangement that the European Commission 'shall take part in the work' of the OECD (Article 13 of the 1960 Paris Convention in conjunction with Protocol 1). Accession to the Organization on International Carriage by Rail (OTIF) is pending.

Full participation is also possible in the case of treaty-regimes. Thus the EU (as such) has joined (or signed) a number of UN Conventions, including the Convention on the Rights of Persons with Disabilities, UN Convention against Corruption, the UN Convention against Transnational Organized Crime and the UN Framework Convention on Climate Change. The Northwest Atlantic Fisheries Organization (NAFO) reveals that it is even possible for the EU to become a member of a treaty-regime without its Member States themselves being members.

In most cases, however, there exists a situation of 'mixity' (see Chapters 2, 3, 6 and 7), based on the fact that many competences are shared between the EU and its Member States. But, as in external relations law in general, the 'principle of sincere cooperation' (Article 4(3) TEU) or as it is often referred to, 'the duty of cooperation' (see Chapter 6), may restrain Member States in their actions, irrespective of the unclear practical implications of the principle in relation to the actions of the EU and its Member States in other international institutions.

P. Eeckhout, *EU External Relations Law*, 2nd edn (Oxford: Oxford University Press, 2011), p. 255

The . . . case law on the duty of co-operation and the Community's experience with work in international organizations suggest that the principle's effectiveness is limited if it is not fleshed out. There is an obvious case for creating some . . . EU treaty language on this crucial principle for mixed external action. There is also an obvious case for basic legal texts on how to conduct co-operation in the framework of international organizations.

The FAO and the WTO are the obvious examples of organizations in which the EU participates as a full member. While as a rule EU membership is still excluded both in the UN itself and in the specialized agencies (Article 4(1) of the UN Charter), the Community did join the FAO in 1991, after the provisions of the FAO Constitution had been amended to allow for the accession of regional economic organizations. From the outset, the division of competences was a difficult issue to handle and was to be based on a Declaration of Competence that had to be submitted by the Community at the time of its application. In addition, EU competences need to be established before each FAO meeting and for each item on the agenda. Without that statement, Member States' competences are presumed.[3] In cases where the EU is entitled to vote, its vote equals the number of votes of the Member States.[4] The requirement of constant statements of competences seems to form an obstacle for an efficient function of the EU in the FAO.[5] In addition, the EU is excluded from the organizational and budgetary affairs of the FAO. Thus, the EU is 'not eligible for election or designation' to bodies with restricted membership, which include the Constitutional, Legal, Financial and Planning Committees.[6] The actual and potential problems which this state of affairs raises will be addressed below. Following up on its FAO membership, the Community joined the CAC in 2003. The CAC was established by the FAO and the World Health Organization (WHO) and provides almost equal voting and participation rights to the EU as the FAO.

The EU's membership of the WTO (see further below),[7] differs in the sense that the Community was one of the founders of the WTO and a major partner in the Uruguay Round that led to the establishment of the WTO. No difference is made between EU and state membership, although here also voting rights may either be used by the EU (in which case the EU vote has the weight of

---

[3] Cf. Constitution of the FAO (CFAO), Article II, para 6.
[4] *Ibid.*, para 10.
[5] P. Eeckhout, *EU External Relations Law*, 2nd edn (Oxford: Oxford University Press, 2011), p. 229.
[6] CFAO, Article II, para 9.
[7] Article XI, para 1 of the 1994 Marrakesh Agreement.

the number of its Member States) or by the individual EU Member States. However, due to the fact that voting rarely takes place in the WTO, the voting rules remain rather theoretical. Nevertheless, competence problems remain a source for a complex participation of both the EU and its Member States in the WTO. In Opinion 1/94 the Court held that the Community did not have an exclusive competence to conclude agreements in the area of trade in services and trade-related aspects of IP rights,[8] two areas which in the form of the GATS and the TRIPS form part of the WTO system (next to the modified GATT). This has not prevented the EU from playing an active role also in relation to these areas. Billet pointed to two reasons for an active role of the Commission even in case where competences are (mainly) in the hands of the Member States: (1) the strongly institutionalized setting of the WTO, in particular in relation to the system of dispute settlement strengthens the position of the Commission 'both internally – vis-à-vis the member States – as well as internationally'; (2) the EU's own decision-making procedure (already implying a strong role of the Commission) as well as the Commission's expertise in the area.[9]

(ii) Observer status

Observer status implies that the EU can attend meetings of a body or an organization, but without voting rights. Furthermore, the presence of an observer can be limited to formal meetings only, after all formal and informal consultations have been conducted with members and relevant parties. In addition, formal interventions may only be possible at the end of the interventions of formal participants, which may have an effect on the political weight of the EU. In areas where the EU does have formal competences, but where the statutes of the particular international institution do not allow for EU membership, this may lead to a complex form of EU involvement. A good example is formed by the ILO. The 1919 ILO Constitution does not allow for the membership of international organizations. The existence of Community competences in the area of social policy nevertheless called for its participation in ILO Conferences. The Community was officially granted an observer status in 1989. The observer status allows the EU (represented by the Commission) to speak and participate in ILO Conferences, to be present at the meeting of the Committees of the Conference and to participate in discussions there. The status also allows for presence at the ILO Governing Body, where the Commission may participate in the Plenary as well as in the committees. However, it cannot become a party to any of the ILO Conventions. This complex division of powers between the EU and its Member States in the ILO was addressed by the Court in Opinion 2/91.

Opinion 2/91, *Convention No 170 ILO on Safety in the Use of Chemicals at Work* [1993] ECR I–1061

5. In any event, although, under the ILO Constitution, the Community cannot itself conclude Convention No 170, its external competence may, if necessary, be exercised through the medium of the Member States acting jointly in the Community's interest.

---

[8] Opinion 1/94, *WTO* [1994] ECR I-5267.
[9] S. Billet, 'From GATT to WTO: Internal Struggle for External Competences in the EU' (2009) 44 *Journal of Common Market Studies*, 5, 899–919, at 901–905.

Hence, in this case the Member States are used to act as agents of the EU to allow the latter to make use of its external competences in this field. Obviously, coordination issues arise, although both the EU and its Member States increasingly see the need of a joint approach (see also Chapter 6). A similar situation is found in relation to the IMO. Only states can become members of the IMO and hence the EU is excluded from membership. Yet, the EU has extensive competences in the area and will have to use its Member States (which are all IMO members) to act on its behalf in cases where competences have been transferred to it. The question of whether the EU had assumed powers from the Member States and in that sense had actually succeeded the Member States in a number of issue areas was excepted by the Court earlier in relation to the GATT,[10] and was answered negatively in relation to the MARPOL 73/78 Convention in the framework of the IMO (see the *Intertanko* case, Chapter 7).[11] It has, however, been made clear by the Court that Member States may not abuse the fact that the Union is not a member of an international organization. In cases of exclusive competence, Member States are not free to act on their own even if the Union is not able to table proposals by itself. Here also, the principle of sincere cooperation (Article 4(3) TEU) should be observed.[12]

Situations like these may indeed be prevented by granting the EU observer status and allowing it to act on behalf of its Member States in areas where it has assumed powers, rather than asking Member States to act on behalf of the Union in areas where they perhaps no longer have powers. Although it remains difficult for international organizations and third states (and occasionally even for Member States) to accept a role of the EU in international institutions, the extensive observer status enjoyed by the EU in the ILO is not unique and can be found in many specialized agencies and programmes of the UN, as well as in the UN's General Assembly and in ECOSOC. With regard to a number of international institutions (including the ICAO, UNESCO, OECD and the Council of Europe) the arrangements have been referred to as 'full participant' status, indicating that the only element that separates the EU from membership is related to the voting rights.

Finally, the EU may even participate in treaty-regimes or informal international networks in areas which are deliberately left to the Member States. Prime examples in this area include the regimes on non-proliferation and on export controls. On the basis of Article 347 TFEU, Member States have always claimed their own competence in relation to commodities related to the maintenance of peace and international security. At the same time this provision calls upon them to ensure that any measures taken in this respect do not prevent the functioning of the internal market and are in line with the CCP. In turn, this forms a reason for the European Commission (not the EU as such) to participate in some of these regimes, as a 'permanent observer' (for instance, in the Zangger Committee to harmonize the interpretation of nuclear export control policies for parties to the Non-Proliferation Treaty (NPT)) or even as a 'full participant' (as in the Australia Group which aims to ensure that exports do not contribute to the development of chemical or biological weapons).

---

[10] Cases 21/72–24/72 *International Fruit Company and Others* v. *Produktschap voor Groenten en Fruit* [1972] ECR 1226.

[11] See also case C-188/07 *Commune de Mesquer* [2008] ECR I-4501.

[12] Case C-45/07 *Commission* v. *Greece (International Maritime Organization)* [2009] ECR I-701.

F. Hoffmeister, 'Outsider or Frontrunner? Recent Developments under International and European Law on the Status of the European Union in International Organizations and Treaty Bodies' (2007) 44 *Common Market Law Review* 41–68[13]

After the breakthrough of Community membership in the FAO in 1991, the status of the European Union has further advanced in other international organizations and treaty bodies. Despite some resistance, inter alia from the United States, the Union has achieved greater visibility within and influence over the activities over several important organizations on the global level (ICAO, WHO, UNESCO). It has also consolidated and further refined its participant status in the Council of Europe and the OECD. It became a member in such diverse organizations as the Hague Conference on international private law and the newly founded Energy Community. On the other hand, the Union also keeps on struggling with the reluctance of some Member States to accept such a role in the transport sector in particular (IMO, Rhine and Danube Commissions) and continues to face a deadlock in some important UN bodies (for example UNHCR).

Against the backdrop of this mixed picture of factual developments, some interesting questions under international law came to the forefront. It could be shown that decisions to grant the status of a "full participant" to the European Union belong to the respective organs of an international organization, as long as they do not intend to regulate the overall status of the Union in the whole organization. In the latter scenario, the decision must be taken by the plenary organ. It also became clear that the Union's membership in treaty bodies will face new challenges when such bodies are not open to all contracting parties, but only to a certain number of elected members. . . .

In a nutshell, the European Union is neither an outsider anymore nor has it become a frontrunner in the multilateral arena. Rather it turns into a respected actor in international organizations and treaty bodies with the same speed as the law develops. Under international law that needs years of skilful multilateral diplomacy, under European law the European Court of Justice may accelerate the process.

5 REPRESENTATION IN INTERNATIONAL INSTITUTIONS

(i) Coordination of positions

In line with his upgraded position (see Chapter 1), the Union's HR for Foreign Affairs and Security Policy has been given a special role.

Article 27(2) TEU

The High Representative shall represent the Union for matters relating to the common foreign and security policy. He shall conduct political dialogue with third parties on the Union's behalf and shall express the Union's position in international organisations and at international conferences.

As we have seen, however, in many areas Member States enjoy individual competences in international institutions. Yet, they do have an obligation to coordinate their positions (under

---

[13] The excerpt has been updated to the post-Lisbon terminology.

the guidance of the HR) and once there is a Union position, the HR or Member States present will have to uphold the Union position.

Article 34(1) TEU

Member States shall coordinate their action in international organisations and at international conferences. They shall uphold the Union's positions in such forums. The High Representative of the Union for Foreign Affairs and Security Policy shall organise this coordination.

In international organisations and at international conferences where not all the Member States participate, those which do take part shall uphold the Union's positions.

In fact, effective multilateralism to a large extent depends on the (coordinated) actions by the Member States. This explains, for instance, why the Treaty stresses the obligations of Member States to uphold the Union's positions in international organizations and at international conferences where not all the Member States participate. The need for coordination between the Union and its Member States (and their diplomatic missions and delegations) in international organizations returns in the obligation for the diplomatic missions of the Member States and the Union delegations to cooperate and contribute to formulating and implementing a common approach (Articles 32 and 35 TEU). Interestingly enough, the Treaty for the first time also mentions 'Union delegations in third countries and at international organizations' which shall represent the Union (Article 221(1) TFEU). However, Member States seem to be somewhat anxious about the developments in this area. In a special Declaration to the Treaty (13) they stated the following:

Declaration No. 13 concerning the common foreign and security policy, OJ 2010 No. C83/343

... the creation of the office of High Representative of the Union for Foreign Affairs and Security Policy and the establishment of an External Action Service, do not affect the responsibilities of the Member States, as they currently exist, for the formulation and conduct of their foreign policy nor of their national representation in third countries and international organisations.

This Declaration underlies the tension between, on one hand, the need to coordinate positions in international organizations and where possible have these presented by an EU representative and, on the other hand, the wish of many Member States to maintain their own visible presence in international institutions.

As explained in Chapter 1, the EEAS plays an important role in the coordination of positions, in particular through the 'Union delegations', which have replaced the Commission delegations. The transformation to 'Embassy-like' delegations proved to be difficult in the case of missions at international bodies such as the UN in New York or the Organization for Security and Cooperation in Europe (OSCE) in Vienna, since the Union still had to work out how to handle EU representation in multilateral forums. However, it is certainly the EU's ambition to expand these powers 'progressively' to other EU delegations as well.[14] This process can be followed in the regular reports on 'EU Diplomatic Representation in third countries' published by the Policy Coordination Division of the EEAS, and has been recently evaluated in the December 2011 report on one year of EEAS. The latter report states that EU delegations 'have progressively taken over the responsibilities held by the rotating presidency for the co-ordination of EU positions and démarches'.[15] The report adds that this evolution has been a 'mixed success'. It argues that the transition 'has gone remarkably smoothly in bilateral delegations and has been welcomed by third countries', though other reports are cautious.[16] As regards EU representation at international organizations, the EEAS evaluation report states that 'the situation has in general been more challenging in multilateral delegations ... given the greater complexity of legal and competence issues'.[17]

Indeed, the unified diplomatic presence for the EU in multilateral forums post-Lisbon has so far proven highly problematic, in spite of the TFEU's specific legal obligation in its Article 220(1) TFEU. As we have seen, this provision requires that the EU 'shall establish all appropriate forms of cooperation' with various international organizations including, but not limited to (Article 220(2) TFEU), the UN, the Council of Europe, the OSCE and the OECD. On the basis of this provision, the Union has already begun to implement its ambitions in terms of presence in multilateral forums.[18] The saga of speaking rights at the UN General Assembly and EU participation in the UN concluded in May 2011 is referred to below.[19]

One particular situation is laid down in Article 218(9) TFEU.

Article 218(9) TFEU

The Council, on a proposal from the Commission or the High Representative of the Union for Foreign Affairs and Security Policy, shall adopt a decision suspending application of an agreement and establishing the positions to be adopted on the Union's behalf in a body set up by an agreement, when that body is called upon to adopt acts having legal effects, with the exception of acts supplementing or amending the institutional framework of the agreement.

[14] See for example: EEAS, *EU Diplomatic Representation in Third Countries – second half of 2011*, 11808/2/11 REV 2 (Brussels, 25 November 2011), and EEAS, *EU Diplomatic Representation in Third Countries – first half of 2012*, 18975/11 (Brussels, 22 December 2011).

[15] EEAS, *Report by the High Representative to the European Parliament, the Council and the Commission*, 22 December 2011, p. 6.

[16] *Ibid.*, p. 7; P. M. Kaczynski, *Swimming in Murky Waters: Challenges in Developing the EU's External Representation* (FII Briefing Paper 88, September 2011), p. 9.

[17] EEAS, *Report by the High Representative to the European Parliament, the Council and the Commission*, 22 December 2011, p. 8.

[18] As regards the Council of Europe, Article 6(2) states that the Union shall accede to the ECHR, a negotiation process which was nearly completed at the time of writing, January 2012.

[19] The EU first sought to upgrade its observer status at the United Nations at the UNGA meeting in September 2010, but after a much publicized failure only managed to do so by May 2011. See Catherine Ashton, *Statement by the High Representative following her call with UN Secretary-General Ban Ki-Moon*, A 162/10 (Brussels, 18 August 2010); also Ashton, *Statement by the High Representative on the adoption of the UN General Assembly Resolution on the EU's participation in the work of the UN*, A 172/11 (Brussels, 3 May 2011).

In 2012 this article was used by the Council as a basis for a Decision 'establishing the position to be adopted on behalf of the European Union with regard to certain regulations to be voted in the framework of the International Organisation for Vine and Wine' (IOV).[20] While the Council may indeed adopt a decision to establish the Union's position in an international organization, in the case of the IOV, the EU itself is not a member. Germany therefore argued that Article 218(9) TFEU was the incorrect legal basis for the adoption of the decision. Article 218(9) concerns in the first instance only the adoption of the positions of the Union in bodies, set up by international agreements, of which the Union is a member. According to Germany, Article 218(9) cannot however be applied in relation to the representation of the Member States in bodies of international organizations in which only the Member States participate by virtue of separate international treaties. Second, Article 218(9) covers only 'acts having legal effects', meaning acts binding under international law. OIV Resolutions are however not acts in that sense.[21]

(ii) Delivery of EU démarches on behalf of the EU and/or its Member States

The above case reflects the tension that may occur in relation to the question who may speak on behalf of the EU. With the EU wishing to establish its unified substantive diplomatic presence in multilateral forums, for some Member States it has become problematic that the EU's legal personality is now explicitly recognized by the Treaty (Article 47 TEU). While prior to the Lisbon Treaty the EU did already conclude many international agreements and could thus be argued to possess *implicit* legal personality (see Chapters 1 and 2), the 'politically constructive ambiguity' of 'European Union' allowed this label to function as a political umbrella term referring to the EC and its twenty-eight Member States. The fact that now Article 47 TEU explicitly gives legal personality to the EU has prompted the UK to deploy the argument that the terminology 'EU' can no longer be utilized to designate 'EC and its Member States' when delivering statements on behalf of the EU in multilateral forums.[22] Certain member States have argued that because the Union's legal personality has explicitly been recognized, 'EU' has become a purely legal concept. Therefore, it allegedly can no longer serve to represent areas covered both by EU and Member State competences as that might lead to competence creep to the Union. The Commission and several Member States strongly opposed this reasoning, which ground to a halt formal 'EU' representation in multilateral forums such as the OSCE and UN during the second half of 2011. During that time, several dozen of EU statements and démarches were blocked over deep disagreement as to who delivers the statement: 'the European Union' or 'the European Union and its Member States'. A temporary ceasefire, though not a permanent solution, was agreed on 24 October 2011 in the form of a document entitled 'General Arrangements for EU Statements'.[23] Through this document the EU wishes to keep competence battles 'internal and consensual'[24] so that the EU achieves 'coherent, comprehensive and unified external representation' in multilateral organizations. However, the time and effort spent on minutiae in Council Conclusions no

---

[20] Council Document No. 11436/2012.
[21] Case C-399/12 *Germany* v. *Council* (case in progress).
[22] Discussion with senior official from a Member State, November 2011.
[23] Council of the European Union, *General Arrangements for EU Statements in Multilateral Organisations*, 16901/11 (Brussels, 24 October 2011).
[24] *Ibid.*, p. 2.

less – ('EU representation will be exercised from behind an EU nameplate')[25] shows how difficult it remains to reach the ambition for the EU as a diplomatic actor to exhibit these three qualities. Notably, the arrangement expresses a rather rigid interpretation of 'international unity' focusing on form rather than substance. This because it requires that each statement made in a multilateral organization requires tracing who is competent for which area, and to ensure that the internal division of competences is adequately reflected *externally*, namely on the statement's cover page and in the body of the text.

The point made by the UK – the EU is the name of the organization of which the Member States are members and can therefore not include those Member States – seems legally correct (see also Chapter 1). Yet, in practice the debates do not strengthen the diplomatic power of the EU as a cohesive force in multilateral diplomacy relations with the substance of the single message being of central importance. What is then notable in light of the single message is that even when there is agreement that the EU shall present a statement on its *own behalf*, according to the arrangement, still, '*Member States may complement statements made on behalf of the EU whilst respecting the principle of sincere cooperation*'.[26] This statement is rather troubling diplomatically and legally: diplomatically, the utility of a Member State also taking the microphone to repeat what the EU delegate has just said (since the duty of cooperation in Article 4(3) TEU would not allow that Member State to say anything that contravenes it) seems rather futile. In international diplomacy one may certainly consider it useful that specific Member States with specific skills, knowledge or historically good diplomatic relations 'back up' EU action, though this is not what is envisaged by the arrangement: it concretely implies that Member States should still be allowed to repeat the same message of the Union, largely for the visibility of their own foreign (etc.) minister. Legally too, the duty of cooperation entails from the Member States that they respect 'the EU institutional process' and accept that their interests be defended 'through the Union' as a consequence of their EU membership.[27] In fact, when the EU has decided to act internationally, in many cases this will actually entail a 'duty to remain silent' on the part of the Member States, even in the area of shared competences.[28] Thus, the arrangement seems to go against pre-existing legal interpretations of shared competence and the duty of cooperation, and seems hardly conducive to the unified diplomatic actor *in substance* which the Lisbon Treaty and EEAS sought to create.

One example may illustrate the concrete impact of this rigid interpretation of Union competence and legal personality from the perspective of unified diplomatic representation.[29] On 22 February 2012, the Council adopted a Decision concluding the 'Memorandum of Cooperation between the European Union and the International Civil Aviation Organization providing a framework for enhanced cooperation, and laying down procedural arrangements related thereto'.[30] The Commission had proposed the negotiation of this Memorandum in June 2009,

---

[25] *Ibid.*, p. 3.

[26] *Ibid.*, p. 3.

[27] Opinion of AG Maduro, Case C-246/07 *Commission* v. *Sweden (PFOS)* [2010] ECR I-3317, paras 49 and 56.

[28] J. Larik and A. Delgado Casteleiro, 'The Duty to Remain Silent: Limitless Loyalty in EU External Relations' (2011) 36 *European Law Review* 524–541.

[29] The content of this box is based on B. Van Vooren and R. A. Wessel, 'The EEAS' Diplomatic Dreams and the Reality of European and International Law' (2013) *Journal of European Public Policy* 1–18.

[30] Council Decision on the conclusion of a Memorandum of Cooperation between the European Union and the International Civil Aviation Organization providing a framework for enhanced cooperation, and laying down procedural arrangements related thereto, DOC 5560/12 (Brussels, 22 February 2012).

and it was authorized to do so by the Transport Council in December 2009. The final document was initialled in September 2010. The purpose of this document was to ensure deep EU involvement in a multilateral organization of which it is not a member, but where it has significant competences. In essence it deals with the situation at issue in Opinion 2/91, where the CJEU has decided that due to absence of EU membership in the ILO, the Member States owed a close duty of cooperation to the Union so as to ensure adequate representation of the common 'Union interest'.[31] There should be no doubt that the Union has a strong legal and political interest to be represented in a singular fashion before the ICAO. Through the completion of the internal aviation market by the mid 1990s, as confirmed by the *Open Skies* judgments of 2002, many of the aspects on civil aviation covered by the 1944 Chicago Convention (safety, security, environment and air traffic management) fall within the scope of EU competence through the application of the *ERTA* doctrine. In keeping with this reality, the EU–ICAO memorandum essentially sets out a regime of closer cooperation through the reciprocal participation in EU and ICAO consultative processes, joint mechanisms for regular dialogue, information-sharing through databases, and so on. From the perspective of the EU Member States, supporting the EU in achieving its Treaty objectives through such a Memorandum in an organization of which it is not a member, is indubitably an expression of their duty of loyalty towards the Union embedded in Article 4(3) TEU.[32] The response of the UK was the following:

Council Decision of 22 February 2012, *supra*, p. 3

The UK will be abstaining on the Decision on Conclusion of a Memorandum of Cooperation between the European Union and the International Civil Aviation Organization. The UK recognises the benefits of the Memorandum of Cooperation, but attaches great importance to the principle of Member State sovereignty in international organisations. The UK is cautious about any measures and processes which could eventually lead to a change of the distribution of competences between the EU and Member States. We would wish to convey these concerns by abstaining on this Decision.

The UK had previously mulled a negative vote, but then decided that abstention would suffice to make their point. In any case, since the legal basis of this Council Decision is Articles 100(2) *iuncto* 218(6) TFEU, the Council adopted this decision by QMV and the adoption of the Memorandum was not blocked. However, it points to a road in EU external representation which ought not be taken. A close look at the substance of the Memorandum of Cooperation shows that it is 'procedural' in nature, by establishing forms of closer cooperation between the EU and the ICAO in areas where it already possesses competence. It thus does not 'expand' EU competence in scope or substance, and one might query what would be the on-the-ground consequences of this 'abstention' – read together with the general arrangement on external representation. In application of QMV it is normal that certain Member States may be outvoted, but the explicit adoption of this statement cannot be permitted to have any further consequences. Indeed, the UK remains bound by the duty to cooperate loyalty embedded in Article 4(3) TEU ('The Member States shall

---

[31] R. Holdgaard, 'The European Community's Implied External Competence after the Open Skies Cases' (2003) 8 *European Foreign Affairs Review* 365–394; European Commission, *Proposal for a Council Decision on the conclusion of a Memorandum of Cooperation between the EU and the ICAO*, Explanatory Memorandum, COM(2011) 107 final, Brussels, 10 March 2011, p. 2.

[32] Opinion 2/91, *Convention No 170 ILO on the safety in the use of chemicals at work* [1993] ECR I-1061.

facilitate the achievement of the Union's tasks and refrain from any measure which could jeopardize the attainment of the Union's objectives.'). Thus, in practice the UK must actively support EU activities in Montréal to implement this Memorandum of Cooperation, and may not undertake any action that would hamper its implementation. Time must now tell whether that will be the case, but the blockage of EU presence in other multilateral forums in the period after the entry into force of the Lisbon Treaty does not bode well.

The question of the effectiveness (or broader: *performance*) of the EU in international institutions has extensively been analysed by political scientists. While effectiveness (in terms of successful goal achievement) may be difficult to measure, there is some agreement that the EU has become a 'relevant' player in international institutions.

K. E. Jørgensen, S. Oberthür and J. Shahin, 'Introduction: Assessing the EU's Performance in International Institutions – Conceptual Framework and Core Findings' (2011) 33 *Journal of European Integration* **599–620**[33]

Overall, the empirical case studies point to a clear trend towards an increasing EU 'relevance' in international institutions. . . .

Without contradicting the overall picture, the case studies display important differences as regards the overall trend between different institutions and policy fields. To start with, instances of a decreasing relevance of the EU in international institutions would appear to be exceptional, requiring rather special circumstances. First, a specific ruling of the European Court of Justice (ECJ) led to less speaking with a common/single voice (although not necessarily less unity in substance) in the 'technical' standard-setting processes in the ILO in the 1990s. Second, the decline of the International Telecommunications Union (ITU) in the 1990s can be considered a prime reason for the declining relevance of the EU in areas of mixed competence with respect to the ITU. In other institutions, movement towards more EU relevance has either been non-existent (NATO), minimal/very limited (UNSC) or slow and cumbersome (World Bank). It is notable that these cases of limited progress all relate to areas traditionally considered particularly sensitive by Member States, namely security policy and finance (with EU presence and relevance in the IMF being similarly low/absent). From this perspective, it may be particularly noteworthy that some progress has been made even in these sensitive policy areas, even including the UN Security Council, which otherwise remains one of the strongholds of Member State competence. EU relevance is far more advanced in other important institutions: Both in the WTO and the international climate change regime, the EU is clearly established and accepted as speaking with a single common voice (represented by the European Commission in the case of trade and, so far, the Council Presidency in the case of climate change) based on elaborate internal practices and procedures for coordination. In the WHO and the ILO (in the more 'political' process of implementation review), there is a clear trend towards more coordination and common representation. . . .

Finally, the cases illustrate that procedures and practices of coordination of EU positions vary and do not display much consistency across institutions. For example, coordination in established (Council) working groups in Brussels (WTO, climate change) is supported by the EU structures and institutions established there (Commission, Council secretariat). In contrast, a more ad hoc approach seems to prevail where coordination primarily relies on arrangements at the seat of relevant international organizations (e.g. Geneva: ILO, WHO; Washington: World Bank). Under these circumstances, coordination relies much on individual Council Presidencies or the collective will of Member States.

---

[33] References to literature have been removed.

6 THE EU IN KEY INTERNATIONAL INSTITUTIONS

(i) The World Trade Organization

Ever since 1968, the EU constitutes a customs union and has been actively involved in the most important trade regime established since the 1960s, namely the GATT.[34] In 1995, the EC – as the only regional trade arrangement – became one of the founding members of the WTO.[35] The CCP (see Chapter 9) falls within the scope of the exclusive competences of the Union, and the European Commission is endowed with extensive functions for the management of this important external policy field, including monitoring the market access strategy, and concluding and negotiating trade agreements with third countries.

The substantive dimension of the WTO is dealt with in Chapter 9. In the present section we aim to point to a number of institutional peculiarities, underlining the complex relationship between the EU (and its Member States) and the WTO. The EU is a full member of the WTO, as are its Member States. While the participation of the EC in the GATT had already paved the way for EU membership of the WTO, the actual negotiations during the Uruguay Round of the WTO in the 1980s and the beginning of the 1990s revealed the complexities and sensitivities on the side of all participants. Again, the key question concerned the division of competences between the EU and its Member States, and the Commission was seen as perhaps attempting to stretch the exclusive competences it enjoyed in the area of goods (the GATT), to services (on the basis of the GATS) and IP (the so-called TRIPS).

Obviously, one of the issues was how to regulate the voting rights within the WTO. After all, the Union could be perceived by third states as an additional EU Member State because of its independent membership. The solution can be found in Article IX of the WTO Agreement.

Article IX of the WTO Agreement

1. The WTO shall continue the practice of decision-making by consensus followed under GATT 1947.[1] Except as otherwise provided, where a decision cannot be arrived at by consensus, the matter at issue shall be decided by voting. At meetings of the Ministerial Conference and the General Council, each Member of the WTO shall have one vote. Where the European Communities exercise their right to vote, they shall have a number of votes equal to the number of their member States[2] which are Members of the WTO. Decisions of the Ministerial Conference and the General Council shall be taken by a majority of the votes cast, unless otherwise provided in this Agreement or in the relevant Multilateral Trade Agreement.[3]
   1. The body concerned shall be deemed to have decided by consensus on a matter submitted for its consideration, if no Member, present at the meeting when the decision is taken, formally objects to the proposed decision.
   2. The number of votes of the European Communities and their member States shall in no case exceed the number of the member States of the European Communities.
   3. Decisions by the General Council when convened as the Dispute Settlement Body shall be taken only in accordance with the provisions of paragraph 4 of Article 2 of the Dispute Settlement Understanding.

---

[34] Since the successful establishment of the customs union in 1968, the EC had a de facto institutional status in the de facto international organization known as the GATT.

[35] For regional trade arrangements in the form of a customs union or free trade area, the relevant provision is Article XXIV of the GATT Agreement. See Article XI of the Agreement establishing the WTO.

The solution is thus quite simple: either the EU or the Member States vote. When the EU votes it gets the number of votes equal to the number of its Member States (that are a member of the WTO). Footnote no. 2 underlines that this way the EU (as a collective) will never have more votes than the number of its Member States. While the negotiations on these issues were difficult, practice revealed that the WTO almost never votes as decisions are generally taken by consensus of the entire membership.

P. Van den Bossche, *The Law and Policy of the World Trade Organization: Text, Cases and Materials* (Cambridge: Cambridge University Press, 2008), p. 145

Although the WTO Agreement provides for the possibility to take decisions by voting, it is exceptional for WTO bodies to vote. In 1999, when discussion on the selection of a new Director-General became deadlocked, some developing countries suggested that the decision on the new Director-General should be taken by vote (as provided for in Article IX:1 of the WTO Agreement). However, this suggestion was not well received, in particular by the developed countries who argued that this was 'contrary to the way things were done in the WTO'. Jackson wrote: the spirit and practice of the GATT has always been to try to accommodate through consensus negotiation procedures the views of as many countries as possible, but certainly to give weight to the views of countries that have power in the trading system. This is not likely to change. In a speech in February 2000 at UNCTAD X in Bangkok, ... Mike Moore the then Director-General, stated: The consensus principle which is at the heart of the WTO system – and which is a fundamental democratic guarantee – is not negotiable.

It is striking that not so much has been regulated concerning the roles of the Commission and the Member States in the WTO, neither at WTO level, nor at the level of the EU itself. There have been attempts to decide on a code of conduct, but no final document has been used in practice. Nevertheless, the provision on CCP was modified and it does give clear indications of the central role of the EU in the WTO because of the broad scope of the CCP.

Article 207 TFEU

1. The common commercial policy shall be based on uniform principles, particularly with regard to changes in tariff rates, the conclusion of tariff and trade agreements relating to trade in goods and services, and the commercial aspects of intellectual property, foreign direct investment, the achievement of uniformity in measures of liberalisation, export policy and measures to protect trade such as those to be taken in the event of dumping or subsidies. The common commercial policy shall be conducted in the context of the principles and objectives of the Union's external action.

Given the exclusive competence of the EU in this area (see Chapter 4), the role of the individual Member States in the WTO is limited (with the notable exception of transport). In fact, the Court's broad definition of 'trade issues' was already made clear in Opinion 1/78 when the question arose of who should negotiate a draft Agreement on Natural Rubber in 1978. Irrespective of the legal battles on the question of who should be at the international negotiating table, Member States seem to have accepted a leading role of the EU and do rely on the Commission's expertise, also in cases where they have an individual standing in dispute settlement in the WTO.

At the time of the negotiations on the WTO Agreement, these fundamental questions never-theless returned. After all, it is one thing to accept a key role of the Commission on an ad hoc basis (as exemplified by the Court Opinions during the 1970s and 1980s), but it is quite another to accept a structural and permanent limitation of traditional state powers in what was to become one of the leading international organizations in the world. While the negotiations during the Uruguay Round revealed the same pragmatism of allowing the Commission to be the key negotiator, with the Council and the Member States closely looking over its shoulder, the Commission in the end nevertheless requested the Court to confirm its exclusive competences in this area.[36] This is perhaps the irony of the EU/MS membership of the EU: the EU Member States have all joined an organization in which their powers, both theoretically (based on the exclusiv-ity of the competence) and practically (given the expertise of the Commission in the area), are very limited indeed.

Yet, in Opinion 1/94 the Court was asked to answer the question of whether the EU (at the time the EC) was exclusively competent to conclude the 1994 WTO Agreement, the argument essentially being that all underlying agreements had in fact trade policy objectives.[37] The WTO Agreement itself can be seen as an umbrella agreement, which – apart from establishing the WTO – tied together a number of agreements. The Court agreed with the Commission with regard to the agreements related to the trade in goods (Annex 1A of the WTO Agreement), but that exclusivity of the Union in relation to the GATS (Annex 1B) could only be established as regards cross-border services. Transport was not to be considered part of the CCP and could therefore also not be automatically included under the heading of exclusive competences; finally, the TRIPS on IP rights could fully be seen as coinciding with the Union's treaty competences in trade policy. This led the Court to conclude that the Member States were also still competent to conclude the GATS and the TRIPS; hence, the joint competence of the EU and its Member States in these areas.[38]

J. Bourgeois, 'The EC in the WTO and Advisory Opinion 1/94: An Echternach Procession' (1995) 32 *Common Market Law Review* 763–787

On 22 December 1994 the Council of the European Union formally approved the conclusion of the Agreement establishing the WTO and the agreements and associate legal instruments including the annexes to the WTO Agreement. According to its Article XIV the WTO Agreement is open for acceptance *inter alia* by "contracting parties to GATT 1947 and the European Communities, which are eligible to become original Members of the WTO". Throughout the whole Uruguay Round negotiation, the European Community has acted as an entity with the European Commission negotiating, assisted by the usual committee of representatives of Member States, called 'the mothers-in-law', and reporting from time to time to the Council to obtain fresh negotiation directives. However, partly as a result of the dispute between the Commission and several Member States on the question whether all matters negotiated

---

[36] P. Van den Bossche, 'The European Community and the Uruquay Round Agreements', in J. H. Jackson and A. O. Sykes (eds.), *Implementing the Uruquay Round* (Oxford: Oxford University Press, 1997), pp. 25–26.

[37] Eeckhout, *EU External Relations Law*, p. 28. See also J. Bourgeois, 'The EC in the WTO and Advisory Opinion 1/94: An Echternach Procession' (1995) 32 *Common Market Law Review* 763; M. Hilf, 'The ECJ's Opinion 1/94 on the WTO – No Surprise, but Wise?' (1995) 6 *European Journal of International Law* 245.

[38] A similar line of reasoning was followed by the Court in Opinion 2/92 *Re Third Revised Decision of the OECD on National Treatment* [1995] ECR I-521 and in Case C-360/93 *Parliament* v. *Council* [1996] ECR I-1195.

in the Uruguay Round come within the EC's exclusive powers under Article 113 EC [now Article 207 TFEU], the EC insisted itself that not only the EC but also its Member States be considered as members of the WTO.

This was admittedly the case in the GATT. Here was, however, a rational explanation for that: the EC Member States were contracting parties to the GATT before the creation of the EC. As the EC progressively took trade policy over from its Member States, this substitution of the Member States by the EC came to be recognized both within the EC and within the GATT. For all practical purposes the EC had become a GATT contracting party in the place of its Member States. The pragmatic acceptance by the other GATT contracting parties of the EC as a single entity replacing its Member States had been obtained without amending the GATT inter alia on the basis of the argument that one should not amend the GATT solely for the purposes of formally substituting the EC for its Member States; this could wait until the GATT was amended for other reasons. The creation of the WTO and the review of the GATT offered such opportunity. The EC missed it. This is the first reason for referring to the Echternach procession.

The second reason is Advisory Opinion 1/94 of the Court of Justice of the European Communities. . . . Opinion 1/94 is likely to have negative effects on the administration on the EC side of the WTO Agreement and its related agreements on the status of the EC within the WTO. . . . With a bit of negotiating skill, other WTO Members will have a field day in exploiting the situations.

It seems fair to say, that – despite these rather pessimistic forecasts – practice revealed a workable situation, in which EU Member States entrusted the Union to the larger extent to take care of their interests, and other WTO members learnt to live with the twenty-eight rather than just one EU member. This might very well be different were the WTO actually to vote on decisions rather than strive for consensus.

(ii) The United Nations

The EU Treaties present the UN and its Charter as the guiding legal framework for the EU in its external relations. Article 3(5) TEU mentions 'respect for the principles of the United Nations Charter' as part of the 'the strict observance and the development of international law' which are to be pursued by the EU. Similar wordings reappear in Article 21 TEU of the general provisions on the Union's external action. In fact, the promotion of 'multilateral solutions to common problems' should be done '*in particular* in the framework of the United Nations'.[39] Finally, as reflected in the preamble to the TFEU, UN law not only guides the external relations of the Union, but also its internal relations with its overseas countries. The Member States announced that they intend to 'confirm the solidarity which binds Europe and the overseas countries and . . . ensure the development of their prosperity, in accordance with the principles of the Charter of the United Nations'.

Over the years, empirical political studies revealed the difficulties of presenting a common EU position in the UN General Assembly. It has been noted that

---

[39] Emphasis added.

national interest [drives] the policies of the EU countries and the processes within the CFSP at the UN. In New York, the CFSP-regime is simply an instrument for intergovernmental dealings between the EU MS . . . There is little room for a single European voice on the East River, i.e. for a truly *common* foreign policy.[40]

More generally, there seems to be some consensus that 'EU cohesion in the UNGA varies over time and by issue area.'[41] Recent attempts to upgrade the position of the EU to a 'full participant' with full rights to speak and make proposals met with opposition in the UNGA.[42] Even more difficult would be to set national sentiments aside in the UN Security Council. Nevertheless, a specific provision aims to ensure that CFSP outcomes are also taken into account by EU members in the UN Security Council:

Article 32(2) TEU

Member States which are also members of the United Nations Security Council will concert and keep the other Member States and the High Representative fully informed. Member States which are members of the Security Council will . . . defend the positions and the interests of the Union, without prejudice to their responsibilities under the provisions of the United Nations Charter.

The Treaty even allows for the possibility that the Union's position is not presented by one of the EU Member States, but by the HR of the Union for Foreign and Security Policy. In that case the Member States which sit on the Security Council shall forward a request to that end to the Security Council. Given the traditionally sensitive nature of the special position of (in particular the permanent) members of the Security Council, this provision can certainly be seen as a further step in facilitating the Union to speak with one voice. Obviously, the ultimate decision to accept a presentation by the HR lies in the hands of the Security Council.

In order to prevent these new diplomatic competences of the Union from affecting the Member States' own powers, they adopted a special Declaration during the Lisbon IGC:

Declaration No. 14 concerning the common foreign and security policy, OJ 2010 No. C83/343

The Conference underlines that the provisions covering the Common Foreign and Security Policy including in relation to the High Representative of the Union for Foreign Affairs and Security Policy and the External Action Service will not affect the existing legal basis, responsibilities, and powers of each member state in relation to the formulation and conduct of its foreign policy, its national diplomatic service, relations with third countries and participation in international organisations, including a member state's membership of the Security Council of the United Nations.

---

[40] M. B. Rasch, *The European Union at the United Nations: The Functioning and Coherence of EU External Representation in a State-Centric Environment* (Leiden/Boston: Martinus Nijhoff Publishers, 2008), p. 301.

[41] G. Birnberg, *The Voting Behaviour of the EU Member States in the UN General Assembly* (PhD Thesis LSE, LSE Theses online), 2009, p. 52.

[42] M. Emerson and J. Wouters, 'The EU's Diplomatic Debacle at the UN: and Now What?' *European Voice*, 23 September 2010.

Irrespective of the interpretative character of this type of Declaration, they can never be used to evade the actual Treaty provisions. Any further development will therefore depend on the use by Member States of the new treaty provisions allowing for a stronger diplomatic representation by the HR (see Chapter 1).

With the coming of age of the EU's CSDP, relations between the EU and the UN have also gained importance in that area. As analysed in Chapter 12, Article 42(1) TEU provides that the Union may use its civilian and military assets missions outside the Union for peacekeeping, conflict prevention and strengthening international security, and again this should be done 'in accordance with the principles of the United Nations Charter'. In fact, the Treaties foresee the possibility of EU missions operating in a UN framework. The preamble of Protocol 10 to the Treaties refers to the fact that 'the United Nations Organization may request the Union's assistance for the urgent implementation of missions undertaken under Chapters VI and VII of the United Nations Charter'. And, Article 1 of the Protocol considers a 'permanent structured cooperation' between able and willing EU Member States necessary 'in particular in response to requests from the United Nations Organization'.

Similarly, UN law forms the legal framework for actions in relation to the new collective defence obligation in Article 42(7) TEU: 'If a Member State is the victim of armed aggression on its territory, the other Member States shall have towards it an obligation of aid and assistance by all the means in their power, in accordance with Article 51 of the United Nations Charter [the provision on (collective) self-defence].'

Also development cooperation (a shared-complementary competence) will have to be based on decisions taken by and in other international organizations, including the UN.

Article 208(2) TFEU

The Union and the Member States shall comply with the commitments and take account of the objectives they have approved in the context of the United Nations and other competent international organisations.

The same holds true for humanitarian aid operations, which are to be 'coordinated and consistent with those of international organisations and bodies, in particular those forming part of the United Nations system' (Article 214(7) TFEU).

The attention to the UN and its principles in the EU Treaties is thus overwhelming. In fact, the UN is referred to nineteen times in the current EU Treaties (including the Protocols and Declarations). Irrespective of the CJEU's judgment in the 2008 *Kadi* case, which seemed to emphasize the Union's own principles (see Chapter 7), the EU obviously regards many of its actions as being part of a global governance programme. With a view to the legal regime governing the EU–UN relations, one may conclude that most of the provisions aim to regulate EU policy in a *substantive*, rather than an *institutional* manner. EU foreign policy is to take place within the limits set by UN law. This holds true for external relations in general, and for CFSP, CSDP and development cooperation in particular. The Treaties do not offer *institutional* improvements to allow the EU and the UN to become 'partners in multilateralism'. The establishment of the EEAS, together with the new provision which allows for the HR to present EU positions in the UN Security Council (alongside her potential role in the General Assembly plenary), at best offer options that may be used by the Member States.

J. Wouters, *The United Nations and the European Union: Partners in Multilateralism*
(Leuven Centre for Global Governance Studies: Working Paper No. 1, 2007)

For several years, high-ranking officials from the European Union have been saying that the EU and the UN are 'natural partners' in multilateralism. Numerous factors feed this opinion. Both organizations find their origins in the same desire to eliminate 'the scourge of war'. A comparison of the principles and purposes moreover affirms the fundamental like-mindedness of the two institutions. . . . Last but not least, the European Union has presented itself as a reliable and even a vital partner for the workings of the United Nations. The figures are telling: together the 27 EU Member States contribute more than 38% of the UN's regular budget (compared to some 22% by the United States and some 20% by Japan), more than two-fifths of the UN peacekeeping budget and around half of all UN Member States' contributions to UN funds and programmes.

The EU is also the largest provider of official development assistance (ODA), accounting for some 54%. Over the last years, EU–UN cooperation has gained new impetus as common ground between the two organizations has expanded – notably through the rapid development of the EU's Common Foreign and Security Policy (CFSP) – to cover matters concerning not only trade and development, humanitarian aid and protection of the environment, but also the promotion of human rights, the fight against terrorism, conflict prevention, crisis management and peacebuilding. In this context, the EU has adopted a new credo of 'effective multilateralism', firmly enshrined in the European Security Strategy of December 2003, which declares that 'strengthening the United Nations, equipping it to fulfil its responsibilities and to act effectively, is a European priority'. . . .

True, in some areas the EU still suffers from a lack of credibility. Thus, despite the surge in Official Development Assistance, EU Member States still dump massive amounts of subsidized agricultural products on the world market, to the detriment of developing countries' national economies. Likewise, continuous lip service to the UN Charter cannot hide the fact that some EU Member States participated in recent military campaigns against the Federal Republic of Yugoslavia and Iraq without authorization from the UN Security Council.

However, when looking at the whole picture of EU–UN cooperation in areas such as environmental protection, human rights promotion, counterterrorism, et cetera, the EU's support for the principles and purposes of the UN outweighs the more questionable effects of some of its policies and of the military actions of some of its Member States. It is therefore safe to assert that the EU and the UN are, indeed, true partners in multilateralism.

7 THE INFLUENCE OF INTERNATIONAL ORGANIZATIONS ON THE EU

As we have seen in Chapter 7, the EU's legal order is traditionally perceived as largely autonomous, not only *internally* (vis-à-vis the Union's own Member States), but also *externally* (in relation to third states and other international organizations). The EU displays a certain 'openness' and does not seem to have a problem with allowing binding international norms to become part of its legal order, either through accepting international obligations or by referring to international agreements in its own Treaties (i.e. the UN Charter, the ECHR or the Geneva Conventions). With the gradual development of its external relations and the increase of external competences (on the basis of both primary law and case law),[43] the EU even revealed its

---

[43] See ECJ, Case 22/70 *Commission* v. *Council (ERTA)* [1971] ECR 263; Joined Cases 21/72 – 24/72 *International Fruit Company and Others* v. *Produktschap voor Groenten en Fruit* [1972] ECR 1226; Opinion 1/75, *Re Understanding on a Local Costs Standard* [1975] ECR 1355.

'dependence' as it had no choice but to accept that in order to be able to play along at the global level, it had to follow the rules of the game (i.e. in accepting global (product or process) standards or UN Security Council Resolutions). As indicated in Chapters 2 and 7, this has consequences for the effects of international obligations of the Union within its own legal order. The interplay between international and European law also may be important to understand the reverse effect: the influence of EU law on the international legal order, and the position the EU occupies in international organizations as explained in the present chapter.

The 'openness' of the EU legal order towards international norms implies the acceptance of an influence of these norms on the EU legal order. This, in turn, obviously puts the autonomy of the EU legal order into perspective. Indeed, over the years the EU has even accepted its 'dependence' on international normative processes. And, increasingly, these normative processes take place within international organizations and other norm-generating bodies.[44]

The strong and explicit link between the EU and a large number of other international organizations raises questions concerning the impact of decisions taken by other international organizations and of international agreements concluded with those organizations (either by the EU itself or by its Member States) on the autonomy of the EU and its Member States. To a certain extent this impact is shaped by the decisions of international (quasi-)judicial bodies, the two most influential ones being the dispute settlement mechanism of the WTO and that of the European Court of Human Rights. It is up to the Court of Justice of the EU to square these decisions with its long-standing and ongoing concern for the autonomy of the EU legal order and its own jurisdiction. The question is to what extent the Court of Justice has accepted being bound by the decisions of any external (quasi-)judicial body, although the influence of the ECHR's case law is settled by the EU Treaty itself (Article 6(3) TEU). In a similar vein, the WTO continues to have a considerable influence on the EU legal order. Both primary and secondary EU law is highly inspired by the GATT 1947; the WTO 1994 and many pieces of EU secondary legislation are either transposing WTO norms or were modified to bring them in line with world trade standards after adverse WTO judicial decisions.

Over the last decade scholars drew attention both to the proliferation of international bodies and to their normative (and at times 'legislative') activities.[45] The complex 'normative web' that is the result of the fact that globalization increasingly demands cooperation between rule-makers, obviously affects the EU as well. Examples include a variety of very different international organizations, with different relations to the EU. We may point to the influence of organizations referred to by the EU Treaties (such as the UN and the Council of Europe), organizations and bodies of which the EU itself is a member (WTO, FAO, G-20), UN specialized agencies (World Intellectual Property Organization (WIPO), FAO, WHO), economic organizations (WTO, OECD), financial organizations and bodies (International Monetary Fund (IMF), G-20, Financial Stability Board (FSB)) as well as organizations of which the activities are related to the (former) 'non-Community' areas of the Union (North Atlantic Treaty Organization (NATO), UN, Council of Europe).

---

[44] Cf. K. E. Jørgensen (ed.), *The European Union and International Organizations* (London and New York: Routledge, 2008), p. 188, who argues that over the last twenty years, the relationship between the European Union and international institutions has become 'more sustained and consistent'.

[45] J. Alvarez, *International Organizations as Law-Makers* (Oxford: Oxford University Press, 2005); A. Follesdal, Wessel and Wouters (eds.), *Multilevel Regulation and the EU: The Interplay between Global, European and National Normative Processes* (Leiden/Boston: Martinus Nijhoff Publishers, 2008); J. Pauwelyn, Wessel and Wouters (eds.), *Informal International Lawmaking* (Oxford: Oxford University Press, 2012).

Indeed, it is in particular areas where the EU does not seem to be in a position to ignore international norms. Thus, the impact of standards of its sister organization, the Council of Europe, can be studied at different levels and in different degrees, from the participation of the EU in Council of Europe conventions to the indirect influence of Council of Europe conventions on the EU legal order. Yet, as a non-member (for the moment) the EU still has a free choice whether or not to accede to the Conventions, and it frequently chooses not to commit itself. Similar situations are to be found in relation to the IMF. The EU is not a member of the IMF but all EU Member States are, which raises the question as to what extent IMF law interacts with and impacts EU law indirectly. A similar question may be raised in relation to the WIPO where the EU is among the most active international organizations.

Whereas the influence of these international organizations may flow from a substantive link with EU policy areas, the impact may even be more profound when the EU is a formal member of an international organization. This is the case in, for instance, the FAO and the CAC in the area of food security and food law. Similar to the situation in the WTO, the EU's membership defines the relationship with the other organization and the question emerges of whether one may note a hierarchical subordination of the EU to those international bodies.

The question of the autonomy of the EU came up in relation to the former EC in particular as it was related to principles of direct effect and supremacy. With the entry into force of the Lisbon Treaty at the end of 2009, the former 'non-Community' parts of the EU have been integrated into the same legal order. The sensitive area of Police and Judicial Cooperation in Criminal Matters (PJCC) is now part of the AFSJ (Chapter 14) and unlike the continuing special position of the common foreign, security and defence policy (CFSP and CSDP; Chapters 11 and 12), this policy field can no longer be said not to form part of the same legal order as the other policies. While one may argue that one of the reasons for the Court to underline the autonomy of the EU legal order (the preservation of its own exclusive jurisdiction)[46] is less valid in relation to CFSP and CSDP because of the limited role of the Court in that area, it is interesting to assess whether we can indeed witness differences. Thus, it is interesting to assess NATO's impact on the EU's legal and institutional design, policy-making and operational experience gathering in the field of security and defence. Also in the other, relatively young, policy field of the Union, the AFSJ, it would not make sense to turn one's back on the international developments. While in the field of criminal law the EU develops its role as a global security actor and makes use of its international engagements in order to develop deeper, autonomous measures in specific fields, cooperation in the field of private international law is characterized by a dichotomous approach, where the thorough participation of the Union in the negotiation of multilateral conventions may lead the Union to avoid external interference in the internal *acquis*.

Obviously, 'influence' is a matter of degree. In this section we use it to denote *the effect of norms created in or by international organizations on EU norms*. One may approach the issue from two sides: the international organization in question should have the capacity or power to exercise its influence (there has to be an institutional and substantive link), and the EU must be willing or compelled to 'receive' the influence. Influence is not a legal concept, and lawyers are not used to working with it (perhaps because it would imply the actual 'measuring' of

---

[46] Cf. Opinion 1/00, *Re Agreement between the European Community and Non-Member States on the establishment of a European Common Aviation Area* [2002] ECR I-3493, para 24.

effects – something that is also beyond the scope of the present book). We therefore rely on insights offered by political science and International Relations (IR) theory.

Costa and Jørgensen reveal that 'under certain circumstances international institutions [indeed] shape both policies and policy-making processes, even in ways sometimes unintended by the EU, or undesired by some Member States'.[47] They point to the fact that in IR-theory, different 'mechanisms' to exert influence have been noticed, which may (1) provide opportunities or constraints to actors, (2) change their ability to influence decision-making by changing the distribution of power, (3) establishing or spreading norms and rules, or (4) creating path dependencies. The emerging picture is a complex set of formal and (sometimes very subtle) informal ways in which international organizations (and other multilateral forums) influence the EU. The degree of influence may then also depend on the 'institutional strength' of the international organization. Some research showed that 'international institutions embodied in toothless non-binding agreements should have less influence on the EU than fully-fledged international institutions including binding treaties and meetings of regular fora'.[48] At the same time, it is well known that 'domestic conditions' are an important factor for the degree of influence.

The emerging picture is a complex set of formal and (sometimes very subtle) informal ways in which international organizations and other multilateral forums (such as the G-20) influence the EU. The degree of the normative influence of international bodies on the EU and its legal order depends on a raft of factors, ranging from the binding obligations resulting from EU membership and full participation in other international organizations, to the voluntary reception or outright rejection of international norms by the EU legislator and Court of Justice. In view of globalization's growing interconnectedness between all sorts of subjects of international law, and the waning economic and financial power of the EU on the international plane, the Court's refusal to take account of international law in order to protect the unity of the internal market becomes increasingly untenable. There is empirical evidence of the intense legal interactions between the EU and most international institutions. This is testimony to the coming of age of the EU as a polity. Whereas stressing its autonomy is necessary to establish the EU's position both vis-à-vis its own Member States and in the global legal order, the Union's further development sets limits on that autonomy. In many policy areas the EU has become a global player, and everything it does cannot be disconnected from the normative processes that take place in other international organizations.

8 THE BROADER PICTURE OF EU EXTERNAL RELATIONS LAW

The main question raised in this chapter was to what extent the EU Treaties regulate the position of the EU in other international institutions. It can be concluded that the Treaties do allow for the EU to be engaged in international institutions and even to become a full member of other international organizations or participate in treaty-regimes, albeit that the Treaties do not at all present the relevant provisions in any coherent fashion. The EU made full use of its possibilities,

---

[47] O. Costa and Jørgensen, 'The Influence of International Institutions on the EU: A Framework for Analysis', in Costa and Jørgensen (eds.), *The Influence of International Institutions on the EU: When Multilateralism Hits Brussels* (Basingstoke: Palgrave Macmillan, 2012).

[48] As paraphrased by Costa and Jørgensen, 'The Influence of International Institutions on the EU'.

but is often hampered either by the rules of the international institution, or reluctance by its own Member States to allow the EU to act on their behalf. A case in point is the EU's position in the UN, an organization that receives abundant attention in the new Treaties, but the substantive rather than institutional innovations are presented in terms of restrictions rather than as opportunities. At the same time, the complex division of competences between the EU and its Member States often blocks the EU from fully taking over.

It is this latter aspect that makes it difficult to speculate about future developments. Obviously, with the increasing external competences, the EU's position in the world becomes more prominent. At the same time international organizations (and their members) find it increasingly difficult to cope with the EU's complexities in the negotiating rooms. The question of who can sit behind which nameplate or who can speak on behalf of the EU may seriously distract everyone, and may even hamper an effective performance of the EU in international organizations or at other international forums.

SOURCES AND FURTHER READING

Alvarez, J., *International Organizations as Law-Makers* (Oxford: Oxford University Press, 2005).

Billet, S., 'From GATT to WTO: Internal Struggle for External Competences in the EU' (2009) 44 *Journal of Common Market Studies*, 5, 899–919.

Birnberg, G., *The Voting Behaviour of the EU Member States in the UN General Assembly* (PhD Thesis LSE, LSE Theses online, 2009).

Bourgeois, J., 'The EC in the WTO and Advisory Opinion 1/94: An Echternach Procession' (1995) 32 *Common Market Law Review* 763–787.

Chiti, E. and Wessel, R. A., 'The Emergence of International Agencies in the Global Administrative Space: Autonomous Actors or State Servants?' in N. D. White and R. Collins (eds.), *International Organizations and the Idea of Autonomy: Institutional Independence in the International Legal Order* (Oxford/New York: Routledge, 2011), pp. 142–159.

Costa, O. and Jørgensen, K. E., 'The Influence of International Institutions on the EU: A Framework for Analysis', in O. Costa and K. E. Jørgensen (eds.), *The Influence of International Institutions on the EU: When Multilateralism Hits Brussels* (Basingstoke: Palgrave Macmillan, 2012).

Delarue, R., 'ILO–EU Cooperation on Employment and Social Affairs', in F. Hoffmeister, J. Wouters and T. Ruys (eds.), *The United Nations and the European Union: An Ever Stronger Partnership* (The Hague: T.M.C. Asser Press, 2006), pp. 93–114.

Eeckhout, P., *EU External Relations Law*, 2nd edn (Oxford: Oxford University Press, 2011).

Emerson, M. and Wouters, J., 'The EU's Diplomatic Debacle at the UN: And Now What?' *European Voice*, 23 September 2010.

Follesdal, A., Wessel, R. A. and Wouters, J. (eds.), *Multilevel Regulation and the EU: The Interplay between Global, European and National Normative Processes* (Leiden/Boston: Martinus Nijhoff Publishers, 2008).

Frid, R., *The Relations between the EC and International Organizations* (The Hague: Kluwer Law International, 1995).

Hilf, M., 'The ECJ's Opinion 1/94 on the WTO – No Surprise, but Wise?' (1995) 6 *European Journal of International Law* 245.

Hoffmeister, F., 'Outsider or Frontrunner? Recent Developments under International and European Law on the Status of the European Union in International Organizations and Treaty Bodies' (2007) 44 *Common Market Law Review* 41–68.

Hoffmeister, F. and Kuijper, P. J., 'The Status of the European Union at the United Nations: Institutional Ambiguities and Political Realities', in F. Hoffmeister, J. Wouters and T. Ruys (eds.), *The United Nations and the European Union: An Ever Stronger Partnership* (The Hague: T.M.C. Asser Press, 2006), pp. 9–34.

Hoffmeister, F., Wouters, J. and Ruys, T. (eds.), *The United Nations and the European Union: An Ever Stronger Partnership* (The Hague: T.M.C. Asser Press, 2006).

Holdgaard, R., 'The European Community's Implied External Competence after the Open Skies Cases' (2003) 8 *European Foreign Affairs Review* 365–394.

Jørgensen, K. E. (ed.), *The European Union and International Organizations* (London and New York: Routledge, 2008).

Jørgensen, K. E., Oberthür, S. and Shahin, J., 'Introduction: Assessing the EU's Performance in International Institutions – Conceptual Framework and Core Findings' (2011) 33 *Journal of European Integration* 599–620.

Jørgensen, K. E. and Wessel, R. A., 'The Position of the European Union in (Other) International Organizations: Confronting Legal and Political Approaches', in P. Koutrakos (ed.), *European Foreign Policy: Legal and Political Perspectives* (Cheltenham/Northampton: Edward Elgar Publishing, 2011).

Kaczynski, P. M., *Swimming in Murky Waters: Challenges in Developing the EU's External Representation* (FII Briefing Paper 88, September 2011).

Larik, J. and Delgado Casteleiro, A., 'The Duty to Remain Silent: Limitless Loyalty in EU External Relations' (2011) 36 *European Law Review* 524–541.

Marchisio, S., 'EU's Membership in International Organizations', in E. Cannizzaro (ed.), *The European Union as an Actor in International Relations* (The Hague/London/New York: Kluwer Law International, 2002), pp. 231–260.

Pauwelyn, J., Wessel, R. A. and Wouters, J. (eds.), *Informal International Lawmaking* (Oxford: Oxford University Press, 2012).

Rasch, M. B., *The European Union at the United Nations: The Functioning and Coherence of EU External Representation in a State-Centric Environment* (Leiden/Boston: Martinus Nijhoff Publishers, 2008).

Sack, J., 'The European Community's Membership of International Organizations' (1995) 32 *Common Market Law Review* 1227–1256.

Schermers, H. G. and Blokker, N. M., *International Institutional Law: Unity in Diversity* (Leiden/Boston: Martinus Nijhoff Publishers, 2011).

Van den Bossche, P., 'The European Community and the Uruguay Round Agreements', in J. H. Jackson and A. O. Sykes (eds.), *Implementing the Uruquay Round* (Oxford: Oxford University Press, 1997).

Van den Bossche, P., *The Law and Policy of the World Trade Organization: Text, Cases and Materials* (Cambridge: Cambridge University Press, 2008).

Van Vooren, B. and Wessel, R. A., 'The EEAS' Diplomatic Dreams and the Reality of European and International Law' (2013) *Journal of European Public Policy* 1–18.

9
Common Commercial Policy

1 CENTRAL ISSUES

- This chapter[1] deals with a policy area that is traditionally seen as forming the heart of EU external relations law. The CCP not only formed the start of the development of EU external relations, it still forms a key example of a policy area in which internal and external policies are inextricably linked.
- In this chapter we will analyse the principles and instruments of the CCP. Irrespective of the scarce references in primary law, the Union has developed several instruments to shape this policy area. We also look at the roles of the Union institutions and the applicable decision-making procedures.
- Finally, this chapter will analyse the relation between the internal market and the external trade, and address the question of how this relationship influenced the development of CCP.

2 INTRODUCTION

The CCP is 'the mother of all EU external relations policies'. In the early days, many authors would even have a tendency to equate EU external relations law to CCP, and still many textbooks would explain basic notions underlying EU external relations law with extensive references to CCP,[2] so as to illustrate the development of the scope of an existing competence. It is true that the existence, nature and scope of external competences (see Chapters 3–5) have largely been defined by reference to early cases in the area of CCP. In this chapter we will occasionally return to these basic notions, but will predominantly look at CCP as an institutional and substantive policy area.

In fact, CCP is not just a key external relations policy, but in substantive terms, it is at the heart of the European integration project and a logical consequence of the interaction between

---

[1] We are indebted to Dr Joris Larik who because of his valuable suggestions and substantive additions may be considered a co-author of parts of this chapter. The usual disclaimer applies.

[2] See P. Eeckhout, *EU External Relations Law*, 2nd edn (Oxford: Oxford University Press, 2011): CCP 'remains the centre-piece of the EU's external policies' (p. 439); P. Koutrakos, *EU International Relations Law* (Oxford: Hart Publishing, 2006), who starts with CCP in the first chapter.

internal and external developments: e.g. the EEC as a customs union and the rules of free trade laid down in the GATT. Indeed, 'European integration itself was launched in the shadow of the pre-existing General Agreement on Tariffs and Trade (GATT), and continues to be shaped within the more comprehensive WTO framework'.[3] Also in quantitative terms, CCP cannot be ignored: most of the agreements concluded between the EU and third states concern trade or at least deal with trade-related issues. Since CCP (unlike for instance CFSP or the AFSJ) has been part and parcel of the European integration process from the outset, a vast amount of legislation and case law exists. In addition, despite the fact that CCP competences are exclusively in the hands of the EU (see Chapter 4), issues of demarcation with Member State powers continue to flare up (see Chapter 5).

According to the European Commission, 'the European Union is the biggest actor in international trade'.[4] It is indeed difficult to overestimate the trade dimensions of the EU's external relations. At the same time there is more to external relations than just trade, and combinations and conflicts with other policy areas (such as CFSP or development cooperation) do occur.

3 PRINCIPLES AND INSTRUMENTS OF THE COMMON COMMERCIAL POLICY

(i) Primary law provisions

The CCP is the external complement to the internal market rules on trade. As early as 1975, the Court of Justice ruled that the CCP had been devised in the Treaties 'in the context of the operation of the Common Market, for the defence of the common interests of the Community, within which the particular interests of the Member States must endeavour to adapt to each other'.[5] Its external nature is reflected in the preamble to the TFEU, which explicitly refers to *international* trade.

> **Preamble TFEU**
>
> DESIRING to contribute, by means of a common commercial policy, to the progressive abolition of restrictions on international trade

As we will see, the contribution of the EU to the 'progressive abolition of restrictions' is not always clear when we take into account the protection of certain industries or consumers in the Member States, as well as the preferences granted only to certain external partners (e.g. in development cooperation). These issues have all sparked disputes at the WTO level, which shows

---

[3] Larik, 'Much More than Trade: The Common Commercial Policy in a Global Context', in M. Evans and Koutrakos (eds.), *Beyond the Established Legal Orders: Policy Interconnections between the EU and the Rest of the World* (Oxford: Hart Publishing, 2011), pp. 13–45 at 16.

[4] European Commission, *International Trade Report*, Special Eurobarometer 357, November 2010, p. 5 (http://trade.ec. europa.eu/doclib/docs/2010/november/tradoc_146948.pdf).

[5] Opinion 1/75, *Re Understanding on a Local Costs Standard* [1975] ECR 1355, at 1363–64.

that the EU is not a docile trade giant, but in fact 'a very active player in trade dispute litigation'.[6] At the same time – and perhaps on a more positive note – the EU considers CCP to be an instrument of foreign policy, and has continuously linked it to development issues, environmental policies or CFSP. This is reflected by the listing of trade policy among the various external action objectives in Article 21 TEU.

Article 21(2) TEU

(e) encourage the integration of all countries into the world economy, including through the progressive abolition of restrictions on international trade . . .

It should therefore come as no surprise that CCP is part of 'The Union's External Action' (Part V TFEU) and finds its basis in Title II of that Part.

Article 206 TFEU

By establishing a customs union in accordance with Articles 28 to 32, the Union shall contribute, in the common interest, to the harmonious development of world trade, the progressive abolition of restrictions on international trade and on foreign direct investment, and the lowering of customs and other barriers.

This provision reflects the 'liberalization objective', which is drafted in mandatory terms ('the Union shall contribute'). This implies that 'Union institutions are bound to formulate the CCP in a way that has positive effects on trade and FDI [Foreign Direct Investment] liberalization'.[7] Article 206 TFEU also points to the direct relationship between the establishment of an internal 'customs union' and the objective of replicating this, at least to some extent, at the global level. This explains why from the outset it was clear that the core of CCP needed to be based on an exclusive competence. After all, any discretion on the side of Member States to enter into trade agreements on an individual basis could seriously harm the very foundations of the internal market. Article 206 TFEU explicitly refers to 'the Union' rather than to the Member States and, thereby, underlines that the development of world trade has shifted from the Member States to the EU. Second, in comparison to its predecessor, Article 206 TFEU not only mentions international trade, but also FDI as forming part of CCP, which indeed turns it into a fully fledged 'commercial policy'.

The underlying principles of CCP are mentioned in Article 207 TFEU (the only other provision specifically on CCP) and are – as we will see further on – elaborated upon in specific instruments.

---

[6] A. Delgado Casteleiro and Larik, 'The "Odd Couple": The Responsibility of the EU at the WTO', in Evans and Koutrakos (eds.), *The International Responsibility of the European Union* (Oxford: Hart Publishing, 2013), pp. 233–255 at 238.

[7] A. Dimopoulos, 'The Effects of the Lisbon Treaty on the Principles and Objectives of the Common Commercial Policy' (2010) 15 *European Foreign Affairs Review* 153–170 at 160.

Article 207(1) TFEU

The common commercial policy shall be based on uniform principles, particularly with regard to changes in tariff rates, the conclusion of tariff and trade agreements relating to trade in goods and services, and the commercial aspects of intellectual property, foreign direct investment, the achievement of uniformity in measures of liberalisation, export policy and measures to protect trade such as those to be taken in the event of dumping or subsidies. The common commercial policy shall be conducted in the context of the principles and objectives of the Union's external action.

The first sentence refers to the so-called principle of uniformity, requiring the adoption of common rules throughout the EU in the field of the CCP in order to prevent distortions of the internal market and to preserve the unity of the EU's position with respect to third countries.

The final sentence underlines that CCP is part and parcel of the Union's external action in general and is to be conducted in the context of the general principles underlying that area. In addition, Article 207(1) TFEU underlines that post-Lisbon, CCP is unambiguously widely defined, encompassing all trade aspects and eliminating previous uncertainties beyond trade in goods. Together with the reference to 'commercial aspects of intellectual property', the CCP is not only linked to the GATT, but also to the two other key WTO Agreements, the GATS and the TRIPS.

Finally, like Article 206 TFEU, Article 207 underlines that FDI falls within the scope of the CCP. FDI usually involves long-term investments and thus it is different from short-term investments. International investment operates in a different way from traditional trade. International trade agreements deal with the exchange of goods and cross-border services between two or more states (or the EU for that matter), whereas international investment agreements aim to protect foreign investment in a specific country. In addition, while trade agreements today often take a (regional) multilateral form, agreements regarding investment continue to exist mostly in a bilateral format. However, it is often difficult to separate the two areas, which makes it important that both are covered by the CCP. Most interestingly perhaps is that since 2009, FDI has been turned into an exclusive competence of the Union. This has serious consequences for the many existing BITs which over the years have been concluded between Member States and third states (see Chapters 2 and 7).

Article 207 TFEU at the same time provides the legal basis for the adoption of 'measures for the implementation of CCP'.

Article 207(2) TFEU

The European Parliament and the Council, acting by means of regulations in accordance with the ordinary legislative procedure, shall adopt the measures defining the framework for implementing the common commercial policy.

We will come back to this below, but it is important to note that this provision applies not only to trade in goods, but also to trade in services and commercial aspects of IP. This empowers the EU's institutions 'by means of regulations' to adopt measures for the implementation of the CCP. A degree of flexibility is reflected in the phrase 'defining the framework'. As we have seen in

Chapter 4, Union CCP competences are exclusive, which implies that the Member States have now transferred their competences in this (extended) area entirely to the Union. These wide-ranging exclusive powers notwithstanding, two safeguards have thus been introduced.

Article 207(6) TFEU

The exercise of the competences conferred by this Article in the field of the common commercial policy shall not affect the delimitation of competences between the Union and the Member States, and shall not lead to harmonisation of legislative or regulatory provisions of the Member States in so far as the Treaties exclude such harmonisation.

The first safeguard merely states the obvious and is in line with the principle of conferral. The second one also seems a bit superfluous, but mainly aims to make sure that trade agreements in services do not lead to a harmonization 'through the backdoor'. Here the 'parallelism between the internal and external actions' returns (see Chapter 3) and reflects the dilemma in CCP. The exclusive competence of the EU to negotiate and conclude international agreements within the scope of the CCP brings about the need to allow the Union to implement these agreements internally. However, this may lead to an extension of the EU's competence to act internally in those areas where competence lies with the Member States. At the same time, allowing the EU to act internationally only in as far as it has the competence to legislate at the internal level would restrict the internal competence of the EU as it could only implement international agreements to the extent that it has the internal power. Consequently, the EU needs to enjoy the power to negotiate and conclude international agreements which fall within the scope of the CCP even if it does not have the power to legislate internally in this respect. This means that the EU's competence can be exclusive at the external level in the areas where it has internally shared competence with the Member States. Obviously, the duty of sincere cooperation between the EU and Member States (see Chapter 6) may minimize the EU's lack of power to implement international agreements in this regard. In addition, the responsibility of the EU to implement these agreements under public international law should encourage the Member States to implement them.[8]

Finally, even if trade forms the core element of the Union's external relations (being part of 'The Union's External Action' in Part V TFEU), CCP is to be formulated and implemented with the general objectives and principles of its external action in mind. These are expressed, next to Article 21 TEU, also in a more succinct form in Article 3(5) TEU (see Chapter 1).

Article 3(5) TEU

In its relations with the wider world, the Union shall uphold and promote its values and interests and contribute to the protection of its citizens. It shall contribute to peace, security, the sustainable development of the Earth, solidarity and mutual respect among peoples, free and fair trade, eradication of poverty and the protection of human rights, in particular the rights of the child, as well as to the strict observance and the development of international law, including respect for the principles of the United Nations Charter.

---

[8] G. Villalta Puig and B. Al-Haddab, 'The Common Commercial Policy after Lisbon: An Analysis of the Reforms' (2011) 36 *European Law Review* 289–301.

A. Dimopoulos, 'The Effects of the Lisbon Treaty on the Principles and Objectives of the Common Commercial Policy' (2010) 15 *European Foreign Affairs Review* 153–170

... the Lisbon Treaty marks a new era for the orientation of the CCP. It signals the transformation of the CCP from an autonomous field of EU external action, subject to its own rules and objectives, into an integrated part of EU external relations, characterized by common values that guarantee unity and consistency in the exercise of Union powers. Within this framework, uniformity and liberalization are no longer the only principles determining the formation of the CCP. EU action in the field shall take into account and pursue the general objectives of EU external relations, thus legitimizing the current practice of adopting CCP measures for achieving other trade and non-trade goals. In particular, the references to fair trade and integration to the world economy next to liberalization illustrate that trade liberalization should not be seen any longer as a self-determining objective, but it should be regarded within the broader context of economic and social development objectives.

In addition, the Lisbon Treaty introduces another, more radical change. It strengthens the commitment of the EU towards gradual trade and FDI liberalization, incorporating in fact a standstill obligation of the EU to retain the existing level of liberalization. Bearing in mind the broader orientation of the CCP towards other potentially conflicting objectives, the task of balancing between liberalization and other objectives acquires a new dimension, as it is set on different institutional foundations. Apart from the plurality of political organs that have a saying in the determination of the CCP, the role of the ECJ engaging into a review of the legality of specific Union measures in light of the objectives they pursue is enhanced. Whether the Court will entrust the task of ensuring the coherent and consistent application of CCP to the political institutions or it will take a more active role remains to be seen.

(ii) Specific instruments and policies

The institutional and substantive rules that make up the CCP have been formalized in different instruments that over the years have placed some flesh on the skeleton presented in the Treaties. These instruments relate, inter alia, to tariffs, trade barriers, market access and anti-dumping measures.

(a) Common Customs Tariff

The Common Customs Tariff (CCT) dates back to 1968 and follows the logic of the internal market: once internal tariffs are removed one needs to agree on a common external tariff to prevent goods entering the internal market through the Member State with the lowest import tariff. These days the CCT can be found in Regulation 2658/87. This Regulation makes a difference between so-called autonomous rates of duty, which were fixed in 1968, and conventional rates that are the result of the negotiations in the WTO.

Domestic authorities are in charge of the application of the CCT. Its application is quite technical and complex and finds its basis in Council Regulation 450/2008 establishing the Community Customs Code. The European Union Customs Union (EUCU) not only consists of all the EU Member States, but also of a number of surrounding countries. EU applicant Turkey and two bordering microstates – Andorra and San Marino – have joined the customs union, as well as Monaco, which is part of the EU customs territory through an agreement with France.

(b) Trade barriers and market access

The free trade rules find their basis in a number of Regulations, the most general one being Regulation 260/2009, which lays down the basic free trade rules and their exceptions. Next to this, separate Regulations deal with specific (groups of) countries (such as North Korea) or specific products (such as textile products). Monitoring of the global rules on free trade is done above all on the basis of the dispute settlement system of the WTO. Yet, this system is only accessible to WTO Member States. The TBR of 1994 is a legal instrument that gives the right to EU enterprises, industries or their associations (as well as the EU Member States) to lodge a complaint with the European Commission which then investigates and determines whether there is evidence of a violation of international trade rules which has resulted in either adverse trade effects or injury. It is aimed at opening third-country markets by eliminating obstacles to trade for the benefit of EU exporters. It not only relates to goods but also to services and IP rights, when the rules concerning these rights have been violated and had an impact on trade between the EU and a third country. Hence, the TBR is designed to ensure that the rights of the EU under international trade agreements can be enforced in cases where third countries 'adopt or maintain' barriers to trade.

Council Regulation 3286/94/EC of 22 December 1994 laying down Community procedures in the field of the common commercial policy in order to ensure the exercise of the Community's rights under international trade rules, in particular those established under the auspices of the World Trade Organization, OJ 1994 No. L349/71

Article 1 Aims

This Regulation establishes Community procedures in the field of the common commercial policy in order to ensure the exercise of the Community's rights under international trade rules, in particular those established under the auspices of the World Trade Organization which, subject to compliance with existing international obligations and procedures, are aimed at:

(a) responding to obstacles to trade that have an effect on the market of the Community, with a view to removing the injury resulting therefrom;

(b) responding to obstacles to trade that have an effect on the market of a third country, with a view to removing the adverse trade effects resulting therefrom.

These procedures shall be applied in particular to the initiation and subsequent conduct and termination of international dispute settlement procedures in the area of common commercial policy.

Article 2 Definitions

1. For the purposes of this Regulation, 'obstacles to trade' shall be any trade practice adopted or maintained by a third country in respect of which international trade rules establish a right of action. Such a right of action exists when international trade rules either prohibit a practice outright, or give another party affected by the practice a right to seek elimination of the effect of the practice in question.

In addition, Articles 8(1), 11(1) and 12(1) of the Regulation make clear that the rules are not intended to protect the interests of individual companies (or even Member States). There also needs to be a Union interest involved for the Commission to be obliged to act.

Commission Staff Working Paper, Report to the Trade Barriers Regulation Committee, Brussels, 10 June 2009, Complaint Submitted by the Remote Gambling Association (RGA)

A. Introduction

On 20 December 2007, the Remote Gambling Association ("RGA") lodged a complaint pursuant to Article 4 of Council Regulation (EC) No 3286/94 (hereinafter the "Trade Barriers Regulation") concerning what was described as the United States' WTO-illegal ban on foreign Internet gambling providers and its allegedly discriminatory enforcement against EU companies. . . .

C. The challenged measures and obstacles to trade

The complaint concerns alleged trade barriers maintained by the US consisting of legislation imposing a ban on internet gambling; the measures taken to enforce that legislation; and the fact that the legislation is enforced in a discriminatory way. The investigation has confirmed that the US applies a prohibition on the cross-border supply of gambling and betting services into the US territory, and that in parallel certain types of remote supply of gambling and betting services are allowed within the US, both on an intrastate and interstate basis. . . .

D. Adverse trade effects

The obstacles to trade identified in the complaint have forced the total withdrawal and/or absence of EU companies from the US market and have significant additional negative effects on their business outside the US. It is evident that the Community enterprises affected by the US measures have suffered, and continue to suffer, adverse effects as a result of the US measures under investigation. Moreover, there is a threat of additional adverse trade effects that could develop into actual adverse trade effects. These adverse trade effects have a material impact on a sector of economic activity and on a region of the Community.

The obstacles to trade can therefore be considered as causing and threatening to cause adverse trade effects, having a material impact on a sector of economic activity and a region of the Community.

E. Community interest

The EU has developed the world's leading internet gaming business. Many of the world's largest companies are licensed in and operate from the UK, Gibraltar, Malta, Ireland and Austria. There are significant back office operations providing technology, marketing and customer service support in other Member States. Although accurate statistics on this sector are not readily available, the sector is economically significant, with an estimate of more than 10,000 staff employed by the internet gaming industry in the EU. . . .

The Global Europe Communication from October 2006 calls for activism in creating open markets and fair conditions for trade abroad. In this context, it is important to ensure that other WTO Members, and in particular the US, observe international trade rules, and the obligations contained in the WTO Agreement.

It can therefore be concluded that it is in the interest of the Community to act in respect of the obstacles to trade identified in this investigation.

Apart from the TBR, market access is aimed to be ensured through a set of other instruments as well, including so-called Market Access Teams: networks of relevant stakeholders who actively engage foreign authorities to remove non-tariff barriers before an actual multilateral dispute arises.[9]

[9] European Commission, *Global Europe: A Stronger Partnership to Deliver Market Access for European Exporters (Market Access Strategy)*, COM(2007) 183, Brussels, 18 April 2007; A. Tiedemann, *EU Market Access Teams: New Instruments to Tackle Non-Tariff Barriers to Trade* (College of Europe EU Diplomacy Paper 9/2009, December 2009).

In relation to development policy (see Chapter 10), CCP and the facilitation of access to the EU market have always played a role in creating leverage for improving for instance human rights or environmental standards. In this vein, CCP allows for trade benefits for developing countries. As we have seen, this seems explicitly required by Article 3(5) TEU, which refers to 'eradication of poverty and the protection of human rights' as elements forming the context in which CCP should be implemented.[10] Although the current Treaties do not make a distinction between different developing countries, CCP had a history of treating the ACP countries differently. It is with these countries that the EU had a special relationship on the bases of a series of international agreements (Yaoundé I in 1963 and II in 1969, the four Lomé Conventions spanning the time from 1975 until 2000, and finally the Cotonou Agreement of 2000 – see further Chapter 10). This special relationship has caused some controversies in the trade relationships with some other countries.

J. Larik, 'Much More than Trade: The Common Commercial Policy in a Global Context', in M. Evans and P. Koutrakos (eds.), *Beyond the Established Legal Orders: Policy Interconnections between the EU and the Rest of the World* (Oxford: Hart Publishing, 2011), pp. 13–45

It is in this context that the *Bananas* dispute arose, which would become the EU's longest-lasting trade dispute. The United States and several Latin American countries challenged the EU's regime for the import, sale and distribution of bananas favouring ACP countries. The [WTO] Appellate Body repeatedly found that the EU's preferential treatment, even after several reconfigurations, violated WTO rules. The EU had exceeded the derogations introduced in the GATT/WTO system favouring developing countries, as well as the special waiver granted to the EU in 1994 for the Lomé Agreement. Recently, the EU agreed to reduce the overall import tariffs for bananas in exchange for a no-litigation commitment from the Latin American countries. Consequently, an eroded preferential banana market organisation for the ACP countries will remain, but in order to adjust to the stiffer competition the EU decided to pay additional financial aid to the ACP countries. While this is arguably a positive move in terms of WTO compliance, it also appears as an implicit acknowledgement of the failure of this particular example of development through trade. More generally, the EU has abandoned its ACP-wide approach for granting trade preferences, and has moved to negotiate WTO compatible bi-regional agreements.

The WTO disputes on bananas arose from the fact that the EU differentiated between the ACP countries and other third countries, some of which were also producers of bananas. Through Regulation 404/93 the EC at the time aimed at protecting both the domestic banana production and the imports of bananas from the ACP countries. The result was that it was much easier for ACP countries to have access to the European market than, say, for Latin American countries. Germany, in an action it had brought before the Court,[11] inter alia, challenged Title IV of the Regulation, which referred to traditional imports of bananas from ACP countries into the Community and the absence of customs duties. Germany also argued that the Regulation was

---

[10] See also Joint Statement by the Council and the representatives of the governments of the Member States meeting within the Council, the European Parliament and the Commission on European Union Development Policy: The European Consensus, OJ 2006 No. C46/1, para 2.

[11] Case C-280/93 *Germany* v. *Council* [1994] ECR I-4973.

adopted in breach of GATT as well as the Banana Protocol. While the case was particularly relevant to determine that Article V GATT was not capable of conferring rights enforceable by individuals before national courts (see further below), in a more substantive sense it also clarified the subdivision of the tariff quota in favour of importers of Community and ACP bananas. These issues had been brought up by Germany by referring to the principle of non-discrimination.

Case C–280/93 *Germany* v. *Council* [1994] ECR I–4973

72. It is therefore clear that before the Regulation was adopted the situations of the categories of economic operators among whom the tariff quota was subdivided were not comparable.
73. It is true that since the Regulation came into force those categories of economic operators have been affected differently by the measures adopted. Operators traditionally essentially supplied by third-country bananas now find their import possibilities restricted, whereas those formerly obliged to market essentially Community and ACP bananas may now import specified quantities of third-country bananas.
74. However, such a difference in treatment appears to be inherent in the objective of integrating previously compartmentalized markets, bearing in mind the different situations of the various categories of economic operators before the establishment of the common organization of the market. The Regulation is intended to ensure the disposal of Community production and traditional ACP production, which entails the striking of a balance between the two categories of economic operators in question.
75. Consequently, the complaint of breach of the principle of non-discrimination must be rejected as unfounded. . . .

[And on the effect of the agreement on the competitive position of economic operators on the German market:]

82. The restriction of the right to import third-country bananas imposed on the economic operators on the German market is inherent in the establishment of a common organization of the market designed to ensure that the objectives of Article 39 of the Treaty are safeguarded and that the Community's international obligations under the Lomé Convention are complied with. The abolition of the differing national systems, in particular the exceptional arrangements still enjoyed by operators on the German market and the protective regimes enjoyed by those trading in Community and traditional ACP bananas on other markets, made it necessary to limit the volume of imports of third-country bananas into the Community. A common organization of the market had to be implemented while Community and ACP bananas were not displaced from the entire common market following the disappearance of the protective barriers enabling them to be disposed of with protection from competition from third-country bananas.
83. The differing situations of banana traders in the various Member States made it necessary, in view of the objective of integrating the various national markets, to establish machinery for dividing the tariff quota among the different categories of traders concerned. That machinery is intended both to encourage operators dealing in Community and traditional ACP bananas to obtain supplies of third-country bananas and to encourage importers of third-country bananas to distribute Community and ACP bananas. It should also in the long term allow economic operators who have traditionally marketed third-country bananas to participate, at the level of the overall Community quota, in the two sub-quotas introduced.

The role of the Court in the development of CCP will be addressed in more detail below, and has also been addressed in Chapters 3 and 4 on competence.

Apart from the preferential treatment of ACP countries (which is now replaced by bi-regional agreements), a so-called GSP also provides preferential access to the EU market for developing countries. This can be done on the basis of the WTO's 1979 'enabling clause'.[12] Specific rules were laid down by the EU in two additional schemes.[13] Firstly, the 'special incentive arrangement for sustainable development and good governance', known as GSP+, incentivizes third countries to comply with a range of international agreements, covering issues from labour standards and human rights to environmental protection, through preferential trade with the EU. Secondly, the 'special arrangement for the least-developed countries', known as 'Everything but Arms' or EBA, is aimed specifically at helping the world's poorest countries through duty-free access to the EU market. One hundred and seventy-six developing countries fall under GSP, forty-nine under EBA, while only sixteen countries have qualified for GSP+. In general, the effects of these arrangements have been said to be limited, not least due to their complexity.[14] In the *EC – Tariff Preferences* dispute, the WTO Appellate Body determined that certain forms of its conditionality were not covered by the enabling clause, which underlines also that these EU preferential treatment regimes run the risk of being countered by the international trade rules.[15]

Next to development, the issue of environmental protection has received more heightened attention in view of the emerging threat of climate change. Both are linked through the notion of sustainable development, which features both in the EU Treaties[16] and in the preambles to the WTO Marrakesh Agreement and the Doha Ministerial Declaration.[17] What role WTO dispute settlement can play here is also uncertain, but in view of the Appellate Body Report in *Shrimp Turtle*,[18] there is scope to consider products being made in an environmentally unfriendly way to be 'unlike' similar products using more environmentally friendly production methods. On the EU side, noteworthy trade-related environmental protection measures include the Regulation on waste shipment,[19] which transposes into EU Law the Basel Convention on the Control of Transboundary Movements of Hazardous Wastes and their Disposal, and the adherence of the Union to the Rotterdam Convention on the PIC Procedure for certain hazardous chemicals and pesticides in international trade.[20] This serves to show that CCP is not always about liberalizing trade, but can indeed also be used to regulate and if necessary restrict it, if this is in the interest of the Union.[21] Another area where the EU has combined trade with environmental protection is

---

[12] GATT, *Decision on Differential and More Favourable Treatment, Reciprocity and Fuller Participation of Developing Countries*, Decision of 28 November 1979, L/4903.

[13] Council Regulation 732/2008/EC of 22 July 2008 applying a scheme of generalised tariff preferences for the period from 1 January 2009 to 31 December 2011, OJ 2008 No. L211/1.

[14] L. Bartels, *Human Rights Conditionality in the EU's International Agreements* (New York: Oxford University Press, 2005), pp. 155–56.

[15] WTO, *European Communities – Conditions for the Granting of Tariff Preferences to Developing Countries*, Appellate Body Report (adopted 20 April 2004), WT/DS246/AB/R.

[16] See Article 3(3) TEU on 'sustainable development of Europe'; Article 3(5) TEU on 'sustainable development of the Earth'; and Article 21(2)(d) TEU on 'sustainable economic, social and environmental development of developing countries'.

[17] WTO, *Ministerial Declaration*, adopted on 14 November 2001, WT/MIN(01)/DEC/1, point 6; see also points 31–33.

[18] WTO, *United States – Import Prohibition of Certain Shrimp and Shrimp Products*, Appellate Body Report (adopted 6 November 1998), WT/DS58/AB/R.

[19] Regulation 1013/2006/EC of the European Parliament and of the Council of 14 June 2006 on shipments of waste, OJ 2006 No. L190/1.

[20] Council Decision 2006/730/EC of 25 September 2006 on the conclusion, on behalf of the European Community, of the Rotterdam Convention on the PIC Procedure for certain hazardous chemicals and pesticides in international trade, OJ 2006 No. L299/23.

[21] See, to this effect, Case C-94/03 *Commission* v. *Council (Rotterdam Convention)* [2006] ECR I-1, para 49.

through the establishment of a regional emissions trading scheme, linked on the global level to the Kyoto Protocol. At the WTO level, however, the *Swordfish* dispute shows that the EU has also not hesitated to launch a complaint against Chile for adopting conservation measures for alleged adverse effects on its trade benefits.[22] Finally, we can recall that environmental conventions also figure among the agreements to be ratified in order to qualify for GSP+.[23]

In Chapter 11 we will address the obvious relation between CCP and 'restrictive measures' (economic sanctions) established on the basis of CFSP. In general, rules on exports are specified in Council Regulation 1061/2009 establishing common rules for exports.

There is no one-size-fits-all model of a trade agreement but in most cases, the EU now tends to negotiate comprehensive FTAs. While bilateral trade agreements may – at first sight – not contribute to a global trade liberalization regime, they are often used as alleged 'stepping stones' to multilateral liberalization. The rules for FTAs are set out in the WTO, specifically in Article XXIV of the GATT and Article V of the GATS. FTAs are designed to create opportunities by: opening new markets for goods and services; increasing investment opportunities; making trade *cheaper* (by eliminating substantially all customs duties); making trade *faster* (by facilitating the transit of goods through customs and setting common rules on technical and sanitary standards); and making the policy environment more *predictable* (by taking joint commitments on areas that affect trade such as IP rights, competition rules and the framework for public purchasing decisions).

Free Trade Agreement between the European Union and its Member States, of the one part, and the Republic of Korea, of the other part, OJ 2011 No. 127/6

HAVE AGREED AS FOLLOWS:
CHAPTER ONE
OBJECTIVES AND GENERAL DEFINITIONS

Article 1.1 Objectives
1. The Parties hereby establish a free trade area on goods, services, establishment and associated rules in accordance with this Agreement.
2. The objectives of this Agreement are:
   (a) to liberalise and facilitate trade in goods between the Parties, in conformity with Article XXIV of the General Agreement on Tariffs and Trade 1994 (hereinafter referred to as 'GATT 1994');
   (b) to liberalise trade in services and investment between the Parties, in conformity with Article V of the General Agreement on Trade in Services (hereinafter referred to as 'GATS');
   (c) to promote competition in their economies, particularly as it relates to economic relations between the Parties;
   (d) to further liberalise, on a mutual basis, the government procurement markets of the Parties;
   (e) to adequately and effectively protect intellectual property rights;
   (f) to contribute, by removing barriers to trade and by developing an environment conducive to increased investment flows, to the harmonious development and expansion of world trade;

---

[22] WTO, *Chile – Measures Affecting the Transit and Importation of Swordfish*, Request for consultations by the European Communities of 19 April 2000, WT/DS193/1. Chile had also brought proceedings against the EU at the ITLOS. While the *ITLOS* case has been discontinued, the WTO proceedings have been suspended due to a provisional arrangement between the two parties.
[23] Council Regulation 732/2008/EC, OJ 2008 No. L211/1, Article 15(2).

(g) to commit, in the recognition that sustainable development is an overarching objective, to the development of international trade in such a way as to contribute to the objective of sustainable development and strive to ensure that this objective is integrated and reflected at every level of the Parties' trade relationship; and

(h) to promote foreign direct investment without lowering or reducing environmental, labour or occupational health and safety standards in the application and enforcement of environmental and labour laws of the Parties.

(c) Trade defence instruments

At first sight, trade defence seem to go against the idea of a free market. But as we have seen, perhaps ironically, to reach the objective of free trade much regulation is needed. The purpose of anti-dumping measures is to prevent the market (or in fact established domestic industry) from being distorted by products that are sold under their so-called 'normal value'. Determining whether sales are sold below value is a critical yet (politically) highly contested process, since it depends on an accurate comparison of data that is inherently hard to compare. The EU's commitment to the liberalization of international trade depends on a level playing field between domestic and foreign producers based on genuine competitive advantages. Hence, like other markets, the EU is keen on using the possibilities to defend free trade that find their basis in Article VI GATT and issued Council Regulation 1225/2009 on 'protection against dumped imports from countries not members of the European Community'. The Commission monitors the application of these instruments, follows up the enforcement of measures and negotiates future international rules with EU trading partners.

Council Regulation 1225/2009/EC of 30 November 2009 on protection against dumped imports from countries not members of the European Community, OJ 2009 No. L343/51

Article 1 Principles

1. An anti-dumping duty may be applied to any dumped product whose release for free circulation in the Community causes injury.

2. A product is to be considered as being dumped if its export price to the Community is less than a comparable price for the like product, in the ordinary course of trade, as established for the exporting country.

3. The exporting country shall normally be the country of origin. However, it may be an intermediate country, except where, for example, the products are merely transhipped through that country, or the products concerned are not produced in that country, or there is no comparable price for them in that country.

4. For the purpose of this Regulation, 'like product' means a product which is identical, that is to say, alike in all respects, to the product under consideration, or in the absence of such a product, another product which, although not alike in all respects, has characteristics closely resembling those of the product under consideration.

The following extract is an example whereby the European Commission decided to impose provisional anti-dumping duties on imports of solar panels and key components such as solar cells and wafers from China. An investigation by the Commission found that Chinese solar panels were being sold to Europe far below their normal market value. This decision taken by the Commission was particularly sensitive for Germany. That Member State has the largest solar panel industry of the Union, and feared that EU-level action would spark a trade war with China with commensurate impact on its industry. The Commission argued that international trade relations are to be conducted on the basis of law, rather than political strong-arming and divide-and-rule tactics by third countries. The day after publication of the extract below, China opened anti-dumping proceedings against European wine imports into that country, which made up two-thirds of its imports in 2012.

European Commission, *EU imposes provisional anti-dumping duties on Chinese solar panels*, 4 June 2013, MEMO/13/497

Whereas the dumping rate is at 88% on average, the anti-dumping duties imposed will only be set at an average of 47.6%, which is required to remove the harm caused by the dumping to the European industry. In addition, a transitional period of two months with a reduced duty level of 11.8% will be introduced as of 6 June. The duty will have to be paid as an "ad valorem" duty; in other words, as a percentage of the import value. It is provisional and imposed in total for a period of maximum six months.

The investigation will now continue. Definitive measures applying for five years, if any, would have to be imposed within 15 months of initiation, i.e. by early December 2013. . . .

The investigation was initiated on 6 September 2012 following a complaint lodged by EU ProSun, an industry association, which claims solar panels from China are being dumped in the EU at prices below market value and causing material injury to the EU photovoltaic industry.

The investigation was carried out within a strict legal framework covering a full analysis of dumping by Chinese exporting companies, injury suffered by the EU photovoltaic industry as a result of that dumping, and the interest of all EU players (Union producers, suppliers of components such as silicon, installers, importers, users and consumers). It showed that:

- there is dumping by the exporting producers in China: Chinese solar panels are sold on the European market far below their normal market value, resulting, on average, in dumping margins of 88%, which means that the fair value of a Chinese solar panel sold to Europe should actually be 88% higher than the price to which it is sold. In some cases, dumping margins of up to 112.6% were found
- material injury has been suffered by the Union industry concerned translated in loss of market shares in the EU, decrease in sales prices and decrease in profitability leading to a number of insolvencies of Union producers
- there is a causal link between the dumping and injury found
- the imposition of measures is not against the Union interest. . . .

How has the duty been calculated?

In general, duty rates are set by reference to the "lesser duty rule". The "lesser duty rule" is a so-called "WTO-plus" commitment of the EU, i.e. which allows the Commission to set a duty at a level lower than the dumping margin when this lower level is sufficient to remove the injury suffered by the Union industry. This fair approach benefits the exporters and goes beyond what is required by our WTO obligations. In practice, the injury margin is the amount "removing the injury", i.e. it aims at increasing prices to a level allowing EU industry to sell at a reasonable profit.

In addition, in view of exceptional circumstances and, in particular, the need to ensure the stability of supply in the short term, it is considered appropriate to phase-in the provisional duties and to introduce them in two steps. A period with a lower duty will ensure sufficient supply to meet all the demand, while allowing the Union industry to adapt to the situation and increase the supply gradually.

Since the EU does not recognise China as a "market economy", India has been chosen as the most appropriate and reasonable analogue country. This choice is not disputed by the Chinese side. In effect, a number of parties – including Chinese – have proposed India and expressed a clear preference over other alternatives such as the USA. ...

By 5 December 2013, the European Commission may propose to the Council (a) to terminate the case without measures or (b) to impose definitive anti-dumping measures for a duration of five years. According to the current rules, the Council can reject the Commission's proposal by simple majority. The final findings will be published in the Official Journal of the European Union.

Apart from the anti-dumping measures, Regulation 597/2009 aims to protect the internal market and its industries from subsidized imports from third states. The EU anti-subsidy rules define a subsidy as 'a financial contribution made by (or on behalf of) a government or public body which confers a benefit to the recipient'. The EU anti-subsidy rules further provide that the EU may impose countervailing duties to neutralize the benefit of such a subsidy only if it is limited to a specific firm, industry or group of firms or industries. Export subsidies and subsidies contingent on the use of domestic over imported goods are deemed to be specific. Subsidies can be used for different purposes, e.g. pursuing domestic and social policies, fostering production or exports, creating jobs, facilitating the creation and expansion of new industries, supporting economic activities that might otherwise fail, etc. However, they may distort competition by making subsidized goods artificially competitive (e.g. cheaper) against non-subsidized goods and thus negatively affecting competitors. In parallel to the aforementioned solar panel anti-dumping investigation, the Commission was from the end of 2012 also carrying out an anti-subsidy investigation.

Council Regulation 597/2009/EC of 11 June 2009 on protection against subsidised imports from countries not members of the European Community, OJ 2009 No. L188/93

Article 1 Principles
1. A countervailing duty may be imposed for the purpose of offsetting any subsidy granted, directly or indirectly, for the manufacture, production, export or transport of any product whose release for free circulation in the Community causes injury.
2. Notwithstanding paragraph 1, where products are not directly imported from the country of origin but are exported to the Community from an intermediate country, the provisions of this Regulation shall be fully applicable and the transaction or transactions shall, where appropriate, be regarded as having taken place between the country of origin and the Community.

The third category of trade defence instruments concerns so-called safeguards. Safeguards are intended for situations in which an EU industry is affected by an unforeseen, sharp and sudden increase of imports. The objective is to give the industry a temporary breathing space to make necessary adjustments – safeguards always come with an obligation to restructure. Unlike anti-dumping and anti-subsidy measures, safeguards do not focus on whether trade is fair or not, so the conditions for imposing them are more stringent. A safeguard investigation may lead to quantitative restrictions on imports of the investigated product (*import* or *tariff quota*) from any non-EU country and surveillance (a system of automatic import licensing). The legal basis for safeguards is different for measures against WTO members (Regulation (EC) No. 260/2009) and non-WTO members (Regulation (EC) No. 625/2009).

The results of the trade defence instruments are presented to the EP on a yearly basis.[24]

4 THE ROLE OF THE INSTITUTIONS AND DECISION-MAKING

(i) The Commission

International agreements concluded in the area of the CCP follow the general procedure laid down in Article 218 TFEU (see Chapter 2). Yet, Article 207(3) mentions a few particularities, which point to the institutions' somewhat different position.

Article 207(3) TFEU

Where agreements with one or more third countries or international organisations need to be negotiated and concluded, Article 218 shall apply, subject to the special provisions of this Article.

The Commission shall make recommendations to the Council, which shall authorise it to open the necessary negotiations. The Council and the Commission shall be responsible for ensuring that the agreements negotiated are compatible with internal Union policies and rules.

The Commission shall conduct these negotiations in consultation with a special committee appointed by the Council to assist the Commission in this task and within the framework of such directives as the Council may issue to it. The Commission shall report regularly to the special committee and to the European Parliament on the progress of negotiations.

It is explicitly mentioned that the Council and the Commission need to make sure that the agreements are compatible with internal policies. There is no choice in the selection of the 'Union negotiator' or the 'negotiating team' (see Article 218 TFEU); negotiations are by definition in the hands of the Commission, in consultation with a special committee through which, in turn, the Council can maintain its influence on the negotiations. Whereas Article 218 gives some freedom to the Council to establish a committee, it seems to be mandatory in relation to the CCP, and in fact it has been part of the system for a long time (previously known as the '133 Committee', named after the former Treaty article; these days as the 'Trade Policy Committee').[25] Finally, the EP is regularly informed during the negotiations (see below).

Despite the expressly mentioned roles of the Council and the EP in the final decision-making, the role of the Commission in CCP cannot be overestimated. Over the years the Commission has built up an extensive (technical) expertise and has been the main EC/EU representative in GATT/

---

[24] See for instance *Report from the Commission to the European Parliament*, 30th Annual Report from the Commission to the European Parliament on the EU's Anti-Dumping, Anti-Subsidy and Safeguard Activities (2011), Brussels, 19 October 2012, COM(2012) 599 final.

[25] Council document 16864/2009, 1 December 2009.

WTO. It is the negotiator of trade agreements and executes trade policy. On the basis of the new *comitology* rules[26] (defining the role of the various Member States' driven committees in the Commission's decision-making procedure), the Commission (and no longer the Council) takes final trade defence measures in the important CCP fields of anti-dumping, anti-subsidy and safeguards (see above).

Finally, the Commission's general competence to initiate an infringement procedure against a Member State is also applicable in relation to CCP matters.[27]

(ii) The Council

Article 207 TFEU

2. The European Parliament and the Council, acting by means of regulations in accordance with the ordinary legislative procedure, shall adopt the measures defining the framework for implementing the common commercial policy. . . .

4. For the negotiation and conclusion of the agreements referred to in paragraph 3, the Council shall act by a qualified majority.

   For the negotiation and conclusion of agreements in the fields of trade in services and the commercial aspects of intellectual property, as well as foreign direct investment, the Council shall act unanimously where such agreements include provisions for which unanimity is required for the adoption of internal rules.

   The Council shall also act unanimously for the negotiation and conclusion of agreements:

   (a) in the field of trade in cultural and audiovisual services, where these agreements risk prejudicing the Union's cultural and linguistic diversity;

   (b) in the field of trade in social, education and health services, where these agreements risk seriously disturbing the national organisation of such services and prejudicing the responsibility of Member States to deliver them.

Together with the EP, the Council is the main decision-making institution – this time in the formation of the 'Trade Council'. Article 207(2) refers to the application of the ordinary legislative procedure for the adoption of 'the measures defining the framework for implementing the common commercial policy'. This may be interpreted as reflecting a distinction between CCP Regulations laying down general legislative provisions concerning trade policy (to be adopted on the basis of the ordinary legislative procedure) and the implementation and application of such provisions in specific cases (not subject to that procedure).[28] In addition, Member States use the above-mentioned Trade Policy Committee to discuss and influence all trade matters.

---

[26] Regulation 182/2011/EU of the European Parliament and of the Council of 16 February 2011 laying down the rules and general principles concerning mechanisms for control by Member States of the Commission's exercise of implementing powers, OJ 2011 No. L55/13.

[27] See for instance, Case C-173/05 *Commission* v. *Italy* [2007] ECR I-4917; and Case 127/87 *Commission* v. *Greece* [1988] ECR 3333.

[28] Eeckhout, *EU External Relations Law*, p. 458.

In terms of voting modalities, the two paragraphs are clear: the Council decides by QMV. Indeed, this follows from the application of the ordinary legislative procedure. Yet, paragraph 4 also mentions an exception to the rule: the Council acts unanimously in the negotiation and conclusion of international agreements in the areas of trade in services and commercial aspects of IP, as well as FDI. The same holds for the areas mentioned in paragraphs 4(a) and (b). The latter points to that fact that it would not make sense to conclude agreements which cannot be implemented by the Member States. Pre-Lisbon, in Opinion 1/08 the CJEU considered that the principle of conferral places limitations on the exclusive competence of the EU in politically sensitive areas. In these cases mixity would form the solution. With former Article 133 TEC having been modified and replaced by Article 207 TFEU, these sensitivities are now catered for by more burdensome procedures and voting prerogatives of the Member States within the Council, while CCP as a whole has become an exclusive Union competence.

Opinion 1/08, *Amendments to EU Schedules of Commitments under GATS* [2009] ECR I-11129

135. The second subparagraph of Article 133(6) EC reflects a concern to prevent trade in such services being regulated by means of international agreements concluded by the Community alone under its external competence in commercial matters. Without in any way excluding a Community competence in that regard, the second subparagraph of Article 133(6) EC requires, however, that that competence which the Community in this instance shares with its Member States be exercised jointly by those States and the Community.

136. It may be observed that, by providing in that way for common action by the Community and its Member States by virtue of their shared competence, the second subparagraph of Article 133(6) EC allows the interest of the Community in establishing a comprehensive, coherent and efficient external commercial policy to be pursued whilst at the same time allowing the special interests which the Member States might wish to defend in the sensitive areas identified by that provision to be taken into account. The requirement of unity in the international representation of the Community calls in addition for close cooperation between the Member States and the Community institutions in the process of negotiation and conclusion of such agreements (see, to that effect, inter alia, Opinion 2/00, paragraph 18 and case-law cited).

137. In view of the foregoing, the various arguments put forward by the Commission and the Parliament to restrict the scope of the second subparagraph of Article 133(6) EC cannot succeed.

This explains the large number of mixed agreements (see Chapter 2) in an area which is considered to be the prime example of exclusivity. At the same time it puts the relevance of the principle of parallelism (see above) into perspective, as harmonization is not possible in areas not foreseen by the Treaty. These days, this is clearly laid down in paragraph 6 of Article 207.

Article 207(6) TFEU

The exercise of the competences conferred by this Article in the field of the common commercial policy shall not affect the delimitation of competences between the Union and the Member States, and shall not lead to harmonisation of legislative or regulatory provisions of the Member States in so far as the Treaties exclude such harmonisation.

This implies that the conclusion of international agreements is not allowed if it would lead to internal harmonization in areas where this was not meant to happen, such as the areas mentioned in Article 6 TFEU. Even in the area of CCP, Opinion 1/08 made clear that parallelism could not lead to disregarding the principle of conferral.

(iii) The European Parliament

As we have seen, and as in most other areas of Union policy, the EP is a co-decider in relation to the CCP. The ordinary legislative procedure applies, which implies that internal measures on CCP issues need the support of a majority in the EP.

Article 207(2) TFEU

The European Parliament and the Council, acting by means of regulations in accordance with the ordinary legislative procedure, shall adopt the measures defining the framework for implementing the common commercial policy.

The EP is kept informed on the negotiations of trade agreements by the Commission on the basis of Article 207(3).

Article 207(3) TFEU

... The Commission shall report regularly to the special committee and to the European Parliament on the progress of negotiations.

This allows for parliamentary scrutiny over trade negotiations. Irrespective of these specific provisions, Article 207(3) TFEU points to the applicability of the general procedure in Article 218 TFEU, which, inter alia, includes the following in relation to the negotiation and conclusion of international agreements (including the ones in the area of CCP; see also Chapter 2):[29]

Article 218 TFEU

6. ... the Council shall adopt the decision concluding the agreement:
   (a) after obtaining the consent of the European Parliament in the following cases: ...
      (v) agreements covering fields to which either the ordinary legislative procedure applies, or the special legislative procedure where consent by the European Parliament is required.
   The European Parliament and the Council may, in an urgent situation, agree upon a time-limit for consent. ...
10. The European Parliament shall be immediately and fully informed at all stages of the procedure.

---

[29] The arrangements are further specified in the Framework Agreement on relations between the European Parliament and the European Commission, OJ 2010 No. L304/47.

Yet, while the requirement of final consent may certainly be helpful, the EP has only a limited role to play during the negotiation process. Obviously, it will be very difficult for the EP to deny its consent or call for amendments after (usually) difficult and complex negotiations have ended. This makes consulting the EP during the negotiation process all the more important, thereby giving the Parliament the possibility of indicating some possible obstacles for its final consent.

The EP's consent is not needed for provisional application of international agreements. Council decisions to authorize the provisional application of an agreement can be taken on a proposal from the Commission alone without the need to ask for prior parliamentary consent (Article 218(3) TFEU). The latter rule is of particular importance in relation to CCP, as indicated by the 'Banana Agreement' between the EU and a number of Latin American states which effectively ended the already mentioned long trade dispute. The EU was only able to conclude this deal with the possibility of putting it into early provisional application in late 2009. The Latin American countries dropped their WTO cases against the EU in return for easier access to the EU market. On 3 February 2011, the EP then gave its consent to the text. Because of the current broad scope of the CCP in combination with its exclusive nature, international trade and investment agreements can be concluded by the Union alone, and consequently do not need to be ratified by the Member States, unless a mixed agreement was concluded. It is therefore up to the EP to exercise the necessary democratic control.

The extract below illustrates the active and proactive role the EP plays in the CCP. In this legally non-binding Resolution, the EP sets out some of its key views on these negotiations conducted by the Commission with the USA. For example, it expressly supports efforts by Member States such as France to exclude audiovisual services from the future EU–US agreement, for fear that European culture be swept away by USA (Hollywood) productions. While this Resolution has no legal effect, at the end of this document the Parliament does not hesitate to remind the reader that it 'will be asked to give its consent to the future TTIP agreement' as required by the TFEU and that therefore 'its positions should therefore be duly taken into account at all stages' of the negotiations of this agreement.

European Parliament Resolution of 23 May 2013 on EU trade and investment negotiations with the United States of America, 2013/2558(RSP)

The European Parliament . . .

A. whereas the EU and the US are the world's two major global traders and investors, accounting together for nearly half of world GDP and one-third of world trade; . . .

E. whereas the global economy faces challenges and the emergence of new actors, and both the EU and the US must exploit the full potential of closer economic cooperation in order to leverage the benefits of international trade in terms of overcoming the economic crisis and achieving a sustained global economic recovery; . . .

H. whereas the EU is convinced that developing and strengthening the multilateral system is the crucial objective; whereas, however, that does not preclude bilateral agreements going beyond WTO commitments and being complementary to multilateral rules, since both regional agreements and free trade agreements lead to increasing harmonization of standards and broader liberalisation favourable to the multilateral trading system;

I. whereas on 12 March 2013 the Commission proposed authorising the opening of negotiations and draft negotiating directives for the consideration of the Council;

1. Believes that the strategic importance of the EU–US economic relationship should be reaffirmed and deepened, and that the EU and the US should design common approaches to global trade, investment and trade-related issues such as standards, norms and regulations, in order to develop a broader transatlantic vision and a common set of strategic goals;

2. Considers that it is crucial for the EU and the US to realise the untapped potential of a truly integrated transatlantic market, in order to maximise the creation of decent jobs and stimulate a smart, strong, sustainable and balanced growth potential; considers this to be particularly timely in the light of the ongoing economic crisis, the state of the financial markets and financing conditions, the high level of public debt, high unemployment rates and modest growth projections on both sides of the Atlantic, and of the benefits offered by a truly coordinated response to these shared problems;

3. Believes that the EU should draw on its vast experience of negotiating deep and comprehensive bilateral trade agreements in order to achieve even more ambitious results with the US;

4. Welcomes the release of the HLWG [High Level Working Group] Final Report and fully endorses the recommendation to launch negotiations for a comprehensive trade and investment agreement;

5. Welcomes the emphasis in the HLWG Final Report on: (i) ambitiously improving reciprocal market access for goods, services, investment and public procurement at all levels of government; (ii) reducing non-tariff barriers (NTBs) and enhancing the compatibility of regulatory regimes; and (iii) developing common rules to address shared global trade challenges and opportunities;

6. Supports the view that, given already-existent low average tariffs, the key to unlocking the potential of the transatlantic relationship lies in the tackling of NTBs, which consist mainly of customs procedures, technical standards, and behind-the-border regulatory restrictions; supports the objective proposed by the HLWG of moving progressively towards an even more integrated transatlantic marketplace;

7. Welcomes the recommendation to explore new means of reducing unnecessary costs and administrative delays stemming from regulation, while achieving the levels of health, safety and environmental protection that each side deems appropriate, or while otherwise meeting legitimate regulatory objectives;

Negotiating mandate

8. Reiterates its support for a deep and comprehensive trade and investment agreement with the US that would support the creation of high-quality jobs for European workers, directly benefit European consumers, open up new opportunities for EU companies, in particular small and medium-sized enterprises (SMEs), to sell goods and provide services in the US, ensure full access to public procurement markets in the US, and improve opportunities for EU investments in the US;

9. Calls on the Council to follow up on the recommendations contained in the HLWG Final Report and to authorise the Commission to start negotiations for a Transatlantic Trade and Investment Partnership (TTIP) agreement with the US;

10. Stresses that the TTIP should be ambitious and binding on all levels of government on both sides of the Atlantic, including all regulators and other competent authorities; stresses that the agreement should lead to lasting genuine market openness on a reciprocal basis and trade facilitation on the ground, and should pay particular attention to structural ways of achieving greater transatlantic regulatory convergence; considers that the agreement should not risk prejudicing the Union's cultural and linguistic diversity, including in the audiovisual and cultural services sector;

11. Considers it essential for the EU and its Member States to maintain the possibility of preserving and developing their cultural and audiovisual policies, and to do so in the context of their existing laws, standards and agreements; calls, therefore, for the exclusion of cultural and audiovisual services, including those provided online, to be clearly stated in the negotiating mandate; ...

17. Emphasises the sensitivity of certain fields of negotiation, such as the agricultural sector, where perceptions of Genetically Modified Organisms (GMOs), cloning and consumer health tend to diverge between the US and the EU; sees an opportunity in enhanced cooperation in agriculture trade, and stresses the importance of an ambitious and balanced outcome in this field; stresses that the agreement must not undermine the fundamental values of either side, for example the precautionary principle in the EU; calls on the US to lift its import ban on EU beef products, as a trust-building measure;

18. Stresses that financial services must be included in the TTIP negotiations, and calls in this context for particular attention to be paid to equivalence, mutual recognition, convergence and extraterritoriality, since these are central considerations for both sides; emphasises that convergence towards a common financial regulatory framework between the EU and US would be beneficial; highlights that whilst market access must be regarded as a positive step, prudential supervisory processes are vital for obtaining proper convergence; stresses that the negative impact of extraterritoriality should be minimised and should not be allowed to detract from a consistent approach to regulating financial services; . . .

The role of Parliament

23. Looks forward to the launch of negotiations with the US, and to following them closely and contributing to their successful outcome; reminds the Commission of its obligation to keep Parliament immediately and fully informed at all stages of the negotiations (before and after the negotiating rounds); is committed to addressing the legislative and regulatory issues that may arise in the context of the negotiations and the future agreement; reiterates its basic responsibility to represent the citizens of the EU, and looks forward to facilitating inclusive and open discussions during the negotiating process; is committed to taking a proactive role in collaborating with its US counterparts when introducing new regulations;

24. Is committed to working closely with the Council, the Commission, the US Congress, the US Administration and the stakeholders to achieve the full economic, social and environmental potential of the transatlantic economic relationship and strengthen EU and US leadership in the liberalisation and regulation of trade and foreign investment; is committed to encouraging a deeper bilateral EU–US cooperation in order to assert the leadership of both in international trade and investment;

25. Recalls that Parliament will be asked to give its consent to the future TTIP agreement, as stipulated by the Treaty on the Functioning of the European Union, and that its positions should therefore be duly taken into account at all stages;

26. Recalls that Parliament will endeavour to monitor the implementation of the future agreement;

(iv) The Court of Justice

This subsection differs from the ones addressing the other institutions in the sense that we will use it to highlight a number of issues on which the role of the Court has been quite decisive with regard to the definition and development of CCP. Because of the fundamental relationship between CCP and the European integration process, a broad range of actors may be affected by the CCP measures, or hope to be able to rely on WTO Agreements. In principle, the EU Courts are competent to deal with CCP on the basis of the general judicial procedures: the action for annulment (Article 263 TFEU), the preliminary reference procedure (Article 267 TFEU) and an action to invoke the contractual liability of the Union (Articles 268 and 340 TFEU). Furthermore, the Member States and the institutions can request the *ex ante* review of a trade agreement by the

Court (Article 218(11) TFEU), as was the case with the WTO Agreements of 1994.[30] The extensive case law may be divided in cases related to commercial policy measures and cases on the effects of GATT/WTO law in the EU legal order, both reflecting the internal/external interface which is so characteristic for the CCP.

(a) CCP measures

The possibility for individuals to bring an action for annulment against a CCP measure (in this case an anti-dumping measure) was confirmed by the Court in *Allied Corporation and Others*.[31] Irrespective of their general legislative nature, the fact that the exporters (of fertilizers) were expressly named in the Regulation caused the Court to rule that the provisions of anti-dumping Regulations could be of direct and individual concern to the producers and exporters. Indeed, many CCP cases concern anti-dumping measures. In *Timex*,[32] this watch producer argued that anti-dumping duties on imports of mechanical wristwatches originating from the (then) Soviet Union were insufficient to protect its interests on the EU market. In this case the measure in question was of direct and individual concern to Timex as this company was involved in initiating the proceedings, and was in fact the only producer that was affected by the dumping of Soviet watches.

Anti-dumping duties are paid by the importers of dumped products and obviously they may disagree with the duties themselves or with their level. Yet, while exporters have occasionally been quite successful in claiming to be directly and individually concerned, this has proven to be more difficult for importers. In *Alusuisse*,[33] the Court found the anti-dumping measure to be of general application as the importers were not listed in the Regulation. Exceptions have been noted when importers were associated with the mentioned exporters, or in a very specific situation,[34] but the general rules seems to be that anti-dumping measures apply generally. Nevertheless, the fact that current Article 263(4) TFEU allows individuals to initiate proceeding against a 'regulatory act' when it is 'of direct concern to them and does not entail implementing measures', may allow for some flexibility. After all, once anti-dumping measures can be qualified as 'regulatory acts', there is no need for individuals to state their individual concern.

(b) Effects of WTO law

The effects of international law in the EU legal order have been addressed in Chapter 7 in general. In this subsection we highlight some specific aspects of the role of the Court in relation to the CCP and, above all, the effects of WTO rules in the Union's legal order.

In principle the competence of the Court extends to CCP issues, and in terms of legal scrutiny and protection the whole regime of Article 263 TFEU applies. The establishment of the WTO (1994), and in particular its quasi-judicial dispute settlement system laid down in the Understanding on Rules and Procedures Governing the Settlement of Disputes (DSU), turned the rather 'member-driven' GATT 1947 trade regime into a more sophisticated, 'rules based' system. This development sparked a number of cases before the ECJ. The leading case is the *Portuguese*

---

[30] Opinion 1/94, *Re World Trade Organization Agreement* [1994] ECR I-5267.
[31] Joined Cases 239/82 & 275/82 *Allied Corporation and Others* v. *Commission* [1984] ECR 1005.
[32] Case 264/82 *Timex* v. *Council and Commission* [1985] ECR 849.
[33] Case 307/81 *Alusuisse* v. *Council and Commission* [1982] ECR 3463.
[34] Case C358/89 *Extramet Industrie* v. *Council* [1991] ECR I-2501.

Textiles case[35] where Portugal challenged a Council Decision concerning the conclusion of an MoU between the Community and Pakistan and India on arrangements in the area of market access for textile products. In this case the ECJ was asked to decide on the direct effect of a WTO Agreement, which the Court denied. While this case was brought to the Court by a Member State, two years later it came to a similar conclusion in answering the question of whether individuals could challenge the legality of EU secondary legislation by invoking a WTO Agreement (*Parfums Dior*).[36]

Case C-149/96 *Portugal* v. *Council* [1999] ECR I-8395

36. While it is true that the WTO agreements, as the Portuguese Government observes, differ significantly from the provisions of GATT 1947, in particular by reason of the strengthening of the system of safeguards and the mechanism for resolving disputes, the system resulting from those agreements nevertheless accords considerable importance to negotiation between the parties.

37. Although the main purpose of the mechanism for resolving disputes is in principle, according to Article 3(7) of the Understanding on Rules and Procedures Governing the Settlement of Disputes (Annex 2 to the WTO), to secure the withdrawal of the measures in question if they are found to be inconsistent with the WTO rules, that understanding provides that where the immediate withdrawal of the measures is impracticable compensation may be granted on an interim basis pending the withdrawal of the inconsistent measure.

38. According to Article 22(1) of that Understanding, compensation is a temporary measure available in the event that the recommendations and rulings of the dispute settlement body provided for in Article 2(1) of that Understanding are not implemented within a reasonable period of time, and Article 22(1) shows a preference for full implementation of a recommendation to bring a measure into conformity with the WTO agreements in question.

39. However, Article 22(2) provides that if the member concerned fails to fulfil its obligation to implement the said recommendations and rulings within a reasonable period of time, it is, if so requested, and on the expiry of a reasonable period at the latest, to enter into negotiations with any party having invoked the dispute settlement procedures, with a view to finding mutually acceptable compensation.

40. Consequently, to require the judicial organs to refrain from applying the rules of domestic law which are inconsistent with the WTO agreements would have the consequence of depriving the legislative or executive organs of the contracting parties of the possibility afforded by Article 22 of that memorandum of entering into negotiated arrangements even on a temporary basis.

41. It follows that the WTO agreements, interpreted in the light of their subject-matter and purpose, do not determine the appropriate legal means of ensuring that they are applied in good faith in the legal order of the contracting parties.

42. As regards, more particularly, the application of the WTO agreements in the Community legal order, it must be noted that, according to its preamble, the agreement establishing the WTO, including the annexes, is still founded, like GATT 1947, on the principle of negotiations with a view to 'entering into reciprocal and mutually advantageous arrangements' and is thus distinguished, from the viewpoint of the Community, from the agreements concluded between the Community and non-member countries which introduce

---

[35] Case C-149/96 *Portugal* v. *Council* [1999] ECR I-8395.

[36] Joined Cases C-300/98 and C-392/98 *Parfums Dior SA* v. *TUK Consultancy BV, and Assco Gerüste GmbH and Rob van Dyk* v. *Wilhelm Layhwer GmbH and Co. KG and Layher BV* [2000] ECR I-11307.

a certain asymmetry of obligations, or create special relations of integration with the Community, such as the agreement which the Court was required to interpret in Kupferberg.

43. It is common ground, moreover, that some of the contracting parties, which are among the most important commercial partners of the Community, have concluded from the subject-matter and purpose of the WTO agreements that they are not among the rules applicable by their judicial organs when reviewing the legality of their rules of domestic law.

44. Admittedly, the fact that the courts of one of the parties consider that some of the provisions of the agreement concluded by the Community are of direct application whereas the courts of the other party do not recognise such direct application is not in itself such as to constitute a lack of reciprocity in the implementation of the agreement (Kupferberg, paragraph 18).

45. However, the lack of reciprocity in that regard on the part of the Community's trading partners, in relation to the WTO agreements which are based on 'reciprocal and mutually advantageous arrangements' and which must ipso facto be distinguished from agreements concluded by the Community, referred to in paragraph 42 of the present judgment, may lead to disuniform application of the WTO rules.

46. To accept that the role of ensuring that Community law complies with those rules devolves directly on the Community judicature would deprive the legislative or executive organs of the Community of the scope for manoeuvre enjoyed by their counterparts in the Community's trading partners.

47. It follows from all those considerations that, having regard to their nature and structure, the WTO agreements are not in principle among the rules in the light of which the Court is to review the legality of measures adopted by the Community institutions.

48. That interpretation corresponds, moreover, to what is stated in the final recital in the preamble to Decision 94/800, according to which 'by its nature, the Agreement establishing the World Trade Organization, including the Annexes thereto, is not susceptible to being directly invoked in Community or Member State courts'.

49. It is only where the Community intended to implement a particular obligation assumed in the context of the WTO, or where the Community measure refers expressly to the precise provisions of the WTO agreements, that it is for the Court to review the legality of the Community measure in question in the light of the WTO rules (see, as regards GATT 1947, Fediol, paragraphs 19 to 22, and Nakajima, paragraph 31).

50. It is therefore necessary to examine whether, as the Portuguese Government claims, that is so in the present case.

51. The answer must be in the negative. The contested decision is not designed to ensure the implementation in the Community legal order of a particular obligation assumed in the context of the WTO, nor does it make express reference to any specific provisions of the WTO agreements. Its purpose is merely to approve the Memoranda of Understanding negotiated by the Community with Pakistan and India.

52. It follows from all the foregoing that the claim of the Portuguese Republic that the contested decision was adopted in breach of certain rules and fundamental principles of the WTO is unfounded.

The sentence in paragraph 47 is particularly important: 'the WTO agreements are not in principle among the rules in the light of which the Court is to review the legality of measures adopted by the Community institutions'. Hence, the changes introduced to the international trade regime by the WTO Agreements notwithstanding, the arguments used by the Court continue to highlight the strong element of 'negotiation' between the parties, the reciprocal and mutually advantageous nature of the WTO, and the fact that allowing for direct effect in the Community would lead to putting the EU at a disadvantage with regard to the application of WTO rules, given the fact that other WTO Member States would not allow it.

But what about decisions by the WTO's DSB? After all, a report by the WTO Appellate Body is 'as judicial and final a pronouncement on compatibility with WTO rules as a state can possibly get under the DSU system, hence consisting of the clearest illustration of the legalisation process of the international economic order'.[37] In *Van Parys*[38] the Court was confronted with this question.

Case C-377/02 *Van Parys* v. *BIRB* [2005] ECR I-1465

39. It is settled case-law in that regard that, given their nature and structure, the WTO agreements are not in principle among the rules in the light of which the Court is to review the legality of measures adopted by the Community institutions (Case C-149/96 Portugal v Council [1999] ECR I-8395, paragraph 47; order of 2 May 2001 in Case C-307/99 OGT Fruchthandelsgesellschaft [2001] ECR I-3159, paragraph 24; Joined Cases C-27/00 and C-122/00 Omega Air and Others [2002] ECR I-2569, paragraph 93; Case C-76/00 P Petrotub and Republica v Council [2003] ECR I-79, paragraph 53 and Case C-93/02 P Biret International v Council [2003] ECR I-10497, paragraph 52).

40. It is only where the Community has intended to implement a particular obligation assumed in the context of the WTO, or where the Community measure refers expressly to the precise provisions of the WTO agreements, that it is for the Court to review the legality of the Community measure in question in the light of the WTO rules (see, as regards GATT 1947, Case 70/87 Fediol v Commission [1989] ECR 1781, paragraphs 19 to 22, and Case C-69/89 Nakajima v Council [1991] ECR I-2069, paragraph 31, and, as regards the WTO agreements, Portugal v Council, paragraph 49, and Biret International v Council, paragraph 53).

41. In the present case, by undertaking after the adoption of the decision of the DSB of 25 September 1997 to comply with the WTO rules and, in particular, with Articles I(1) and XIII of GATT 1994, the Community did not intend to assume a particular obligation in the context of the WTO, capable of justifying an exception to the impossibility of relying on WTO rules before the Community Courts and enabling the Community Courts to exercise judicial review of the relevant Community provisions in the light of those rules.

42. First, it should be noted that even where there is a decision of the DSB holding that the measures adopted by a member are incompatible with the WTO rules, as the Court has already held, the WTO dispute settlement system nevertheless accords considerable importance to negotiation between the parties (Portugal v Council, paragraphs 36 to 40).

43. Thus, although, in the absence of a resolution mutually agreed between the parties and compatible with the agreements in question, the main purpose of the dispute settlement system is in principle, according to Article 3(7) of the understanding, to secure the withdrawal of the measures in question if they are found to be inconsistent with the WTO rules, that provision provides, however, that where the immediate withdrawal of the measures is impracticable, compensation may be granted or the application of concessions or the enforcement of other obligations may be suspended on an interim basis pending the withdrawal of the inconsistent measure (see, to that effect, Portugal v Council, paragraph 37).

44. It is true that, according to Articles 3(7) and 22(1) of the understanding, compensation and the suspension of concessions or other obligations are temporary measures available in the event that the recommendations and rulings of the DSB are not implemented within a reasonable period of time, the

---

[37] Koutrakos, *EU International Relations Law*, p. 285.
[38] Case C-377/02 *Van Parys* v. *BIRB* [2005] ECR I-1465.

latter of those provisions showing a preference for full implementation of a recommendation to bring a measure into conformity with the WTO agreements in question (Portugal v Council, paragraph 38).

45. However, Article 22(2) provides that, if the Member concerned fails to enforce those recommendations and decisions within a reasonable period, if so requested, and within a reasonable period of time, it is to enter into negotiations with any party having invoked the dispute settlement procedures with a view to agreeing compensation. If no satisfactory compensation has been agreed within 20 days after the expiry of the reasonable period, the complainant may request authorisation from the DSB to suspend, in respect of that member, the application of concessions or other obligations under the WTO agreements.

46. Furthermore, Article 22(8) of the understanding provides that the dispute remains on the agenda of the DSB, pursuant to Article 21(6) of the understanding, until it is resolved, that is until the measure found to be inconsistent has been 'removed' or the parties reach a 'mutually satisfactory solution'.

47. Where there is no agreement as to the compatibility of the measures taken to comply with the DSB's recommendations and decisions, Article 21(5) of the understanding provides that the dispute shall be decided 'through recourse to these dispute settlement procedures', including an attempt by the parties to reach a negotiated solution.

48. In those circumstances, to require courts to refrain from applying rules of domestic law which are inconsistent with the WTO agreements would have the consequence of depriving the legislative or executive organs of the contracting parties of the possibility afforded by Article 22 of that memorandum of reaching a negotiated settlement, even on a temporary basis (Portugal v Commission, paragraph 40).

49. In the dispute in the main proceedings, it is apparent from the file that:
   - after declaring to the DSB its intention to comply with the DSB's decision of 25 September 1997, the Community amended its system for imports of bananas upon the expiry of the period allocated to it for that purpose;
   - as a result of the challenge by the Republic of Ecuador to the compatibility with the WTO rules of the new system of trade with third States arising from Regulation No 1637/98, the matter was referred to an ad hoc panel pursuant to Article 21(5) of the understanding and that panel held in a report adopted by the DSB on 6 May 1999 that that system continued to infringe Articles I(1) and XIII of GATT 1994;
   - in particular, the United States of America was authorised, in 1999, pursuant to Article 22(2) of the understanding and following an arbitration procedure, to suspend concessions to the Community up to a certain level;
   - the Community system was the subject of further amendments introduced by Regulation No 216/2001, applicable with effect from 1 April 2001 pursuant to the second paragraph of Article 2;
   - agreements were negotiated with the United States of America on 11 April 2001 and with the Republic of Ecuador on 30 April 2001, with a view to bringing the Community legislation into conformity with the WTO rules.

50. Such an outcome, by which the Community sought to reconcile its obligations under the WTO agreements with those in respect of the ACP States, and with the requirements inherent in the implementation of the common agricultural policy, could be compromised if the Community Courts were entitled to judicially review the lawfulness of the Community measures in question in light of the WTO rules upon the expiry of the time-limit, in January 1999, granted by the DSB within which to implement its decision of 25 September 1997.

51. The expiry of that time-limit does not imply that the Community had exhausted the possibilities under the understanding of finding a solution to the dispute between it and the other parties. In those circumstances, to require the Community Courts, merely on the basis that that time-limit has expired,

to review the lawfulness of the Community measures concerned in the light of the WTO rules, could have the effect of undermining the Community's position in its attempt to reach a mutually acceptable solution to the dispute in conformity with those rules.

52. It follows from the foregoing considerations that Regulation No 1637/98 and the regulations in issue in the main proceedings adopted to apply it, cannot be interpreted as measures intended to ensure the enforcement within the Community legal order of a particular obligation assumed in the context of the WTO. Neither do those measures expressly refer to specific provisions of the WTO agreements.

53. Second, as the Court held in paragraphs 43 and 44 of its judgment in Portugal v Council, to accept that the Community Courts have the direct responsibility for ensuring that Community law complies with the WTO rules would deprive the Community's legislative or executive bodies of the discretion which the equivalent bodies of the Community's commercial partners enjoy. It is not in dispute that some of the contracting parties, which are amongst the most important commercial partners of the Community, have concluded from the subject-matter and purpose of the WTO agreements that they are not among the rules applicable by their courts when reviewing the legality of their rules of domestic law. Such lack of reciprocity, if admitted, would risk introducing an anomaly in the application of the WTO rules.

Key elements are to be found in paragraphs 50 and 51, where the Court basically argues again that a judicial review possibility level would undermine the negotiating position of the Community. In addition (paragraph 53), a role for the Court would not be in line with the principle of reciprocity and 'would risk introducing an anomaly in the application of the WTO rules'.

In both *Portuguese Textiles* and *Van Parys* the Court refers to earlier case law related to GATT 1947. This case law forms the basis for the rulings in the WTO era. Indeed, the question of the effect of the GATT rules in the Community legal order had already arisen at the beginning of the 1970s. In *International Fruit Company*[39] the Court confirmed that the Community was bound by the GATT (as it had assumed the rights previously exercised by the Member States), but concluded that the Agreement was not capable of conferring rights enforceable before national courts. In other words: no direct effect of the GATT. The argumentation has been criticized quite extensively over the years, and mainly related to the specific nature of the agreement which was characterized by a 'great flexibility'. This flexibility was caused by a number of specific characteristics of the GATT: the duty of contracting parties to engage in consultations on any issue pertaining to the operation of GATT and their right to engage in further consultation if a satisfactory solution was not reached; the settlement of a conflict provided for written recommendations or proposals to be given sympathetic considerations, consultations between the parties, authorization to suspend the application of parts of GATT and, in that case, the right to withdraw from the Agreement; and the possibility of derogation by means of unilateral suspension of GATT obligations in the event or the threat of serious damage. All in all, this precluded individuals from challenging the legality of Community legislation in the light of GATT.

The special nature of GATT not only made it impossible for individuals to challenge Community law, but also national law on the basis of alleged violations of international trade rules,

---

[39] Joined Cases 21–24/72 *International Fruit Company NV and Others* v. *Produktschap voor Groenten en Fruit* [1972] EC 1226.

as was made clear in a number of Italian cases.[40] Moreover, as we have seen in the case of Germany challenging Regulation 404/93, the Court's line of argumentation extended to actions by Member States against Community acts. This also means, as the Court found in *FIAMM*,[41] that companies or individuals in the EU cannot claim damages for being adversely affected by countermeasures authorized by the DSB for WTO law-inconsistent behaviour on the part of the EU.

The rule that provisions of GATT 1947 may not be relied upon by individuals or Member States in order to challenge the validity of EU measures in either national courts or the EU Courts obviously limited the role of the Court itself in scrutinizing EU rules in the light of the global trade agreements.

Joined Cases 21/72–24/72 *International Fruit Company and Others* v. *Produktschap voor Groenten en Fruit* [1972] ECR 1226

19. It is also necessary to examine whether the provisions of the general agreement confer rights on citizens of the Community on which they can rely before the courts in contesting the validity of a Community measure.

20. For this purpose, the spirit, the general scheme and the terms of the General Agreement must be considered.

21. This agreement which, according to its preamble, is based on the principle of negotiations undertaken on the basis of "reciprocal and mutually advantageous arrangements" is characterized by the great flexibility of its provisions, in particular those conferring the possibility of derogation, the measures to be taken when confronted with exceptional difficulties and the settlement of conflicts between the contracting parties.

22. Consequently, according to the first paragraph of Article XXII "each contracting party shall accord sympathetic consideration to, and shall afford adequate opportunity for consultation regarding, such representations as may be made by any other contracting party with respect to ... All matters affecting the operation of this agreement".

23. According to the second paragraph of the same Article, "the contracting parties" – this name designating "the contracting parties acting jointly" as is stated in the first paragraph of Article XXV – "may consult with one or more contracting parties on any question to which a satisfactory solution cannot be found through the consultations provided under paragraph (1)".

24. If any contracting party should consider "that any benefit accruing to it directly or indirectly under this agreement is being nullified or impaired or that the attainment of any objective of the agreement is being impeded as a result of", inter alia, "the failure of another contracting party to carry out its obligations under this agreement", Article XXIII lays down in detail the measures which the parties concerned, or the contracting parties acting jointly, may or must take in regard to such a situation.

25. Those measures include, for the settlement of conflicts, written recommendations or proposals which are to be "given sympathetic consideration", investigations possibly followed by recommendations, consultations between or decisions of the contracting parties, including that of authorizing certain

---

[40] Case 266/81 *SIOT* v. *Ministero delle Finanze* [1983] ECR 731. Similar arguments were used in subsequent cases, such as Joined Cases 267/81, 268/81 & 269/81 *Amministrazione delle Finanze dello Stato* v. *Società Petrolifera Italiana SpA (SPI) and SpA Michelin Italiana (SAMI)* [1983] ECR 801; and Case C-469/93 *Amministrazione delle Finanze dello Stato* v. *Chiquita Italia* [1995] ECR I-4533.

[41] Joined Cases C-120/06 & C-121/06 *FIAMM and Others* v. *Council and Commission* [2008] ECR I-6513.

contracting parties to suspend the application to any others of any obligations or concessions under the General Agreement and, finally, in the event of such suspension, the power of the party concerned to withdraw from that agreement.

26. Finally, where by reason of an obligation assumed under the General Agreement or of a concession relating to a benefit, some producers suffer or are threatened with serious damage, Article XIX gives a contracting party power unilaterally to suspend the obligation and to withdraw or modify the concession, either after consulting the contracting parties jointly and failing agreement between the contracting parties concerned, or even, if the matter is urgent and on a temporary basis, without prior consultation.

27. Those factors are sufficient to show that, when examined in such a context, Article XI of the General Agreement is not capable of conferring on citizens of the Community rights which they can invoke before the courts.

Irrespective of the basic starting point, the role of the Court has been quite extensive regarding the relation between GATT/WTO and the EU legal order, and some key examples reveal that the rule is not as clear-cut as may be argued on the basis of *International Fruit*. In *Fediol*[42] the Court argued that the flexibility of the GATT rules did not prevent it from interpreting the Agreement in order to assess the consistency of a specific commercial practice with its provisions. In the concrete case, the applicant had a right to challenge a Commission decision in view of the GATT by virtue of the very detailed procedure in Regulation 2641/84 and its explicit reference to the GATT. In *Nakajima*[43] the Court was asked whether a Council Regulation (the 'Basic Regulation')[44] violated the Anti-Dumping Code annexed to GATT 1947. In this case the Court argued that 'direct effect' was not the issue as the Basic Regulation was only challenged in an incidental manner. Consequently, review of legality is possible with a reference to the GATT. *Fediol* and *Nakajima* did not change the principle in *International Fruit*, but rather pointed to the fact that, in these strictly defined cases, the GATT rules were to be seen as part of the Community legal order, which made it unnecessary to address the question of whether these rules could be relied upon by individuals. Finally, the Court has argued that the provisions of international agreements should be read into Community legislation as far as possible.[45]

The effects of WTO law in the EU legal order can be summarized as follows: as the general rule, the provisions of WTO Agreements cannot be invoked by either Member States (*Portuguese Textiles*) or individuals (*Parfums Dior*) to challenge the legality of EU secondary legislation. This general rule holds also in the case even when the DSB decided that an EU measure is incompatible with the WTO rules (*Van Parys*). However, by way of exception, EU measures may be challenged in the light of a WTO rule if it can be established that the latter was to be implemented by that particular measure (*Nakajima*) or when an EU measure makes an express reference to that WTO rule (*Fediol*).

Obviously, the limited role the Court can play here may be criticized as it excludes parts of the exercise of CCP from scrutiny by the Court, and may be seen to condone certain violations of

---

[42] Case 70/87 *Fediol* v. *Commission* [1989] ECR 1781.
[43] Case C-69/89 *Nakajima* v. *Council* [1991] ECR I-2069.
[44] Regulation 2423/88/EEC of 11 July 1988 on protection against dumped or subsidized imports from countries not members of the European Economic Community, OJ 1988 No. L209/1.
[45] Case C-61/94 *Commission* v. *Germany* [1996] ECR I-3989 (*International Dairy Arrangement* case).

international law by the EU, which is at odds with its self-imposed pledge to the 'strict observance' of international law (Article 3(5) TEU).

5 DEVELOPMENT OF THE CCP: THE INTERNAL MARKET AND EXTERNAL TRADE

The origins of CCP can be found in the liberalization of trade in goods. Gradually the scope of CCP expanded to trade in services and trade-related aspects of IP rights. Yet, competences in the latter areas were shared with the Member States, and in Opinion 1/94 on the WTO Agreements the Court held that the EU could conclude the GATS and the TRIPS only together with its Member States (see Chapter 4). As we have seen, current Article 207(1) TFEU provides for a comprehensive set of competences of the Union in the area of trade, including GATS and TRIPS aspects, and thus reduces the need for the Union to rely on mixed agreements. The development of CCP, however, can only be properly understood when taking into account that it was being shaped from the very outset by, on the one hand, the evolution of the international trade regime, and on the other hand by the process of economic integration in Europe, most notably the advances towards the internal market. Thus, CCP is at the same time the EU's voice in the international trading order as well as 'a necessary corollary for the maintenance of its internal market'.[46] Arguably more than any other EU policy, CCP exemplifies that in the contemporary world, internal and external policies are inextricably intertwined.

(i) The internal market and GATT/WTO

As indicated in the introduction to this chapter, the establishment and further evolution of CCP reflects the strong relationship between internal and external aspects of economic integration. This was explicitly acknowledged by the Court in Opinion 1/75.

Opinion 1/75, *Re Understanding on a Local Costs Standard* [1975] ECR 1355

In the course of the measures necessary to implement the principles laid down in the abovementioned provisions, particularly those covered by Article 113 of the Treaty [now Art. 207 TFEU], concerning the common commercial policy, the Community is empowered, pursuant to the powers which it possesses, not only to adopt internal rules of Community law, but also to conclude agreements with third countries pursuant to Article 113(2) and Article 114 of the Treaty [Articles 206, 207 TFEU].

A commercial policy is in fact made up by the combination and interaction of internal and external measures, without priority being taken by one over the others. Sometimes agreements are concluded in execution of a policy fixed in advance, sometimes that policy is defined by the agreements themselves.

Such agreements may be outline agreements, the purpose of which is to lay down uniform principles. Such is the case with the understanding on local costs: it does not have a specific content adapted to particular export credit transactions; it merely lays down a standard, sets out certain exceptions, provides, in exceptional circumstances, for derogations and, finally, lays down general provisions. Furthermore, the

---

[46] Larik, 'Much More than Trade', p. 16.

> implementation of the export policy to be pursued within the framework of a common commercial policy does not necessarily find expression in the adoption of general and abstract rules of internal or Community law. The common commercial policy is above all the outcome of a progressive development based upon specific measures which may refer without distinction to 'autonomous' and external aspects of that policy and which do not necessarily presuppose, by the fact that they are linked to the field of the common commercial policy, the existence of a large body of rules, but combine gradually to form that body.

These days the competence to conclude agreements in the area of CCP is explicitly mentioned in Article 207 TFEU (see also Chapter 2), but it was indeed the 'combination and interaction of internal and external measures' which turned CCP into one of the key policy areas of the Union. In this context, it should not be forgotten that when the original six Member States signed the Treaty of Rome in 1957, the GATT had been in existence for a decade, to which the six were already party. Therefore, the EU (at the time still the Communities) came to succeed the Member States, by virtue of CCP, in exercising the rights and duties under the GATT, as confirmed by the ECJ in *International Fruit* (see above).

As a regional trading bloc, an initial question concerned whether European integration itself was consistent with the pre-existing rules at the international level. Article XXIV GATT allows for customs unions under certain circumstances, since they do represent exceptions to the general trade principles of MFN treatment and non-discrimination. It was not with the Schuman Plan in mind that this exception was introduced, but instead due to an envisaged FTA between the United States and Canada, which was however never ratified.[47] Nonetheless, 'the EEC's common market was modelled partly on the GATT, and many of the EC Treaty provisions clearly reflect this'.[48] Under Article XXIV, substantially all the trade within the customs union has to be liberalized, and the level of customs duties with the other trading partners should on the whole not be raised. However, whether the EU and its advancing Common Market, as it was known at the time, was compatible with Article XXIV has never been put to a test, either by means of dispute settlement or through the Committee on Regional Trade Agreements (CRTA).

With regard to the linkages between the internal market and the WTO, the enlargement of the EU from six founding members to now twenty-eight members is also noteworthy. Enlargement can well be considered the area in which the EU has had the most tangible impact on domestic policy. Using the attraction of access to the prosperous EU market, it has incentivized candidate states to effect wide-ranging reforms in order to comply with the *acquis communautaire*. This, however, has an important trade dimension as well. By virtue of pre-accession agreements with the candidate countries, which usually include the granting of trade preferences to them, and their subsequent integration into the Union (and under its CCP), trade is reinforced within the Union, but is at the same time diverted from the rest of the world.

---

[47] See K. Chase, 'Multilateralism Compromised: The Mysterious Origins of GATT Article XXIV' (2006) 5 *World Trade Review* 1–30.

[48] G. de Búrca and J. Scott, 'The Impact of the WTO on EU Decision-Making', in de Búrca and Scott (eds.), *The EU and the WTO: Legal and Constitutional Issues* (Oxford/Portland: Hart Publishing, 2001), p. 2.

(ii) Protecting the internal market

As we have seen earlier in the form of trade defence instruments such as anti-dumping measures, the CCP also plays a crucial role in defending the internal market from external influences which are seen as harmful to it. In attempting to maintain a level playing field also with respect to the outside world, these instruments can be understood as complementing competition and state aid policy within the Union. However, WTO rules have also a word in the application of such internal policies. Concerning subsidies, the WTO Agreement on Subsidies and Countervailing Measures provides definitions of specific categories which are either prohibited altogether or can be challenged through dispute settlement or so-called countervailing measures. Such a question of subsidization sparked the *Large Civil Aircraft* disputes between the United States and the EU, in which both sides accused the other of subsidizing their major civil aviation companies.[49] In view of the fact that Boeing and Airbus (as part of EADS) are also involved in the production of defence equipment, i.e. military aircraft, and given that awarding such projects to them might be seen as masked subsidies, it cannot be denied that 'this matter is all but exclusively civil, and relates to the EU's efforts for armaments cooperation',[50] and thus, albeit indirectly, to the CSDP.

To take another example, the EU market is also to be protected from products which are considered harmful to the European consumers. The issue of trade restrictions based on health concerns is addressed in the WTO framework by the Agreement on Sanitary and Phytosanitary Measures (SPS). Under this agreement, the EU found itself being sued by its trading partners, notably the US, in widely publicized disputes such as *Beef Hormones*[51] and those concerning genetically modified organisms (GMOs). These disputes raise fundamental questions about the interpretation of the so-called precautionary principle and the use of scientific evidence by the WTO Appellate Body. These controversies serve to show that the internal market and its relations with the outside world are far from being matters of only technical relevance, but can indeed become highly politicized. In the extract from the EP on trade negotiations with the USA, we find express reference to these diverging transatlantic views, and which carry the real potential to scupper EU–US negotiations.

(iii) Extending the internal market

In addition to enlarging the EU and the protection of its market, the EU has also partially extended the internal market beyond its own Member States, which also is not without effect on international trade. In the case of countries where accession is geographically excluded or where it proves politically difficult, the Union has devised ways to integrate these largely into the internal market and bind them to its rules, without giving them a vote in the Union's own legislative processes. This is the case with the countries of the EEA, i.e. Iceland, Liechtenstein and Norway, but also with Switzerland and Turkey. Also the post-enlargement neighbourhood of the

---

[49] WTO, *United States – Measures Affecting Trade in Large Civil Aircraft*, Request for Consultations by the European Communities of 12 October 2004, WT/DS317/1; WTO, *European Communities and Certain Member States – Measures Affecting Trade in Large Civil Aircraft*, Request for Consultations by the United States of 12 October 2004, WT/DS316/1.
[50] Larik, 'Much More than Trade', p. 20.
[51] WTO, *European Communities – Measures Concerning Meat and Meat Products (Hormones)*, Appellate Body Report (adopted 13 February 1998) WT/DS26/AB/R, WT/DS48/AB/R.

EU has been promised a so-called 'stake in the EU's Internal Market'[52] or, as former European Commission President Prodi put it, 'sharing everything with the Union but institutions'.[53] The attraction of access to the internal market, and the way the EU uses it, highlight that it is not only 'a formidable power *in* trade' but indeed a 'power *through* trade'.[54]

6 THE BROADER PICTURE OF EU EXTERNAL RELATIONS LAW

This chapter addressed the key role of the CCP in the EU's external relations regime. From the outset, the main starting points of EU external relations law have been defined on the basis of developments in the area of CCP. This role as a 'driving force' behind the development of the Union's external relations flows from the fact that trade internal market issues were (and still are) closely related to external trade issues. At the same time there are few areas in which such a direct link exists with global developments and agreements. Indeed, both the existence and further development of the GATT, and later the WTO, have had a large impact on the CCP – and vice versa.

While trade issues remain a key element of the Union's external relations, we have seen that similar developments have taken place in other policy areas. The Lisbon Treaty in particular presents EU external action in a more coherent fashion, and trade issues are more frequently linked to other external policy areas.

F. Hoffmeister, 'The European Union's Common Commercial Policy a year after Lisbon – Sea Change or Business as Usual?', in P. Koutrakos (ed.), *The European Union's External Relations a Year after Lisbon* (The Hague: CLEER Working Papers 2011/3), pp. 83–95

Experience from the first Lisbon year may lead to three provisional conclusions.

First, we witness a clear modernisation of the EU's trade policy. The enlarged scope and the new institutional set-up on trade-defence measures will allow the EU to be more effective in pursuing its interests. After all, as the Community method had been particularly successful in the commercial field, it was high time to keep up with international developments. Being invested with clear competences on services, intellectual property rights and investment, the EU got stronger, and giving the Commission the power to decide on trade-defence measures both at provisional and at final stage, makes the EU more resilient against foreign pressure previously exercised on Member States in sensitive anti-dumping or anti-subsidy cases.

Second, there are signs of an increased politicisation of trade policy. The formal link to broader foreign policy goals and the institutional task of the High-Representative of the Union to ensure consistence of the EU's external action, including trade, may lead to a situation where non-trade considerations may play a bigger role in the decision-making. A number of examples have already been identified in the first year.

---

[52] European Commission, *European Neighbourhood Policy Strategy Paper*, COM(2004) 373 final, Brussels, 12 May 2004, p. 3.

[53] R. Prodi, *A Wider Europe – A Proximity Policy as the Key to Stability*, Sixth ECSA World Conference, Speech/02/619 (2002), Brussels, 5–6 December 2002, p. 6.

[54] S. Meunier and K. Nicolaïdis, 'The EU as a Trade Power', in C. Hill and M. Smith (eds.), *International Relations and the European Union*, 2nd edn (Oxford: Oxford University Press, 2011), Chapter 12, pp. 275–298.

Third, and probably most importantly, trade policy has been democratised. The role of the European Parliament in both internal legislation and in exercising scrutiny over trade agreements adds greatly to the legitimacy of this policy. And the Parliament has exercised its new powers in a measured manner, both working hard on domestic legislation and having approved the first major trade deal for years, i.e. the EU–Korea FTA with a large majority. Whether these aspects of modernisation, politicisation and democratisation amount to a sea change is, however, hard to assess after only one year.

SOURCES AND FURTHER READING

Bartels, L., *Human Rights Conditionality in the EU's International Agreements* (New York: Oxford University Press, 2005).

Bartels, L., 'The Trade and Development Policy of the European Union', in M. Cremona (ed.), *Developments in EU External Relations Law* (Oxford: Oxford University Press, 2008), pp. 128–171.

Chase, K., 'Multilateralism Compromised: The Mysterious Origins of GATT Article XXIV' (2006) 5 *World Trade Review* 1–30.

Cremona, M., 'The External Dimension of the Internal Market: Building (on) the Foundations', in C. Barnard and J. Scott (eds.), *The Law of the Single European Market: Unpacking the Premises* (Oxford/Portland: Hart Publishing, 2002), pp. 351–394.

De Búrca, G. and Scott, J., 'The Impact of the WTO on EU Decision-Making', in G. de Búrca and J. Scott (eds.), *The EU and the WTO: Legal and Constitutional Issues* (Oxford/Portland: Hart Publishing, 2001).

Delgado Casteleiro, A. and Larik, J., 'The "Odd Couple": The Responsibility of the EU at the WTO', in M. Evans and P. Koutrakos (eds.), *The International Responsibility of the European Union* (Oxford: Hart Publishing, 2013), pp. 233–255.

Dimopoulos, A., 'The Effects of the Lisbon Treaty on the Principles and Objectives of the Common Commercial Policy' (2010) 15 *European Foreign Affairs Review* 153–170.

Eeckhout, P., *EU External Relations Law*, 2nd edn (Oxford: Oxford University Press, 2011).

Hoffmeister, F., 'The European Union's Common Commercial Policy a Year after Lisbon – Sea Change or Business as Usual?', in P. Koutrakos (ed.), *The European Union's External Relations a Year after Lisbon* (The Hague: CLEER Working Papers 2011/3), pp. 83–95.

Koutrakos, P., *EU International Relations Law* (Oxford: Hart Publishing, 2006).

Larik, J., 'Much More than Trade: The Common Commercial Policy in a Global Context', in M. Evans and P. Koutrakos (eds.), *Beyond the Established Legal Orders: Policy Interconnections between the EU and the Rest of the World* (Oxford: Hart Publishing, 2011), pp. 13–45.

Meunier, S. and Nicolaïdis, K., 'The EU as a Trade Power', in C. Hill and M. Smith (eds.), *International Relations and the European Union*, 2nd edn (Oxford: Oxford University Press, 2011), Chapter 12, pp. 275–298.

Tiedemann, A., *EU Market Access Teams: New Instruments to Tackle Non-Tariff Barriers to Trade* (College of Europe EU Diplomacy Paper 9/2009, December 2009).

Villalta Puig, G. and Al-Haddab, B., 'The Common Commercial Policy after Lisbon: An Analysis of the Reforms' (2011) 36 *European Law Review* 289–301.

10

EU development policy

1 CENTRAL ISSUES

- Development cooperation policy is as old as the European integration project itself. Objectives in this policy area have evolved from associating EEC Member States' colonies with focus on trade and aid, to a progressively broader development agenda incorporating human rights, sustainable development aspects such as environment and social issues, and most recently links to (common foreign and) security policy.
- EU development policy can be defined through the three C's which have been expressly incorporated into the competence-conferring provisions of the TFEU: complementarity, coherence and coordination.
- Complementarity is laid down generally in Article 208(1) TFEU, and broadly implies that the exercise of EU and Member State competences shall complement and reinforce each other. From the perspective of the nature of the EU's development competence, it means that EU action does not pre-empt Member State action (Article 4(4) TFEU), thereby making coherence and coordination between these levels crucial.
- Coherence is also contained in Article 208 TFEU and is composed of three aspects: first, coherence of EU development cooperation with the more general principles and objectives of EU external relations (Article 21 TEU); secondly, poverty reduction as the primary policy objective providing intra-policy focus on how diverse development initiatives cohere to the central goal; thirdly, the obligation to take account of development objectives in other policies which are likely to affect developing countries.
- Coordination is laid down in Article 210 TFEU, and entails that EU and Member States must proactively collaborate and consult in order to ensure complementarity and coherence of their respective EU development policies. Article 210 TFEU gives the Commission a central role in ensuring coordination of EU and Member State development cooperation initiatives.

2 THE THREE C'S OF EU DEVELOPMENT POLICY: COMPLEMENTARY, COHERENT AND COORDINATED

Article 208 TFEU

1. Union policy in the field of development cooperation shall be conducted within the framework of the principles and objectives of the Union's external action. The Union's development cooperation policy and that of the Member States *complement* and reinforce each other.

   Union development cooperation policy shall have as its primary objective the reduction and, in the long term, the eradication of poverty. *The Union shall take account of the objectives of development cooperation in the policies that it implements which are likely to affect developing countries.*[1]

2. The Union and the Member States shall comply with the commitments and take account of the objectives they have approved in the context of the United Nations and other competent international organisations.

Article 209 TFEU

1. The European Parliament and the Council, acting in accordance with the ordinary legislative procedure, shall adopt the measures necessary for the implementation of development cooperation policy, which may relate to multiannual cooperation programmes with developing countries or programmes with a thematic approach.

2. The Union may conclude with third countries and competent international organisations any agreement helping to achieve the objectives referred to in Article 21 of the Treaty on European Union and in Article 208 of this Treaty.

   The first subparagraph shall be without prejudice to Member States' competence to negotiate in international bodies and to conclude agreements.

3. The European Investment Bank shall contribute, under the terms laid down in its Statute, to the implementation of the measures referred to in paragraph 1.

Article 210 TFEU

1. In order to promote the *complementarity* and efficiency of their action, the Union and the Member States shall *coordinate* their policies on development cooperation and shall consult each other on their aid programmes, including in international organisations and during international conferences. They may undertake joint action. Member States shall contribute if necessary to the implementation of Union aid programmes.

2. The Commission may take any useful initiative to promote the *coordination* referred to in paragraph 1.

---

[1] Emphasis added.

> ### Article 211 TFEU
>
> Within their respective spheres of competence, the Union and the Member States shall cooperate with third countries and with the competent international organisations.

The essential features of EU development policy as they permeate these provisions are traditionally captured in the three C's: complementarity, coherence and coordination.[2] They imply:

(1) that the policy vis-a-vis developing countries and other policies must be coherent, (2) that Union policy and Member State policies in the area of development cooperation must be complementary, and (3) that the Union and the Member States are obliged to coordinate their efforts in the field of development cooperation.[3]

The three C's have legal significance since the articles conferring development competence on the EU have been drafted incorporating them as fundamental legal and policy dimensions of EU development cooperation:

- *Complementarity*: Article 208(1) TFEU expresses that EU and Member State competences shall complement and reinforce each other. This article is closely linked to Article 4(4) TFEU which states that in the areas of development cooperation and humanitarian aid, the Union shall have competence to carry out activities and conduct a common policy; but that the exercise of that competence shall not result in Member States being prevented from exercising theirs. In other words, complementarity to a large extent concerns the *nature* of EU competence in the areas of development policy (and humanitarian aid) and more generally views the EU and national levels as positively and mutually reinforcing. Complementarity is different from subsidiarity because the two levels are equally appropriate to exercise competences in the same area simultaneously.
- *Coherence*: Article 208(1) and (2) TFEU both express the need for coherence in different ways: it makes a link to the general principles and objectives of EU external action (e.g. Article 21 TEU), states that other EU policies likely to affect developing countries must take account of development policy, and Article 208(2) requires that the EU and its Member States 'shall' take account of objectives approved at the UN and other competent international organizations. Defining coherence in the abstract is notoriously difficult as much depends on the perspective of the viewer.[4] In general, it may be viewed as avoidance of conflicts and creation of positive synergy within EU development policy itself, between development and other policies, and between all relevant norms, actors and instruments active in these domains.[5]

---

[2] For the results of the EU initiative evaluating the three C's of EU development policy, see www.three-cs.net (last accessed 13 June 2013).

[3] M. Broberg, 'What Is the Direction for the EU's Development Cooperation after Lisbon? A Legal Examination' (2011) 16 *European Foreign Affairs Review* 539–557 at 543.

[4] B. Van Vooren, *EU External Relations Law and the European Neighbourhood Policy: A Paradigm for Coherence* (Abingdon/New York: Routledge, 2012), p. 289.

[5] *Ibid.*, p. 69.

- *Coordination*: Article 210 TFEU lays down the obligation of coordination between the EU and Member State in the implementation of their development policies, with a specific right of initiative for the Commission to attain this objective. Coordination is the action-orientated dimension towards ensuring coherent and complementary policies, and can be defined as 'activities of two or more development partners that are intended to mobilise aid resources or to harmonize their policies, programmes, procedures and practices so as to maximise the development effectiveness of aid resources'.[6] The coordination dimension thus focuses on various forms of consultation, cooperation and collaboration at all levels, from the international to the sub-national in setting out priorities, good practices, policies, etc.

The objectives of EU development policy are made explicit in the second indent of Article 208(1) TFEU. In a concise fashion, that provision states that the primary objective is to reduce, and in the long term eradicate poverty. Prior to the Lisbon Treaty the objectives of EU development policy were actually formulated far more elaborately in the former Article 177 of the EC Treaty. The objectives of EU development policy that were previously found in Article 177 EC Treaty have now been moved to Article 21 of the TEU, namely 21(2) paragraphs (b), (d), (e), and to a certain extent paragraph (f). These textual interventions in EU primary law were made exactly because of the increased emphasis on coherence. On the one hand, placing poverty reduction dead centre to EU development policy provides coherence by focusing on one single target, rather than a more diffuse set of 'issues which are all important'. On the other hand, placing objectives such as sustainable development and incorporation of developing countries into the world economy into the general provision Article 21 TEU implies that the EU must not only pursue them through development cooperation, but through all its policies, including CCP, transport policy, agricultural policy, and so on.

The principles, scope and substance of EU development policy have grown and evolved organically over the past six decades, and a brief historic introduction starting from the Treaty of Rome is indispensable to understand the operation of the three C's in EU development policy today.

3 A BRIEF HISTORY OF EU DEVELOPMENT POLICY

(i) A succession of treaties and conventions: Rome, Yaoundé, Lomé and Cotonou

The Schuman Declaration of 9 May 1950 underlined that the proposed integration project had a calling in the field of development cooperation. It stated that the pooling of coal and steel would free up resources which would allow the Community 'to pursue the achievement of one of its essential tasks, namely, the development of the African continent'. Whereas ECSC finally had no such provisions, the 1957 Rome Treaty – under French pressure which viewed France and its colonies as a cultural unity ('Eurafrica')[7] – stated in Article 3(r) that one of the activities of the Community was 'the association of the overseas countries and territories (OCTs) in order to

---

[6] P. Hoebink (ed.), *The Treaty of Maastricht and Europe's Development Co-operation, Studies in European Development Co-operation Evaluation No. 1* (Amsterdam: Aksant Academic Publishers, 2005), p. 5.

[7] L. Bartels, 'The Trade and Development Policy of the European Union', in M. Cremona (ed.), *Developments in EU External Relations Law* (Oxford: Oxford University Press, 2008), p. 130; Broberg, *The EU's Legal Ties with its Former Colonies – When Old Love Never Dies* (DIIS Working Paper 2011:01), p. 10.

increase trade and promote jointly economic and social development'. This association meant that the Member States applied to trade with the OCTs 'the same treatment as they accord each other' under the Rome Treaty.[8] Thus, the gradual elimination of duties and quantitative restrictions which characterized the creation of the common market was largely applied to the associated entities as well.[9] Beyond the trade aspect of the relationship, the Member States made commitments in the field of investments and notably the provision of development aid. In terms of its scope, development cooperation in the early years thus had a narrow focus on aid and trade.[10]

Decolonization of the African continent took place in the years immediately following the entry into force of the Rome Treaty. As a consequence, relations with the newly sovereign nations could no longer be conducted on the basis of Part IV of the Rome Treaty, but would be founded on a succession of multilateral framework treaties.

M. Broberg, *The EU's Legal Ties with its Former Colonies – When Old Love Never Dies* (DIIS Working Paper 2011:01), p. 10

... in the years following the creation of the EEC most of these [OCTs] gained independence requiring a redefinition of the framework regulating the relationship between the former colonies and the EEC. Hence, in 1964 the first Yaoundé Convention came into force. This was followed, first, by the second Yaoundé Convention and, subsequently, by the so-called Lomé Conventions. In 2000 the fourth Lomé Convention was replaced by the Cotonou Partnership Agreement which will remain in force until 2020. Since the first Yaoundé Convention the number of (non-European) countries covered by the legal scheme has grown from 18 originally to 79 today. The majority are former French and British colonies in Africa, but former colonies in the Caribbean and the Pacific are also parties to the Agreement – hence the name African, Caribbean and Pacific countries (widely referred to as ACP countries).

The first Yaoundé Convention was signed in 1963 between eighteen African countries which were mostly newly independent French colonies referred to as the 'Associated African States' (AAS) and the EEC and its Member States.[11] This was followed by the second Yaoundé Convention in 1969. Both were based on two fundamental principles: free trade[12] and 'financial and technical co-operation', e.g. development aid.[13] In Title I concerning trade, it is clear that this convention continued the direction taken with the Rome Treaty on customs duties and quantitative restrictions, with specific treatment for coffee, bananas and the CAP.[14]

---

[8] Article 132(1) TEC-Rome.

[9] Bartels, 'The Trade and Development Policy of the European Union', p. 133.

[10] Broberg, 'What Is the Direction for the EU's Development Cooperation after Lisbon?', p. 540.

[11] Convention of Association between the European Economic Community and the African and Malagasy States associated with that Community and annexed documents signed at Yaoundé on 20 July 1963. Available from: http://aei.pitt.edu/id/eprint/4221 last accessed 13 May 2013).

[12] Title I Yaoundé Convention.

[13] Title II Yaoundé Convention. See Commission of the European Communities, *The Second Yaoundé Convention – Great Possibilities for Private Investment in Africa* (Commission Working Document, 1971), p. 5.

[14] See Articles 2 and 11 Yaoundé I Convention. Article 2(3) Yaoundé I reads: 'Imports from third countries of unroasted coffee into the Benelux countries on the one hand, and of bananas into the Federal Republic of Germany on the other hand, shall be subject to the terms set out respectively, as to unroasted coffee, in the Protocol this day concluded between the Member States and as to bananas, in the Protocol concluded on 25 March 1957 between the Member States and in the Declaration annexed to this Convention.'

L. Bartels, 'The Trade and Development Policy of the European Union', in M. Cremona (ed.), *Developments in EU External Relations Law* (Oxford: Oxford University Press, 2008), p. 137

One of the striking features of these trade arrangements [Yaoundé] was their emphasis on reciprocal trade liberalization. In modern times, reciprocity in trade relations is justified on both economic and political economy grounds: put simply, it gives the country granting the trade concessions a means of extracting trade concessions from the other party ... At the time of the Yaoundé Conventions, however, the main reasons given for reciprocity were ideological. First, it was said that only with mutual obligations could Africa negotiate as an 'equal' with Europe; second that these obligations went 'beyond' more contractual relations; and third, that these obligations were essential to ensure that Africa did not fall under the sway of a (non-French) economic power. .... A practical effect to these preferences ... was to benefit the (mainly) French exporters, who tended to be monopolists, and therefore able to keep prices high despite their low exports costs. [Reciprocity] was a concept hard to identify in practice.

In the field of international trade, the Yaoundé Contracting Parties agreed to keep each other informed, and when requested there could be consultation for the purpose of giving effect to the Convention.[15] Institutionally, the Convention set up an Association Council, a Parliamentary Conference and a Court of Arbitration.[16] Under the first convention, development aid commitments were carried out through the first European Development Fund (EDF) to which the Member States provided the necessary funds,[17] and the EIB undertook to provide loans out of its own resources.[18] All economic sectors could benefit from aid under these instruments but funds were primarily directed at industry, tourism, agriculture, socio-economic infrastructure (schools, roads, hospitals, etc.) and export promotion.[19] Development cooperation under the Yaoundé regime was still very much characterized by its government-to-government nature,[20] which would slowly change in subsequent conventions in line with evolving perceptions of development policy and cooperation.

The two Yaoundé Conventions were subsequently replaced by the Lomé Conventions entering into force in 1975, 1981, 1986 and 1990; and were concluded as EEC Member State mixed agreements like Yaoundé. The backdrop to these new agreements is important: the first EEC enlargement which included the United Kingdom and thus a new perspective on international development, and the oil crisis which created a fear of shortages of raw materials, all combined with a desire to hold on to valued overseas markets and a sense of responsibility for the colonial past.[21] In terms of market access, the central change with the preceding Yaoundé legal regime

---

[15] Article 12 Yaoundé I Convention.

[16] No case was ever decided before this tribunal. See Bartels, 'The Trade and Development Policy of the European Union', note 1, p. 135.

[17] The EDF was kept separate from the EC budget because of lack of enthusiasm on the part of other Member States to fund former French colonies. In principle the EDF allows each Member State to decide how much it is willing to contribute under the applicable convention (see further below). To the EDF France and Germany contributed roughly one-third each. See Commission, 'The Second Yaoundé Convention', note 3, 7.

[18] Article 16 Yaoundé I Convention.

[19] Commission of the European Communities, *The Second Yaoundé Convention – Great Possibilities for Private Investment in Africa* (Commission Working Document, 1971), p. 7.

[20] *Ibid.*, p. 18.

[21] European Commission, *Green Paper on relations between the EU and the ACP countries on the eve of the 21st century – Challenges and options for a new partnership*, COM(96) 570 final, Brussels, 20 November 1996, p. 9.

was the inclusion of the principle of *non-reciprocal* trade preferences, mainly under the pressure of the twenty-seven other nations joining the Yaoundé associates of which twenty-one were Commonwealth nations due to the UK's accession to the EEC.[22]

European Commission, *Information Note, Development and Cooperation*, 1975, 99/75 F (translated from French)

Title I of the Convention concerning commercial cooperation has certainly posed the most arduous problems to the negotiators, with the EEC and ACP countries being each other's primary commercial partners. . . . The diversity of situations, traditions and wishes of the different partners, including that of the Community, seemed a priori in opposition. In the end the negotiators succeeded in surmounting these difficulties and [basing] – in spite of everything – their future commercial relations on a just and certain basis, with the needed flexibility for ensuring an application without ambiguity of the provisions of the Convention.

1. The non-reciprocity of the commercial obligations.

   This principle has been one of the major innovations of the Lomé Convention. Justified by the different levels of development, it implies that the ACP Countries are not held to subscribe to obligations corresponding to those of the Community in relation to products originating in the latter. . . . Nevertheless, the ACP Countries, as regards their commercial relations with the Community, have committed to not discriminate between the Member States, and to accord to the Community a treatment not less favourable to that which they give to the most favoured nation. . . . However, the Community has accepted that MFN shall not apply between the ACP nations, or between them and other developing nations. For example, when a Caribbean Country concludes an agreement with a Latin American Nation, it is free to accord commercial advantages which it does not provide to the Community.

Non-reciprocity therefore means that with Lomé, the Community demanded that it be treated equally to other non-developing nations, but that no obligations of reciprocity existed as regards other developing nations. Under Lomé the Community continued to provide financial and technical assistance to the ACP countries on the basis of EDF and EIB funding.[23] The list of types of projects which could be covered by Community aid had a similar focus to that under Yaoundé,[24] but was in fact wider and more diverse: rural development, industrialization, energy, mining, tourism, socio-economic infrastructure, structural improvement to agriculture, technical cooperation, sales promotion, support to SMEs, and grassroots micro projects. Institutionally, Lomé reformed the previous governing bodies into an EEC–APC Council of Ministers, a Committee of Ambassadors and a Consultative Assembly.[25]

---

[22] Bartels, 'The Trade and Development Policy of the European Union', p. 147. Certain East African countries entered into an agreement with the EEC in 1968.

[23] Commission of the European Communities, *Information Note, The Convention of Lomé, Europe/Africa, Caribbean, Pacific*, 1976, No. 129/76, p. 31; Commission of the European Communities, *Information Note, The ACP–EEC Convention of Lomé: One year after its entry into force*, Brussels, March 1977, p. 6 (on the Stabex system, which meant to stabilize export earnings, and which was introduced with the Lomé Conventions).

[24] Article 46 Lomé Convention.

[25] Commission of the European Communities, *Information Note, The Convention of Lomé, Europe/Africa, Caribbean, Pacific*, 1976, No. 129/76, p. 69.

Between Lomé I and II little changed, but a notable shift occurred in Lomé III and IV: the incorporation of human rights into EEC relations with the ACP countries, and a general broadening of development cooperation beyond trade and aid. Compared to Lomé II, the third Convention now included a reference to human rights in the preamble: 'Reaffirming their adherence to the principles of the [UN Charter] and their faith in fundamental human rights, in the dignity and worth of the human person, in the equal rights of men and women and of nations large and small.' Lomé III was also different in the sense that its first part was no longer trade, followed by investment, technical cooperation, etc., but that it had an introductory part which described in more general terms the political objectives and underlying principles of cooperation.[26] Article 1 of Chapter 1 of Lomé III thus made explicit that the agreement was to promote and expedite the economic, cultural and social development of ACP states. Both elements were indicative of a broadening scope of development cooperation beyond trade and aid, and towards a broader notion of sustainable development which implied focus on areas such as environmental protection and debt relief.[27] Lomé IV continued that reorientation, in particular with its new Article 5 which stated that 'cooperation shall be directed towards development centred on man, the main protagonist and beneficiary of development, which thus entails respect for and promotion of all human rights'. In 1995, Lomé IV bis was the result of a review of the earlier agreement, placing further emphasis on political, security and social content as well as cooperation in a decentralized fashion with a greater role for civil society.

By the mid 1990s it was argued that the various agreements which regulated the EC–ACP relationship for around thirty-five years were mostly significant in principle rather than in practice.[28] In particular as regards trade, the significance of these agreements was progressively diminished through successive tariff reductions following from multilateral GATT negotiations. The Cotonou agreement which replaced Lomé IV was signed in 2000, and was concluded between the Union and seventy-seven ACP countries for a period of twenty years. Because of disappointment in the results of Lomé and a host of other reasons, the EU clearly sought a radical change with what existed beforehand.[29] This was initially not well received by ACP countries. Even if most still belonged to the category of 'Least-Developed Countries' after decades of Lomé, most ACP States argued that they would have been worse off without Lomé cooperation.[30]

K. Arts, 'ACP–EU Relations in a New Era: The Cotonou Agreement' (2003) 40 *Common Market Law Review* 95–116 at 96

The end of the Cold War, the creation of the World Trade Organization (WTO), a stronger emphasis on privatization, liberalization and on the need to allow for full participation of non-State actors in development (cooperation) processes, the challenges posed by the concept of sustainable development,

---

[26] Commission of the European Communities, *Information Note, The Third Lomé Convention – Improvements and Innovations in Relation to Lomé II*, Brussels, November 1984, p. 1.

[27] Broberg, 'What Is the Direction for the EU's Development Cooperation after Lisbon?', p. 542.

[28] M. Sissoko, L. Osuji, W. Cheng, 'Impacts of the Yaoundé and Lomé Conventions on EC–ACP Trade' (1998) 1 *The African Economic and Business Review* 6–24, 21.

[29] Commission Communication, *Guidelines for the negotiation of new cooperation agreements with the African, Caribbean and Pacific (ACP) countries*, COM(97) 537 final, Brussels, 29 October 1997, pp. 3–5.

[30] K. Arts, 'ACP–EU Relations in a New Era: The Cotonou Agreement' (2003) 40 *Common Market Law Review* 95–116 at 96.

and the outburst of armed conflict and humanitarian crises in a considerable number of ACP countries drastically changed the (largely external) environment within which ACP–EU cooperation found itself. . . . For the European Union, the combination of the disappointing Lomé performance record until then, the changes in the external environment . . . and a number of internal circumstances provided strong incentives in favour of drastic modification of the traditional Lomé arrangements. These internal circumstances included, most notably: the overall declining political priority for maintaining a highly favourable package for the ACP, given the enlargement process and security and migration challenges closer to home in Central and Eastern Europe and around the Mediterranean; a certain degree of "aid fatigue" in traditional donor countries; and the serious managerial and competence problems in the European Commission.

The 1996 Commission Green Paper which prepared the ground for a follow-up to the Lomé Conventions listed a substantive number of major problems with Lomé which needed to be resolved.

European Commission, *Green Paper on relations between the EU and the ACP countries on the eve of the 21st century – Challenges and options for a new partnership*, COM(96) 570 final, Brussels, 20 November 1996

- The foundations of future partnership: . . . the EU tended to adopt unilateral interventionist approaches that were not conducive to ACP internalization of development policies or to each side accepting its own responsibilities . . .
- The EU's priorities and resource allocation criteria: If no clear priorities can be discerned from the breakdown of resource allocation by country over the last few decades it is largely because the various instruments created have all added their own specific goals to the list . . .
- Aid conditionality and selectiveness. . . . The effect of "conditionality" is to give more weight to performance-related criteria in resource allocation, but a consistent, universal approach to the issue has yet to be defined. . . .
- A new trade chapter. While the trade preferences enshrined in the Lomé Convention have a significant value,[31] not only in terms of concrete concessions but also as regards the basic principles underpinning the trade partnership between both parties (non-reciprocity, stability and contractuality), it is widely considered that, in general, the impact of the Lomé trade preferences has not been sufficient to enhance growth and increase diversification.

Some of the trends and features of the new global context, such as multilateral and regional liberalization, will have to be taken into account, in particular the need to comply with WTO rules. . . .
- Rethinking aid and aid instruments: The impact of Community aid is less than the sum of its parts because of the way the Community has accumulated aid instruments, each one with its own rationale.

---

[31] Emphasis in original. The Commission thereby wished to underline that regardless of the significance of trade preferences granted to the ACP having declined in value, this still remained important. See J. A. McMahon, 'Negotiating in a Time of Turbulent Transition: The Future of Lomé' (1999) 36 *Common Market Law Review* 599–624 at 600.

> Adopting a thematic approach and refocusing Community assistance on sectoral policies and agreed reforms should help make aid more efficient and increase its impact on economic and social conditions in ACP countries. . . .

The Cotonou Agreement entailed significant changes in at least four important areas.

1. It further strengthened the political dimension of the new partnership which among others entailed a strengthened conditionality and the incorporation of broader objectives such as peace and stability, and a stable and democratic environment.[32]
2. Poverty alleviation was made the cornerstone of the new partnership. Legally this entailed entrenching the wider focus on sustainable development (as reflected in the new EU development competence introduced by the Maastricht Treaty)[33] by including social, human and environmental objectives alongside the more traditional focus on trade.
3. This certainly did not diminish the importance of trade in the relationship with ACP, but a qualitative change did take place. As a consequence of the limited impact of Lomé to stimulate economic development, and due to the WTO-incompatibility of the EU's preferential banana regime for ACP countries, Cotonou was based on a new footing of progressive reintroduction of reciprocal preferences for all but the least developed ACPs. Cotonou would function as the framework agreement, and the ACPs were expected to negotiate free trade-orientated Economic Partnership Agreements (EPAs) with the Community.[34]
4. Cotonou would introduce a considerable element of geographical differentiation. This reflected an acceptance that there were significant differences among the seventy-seven ACP nations, combined with an EU-centric view that regional integration is key to stimulating long-lasting and stable economic growth. As a consequence EPAs would be negotiated with specific regional groupings, which has been a significant source of controversy. Overall, the EPAs have been conceived by the EU as comprehensive FTAs which also aim to improve the third countries' business environment by focusing on competition law, transparency, IP, and so on. However, large question marks existed over the ACP countries' institutional capacity to support such comprehensive trade agreements. Furthermore, there has been significant disagreement between EU and ACP countries as to the link between trade liberalization and the need for financial aid in these agreements. Finally, the EU has been subject to significant critique for its artificial creation of regional groupings which do not necessarily reflect actual reality as regards regional integration.[35]

The Cotonou agreement was negotiated for a period of twenty years, with a revision every five years. At the end of its lifespan, it requires that its parties shall enter into negotiations on its future eighteen months before its expiry, meaning that negotiations can be expected to commence in 2018.

---

[32] Article 98.
[33] Article 177 EC Treaty pre-Lisbon.
[34] Arts, 'ACP–EU Relations in a New Era: The Cotonou Agreement', p. 111.
[35] M. Meyn, 'Economic Partnership Agreements: A "Historic Step" Towards a "Partnership of Equals"?' (2008) 26 *Development Policy Review* 515–528 at 519.

G. Rye Olsen, 'Coherence, Consistency and Political Will in Foreign Policy: The European Union's Policy towards Africa' (2008) 9 *Perspectives on European Politics and Society* 157–171 at 167

... the motives and reasons for launching the ideas to establish the EPAs were closely related to a political wish of the EU to be in line with the WTO and to be in agreement with its aim to promote trade liberalisation. WTO compliance is 'at the very centre of the present post-Lomé' negotiations because the EU puts them there. ... [T]he use of the WTO is a 'strategic attempt by the EU to externalise responsibility for its own policy'. On the other hand, the European Union sees the regional trade arrangements as a mechanism to promote development via trade liberalisation. It is an assumption that trade liberalisation will result in more trade and thus contribute to increased economic growth, which may lead to reduced poverty. At least, it is worth noting that one of the topics which were dealt with during the negotiations on establishing the EPAs was exactly how to promote development by means of trade. So if the future will show that the EPAs and free trade promote development, it is possible to argue that the trade policy of the Union buttresses the aim of its development aid policy. If on the other hand, the critics are shown to be right in their negative evaluation of the possible consequences of the EPAs, it is necessary to conclude that the trade policy is inconsistent and incoherent with the aims of several of the other policy instruments.

The historical overview is important to keep in mind when analysing the legal aspects of the three C's in EU development cooperation policy. In the preceding paragraphs, we have high-lighted the intimate linkage between development and trade. However, as time progressed, the scope of development policy became progressively wider to include human rights, social and environmental concerns. The objectives of EU development policy and the instruments to implement them have evolved significantly: the oscillation of reciprocal and non-reciprocal trade arrangements, the shift in focus on governments to civil society, and so on. Finally, the relationship with the Member States is important too: on the one hand the Member States upload their interests to the EU level, while they simultaneously maintain their own individual develop-ment policies. These and other concerns are to this day captured by the notions of comple-mentarity, coherence and coordination.

(ii) Complementarity of EU development policy: position of the Member States

In legal terms, the complementarity of development policy concerns the nature of EU compe-tence. As indicated in Chapter 4, shared competences which are non-pre-emptive and comple-mentary are the exception, and their effect is defined in Article 4(3) TFEU for research, technological development and space policy, and in Article 4(4) TFEU for development and humanitarian aid. The difference between these provisions is that the latter indicates that the EU can develop a 'common policy and carry out activities' whereas Article 4(3) TFEU merely points to 'carrying out activities'. In both cases, these paragraphs indicate that 'the exercise of that competence shall not result in Member States being prevented from exercising theirs'. Articles 208(1) and 214(1) TFEU in the sphere of development policy and humanitarian aid respectively, define this coexistence in a more positive, constructive fashion as 'complementing and reinfor-cing' each other. The purpose of defining these policy areas in this fashion is that there is a 'bias towards action', or even a 'the more the better' approach in these fields. The consequence of this peculiar legal nature of EU external competence is that EU Member State coexistence in development takes on a form rather different from that in pre-emptive shared competences. This is specifically reflected in the approach taken by the Court to EU and Member State action in this policy domain. In the *Bangladesh* and *EDF* cases, the Court expressly exhibited a tolerant approach to the interconnection between intergovernmental and supranational approaches to organizing and exercising the complementary competences of the Union and the Member States.

A. Ward, 'Community Development Aid and the Evolution of the Inter-Institutional Law of the European Union', in A. Dashwood and C. Hillion (eds.), *The General Law of EC External Relations* (London: Sweet and Maxwell, 2000)

[These cases] addressed whether or not there are circumstances in which the EC Treaty prevents the Member States from taking independent, collective action in coming to decisions concerning the donation of aid, and binds them instead to recourse to Community institutional structure. The cases also made it clear that Member States are entitled to second the services of the EU institutions in formulating and implementing decisions that are made in intergovernmental fora. In addition, the rulings discuss the entitlement of the ECJ to review the legality of Council acts that are taken outside the EC institutional framework.

In the *Bangladesh* case, Parliament sought the annulment of an act adopted by the Council which was to grant special aid to Bangladesh,[36] and the means adopted by the Commission to implement that act. Specific to that act was that it was not adopted by the Council as an institution of the Union, but as 'the Member States meeting in Council', even though they decided 'on the basis of a Commission proposal' to grant aid to Bangladesh, which it would execute 'under a Community action'.[37] This means that the Member States were not acting in their capacity as members of the Council, but as representatives of their governments collectively exercising the powers of the Member States.[38] The EP submitted that the act really constituted an act of the Council since the document was entitled 'Council conclusions' since all Foreign Ministers were present. Therefore, it infringed the budgetary prerogatives of Parliament as well as the institutional balance as laid down in the EC Treaty. Parliament submitted a number of arguments to underline the 'Community' nature of the act, which the Court all refuted. The CJEU founded its reasoning upon the nature of the competence as complementary, and gave the Member States and institutions a good amount of freedom to organize development policy:

---

[36] This case concerned what is presently Article 214 TFEU, the EU's competence in humanitarian aid, as no distinct competence existed at the time of that judgment. Given the identical complementary nature of EU development and humanitarian competencies, the findings apply equally to the former competence.

[37] C-181/91 & C-248/91 *Parliament* v. *Council and Commission (Bangladesh)* [1993] ECR I-3685, para 2.

[38] *Ibid.*, para 12. The Council argued that therefore the action was inadmissible, but the Court maintained that an action for annulment is available in the case of all measures adopted by the institutions, whatever their nature or form, which are intended to have legal effects. See para 13 and also Case 22/70 *Commission* v. *Council (ERTA)* [1971] ECR 263.

C-181/91 & C-248/91 *Parliament* v. *Council and Commission (Bangladesh)* [1993] ECR I-3685

16. ... it should be pointed out that the Community does not have exclusive competence in the field of humanitarian aid, and that consequently the Member States are not precluded from exercising their competence in that regard collectively in the Council or outside it.

17. In support of its application, Parliament relies firstly on the reference made in the contested act to the Commission's proposal. In its opinion, that reference shows that, in view of the procedure which led to the act's adoption, it was the Council, not the Member States, which acted in this case.

18. That argument is not conclusive. Not all proposals from the Commission necessarily constitute proposals within the meaning of Article 149 of the Treaty. Their legal character must be assessed in the light of all the circumstances in which they were made. They may just as well constitute mere initiatives taken in the form of informal proposals.

19. Secondly, Parliament observes that, according to the description of the act, the special aid was to be administered by the Commission. According to the fourth indent of Article 155 of the Treaty, however, powers of implementation may be conferred on the Commission only by a decision of the Council.

20. That argument cannot be accepted either. The fourth indent of Article 155 of the Treaty does not prevent the Member States from entrusting the Commission with the task of coordinating a collective action undertaken by them on the basis of an act of their representatives meeting in the Council.

The objective of the Parliament's arguments was to more fully 'communautarize' action in development policy, and thereby ensure its own (budgetary) role in the process. In this case the Commission had made a proposal on aid to Bangladesh, and left Member States a choice to provide contributions either to the EC which the Commission would then administer, or bilaterally to Bangladesh. The Court found that such a proposal does not necessarily 'start up' a Union (legislative) process. They may also be informal policy proposals of which legal consequences ought to be assessed in their own right.[39] More generally, the Court finds that the role of the Commission is not limited by the Treaty. It may function as an organ/institution of the EU as a legal person, but the Treaties do not exclude it providing services which are more akin to that of a 'secretariat of an international organization' being requested to support a collective of Member States. This approach of the Court can be seen as an expression of the idea of 'mutually reinforcing and complementary' EU and Member State competence, and the corollary need for coordination. The relevant actors are free to exercise and coordinate their respective powers on a supranational or intergovernmental basis as they deem most appropriate.

For many years the notion of 'Member States in Council' was a relative oddity. However this changed with the Lisbon Treaty since the pressure of Member States who wish to be seen to act as sovereigns, yet reap the benefit of EU-level collaboration, has led to the revival of this concept. This has not been to the liking of the Commission, which has filed infringement proceedings against the Council.[40] In a case concerning the negotiation for a Convention on broadcasting in the Council of Europe context, the Member States gave a negotiation mandate to the Commission as the Council (exercising EU-implied external competence) and as the Member States in

---

[39] For more on soft law and its role in developing EU external relations, see Chapter 15.

[40] C-114/12 *Commission* v. *Council* (Case in progress) and C-28/12 *Commission* v. *Council* (Case in progress).

Council (exercising their own retained competence). The Commission argues that Member States in Council are not competent to give a negotiation mandate to the Commission, only the Council; and more generally, the Commission argues that the Council, by acting jointly with the Member States, undermines the standing of the Union and weakens the institutional framework of the Union.[41]

A few months after the *Bangladesh* judgment, in the *EDF* case, Parliament sought the annulment of a Financial Regulation of July 1991 applicable to development finance cooperation under the Fourth Lomé Convention.[42] To implement financing commitments under that Convention, the Member States meeting within the Council had adopted the instrument setting up a seventh EDF,[43] which in turn would be implemented through a financial Regulation adopted according to a procedure which did not include Parliament. The latter institution thus sought a Declaration from the Court that development aid under the Lomé Convention was Community expenditure, and therefore had to be governed by financial Regulations implemented according to the correct EEC Treaty procedure (consultation of Parliament).[44] In short, Parliament argued that the institutional balance within the Treaties had been impinged. The Court tackled this question by first examining who had undertaken financial commitments towards third countries under the Lomé Convention (EC or Member States), and secondly who was subsequently responsible for the performance of those obligations. In both instances, the answer was essentially derived from the complementary nature of EU development competence. The EU and the Member States can choose which of them, or both jointly, undertakes an international commitment in this sphere, and subsequently they can choose which of them, or both jointly, is responsible for carrying out their financing obligations. In this instance they chose to do so through the EDF.

Case C-316/91 *Parliament* v. *Council (EDF)* [1994] ECR I-625

21. The Parliament argues that it follows from the very words of Article 231 of the [Lomé Convention] that the Community as such has undertaken vis-à-vis the ACP States ... an obligation of international law distinct from those undertaken by the Member States. ...

24. The question as to who has entered into a commitment vis-à-vis the ACP States must be dissociated from the question whether it is for the Community or its Member States to perform the commitment entered into. The answer to the first question depends on an interpretation of the Convention and on how in Community law powers are distributed between the Community and its Member States in the relevant field, while the answer to the second question depends only on how those powers are distributed.

25. It is appropriate first to consider the distribution of powers between the Community and its Member States in the field of development aid.

26. The Community's competence in that field is not exclusive. The Member States are accordingly entitled to enter into commitments themselves vis-à-vis non-member States, either collectively or individually, or even jointly with the Community.

---

[41] C-114/12, Action brought on 1 March 2012, *Commission* v. *Council*, Application, OJ 2012 C138/5.
[42] C-316/91 *Parliament* v. *Council (EDF)* [1994] ECR I-625, para 1.
[43] *Ibid.*, para 2.
[44] *Ibid.*, para 3.

27. ... that finding is supported by the new Title XVII of the EC Treaty, inserted by the Treaty on European Union, Article 130x of which provides for the Community and the Member States to coordinate their policies on development cooperation and to consult each other on their aid programmes and for the possibility of joint action.

28. It is appropriate next to interpret the Convention in order to identify the parties which have entered into commitments.

29. The Convention was concluded, according to its preamble and Article 1, by the Community and its Member States of the one part and the ACP States of the other part. It established an essentially bilateral ACP–EEC cooperation. In those circumstances, in the absence of derogations expressly laid down in the Convention, the Community and its Member States as partners of the ACP States are jointly liable to those latter States for the fulfilment of every obligation arising from the commitments undertaken, including those relating to financial assistance.

30. Although Article 231 of the Convention, like Article 1 of the Financial Protocol, uses the phrase "the Community's financial assistance", it is nonetheless the case that several other provisions use the term "Community" in order to denote the Community and its Member States considered together. ...

33. It follows from the above that, in accordance with the essentially bilateral character of the cooperation, the obligation to grant "the Community's financial assistance" falls on the Community and on its Member States, considered together.

34 As for the question whether it is for the Community or for its Member States to perform that obligation, it should be noted, as stated above at paragraph 26, that the competence of the Community in the field of development aid is not exclusive, so that the Member States are entitled collectively to exercise their competence in that field with a view to bearing the financial assistance to be granted to the ACP States.

35. It follows that the competence to implement the Community's financial assistance provided for by Article 231 of the Convention and Article 1 of the Financial Protocol is shared by the Community and its Member States and that it is for them to choose the source and methods of financing. ...

38. It follows that the expenditure necessary for the Community's financial assistance provided for in Article 231 of the Convention and Article 1 of the Financial Protocol is assumed directly by the Member States and distributed by a Fund which they have set up by mutual agreement, with the administration of which the Community institutions are associated by virtue of that agreement.

4 COHERENCE IN EU DEVELOPMENT POLICY: EVOLVING SCOPE AND LINK WITH OTHER POLICIES

(i) 'Policy Coherence for Development': legal and policy dimensions

In development cooperation, coherence has significant legal and political implications. In legal terms, the principle has a firm footing in Article 208(1) TFEU. According to this provision there are three distinct aspects to coherence in this policy area: first, coherence of EU development cooperation with the more general principles and objectives of EU external relations (e.g. linking to Article 21 TEU); second, poverty reduction as the primary policy objective providing intra-policy focus as to how different initiatives cohere to the central goal; third, the obligation to take account of development objectives in other policies which are likely to affect developing countries. These legal obligations attract regular and significant attention in EU policy-making through the process called 'Policy Coherence for Development (PCD).[45] PCD was formalized in the 2005 European Consensus as a way of strengthening work towards achieving the MDGs,[46] and was particularly focused on linkages between development and other EU policies. According to the Commission:

the impact of EU non-aid policies on developing countries should not be underestimated, and neither should their potential to make a positive contribution to the development process in these countries. EU policies in areas such as trade, agriculture, fisheries, food safety, transport and energy have a direct bearing on the ability of developing countries to generate domestic economic growth.[47]

European Commission, *EU 2011 Report on Policy Coherence for Development*, SEC(2011) 1627 final, Brussels, 15 December 2011, p. 9

Policy Coherence for Development (PCD) has, since 2005, become a permanent and significant pillar of the EU effort to enhance the impact of external assistance and to better tailor and weigh the external effects of EU non-development policies in our partner countries. In 2011, the Policy Coherence for Development agenda is more ambitious than ever. In addition to the strengthened legal basis for PCD in the Lisbon Treaty, thereby confirming its important place in EU development policy, policy coherence requires special attention and active participation of all actors (i.e. EU institutions, Member States' administrations and civil society) to ensure real results. It is equally important to promote PCD both at EU and at national levels. . . .

The Council, in its Conclusions of 2005, instructed the European Commission to monitor progress in the EU and all Member States and to produce a report every two years. This is the third biennial report on PCD progress prepared by the Commission. It aims to report: a) on progress made by the EU and its Member States in making their policies more coherent with development cooperation objectives, focusing on those sectors identified as priority challenges for the PCD exercise, b) on the recent activities to ensure better monitoring and implementation of the PCD process, and c) on the main lessons learned and challenges ahead.

The present document focuses specifically on the actions taken, progress made and priorities pursued by EU institutions and Member States during the period 2009–2011. In preparation for this report, Member States, the Commission services and the European External Action Service were asked to respond to a questionnaire. Twenty-five replies were received from the Member States between April and September 2011. Based on these findings, the document also identifies the main challenges and outstanding issues for the next period.

The main legal implications of PCD are found in the scope of EU competence and the choice of legal basis. In the competence chapters of this book we have seen that in the Treaty of Rome, the EEC was only conferred two substantive competences in the external field, namely CCP[48] and

---

[45] Communication from the Commission, *Policy Coherence for Development – Accelerating progress towards attaining the Millennium Development Goals*, COM(2005) 134 final, Brussels, 12 April 2005.

[46] Looking beyond 2015 – which is when new targets replacing the MDGs are expected to be set – PCD will continue to play a significant role given the breadth in scope of current-day development policy. To that end the Rio+20 Conference in June 2012 launched the new term of SDGs to guide the post-2015 development pathway. See Resolution of the UN General Assembly, *The Future we want*, 66th session DOC 66/228, Outcome document in Annex.

[47] Communication from the Commission, *Policy Coherence for Development*, pp. 3–4.

[48] Article 113 EC-Rome.

AAs.[49] As the nature of international trade relations began to change, the EEC sought to incorporate development concerns into its international trade policies, which led to early case law on the scope of CCP and the expansive approach of the Court of Justice. With new competences being conferred from the SEA onwards, the CJEU more carefully worked towards a 'balance of competences'. In Chapter 5 of this book we then examined the intricate relationship between diverse competence-conferring provisions, the scope of these competences, the obligation to take into account objectives from other policy areas, and the challenges with regard to establishing the appropriate legal basis. In the following subsections, we will build on this knowledge, and highlight two legal aspects of coherence as they apply in relation to development policy: first, the incorporation of human rights conditionality in development policy; second, the relationship between development policy and security (CFSP) concerns.

(ii) EU development policy and human rights conditionality

In the succession of treaties from Yaoundé through Lomé to Cotonou, a progressive dynamic of politicization and broadening the scope of the agreements beyond aid and trade has taken place. The inclusion of human rights first happened in 1986 with their addition to the preamble of Lomé III, subsequently included in the body of Lomé IV in Article 5 in 1990. This evolution reflects EU internal developments, as in the EU Treaties references to human rights were first explicitly introduced by the SEA (1986). The SEA, in the preamble, expressed the 'awareness' of the responsibility incumbent upon Europe in its external relations to assume responsibility for promoting the principles of democracy, the rule of law and respect for human rights. With the Treaty of Maastricht in 1992, respect and promotion of these principles was made one of the general objectives of development cooperation policy (Article 130(u) TEC-Maastricht).[50] This treaty-based obligation served as foundation to the Commission's efforts to elevate the respect for human rights by the parties to its international agreements to an essential element of that agreement. These developed into 'essential element clauses', meaning that effective observance of human rights and real progress towards democracy are preconditions for commitments contained in that EU trade or association treaty with the third country.[51] It is therefore generally referred to as 'conditionality'.[52] From the perspective of EU external competence, the question then arose whether that meant that the EU de facto pursued 'an external human rights policy' through incorporation of such clauses, or whether the incorporation of human rights into external development instruments could indeed be said to simply be an element of EU development competence.

Communication from the Commission, *On the inclusion of respect for democratic principles and human rights in agreements between the Community and third countries*, COM(95) 216 final, Brussels, 23 May 1995

The Community's growing commitment to the promotion of human rights and democratic principles is reflected in the evolving nature of the references to these issues in the relevant agreements. . . . In this way

---

[49] Article 238 EC-Rome.
[50] Cremona, 'Human Rights and Democracy Clauses in the EC's Trade Agreements', in D. O'Keeffe and N. Emiliou (eds.), *The European Union and World Trade Law: After the GATT Uruguay Round* (Chichester/New York: Wiley, 1996), pp. 62–77.
[51] *Ibid.*, p. 64.
[52] A method which is now more generally applicable in EU external relations, extending also beyond fundamental rights.

the European Community and its Member States tangibly demonstrated their commitment to human rights in their relations with third countries. In the ensuing three years, this stance was confirmed as such references gradually began to appear in cooperation agreements, defining respect for democratic principles and human rights as one of the foundations of the parties' relations.

However, Article 5 of Lomé IV and similar articles in other agreements do not provide a clear legal basis to suspend or denounce agreements in cases of serious human rights violations or interruptions of democratic process.

It is for this reason that a clause defining democratic principles and human rights as an "essential element" of the agreements with Brazil, the Andean Pact countries, the Baltic States and Albania was introduced in 1992 (see Annex 1-1).

This is a substantial innovation, in that:
- it makes human rights the subject of common interest, part of the dialogue between the parties and an instrument for the implementation of positive measures, on a par with the other key provisions;
- it enables the parties, where necessary, to take restrictive measures in proportion to the gravity of the offence.

The inclusion of essential element clauses in agreements which could be used to suspend the other provisions they contain, gave rise to the 1994 *Portugal* v. *Council* case.[53] Portugal argued that the EC–India Partnership and Development Agreement which had been founded on trade and development legal bases, required the inclusion of the flexibility clause (current Article 352 TFEU) because the development competence allegedly did not suffice to support the inclusion of human rights as an essential element of the agreement. Portugal considered that respect for human rights could at most be a general objective of the cooperation agreement if based on the development competence alone. It therefore argued that the development competence could not support the evolution between Lomé IV and subsequent agreements, and that action suspending the agreement for human rights violations could be undertaken only with recourse to the flexibility clause. Conversely, the Council argued that action could be taken without using that provision, and the Danish government argued that the flexibility clause would be the proper legal basis if the agreement would have as its *sole* purpose to safeguard human rights. The Court sided with the Council drawing on an argument that reflects the coherence rationale of EU development policy as embedded in the Treaties. The fact that respect for human rights in development has to be 'taken into account' (ex Article 177 TEC, current Article 208(1) TFEU) entails that it is possible for the EU to give substantive meaning to that provision without needing recourse to the flexibility clause. As we have seen in Chapter 5, the Court's approach was one of seeking to guarantee the *effet utile* of the competence conferred upon the EU: it would not make sense for the drafters of the Treaties to refer to human rights in the competence-conferring provision, if no real-world action could be taken on their basis.

[53] C-268/94 *Portugal* v. *Council* [1996] ECR I-6177.

Case C-268/94 *Portugal* v. *Council* [1996] ECR I-6177

23. By declaring that 'Community policy ... shall contribute to the general objective of developing and consolidating democracy and the rule of law, and to that of respecting human rights and fundamental freedoms', [current Article 21 TEU] requires the Community to take account of the objective of respect for human rights when it adopts measures in the field of development cooperation.

24. The mere fact that Article 1(1) of the Agreement provides that respect for human rights and democratic principles 'constitutes an essential element' of the Agreement does not justify the conclusion that that provision goes beyond the objective stated in [Article 208 TFEU]. The very wording of the latter provision demonstrates the importance to be attached to respect for human rights and democratic principles, so that, amongst other things, development cooperation policy must be adapted to the requirement of respect for those rights and principles.

In Chapter 5 we have seen that there is a fine line between 'taking into account' a given policy objective, and pursuing such an objective in its own right which requires a separate legal basis. We have seen that the Court approaches this question both in the context of establishing the scope of a given EU competence, as well as in the closely related issue of correct legal basis. In EU development policy the Court has been faced with this question most recently in the context of the security–development nexus.

(iii) The relationship between development and security policy

R. Youngs, 'Fusing Security and Development: Just Another Euro-Platitude?' (2008) 30 *Journal of European Integration* 420

The European Union has routinely and increasingly asserted that it pursues security and development as mutually enhancing policy objectives. ... European policy makers proclaim a two-way link between development and security to be an increasingly core tenet of EU foreign policy. ... The link occupies centre stage within the EU's seminal policy coherence for development (PCD) commitments and is ostensibly integral to the generic design of European policies towards "fragile states". While widely praised, this rhetorical commitment to link development and security is in itself unremarkable: would anyone contend that insecurity and raging conflict were good for development, or conversely poverty good for conflict mitigation? The pertinent issue is whether it has actually changed anything in terms of policy. Has development policy become more security-sensitive? Has security policy incorporated concrete development components? Or is this strand of PCD simply a question of assuming that anything beneficial for development is good for security, and vice versa?

The security–development nexus has a policy and a legal dimension. From the policy side, the question revolves around the two-way relationship between a safe and secure environment and long-term progressive socio-economic development. From a legal perspective, the security–development relationship raises the question as to whether the EU ought to adopt a given initiative within the context of CFSP or its development competence – each with significantly different EU institutional structures, financial resources and diverse roles for the Member States.

To summarize it succinctly, stabilizing or preventing armed conflict in the short term is commonly addressed through the EU's CFSP (see Chapter 11), whereas longer-term socio-economic development falls within the realm of Article 208 TFEU. Quite evidently, however, initiatives that stimulate security will aid long-term development, and initiatives that support development will aid security in a given region. In light of this need for coherent development initiatives (PCD), the question which arises is similar to that on human rights above: to what extent do security initiatives fall within the scope of EU development competence? In recent pre-Lisbon case law, the Court of Justice has affirmed the wide scope of EU development policy in relation to a dispute on a border management project in the Philippines,[54] and in a case concerning EU support to ECOWAS to combat the illegal dissemination of small arms and weapons (see also Chapters 5 and 11).[55] In these cases of 2007 and 2008, the Court of Justice confirmed that development cooperation has developed to a very broad policy field which meant that security-orientated measures could also be adopted by the Union under its development competence, as long as they were focused on the socio-economic objectives of EU development policy (the eradication of poverty).

With the *Philippine Border Mission* case, the Parliament sought to annul the Commission Decision approving a project concerning the security of the borders of the Philippines. The contested Decision was based on Regulation No. 443/92 organizing financial and technical cooperation with the Asian and African countries, predating the entry into force of the Maastricht Treaty by little over a year. This Regulation had since been replaced by Regulation (EC) 1905/2006, valid until replaced by a new financing instrument after 2013.[56] The 2006 Regulation stated that the old Regulation continued to apply for legal acts and commitments of the pre-2007 budget years, and the contested decision was to be financed from the 2004 budget. As regards objectives, the contested decision clearly stated that 'the overall objective of the proposed project is to assist in the implementation of the UNSCR 1373 (2001) in the fight against terrorism and international crime'.[57] Parliament submitted that the Commission exceeded its implementing powers because the reasons for that decision were clearly based on considerations connected with the fight against terrorism and international crime, thereby going beyond the framework set out by Regulation No. 443/92 which serves as its basis.[58] The Commission made two counter-arguments: one regarding the specific objective of the instrument,[59] and the other regarding the general scope of EU development policy. For present purposes the second is solely pertinent.

---

[54] C-403/05 *Parliament* v. *Commission (Philippine Border Mission)* [2007] ECR I-9045.

[55] C-91/05 *Commission* v. *Council (Small Arms/ECOWAS)* [2008] ECR I-3651.

[56] Regulation 1905/2006/EC of the European Parliament and of the Council of 18 December 2006 establishing a financing instrument for development cooperation, OJ 2006 No. L378/41.

[57] C-403/05 *Parliament* v. *Commission (Philippine Border Mission)* [2007] ECR I-9045, para 16. United Nations Security Council Resolution 1373 (2001) of 28 September 2001 was adopted immediately in the wake of the 9/11 terrorist attacks in the USA.

[58] C-403/05 *Parliament* v. *Commission (Philippine Border Mission)* [2007] ECR I-9045, para 39.

[59] See paras 43 and 44. Essentially, the Commission sought to argue that combating international terrorism was not the dominant aim of the contested Decision, but combating trafficking in drugs and human beings, which more generally creates conditions conducive to economic development. It thereby sought to steer the objectives of the instrument away from a predominant 'security-focus' to ensure that the instrument remained within the scope of Regulation 443/92.

C-403/05 *Parliament* **v.** *Commission (Philippine Border Mission)* **[2007] ECR I-9045**

45. Relying on the general framework and evolution of development policy over recent years the Commission then explains that the strengthening of institutions, which is one of the horizontal aspects essential to sustainable development, henceforth forms an integral part of Community cooperation policies. That follows also from a reading of Articles 177 EC and 181a EC, in which the terms employed show that assistance may be given in fields not expressly referred to, such as, in particular, mine-clearance or the decommissioning of light weapons.

46. Whilst recognising that it has no independent powers in respect of anti-terrorism, the Commission points out that Regulation No 443/92 is a financial instrument at the service of a global policy, so that, in determining its scope, it is appropriate to show a certain flexibility and to take account, in particular, of the general policy framework.

The Court thus had to answer the question whether the scope of EU development policy of the early 2000s had developed and widened to the extent that EU development measures can support and 'take into account' international efforts combating terrorism.

C-403/05 *Parliament* **v.** *Commission (Philippine Border Mission)* **[2007] ECR I-9045**

55. In order to rule upon the Parliament's action, it is appropriate, therefore, to determine whether an objective such as that pursued by the contested decision, relating to the fight against terrorism and international crime, comes within the scope of Regulation No 443/92.

56. Admittedly, Articles 177 EC to 181 EC, inserted by the EU Treaty and dealing with cooperation with developing countries, refer not only to the sustainable economic and social development of those countries, their smooth and gradual integration into the world economy and the campaign against poverty, but also to the development and consolidation of democracy and the rule of law, as well as to respect for human rights and fundamental freedoms, whilst complying fully with their commitments in the context of the United Nations and other international organisations.

57. In addition, it follows from the Joint statement of the Council and the representatives of the governments of the Member States meeting within the Council, the European Parliament and the Commission on European Union Development Policy entitled 'The European Consensus' (OJ 2006, C 46, p. 1) that there can be no sustainable development and eradication of poverty without peace and security and that the pursuit of the objectives of the Community's new development policy necessarily proceed via the promotion of democracy and respect for human rights.

58. The Community legislature thus decided, in repealing Regulation No 443/92 by Regulation (EC) No 1905/2006 of the European Parliament and of the Council of 18 December 2006 establishing a financing instrument for development cooperation (OJ 2006 L 378, p. 41), to strengthen the development policy framework in order to improve its effectiveness. In that respect, Regulation (EC) No 1717/2006 of the European Parliament and of the Council of 15 November 2006 establishing an Instrument for Stability (OJ 2006 L 327, p. 1) establishes Community assistance, complementary to that provided for under external assistance, by contributing, among other things, to preventing the fragility of the States concerned. Under the sixth recital in the preamble to that regulation, account must be taken of the European Council Declaration on Combating Terrorism of 25 March 2004, in which it called for counter-terrorist objectives to be integrated into external assistance programmes. Under Article 4(1)(a) of that regulation the

Commission was thenceforth empowered to administer technical and financial assistance in the field of strengthening the capacity of authorities involved in the fight against terrorism and organised crime, by giving priority, inter alia, to supporting measures concerning the development and strengthening of counter-terrorism legislation, of customs law and of immigration law.

59. The fact remains that it is common ground that Regulation No 443/92 contains no express reference to the fight against terrorism and international crime. In that same respect, it must be pointed out that the proposal for amendment of Regulation No 443/92, presented by the Commission in 2002 (COM 2002/0340 final of 2 July 2002) and intended to insert in the scope of that regulation, among other things, the fight against terrorism, failed. . . .

68. It follows from all the foregoing that the contested decision pursues an objective concerning the fight against terrorism and international crime which falls outside the framework of the development cooperation policy pursued by Regulation No 443/92, so that the Commission exceeded the implementing powers conferred by the Council in Article 15 of that regulation.

The Court starts from the observation that the competences inserted into the EC Treaty in Maastricht are quite broad. They also include objectives relating to democracy, rule of law and human rights, although the connection of development to security is not explicit in EU primary law as it stood in 1992. Given that the contested instrument was adopted in the implementation of the old Regulation based on the Treaties as they stood then, the scope of EU development policy should be read in light of its specific point in time, and security objectives did not fall within the scope of EU development competence. It is then important that the CJEU expressly accepts that the scope of EU powers has since developed. In the excerpt above, it supports this evolutive interpretation of the scope of EU development powers with reference to a number of political and legal developments. Importantly, the CJEU does not accept that the Commission, as an implementing institution, can independently establish the evolving scope of EU development powers, but this clearly falls to the EU legislative bodies. Although the Lisbon Treaty has since reshuffled the objectives of EU external relations (see Chapter 1), the principle still stands: EU development policy is wide in scope, and can take into account security-related initiatives in the function of eradicating poverty (Article 208 (1) TFEU).

In the *ECOWAS* judgment the Court was again faced with having to establish the scope of EU development policy, confirming its wide scope established in the *Philippine Border Mission* case. The case nonetheless deserves attention, since it was a politically high-profile clash between the Member States on the one hand, and the Commission and Parliament on the other hand.

The dispute originated between the Commission and the Council concerning financial and technical assistance to the ECOWAS. From a policy perspective, the objective was legally to formalize into a binding treaty a pre-existing moratorium on the trade in small arms and light weapons. The Council adopted a Decision providing funds to ECOWAS with that objective in mind, and did so on a CFSP legal basis. However, the Commission was of the opinion that such action fell within the sphere of development cooperation. In *ECOWAS*, the Court similarly defined the broad scope of EU development policy, utilizing the European Consensus,[60] a statement of the Development Council on the threat of small arms to global

---

[60] C-91/05 *Commission v. Council (Small Arms/ECOWAS)* [2008] ECR I-3651, para 66.

stability, and a statement of the European Council on combating the illicit spread of small arms and light weapons.[61]

C-91/05 *Commission* v. *Council (Small Arms/ECOWAS)* [2008] ECR I-3651

69. For example, on 21 May 1999, the 'development' Council of the European Union adopted a resolution on small arms in which it presented the proliferation of those weapons as a problem of global proportions which, in particular in crisis zones and countries where the security situation is unstable, has been an obstacle to peaceful economic and social development. More recently, in the European Union strategy to combat illicit accumulation and trafficking of small arms and light weapons adopted by the European Council on 15 and 16 December 2005 (Council document No 5319/06 PESC 31 of 13 January 2006), the European Council referred, among the consequences of the illicit spread of small arms and light weapons, in particular to those relating to the development of the countries concerned, that is, the weakening of State structures, displacement of persons, collapse of health and education services, declining economic activity, reduced government resources, the spread of pandemics, damage to the social fabric and, in the long term, the reduction or withholding of development aid, while adding that those consequences constitute, for sub-Saharan Africa, the region principally affected, a key factor in limiting development.

70. Equally, [the European Consensus] refers, in paragraph 37, to insecurity and violent conflict as amongst the biggest obstacles to the achievement of the Millennium Development Goals, agreed by the United Nations, while mentioning, in that context, the fight against the uncontrolled proliferation of small arms and light weapons.

In delineating the CFSP from EU development policy, the Court thus found that the intimate relationship between socio-economic development and the security and stability of developing nations means the following: a concrete measure aiming to combat the proliferation of small arms and light weapons may be adopted by the Union under its development cooperation competence, if that measure by virtue both of its aim and its content falls within the socio-economic objectives of development policy and it does not pursue a security objective in itself.[62] While the broadening scope of development cooperation stands, the Treaty of Lisbon has made significant changes to the Treaty structure which also impact EU development competence. We refer to Chapter 5 for the analysis of how Lisbon has reorientated established case law on scope and choice of legal basis. Notably, the Lisbon Treaty placed greater emphasis on coherence by linking various external objectives in Article 21 TEU (see Chapter 1), aiming to avoid competence conflicts and instead focus energy on the substance of policy-making. The example below illustrates that dual CFSP–development legal bases have now become a possibility (see also Chapter 11, CFSP).

Council Decision 2012/308/CFSP of 26 April 2012 on the accession of the European Union to the Treaty of Amity and Cooperation in Southeast Asia, OJ 2012 No. L154/1

THE COUNCIL OF THE EUROPEAN UNION,

Having regard to the Treaty on European Union, and in particular Article 37 in conjunction with Article 31(1) thereof,

---

[61] *Ibid.*, paras 69–70.
[62] *Ibid.*, para 71.

Having regard to the Treaty on the Functioning of the European Union, and in particular Articles 209 and 212 in conjunction with Article 218(6)(a) and Article 218(8), second subparagraph, thereof,

Having regard to the joint proposal of the High Representative of the Union for Foreign Affairs and Security Policy and of the European Commission,

Having regard to the consent of the European Parliament,

Whereas:

(1) The Treaty of Amity and Cooperation in Southeast Asia ('the Treaty') was signed on 24 February 1976 by the Republic of Indonesia, Malaysia, the Republic of the Philippines, the Republic of Singapore and the Kingdom of Thailand. Since the date of signature, the following countries have also become signatories of the Treaty: Brunei Darussalam, the Kingdom of Cambodia, the Lao People's Democratic Republic, Burma/Myanmar, the Socialist Republic of Vietnam, the Independent State of Papua New Guinea, the People's Republic of China, the Republic of India, Japan, the Islamic Republic of Pakistan, the Republic of Korea, the Russian Federation, New Zealand, Mongolia, the Commonwealth of Australia, the French Republic, the Democratic Republic of East Timor, the People's Republic of Bangladesh, the Democratic Socialist Republic of Sri Lanka, the Democratic People's Republic of Korea, the United States of America, the Republic of Turkey and Canada.

(2) The Treaty aims to promote peace, stability and cooperation in the region. To this end, it calls for the settlement of disputes by peaceful means, the preservation of peace, the prevention of conflicts and the strengthening of security in Southeast Asia. Hence, the rules and principles set out in the Treaty correspond to the objectives of the Union's common foreign and security polity.

(3) Furthermore, the Treaty provides for enhancing cooperation in economic, trade, social, technical and scientific fields as well as for the acceleration of economic growth in the region by promoting a greater utilisation of the agriculture and industries of the nations in Southeast Asia, the expansion of their trade and the improvement of their economic infrastructure. Therefore, the Treaty promotes cooperation with the developing countries of that region as well as economic, financial and technical cooperation with countries other than developing countries.

(4) The Council, at its meeting of 4–5 December 2006, authorised the Presidency and the Commission to negotiate the Union's and the European Community's accession to the Treaty.

(5) By letter dated 7 December 2006, the Union and the European Community informed Cambodia, in its capacity of ASEAN Coordinator for relations with the Union, of its decision to apply for accession to the Treaty subject to the understandings expressed in the letter.

(6) On 28 May 2009, Thailand, then Chair of ASEAN, declared the consent of all the States in Southeast Asia to the accession to the Treaty by the Union and the European Community, subject to the entry into force of the Third Protocol to the Treaty.

(7) The Third Protocol to the Treaty, signed on 23 July 2010, provides for the accession of regional organisations to the Treaty.

(8) The Union should therefore accede to the Treaty following the entry into force of the Third Protocol to the Treaty,

HAS ADOPTED THIS DECISION:

Article 1

The accession of the Union to the Treaty of Amity and Cooperation in Southeast Asia is hereby approved on behalf of the Union.

The texts of the Treaty and its three amending Protocols, as well as the Instrument of Accession to the Treaty by the Union, are attached to this Decision.

Article 2

The Council hereby authorises the High Representative of the Union for Foreign Affairs and Security Policy to sign and deposit the Instrument of Accession to the Treaty on behalf of the Union.

Article 3

This Decision shall enter into force on the day of its adoption.

Done at Luxembourg, 26 April 2012.

For the Council

The President

Evidently, the question of legal basis is but a narrow aspect of the security–development nexus in EU development cooperation. The fact that dual legal bases may be utilized for an international instrument implies a policy connection between development and security matters. It is contested whether this link is actually desirable, and the extent to which it is a two-way street is also put into question.

A. Hadfield, 'Janus Advances? An Analysis of EC Development Policy and the 2005 Amended Cotonou Partnership Agreement' (2007) 12 *European Foreign Affairs Review* 39–66

There is no lack of evidence that the development–security nexus has emerged in consequence of poverty-insecurity dilemmas around the world. It may indeed form part of a strategy in tackling the challenges of frail states. Equally, constructing a development policy with robust security components instantly strengthens the viability and seriousness of EU foreign policy, components that have in the past been sorely lacking. A securitized development policy unites the foreign policy interests of many EU Member States and certainly 'offers a focus for European policy more generally to be a "force for good" in the world'. Indeed, as Clive Hamilton has suggested, 'a bleeding heart is a good complement to, but no substitute for, a hard-headed analysis of social structure and the deployment of power'. In other words, the efficacy of development intervention must balance the ideals. The inclusion of anti-terrorist and WMD non-proliferation provisions in a development treaty [the revised Cotonou agreement after 2005, ed.] is, however, a bridge too far, and may ultimately have a distorting effect upon development policy in general, and prove a source of confusion among ACP states over the 'hierarchy of interests' promulgated in multilateral aid treaties. Worse, anti-WMD provisions and their accompanying minutiae of compliance, observation, timetables and funding may well distract from valid security–development challenges faced by ACPs and other developing states. The political symbolism of Cotonou as a platform of EC external action now outweighs its original geographic or economic objectives. The addition of security provisions has had a damaging effect on the EC's development objectives but arguably adds to the robustness (if not the coherence) of overall EU foreign policy ... Holland and others have suggested the EU foreign policy should over time absorb national preferences; while this appears unlikely in the present, a strengthened development-fed foreign policy has already made its presence felt and would be better managed as an area of exclusive EU competence to guarantee both legitimacy and effectiveness. Operating on the understanding that – as per the [European Consensus on Development] – 'security and development are important and complementary aspects of EU relations with third countries', the EU has harnessed both the central components of securitized development and the subsequent benefits of a more robust foreign policy. A truer consensus would perhaps suggest that the securitization of development should be matched by 'developmentalized' security policies. Only in this way can the Janus-faced tensions of EC/EU development policy be resolved.

5 VERTICAL AND HORIZONTAL COORDINATION IN EU DEVELOPMENT POLICY

(i) Introduction

Coordination is the operative arm of the other two C's, complementarity and coherence. The conferral of a complementary EU development competence implies that the Member States remain fully competent to deploy initiatives in this domain alongside the EU, without one excluding the other. This 'bias towards action' makes vertical coordination of EU and Member State action all the more imperative. It is for that reason that Article 210 TFEU contains an explicit obligation to coordinate and consult, with a distinct role for the Commission to promote complementarity and efficiency of EU–Member State action. The notion of coherence then overlaps with complementarity in that it evidently implies positive synergies between the EU and national levels. Coherence is however more than that, and it also has an important horizontal component. As we have seen, the scope of EU development policy is wide, and legal obligations exist to take into account objectives from other EU policies as well. Thus, intra-EU coordination between different institutions and bodies or within institutions is crucial. This includes a range of relationships such as the Council–Commission–Parliament relationship in legislative work (Article 209 TFEU), but most crucially the Commission–EEAS relationship at the implementing level and also intra-organizational relations such as those between Commission DGs (e.g. DG Trade–DG Development and Cooperation (DevCo). In sum, complementarity and coherence in practice requires coordination between all actors involved. We will examine the vertical and horizontal dimensions by looking at the way EU development policy is financed and implemented in practice.

(ii) Multi-track financing of development cooperation: EDF and EU budget

The challenge to coordinate EU and Member State efforts is best illustrated through the important non-legally binding document from 2006 known as the European consensus on development. Published in the C series of the Official Journal, the full name of this soft legal document is: 'Joint Statement by the Council and the representatives of the governments of the Member States meeting within the Council, the European Parliament and the Commission on European Union Development Policy: "The European Consensus"'.[63] The stated objective of this document is to increase aid effectiveness by setting out a common vision that 'guides the action

---

[63] Title as quoted, OJ 2006 No. C46/1.

of the EU, both at its Member States and Community levels' towards achieving the MDGs. From a legal perspective, the title of the document indicates that the Member States participated as the Council – an institution of the EU – but also as sovereign nations exercising their retained competence. They signed up to the European Consensus to set out a common vision together with the Commission and EP as institutions of the EU as international organization. By rising above legal dividing lines, this document meant to coordinate the three dominant streams of development assistance that make up *European* (as opposed to EU) development cooperation: funds from Member State budgets disbursed in accordance with national rules and policy priorities; funds from the EU budget disbursed in accordance with EU development policy priorities (Article 208 TFEU); funds from the Member State budgets which are pooled in an EDF and disbursed in accordance with the priorities jointly agreed in the Cotonou Agreement with the ACP countries (specifically mentioned in former Article 179(3) TEC, omitted from the Lisbon Treaty).

M. Broberg, *Governing by 'Consensuses' – On the Legal Regulation of the EU's Development Cooperation Policy* (DIIS Working Paper 2010:23), pp. 6–7

As a rule the Union's expenses are financed via its budget. Such expenditure presupposes the prior adoption of a legally binding Union act forming the legal basis for the expenditure in accordance with the Union's financial regulation. However, the Union's development cooperation policy only partially follows this scheme, since to a large extent development assistance to the ACP countries is financed via the European Development Fund (EDF) instead of via the Union's budget. There are historical reasons for this and on several occasions the Commission has proposed integrating all development assistance in the budget. Such integration would lead to a different allocation of the Member States' financing of assistance to the ACP countries and would give the Commission greater power in this field. Perhaps this is part of the explanation why the EDF continues to exist. The EDF is financed by the Member States, has its own financial rules and is governed by a special committee. The continuing existence of the EDF means that the European Union's development assistance flows via two main channels, namely the budget and the EDF.

The EDF is an instrument funded outside the EU budget, consisting of financial contributions by the EU Member States. These contributions are calculated as a percentage of the entire value of the EDF, and according to a specific contribution key. For example, the eleventh EDF for 2014–2020 is expected to be worth around 34 billion euros, of which Germany would contribute about 20 per cent, and Bulgaria would contribute around 0.2 per cent.[64] The funds are provided on an intergovernmental basis, yet the Commission has a significant role since it is responsible for administering the Fund in line with an Implementing Regulation which is adopted for each EDF period. The Member States play a role in EDF governance through a

---

[64] Regulation 966/2012/EU/Euratom of the European Parliament and of the Council of 25 October 2012 on the financial rules applicable to the general budget of the Union and repealing Council Regulation (EC, Euratom) No. 1605/2002, OJ 2012 No. L298/1.
See Commission Communication, *Preparation of the multiannual financial framework regarding the financing of EU cooperation for African, Caribbean and Pacific States and Overseas Countries and Territories for the 2014–2020 period (11th European Development Fund)*, COM(2011) 837 final, Brussels, 7 September 2011, p. 9.

Committee which consists of representatives of the Member States set up at the Commission. This EDF committee is chaired by a Commission representative, and for each EDF it adopts rules of procedure which specify when it meets and renders decisions in line with the pertinent Implementing Regulation.[65] While the EDF has been in existence since the early days of the EEC, incorporation into the EU budget has been on the agenda for some time. The first EDF was launched in 1959, with the tenth EDF having run from 2008 to 2013, and the eleventh EDF will possibly be the last. In its Communication pertaining to the negotiations for the 2014–2020 multiannual financial framework, the Commission stated that it was not yet appropriate to propose that the EDF be integrated into the EU budget ('EDF budgetisation'). However, it foresaw that this would occur at the end of the next Multi-Annual Financial Framework (MFF) in 2020, which would then coincide with the expiry of the Cotonou Agreement.

The second channel through which the EU provides financing for its development policy is through the EU budget. Here the EU adopts a set of legally binding instruments via the ordinary legislative procedure (Article 209 TFEU) through which funds are administered in accordance with the general budgetary rules of the EU's Financial Regulation.[66] These legally binding acts – usually Regulations – are adopted for the duration of the seven-year MFF, e.g. 2007–2013, and now 2014–2020, in parallel to the EDF. In their scope of application and objectives for which funds are allocated, a distinction is made between geographic and thematic instruments. For the previous MFF, the EU had adopted the following instruments:[67]

- Geographic: Development Cooperation Instrument (DCI) and European Neighbourhood and Partnership Instrument (ENPI).
- Thematic: European Instrument for Democracy and Human Rights (EIDHR), Instrument for Stability (IfS), Instrument for Pre-Accession Assistance (IPA), Instrument for Cooperation with Industrialized Countries, Instrument for Nuclear Safety Cooperation and the EU Food Facility.

In December 2011 the Commission published its proposals for updated versions of the above-mentioned instruments for the MFF 2014–2020. The Communication was entitled 'Global Europe: A new approach to financing EU external action', and was published jointly by the Commission and High Representative. The premise of this instrument is that the EU has changed and that the EU's global environment has transformed as well. The communication places

---

[65] For the tenth EDF: Council Decision 2008/215/EC of 18 February 2008 adopting the rules of procedure for the European Development Fund Committee, OJ 2008 No. L78/35.

[66] Broberg, *Governing by 'Consensuses' – On the Legal Regulation of the EU's Development Cooperation Policy* (DIIS Working Paper 2010:23), pp. 6–7.

[67] Regulation 1905/2006/EC of 18 December 2006 establishing a financing instrument for development cooperation, OJ 2006 No. L378/41; Regulation 1638/2006/EC of 24 October 2006 laying down general provisions establishing a European Neighbourhood and Partnership Instrument, OJ 2006 No. L310/1; Regulation 1085/2006/EC of 17 July 2006 establishing an Instrument for Pre-Accession Assistance (IPA), OJ 2006 No. L210/82; Regulation 1717/2006/EC of 15 November 2006 establishing an Instrument for Stability, OJ 2006 No. L327/1; Regulation 1889/2006/EC of 20 December 2006 on establishing a financing instrument for the promotion of democracy and human rights worldwide, OJ 2006 No. L386/1; Regulation 1337/2008/EC of 16 December 2008 establishing a facility for rapid response to soaring food prices in developing countries, OJ 2008 No. L354/62; Council Regulation 382/2001/EC of 26 February 2001 concerning the implementation of projects promoting cooperation and commercial relations between the European Union and the industrialised countries of North America, the Far East and Australasia, OJ 2001 No. L57/10; Council Regulation 300/2007/Euratom of 19 February 2007 establishing an Instrument for Nuclear Safety Cooperation, OJ 2007 No. L81/1.

emphasis on new kinds of challenges as regards economy, climate and scarce resources, while simultaneously pointing to the shift in power in the global arena (BRICS countries). Internally too, the EU has changed since the previous instruments were adopted, and the Communication states that the Lisbon Treaty offers new opportunities through the overarching external objectives in Article 21 TEU and the establishment of the EEAS and EU delegations. At the time this book went to press the final texts for the 2014–2020 period had not yet been adopted because negotiations on the MFF had been long and arduous. As with the last MFF, the final version of these instruments is likely to appear in the last days of December 2013. Indicatively, from the Commission proposal it was clear that previous financing instruments would broadly continue to exist but in adapted form to take account of the new EU internal and external environments. It illustrates how coordination, coherence and complementarity are intertwined in the day-to-day practice of EU development cooperation.

Joint Communication of the Commission and High Representative, *Global Europe: A new approach to financing EU external action*, COM(2011) 865 final, Brussels, 7 December 2011

The emphasis for the post-2013 period will be on adapting the EU's methods of designing, programming and delivering external assistance to the new political, economic and institutional realities while building on what has proven to be successful so far. Addressing short-, mid- and long-term challenges on a variety of issues and mobilising a mix of external instruments at EU and Member State level will require particular efforts ensuring overall policy coherence in our engagement with our partners in the pursuit of a comprehensive EU approach. The proposed revision of the programming process will ensure greater consistency between the different areas of EU external action and a more result-driven approach, while allowing flexibility to respond to political priorities.

The new generation of external instruments will facilitate political dialogue, negotiations and implementation of existing and future agreements with our partners in support of an overall political strategy for that country. In this framework, policy coherence for development remains a key priority. . . .

The EU must seek to target its resources where they are needed most and where they could make the most difference. A more differentiated approach to partnerships and aid allocation driven by the country context is a core principle of this proposal. The EU should continue to recognise the particular importance of supporting development in its own neighbourhood and in Sub-Saharan Africa. On the other hand, many countries are graduating from EU development assistance because they are capable of funding their own development. Assistance will be allocated on the basis of country needs, capacities, commitments, performance and potential EU impact. The specific needs of countries in vulnerable, fragile, conflict-affected and crisis situations will be a priority. . . .

Overall, EU external instruments will take greater account of human rights, democracy and good governance when it comes to allocating external assistance to partner countries. With enlargement and neighbouring countries, country allocations and delivery of assistance should be more closely linked to progress in implementing reforms. For developing countries, the EU will strengthen mutual accountability in respect of commitments and the fulfilment of objectives as agreed with partner countries. . . . In line with the Lisbon Treaty provisions, the new instruments will implement new mechanisms to ensure more democratic debate on EU external assistance through a stronger involvement of the European Parliament. An example of this is the use of delegated acts, which can increase the flexibility of external instruments. Democratic scrutiny over the European Development Fund (EDF) will also be improved by bringing it into line with the Development Cooperation Instrument, while taking into account the specificities of the instrument.

(iii) Executing EU development policy: the Commission and EEAS

The financing instruments to support EU development are adopted for a seven-year window covering the MFF. Thereafter the Union must utilize these macroscopically orientated financing instruments to set more specific policy priorities and targets with shorter time spans. In turn, these are to be concretized and implemented through on-the-ground projects. This process of EU development policy-making encompasses three phases: (1) management, (2) programming and (3) implementing EU development policy. In the pre-Lisbon context it was the Commission that oversaw this process, whereas in the post-Lisbon era a complex division of tasks exists between the EEAS and the Commission (specifically DG DevCo). This division of tasks is based on their respective roles as laid down in Articles 17 and 27(3) TEU, and has been specified in Article 9 of the Council Decision establishing the EEAS (see also Chapter 1). Note that following the adoption of new financing instruments at the end of 2013, an updated version of the EEAS Council Decision will be published during the spring of 2014.

Article 9, Council Decision 2010/427/EU establishing the organisation and functioning of the European External Action Service (2010 version), OJ 2010 No. L201/30

1. The management of the Union's external cooperation programmes is under the responsibility of the Commission without prejudice to the respective roles of the Commission and of the EEAS in programming as set out in the following paragraphs.
2. The High Representative shall ensure overall political coordination of the Union's external action, ensuring the unity, consistency and effectiveness of the Union's external action, in particular through the following external assistance instruments:
   - the Development Cooperation Instrument,
   - the European Development Fund,
   - the European Instrument for Democracy and Human Rights,
   - the European Neighbourhood and Partnership Instrument,
   - the Instrument for Cooperation with Industrialised Countries,
   - the Instrument for Nuclear Safety Cooperation,
   - the Instrument for Stability, regarding the assistance provided for in Article 4 of Regulation (EC) No 1717/2006.
3. In particular, the EEAS shall contribute to the programming and management cycle for the instruments referred to in paragraph 2, on the basis of the policy objectives set out in those instruments. It shall have responsibility for preparing the following decisions of the Commission regarding the strategic, multiannual steps within the programming cycle:
   (i) country allocations to determine the global financial envelope for each region, subject to the indicative breakdown of the multiannual financial framework. Within each region, a proportion of funding will be reserved for regional programmes;
   (ii) country and regional strategic papers;
   (iii) national and regional indicative programmes.

In accordance with Article 3, throughout the whole cycle of programming, planning and implementation of the instruments referred to in paragraph 2, the High Representative and the EEAS shall work with the relevant members and services of the Commission without prejudice to Article 1(3).

All proposals for decisions will be prepared by following the Commission's procedures and will be submitted to the Commission for adoption.

[The article continues to set out a specific modus operandi for each listed instrument.]

In the three execution phases of development policy, the Commission is responsible for the 'management' of external development cooperation, whereas the EEAS and Commission share roles in the 'programming' phase. The 'implementation' phase again befalls the Commission. The line between management and programming can be difficult to draw, whereas implementation is perhaps the most straightforward to delineate: the implementation phase concerns the actual delivery of aid in an efficient and effective way, usually through a project or sector approach, or straightforward budget support.[68] The line between management and programming, and the role of the EEAS and Commission therein, has been explained in the extract below.

S. Blockmans, M. Cremona, D. Curtin, G. de Baere, S. Duke, C. Eckes, C. Hillion, B. Van Vooren, R. Wessel and J. Wouters, *EEAS 2.0 – A Legal Commentary on Council Decision 2010/427/EU establishing the Organisation and Functioning of the European External Action Service* (SIEPS Working Paper 2013:1), pp. 92–93

In the context of (business) administration, "management" is the process of dealing with or controlling things or people; the responsibility for and control of a company or organisation. Management in all business and organisational activities is the act of getting people together to accomplish desired goals and objectives using available resources efficiently and effectively. Management comprises designing, planning, organising, staffing, leading or directing, and controlling an organisation (a group of one or more people or entities) or effort for the purpose of accomplishing a goal.

According to Article 9(1) [of the Council Decision establishing the EEAS], the management of the EU's external cooperation programmes is "under" the responsibility of the Commission "without prejudice to the respective roles of the Commission and of the EEAS in programming". Thus, the Commission retains overall responsibility for dealing with and controlling the Union's external cooperation programmes, whereas it shares the role of "programming", i.e. designing, scheduling, or planning the EU's external cooperation programmes (only an element of the wider concept of "management"), with the EEAS. In short, the basic prescript, namely that during the whole process of planning and implementation both parts of the organisation should work together and that all proposals for decision have to be prepared through the Commission procedures and submitted to the Commission (Article 9(3)), has remained unchanged. ... In its contribution to the Union's external cooperation programmes, the EEAS is expected to work towards ensuring that the programmes fulfil the objectives for external action as set out in Article 21 TEU, in particular in paragraph (2)(d) thereof, and that they respect the objectives of the Union's development policy in line with Article 208 TFEU.

---

[68] The project approach entails funding projects of civil society or private actors with a clearly specified objective in a given time period. The sector approach is broader by focusing on working with partner governments and other donors or stakeholders to coordinate longer-term outcomes and financing for a given sector.

Programming is the decision-making process whereby strategy, budget and priorities for spending aid in non-EU countries is drawn up. During the MFF 2007–2013 this occurred through three kinds of instruments: first, the general strategy papers per country or region covering the whole period of seven years; second, the more detailed indicative programmes (national or regional) which cover half the period of the MFF (2007–2009 and 2010–2013); third, the detailed annual action programmes for each year of the programming period. Looking to the next MFF and new development cooperation instruments, the joint EEAS–Commission Communication 'Global Europe' has made a number of proposals to strengthen the three C's throughout the forthcoming programming cycle.

Joint Communication of the Commission and High Representative, *Global Europe: A new approach to financing EU external action*, COM(2011) 865 final, Brussels, 7 December 2011, pp. 6–7

5 A Revised and Simplified Programming Process

A major innovation in this revision of EU external instruments is in the changes proposed for the programming process. The Lisbon Treaty sets out a clear obligation for the EU and its Member States to coordinate their policies on external action, including development cooperation

5.1 Agreeing on comprehensive joint EU strategies

To achieve this goal and to generate more impact and visibility in their relationships with third countries, the EU and Member States need to have a clear shared strategy in their relations with a partner country or region. In appropriate cases, this could mean drafting a Joint Framework Document (JFD) on the basis of a joint analysis. A JFD would integrate all aspects of EU external action and all EU tools/instruments to achieve an adequate balance between flexibility and predictability as well as between short-, medium- and long-term objectives. The JFD would define strategic lines of action, and a broad policy mix referring to the EU and Member States instruments and policies to be used in a country or region taking into account diplomatic and political aspects (Common Foreign and Security Policy, political dialogue, democracy and human rights, etc.), development cooperation, humanitarian aid, security, and the external projection of internal policies.

The previously discussed security–development nexus provides good insight into the impact of the new EEAS on policy-making in EU development cooperation policy. The excerpt below is of course an assessment written during the early days of the EEAS, where the pertinent actors were still hammering out a new modus vivendi. The post-2013 financing instruments can be expected to be more attuned to this new institutional setting.

H. Merket, 'The European External Action Service and the Nexus between CFSP/CSDP and Development Cooperation' (2012) 17 *European Foreign Affairs Review* 650–651

Both insiders and outsiders agree that the EU's commitment to the nexus between development cooperation and CFSP/CSDP has not achieved the aspired level of cooperation and coordination between security and development strategies, initiatives and actors. While the European External Action Service was not established with the specific objectives of the security–development nexus in mind, its aims of enhanced effectiveness, visibility and consistency of EU external action indirectly raise expectations for this particular interface. The more so because it integrates – for the first time in the EU's history – staff from the Commission, the Council and the Member States, with both security and development-oriented portfolios. Against this background, this article has aimed to analyse whether and how the EEAS can help the EU to overcome the hurdles it faces in implementing the security–development alliance.

First, as a central policy interlocutor with a heterogeneous composition the EEAS could finally put the rhetoric of coordination into practice. Its setting enables a decentralized and cross-fertilizing exchange of experience-based knowledge in a network of security and development-oriented actors. Second, the analysis of EEAS Decision 2010/427/EU demonstrated that the Union's foreign service has been assigned with responsibilities in the decision-making processes of the various instruments in the EU's security–development armamentarium. In this manner, the EEAS to a certain extent pools together the EU's scattered resources and could make an end to the diffused institutional responsibility. However, while the EEAS offers opportunities to close the gap between security and development polices, the Lisbon Treaty did not make an end to the legal divide itself. The challenge will therefore be to ensure that the EEAS is more than a mere juxtaposition of its constituent parts and does not internalize old rivalries and challenges of delimitation. [Finally], the EEAS is only a service and does not dispose of genuine decision-making powers. The extent to which its benefits are reaped therefore depends on the constant cooperation with the EU's traditional external actors, in particular the Commission and the Member States, and their willingness to make use of the framework offered by the EEAS. In the process of working out the practical implications of the vague and often dubious provisions of the EEAS Decision, it remains to be seen how willing the latter will be to give up certain prerogatives in the external sphere.

6 THE BROADER PICTURE OF EU EXTERNAL RELATIONS LAW

EU development policy is a mature policy field as old as European integration itself. As a result the legal principles, institutions and instruments that underpin it have been progressively shaped through the interaction between European integrative processes, concrete policy needs and law as a structuring element. The complementary nature of EU development policy is exemplary of this interaction and the broader context of EU external relations law. During the early years of the Treaty of Rome, mainly France pushed its development interests through the supranational level in the form of associating certain third States with the EEC. This did not pre-empt Member State development initiatives, and laid the basis for 'the other two C's', namely the need for coherence and coordination between the two levels. The EDF soon became an interesting peculiarity of EC development cooperation exhibiting all three C's: funds of the Member States were being pooled on an intergovernmental basis (complementarity), with a central management role for the Commission (coordination), with jointly agreed policy objectives but without actually integrating the funds into the EU budget (coherence). In the early 1990s Parliament sought to push budgetization through judicial means, which would have extended its role in EU budgetary matters over (the quantitatively significant) EDF funds as well. However, the Court was unreceptive and expressly confirmed the complementary nature of this competence. Eventual budgetization is likely however. During the negotiations on the 2014–2020 MFF, the Commission certainly would have wished to propose the integration of EDF funding into the EU budget structures, arguing that this would streamline funding procedures, ease coordination efforts and substantive coherence between initiatives and increase transparency in the provision of EU development aid. However, the Commission did not make such a proposal because Member States were not yet prepared to make that step. It announced that it would make that proposal towards the revision of the Cotonou agreement by 2020.

SOURCES AND FURTHER READING

Arts, K., 'ACP–EU Relations in a New Era: The Cotonou Agreement' (2003) 40 *Common Market Law Review* 95–116.

Arts, K. and Dickson, A. K. (eds.), *EU Development Cooperation – From Model to Symbol* (Manchester: Manchester University Press, 2004).

Bartels, L., 'The Trade and Development Policy of the European Union', in M. Cremona (ed.), *Developments in EU External Relations Law* (Oxford: Oxford University Press, 2008), pp. 128–171.

Blockmans, S., Cremona, M., Curtin, D., de Baere, G., Duke, S., Eckes, C., Hillion, C., Van Vooren, B., Wessel, R. and Wouters, J., *EEAS 2.0 – A Legal Commentary on Council Decision 2010/427/EU establishing the Organisation and Functioning of the European External Action Service* (SIEPS Working Paper 2013:1).

Broberg, M., *Governing by 'Consensuses' – On the Legal Regulation of the EU's Development Cooperation Policy* (DIIS Working Paper 2010:23).

Broberg, M., *The EU's Legal Ties with its Former Colonies – When Old Love Never Dies* (DIIS Working Paper 2011:01).

Broberg, M., 'What Is the Direction for the EU's Development Cooperation after Lisbon? A Legal Examination' (2011) 16 *European Foreign Affairs Review* 539–557.

Carbone, M. (ed.), *Policy Coherence and EU Development Policy* (Abingdon/New York: Routledge, 2009).

Carbone, M., 'Au-delà de l'aide: la Cohérence des Politiques de Développement de l'Europe' (2012) *Revue Internationale de Politique de Développement*, 3, 197–212.

Carbone, M., 'Preserving Policy Autonomy: EU Development Cooperation from Maastricht to Lisbon', in F. Laursen (ed.), *The EU's Lisbon Treaty: Institutional Choices and Implementation* (Farnham/Burlington: Ashgate, 2012), pp. 229–242.

Cremona, M., 'Human Rights and Democracy Clauses in the EC's Trade Agreements', in D. O'Keeffe and N. Emiliou (eds.), *The European Union and World Trade Law: After the GATT Uruguay Round* (Chichester/New York: Wiley, 1996), pp. 62–77.

Hadfield, A., 'Janus Advances? An Analysis of EC Development Policy and the 2005 Amended Cotonou Partnership Agreement' (2007) 12 *European Foreign Affairs Review* 39–66.

Hoebink, P. (ed.), *The Treaty of Maastricht and Europe's Development Co-operation*, Studies in European Development Co-operation Evaluation No. 1 (Amsterdam: Aksant Academic Publishers, 2005).

McMahon, J. A., 'Negotiating in a Time of Turbulent Transition: The Future of Lomé' (1999) 36 *Common Market Law Review* 599–624.

Merket, H., 'The European External Action Service and the Nexus between CFSP/CSDP and Development Cooperation' (2012) 17 *European Foreign Affairs Review* 625–651.

Meyn, M., 'Economic Partnership Agreements: A "Historic Step" Towards a "Partnership of Equals"?' (2008) 26 *Development Policy Review* 515–528.

Olsen, G. R., 'Coherence, Consistency and Political Will in Foreign Policy: The European Union's Policy towards Africa' (2008) 9 *Perspectives on European Politics and Society* 157–171.

Sissoko, M., Osuji, L. and Cheng, W., 'Impacts of the Yaoundé and Lomé Conventions on EC–ACP Trade' (1998) 1 *The African Economic and Business Review* 6–24.

Van Vooren, B., *EU External Relations Law and the European Neighbourhood Policy: A Paradigm for Coherence* (Abingdon/New York: Routledge, 2012).

Ward, A., 'Community Development Aid and the Evolution of the Inter-Institutional Law of the European Union', in A. Dashwood and C. Hillion (eds.), *The General Law of EC External Relations* (London: Sweet and Maxwell, 2000).

Youngs, R., 'Fusing Security and Development: Just Another Euro-Platitude?' (2008) 30 *Journal of European Integration* 419–437.

11

Common Foreign and Security Policy

1 CENTRAL ISSUES

- The Union's foreign and security policy is based on a set of compromises. From the outset, Member States have been hesitant to hand over powers in this area. Yet, the strong links with other policies as well as the single institutional structure caused an integration of CFSP into the Union legal order. While its distinct nature remains clearly visible, CFSP has become part and parcel of the EU's external relations regime.
- In this chapter we will address the historical explanations for the current place of CFSP in the EU legal order. We will analyse the attempts to start political cooperation before the 1990s and will assess the current provisions in that context. We will also address the role of the institutions (including the role of the CJEU) in CFSP as well as the decision-making procedures. Finally, we will assess the legal nature and function of the CFSP instruments.

2 INTRODUCTION

The CFSP of the EU has for decades been the 'odd one out'. It emerged separately from the EEC in an incremental, pragmatic fashion at the beginning of the 1970s. The process was stimulated through the realization that the coordination of the different foreign policies of the (six, then nine, etc.) Member States was helpful, and occasionally even necessary, for the Community to pursue its goals. At present CFSP objectives have become an integral part of the overall objectives of the Union. Thus, this policy area has developed from a purely intergovernmental form of information exchange, coordination and cooperation in the days of the EPC, to an EU competence in its own right and an area in which the Member States have accepted significant forms of institutionalization and legalization. The integration of CFSP policy goals is clearly visible in the Treaty when we look at the general statement of values which include peace and security, and the protection of EU citizens:

Article 3(5) TEU

In its relations with the wider world, the Union shall uphold and promote its values and interests and contribute to the protection of its citizens. It shall contribute to peace, security, the sustainable development of the Earth, solidarity and mutual respect among peoples, free and fair trade, eradication of poverty and the protection of human rights, in particular the rights of the child, as well as to the strict observance and the development of international law, including respect for the principles of the United Nations Charter.

Yet, the integration is not complete. Even after the Lisbon Treaty, the CFSP remains 'distinct' from the general former 'Community logic'. Most notably, the CFSP (and CSDP) are the only substantive policy domains found in the TEU, whereas other policies are found in the TFEU.

Article 24(1) TEU

The common foreign and security policy is subject to specific rules and procedures.

Indeed, in many aspects the nature of CFSP still differs from other 'common' policies, such as the CCP (Article 207 TFEU) or the CAP. Over the years, Member States have shown a willingness to cooperate in CFSP, but remained reluctant to actually transfer competences. This makes it difficult to establish the *nature* of competence the EU has under CFSP (see Chapter 4), yet, the existence of a competence is beyond any doubt.

Article 2(4) TFEU

The Union shall have competence, in accordance with the provisions of the Treaty on European Union, to define and implement a common foreign and security policy . . .

This provision indicates that CFSP has moved beyond intergovernmentalism: i.e. an actual competence as such has been *conferred* upon the Union rather than existing as a mere cooperative framework for Member State competences. Nonetheless, the *nature* of the competence remains unclear. CFSP is not mentioned in Articles 3–6 TFEU under either of the categories: exclusive competences, shared competences or supporting, coordinating or supplementing competences. It would probably come closest to the field of complementary competence as observed in the field of development: both the Union and the Member States have roles to play, strong coordination is legally required and politically desirable, yet it remains questionable that activities of the Union would pre-empt Member State action. The *sui generis* nature of CFSP is usually related to a number of elements which are lacking when compared to most other Union policy areas: the different roles of the European Commission and the EP in the decision-making process, the impossibility of the Court to rule on most CFSP decisions and Treaty provisions, the different effects of CFSP decisions in the domestic legal orders of the Member States, and the different nature of the instruments themselves.

3 THE NATURE OF CFSP

On 7 February 1992, the Member States of the EEC entered a new phase in the ongoing process of intensifying their political cooperation. In signing the TEU they officially embraced foreign and security cooperation as an inextricable component of what from that moment on was to referred to as the 'European Union' (see Chapter 1). CFSP was – from the entry into force of the Treaty on 1 November 1993 – to be seen as one of the areas that would serve as the justification for the establishment of that Union.

This CFSP did not, however, appear out of the blue, and its origins date back to the 1950s.[1] The history of CFSP reveals an ongoing struggle to reach an agreement between the members of the EEC on political cooperation alongside their economic cooperation and, above all, on the legal institutional relationship between the economic and political policy domains. The purpose of the present section is to explain many of the choices made in the current CFSP provisions as well as the special position CFSP still has within the Union. The foreign, security and defence policy is the only policy area that finds its legal basis in the TEU and not in the TFEU. This can only be understood through examining the origins of integrative efforts in this policy field.

(i) The position of the CFSP in the Treaty

The 2009 Lisbon Treaty made an end to the so-called 'pillar structure' (see below). Since the entry into force of that Treaty and the resulting new TEU, CFSP is no longer 'the second pillar' of the Union, but an integral part of the single legal person that is the EU. While CFSP is occasionally referred to in the first parts of the TEU in relation to the role of the institutions, the main provisions are to be found in Title V TEU, entitled 'General Provisions on the Union's External Action and Specific Provisions on the Common Foreign and Security Policy'. The 'specific provisions' to which the Treaty refers, are then laid down in Chapter 2 of Title V. This structure underlines that CFSP is special, but nonetheless clearly integrated into the overall 'external action' of the Union. CFSP has a wide scope and, at first glance, seems to cover all foreign policy dimensions of the Union.

Article 24(1) TEU

The Union's competence in matters of common foreign and security policy shall cover all areas of foreign policy and all questions relating to the Union's security, including the progressive framing of a common defence policy that might lead to a common defence.

In principle, nothing in foreign affairs is excluded and all aspects may become subject to common policy action or rules. At the same time a reference is made to the fact that the regular decision-making procedures that are applicable to other policy areas do not apply to CFSP.

---

[1] One may even go back as far as 19 September 1946, when Winston Churchill stressed the need to establish 'a kind of United States of Europe'; or, to 7 May 1948 when the so-called 'Congress of Europe' called for the establishment of a political and economic union in Europe.

> ## Article 24(1) TEU
>
> ... The common foreign and security policy is subject to specific rules and procedures

Chapter 2 of Title V thus provides the *lex specialis* for CFSP, and the key differences as regards the institutional balance and the role of the CJEU in CFSP are summarized in Article 24 TEU.

> ## Article 24(1) TEU
>
> The common foreign and security policy is subject to specific rules and procedures. It shall be defined and implemented by the European Council and the Council acting unanimously, except where the Treaties provide otherwise. The adoption of legislative acts shall be excluded. The common foreign and security policy shall be put into effect by the High Representative of the Union for Foreign Affairs and Security Policy and by Member States, in accordance with the Treaties. The specific role of the European Parliament and of the Commission in this area is defined by the Treaties. The Court of Justice of the European Union shall not have jurisdiction with respect to these provisions, with the exception of its jurisdiction to monitor compliance with Article 40 of this Treaty and to review the legality of certain decisions as provided for by the second paragraph of Article 275 of the Treaty on the Functioning of the European Union.

CFSP is characterized by different voting rules, different instruments, a different role for the institutions and a very limited role for the Court of Justice. In the subsequent sections in the chapter we will analyse these aspects in more detail. Because of Article 24 TEU, some authors have argued that the current situation is not so different from what we have seen in the past, and that CFSP is still largely intergovernmental which implies the continuation of the 'second pillar' even if it is less visible than it used to be.[2]

> ### B. Van Vooren, *EU External Relations Law and the European Neighbourhood Policy: A Paradigm for Coherence* (Abingdon/New York: Routledge, 2012), pp. 53–54
>
> The Lisbon Treaty contains a large number of other innovations pertinent to coherent EU external relations, including the single legal personality and a further reformulation of the non-affect clause between the CFSP in the TEU and other external policies in the TEU. ... The Union has certainly come a long way since the 1957 Treaty of Rome and the 1970 Davignon Report. The CFSP is now a mature part of external relations of the Union as a whole, with its objectives figuring side by side to former Community objectives in Art 21 TEU. Institutionally, too, the creation of the European External Action Service in support of the HR/VP is in stark contrast to the earliest apprehension of giving EPC any kind of permanent secretariat for fears that this might lead to the crumbling of national sovereignty. Hence, the Lisbon Treaty has brought about a number of important innovations towards coherent EU external relations. However, as all the treaty changes that preceded it, this document is evolutionary rather than revolutionary. While the

---

[2] For example, R. Whitman and A. Juncos, 'The Lisbon Treaty and the Foreign, Security and Defence Policy: Reforms, Implementation and the Consequences of (Non-)Ratification' (2009) 14 *European Foreign Affairs Review* 25–46.

external action service may over time prove to be the seed that leads to a single external policy for the Union properly-so-called, the fragmented legal foundation to EU external relations remains – for the time being – firmly in place.

Even if the CFSP is subject to special procedures and utilizes a specific toolbox of instruments, the Treaty aims to avoid conflict and seeks consistency in 'EU' external relations, as is apparent through the following provisions[3] (see also Chapter 1):

Article 13 TEU

The Union shall have an institutional framework which shall aim to promote its values, advance its objectives, serve its interests, those of its citizens and those of the Member States, and ensure the *consistency*, effectiveness and continuity of its policies and actions.

Article 16(6) TEU

The General Affairs Council shall ensure *consistency* in the work of the different Council configurations [and it] shall elaborate the Union's external action on the basis of strategic guidelines laid down by the European Council and ensure that the Union's action is *consistent.*

In relation to the external relations in particular, Article 18(4) lays the same task in the hands of the HR for the Union's foreign and security policy as (s)he 'shall ensure the consistency of the Union's external action'. In the most elaborate fashion, the demand for consistency returns in the following provision:

Article 22(3) TEU

The Union shall ensure *consistency* between the different areas of its external action and between these and its other policies. The Council and the Commission, assisted by the High Representative of the Union for Foreign Affairs and Security Policy, shall ensure that *consistency* and shall cooperate to that effect.

C. Hillion, 'Tous pour un, un pour tous! Coherence in the External Relations of the European Union', in M. Cremona (ed.), *Developments in EU External Relations Law* (Oxford: Oxford University Press, 2008), pp. 10–36[4]

'[C]onsistency', understood as absence of legal contradiction, is an essential element of coherence. Such consistency is ensured notably through the observance of EU rules on distribution of powers, and thanks to

---

[3] Emphasis added.
[4] The text was slightly adapted towards post-Lisbon language. See Chapter 7 for a more elaborate analysis of the duty of cooperation.

mechanisms to handle conflicts between acts adopted by each actor of the EU system of external relations. In the Member States–EU interface, the principles of the attribution of powers and primacy of EU law play a key role in ensuring consistency ... Importantly, consistency between the actions of the Member States ... is guaranteed by the Council and thus by the Member States themselves, given the limited supranational nature of the CFSP ...

[C]oherence in EU external relations does not only depend on the absence of legal contradiction between the different instruments of EU external action. Coherence also stems from the *degree of cooperation* between the different actors in the system, and particularly between the Member States, on the one hand, and the Union's institutions on the other; as well as cooperation between the institutions themselves when acting in the different EU procedural frameworks. In its respective field of power, each actor is bound by a multifarious principle of cooperation. In essence, this principle entails procedural obligations, whose purpose is to ensure that each actor's competence is exercised with the ultimate purpose of contributing to the general Union's objective of asserting its identity on the international scene. Rather than aiming at policing the boundaries between the different areas of competences, the duty of cooperation aims at moderating the implications of such division. It has a more positive undertone, suggesting that the Union's external action is not a zero sum game.

(ii) The choice for the correct legal basis

In Chapters 3 to 5 we have seen the legal complexity which is the consequence of the principle of conferred powers: it is a legal requirement that any and all EU action be based on a legal basis in the TEU or TFEU. The centre-of-gravity test was developed in order to make the 'correct' choice as to whether an initiative falls within one or the other policy domain. However, in policy reality such neat separations are often very difficult to make: trade and environmental issues can be interlinked, as can development and security. In fact, as we have seen also in Chapter 10 on development, the Treaty-mandated consistency requirement actually calls for a proactive approach to combining different areas of external action. Yet, especially in the field of CFSP, the diverging decision-making procedures make it difficult to combine a CFSP legal basis with one in another (TFEU) policy area. This is a significant legal obstacle to comprehensive external action. Here we examine the legal basis aspect to this complexity, and further in this chapter we examine one of the key institutional innovations to resolve this tension: the EEAS.

In the pre-Lisbon version of the TEU, choices for the correct legal basis were to be made on the basis of (former) Article 47 TEU. This so-called 'non-affect clause' had as its main purpose to 'protect' the *acquis communautaire* from incursion by the special CFSP method, and provided that 'nothing in [the TEU] shall affect the Treaties establishing the European Communities or the subsequent Treaties and Acts modifying and supplementing them'.

The landmark case at that time was *ECOWAS* (or *Small Arms and Light Weapons*; also discussed in Chapters 5 and 10).[5] As this case clearly reveals the dilemmas as well as the institutional turf battles behind the choice of legal basis in this policy area, it deserves some more attention and remains partially pertinent after the Lisbon Treaty reformulated Article 47 TEU into the new Article 40 TEU. The case provided the first opportunity for the Court of Justice

---

[5] Case C-91/05 *Commission* v. *Council (Small Arms/ECOWAS)* [2008] ECR I-3651.

to speak out on a legal base conflict between the first (EC) and second (CFSP) pillars,[6] and to shed some light on the distribution of competence between the EC and the EU qua CFSP.[7] In the event, the Grand Chamber of the Court found that by using a CFSP Decision on the EU support to ECOWAS in the fight against the proliferation of small arms and light weapons (SALW), the Council had encroached upon the EC competence in the field of development cooperation, thus violating the provisions of Article 47 TEU. We recommend that the reader also examine this judgment in light of Chapter 10 on development policy, and specifically the widening scope of EU development policy and its relationship to security-orientated policy initiatives.

Case Study: Development Cooperation or Security Policy? The *ECOWAS* case[8]

In 2005, the Commission challenged the legality of two acts which the Council adopted in the context of Title V TEU, namely a CFSP Joint Action (2002/589/CFSP) "on the European Union's contribution to combating the destabilising accumulation and spread of small arms and light weapons", and the implementing decision (2004/833/CFSP) "with a view to a European Union contribution to ECOWAS in the framework of the Moratorium on Small Arms and Light Weapons". The Joint Action thus laid down the general EU policy in combating the proliferation of small arms and light weapons, while the 2004 Decision was one of its specific applications, here to the ECOWAS by supporting the latter in its fight against such proliferation.

Although the Commission did not protest at the time the Joint Action was adopted in 2002, the subsequent Council decision relating to ECOWAS was seen as a step too far. Obviously the Council crossed a boundary and thus violated any understanding it may have had with the Commission on competence division in the area of development cooperation and security. One of the reasons was that the Commission was preparing a proposal to finance operations in the field of conflict resolution and peace-building, and a considerable part of these finances was earmarked for the ECOWAS project to control light weapons.[9] The initiative of the Commission was envisaged as an implementation of the Cotonou Agreement concluded between the EC and its Member States, and a group of African, Caribbean and Pacific states on 23 June 2000, which came into force on 1 April 2003.[10]

Possible Commission and/or Community involvement in the field were indeed envisaged in the CFSP Joint Action of 2002. Hence, according to Article 8 "The Council notes that the Commission intends to direct its action towards achieving the objectives and the priorities of this Joint Action, where appropriate by pertinent Community measures." Indeed, Art. 1(1) stipulated that:

"The Council and the Commission shall be responsible for ensuring the consistency of the Union's activities in the field of small arms, in particular with regard to its development policies. For this purpose,

---

[6] The Court has in the past only been asked to test the compatibility of 'third pillar' measures with Article 47 TEU: Case C-170/96 *Commission* v. *Council (Airport transit visa)* [1998] ECR I-2763, paras 15–16; Case C-176/03 *Commission* v. *Council (Environmental Crimes)* [2005] ECR I-7879; Case C-440/05 *Commission* v. *Council (Ship-Source Pollution)* [2007] ECR I-9097.

[7] In Cases T-349/99 *Miskovic* and T-350/99 *Karic* (removed from the register), the CFI missed the opportunity when the Council amended the decision challenged by two individuals who had been refused visas on the basis of a CFSP act.

[8] Partly based on C. Hillion and R. A. Wessel, 'Restraining External Competences of EU Member States under CFSP', in M. Cremona and B. de Witte (eds.), *EU Foreign Relations Law: Constitutional Fundamentals* (Oxford: Hart Publishing, 2008), pp. 79–121.

[9] See Opinion of AG Mengozzi in Case C-91/05 *Commission* v. *Council (Small Arms/ECOWAS)* [2008] ECR I-3651, para 23.

[10] OJ 2000 No. L317/3; on behalf of the Community signed by the Council; Decision 2003/159/EC of the Council of 19 December 2002, OJ 2003 No. L65/27.

Member States and the Commission shall submit any relevant information to the relevant Council bodies. The Council and the Commission shall ensure implementation of their respective action, each in accordance with its powers."

Moreover, Article 3 of the ECOWAS Decision endowed the Commission with a specific task:

"The Commission shall be entrusted with the financial implementation of this Decision. To that end, it shall conclude a financing agreement with ECOWAS on the conditions for use of the European Union contribution, which shall take the form of a grant. Amongst other things, this grant shall cover, over a period of 12 months, salaries, travel expenses, supplies and equipment necessary for setting up the Light Weapons Unit within the ECOWAS Technical Secretariat and converting the Moratorium into a Convention on small arms and light weapons between the ECOWAS Member States."

In the discussion of the proposed ECOWAS decision at Coreper level, the Commission suggested that the underlying Joint Action should not have been adopted, and that the whole project should have been financed out of the European Development Fund in the framework of the Cotonou Agreement. The Commission further contended that the Joint Action fell under the Community's development policy, protected by Article 47 TEU.[11] On 21 February 2005, it eventually requested the Court to annul the ECOWAS Decision and to declare illegal, and hence inapplicable, the 2002 Joint Action.

As defendant, the Council was supported by numerous intervening Member States, namely Spain, France, the Netherlands, Sweden, Denmark and the United Kingdom. While there was no objection to the Court's jurisdiction to review the CFSP decision for the purpose of ascertaining whether it had encroached upon Community powers, the Council, the Spanish and UK governments nevertheless submitted that the Court had no jurisdiction to consider the plea of illegality of the 2002 Joint Action on the basis of Article 241 EC. As to the main action, the Council and the intervening Member States argued that the fight against accumulation and proliferation of small arms and light weapons did not fall within the Community competences. Article 47 TEU could not therefore be infringed.

The parties also disagreed on the function of Article 47 TEU, and on the distribution of competence between the EC and the EU it is meant to guarantee. The Commission, supported by the Parliament, considered that Article 47 TEU establishes a '"fixed" boundary between the competences of the Community and those of the Union. Hence in areas of shared competence, while Member States retain their ability to act by themselves, individually or collectively, to the extent that the Community has not exercised its competence, the same cannot be said for the Union. Under Article 47 TEU, the EU does not enjoy the same complementary competence, but must respect the powers attributed to the Community, whether exclusive or not, even if they have not been exercised. Accordingly, there is an "encroachment upon Community competences whenever the Council adopts, in the framework of the CFSP, an act which could properly have been adopted on the basis on the EC Treaty" (Par. 36).

By contrast, the Council's view of Article 47 TEU was that it aims to guard the balance of powers established by the Treaties, and not to protect the competences conferred upon the Community to the detriment of those enjoyed by the Union. Hence, Article 47 does not establish a fixed boundary between Community and Union competences. It is instead necessary to take account of the nature of the power conferred on the Community in the sector concerned, *in casu* the complementary character of Community competence in the field of development cooperation, when determining whether the provisions of Article 47 TEU have been infringed. The United Kingdom further contended that "in order to regard a measure based on the EU Treaty as contrary to Article 47 EU, it is necessary, first, that the

---

[11] See Opinion of AG Mengozzi, in Case C-91/05 *Commission* v. *Council (Small Arms/ECOWAS)* [2008] ECR I-3651, para 23.

Community be competent to adopt a measure having the same purpose and the same content. Second, the measure based on the EU Treaty must encroach on a competence conferred upon the Community by preventing or limiting the exercise of that competence, thus creating a pre-emptive effect on Community competence". An effect which, according to the UK, was impossible in an area such as development cooperation, given that the Community has concurrent competences (Par. 44).

The Court recognises the 'peace and security' – and thus the CFSP – dimension of the ECOWAS Decision, and more generally of the fight against the spread of small arms and light weapons (SALW). Hence, at para 95, the judges hold that:

"Contrary to what is submitted by the Commission and the Parliament, it cannot be denied that the contested decision, to the extent that it aims to prevent further accumulation of small arms and light weapons in West Africa capable of destabilising that region, forms part of a general perspective of preserving peace and strengthening international security."

However, the contested decision is *also* found to relate to development cooperation. The dual dimension of the contested Decision is notably substantiated by the connections between the fight against the proliferation of SALW and the economic and social development of the countries concerned, which were expressly made by the EU institutions, notably in the preamble of the initial Joint Action of which the contested 2002 JA is the successor. Hence, "from the outset", the EU fight against proliferation of SALW has been placed within the "dual perspective" of preservation of peace and international security on the one hand, and safeguarding development perspective on the other (Par. 85).

In view of the aim of the contested decision, the Court finds that the decision to make funds available and to give technical assistance to a group of developing countries in order to draft a convention "is capable of falling both under development cooperation policy and the CFSP". Added to the established possibility to implement the objective of the campaign both by CFSP and Community measures, the Court opines that "it follows ... that, taking account of its aim and its content, the contested decision contains two components, neither of which can be considered to be incidental to the other, one falling within Community development cooperation policy and the other within the CFSP" (Par. 108).

Given that "Article 47 EU precludes the Union from adopting, on the basis of the EU Treaty, a measure which could properly be adopted on the basis of the EC Treaty", the Court concludes that the Council infringed Article 47 TEU by adopting the contested Decision on the basis of Title V TEU and therefore annuls that Decision.

The result of the *ECOWAS* case was that the Council's CFSP Decision was annulled because it also included aspects of development cooperation, an area that was not covered by the CFSP legal basis. Post-Lisbon, the pillars no longer exists and Article 47 has been replaced by current Article 40 TEU. This provision reflects the post-Lisbon focus on coherent EU external relations, and is therefore more balanced between the TFEU policy fields and CFSP. In substantive terms, it essentially reflects the method whereby the correct legal basis is found through establishing the centre of gravity of the decision at stake (see Chapter 5).

Article 40 TEU

The implementation of the common foreign and security policy shall not affect the application of the procedures and the extent of the powers of the institutions laid down by the Treaties for the exercise of the Union competences referred to in Articles 3 to 6 of the Treaty on the Functioning of the European Union.

Similarly, the implementation of the policies listed in those Articles shall not affect the application of the procedures and the extent of the powers of the institutions laid down by the Treaties for the exercise of the Union competences under this Chapter.

In other words: in adopting CFSP decisions the Council should be aware of the external policies in the TFEU, *and* vice versa. Despite its 'balanced' approach, Article 40 implies that foreign policy measures are excluded once they would interfere with exclusive powers of the Union, for instance in the area of CCP. This may seriously limit the freedom of the Member States in the area of restrictive measures (see below) or the export of 'dual goods' (commodities which can also have a military application).[12]

The current text of Article 40 TEU forces the Court to take a different view on the relationship between CFSP and other areas of external action. No longer should an automatic preference be given to a non-CFSP legal basis whenever this is possible. In a 2012 judgment, the Court was given the opportunity to come back to this issue. In Case C-130/10 *European Parliament* v. *Council of the European Union*, the EP challenged a Council Regulation imposing certain specific restrictive measures directed against certain persons and entities associated with Usama bin Laden. The Court confirmed the following:

JUDGMENT OF THE COURT (Grand Chamber)
19 July 2012
In Case C-130/10,
ACTION for annulment under Article 263 TFEU, brought on 9 March 2010,
European Parliament* v. *Council of the European Union

44. With regard to a measure that simultaneously pursues a number of objectives, or that has several components, which are inseparably linked without one's being incidental to the other, the Court has held that, where various provisions of the Treaty are therefore applicable, such a measure will have to be founded, exceptionally, on the various corresponding legal bases (see, in particular, Parliament v Council, paragraph 36 and case-law cited).

45. None the less, the Court has held also, in particular in paragraphs 17 to 21 of Case C-300/89 Commission v Council [1991] ECR I-2867 ('Titanium dioxide'), that recourse to a dual legal basis is not possible where the procedures laid down for each legal basis are incompatible with each other (see, in particular, Parliament v Council, paragraph 37 and case-law cited).

46. If it was in the context of the cooperation procedure that the Court found, in Titanium dioxide, an incompatibility between that procedure, provided for by one of the two legal bases concerned in that

---

[12] Council Regulation 1334/2000/EC setting up a Community regime for the control of exports of dual-use items and technology, OJ 2000 No. L159/1; in the meantime replaced by Council Regulation 428/2009/EC setting up a Community regime for the control of exports, transfer, brokering and transit of dual-use items, OJ 2009 No. L134/1. Exception was only made for certain services considered not to come under the CCP competence. For these services (again) a CFSP measure was adopted: Council Joint Action 2000/401/CFSP concerning the control of technical assistance related to certain military end-uses, OJ 2000 No. L159/216.

judgment, and the Council's acting unanimously after merely consulting the European Parliament, provided for by the other, the Court has, nevertheless, in its subsequent decisions adopted a similar approach in connection with the procedure under Article 251 EC, known as 'the co-decision procedure' (see, to this effect, Case C-178/03 Commission v Parliament and Council [2006] ECR I-107, paragraphs 58 and 59, and Parliament v Council, paragraphs 76 to 79). Such an approach is still valid, after the entry into force of the Treaty of Lisbon, in the context of the ordinary legislative procedure.

47. In this instance, while Article 75 TFEU provides for application of the ordinary legislative procedure, which entails qualified majority voting in the Council and the Parliament's full participation in the procedure, Article 215(2) TFEU, for its part, entails merely informing the Parliament. In addition, recourse to Article 215(2) TFEU, unlike recourse to Article 75 TFEU, requires a previous decision in the sphere of the CFSP, namely, a decision adopted in accordance with Chapter 2 of Title V of the EU Treaty, providing for the adoption of restrictive measures such as those referred to in that provision. As a general rule, adoption of such a decision calls for unanimous voting in the Council acting alone.

48. Differences of that kind are such as to render those procedures incompatible.

So, at least one element of the pillars remained the same: the different decision-making procedures and legal instruments render combinations of CFSP and other legal basis difficult (see also below, section (ii)(c)). At the same time, the Court underlined its view (previously also presented in *Parliament* v. *Council* and case law referred to there)[13] that recourse to a dual legal basis is not possible where the procedures laid down for each legal basis are incompatible with each other (see Chapter 5).

B. Van Vooren, 'The Small Arms Judgment in an Age of Constitutional Turmoil' (2009) 14 *European Foreign Affairs Review*, 1, 231–248

... whereas current Article 47 TEU states that 'nothing in the TEU shall affect the EC Treaty', the new Article 40 TEU makes that clause work reciprocally: nothing in the CFSP shall affect the former EC competences, such as development cooperation; and the former EC competences shall not affect the CFSP. Additionally, this Article 40 TEU-new must be read in tandem with Articles 1 TEU-new and 1.2 TFEU which state that both treaties 'shall have the same legal value'. Consequently, even though the era between the Single European Act and the Lisbon Treaty saw a progressively stronger emphasis on the 'supplementary' nature of Union policies [such as CFSP] (Art. 1 TEU-old) and a hierarchical interpretation of Article 47 TEU gradually crept in; the post-Lisbon version of this article eradicates any doubt in this regard. Indeed, under this setting, the Commission's view of "Everything that can be done through EC policies should not be done through the CFSP" is no longer tenable, nor is the Court's hierarchical conflict rule: both Union competences are of equal value, and one is no longer supplementary to the other.

... when security and development objectives are pursued equally, without one being incidental to the other, the 'Community' legal base [e.g. TFEU] would no longer mechanically prevail ... Thus, in a context where a hierarchy is simply excluded, and the Union has a duty to take into account objectives of other policy areas, the Court would indeed have to apply different legal constructs to ensure that neither the CFSP nor the development policy of the Union are 'affected'.

[13] Case C-155/07 *Parliament* v. *Council (EIB Guarantees)* [2008] ECR I-8103.

... one can argue that the ECJ's approach to the new Article 40 TEU-new would consist of the combination of: *Firstly,* the emphasis on the duty of consistency so as to avoid picking apart the Union external action instrument before it; and *secondly,* the centre of gravity reasoning but with judicial review limited to cases where obligations are sufficiently extensive, e.g. going beyond the integration requirement, so as to require separate legal bases.

(iii) Explaining the nature of CFSP

The specific rules and procedures, the non-exclusionary (parallel) *nature* of the competence reminiscent of complementary competences in development policy, and the fact that CFSP is the only policy area that finds its basis in the TEU rather than the TFEU, can only be explained when we take the development of this policy area into account. While these days we are used to Member States coordinating their foreign and security policy and to a Union with competences in that area, CFSP has come a long way – one that is characterized more by 'muddling through' than by a clear willingness of Member States to make it work. The current CFSP has developed out of the former EPC, which in turn was an answer to failed attempts in the 1950s and 60s to establish an institutionalized cooperation in the area of foreign and security policy.

(a) The European Defence Community and the European Political Community

The ECSC, signed on 18 April 1951, was one of the outcomes of the plan of the French Foreign Minister, Robert Schuman, to secure peace in Europe through economic cooperation. It led to a common market for coal and steel, supervised by a 'High Authority', with six participating countries (the German Federal Republic, France, Italy and the three Benelux countries). Upon further proposals from the Belgian statesman Paul Henri Spaak, the conclusion of the ECSC Treaty resulted in two additional Treaties on 25 March 1957: the Treaty establishing the EEC and the Treaty establishing an EAEC.

Apart from these developments in economic cooperation, two attempts in particular aimed at integration in other fields as well. Following the Schuman Plan of 9 May 1950, proposals for a CFSP *avant la lettre* reached the stage of elaborate draft Treaties. In 1950 the Korean conflict triggered a number of politicians to come up with proposals for European defence cooperation. In August of that year, Winston Churchill launched the idea of a European Army under a European Minister of Defence. This proposal was followed by a plan by the French Minister of Defence René Pleven, in October 1950. The Pleven Plan partly accepted the British proposal, but proposed to embed the European Ministry of Defence in an institutional structure comparable to that of the ECSC. This plan found its way into the Treaty establishing the European Defence Community (EDC), which was signed by the ECSC Member States on 27 May 1952.[14] The EDC would make possible the German rearmament and the new European Army would operate within the framework of the Atlantic Alliance. Apart from a collective defence clause (Article 2) as the core of the Treaty, the institutional system was comparable to the system used in the ECSC: the Treaty introduced a Commission ('*Commissariat*'), a Council, an Assembly and a Court. In the

---

[14] *Traité instituant la Communauté Européenne de Défense,* signed in Paris, 27 May 1952.

latter two cases the institutions were to be 'borrowed' from the ECSC meaning that there would be a clear linkage between the political and economic integration projects. Notably, according to the first Article of the EDC Treaty, the Community would have a 'supranational character': it would have common institutions, common armed forces and a common budget. The Commissariat as well as the Council could take decisions by a majority of its members (Articles 24 and 39) and the legal personality of the Community was undisputed (Article 7).

Regardless of the fact that the Treaty was signed, political objections were still apparent and ranged from criticism regarding the absence of a European defence policy and a connected foreign policy, to the weak democratic character of the EDC. In an attempt to meet these objections the six Foreign Ministers, on 10 September 1952, requested the Parliamentary Assembly (as foreseen in the Treaty) to draft a Statute for a European Political Community. Under the leadership of Paul Henri Spaak the 'ad hoc Assembly' produced the Statute in March 1953. The institutions of the European Political Community were to take over the powers of the existing ECSC and the future EDC and like these organizations, the European Political Community was presented as being 'supranational'. This Statute – also labelled: the draft Treaty establishing the EC – inter alia included provisions on a *coordinated* foreign policy, which might in time become a *common* policy. Together with the ECSC and the EDC, the EC was to form a 'legal union' (Article 5). According to its Article 4, the Community would possess legal personality.

However, in 1954 the French *Assemblée Nationale* resolved to adjourn the debate on the acceptance of the EDC Treaty, which also meant the end of the Statute on a European Political Community. The reasons for this included the objections of a strong coalition of communists and Gaullists, a fear of a confrontation with growing German power within an EDC in which the United Kingdom would not participate,[15] and changes in the international situation (including the death of Joseph Stalin and the Korean Armistice in 1953). Despite the setback in European integration resulting from the decision of the French Parliament, a solution was found to make possible the admission of Germany to the Atlantic Alliance. The Brussels Treaty on Economic, Social and Cultural Collaboration and Collective Self-Defence[16] between the United Kingdom, France and the Benelux countries was modified, which provided, inter alia, for the creation of the Western European Union (WEU) and the accession of Germany and Italy. Germany was allowed to proceed with rearmament under certain strict conditions, and at the same time the way was paved for the accession of Germany and Italy to NATO.

Nevertheless, attempts to create a common foreign policy and a common defence policy alongside the cooperation between the then six members in the EEC had not ceased. Meetings between French President Charles de Gaulle and the German Chancellor Konrad Adenauer in 1958 resulted in a new plan for political cooperation between the six. The Dutch in particular rejected the idea of permanent (and probably French-led) forms of cooperation that could undermine concepts like the Free Trade Association (which led to the European Free Trade Agreement (EFTA) in 1960). But negotiations continued and in 1959, the EEC Foreign Ministers agreed to hold regular meetings every three months 'on matters of international policy', covering both 'the political implications of the activities of the European Communities and

---

[15] Because of the proposed strong link with the ECSC of which the United Kingdom was not a member.
[16] Signed at Brussels on 17 March 1948. The Protocol Modifying and Completing the Brussels Treaty was signed in Paris on 23 October 1954 (entry into force on 6 May 1955).

other problems'.[17] The outline of a formal ('intergovernmental') political union was presented by de Gaulle in 1960:

President Charles de Gaulle, 5 May 1960

To help to build Western Europe into a political, economic, cultural and human grouping, organized for action and for defence: this is the aim of the French Government ... Of course it is necessary that the nations which become associated do not cease to be themselves, and that the path to be followed should be that of an organized cooperation between states, while waiting to achieve perhaps an imposing confederation.[18]

De Gaulle intended to include the future goal of a 'confederation' in the final communiqué, which caused immediate and specific opposition from the Dutch for reasons explained below. Adenauer finally convinced de Gaulle to replace the word 'confederation' with 'organized cooperation' and to avoid all references to defence matters. The conference finally agreed on the foundation of a committee, the Fouchet Committee, to study further all possible aspects of future political cooperation.

One of the main structural problems for the Dutch government was the French domination and the (related) British absence in the negotiations. The latter problem became known as the '*préalable anglais*' and meant that British membership of the economic and political frameworks was perceived as a precondition for progress. The Dutch (and later also Belgian) position did not prevent France from presenting a draft treaty for a 'Union of States' which had as its aim to make possible cooperation in cultural and scientific matters and to adopt a common foreign policy and a common defence policy (the 'first Fouchet Plan'). In the 1961 version the French specified that the common defence policy 'would contribute to the strengthening of the Atlantic Alliance', that there would be an attempt 'to associate the European Parliament more closely to the definition and execution of the common policies' and that the Community structures would be respected. An independent Secretary-General was to represent the Union. Dutch and Belgian objections were met with a German compromise formula in which Britain would be closely informed about the process, and that membership of the Union would be automatic for those countries which joined the EEC.

Nevertheless, de Gaulle decided to present a new proposal, known as Fouchet II, in which a reference to cooperation with NATO, supranational goals of the revision clause and the provision for a Secretary-General were dropped. Moreover, Fouchet II provided that the accession of new members would be decided unanimously by the Council, the EP would only have advisory powers and 'economics' was mentioned as one of the subjects of consultation between the participants (thus encroaching upon the competences of the EEC Commission). With this proposal de Gaulle caused a serious rift between France and the other five states, which motivated the Netherlands and Belgium to block and end the Fouchet process at a meeting on 17 April 1962.

---

[17] See *Towards Political Union. A selection of documents with a foreword by Mr. Emilio Battista*, European Parliament, Political Committee, January 1964 [EU European Parliament Document], p. 5.

[18] As quoted by H. Mayer, 'Germany's Role in the Fouchet Negotiations' (1996) 2 *Journal of European Integration History*, 2, 39–59 at 43.

(b) From EPC to a common foreign and security policy

The 'failure of Fouchet' caused the six to desist from presenting new proposals on political cooperation for some time. However, after the departure of President de Gaulle in 1969, the meeting of the HoSG in The Hague in December of that year decided that their Foreign Ministers should again investigate the possibilities for closer political cooperation. On 20 July 1970 this resulted in the *Davignon Report*, which was adopted by the European Council in Luxembourg on 23 October 1970.[19] This *Luxembourg Report* is usually seen as the constitutive document of EPC, and hence as the origin of CFSP.

Its main purpose was to intensify political cooperation by introducing meetings of the Foreign Ministers (twice a year) and creating a Political Committee (consisting of the Political Affairs Directors of the national Foreign Ministries; three times a year). Moreover, specialized working groups on specific issues of potential common interest were created. The first meeting in the framework of EPC took place in Munich in 1970. These meetings were completely separate from the meetings of the EEC Council of Ministers in Brussels. EPC meetings preferably took place in the capital of the state holding the Presidency of the EEC. Despite the explicit attempts to keep the political cooperation isolated from the cooperation within the context of the EEC Treaty, the need for some consistency was acknowledged. In the *Luxembourg Report* a reference to the Commission was included: '[s]hould the work of the Ministers affect the activities of the European Communities, the Commission will be invited to make known its views'. Notice in the extract below that 'concertation' in the area of foreign policy is seen as an important driver for political integration towards 'European Union'. The drafters of the *Luxembourg Report* thus expressly argue that European citizens will derive some sense of commonality and togetherness from a joint approach in their foreign policies, towards what later became the Maastricht Treaty (EU).

The 1970 Luxembourg Report ('Davignon Report'): The Start of European Political Cooperation

6. The Ministers ... considered that their proposals should be based on three facts, in order to ensure consistency with the continuity and political purpose of the European design which were emphasized so forcefully by the Hague Conference.

7. The first fact is that, in line with the spirit of the Preambles to the Treaties of Paris and Rome, tangible form should be given to the will for a political union which has always been a force for the progress of the European Communities.

8. The second fact is that implementation of the common policies being introduced or already in force requires corresponding developments in the specifically political sphere, so as to bring nearer the day when Europe can speak with one voice. Hence the importance of Europe being built by successive stages and the gradual development of the method and instruments best calculated to allow a common political course of action.

9. The third and final fact is that Europe must prepare itself to discharge the imperative world duties entailed by its greater cohesion and increasing role.

---

[19] The EPC Reports are reproduced in the *Bulletin EC* in the respective years. For the *Luxembourg Report*, see *Bulletin EC* 11-1970, p. 9.

10. Current developments in the European Communities make it necessary for the Member States to step up their political cooperation and, in the initial stage, to provide themselves with ways and means of harmonizing their views in the field of international politics.

The Ministers therefore felt that foreign policy concertation should be the object of the first practical endeavours to demonstrate to all that Europe has a political vocation. The Ministers are, in fact, convinced that progress here would be calculated to promote the development of the Communities and give Europeans a keener awareness of their common responsibility.

After the adoption of the 1970 *Luxembourg Report*, EPC developed incrementally, and established customs were codified on an ad hoc basis in new reports. These reports were adopted by the HoSG or the Foreign Ministers of the EPC states, and presented as 'Communiqués' or 'Reports'.[20] Thus, the *Copenhagen Report* (23 July 1973) reflected an increase in the meetings of the Foreign Ministers to four times a year, and of the Political Committee as often as necessary (in practice once a month). It also formally introduced the COREU network (Correspondence Européenne), a special telex-network between the participating states of which a modernized version is still in existence today. Furthermore, the adoption of common positions was presented as an objective of the EPC. Consistency in the overall European external relations was still one of the key issues. After the Declaration of the Paris Summit of 1972 that '[o]n matters which have a direct bearing on Community activities, close contact will be maintained with the Institutions of the Community', the Copenhagen Report stipulated:

The Political Cooperation machinery which is responsible for dealing with questions of current interest and where possible for formulating common medium and long-term positions, must do this keeping in mind, *inter alia*, the implications for and the effects of, in the field of international politics, Community policies under instruction.

The need for consistency of Community and EPC policies became increasingly apparent due to the successful development of the EPC. The necessary contacts with the Community were ensured in three ways: (1) the Commission could make its views known in accordance with current practice; (2) the Presidency could inform the Council (via the President of the permanent representatives); and (3) the Council could instruct EPC to study the political aspects of problems under examination in the Community.[21]

The third step in the progressive development of EPC was the *London Report*, adopted in 1981. Again this report codified some developments in the EPC on enhanced relations with the Community institutions. Apart from a reference to contacts with the EP, the Foreign Ministers underlined the importance of the coordination of EPC and Community policies. Upon the initiative of the new French Foreign Minister, Claude Cheysson, himself a former Commissioner responsible for development cooperation, the London Report called for a full association of the Commission with political cooperation at all levels since previously the Commission was

[20] An extensive survey of these reports and their legal status is given in Th. Jürgens, *Die Gemeinsame Europäische Außen- und Sicherheidspolitik* (Cologne: Carl Heymanns Verlag, 1994).

[21] S. Nuttall, 'European Political Cooperation and the Single European Act' (1985) 5 *Year of European Law* 203–232.

dependent on an explicit invitation to EPC meetings at all levels. The full association included the establishment of a direct link to the COREU network. The reasons for the enhanced coordination were presented in the Report and Foreign Ministers agreed on the following:

London Report on EPC, 13 October 1981

... that further European integration, and the maintenance and development of Community policies in accordance with the Treaties, will be beneficial to a more effective coordination in the field of foreign policy, and will expand the range of instruments at the disposal of the Ten. [The Presidency shall] ensure that the discussion of the Community and Political Cooperation aspects of certain questions is coordinated if the subject matter requires this.

Despite the ongoing enmeshment of Community and EPC policies in practice, some Member States from time to time tried to strengthen the EPC and to link it more closely to the Community. An outstanding example in this respect concerned the initiative by the Foreign Ministers of Germany and Italy, Hans-Dietrich Genscher and Emilio Colombo, in 1981, to take a further step towards the realization of a 'European Union'. Apart from proposals which were aimed at bridging the artificial gap between the EPC and the Community, they proposed to bring security issues within the realm of the EPC. However, the Genscher–Colombo initiative proved to be unacceptable for most other participating states. The result was the *Solemn Declaration on European Union* (Stuttgart, 19 June 1983),[22] a considerably toned down version of the original proposal by Genscher and Colombo.

The disappointment on the side of the more integrationist Member States regarding the text of the *Solemn Declaration* of Stuttgart, and the Draft Treaty on European Union,[23] adopted by the first directly elected EP in February 1984, inspired them to convince the European Council at Fontainebleau in June 1984 to set up an ad hoc committee of personal representatives of Heads of State or Government (the 'Dooge Committee') to prepare an IGC. The report of the Dooge Committee was finalized in March 1985, but still reflected the fundamental differences between the Member States on the future character of the EPC.

In February 1986, the EPC was at last provided with an official basis in the SEA, but the fundamental differences between opposing camps proved to be insurmountable. The SEA mirrored the traditional diverging views of the Member States on European integration. On the one hand, the EPC was placed with the Community within one *single* document, but on the other hand it remained clearly separated from the Community legal order. The provisions on the EPC in Title III SEA reflected the political cooperation as it had developed in the years before. The 'High Contracting Parties' (instead of 'Member States')[24] still dealt with the EPC outside the Community institutional structure. The consistency problem found its way into Article 30(5): '[t]he external policies of the European Community and the policies agreed in

---

[22] *Bulletin EC* 6-1983 at 26.

[23] OJ, 1984 No. C77/53. In this treaty – often referred to as the *Spinelli Report* – the competences of the Community were stretched far enough to, inter alia, include the EPC. In the EP the Draft Treaty still functions as an important reference document with a possible future goal.

[24] Title III does however show some inconsistencies in this respect. Article 30, paras 10(a), (b) and (d) do use the term 'Member States'.

European Political Cooperation must be consistent. The Presidency and the Commission, each within its own sphere of competence, shall have special responsibility for ensuring that such consistency is sought and maintained'.

B. Van Vooren, *EU External Relations Law and the European Neighbourhood Policy: A Paradigm for Coherence* (Abingdon/New York: Routledge, 2012), pp. 30–31

Throughout the initial two and a half decades of rapprochement between the Member States in EPC and the Community, the process had been one of finding procedural solutions to increase practical intimacy of the different regimes so as to ensure coherent outcomes. The effort has consistently been a two-pronged one: On the one hand, the two spheres of authority needed to be separated, with non-affect clauses signalling this, and, on the other, there needed to be the construction of procedural and substantial bridges between them. In all those arrangements, it seems that the sustenance of 'separateness' at the constitutional level was the main driving force, while recognizing that at the practical level interaction was unavoidable. Consequently the relationship was not discussed in terms of hierarchy: the Presidency and the Commission together, equally and within their own spheres of competence, would seek to ensure consistency in decision making. Above all, the drafters sought to avoid the impression that EPC was being assimilated to the Community, while appeasing the desires of the more integration-minded EC Member States. Additionally, the rapprochement between Member States' foreign policies through EPC and the Communities between the Davignon Report and the Single European Act saw an increasing sense of obligation, and from the SEA onwards, a legal nature of the EPC body of rules. At first, the series of soft legal EPC reports was the only instrument through which the 'spirit of coordination' in foreign policy could be created, but EPC also showed that it lacked the strength to organize Member States' foreign policies in a coherent fashion at various crisis moments during its existence. . . . [G]rand language of integration was already present in the Davignon Report, but achievements and innovations in EPC towards political Union were driven by practical necessity: the Yom Kippur War, the Tehran hostage situation, the Union of Soviet Socialist Republics' (USSR) invasion of Afghanistan, the Polish Crisis . . . That dynamic remains visible [in subsequent years] as the birth of the CFSP was being negotiated against the backdrop of the collapse of the USSR, German reunification and the Gulf War, and would further develop as war raged in the former Yugoslavia.

With the collapse of communism in Central and Eastern Europe, the need for a stronger EPC became apparent and formed the main reason in December 1990 for starting an IGC on Political Union alongside the already planned conference on economic and monetary cooperation. The relation that existed between EPC and the European Communities was maintained in the TEU, signed on 7 February 1992 and came into force on 1 November 1993. The concept of a CFSP, as initially formulated by Chancellor Helmut Kohl and President François Mitterand,[25] was included in the new Treaty without any in-depth discussion of its meaning and its implications. The contrast with the debate on the implications of the Economic and Monetary Union (EMU) was obvious. Despite some attempts by the Dutch government during its Presidency in 1991 to

---

[25] See the letter of Chancellor Kohl and President Mitterand to the Irish Presidency, 19 April 1990 in R. Corbett, *The Treaty of Maastricht: From Conception to Ratification: A Comprehensive Reference Guide* (Harlow, Essex: Longman Group UK, 1993).

realize the opposite, CFSP was not included as part of the Community legal order.[26] As another compromise in the continuous battle between states that favoured a more integrated Europe, and those who tried to hold on to intergovernmental cooperation as much as possible, the structure of the EU was bound to become the subject of criticism.

D. Curtin, 'The Constitutional Structure of the Union: A Europe of Bits and Pieces' (1993) 30 *Common Market Law Review* 17–69

The Union as established in the Maastricht Treaty reveals a highly convoluted structure. It does not, as might have been expected, simply take the place of the existing Communities or elevate the latter into the 'Union'. Nevertheless, to a certain extent the focal point can be said to be the existing three Communities (not merged into one) and the *acquis communautaire* enshrouding them. The three existing Communities continue to exist as separate legal persons and embrace within themselves a variety of institutional schemes. Some distance away and standing alone and apart (except for a scattering of 'passerelles' or one-way bridges) from the three 'Community' supports are two distinct 'pillars', one on foreign and security policy (hereafter: CFSP) and the other a motley combination of home affairs and judicial cooperation (hereafter: CJHA). The main structural attachment which these two pillars have with the Community structure as such is by means of a loose, tarpaulin-like structure (under the heading of an undefined 'European Union') suspended artificially and tenuously above both the loose pillars and the Community as such. The CFSP pillar already existed and was expanded upon. Significant in this respect is the reliance placed on the Western European Union (WEU) which is categorized as "an integral part of the development of the Union" and which is empowered to elaborate and implement decisions and actions of the Union which have defence implications – despite the fact that two Member States do not belong to the WEU. The new crutch added to support some of the weight of the tarpaulin is the pillar of CJHA, a hybrid nonvertical pillar which materially intersects with the existing Community EC competences in some important respects.

Insofar as they all shelter under the one 'umbrella' the three main pillars can indeed be said to form an entity as such. But it is a notional entity. The popular analogy which has been coined, that of the construction of a 'temple' (comprised by the three pillars), implies a degree of architectural stability and aesthetic finish which is both inaccurate and pretentious. True, the 'Union' as such does have the outward shell, in part, of a Constitution – in particular its general principles at the beginning – but this is a *trompe l'oeil*. They are not even justiciable, but exist in a state of suspended animation.

The three-pillar structure, placing CFSP in a separate (second) 'pillar', apart from the three European Communities in the first pillar and the provisions on cooperation in the field of JHA in the third, became a justification for separate analyses of the three pillars. In the early days after the signing of the TEU, the pillar structure was the form in which the Union was perceived (and subsequently criticized) by many authors. At the same time, however, more recent literature pointed to the fact that the 'bits and pieces' which together form the entity referred to as the EU, were more connected than many observers were willing to admit in the early days, and that the

---

[26] See First Dutch Draft Treaty Proposal from the Dutch Presidency, 30 September 1991, in F. Laursen and S. Vanhoonacker (eds.), *The Intergovernmental Conference on Political Union: Institutional Reforms, New Policies and International Identity of the European Community* (Maastricht: EIPA, 1992), pp. 407–412.

metaphor of the Greek temple may not have been the best way of describing what the Union at that time was about.[27]

The Treaty of Amsterdam of 2 October 1997 (entry into force on 1 May 1999) purported to modify both the Community Treaties and the 1992 TEU. Apart from renumbered articles, the structure of the TEU remains largely the same, albeit that the former third pillar cooperation (JHA) was renamed PJCC, and some policy areas were 'rehoused' within the body of the EC Treaty. The CFSP provisions were renumbered from Articles J–J.11 to Articles 11–28.

Despite the fact that the 1986 SEA did not introduce a new name for the combined EC and EPC cooperation, the structure of the TEU at the time was not too different from the one presented in the SEA, and the form of cooperation chosen for CFSP still lacked clarity. Title V 1992 TEU presents CFSP as a more or less autonomous set of rules, intended to lead to a policy which, prima facie, was not by definition connected to the external policy of the Community, which was clearly not to be equalled with the national policies of the Member States, but which was nevertheless part of a new EU.

B. Van Vooren, *EU External Relations Law and the European Neighbourhood Policy: A Paradigm for Coherence* (Abingdon/New York: Routledge, 2012), pp. 39–40

The Maastricht Treaty was not the watershed in creating a single external European Voice, but labelled the box which would require further maturation to fill its lack of substance. A balanced assessment is therefore in place. The CFSP of Maastricht was certainly no longer the purely intergovernmental EPC as initially foreseen in the Davignon Report, but certainly not yet the distinct policy branch of the Union it would become subsequent to ratification of the Lisbon Treaty. First, ... external political events and internal political agendas of some Member States had made the CFSP 'somewhat more' integrated in the overall structure of political Union. For example, integrating the Council General Secretariat and the EPC secretariat laid the foundation for a foreign policy with a home-base in Brussels. Second, the CFSP became more 'legalized', with the agreed outcomes from now on appearing in the L series of the Official Journal. Where it became less of a self-sustaining group of diplomats aligning their countries' views only when consensus seemed possible, the 'legalization' of the CFSP is a process which would gain pace in subsequent years and treaty revisions. More and more the CFSP would develop a personality in its own right, separate from the EC or Member States, a 'third regime' of which later the High Representative (HR)/Secretary General of the Council Secretariat would become the embodiment. However, these developments were only embryonic at the time of Maastricht, and the CFSP did not yet have a legally separate existence from the Member States. G. Bono comprehensively captured it by stating that an 'association of States' had been 'established by Treaty which was not a full international organization, but which had a constitution, common organs, own objectives, legal norms, practices, and which enjoyed certain autonomy from the Member States'.

---

[27] See for instance: de Witte, 'The Pillar Structure and the Nature of the European Union: Greek Temple or French Gothic Cathedral?', in T. Heukels, N. Blokker and M. Brus (eds.), *The European Union after Amsterdam: A Legal Analysis* (The Hague: Kluwer Law International, 1998), pp. 51–68.

4 MEMBER STATE OBLIGATIONS UNDER CFSP

(i) The information and consultation obligation

> **Article 25 TEU**
>
> The Union shall conduct the common foreign and security policy by: ...
>
> (c) strengthening systematic cooperation between Member States in the conduct of policy.

The concept of *systematic cooperation* directly builds on the system of EPC, in which it was agreed that the participating states 'undertake to inform and consult each other on any foreign policy matters of general interest'.[28] It is this systematic cooperation that in fact formed the core of EPC from 1970–1993. In CFSP it still serves as the key notion, in the absence of which it would be impossible for the Union to define and implement a foreign and security policy. The systematic cooperation referred to in the list of CFSP means in Article 25 TEU is to be established in accordance with Article 32, which contains the actual procedural obligations. In principle, the scope of issues to which the systematic cooperation applies is not subject to any limitation regarding time or space.

> **Article 32 TEU**
>
> Member States shall inform and consult one another within the European Council and Council on any matter of foreign and security policy

Nevertheless, Article 32 immediately fills this lacuna in adding a few important extra words:[29]

> **Article 32 TEU**
>
> ... on *any matter* of foreign and security policy *of general interest.*

The European Council has not provided any further specification of 'general interest' in Article 32. This seriously limits the information and consultation obligation in the first part of this article: on the one hand, Member States are obliged to inform and consult one another, whereas on the other hand they are given the individual discretion to decide whether or not a matter is of 'general interest'. The principle of conferral (Article 5 TEU) implies that whatever has not been attributed to the organization remains with the Member States. Hence, once Member States do not agree that a matter is of general interest (for instance because one Member States considers it to be of national interest only), it becomes very hard for the Union to develop a policy in that area. The link to EPC provides important context as it implies that 'general interest' is to be interpreted broadly: in 1970

---

[28] See SEA (1986) Article 30, para 2(a).
[29] Emphasis added.

governments committed to consult each other 'on all major questions of foreign policy' which in 1973 was widened to questions concerning the 'European interest'. Thus, the broader notion of 'any matter of general interest' is constraining only in the sense that it refers to foreign policy issues which are of interest to more than one EU Member State. However, today there are very few foreign policy issues that really do only concern a single Member State. Therefore, it can be asserted that the Member States are indeed under a broad obligation to inform and consult one another. Through the information and consultation obligation the Member States ordered themselves to use it as one of the means to attain the CFSP objectives in Article 24 and 21 TEU. The procedures stipulated in Article 32 only reflect the methods by which the Member States implement CFSP. Moreover, as we have seen, the content of the norm does not provide any other conditions than that the issue should be of general interest.

Taking into account the nature of the information and consultation obligation, it is rather unfortunate that the Treaty does not further define the obligation. Yet, there are no reasons to assume that the notion of consultation as used in Article 32 deviates from these general definitions, which leads us to conclude that the EU Member States are to refrain from making national positions on CFSP issues of general interest public before they have discussed these positions in the framework of the CFSP cooperation. Informing and consulting one another should take place 'within the European Council and the Council'. Keeping in mind the requirement of *systematic* cooperation, this should not be interpreted as only within those institutions. Cooperation within the preparatory organs (PSC, COREPER, and working parties – *infra*), as well as bilateral and multilateral consultations and cooperation (both in Brussels, in third states or international organizations such as the UN) are equally covered by this obligation. In fact, as we will see, it is in these bodies that the actual systematic cooperation takes place. A second reason not to limit the cooperation to meetings of the Member States in the Council may be found in Article 34. According to this provision, Member States shall coordinate their action in international organizations and at international conferences as well. Even when not all Member States are represented in an international organization or an international conference, the ones that do participate are to keep the absent states informed of any matter of common interest (see also Chapter 8).

It can be asserted that over the years the CFSP cooperation at all levels has become more intense, automatic and systematic. The 'European reflex' has become part of the decision-making culture in national ministries; traditional national reservations ('*domaines réservés*') have decreased in number as well as in intensity; and new issues have become part of the CFSP agenda (like developments and actions in Africa). The flip-side, however, is that the larger Member States in particular tend to ignore the information and consultation procedures whenever sensitive policy issues are at stake (such as with Libya in 2011, Syria in 2012–13 . . .). In cases like these they take individual positions and diplomatic initiatives or opt for cooperation in the framework of another international organization. This paradoxical situation reveals that CFSP has become part of the day-to-day policy-making in the national ministries as well as in Brussels, but that important or sensitive issues may also still be dealt with nationally or in other forums.

(ii) The loyalty obligation

The conclusions in the previous section on the mandatory nature of the systematic cooperation are supported by a more general 'loyalty obligation':

> **Article 24(3) TEU**
>
> The Member States shall support the Union's external and security policy actively and unreservedly in a spirit of loyalty and mutual solidarity and shall comply with the Union's action in this area.
>
> The Member States shall work together to enhance and develop their mutual political solidarity. They shall refrain from any action which is contrary to the interests of the Union or likely to impair its effectiveness as a cohesive force in international relations.
>
> The Council and the High Representative shall ensure compliance with these principles.

In order to further define the kinds of action this requires of the Member States, we may find inspiration in the comparable and more general provision in Article 4(3) TEU, which lays down the 'principle of sincere cooperation' (see Chapter 6). Like Article 4(3), the specific CFSP provision contains a *positive* obligation for the Member States to develop the Union's policy actively in the indicated area. In addition, the loyalty obligation contains the *negative* obligation not to undertake 'any action which is contrary to the interests of the Union or likely to impair its effectiveness as a cohesive force in international relations'. The comparison of the CFSP loyalty obligation with the principle of sincere cooperation in Article 3(4) reveals its potential impact. The latter article is often seen as the basis of the constitutional nature of Union law, and it has been frequently used by the Court of Justice in its case law. As seen in Chapter 6, the Commission particularly has utilized the duty of cooperation very effectively to ensure that Member States do not deviate from 'the Union interest' in their own external relations. In the same vein, far-reaching obligations – if applicable to CFSP – could significantly limit the freedom of the Member States. Given that the CFSP is an integral part of the EU legal order, there should be little doubt that in substance the Member States owe their loyalty to the EU in this policy domain as well. However, enforcement of any such legal obligations is limited. Indeed, the absence of any jurisdiction of the Court of Justice to enforce the duty of cooperation *within* CFSP (see below) renders the question whether the case law of Article 4(3) TEU is equally applicable in relation to the CFSP loyalty obligation somewhat abstract and theoretical. Nonetheless, politically it may certainly provide a tool and point of reference for the Council to check on the actions of the Member States which form its constituent members.

5 CFSP DECISION-MAKING AND THE ROLE OF THE INSTITUTIONS

An analysis of the competences and obligations of the institutions concerning decision-making will reveal the extent to which Member States have agreed to replace their national foreign and security policies by a policy of the EU. On the basis of an analysis of the objectives of the CFSP it may already be concluded that the CFSP is not intended to cover all areas of foreign and security policy in the sense that national policies are to converge in one single Union policy.

The institutions responsible for the CFSP do not differ from the ones in other policy areas (see Chapter 1). Indeed, the preamble of the TEU refers to a 'single institutional framework', and Article 13 TEU on the institutions does not exclude any policy area. Yet, the role of the institutions and the balance between them is clearly different, and a number of organs are specifically relevant for the CFSP.

The provision in Article 24 TEU that 'the adoption of legislative acts shall be excluded', implies that CFSP decisions are not adopted on the basis of the legislative procedure, which is, inter alia, characterized by a Commission initiative, co-decision by the EP and QMV. As we will see, neither of these elements forms part of CFSP decision-making.

(i) The European Council

Apart from its general role described in Article 15 TEU, the European Council has a leading role in the formulation of the CFSP.

> **Article 22 TEU**
>
> . . . the European Council shall identify the strategic interests and objectives of the Union. It . . . shall act unanimously on a recommendation from the Council, adopted by the latter under the arrangements laid down for each area. Decisions of the European Council shall be implemented in accordance with the procedures provided for in the Treaties.

> **Article 26 TEU**
>
> [T]he European Council shall identify the Union's strategic interests, determine the objectives of and define general guidelines for the common foreign and security policy, including for matters with defence implications. It shall adopt the necessary decisions.

The competences of the European Council in implementing the CFSP are thus indirect: they make possible or facilitate the decision-making by the Council of Ministers. Its decisions form the basis for the CFSP decisions taken by the Council. In the pre-Lisbon era, the European Council could also adopt Common Strategies, on the basis of which the Council could then adopt further decisions through a different voting procedure (QMV) in the Council. The Common Strategy no longer exists as an instrument, though the procedure remains in place (see below).

The permanent President of the European Council was introduced by the Lisbon Treaty.

> **Article 15(6) TEU**
>
> The President of the European Council shall, at his level and in that capacity, ensure the external representation of the Union on issues concerning its common foreign and security policy, without prejudice to the powers of the High Representative of the Union for Foreign Affairs and Security Policy.

This person may convene an extraordinary meeting of the European Council in order to define the strategic lines of the Union's policy if international developments so require (Article 26(1) TEU). The example below is an extract of the extraordinary European Council convened to concert the European response to the Arab Spring of 2011. Below the diplomatically formulated language, the reader will find some indication of what action the EU will undertake in its CFSP, and which actors will be responsible for its implementation. For example, in paragraph 6 there is some indication of the preparations for the 'no fly zone' enforced by several Member States in collaboration with NATO (e.g. not the EU) during the summer of 2011, which eventually led to the fall of the Libyan regime.

Declaration of the Extraordinary European Council of 11 March 2011, EUCO 7/1/11 REV 1

1. The European Council met today in an extraordinary session to discuss developments in Libya and the Southern Neighbourhood region and set the political direction and priorities for future EU policy and action.
2. Democratic uprisings are bringing dramatic changes to the Southern Neighbourhood, creating a new hope and opportunity to build a future based on democracy, pluralism, the rule of law, human rights, and social justice. Progress and democracy go hand in hand. The European Council salutes the courage demonstrated by the people of the region and reaffirms that it is for them to decide their future, through peaceful and democratic means....
5. The European Council supports the democratic transition in Egypt. It welcomes the timely delivery of the first proposals for amending the constitution and encourages the Egyptian authorities to continue in their commitment to political reform and to create an environment for thorough democratic transition, including by lifting the state of emergency. The European Union is ready to mobilise its full support in line with the priorities of the Egyptian people and has started a dialogue with the recently appointed Egyptian government.
6. The situation in Libya remains a cause for grave concern. We express our strong solidarity with the Libyan people and the victims. We firmly condemn the violent repression the Libyan regime applies against its citizens and the gross and systematic violation of human rights. We welcome UN Security Council Resolution 1970 and the referral of the situation in Libya to the International Criminal Court. The use of force, especially with military means, against civilians is unacceptable and must stop immediately. The safety of the people must be ensured by all necessary means. The European Council expresses its deep concern about attacks against civilians, including from the air. In order to protect the civilian population, Member States will examine all necessary options, provided that there is a demonstrable need, a clear legal basis and support from the region. Those responsible will be held accountable and face grave consequences. We will work with the United Nations, the Arab League, the African Union and our international partners to respond to the crisis. We call for the rapid holding of a summit between the Arab League, the African Union and the European Union.

(ii) The Council

The Council can be regarded as the main CFSP decision-making institution.

Article 26(2) TEU

The Council shall frame the common foreign and security policy and take the decisions necessary for defining and implementing it on the basis of the general guidelines and strategic lines defined by the European Council.

More concrete provisions (Articles 28 and 29 TEU) stipulate that '[t]he Council shall adopt decisions'. Moreover, the Council decides on the voting procedures, and it reviews the principles and objectives of the decisions in order to allow for possible national derogations. Usually CFSP decisions will be taken by the General Affairs Council, consisting of the Ministers for Foreign Affairs of the Member States.

Unanimity continues to form the basis for CFSP decisions, 'except where the Treaties provide otherwise' (Article 24(1) TEU). Yet, a number of exceptions are provided by the Treaty, allowing for the use of QMV under CFSP. Some exceptions already existed pre-Lisbon and recur in Article 31(2) TEU, which allows for QMV:

- when adopting a decision defining a Union action or position on the basis of a decision of the European Council relating to the Union's strategic interests and objectives, as referred to in Article 22(1);
- when adopting any decision implementing a decision defining a Union action or position;
- when appointing a special representative in accordance with Article 33.

In addition it is now possible for the Council to adopt measures by QMV following a proposal submitted by the HR (Article 31(2) TEU). Such proposals should, however, follow a specific request by the European Council, in which, of course, Member States can foreclose the use of QMV. In addition QMV may be used for setting up, financing and administering a start-up fund to ensure rapid access to appropriations in the Union budget for urgent financing of CFSP initiatives (Article 41(3) TEU). This start-up fund may be used for crisis management initiatives as well, which would potentially speed up the financing process of operations.[30] Overall, however, it is clear that any action on the part of the EU will in the end continue to depend on the consent of its Member States.

In most cases CFSP Decisions are adopted without any debate in the Council; they have been prepared by the Council's subsidiary organs and a consensus has already been established between the representatives of the Ministers for Foreign Affairs. When decisions are taken by the General Affairs Council, the issues do not appear on the agenda out of the blue. In most cases the draft decisions have thus already followed a long path through the various subsidiary organs of the Council. Some of these preparatory and implementing organs have an express treaty basis, while others have been set up by the Council itself. According to Article 240 TFEU, the COREPER[31] is responsible for preparing the work of the Council and for carrying out the tasks assigned to it by the Council. Regardless of the fact that COREPER is nowhere explicitly mentioned in the CFSP provisions,[32] its competences in this area are beyond any doubt, since Article 38 TEU provides that the PSC shall act 'without prejudice to Article 240 TFEU'. As we have seen in Chapter 1, there are two COREPER configurations. COREPER II consists of EU Member State representatives at ambassadorial level and deals with political, commercial, economic or institutional matters, and is thus generally pertinent for CFSP.

---

[30] See also DG for External Policies of the Union, Policy Department, *The Lisbon Treaty and its Implications for CFSP/ESDP* (Briefing Paper, European Parliament, February 2008), p. 3. Nevertheless, for some Member States, resort to the EU budget may remain attractive, even if this means delaying the EU's response. See Whitman and Juncos, 'The Lisbon Treaty and the Foreign, Security and Defence Policy'.

[31] This French abbreviation is used in English texts as well.

[32] Contrary to the Luxembourg Draft Treaty of 18 June 1991, which stipulated in Article D of the CFSP provisions: 'The Permanent Representatives Committee shall be responsible for preparing Council meetings and shall carry out the instructions given to it by the Council.' Laursen and Vanhoonacker (eds.), *The Intergovernmental Conference on Political Union*, p. 400.

Over the years, this PSC has developed into the key preparatory and implementing organ for the CFSP and CSDP. This body has its origin in EPC, where a 'Political Committee' was created.[33] This committee consisted of the Political Directors of the national Foreign Ministries. The current PSC is a standing committee, composed of representatives from the Member States. It

Article 38 TEU

It shall monitor the international situation in the areas covered by the common foreign and security policy and contribute to the definition of policies by delivering opinions to the Council at the request of the Council or of the High Representative of the Union for Foreign Affairs and Security Policy or on its own initiative. It shall also monitor the implementation of agreed policies, without prejudice to the powers of the High Representative.

The PSC is also a key actor in the Union's security and defence policy (see further Chapters 1 and 12).

As in all other areas, CFSP decisions are prepared in working groups or working parties (composed of representatives of the Member States and the Commission). The preparatory bodies are installed by the Council and have an important function during the first phase of the decision-making process. According to Article 19(3) of the Council's Rules of Procedure, the main task of the working groups is to carry out certain preparatory work or studies defined in advance. These may include all possible 'CFSP output', ranging from *démarches* to decisions in the form of Joint Actions. The Secretariat prepares reports of the discussions of the working group meetings, which are circulated to all delegations through the COREU network. On all CFSP matters the working groups report to the PSC.

(iii) The High Representative and the EEAS

As indicated in Chapter 1, unlike other Council configurations, in its configuration as FAC the Council is chaired not by Member State representatives, but by the HR (Article 18(3) TEU). Indeed, the original dominant role of the Member States in CFSP is mitigated on a number of occasions. Before Lisbon, most proposals in the area of CFSP came from Member States, with the Presidency having a particularly active role. Article 30(1) TEU lays down the new general rule:

Article 30(1) TEU

Any Member State, the High Representative of the Union for Foreign Affairs and Security Policy, or the High Representative with the Commission's support, may refer any question relating to the common foreign and security policy to the Council and may submit to it initiatives or proposals as appropriate.

It is in particular this new role of the Commission that may trigger new possibilities for the EU in its external affairs. Whereas the Commission so far has largely refrained from making use of its competence to submit proposals on issues in the area of foreign, security or defence policy (Article 22 TEU), the creation of the competence to submit joint proposals with the HR may enhance its commitment to this area.

---

[33] The Political Committee was introduced by the *Davignon Report* in 1970 and gained a legal treaty basis in Article 30, para 10(c) of the SEA (1986). Usually the French abbreviation of *Comité Politique* is used.

Article 27 TEU

1. The High Representative of the Union for Foreign Affairs and Security Policy, who shall chair the Foreign Affairs Council, shall contribute through his proposals to the development of the common foreign and security policy and shall ensure implementation of the decisions adopted by the European Council and the Council.
2. The High Representative shall represent the Union for matters relating to the common foreign and security policy. He shall conduct political dialogue with third parties on the Union's behalf and shall express the Union's position in international organisations and at international conferences.
3. In fulfilling his mandate, the High Representative shall be assisted by a European External Action Service. This service shall work in cooperation with the diplomatic services of the Member States and shall comprise officials from relevant departments of the General Secretariat of the Council and of the Commission as well as staff seconded from national diplomatic services of the Member States. The organisation and functioning of the European External Action Service shall be established by a decision of the Council. The Council shall act on a proposal from the High Representative after consulting the European Parliament and after obtaining the consent of the Commission.

The pivotal position of the HR is strengthened by the fact that the person holding the position at the same time acts as a member (and even a vice-president) of the Commission (Article 17, paragraphs 4 and 5). The potential impact of this combination on the role of the EU in international affairs lies in the fact that there could be a more natural attuning of different external policies, in particular where borders between policies are fuzzy, such as in crisis management. At the same time – as indicated above – the continued separation between CFSP and other Union issues may very well lead to a need for different legal bases for decisions, and hence for the use of distinct CFSP and other Union instruments. This holds true not only for the outcome of the decision-making process, but also for the process itself, in which sincere cooperation between the Council and the Commission, supported by the HR/VP and the new and hybrid EEAS (see Chapter 1), will remain of crucial importance. In fact, while extensively referring to the role of the EEAS in relation to CFSP, the 2010 EEAS Decision is clearly aimed at combining the different dimensions of the EU's external relations.

Council Decision 2010/427/EU of 26 July 2010 establishing the organisation and functioning of the European External Action Service, OJ 2010 No. L201/30

Article 2 – Tasks

1. The EEAS shall support the High Representative in fulfilling his/her mandates as outlined, notably, in Articles 18 and 27 TEU:
   - in fulfilling his/her mandate to conduct the Common Foreign and Security Policy ('CFSP') of the European Union, including the Common Security and Defence Policy ('CSDP'), to contribute by his/her proposals to the development of that policy, which he/she shall carry out as mandated by the Council and to ensure the consistency of the Union's external action,

Indeed, a successful CFSP depends on successful leadership, and the position of the HR has clearly been strengthened by the last treaty modification (see also Chapter 1).

A. Missiroli, 'The New EU Foreign Policy System after Lisbon: A Work in Progress' (2010) 15 *European Foreign Affairs Review* 427–452

The cornerstone of the new EU system in the domain of external action is the creation of the position of HR of the Union for Foreign Affairs and Security Policy.

This is a hybrid institutional figure combining: (a) the pioneering role previously played by Javier Solana as HR for CFSP (1999–2009); (b) that of a Vice-President (VP) of the Commission in charge of external relations and coordinating other relevant portfolios; and (c) the role hitherto played by the Foreign Minister of the country holding the rotating EU Presidency – which includes chairing the Council formation dealing with Foreign Affairs at large (Articles 17–18 TEU).

To these various responsibilities in the Common Foreign and Security Policy/European Security and Defence Policy (CFSP/ESDP; now Common Security and Defence Policy (CSDP)) area should be added chairing the Boards of *domain relevant* agencies such as the European Defence Agency (EDA), the EU Satellite Centre (EUSC), the EU Institute for Security Studies (EUISS), and the European Security and Defense College (ESDC). . . .

Finally, the new HR/VP has a legal right of initiative both as HR only (in strictly CFSP matters) and as double-hatted VP (Article 22.2 TEU). Similarly, the HR/VP has also dual loyalties and accountabilities, appointed as s/he is first by the European Council (as HR) then, as a member (and VP) of the new Commission, by the European Parliament. Such a multi-hatted position represents a unique opportunity to bring coherence to the Union's 'foreign policy' – but also a daunting challenge for the post holder, especially the first one. When Baroness Catherine Ashton accepted the European Council's nomination to the HR/VP post on 19 November 2009, she probably did not realize how intractable the job description was to become. A few months into it, she must now be aware of the urgent need to put in place a structure that would allow her to delegate administrative, operational, and even representational tasks to a number of deputies (de facto if not de jure), leaving her more free to concentrate on policy coordination and strategic leadership.

Article 27 (3) states that in fulfilling his mandate, the High Representative shall be assisted by a European External Action Service (EEAS). This is the only reference anywhere in the TEU or TFEU to this new body in the EU external relations set-up. The legal nature of the EEAS can best be described as *sui generis*, for lack of a better categorization.

B. Van Vooren, 'A Legal Institutional Perspective on the European External Action Service' (2011) 48 *Common Market Law Review* 475–502 at 500–501

The new diplomatic service is formally dissimilar from an EU institution or an EU regulatory agency, yet an EU institution for the purposes of budget and staff, with powers that formally resemble but substantively go beyond those of EU agencies. The diplomatic service does not have legal personality, but does possess functional legal capacity to assist the High Representative. The notion of assistance [in relation to the HR is] broadly defined. In combination with the EEAS' rather extensive policy discretion, the service was argued to be a significant actor in the EU external policy-making. Crucially however, the EEAS has not been delegated powers of the EU institutions, cannot take individually legally binding decisions, and has not been conferred any powers to shape EU external policy-making with legal effect. . . . [This] led us to characterize the EEAS as being functionally akin to

Commission Directorates General, without the legal advantage of being part of an institution with decision-making powers proper, accountable to Parliament, while being placed under the HR's authority with a broad mandate of support within the chalk lines set by the Council and European Council.

(iv) The European Commission

The limited formal competences of the Commission in the CFSP area have not led to the Commission being completely passive in this field. From the outset, the Commission has been represented at all levels in the CFSP structures. Within the negotiating process in the Council, the Commission is a full negotiating partner as in any Working Party or Committee (including the PSC). The President of the Commission attends European Council and other ad hoc meetings. The Commission is in fact the '29th Member State' at the table; it safeguards the *acquis communautaire* and ensures the consistency of the action of the Union other than CFSP. In the implementation of CFSP Decisions the Commission's role is however formally non-existent as delegation of executive competences from the Council to the Commission is prevented by the fact that CFSP acts are not legislative acts (Article 29 TFEU). Nevertheless, practice from the outset showed an involvement of the Commission in the implementation of CFSP Decisions, not in the least because other measures were in some cases essential for an effective implementation of CFSP policy decisions. Regardless of these competences of the Commission under CFSP, it is not difficult to conclude that this institution is nowhere near the pivotal position it occupies in the other areas of the Union. Although it is not formally excluded by Article 17 TEU, the Commission lacks its classic function as a watchdog under CFSP. The absence of an exclusive right of initiative also denies the Commission another indispensable role it has in other areas.

(v) The role of the European Parliament: a democratic deficit in CFSP?

The SEA (1986) already provided for the right of Parliament to be closely associated with EPC and to be informed by the Presidency.[34] This provision found its way into the TEU and in its current version reads as follows:

Article 36 TEU

The High Representative of the Union for Foreign Affairs and Security Policy shall regularly consult the European Parliament on the main aspects and the basic choices of the common foreign and security policy and the common security and defence policy and inform it of how those policies evolve. He shall ensure that the views of the European Parliament are duly taken into consideration.

Special representatives may be involved in briefing the European Parliament.

The European Parliament may address questions or make recommendations to the Council or the High Representative. Twice a year it shall hold a debate on progress in implementing the common foreign and security policy, including the common security and defence policy.

---

[34] SEA (1986), Article 30(4).

Here too, the differences with regard to most other Union policy areas are obvious. The main difference lies in the fact that with regard to CFSP parliamentary influence is not directed towards a concrete decision (as is the case in other procedures), but only towards 'the main aspects and the basic choices' of CFSP. Moreover, it is not the institution which actually takes the decision that is ordered to consult the EP, but the HR. The formal influence of the EP is therefore limited to the general policy lines and does not include influence on the actual decisions which are their result. The obligation of the Commission to inform the EP regularly is of course put into perspective when the modest involvement of the Commission in CFSP is taken into consideration. Yet, as outlined in Chapter 1, the EP is an active player in CFSP and external relations in general. Through its reports, debates and crucially by using its budgetary powers, it has been able to influence CFSP on critical occasions.

(vi) The Court of Justice of the European Union

Limited parliamentary control may to some extent be compensated by judicial control. With respect to CFSP, however, the powers of the Court of Justice are largely excluded by the treaty provisions. Most Member States argued that foreign policy be shielded from what some perceived to be 'judicial activism'; this resulted in a denial of the Court's competences in the area of CFSP. Articles 24 TEU and 275 TFEU provide the following:

Article 24(1) TEU

... The Court of Justice of the European Union shall not have jurisdiction with respect to these provisions, with the exception of its jurisdiction to monitor compliance with Article 40 of this Treaty and to review the legality of certain decisions as provided for by the second paragraph of Article 275 of the Treaty on the Functioning of the European Union.

Article 275 TFEU

The Court of Justice of the European Union shall not have jurisdiction with respect to the provisions relating to the common foreign and security policy nor with respect to acts adopted on the basis of those provisions.

The exclusion of the Court has been part and parcel of CFSP from the outset.[35] It was already in line with the preference of most Member States at the time of the Maastricht IGC because of possible integrative actions by the Court in this sensitive area. Even the Commission's opinion reflected a clear reserve as it pointed at the highly political and sensitive dimensions 'des actions mises en œuvre au cours de l'exercice de la politique étrangère ou de sécurité commune, qui ne sont pas soumises, en règle générale, au contrôle judiciaire'.[36] In fact, when the Maastricht

---

[35] It was affirmed by the Court almost immediately in Case C-167/94 *Grau Gomis and Others* [1995] ECR I-1023.

[36] 'Actions implemented during the course of foreign policy or common security, which are not subject, in general, to judicial review.' Working Document of the Commission SEC (91) 500, 15 May 1991, p. 41.

Treaty was being drafted, excluding jurisdiction of the CJEU was a crucial argument leading to the formation of the 'second pillar', with only the Netherlands at that time favouring judicial oversight in this domain. Under their Presidency during the IGC, they had proposed to allow the Court to 'review ... the legality of the application of the procedures for deciding upon the joint action referred to in this Title of the Treaty'. This provision lacked the necessary consensus and it did not make it to the final draft.

This is not to say that these days the CFSP provisions are not at all relevant for the ECJ. The second part of Article 275 TFEU mentions two situations in which the Court shall have jurisdiction.

Article 275 TFEU

... However, the Court shall have jurisdiction to monitor compliance with Article 40 of the Treaty on European Union and to rule on proceedings, brought in accordance with the conditions laid down in the fourth paragraph of Article 263 of this Treaty, reviewing the legality of decisions providing for restrictive measures against natural or legal persons adopted by the Council on the basis of Chapter 2 of Title V of the Treaty on European Union [the specific provisions on CFSP].

Article 40 TEU, in turn, regulates the relation between CFSP and the other areas of external action.

Article 40 TEU

The implementation of the common foreign and security policy shall not affect the application of the procedures and the extent of the powers of the institutions laid down by the Treaties for the exercise of the Union competences referred to in Articles 3 to 6 of the Treaty on the Functioning of the European Union.

Similarly, the implementation of the policies listed in those Articles shall not affect the application of the procedures and the extent of the powers of the institutions laid down by the Treaties for the exercise of the Union competences under this Chapter [The Chapter on *Specific Provisions on the Common Foreign and Security Policy*].

As indicated before, this provision calls for a balanced choice for either a CFSP or another legal basis of decisions. Conflicts on this issue can be brought before the Court, and as we have seen in the *ECOWAS* case, the predecessor of Article 40 (Article 47) TEU has indeed been used by the Court. These observations underline that the Court of Justice is the ultimate arbiter to decide where the line of demarcation between the Union's issue areas lies.

Irrespective of the focus on demarcation, earlier cases already made clear that in certain constitutional areas, the Court opted for a Union-wide application of rules that were formally made for parts of the Union. Thus, the Court made clear that wherever access of information is concerned, no distinction is made on the basis of the content of the requested document (*Swedish Union of Journalists* case).[37] Despite the fact that the case concerned access to a JHA document,

---

[37] Case T-174/95 *Svenska Journalistförbundet* v. *Council* [1998] ECR II-2289. More implicitly this was already accepted by the Court in Case T-194/94 *Carvel and Guardian Newspapers* v. *Council* [1995] ECR II-2765.

the language used in the judgment enables it to be applied to CFSP as well. The (General) Court based its argument on Decision 93/731 on public access to Council documents,[38] and it argued that this Decision 'expressly provides that it is to apply to all Council documents [and that it] therefore applies irrespective of the contents of the documents requested'. Similarly, the Court argued that judicial protection was to be applied Union-wide. It referred to Article 6 TEU and concluded:

Case C-355/04 P *Segi and Others* v. *Council* [2007] ECR I-1657, para 51

[T]he Union is founded on the principle of the rule of law and it respects fundamental rights as general principles ... It follows that the institutions are subject to review of the conformity of their acts with the treaties and the general principles of law, just like the Member States when they implement the law of the Union.

In a way, these cases underline the possibility of what may be termed 'indirect scrutiny'. We addressed this in Chapter 7 in discussing the *Kadi* case, where the Court addressed the 'bridge' between CFSP and former EC law. In the end, it scrutinized the EC Regulation implementing the CFSP measure which in turn had transposed the UN Security Council Resolution into the EU legal order against the yardstick of the fundamental rights guaranteed by the 'autonomous' EC legal order. This allowed for an indirect scrutiny of a CFSP Common Position which formed the basis for the EC Regulation at stake. More recently – post-Lisbon – the Court seemed to have underlined the idea that CFSP decisions and other EU decisions form part of one legal order, irrespective of its inability to scrutinize most of the CFSP actions.[39]

Apart from Article 40 situations and general constitutional issues, such as access to documents or judicial protection, the Treaty now provides for an additional situation in which the Court enjoys jurisdiction in relation to CFSP. The Court is competent to rule on proceedings, brought in accordance with the conditions laid down in the fourth paragraph of Article 263 TFEU, to review the legality of decisions providing for restrictive measures against natural or legal persons.

Article 263(4) TFEU

Any natural or legal person may, under the conditions laid down in the first and second paragraphs, institute proceedings against an act addressed to that person or which is of direct and individual concern to them, and against a regulatory act which is of direct concern to them and does not entail implementing measures.

This provision, which finally gives the Court the possibility to scrutinize a CFSP measure *directly*, is the result of the proliferation of sanctions targeted at individuals in the (global) fight against terrorism. The implication is that, even if the restrictive measure is only laid down

---

[38] OJ 1993 No. L340/43.

[39] Case C-548/09 P *Bank Melli Iran* v. *Council*, 16 November 2011, n.y.r., para 100: 'Security Council resolutions and Council common positions and regulations originate from distinct legal orders.'

in CFSP measures, the Court has jurisdiction once the plaintiff is directly and individually concerned (see section 6 below for an example). Prior to the entry into force of the Lisbon Treaty, the Court was already confronted with complaints by individuals or entities as a consequence of an adopted CFPS decision. In *Segi*[40] the CJEU had to express itself on a common position listing a Basque group, Segi, as a terrorist organization. The common position had been based on both Article 15 TEU pre-Lisbon (a CFSP provision), and Article 34 TEU pre-Lisbon (on police and judicial cooperation in criminal matters; former third pillar). The Court addressed the reviewability of the measure solely referring to its third pillar basis, and against the background that the Treaty (Article 35 TEU pre-Lisbon) seemed to exclude judicial scrutiny for common positions. In this respect, however, the situation was equal for CFSP common positions. Therefore, the findings of the Court appeared to be applicable also to CFSP measures, especially to common positions.[41]

While recent case law indicates that the Court of Justice is increasingly seen as the Court of the European Union (compare perhaps also the name change from 'European Court of Justice' to 'Court of Justice of the European Union'), it remains clear that the current regime regarding legal protection reveals a number of shortcomings. The most obvious lack of judicial control is apparent when competences and decision-making procedures *within* the CFSP legal order are at stake. In that case, there are no possibilities for the Court to scrutinize either the decision-making procedures or the legal basis chosen for a CFSP decision. This means, for instance, that neither the Commission, nor the EP can commence a procedure before the Court in cases where the Council has ignored their rights and competences in CFSP decision-making procedures where CFSP as a legal basis is not disputed. As far as the legal basis for decisions is concerned, there are no possibilities for the institutions or the Member States to request the opinion of the Court. It is important to note that this brings about a situation in which the interpretation and implementation of the CFSP provisions (including the procedures to be followed, or the duty of cooperation) is left entirely to the Council. Keeping in mind their preference for 'intergovernmental' cooperation where CFSP is concerned, it may be understandable that Member States at the time of the negotiations had the strong desire to prevent a body of 'CFSP law' coming into being by way of judicial activism on the part of the ECJ. However, it is less understandable that they were also reluctant to allow for judicial control of the *procedural* arrangements they explicitly agreed upon, although it is acknowledged that it may be difficult to unlink procedures and content. Similarly, it remains unclear why the ECJ should not have general jurisdiction to rule on the question of whether CFSP acts respect human rights.[42]

---

[40] Case C-355/04 *P Segi and Others* v. *Council* [2007] ECR I-1657.

[41] S. Griller, 'The Court of Justice and the Common Foreign and Security Policy', in A. Rosas, E. Levits and Y. Bot (eds.), *Court of Justice of the European Union – Cour de Justice de l'Union Européene, The Court of Justice and the Construction of Europe: Analyses and Perspectives on Sixty Years of Case-Law – La Cour de Justice et la Construction de l'Europe: Analyses et Perspectives de Soixante Ans de Jurisprudence* (The Hague: T.M.C. Asser Press, 2013), pp. 675–692 at 685.

[42] See also M. Brkan, 'The Role of the European Court of Justice in the Field of Common Foreign and Security Policy after the Treaty of Lisbon: New Challenges for the Future', in P. J. Cardwell (ed.), *EU External Relations Law and Policy in the Post-Lisbon Era* (The Hague: T.M.C. Asser Press, 2012), pp. 97–115 at 100.

**S. Griller, 'The Court of Justice and the Common Foreign and Security Policy',
in A. Rosas, E. Levits and Y. Bot (eds.),** *Court of Justice of the European Union – Cour de
Justice de l'Union Européene, The Court of Justice and the Construction of Europe:
Analyses and Perspectives on Sixty Years of Case-Law – La Cour de Justice et la
Construction de l'Europe: Analyses et Perspectives de Soixante Ans de Jurisprudence*
(The Hague: T.M.C. Asser Press, 2013), pp. 675–692

... the Court's case-law in this area, and, moreover, the scarcity of such case-law especially
during the first decades following the establishment of the Court, can only be correctly assessed
against the background of the very special legal status of this policy field over time. Addressing this
development is therefore indispensable. Respecting at the same time the premise implies to live
with abbreviations.

During the first decades of the European Communities' existence, the Treaties were completely
silent on CFSP. This was in essence due to the underlying assumption that this policy field had remained
with the Member States and hence outside the scope of EC law. For the ECJ, however, this triggered, inter
alia, the question of whether CFSP matters were 'carved out' from EC competences, or whether, by
contrast, they had to be brought in line with legal requirements flowing from overlapping areas, especially
Common Commercial Policy (CCP).

It was not before the second half of the 1980s that CFSP found its way into the text of Primary law,
namely through Article III ('Treaty provisions on European co-operation in the sphere of foreign policy') of
the Single European Act (SEA 1986). The SEA established an intergovernmental 'framework of European
Political Co-operation' (EPC), comprising the Ministers for Foreign Affairs, and a member of the
Commission meeting at least four times a year. However, neither legally binding decisions nor legal
scrutiny by the ECJ were foreseen.

These provisions were repealed by the Treaty of Maastricht (1992) which created the European Union
including its intergovernmental 'second pillar': Title V of the Treaty on European Union (TEU), headed
'Provisions on a common foreign and security policy'. The second – and also the third pillar – contrasted
with the supranational 'first pillar'. One of the resulting characteristics was that the TEU exempted the
provisions on CFSP from the 'powers of the Court of Justice'. By contrast, the Court had to monitor
compliance with the 'priority-clause' 3 in favour of EC law, stating that 'nothing in this Treaty shall affect
the Treaties establishing the European Communities or the subsequent Treaties and Acts modifying or
supplementing them'. ...

It remains to be seen which consequences the ECJ will draw from the fact that, despite this
continuity, the systematic context of the provisions on CFSP was considerably altered by the Treaty of
Lisbon. The Treaty arguably establishes a unified EU legal order including the CFSP, while explicitly
retaining some specific intergovernmental features for this policy field. The latter is true especially
regarding organs, law-making procedures, and sources of secondary law. Direct effect and supremacy,
however, remain unclear. Integrating the CFSP into the new environment without clearly excluding
these features might support the conclusion that the Lisbon Treaty levels the legal force of CFSP law –
both primary and secondary – with that of other EU law. That would considerably reduce the
intergovernmental nature of the post-Lisbon CFSP. However, there are also arguments to the contrary,
and the prevailing view in the literature appears to be that, as far as constitutional specificities are
concerned, 'nothing has changed' compared to pre-Lisbon.

6 CFSP INSTRUMENTS

Article 26(2) TEU entails a general competence for the Council to 'frame the common foreign and security policy and take the decisions necessary for defining and implementing it on the basis of the general guidelines and strategic lines defined by the European Council'. A combination of this provision and the more specific legal bases allows for the Council to adopt different CFSP legal and political instruments. One political instrument is the Declaration. Declarations are usually issued by the HR on behalf of the EU and may concern all areas of CFSP where a political statement is needed towards third states.

Article 25 TEU

The Union shall conduct the common foreign and security policy by:
(a) defining the general guidelines;
(b) adopting decisions defining:
  (i) actions to be undertaken by the Union;
  (ii) positions to be taken by the Union;
  (iii) arrangements for the implementation of the decisions referred to in points (i) and (ii);
  and by
(c) strengthening systematic cooperation between Member States in the conduct of policy.

The general guidelines are adopted by the European Council to lay down the strategies of the Union in relation to a particular third state, region or theme (Article 26(1) TEU). On the basis of the same provisions Decisions may also be adopted by the European Council,[43] but in relation to CFSP issues these usually take the form of 'Conclusions'.

(i) Informal instruments

CFSP is often shaped on the basis of Declarations, which are usually reactions to world events (earthquakes, conflicts, or serious human rights violations) and are relative easy to draft and to agree on. Although they lack a specific legal basis, the Council confirmed that the political impact of Declarations may go beyond that of formal decisions. Indeed, Declarations may come close to generally phrased formal decisions. On the other hand, although Declarations may be used for policy orientations vis-à-vis a third state, they lack an operational framework, which ultimately calls for a formal legal act to implement that policy.

Declaration by the High Representative Catherine Ashton on behalf of the European Union on Libya, Brussels, 23 February 2011, 6966/1/11 REV 1, PRESSE 36

The European Union expresses its grave concern by the situation unfolding in Libya. We strongly condemn the violence and use of force against civilians and deplore the repression against peaceful

---

[43] See for instance European Council Decision 2011/199/EU of 25 March 2011 amending Article 136 of the Treaty on the Functioning of the European Union with regard to a stability mechanism for Member States whose currency is the euro, OJ 2011 No. L91/1.

demonstrators which has resulted in the deaths of hundreds of civilians. These brutal mass violations of human rights are unacceptable.

The EU reiterates its call for an immediate end to the use of force and for steps to address the legitimate demands of the population, including through national dialogue. All restrictions of freedom of expression, including the internet, and of peaceful assembly must be lifted immediately. The will of the people in Libya must be respected and the EU stands by them.

We welcome the UN Security Council statement of 22 February 2011, which calls on the Government of Libya to meet its responsibility to protect its population and which calls on the Libyan authorities to respect human rights and international humanitarian law. We also welcome the Arab League statement of 22 February.

Immediate access should be provided for international human rights monitors and humanitarian agencies. The EU is ready to supply humanitarian aid where needed.

The EU also urges the Libyan authorities to ensure the safety of all foreign nationals, and to facilitate the departure of those wishing to leave the country.

The EU also welcomes the UN Security Council's call for a transparent, credible and independent investigation into events in Libya and the holding of a special session of the UN Human Rights Council on 25 February.

In this context, the EU stresses that those responsible for the brutal aggression and violence against civilians will be held to account. The EU has decided to suspend negotiations with Libya on the EU–Libya Framework Agreement and is ready to take further measures.

The Candidate Countries Croatia*, the former Yugoslav Republic of Macedonia*, Montenegro* and Iceland[+], the Countries of the Stabilisation and Association Process and potential candidates Albania, Bosnia and Herzegovina, Serbia, and the EFTA countries Liechtenstein and Norway, members of the European Economic Area, as well as the Republic of Moldova and Georgia align themselves with this declaration.

* Croatia, the former Yugoslav Republic of Macedonia and Montenegro continue to be part of the Stabilisation and Association Process.

[+] Iceland continues to be a member of the EFTA and of the European Economic Area.

In practice, CFSP systematic cooperation has also proved important with regard to the so-called 'political dialogues' with third countries. Political dialogues as such cannot be found in the TEU, but are established on the basis of general association treaties, Decisions, Declarations, or simply on the basis of an exchange of letters. Political dialogues take place in the framework of CFSP.

Dialogue meetings can take place at different levels. The highest level is that of the HR or the Presidency (together with the President of the Commission). Lower levels are the ministerial level, the level of political directors, the senior official or expert level and the parliamentary level. Due to agenda difficulties there is a growing tendency to send lower deputies to dialogue meetings. Thus the ministers often send junior ministers, and political directors increasingly send deputy political directors or even more junior officials.

(ii) Legal acts

(a) CFSP decisions as legal acts?

CFSP legal acts cannot be adopted in the form of Regulations or Directives, but only as 'Decisions'. This is again a striking difference compared to other Union policy areas. At the same time, the CFSP 'Decisions' are not to be equated with the 'Decisions' in Article 288 TFEU. Although they are qualified as 'legal acts' (or '*actes juridiques*' in the CFSP Annual Reports, for instance) they have not been adopted on the basis of a legislative procedure. Prior to the entry into force of the Lisbon Treaty, the Council had a choice between Joint Actions and Common Positions. The former TEU stated that 'Joint Actions shall address specific situations where operational action by the Union is deemed to be required'. At the same time, 'Common Positions shall define the approach of the Union to a particular matter of a geographical or thematic nature'. The difference between the two instruments has never been very clear, and considering the fact that the legal consequences of both instruments did not clearly differ, the sensible decision was made to replace both instruments by the current 'Decisions'.

Article 25 TEU now makes a distinction between decisions defining: (i) actions to be undertaken by the Union; and (ii) positions to be taken by the Union. Hence, both actions and positions can be laid down in the form of a CFSP Decision. At the same time Decisions can be used for '(iii) arrangements for the implementation of the decisions referred to in points (i) and (ii)'. Again this follows the practice that all implementing, modifying or repealing decisions take the shape of a CFSP Decision.

Over the years, CFSP Decisions have been used to regulate various issues. Regardless of some failed attempts to include a list of possible issue areas to be covered by the CFSP in the text of the Treaty, the 'common interests' which were to be a source of CFSP Decisions, were to some extent defined by the European Council in Lisbon in the early days of CFSP.[44] The European Council acknowledged that the need for a common policy may exist even if an interest is of more importance to some Member States than to others. In the determination of the common interests, consideration should be given to a number of factors: (1) the geographical proximity of a given region or country; (2) an important interest in the political and economic stability of a region or country; and (3) the existence of threats to the security interests of the Union. The European Council identified a number of geographical areas in which Joint Actions could be undertaken in the short term: Central and Eastern Europe (in particular Russia, the former Soviet Republics and the area of the former Yugoslavia); and the Maghreb and the Middle East. Furthermore, however, consistent and coordinated external activities are to be developed with almost every other region in the world: Africa, Latin America, the Caribbean, Asia, the United States of America, Canada and Japan. According to the European Council, from the entry into force of the TEU, the 'security dimension' could cover: (1) the OSCE process; (2) the policy of disarmament and arms control in Europe, including confidence-building measures; (3) nuclear non-proliferation issues; and (4) the economic aspects of security, in particular control of the transfer of military technology to third countries and control of arms exports.[45]

---

[44] Lisbon European Council (1992), 26 and 27 June, Annex 1.

[45] See also the Council's Report on Joint Action and the Development of the Common Foreign and Security Policy in the Field of Security, adopted on 7 December 1992. It is interesting to note that both Luxembourg and the Netherlands had identified nine areas suitable for Joint Action after the entry into force of the Treaty – however, they never found their way into the actual drafts presented by these countries. The areas included were: industrial and technological cooperation in the area of armaments; the transfer to third countries of military technologies and the control on exports of armaments; non-proliferation issues; armaments control, and reduction and confidence building measures (in particular in the OSCE framework); participation in peace-keeping operations in the framework of the United Nations; participation in humanitarian intervention; issues related to the OSCE; and transatlantic relations. See *Europe Documents*, No. 1722/1723 (5 July 1991), p. 26 and No. 1746/1747 (20 November 1991), p. 23.

A limitation regarding the use of the instrument may be found in the general guidelines from the European Council.

> ### Article 26(2) TEU
>
> The Council shall frame the common foreign and security policy and take the decisions necessary for defining and implementing it *on the basis of the general guidelines and strategic lines defined by the European Council.*[46]

At the same time, Council Decisions only seldom refer to European Council guidelines, and the competence of the Council in practice seems to be quite autonomous. In fact, the frequency of European Council meetings would seriously hamper an effective CFSP implementation by the Council.

When we take a first look at the contents of CFSP Decisions, the main objectives seem to be 'political' (reinforcing democracy and respect for human rights) and 'diplomatic' (preventing and solving conflicts, coordinating emergency situations). In addition, 'economic' objectives (support of economic reforms, regional development) and 'legal' objectives (supporting the development of the rule of law and good governance) can be discovered.

These established characteristics of the CFSP Decisions certainly clarify their nature to some extent. The question, however, is whether an analysis of the *procedure* to adopt Decisions may shed some additional light on the nature of the *instrument*.

According to Article 28(1) TEU, whenever CFSP Decisions are adopted, '[t]hey shall lay down their objectives, scope, the means to be made available to the Union, if necessary their duration, and the conditions for their implementation'. CFSP Decisions can therefore not be adopted half-heartedly; the 'objectives', the 'scope' and the 'available means' will have to be defined. In practice the Decisions are less extensive than one would expect on the basis of this provision. Usually the requirements are only *implicitly* included in the decision. In the early days in particular, the 'objectives' – which were referred to as 'general and specific objectives' in the 1992 Treaty – were to be found in sentences like 'in order to work for the conclusion of a comprehensive peace in the Middle East'.[47] While more recent Decisions occasionally devote more space to the reasons behind their adoption (in the preamble) and to concrete objectives (often in Article 1 of the operational part), the objectives and background are usually not extensively presented. Thus, a decision 'concerning restrictive measures directed against certain persons, entities and bodies threatening the peace, security or stability of the Republic of Guinea-Bissau' may simply refer to: 'the seriousness of the current situation in the Republic of Guinea-Bissau' as a reason for the Council to:

> ### Council Decision 2012/237/CFSP of 3 May 2012 concerning restrictive measures directed against certain persons, entities and bodies threatening the peace, security or stability of the Republic of Guinea-Bissau, OJ 2012 No. L119/43
>
> adopt measures targeting those who seek to prevent or block a peaceful political process or who take action that undermines stability in the Republic of Guinea-Bissau, in particular those who played a leading role in the mutiny of 1 April 2010 and the coup d'état of 12 April 2012 and who aim, through

---

[46] Emphasis added.
[47] Council Decision 94/276/CFSP of 19 April 1994 on a joint action adopted by the Council on the basis of Article J (3) of the Treaty on European Union, in support of the Middle East peace process, OJ 1994 No. L119/1.

their actions, at undermining the rule of law, curtailing the primacy of civilian power and furthering impunity and instability in the country.

Decisions usually refer to the scope, the means and the duration, albeit that additional decisions are needed for their actual implementation. These 'implementing' decisions are then based both on the Treaty legal basis (usually Article 29 TEU) and the original Decision.

From the outset, the binding nature of CFSP Decisions has puzzled academics and practitioners alike. The main reason would be the very limited role of the CJEU in relation to adopted CFSP Decisions. Yet – and apart from the indeed limited legal supervision – the obligatory force of CFSP Decisions is quite clear, even if the text does not use the word 'bind' but rather 'commit':

Article 28(2) TEU

Decisions referred to in paragraph 1 shall commit the Member States in the positions they adopt and in the conduct of their activity.

Hence, CFSP Decision Actions, once adopted, limit the freedom of Member States in their individual policies. Member States are not allowed to adopt positions or otherwise to act contrary to the Decisions. They have committed themselves to adapting their national policies to the agreed Decisions. It is tempting to make comparisons with EU Regulations, which also demand the unconditional obedience of Member States once they are adopted. But, the Treaty text alone does not support reading the CFSP Decisions along the same lines as the instruments used in Article 288 TFEU – in particular where the addressees of the obligations or the direct applicability are concerned. A comparison with the legal instrument of 'Directives' equally reveals glaring differences, for example regarding the implementation period of Directives.

Apart from Article 28(2), the binding nature of CFSP Decisions may be derived from Article 29 TEU, which forms the legal basis for most CFSP Decisions.

Article 29 TEU

The Council shall adopt decisions which shall define the approach of the Union to a particular matter of a geographical or thematic nature. *Member States shall ensure that their national policies conform to the Union positions.*[48]

The nature of Article 29 TEU Decisions as concrete norms of conduct demanding a certain unconditional behaviour from the Member States, is underlined by the strict ways in which exceptions are allowed. A first possibility to depart from adopted CFSP Decision Actions is offered by Article 28(1), which is similar to, but at the same time clearly departs from, the *rebus sic stantibus* rule as presented in Article 62 VCLT.[49]

---

[48] Emphasis added.

[49] VCLT Article 62, para 1(a) and (b). The criteria to invoke this provision justifiably include: the fundamental change of circumstances was not foreseen by the parties and (a) the existence of those circumstances constituted an essential basis of the consent of the parties to be bound by the treaty; and (b) the effect of the change is radically to transform the extent of obligations still to be performed under the treaty.

Article 28(1) TEU

Where the international situation requires operational action by the Union, the Council shall adopt the necessary decisions. They shall lay down their objectives, scope, the means to be made available to the Union, if necessary their duration, and the conditions for their implementation.

If there is a change in circumstances having a substantial effect on a question subject to such a decision, the Council shall review the principles and objectives of that decision and take the necessary decisions.

So, even if the original circumstances constitute an essential basis of the consent of the parties to be bound, or the effect of the change is radically to transform the extent of obligations still to be performed, Member States may not invoke the change in circumstances as a ground for not living up to the particular Decision. In that sense the CFSP provision cannot be regarded as a *clausula rebus sic stantibus*: even a change in circumstances may not be invoked by the Member State as a reason to neglect the adopted Decision. It is up to the Council to decide on possible modifications. Pending the decision of the Council, no deviations from the Decision are allowed.

The idea that CFSP Decisions, which are adopted by the Council, can only be modified or terminated by that institution, is furthermore emphasized by the subsequent paragraphs of Article 28.

Article 28(3) TEU

Whenever there is any plan to adopt a national position or take national action pursuant to a decision as referred to in paragraph 1, information shall be provided by the Member State concerned in time to allow, if necessary, for prior consultations within the Council. The obligation to provide prior information shall not apply to measures which are merely a national transposition of Council decisions.

The rationale behind this provision is obvious: it creates a procedure to identify potential conflicting national policies at an early stage. The procedure is in the interest of the Member States themselves; it prevents the adoption of national policies which, because of a conflict with a CFSP Decision, would run the risk of being in violation of Article 28(2) TEU.

Member States are not obliged to refer national implementation measures to the Council. However, when they have major difficulties in implementing a CFSP Decision, paragraph 5 stipulates that these should be referred to the Council, which shall discuss them and seek appropriate solutions.[50] The inviolability of adopted CFSP Decisions is underlined by the rule, formulated in the last sentence of paragraph 5, that '[s]uch solutions shall not run counter to the objectives of the decision ... or impair its effectiveness'. While the wording of paragraph 5 is in general quite clear, the question emerges why this procedure is related to 'major' difficulties only.

---

[50] The United Kingdom initially proposed a withdrawal clause in case of vital national interests. The majority of the Member States, however, were against such a clause, which would certainly erode the very nature of the Joint Action. The provision in the Luxembourg Draft Treaty of 1991 already reflected the current provision (Article K, paragraph 4).

What if a Member State encounters problems with the implementation of a minor part of the Decision only? Obviously, there would be no obligation to refer the case to the Council. Nevertheless we have seen that a Decision commits the Member States; there is no ground for reading paragraph 2 as 'Decision Actions commit the Member States *to the largest possible extent*'. This, together with the loyalty obligation discussed above, leads to the conclusion that the discretion offered to the Member States to decide whether or not their implementation problems need to be brought to the attention of the Council, is limited. In case of any controversies concerning this issue, it seems to be up to the Council to seek an appropriate solution.

Does it follow from the fact that CFSP Decisions are binding that Member States may *never* avoid the obligations laid down in the Decision in question? The CFSP provisions in fact include one quite explicit exception:

Article 28(4) TEU

In cases of imperative need arising from changes in the situation and failing a review of the Council decision as referred to in paragraph 1, Member States may take the necessary measures as a matter of urgency having regard to the general objectives of that decision. The Member State concerned shall inform the Council immediately of any such measures.

While this provision again comes close to the *rebus sic stantibus* rule in Article 62 VCLT, the criteria to be met are strict: (1) there must be a case of *imperative need*; (2) the situation must have been changed; (3) the Council has not (yet) come up with a decision to solve the matter; (4) measures will have to be *necessary*; and (5) must be taken as a *matter of urgency*; (6) the general objectives of the Decision should be taken into consideration; and (7) the Council shall be immediately informed.

P. van Elsuwege, 'EU External Action after the Collapse of the Pillar Structure: In Search of a New Balance between Delimitation and Consistency' (2010) 47 *Common Market Law Review* 987–1019

Whereas "mutual (political) solidarity" is not a traditional normative legal concept, Article 28(2) (ex 14, as amended) TEU specifies that CFSP decisions "commit the Member States in the positions they adopt and in the conduct of their activity". As a corollary, it can thus be argued that also in the field of CFSP the sovereignty of the Member States has been limited. However, this does not mean that all characteristics of the old Community legal order, in particular those of pre-emption, direct effect and primacy, automatically apply to the area of CFSP. A general application of those principles would place the national courts in a precarious position. They would be obliged to set aside national provisions in favour of CFSP decisions without having a possibility to seek guidance from the Court of Justice under the preliminary ruling procedure.

Arguably, such a situation would be detrimental for the uniform application of EU law. The exclusive jurisdiction of the Court of Justice and, in particular, its task "to ensure uniform interpretation of the treaty by national courts and tribunals" is indeed a key element of the closely connected concepts of direct effect and primacy. In the absence of such a role for the Court of Justice in CFSP affairs, the appropriateness of those principles to define the relationship between CFSP acts and national law is questionable.

Council Decision 2011/137/CFSP of 28 February 2011 concerning restrictive measures in view of the situation in Libya, OJ 2011 No. L58/53

THE COUNCIL OF THE EUROPEAN UNION,

Having regard to the Treaty on European Union, and in particular Article 29 thereof,

Whereas:

(1) On 23 February 2011, the European Union expressed its grave concern regarding the situation unfolding in Libya. The EU strongly condemned the violence and use of force against civilians and deplored the repression against peaceful demonstrators.

(2) The EU reiterated its call for an immediate end to the use of force and for steps to address the legitimate demands of the population.

(3) On 26 February 2011, the United Nations Security Council ("the Security Council") adopted Resolution 1970 ("UNSCR 1970 (2011)") which introduced restrictive measures against Libya and against persons and entities involved in serious human rights abuses against persons in Libya, including by being involved in attacks, in violation of international law, on civilian populations and facilities.

(4) In view of the seriousness of the situation in Libya, the EU considers it necessary to impose additional restrictive measures.

(5) In addition, further Union action is needed in order to implement certain measures.

HAS ADOPTED THIS DECISION:

Article 1

1. The direct or indirect supply, sale or transfer of arms and related material of all types, including weapons and ammunition, military vehicles and equipment, paramilitary equipment and spare parts for the aforementioned, as well as equipment which might be used for internal repression, to Libya by nationals of Member States or from or through the territories of Member States or using their flag vessels or aircraft, shall be prohibited whether originating or not in their territories.

2. It shall be prohibited to:
   (a) provide, directly or indirectly, technical assistance, training or other assistance, including the provision of armed mercenary personnel, related to military activities or to the provision, maintenance and use of items referred to in paragraph 1, to any natural or legal person, entity or body in, or for use in, Libya;
   (b) provide, directly or indirectly, financial assistance related to military activities or to the provision, maintenance and use of items referred to in paragraph 1, to any natural or legal person, entity or body in, or for use in, Libya;
   (c) participate, knowingly and intentionally, in activities, the object or effect of which is to circumvent the prohibitions referred to in points (a) or (b).

Article 2

1. Article 1 shall not apply to:
   (a) the supply, sale or transfer of non-lethal military equipment or of equipment which might be used for internal repression, intended solely for humanitarian or protective use;
   (b) other supply, sale or transfer of arms and related material;
   (c) the provision of technical assistance, training or other assistance, including personnel, related to such equipment;

(d) the provision of financial assistance related to such equipment; as approved in advance, where appropriate, by the Committee established pursuant to paragraph 24 of UNSCR 1970 (2011) ("the Committee").

2. Article 1 shall not apply to the supply, sale or transfer of protective clothing, including flak jackets and military helmets, temporarily exported to Libya by UN personnel, personnel of the European Union or its Member States, representatives of the media and humanitarian and development workers and associated personnel for their personal use only.

Article 3

The procurement by nationals of Member States, either using their flag vessels or aircraft, of the items referred to in Article 1(1) from Libya shall be prohibited, whether or not originating in the territory of Libya.

Article 4

1. Member States shall inspect, in accordance with their national authorities and legislation and consistent with international law, in particular the law of the sea and relevant international civil aviation agreements, all cargo to and from Libya, in their territory, including their seaports and airports, if they have information that provides reasonable grounds to believe that the cargo contains items the supply, sale, transfer or export of which is prohibited under this Decision.

2. Member States shall, upon discovery, seize and dispose of (such as through destruction, rendering inoperable, storage or transferring to a State other than the originating or destination States for disposal) items whose supply, sale, transfer or export is prohibited under this Decision.

3. Member States shall cooperate, in accordance with their national legislation, with inspections and disposals undertaken pursuant to paragraphs 1 and 2.

4. Aircrafts and vessels transporting cargo to and from Libya shall be subject to the requirement of additional pre-arrival or pre-departure information for all goods brought into or out of a Member State.

Article 5

1. Member States shall take the necessary measures to prevent the entry into, or transit through, their territories of:
   (a) persons listed in Annex I to UNSCR 1970 (2011), and additional persons designated by the Security Council or by the Committee in accordance with paragraph 22 of UNSCR 1970 (2011), as listed in Annex I;
   (b) persons not covered by Annex I involved in or complicit in ordering, controlling, or otherwise directing, the commission of serious human rights abuses against persons in Libya, including by being involved in or complicit in planning, commanding, ordering or conducting attacks, in violation of international law, including aerial bombardments, on civilian populations and facilities, or acting for or on their behalf or at their direction, as listed in Annex II.

2. Paragraph 1 shall not oblige a Member State to refuse its own nationals entry into its territory.

3. Paragraph 1(a) shall not apply where the Committee determines that:
   (a) travel is justified on the grounds of humanitarian need, including religious obligation; or
   (b) an exemption would further the objectives of peace and national reconciliation in Libya and stability in the region;

4. Paragraph 1(a) shall not apply where:
   (a) entry or transit is necessary for the fulfilment of a judicial process; or

(b) a Member State determines on a case-by-case basis that such entry or transit is required to advance peace and stability in Libya and the Member State subsequently notifies the Committee within forty-eight hours after making such a determination.

5. Paragraph 1(b) shall be without prejudice to the cases where a Member State is bound by an obligation of international law, namely:

(a) as a host country to an international intergovernmental organisation;

(b) as a host country to an international conference convened by, or under the auspices of, the UN;

(c) under a multilateral agreement conferring privileges and immunities; or

(d) under the 1929 Treaty of Conciliation (Lateran pact) concluded by the Holy See (State of the Vatican City) and Italy.

6. Paragraph 5 shall be considered as applying also in cases where a Member State is host country to the Organisation for Security and Cooperation in Europe (OSCE).

7. The Council shall be duly informed in all cases where a Member State grants an exemption pursuant to paragraphs 5 or 6.

8. Member States may grant exemptions from the measures imposed under paragraph 1(b) where travel is justified on the grounds of urgent humanitarian need, or on grounds of attending intergovernmental meetings, including those promoted by the Union, or hosted by a Member State holding the Chairmanship in office of the OSCE, where a political dialogue is conducted that directly promotes democracy, human rights and the rule of law in Libya.

9. A Member State wishing to grant exemptions referred to in paragraph 8 shall notify the Council in writing. The exemption shall be deemed to be granted unless one or more Council members raise an objection in writing within two working days of receiving notification of the proposed exemption. Should one or more Council members raise an objection, the Council, acting by a qualified majority, may decide to grant the proposed exemption.

10. In cases where, pursuant to paragraphs 5, 6, and 8, a Member State authorises the entry into, or transit through, its territory of persons listed in the Annex, the authorisation shall be limited to the purpose for which it is given and to the persons concerned thereby.

Article 6

1. All funds, other financial assets and economic resources, owned or controlled, directly or indirectly, by:

(a) persons and entities listed in Annex II to UNSCR 1970 (2011), and additional persons and entities designated by the Security Council or by the Committee in accordance with paragraph 22 of UNSCR 1970 (2011), or by individuals or entities acting on their behalf or at their direction, or by entities owned or controlled by them, as listed in Annex III;

(b) persons and entities not covered by Annex III involved in or complicit in ordering, controlling, or otherwise directing, the commission of serious human rights abuses against persons in Libya, including by being involved in or complicit in planning, commanding, ordering or conducting attacks, in violation of international law, including aerial bombardments, on civilian populations and facilities, or by individuals or entities acting on their behalf or at their direction, or by entities owned or controlled by them, as listed in Annex IV, shall be frozen.

2. No funds, other financial assets or economic resources shall be made available, directly or indirectly, to or for the benefit of, natural or legal persons or entities referred to in paragraph 1.

3. Exemptions may be made for funds, financial assets and economic resources which are:

(a) necessary for basic expenses, including payment of foodstuffs, rent or mortgage, medicines and medical treatment, taxes, insurance premiums, and public utility charges;

(b) intended exclusively for payment of reasonable professional fees and reimbursement of incurred expenses associated with the provision of legal services in accordance with national laws; or

(c) intended exclusively for payment of fees or service charges, in accordance with national laws, for routine holding or maintenance of frozen funds, other financial assistance and economic resources;

after notification by the Member State concerned to the Committee, where appropriate, of the intention to authorise access to such funds, other financial assets or economic resources and in the absence of a negative decision by the Committee within five working days of such notification.

4. Exemptions may also be made for funds and economic resources which are:

(a) necessary for extraordinary expenses, after notification by the Member State concerned to the Committee, where appropriate, and approval by the Committee; or

(b) the subject of a judicial, administrative or arbitral lien or judgement, in which case the funds, other financial assets and economic resources may be used to satisfy that lien or judgement provided that the lien or judgement was entered before the date of adoption of UNSCR 1970 (2011), and is not for the benefit of a person or entity referred to in paragraph 1, after notification by the Member State concerned to the Committee, where appropriate;

5. Paragraph 1 shall not prevent a designated person or entity from making payment due under a contract entered into before the listing of such a person or entity, provided that the relevant Member State has determined that the payment is not directly or indirectly received by a person or entity referred to in paragraph 1 and after notification by the relevant Member State to the Committee, where appropriate, of the intention to make or receive such payments or to authorise the unfreezing of funds, other financial assets or economic resources for this purpose, 10 working days prior to such authorisation.

6. Paragraph 2 shall not apply to the addition to frozen accounts of:

(a) interest or other earnings due on those accounts; or

(b) payments due under contracts, agreements or obligations that arose before the date on which those accounts became subject to restrictive measures;

provided that any such interest, other earnings and payments continue to be subject to paragraph 1.

Article 7

No claims, including for compensation or any other claim of this kind, such as a claim of set-off or a claim under a guarantee, in connection with any contract or transaction the performance of which was affected, directly or indirectly, wholly or in part, by reason of measures decided upon pursuant to UNSCR 1970 (2011), including measures of the Union or any Member State in accordance with, as required by or in any connection with, the implementation of the relevant decisions of the Security Council or measures covered by this Decision, shall be granted to the designated persons or entities listed in Annexes I, II, III or IV, or any other person or entity in Libya, including the Government of Libya, or any person or entity claiming through or for the benefit of any such person or entity.

Article 8

1. The Council shall implement modifications to Annexes I and III on the basis of the determinations made by the Security Council or by the Committee.

2. The Council, acting on a proposal from Member States or from the High Representative of the Union for Foreign Affairs and Security Policy, shall establish the lists in Annexes II and IV and adopt modifications thereto.

Article 9

1. Where the Security Council or the Committee lists a person or entity, the Council shall include such person or entity in Annexes I or III.
2. Where the Council decides to subject a person or entity to the measures referred to in Articles 5(1)(b) and 6(1)(b), it shall amend Annexes II and IV accordingly.
3. The Council shall communicate its decision to the person or entity referred to in paragraphs 1 and 2, including the grounds for listing, either directly, if the address is known, or through the publication of a notice, providing such person or entity an opportunity to present observations.
4. Where observations are submitted, or where substantial new evidence is presented, the Council shall review its decision and inform the person or entity accordingly.

Article 10

1. Annexes I, II, III and IV shall include the grounds for listing of listed persons and entities concerned, as provided by the Security Council or by the Committee with regard to Annexes I and III.
2. Annexes I, II, III and IV shall also contain, where available, the information necessary to identify the persons or entities concerned, as provided by the Security Council or by the Committee with regard to Annexes I and III. With regard to persons, such information may include names, including aliases, date and place of birth, nationality, passport and ID card numbers, gender, address if known, and function or profession. With regard to entities, such information may include names, place and date of registration, registration number and place of business. Annexes I and III shall also include the date of designation by the Security Council or by the Committee.

Article 11

In order to maximise the impact of the measures laid down in this Decision, the Union shall encourage third States to adopt similar restrictive measures.

Article 12

1. This Decision shall be reviewed, amended or repealed as appropriate, notably in the light of relevant decisions by the Security Council.
2. The measures referred to in Articles 5(1)(b) and 6(1)(b) shall be reviewed at regular intervals and at least every 12 months. They shall cease to apply in respect of the persons and entities concerned if the Council determines, in accordance with the procedure referred in Article 8(2), that the conditions for their application are no longer met.

Article 13

This Decision shall enter into force on the date of its adoption.
Done at Brussels, 28 February 2011.
For the Council
The President
Fellegi T.

ANNEX I
List of persons referred to in Articles 5(1)(a) . . .

6. QADHAFI AL-DAM, Sayyid Mohammed

Date of birth:1948. Place of birth: Sirte, Libya.
   Cousin of Muammar QADHAFI. In the 1980s, Sayyid was involved in the dissident assassination campaign and allegedly responsible for several deaths in Europe. He is also thought to have been involved in arms procurement.
   Date of UN designation: 26.2.2011.

7. QADHAFI, Aisha Muammar

Date of birth: 1978. Place of birth: Tripoli, Libya.
   Daughter of Muammar QADHAFI. Closeness of association with regime.
   Date of UN designation: 26.2.2011.

8. QADHAFI, Hannibal Muammar

Passport number: B/002210. Date of birth: 20.09.1975. Place of birth: Tripoli, Libya.
   Son of Muammar QADHAFI. Closeness of association with regime.
   Date of UN designation: 26.2.2011.

9. QADHAFI, Khamis Muammar

Date of birth: 1978. Place of birth: Tripoli, Libya.
   Son of Muammar QADHAFI. Closeness of association with regime. Command of military units involved in repression of demonstrations.
   Date of UN designation: 26.2.2011.

10. QADHAFI, Mohammed Muammar

Date of birth: 1970. Place of birth: Tripoli, Libya.
   Son of Muammar QADHAFI. Closeness of association with regime.
   Date of UN designation: 26.2.2011.

11. QADHAFI, Muammar Mohammed Abu Minyar

Date of birth: 1942. Place of birth: Sirte, Libya.
   Leader of the Revolution, Supreme Commander of Armed Forces. Responsibility for ordering repression of demonstrations, human rights abuses.
   Date of UN designation: 26.2.2011.

12. QADHAFI, Mutassim

Date of birth: 1976. Place of birth: Tripoli, Libya.

National Security Adviser. Son of Muammar QADHAFI. Closeness of association with regime.
Date of UN designation: 26.2.2011.

13. QADHAFI, Saadi

Passport number: 014797. Date of birth: 25.05.1973. Place of birth: Tripoli, Libya.
Commander Special Forces. Son of Muammar QADHAFI. Closeness of association with regime.
Command of military units involved in repression of demonstrations.
Date of UN designation: 26.2.2011.

14. QADHAFI, Saif al-Arab

Date of birth: 1982. Place of birth: Tripoli, Libya.
Son of Muammar QADHAFI. Closeness of association with regime.
Date of UN designation: 26.2.2011.

15. QADHAFI, Saif al-Islam

Passport number: B014995. Date of birth: 25.06.1972. Place of birth: Tripoli, Libya.
Director, Qadhafi Foundation. Son of Muammar QADHAFI. Closeness of association with regime.
Inflammatory public statements encouraging violence against demonstrators.
Date of UN designation: 26.2.2011.

(b) International agreements

CFSP Decisions are primarily intended to commit the Member States. They lay down the concrete rules that were agreed on in foreign policy and thereby aim to restrain Member States in the conduct of their foreign policy activities. To engage in legal relationships with third states or other international organizations, the EU needs to conclude international agreements. As we have seen in Chapter 2 these agreements can also be concluded in relation to CFSP issues. Whereas the Treaties reveal one procedure only, Article 218 TFEU lists a number of modifications once we deal with agreements that 'relate exclusively to the CFSP'. As indicated, such CFSP agreements are authorized, adopted and concluded by unanimity, rather than by QMV (the default voting procedures for other agreements). Second, in case of CFSP agreements, and despite its increased role in relation to other international agreements, the EP is not even consulted. Note here that the interpretative breadth provided as to when an agreement relates 'exclusively' to CFSP may provide space for future litigation. Third, the opening of negotiations is not recommended by the Commission, but proposed by the HR. And, finally, the ECJ has no jurisdiction in relation to CFSP agreements, apart from situations where they influence non-CFSP provisions.

These diverging procedural requirements make it difficult, although not impossible, for the Union to combine CFSP and other issues in one single international agreement. The example below combines a CFSP legal basis with that of development (Article 209 TFEU) and economic, financial and technical cooperation with third countries (Article 212 TFEU).

Most international agreements in the area of foreign policy fall under the CSDP (see Chapter 12).

(c) Restrictive measures

Article 215 TFEU

1. Where a decision, adopted in accordance with Chapter 2 of Title V of the Treaty on European Union, provides for the interruption or reduction, in part or completely, of economic and financial relations with one or more third countries, the Council, acting by a qualified majority on a joint proposal from the High Representative of the Union for Foreign Affairs and Security Policy and the Commission, shall adopt the necessary measures. It shall inform the European Parliament thereof.
2. Where a decision adopted in accordance with Chapter 2 of Title V of the Treaty on European Union so provides, the Council may adopt restrictive measures under the procedure referred to in paragraph 1 against natural or legal persons and groups or non-State entities.
3. The acts referred to in this Article shall include necessary provisions on legal safeguards.

Restrictive measures – usually referred to as 'economic sanctions' – form a classic example of substantive CFSP (see above the Libyan example). They are a combination of economic and political policies in the sense that a political goal is being achieved by economic means. This explains why in the pre-Lisbon era a two-step system was invented to allow for a smooth cooperation between the CFSP and Community decision-making machineries: economic sanctions could only be adopted on the basis of the Community Treaty after a political decision to that end was taken in the form of a CFSP Decision.

These days, the two-step system is still present in the wordings of Article 215 TFEU: first a CFSP Decision is adopted, providing for sanctions. This is then (to be) followed by measures adopted by the Council following the procedure in Article 215. While this procedure involves many other actors (the HR, the Commission and the EP) it is interesting to note that the Council nevertheless seems to be under an obligation to deliver ('the Council shall adopt'). This may put a certain pressure on those involved, but obviously there may be some freedom to decide on the exact content of the 'measures'. Furthermore, while Council members may have taken the CFSP decision by unanimity, they would have the opportunity to vote against the measures during the second step. In practice, this would seem to be a theoretical option only as this is an area where the dual role of the HR may be particularly helpful: first as a chairman of the FAC adopting the CFSP decision, and afterwards as the key initiator of the restrictive measures.

Article 275 makes clear that sanctions can be directed both towards states and towards natural or legal persons and groups or non-state entities. If sanctions against non-state entities or persons are envisaged, this should already be made clear in the CFSP Decision (see Article 215(2)).

Apart from these types of sanctions, the Treaty foresees another situation in Article 75 TFEU, which relates to the AFSJ (see Chapter 14).

Article 75 TFEU

Where necessary to achieve the objectives set out in Article 67, as regards preventing and combating terrorism and related activities, the European Parliament and the Council, acting by means of regulations in accordance with the ordinary legislative procedure, shall define a framework for administrative measures with regard to capital movements and payments, such as the freezing of funds, financial assets or economic gains belonging to, or owned or held by, natural or legal persons, groups or non-State entities.

The Council, on a proposal from the Commission, shall adopt measures to implement the framework referred to in the first paragraph.

The acts referred to in this Article shall include necessary provisions on legal safeguards.

This provision explicitly relates to 'the objectives set out in Article 67', which lists the goals and background of the AFSJ. Furthermore, Article 75 makes clear that the sanctions are directed at natural or legal persons, groups or non-state entities; in other words – not towards states. The provision is therefore the correct legal basis for financial or administrative sanctions against (potential) terrorists, individuals or groups facilitating terrorism. The available separate procedure allows for anti-terrorism measures to be adopted quickly and without delay (on the basis of a one-step procedure).

The distinction between Article 75 and Article 215 was clarified by the Court in 2012. Now that the objective of combating terrorism is expressly laid down in a specific provision (Article 75, relating to the AFSJ), can anti-terrorism sanctions directed towards individuals and groups also be taken in the area of CFSP?

Case C–130/10 *European Parliament* v. *Council of the European Union*, 19 July 2012

1. By its action, the European Parliament asks the Court to annul Council Regulation (EU) No 1286/2009 of 22 December 2009 amending Regulation (EC) No 881/2002 imposing certain specific restrictive measures directed against certain persons and entities associated with Usama bin Laden, the Al-Qaeda network and the Taliban (OJ 2009 L 346, p. 42, 'the contested regulation'). . . .

10. In support of its action for annulment, the Parliament raises two pleas in law. By the first and principal plea, it claims that the contested regulation is wrongly based on Article 215 TFEU, when the correct legal basis is Article 75 TFEU. By the second plea, raised in the alternative, it maintains that the conditions for recourse to Article 215 TFEU were not satisfied. . . .

47. In this instance, while Article 75 TFEU provides for application of the ordinary legislative procedure, which entails qualified majority voting in the Council and the Parliament's full participation in the procedure, Article 215(2) TFEU, for its part, entails merely informing the Parliament. In addition, recourse to Article 215(2) TFEU, unlike recourse to Article 75 TFEU, requires a previous decision in the sphere of the CFSP, namely, a decision adopted in accordance with Chapter 2 of Title V of the EU Treaty, providing for the adoption of restrictive measures such as those referred to in that provision. As a general rule, adoption of such a decision calls for unanimous voting in the Council acting alone.

48. Differences of that kind are such as to render those procedures incompatible.

49. It follows from the foregoing that, even if the contested regulation does pursue several objectives at the same time or have several components indissociably linked, without one's being secondary to the other, the differences in the procedures applicable under Articles 75 TFEU and 215(2) TFEU mean that it is not possible for the two provisions to be cumulated, one with the other, in order to serve as a twofold legal basis for a measure such as the contested regulation. . . .

55. It is necessary to examine the wording of Article 215 TFEU, the context of which that provision forms part and the objectives it pursues, in relation to those pursued by Article 75 TFEU, before determining, in

the light of the purpose and content of the contested regulation, whether Article 215(2) TFEU constitutes the correct legal basis for the regulation.

56. Article 215 TFEU appears in Title IV, entitled 'Restrictive measures', of Part Five of the FEU Treaty on external action by the Union.

57. Article 215(1) concerns the adoption of measures necessary for the interruption or reduction, in part or completely, of economic and financial relations with one or more third countries. In this context, Article 215(2) concerns the adoption by the Council of 'restrictive measures ... against natural or legal persons and groups or non-State entities', without specifically referring to the combating of terrorism and without limiting those measures to those measures alone that concern capital movements and payments.

58. Moreover, Article 215(2) TFEU, unlike Article 75 TFEU, provides, as mentioned at paragraph 47 above, that it may not be used until a decision under the CFSP has provided for the adoption of restrictive measures against natural or legal persons, groups or non-State entities. For its part, Article 75 TFEU states that it may be used where necessary to achieve the objectives set out in Article 67 TFEU, that is to say, in connection with creating an area of freedom, security and justice.

59. In this regard, it is to be borne in mind that, at paragraph 197 of *Kadi and Al Barakaat International Foundation* v *Council and Commission*, the Court considered that a bridge had been constructed between the actions of the Community involving economic measures under Articles 60 EC and 301 EC and the objectives of the EU Treaty, as it stood before the Treaty of Lisbon entered into force, in the sphere of external relations, including the CFSP. Article 215 TFEU expressly provides such a bridge, but this is not the case with Article 75 TFEU, which creates no link with decisions taken under the CFSP.

60. As regards combating terrorism and its funding, it is to be noted that there is nothing in Article 215 TFEU to indicate that measures designed to combat them, taken against natural or legal persons, groups or non-State entities, could not constitute restrictive measures provided for in subparagraph 2 of that article. It is to be observed here that, although neither Article 60 EC nor Article 301 EC referred expressly to combating terrorism, those two provisions did, none the less, constitute the legal basis for the adoption, before the Treaty of Lisbon entered into force, of restrictive measures designed to combat that phenomenon (see, inter alia, in this respect, the measures at issue in *Kadi and Al Barakaat International Foundation* v *Council and Commission*).

61. While admittedly the combating of terrorism and its financing may well be among the objectives of the area of freedom, security and justice, as they appear in Article 3(2) TEU, the objective of combating international terrorism and its financing in order to preserve international peace and security corresponds, nevertheless, to the objectives of the Treaty provisions on external action by the Union. ...

65. It follows from the foregoing that Article 215(2) TFEU may constitute the legal basis of restrictive measures, including those designed to combat terrorism, taken against natural or legal persons, groups or non-State entities by the Union when the decision to adopt those measures is part of the Union's action in the sphere of the CFSP.

7 THE BROADER PICTURE OF EU EXTERNAL RELATIONS LAW

The image of CFSP as a purely 'intergovernmental' form of international cooperation is not supported by the treaty provisions. Regardless of the prima facie broad scope of CFSP on the basis of its objectives (which indeed seem to cover almost every conceivable area of foreign and security policy), it is not to be seen as a *common policy* in the same way as the concept is used in, for instance, the CAP or CCP. The non-exclusive nature of CFSP is paramount. The competences of the institutions, the obligations of the Member States and the decision-making procedures all reflect the intention of the states to create a common policy that would not unconditionally *replace* the national policies of the individual states, but that would only emerge *where and when possible*. Despite concrete obligations aiming at the establishment of a common policy, a number of vague notions ('important common interests', 'general interest', 'reasons of national policy') allow for a large margin of appreciation on the part of the Member States. Whenever a common policy does not prove possible, Member States are free to pursue their own national foreign policies.

Even adopted Decisions – as the key binding CFSP legal instruments – do not deprive the Member States of all their rights to maintain national policy in the areas covered by the CFSP decisions. Practice reveals that most decisions have a narrow scope only, allowing for parallel national policies in the same issue area. And, even within the scope of the CFSP decisions, Member States have possibilities to lay emphasis on certain national preferences and implementation modalities. While an analysis of the origins of CFSP and the subsequent developments indeed reveal a certain preference for 'intergovernmental' cooperation on the part of most Member States, the conclusions of this chapter have shown that CFSP has developed into a fully fledged – though peculiar – competence of the EU. A number of CFSP features do indicate serious constraints on the Member States in executing their foreign policy as well as on the EU institutions involved.

SOURCES AND FURTHER READING

Brkan, M., 'The Role of the European Court of Justice in the Field of Common Foreign and Security Policy after the Treaty of Lisbon: New Challenges for the Future', in P. J. Cardwell (ed.), *EU External Relations Law and Policy in the Post-Lisbon Era* (The Hague: T.M.C. Asser Press, 2012), pp. 97–115.

Corbett, R., *The Treaty of Maastricht: From Conception to Ratification: A Comprehensive Reference Guide* (Harlow, Essex: Longman Group UK, 1993).

Curtin, D., 'The Constitutional Structure of the Union: A Europe of Bits and Pieces' (1993) 30 *Common Market Law Review* 17–69.

De Witte, B., 'The Pillar Structure and the Nature of the European Union: Greek Temple or French Gothic Cathedral?', in T. Heukels, N. Blokker and M. Brus (eds.), *The European Union after Amsterdam: A Legal Analysis* (The Hague: Kluwer Law International, 1998), pp. 51–68.

Griller, S., 'The Court of Justice and the Common Foreign and Security Policy', in A. Rosas, E. Levits and Y. Bot (eds.), *Court of Justice of the European Union – Cour de Justice de l'Union Européene, The Court of Justice and the Construction of Europe: Analyses and Perspectives on Sixty Years of Case-Law – La Cour de Justice et la Construction de l'Europe: Analyses et Perspectives de Soixante Ans de Jurisprudence* (The Hague: T.M.C. Asser Press, 2013), pp. 675–692.

Hillion, C., 'Tous pour un, un pour tous! Coherence in the External Relations of the European Union', in M. Cremona (ed.), *Developments in EU External Relations Law* (Oxford: Oxford University Press, 2008), pp. 10–36.

Hillion, C. and Wessel, R. A., 'Restraining External Competences of EU Member States under CFSP', in M. Cremona and B. de Witte (eds.), *EU Foreign Relations Law: Constitutional Fundamentals* (Oxford: Hart Publishing, 2008), pp. 79–121.

Jürgens, Th., *Die Gemeinsame Europäische Außen- und Sicherheitspolitik* (Cologne: Carl Heymanns Verlag, 1994).

Keukeleire, S., *Het Buitenlands beleid van de Europese Unie* (Deventer: Kluwer, 1998).

Laursen, F. and Vanhoonacker, S. (eds.), *The Intergovernmental Conference on Political Union: Institutional Reforms, New Policies and International Identity of the European Community* (Maastricht: EIPA, 1992).

Mayer, H., 'Germany's Role in the Fouchet Negotiations' (1996) 2 *Journal of European Integration History*, 2, 39–59.

Missiroli, A., 'The New EU Foreign Policy System after Lisbon: A Work in Progress' (2010) 15 *European Foreign Affairs Review* 427–452.

Neville-Jones, P., 'The Genscher–Colombo Proposals on European Union' (1983) 20 *Common Market Law Review* 657–699.

Nuttall, S., 'European Political Cooperation and the Single European Act' (1985) 5 *Year of European Law* 203–232.

Stein, E., 'European Foreign Affairs System and the Single European Act of 1986', in W. F. Ebke and J. J. Norton (eds.), *Festschrift in Honor of Sir Joseph Gold* (Heidelberg: Verlag Recht und Wirtschaft, 1990).

Van Elsuwege, P., 'EU External Action after the Collapse of the Pillar Structure: In Search of a New Balance between Delimitation and Consistency' (2010) 47 *Common Market Law Review* 987–1019.

Van Vooren, B., 'A Legal Institutional Perspective on the European External Action Service' (2011) 48 *Common Market Law Review* 475–502.

Van Vooren, B., *EU External Relations Law and the European Neighbourhood Policy: A Paradigm for Coherence* (Abingdon/New York: Routledge, 2012).

Van Vooren, B., 'The Small Arms Judgment in an Age of Constitutional Turmoil' (2009) 14 *European Foreign Affairs Review*, 1, 231–248.

Wessel, R. A., *The European Union's Foreign and Security Policy: A Legal Institutional Perspective* (The Hague: Kluwer Law International, 1999).

Whitman, R. and Juncos, A., 'The Lisbon Treaty and the Foreign, Security and Defence Policy: Reforms, Implementation and the Consequences of (Non-)Ratification' (2009) 14 *European Foreign Affairs Review* 25–46.

12

Common Security and Defence Policy

1 CENTRAL ISSUES

- For almost fifty years, security and defence cooperation was excluded from the EU and in fact enjoyed 'taboo status'. Member States were hesitant to hand over powers in this sensitive area to the 'supranational' EC and many preferred to give priority to cooperation in NATO. Yet, since the beginning of the third millennium, CSDP has developed into a fully fledged policy, as part of the CFSP (see Chapter 11), but increasingly as a stand-alone policy field with its own rules, procedures and bodies.
- This chapter will address decision-making in CSDP as well as the role of the institutions and the available legal instruments. We will also go back in time to trace the origins of CSDP, in order to explain its current nature. Over twenty-five missions have been established since the creation of CSDP, and in this chapter we will look at the different types of missions as well as at their (international) legal ramifications.

2 INTRODUCTION

In the previous chapter we referred to the origins of the Union's foreign, security and defence policy. As we have seen, during the 1950s and 1960s far-reaching proposals were tabled to establish a common defence policy with supranational features. These proposals were never accepted, and a security and defence policy developed partly as part of the CFSP and partly autonomously. Over the last decade, the EU has launched over twenty-five civilian missions and military operations on three continents deployed in response to crises, ranging from post-tsunami peace-building in Aceh, to protecting refugees in Chad, to fighting against piracy in and around Somalian waters. The CSDP has developed into a major policy area in EU external relations. Like CFSP, it is formed on the basis of specific rules and procedures, but at the same time we have witnessed a development from a largely inter-governmental policy area to a 'Brussels-based' cooperation in which EU preparatory organs play a leading role.

The 'Provisions on the Common Security and Defence Policy' are laid down in Section 2 of Chapter 2 TEU called 'Specific Provisions on the Common, Foreign and Security Policy'. This underlines that CSDP can be seen as forming part of CFSP.

> ### Article 42(1) TEU
>
> The common security and defence policy shall be an integral part of the common foreign and security policy.

Since both CFSP and CSDP deal with 'security' and that concept is not defined by the Treaty, it has always been unclear where to draw the line. In the 1992 Maastricht Treaty objectives it was implied that there is a difference between the security of the Union and the security of the Member States, since the objective originally read 'to strengthen the security of the Union and its Member States in all ways'. Thus, the objective was not only aimed at strengthening the security of the Union, but also at the security of individual Member States. Nevertheless, the apparent confusion raised by this distinction must have been the reason to delete that reference. These days, the objectives in Article 21(2) TEU simply state that the Union shall 'safeguard its values, fundamental interests, security, independence and integrity'.

What then, is meant by 'security'? The Treaty provisions do not provide reasons to limit this concept to *military* security. Obviously different dimensions of security are acknowledged, including, for instance, environmental and economic security, international crime and terrorism. These aspects of security were originally mentioned by the 1992 European Council in Lisbon which outlined the future development of CFSP.[1] It may be argued that it is exactly these non-military or at least *internal* dimensions of security, in particular in relation to the 'protection of European citizens' in Article 3(5) TEU, that are intended in this objective since another objective explicitly deals with the international dimension: to 'preserve peace, prevent conflicts and strengthen *international* security'.[2]

Indeed, keeping in mind the assertion of Robert Schuman as reflected in his Declaration of 9 May 1950, that the creation of a High Authority would 'make it plain that any war between France and the Federal Republic of Germany becomes, not merely unthinkable, but materially impossible', a role for the Union as an internal stabilizer should not be ruled out as well. In this interpretation 'security' should at least also be seen as meaning 'internal security'. Since the first drafts of the TEU, the objectives included a reference to the eventual framing of a defence policy,[3] which strengthens the idea that the security concept is also directed at security between the Member States. After all, this security would be ultimately guaranteed when a common defence policy existed. This holistic approach to security seems to be confirmed by the Treaty.

---

[1] Lisbon European Council, 26 and 27 June 1992, Annex 1: Report to the European Council in Lisbon on the likely development of the common foreign and security policy (CFSP) with a view to identifying areas open to joint action vis-à-vis particular countries or groups of countries, *Bulletin EC* 6-1992.

[2] Emphasis added.

[3] 'To strengthen the security of the Union and its Member States in all ways, including, eventually, the framing of a defence policy'; Draft Treaty on the Union from the Luxembourg Presidency, 18 June 1991; and First Draft Treaty Proposal from the Dutch Presidency, 30 September 1991; in F. Laursen and S. Vanhoonacker (eds.), *The Intergovernmental Conference on Political Union: Institutional Reforms, New Policies and International Identity of the European Community* (Maastricht: EIPA, 1992), pp. 358 and 407.

> **Article 24(1) TEU**
>
> The Union's competence in matters of common foreign and security policy shall cover ... all questions relating to the Union's security, including the progressive framing of a common defence policy that might lead to a common defence.

In light of this vague definition by the Treaties, practice reveals that CFSP is linked mostly to the practice of 'Foreign Affairs Ministries' which includes diplomacy, political dialogues and the like, whereas CSDP would be the responsibility of the Defence Ministries. This would also draw a relatively clear line of division between 'military security' (CSDP) and other forms of security (CFSP). This chapter will, however, reveal that the different provisions on security and defence policy are far from clear. Obviously, they can again be seen as compromises between states in favour of more integration in this area and states that are afraid of losing control.

3 DECISION-MAKING IN CSDP

(i) The substantive CSDP treaty provisions

Title V, Chapter 2, Section 2 of the TEU lists the 'Provisions on the Common Security and Defence Policy'. The 'external' nature of this policy is underlined by the first provision in this section.

> **Article 42(1) TEU**
>
> The common security and defence policy shall be an integral part of the common foreign and security policy. It shall provide the Union with an operational capacity drawing on civilian and military assets. The Union may use them on missions outside the Union for peace-keeping, conflict prevention and strengthening international security in accordance with the principles of the United Nations Charter. The performance of these tasks shall be undertaken using capabilities provided by the Member States.

The way CSDP functions is that Member States provide the Union with certain civil and military assets, which the Union may then use on missions outside the Union. CSDP is thus intended to allow the Union to play a distinct role as a regional and global security actor, separate from that of the Member States. This is underlined by Article 43, which outlines more specifically when CSDP can be used. The references to 'joint disarmament operations', 'military advice and assistance tasks', 'post-conflict stabilisation' and 'the fight against terrorism' in Article 43(1) are newly introduced by the Lisbon Treaty and allow the Union to develop its security and defence policy further, beyond what was previously possible. Though some of this terminology is relatively wide, it is clear that the purposes for which the Union may use military assets are limited, and by no means equal to those of a state.

Article 43(1) TEU

The tasks referred to in Article 42(1), in the course of which the Union may use civilian and military means, shall include joint disarmament operations, humanitarian and rescue tasks, military advice and assistance tasks, conflict prevention and peace-keeping tasks, tasks of combat forces in crisis management, including peace-making and post-conflict stabilisation. All these tasks may contribute to the fight against terrorism, including by supporting third countries in combating terrorism in their territories.

(ii) A common defence policy and the solidarity clause

Crisis management may also be needed in relation to an attack on the Union itself. However, with regard to the 'defence' part of CSDP, the Treaty remains ambiguous.

Article 42(2) TEU

The common security and defence policy shall include the progressive framing of a common Union defence policy. This will lead to a common defence, when the European Council, acting unanimously, so decides.

Despite the careful wording of this provision in line with earlier versions, the Treaty does offer reasons to conclude that something has changed. First of all – and despite the claim that a 'common defence' is not yet included in CSDP – another paragraph in this article is suddenly quite clear on the defence dimension of CSDP.

Article 42(7) TEU

If a Member State is the victim of armed aggression on its territory, the other Member States shall have towards it an obligation of aid and assistance by all the means in their power, in accordance with Article 51 of the United Nations Charter. This shall not prejudice the specific character of the security and defence policy of certain Member States.

Taking into account that according to the Helsinki (1999) and Laeken (2001) Declarations, 'the development of military capabilities does not imply the creation of a European army', it is unclear what it is the European Council will have to decide on (Article 42(2) TEU). Some argue that this provision does not impose strict obligations for all Member States, and certainly entails an obligation which is weaker than the commitments for collective security made in the context of NATO. This would be confirmed by the second part of paragraph 7 which adds an important dimension in this respect.

Article 42(7) TEU

... Commitments and cooperation in this area shall be consistent with commitments under the North Atlantic Treaty Organisation, which, for those States which are members of it, remains the foundation of their collective defence and the forum for its implementation.

While this would indeed allow the certain states (Austria, Finland, Ireland and Sweden) not to participate in measures of self-defence taken in accordance with Article 51 UN Charter, the collective defence obligation does not really differ from Article 5 of the NATO Treaty.[4] What is different, however, is that both NATO and the WEU started their life as collective defence organizations and only became engaged in other security operations later. The EU seems to follow the reverse path, by concentrating on external crisis management before establishing a mechanism to defend its own Member States.

Nevertheless, the sense that something similar to a collective defence obligation has been created (although somewhat hidden in paragraph 7 of Article 42) becomes stronger when the so-called 'solidarity clause' is taken into account. This clause flowed from the 'Declaration on Solidarity against Terrorism',[5] which was issued by the European Council after the Madrid terrorist attacks in March 2004, although the Declaration does not refer to a role for the Union as such, but to the 'Member States acting jointly'. It is somewhat peculiar that this solidarity clause is separated from the collective defence clause and is included in the TFEU rather than together with the CSDP provisions in the TEU. The clause does not restrict common defence to 'armed aggression', but in fact extends the obligation to terrorist attacks as well.

Article 222 TFEU

1. The Union and its Member States shall act jointly in a spirit of solidarity if a Member State is the object of a terrorist attack or the victim of a natural or man-made disaster. The Union shall mobilise all the instruments at its disposal, including the military resources made available by the Member States, to:
   (a) prevent the terrorist threat in the territory of the Member States;
      - protect democratic institutions and the civilian population from any terrorist attack;
      - assist a Member State in its territory, at the request of its political authorities, in the event of a terrorist attack;
   (b) assist a Member State in its territory, at the request of its political authorities, in the event of a natural or man-made disaster.
2. Should a Member State be the object of a terrorist attack or the victim of a natural or man-made disaster, the other Member States shall assist it at the request of its political authorities. To that end, the Member States shall coordinate between themselves in the Council.
3. The arrangements for the implementation by the Union of the solidarity clause shall be defined by a decision adopted by the Council acting on a joint proposal by the Commission and the High Representative of the Union for Foreign Affairs and Security Policy. The Council shall act in accordance with Article 31(1) of the Treaty on European Union where this decision has defence implications. The European Parliament shall be informed.

---

[4] Article 5 of the NATO Treaty reads: 'The Parties agree that an armed attack against one or more of them in Europe or North America shall be considered an attack against them all and consequently they agree that, if such an armed attack occurs, each of them, in exercise of the right of individual or collective self-defence recognised by Article 51 of the Charter of the United Nations, will assist the Party or Parties so attacked by taking forthwith, individually and in concert with the other Parties, such action as it deems necessary, including the use of armed force, to restore and maintain the security of the North Atlantic area.'

Compare also Article V of the former modified Brussels Treaty (WEU): 'If any of the High Contracting Parties should be the object of an armed attack in Europe, the other High Contracting Parties will, in accordance with the provisions of Article 51 of the Charter of the United Nations, afford the Party so attacked all the military and other aid and assistance in their power.'

[5] Brussels European Council 25–26 March 2004, Presidency Conclusions.

While the wording of the solidarity clause leaves room for both the Member States and the Council regarding the type and scope of their reaction, it may be seen as an innovation to the previous legal regime, where no obligations for the Member States or competences of the Council formed part of the Treaties.

(iii) The institutionalization of CSDP

As CSDP can be seen as forming part of CFSP, the decision-making takes place along similar lines. Decisions are taken by the Council.

Article 42(4) TEU

Decisions relating to the common security and defence policy, including those initiating a mission as referred to in this Article, shall be adopted by the Council acting unanimously on a proposal from the High Representative of the Union for Foreign Affairs and Security Policy or an initiative from a Member State. The High Representative may propose the use of both national resources and Union instruments, together with the Commission where appropriate.

Council Decision 2013/34/CFSP of 17 January 2013 on a European Union military mission to contribute to the training of the Malian Armed Forces (EUTM Mali), OJ 2013 No. L14/19

THE COUNCIL OF THE EUROPEAN UNION,

Having regard to the Treaty on European Union, and in particular Articles 42(4) and 43(2) thereof,

Having regard to the proposal from the High Representative of the Union for Foreign Affairs and Security Policy,

... HAS ADOPTED THIS DECISION:

Article 1 Mission

1. The Union shall conduct a military training mission (EUTM Mali), to provide, in the South of Mali, military and training advice to the Malian Armed Forces (MAF) operating under the control of legitimate civilian authorities, in order to contribute to the restoration of their military capacity with a view to enabling them to conduct military operations aiming at restoring Malian territorial integrity and reducing the threat posed by terrorist groups. EUTM Mali shall not be involved in combat operations.
2. The objective of EUTM Mali shall be to respond to the operational needs of the MAF through the provision of:
    (a) training support for the benefit of the MAF;
    (b) training and advice on command and control, logistical chain and human resources, as well as training on International Humanitarian Law, protection of civilians and human rights.
3. EUTM Mali shall aim at strengthening conditions for proper political control by legitimate civilian authorities of the MAF.
4. The activities of EUTM Mali shall be conducted in close coordination with other actors involved in the support to the MAF, in particular the United Nations (UN) and the Economic Community of West African States (ECOWAS). ....

Article 5 Political control and strategic direction

1. Under the responsibility of the Council and of the HR, the PSC shall exercise the political control and strategic direction of EUTM Mali. The Council hereby authorises the PSC to take the relevant decisions in accordance with Article 38 TEU. This authorisation shall include the powers to amend the planning documents, including the Mission Plan, and the Chain of Command. It shall also include the powers to take decisions on the appointment of the subsequent EU Mission Commanders. The powers of decision with respect to the objectives and termination of EUTM Mali shall remain vested in the Council.
2. The PSC shall report to the Council at regular intervals.
3. The PSC shall, at regular intervals, receive reports from the chairman of the EU Military Committee (EUMC) regarding the conduct of EUTM Mali. The PSC may invite the EU Mission Commander to its meetings, as appropriate.

Article 6 Military direction

1. The EUMC shall monitor the proper execution of EUTM Mali conducted under the responsibility of the EU Mission Commander.
2. The EUMC shall, at regular intervals, receive reports from the EU Mission Commander. It may invite the EU Mission Commander to its meetings, as appropriate.
3. The chairman of the EUMC shall act as the primary point of contact with the EU Mission Commander. ....

Article 12 Entry into force and termination

1. This Decision shall enter into force on the date of its adoption.
2. The mandate of EUTM Mali shall end 15 months after the adoption of the Council Decision to launch EUTM Mali.
3. This Decision shall be repealed as from the date of closure of the Mission Headquarters in accordance with the plans approved for the termination of EUTM Mali, and without prejudice to the procedures regarding the audit and presentation of the accounts of EUTM Mali, laid down in Decision 2011/871/CFSP.
   Done at Brussels, 17 January 2013.
   For the Council
   The President
   C. ASHTON

Both the HR and the Member States may take the initiative for a decision. A difference with CFSP is that the HR cannot work together with the Commission on an initiative, and neither is it possible to decide on the basis of QMV (not even in the case of implementing decisions). These rules underline the preference of most Member States to keep CSDP as intergovernmental as possible. Yet, the role of some organs no doubt points to a serious institutionalization of this policy area. Apart from the HR, which according to Article 43(2) 'shall ensure coordination of the civilian and military aspects of [the Petersberg] tasks', the PSC has been granted a pivotal role in CSDP. Irrespective of the fact that it is hardly mentioned in the CSDP section, the PSC has developed into the centre around which all CSDP actions converge.

A. E. Juncos and C. Reynolds, 'The Political and Security Committee: Governing in the Shadow' (2007) 12 *European Foreign Affairs Review* 127–147

In the event of . . . a crisis, the PSC constitutes the key strategic actor leading the formulation and implementation of a CSDP operation. According to the EU's crisis management procedures, all available information relating to the ongoing crisis should be forwarded to the PSC which will subsequently be convened in order to agree on a Crisis Management Concept. At this stage, coordination with the Member States, NATO, the Commission and other institutional actors such as the EU Military Committee is crucial. The PSC is also at the core of the process leading to the drafting of the relevant Decision, Concept of Operations and Operational Plan which together constitute the key documents guiding the implementation of the operation on the ground. Given the nature of crisis management, these phases often take place simultaneously. Once agreed at the PSC, these documents are forwarded to the Council essentially to be rubber-stamped since it is rare that the Council will reopen issues that have been already approved by the PSC.

The Decision will charge the PSC with the political control and strategic direction of the crisis management operation in question. Such control is exerted via a required six-monthly review process, with all actors involved reporting to the PSC on the operation's progress. The Commission and the High Representative, assisted by the EU Special Representative on the ground – if there is one present – also participate in this process. At the end of the operation's mandate the PSC will recommend to the Council its continuation, refocusing or termination. It ought to be noted, however, that ultimately the PSC's precise role in such operations remains dependent upon the amount and quality of information shared by the Member States via their representatives in the Committee or other EU-level institutions (mainly the Policy Unit and the Situation Centre).

Suffice to say, therefore, that the scale of the PSC's responsibility is potentially enormous and grows with the increasing outreach of the CSDP itself. Every new mission and new policy results in an increasing workload for the Committee and its extensive range of working groups. This has reached the point that, as one ambassador put it, "there is now no foreign policy topic that is not covered in the PSC".

*In this excerpt 'ESDP' was replaced by 'CSDP'

The institutionalization of CSDP included the creation of a number of specific organs, some of which do not have an explicit treaty basis. The European Council (Nice, December 2000) decided to establish permanent political and military structures. Apart from the PSC, which meets at the ambassadorial level as the preparatory body for the Council to keep track of the international situation, help to define policies within CFSP and CSDP and prepare a coherent EU response to a crisis, CSDP depends on a number of other organs.

The European Union Military Committee (EUMC) is the highest military body set up within the Council. It is composed of the Chiefs of Defence of the Member States, who are regularly represented by their permanent military representatives. The EUMC provides the PSC with advice and recommendations on all military matters within the EU.

In parallel with the EUMC, the PSC is advised by a Committee for Civilian Aspects of Crisis Management (CIVCOM). This committee provides information and drafts recommendations, and gives its opinion to the PSC on civilian aspects of crisis management.

The Crisis Management and Planning Directorate (CMPD) contributes to the objectives of the EEAS, the CSDP and a more secure international environment by the political-strategic planning of CSDP civilian missions and military operations, ensuring coherence and effectiveness of those actions as part of the EU comprehensive approach to crisis management, and developing CSDP partnerships, policies, concepts and capabilities.

The European Union Military Staff (EUMS) is part of the EEAS and composed of both military and civilian experts seconded to the EEAS by Member States and officials of the EEAS. The EUMS is the source of military expertise within the EEAS and works under the direction of the Military Committee and Member States' Chiefs of Defence, and under the direct authority of the HR/VP of the European Commission. The EUMS is an integral element of the EEAS Comprehensive Approach, coordinates military actions and focuses on operations and the creation of military capabilities. The EUMS ensures the availability of the military instrument with all its domains as one integrated organization. If called upon, the EUMS will support their civilian colleagues with their broad range of expertise, for example, planning, intelligence, medical, engineering, infrastructure, transport, communications, IT, education, exercises and lessons learnt. Added to this is the ability of the EUMS to act quickly as one integrated entity for the broad range of military options, including complex Combined Joint Operations.

The Civilian Planning and Conduct Capability (CPCC), which is also part of the EEAS, is the permanent structure responsible for an autonomous operational conduct of civilian CSDP operations. Under the political control and strategic direction of the PSC and the overall authority of the HR, the CPCC ensures the effective planning and conduct of civilian CSDP crisis management operations, as well as the proper implementation of all mission-related tasks.

Apart from these bodies, the Satellite Centre and the Institute for Security Studies (ISS) were transferred from the WEU to the EU by taking over the personnel contracts and the agreements with other organizations. The Satellite Centre (in Torrejón de Ardoz, Spain) supports CSDP by supplying satellite images; the ISS (in Paris) does academic research on topics relevant for the development of CSDP.

One body is explicitly mentioned in the Treaty, the European Defence Agency (EDA). Its role is defined as follows:

Article 42(3) TEU

The European Defence Agency shall identify operational requirements, shall promote measures to satisfy those requirements, shall contribute to identifying and, where appropriate, implementing any measure needed to strengthen the industrial and technological base of the defence sector, shall participate in defining a European capabilities and armaments policy, and shall assist the Council in evaluating the improvement of military capabilities.

It is further defined in Protocol 10 on permanent structured cooperation established by Article 42 TEU.

Article 3 Protocol 10, OJ 2010 No. C83/277

The European Defence Agency shall contribute to the regular assessment of participating Member States' contributions with regard to capabilities, in particular contributions made in accordance with the criteria to be established, *inter alia*, on the basis of Article 2, and shall report thereon at least once a year. The assessment may serve as a basis for Council recommendations and decisions adopted in accordance with Article 46 of the Treaty on European Union.

The EDA has thus been given a central role in defining and coordinating the available military capabilities.

Some of the shortcomings in early EU crisis management seemed to relate to the ad hoc implementation of CSDP (see below). The current regime aims to counter this with the introduction of some form of institutionalization of procedures, formats and (civil and military) capabilities. First of all, a new form of ad hoc flexibility is introduced:

Article 44(1) TEU

The Council may entrust the implementation of a task to a group of Member States which are willing and have the necessary capability for such a task. Those Member States, in association with the High Representative of the Union for Foreign Affairs and Security Policy, shall agree among themselves on the management of the task.

This allows the Union to implement CSDP by sub-contracting it to '*coalitions of the able and willing*'. An early example of this arrangement can be found in Operation Artemis, in which France took the initiative to form a group of EU Member States and other states to assist the UN operation MONUC in the Democratic Republic of Congo.

A second form of institutionalization may be found in relation to the notion of '*permanent structured cooperation*'.[6]

Article 42(6) TEU

Those Member States whose military capabilities fulfil higher criteria and which have made more binding commitments to one another in this area with a view to the most demanding missions shall establish permanent structured cooperation within the Union framework.

The permanent structured cooperation is further elaborated by Article 46 and by Protocol 10 (see above). According to this Protocol the permanent structured cooperation can be seen as an institutionalized form of cooperation in the field of defence policy between able and willing Member States. In that sense it may be regarded as a special form of enhanced cooperation, although the term is not used.

Article 1, Protocol 10, OJ 2010 No. C83/276

The permanent structured cooperation referred to in Article 42(6) of the Treaty on European Union shall be open to any Member State which undertakes, from the date of entry into force of the Treaty of Lisbon, to:

(a) proceed more intensively to develop its defence capacities through the development of its national contributions and participation, where appropriate, in multinational forces, in the main European

---

[6] S. Biscop, 'Permanent Structured Cooperation and the Future of the ESDP: Transformation and Integration' (2008) 13 *European Foreign Affairs Review*, 431–448.

equipment programmes, and in the activity of the Agency in the field of defence capabilities development, research, acquisition and armaments (European Defence Agency), and

(b) have the capacity to supply by 2010 at the latest, either at national level or as a component of multinational force groups, targeted combat units for the missions planned, structured at a tactical level as a battle group, with support elements including transport and logistics, capable of carrying out the tasks referred to in Article 43 of the Treaty on European Union, within a period of five to 30 days, in particular in response to requests from the United Nations Organisation, and which can be sustained for an initial period of 30 days and be extended up to at least 120 days.

Obviously, no reference is made to the creation of a 'European army'. Any explicit hints in that direction would have been unacceptable for certain Member States. Nevertheless, the tasks of the participating Member States come close to at least a harmonization of the different national defence policies. According to Article 2 of the Protocol on Permanent Structured Cooperation, Member States have accepted concrete assignments.

Article 2, Protocol 10, OJ 2010 No. C83/276

To achieve the objectives laid down in Article 1, Member States participating in permanent structured cooperation shall undertake to:

(a) cooperate, as from the entry into force of the Treaty of Lisbon, with a view to achieving approved objectives concerning the level of investment expenditure on defence equipment, and regularly review these objectives, in the light of the security environment and of the Union's international responsibilities;

(b) bring their defence apparatus into line with each other as far as possible, particularly by harmonising the identification of their military needs, by pooling and, where appropriate, specialising their defence means and capabilities, and by encouraging cooperation in the fields of training and logistics;

(c) take concrete measures to enhance the availability, interoperability, flexibility and deployability of their forces, in particular by identifying common objectives regarding the commitment of forces, including possibly reviewing their national decision-making procedures;

(d) work together to ensure that they take the necessary measures to make good, including through multinational approaches, and without prejudice to undertakings in this regard within the North Atlantic Treaty Organisation, the shortfalls perceived in the framework of the 'Capability Development Mechanism';

(e) take part, where appropriate, in the development of major joint or European equipment programmes in the framework of the European Defence Agency.

Moreover, the 'Headline Goal 2010' includes the establishment of so-called '*battlegroups*': 'force packages at high readiness as a response to a crisis either as a stand-alone force or as part of a larger operation enabling follow-on phases'.[7] On decision-making, the ambition of the EU is to be able to take the decision to launch an operation within five days of the approval of the so-called Crisis Management Concept by the Council. On the deployment of forces, the ambition is

---

[7] Headline Goal 210, approved by the General Affairs and External Relations (GAER) Council on 17 May 2004; endorsed by the European Council of 17 and 18 June 2004.

that the forces start implementing their mission on the ground, no later than ten days after the EU decision to launch the operation. In December 2008, the Council adopted a 'Declaration on Strengthening Capabilities' in which a number of additional measures were agreed on to ensure that the Union will have sufficient military and civilian capabilities to 'enhance its contribution to international peace and security'.[8] In practice all these efforts seem to come close to what could be called an 'army', irrespective of the fact that – for political reasons – the documents stressed that the concept would not amount to 'the creation of a European army'. Interestingly enough, this phrase did not return in the Lisbon Treaty.

> ### P. Koutrakos, *The EU Common Security and Defence Policy* (Oxford: Oxford University Press, 2013), pp. 101–102
>
> The existence of this dense institutionalized framework may give the impression that the Union has developed a fully operational structure within which the practicalities of every military mission would be addressed automatically as a matter of course. However, this is not the case. For instance, the EU has no permanent military headquarters where the conduct of the operation would be planned and monitored. Instead, every time the Union decides on a military mission, the choice of where the headquarters would be based is made on an ad hoc basis. In cases where the military mission is carried out with recourse to NATO capabilities, the operational headquarters of the mission are in the NATO Allied Command Operations, based in Mons, Belgium. If no NATO assets are relied upon, the choice is made among five locations offered by five Member States, namely the United Kingdom, Italy, France, Germany, and Greece. The State whose headquarters are chosen as the mission's Operational Headquarters becomes the Framework State for the mission. A third possibility has emerged recently and is an Operations centre based in Brussels, which may be activated following a Council Decision and in relation to a specific mission of a joint military and civil character. This Centre, which is envisaged to reach full capacity within twenty days and which would be staffed by EUMS personnel along with other staff from the EEAS has been activated once. While this has not been a permanent feature of CSDP practice so far, it is not inconceivable that reliance upon the centre might become more deeply entrenched.
>
> The establishment of permanent EU Operational Headquarters has been a thorny issue. It is viewed by many as necessary for both reflecting the prominence of CSDP in the Union's external action and facilitating the smooth conduct of missions. However, the establishment of such Headquarters in Brussels, where the main EU institutions are also based, has also been seen as indicative of integration in an area where Member States are not only keen to be in control, but are also just as keen to be seen to be in control. Yet again, it becomes clear that, in this sensitive field, semantics matter. Furthermore, the establishment of autonomous EU headquarters may be seen as antagonistic to, and potentially undermining, NATO.

(iv) CSDP Decisions and international agreements

In legal terms, CSDP takes shape in the form of Decisions and international agreements. As according to Article 42(1) TEU, 'The common security and defence policy shall be an integral part of the common foreign and security policy', most CFSP rules apply to CSDP as well, and Article 28 TEU can be used as a legal basis for CSDP Decisions.

---

[8] Declaration on Strengthening Capabilities, Brussels, 11 December 2008.

> **Article 28(1) TEU**
>
> Where the international situation requires operational action by the Union, the Council shall adopt the necessary decisions. They shall lay down their objectives, scope, the means to be made available to the Union, if necessary their duration, and the conditions for their implementation.

In addition, the adoption of CSDP Decisions is regulated in Articles 42(4) and 43(2) TEU, which serve as specific legal bases (see also the example below).

> **Article 42(4) TEU**
>
> Decisions relating to the common security and defence policy, including those initiating a mission as referred to in this Article, shall be adopted by the Council acting unanimously on a proposal from the High Representative of the Union for Foreign Affairs and Security Policy or an initiative from a Member State. The High Representative may propose the use of both national resources and Union instruments, together with the Commission where appropriate.

Article 43(2) underlines the role of the Council and points to a specific task of the HR.

> **Article 43(2) TEU**
>
> The Council shall adopt decisions ... defining their objectives and scope and the general conditions for their implementation. The High Representative of the Union for Foreign Affairs and Security Policy, acting under the authority of the Council and in close and constant contact with the Political and Security Committee, shall ensure coordination of the civilian and military aspects of such tasks.

As CSDP is part of CFSP, it is again clear that other EU legal instruments (Regulations, Directives) cannot be used for CSDP issues. Yet – as in CFSP – the legal nature of CSDP Decisions is beyond any doubt and all Decisions are published in the L (Legislation) version of the Official Journal.

> **Council Decision 2012/392/CFSP of 16 July 2012 on the European Union CSDP mission in Niger (EUCAP Sahel Niger), OJ 2012 No. L 187/48**
>
> THE COUNCIL OF THE EUROPEAN UNION,
>
> Having regard to the Treaty on European Union and in particular Article 28, Article 42(4) and Article 43(2) thereof,
>
> Having regard to the proposal from the High Representative of the Union for Foreign Affairs and Security Policy,
>
> Whereas:
>
> (1) On 21 March 2011, the Council welcomed the European Union Strategy for Security and Development in the Sahel, underlining that the Union has a longstanding interest in reducing insecurity and improving development in the Sahel region. More recently, the intensification of terrorist actions and the

consequences of the conflict in Libya have increased the urgency of protecting Union citizens and interests in the region and preventing the extension of those threats to the Union, while helping to reduce regional security threats.

(2) On 23 March 2012, the Council approved the Crisis Management Concept for a possible common security and defence policy (CSDP) civilian mission in the Sahel.

(3) On 1 June 2012, the Prime Minister of Niger addressed to the High Representative of the Union for Foreign Affairs and Security Policy (HR) an invitation letter with regard to the planned CSDP mission, welcoming the Union's CSDP deployment with the aim of reinforcing the capacities of the Nigerien Security Forces, in particular to fight terrorism and organised crime in an effective, coherent and coordinated manner.

(4) The Watch-Keeping Capability should be activated for EUCAP Sahel Niger.

(5) EUCAP Sahel Niger will be conducted in the context of a situation which may deteriorate and could impede the achievement of the objectives of the Union's external action as set out in Article 21 of the Treaty on European Union (TEU),

HAS ADOPTED THIS DECISION:

Article 1 Mission

The Union hereby establishes a European Union CSDP mission in Niger to support the capacity building of the Nigerien security actors to fight terrorism and organised crime (EUCAP Sahel Niger).

Article 2 Objectives

In the context of the implementation of the European Union Strategy for Security and Development in the Sahel, EUCAP Sahel Niger shall aim at enabling the Nigerien authorities to implement the security dimension of their own Strategy for Security and Development, as well as at improving regional coordination in tackling common security challenges. In particular, EUCAP SAHEL Niger shall aim at contributing to the development of an integrated, multidisciplinary, coherent, sustainable, and human rights-based approach among the various Nigerien security actors in the fight against terrorism and organised crime.

Article 3 Tasks

1. In order to fulfil the objectives set out in Article 2, EUCAP Sahel Niger shall:
   (a) advise and assist in the implementation of the security dimension of the Nigerien Strategy for Security and Development at national level, complementary to other actors,
   (b) support the development of comprehensive regional and international coordination in the fight against terrorism and organised crime,
   (c) strengthen the rule of law through the development of the criminal investigation capacities, and in this context develop and implement adequate training programmes,
   (d) support the development of Nigerien Security Forces' sustainability,
   (e) contribute to the identification, planning and implementation of projects in the security field.
2. EUCAP Sahel Niger shall initially focus on the activities mentioned in paragraph 1 which contribute to improving the control of the territory of Niger, including in coordination with the Nigerien Armed Forces.
3. EUCAP Sahel Niger shall not carry out any executive function. . . .

Article 9 Political control and strategic direction

1. The PSC shall exercise, under the responsibility of the Council and of the HR, political control and strategic direction of EUCAP Sahel Niger. The Council hereby authorises the PSC to take the relevant decisions in accordance with the third paragraph of Article 38 TEU. This authorisation shall include the powers to appoint a Head of Mission, upon a proposal of the HR, and to amend the Concept of Operations Plus (CONOPS Plus) and the Operation Plan (OPLAN). The powers of decision with respect to the objectives and termination of the EUCAP Sahel Niger shall remain vested in the Council.
2. The PSC shall report to the Council at regular intervals.
3. The PSC shall receive, on a regular basis and as required, reports by the Civilian Operation Commander and the Head of Mission on issues within their areas of responsibility.

Article 10 Participation of third States

1. Without prejudice to the decision-making autonomy of the Union and its single institutional framework, third States may be invited to contribute to EUCAP Sahel Niger, provided that they bear the cost of the staff seconded by them, including salaries, all risk insurance cover, daily subsistence allowances and travel expenses to and from Niger, and that they contribute to the running costs of EUCAP Sahel Niger, as appropriate.
2. Third States contributing to EUCAP Sahel Niger shall have the same rights and obligations in terms of the day-to-day management of EUCAP Sahel Niger as Member States.
3. The Council hereby authorises the PSC to take the relevant decisions on acceptance of the proposed contributions and to establish a Committee of Contributors.
4. Detailed arrangements regarding the participation of third States shall be covered by agreements concluded in accordance with Article 37 TEU and additional technical arrangements as necessary. Where the Union and a third State conclude or have concluded an agreement establishing a framework for the participation of that third State in Union crisis-management operations, the provisions of that agreement shall apply in the context of EUCAP Sahel Niger. . . .

Article 13 Financial arrangements

1. The financial reference amount intended to cover the expenditure related to EUCAP Sahel Niger for the first 12 months shall be EUR 8700000. The financial reference amount for the subsequent periods shall be decided by the Council.
2. All expenditure shall be managed in accordance with the rules and procedures applicable to the general budget of the Union.
3. Nationals of participating third States and of host and neighbouring countries shall be allowed to tender for contracts. Subject to the Commission's approval, the Head of Mission may conclude technical arrangements with Member States, participating third States, and other international actors regarding the provision of equipment, services and premises to EUCAP Sahel Niger.
4. The financial arrangements shall respect the operational requirements of EUCAP Sahel Niger including compatibility of equipment and interoperability of its teams.
5. The Head of Mission shall report fully to, and be supervised by, the Commission on the activities undertaken in the framework of his/her contract.
6. The expenditure related to EUCAP Sahel Niger shall be eligible as of the date of adoption of this Decision.

Article 14 Consistency of the Union's response and coordination

1. The HR shall ensure the consistency of the implementation of this Decision with the Union's external action as a whole, including the Union's development programmes.

2. Without prejudice to the chain of command, the Head of Mission shall act in close coordination with the Union's delegation in Niamey to ensure the consistency of Union action in Niger.

3. The Head of Mission shall coordinate closely with Member States' Heads of Missions present in Niger. . . .

Article 16 Entry into force and duration

This Decision shall enter into force on the day of its adoption.

It shall apply for a period of 24 months.

Done at Brussels, 16 July 2012.

For the Council

The President

S. Aletraris

As underlined by this Decision as well, the PSC is usually given a key role and is authorized by the Council to 'take the relevant decisions in accordance with the third paragraph of Article 38 TEU'. Indeed, many (subsequent) CSDP Decisions are therefore not taken by the Council itself, but by the PSC.

Political and Security Committee Decision EUPOL AFGHANISTAN/1/2012 (2012/456/CFSP) of 10 July 2012 on the appointment of the Head of Mission of the European Union Police Mission in Afghanistan (EUPOL AFGHANISTAN), OJ 2012 No. L208/17

THE POLITICAL AND SECURITY COMMITTEE,

Having regard to the Treaty on European Union, and in particular the third paragraph of Article 38 thereof,

Having regard to Council Decision 2010/279/CFSP of 18 May 2010 on the European Union Police Mission in Afghanistan (EUPOL AFGHANISTAN) [1] and in particular Article 10(1) thereof,

Whereas:

(1) Pursuant to Article 10(1) of Decision 2010/279/CFSP, the Council authorised the Political and Security Committee, in accordance with Article 38 of the Treaty, to take the relevant decisions for the purpose of political control and strategic direction of the EUPOL AFGHANISTAN mission, including the decision to appoint a Head of Mission.

(2) The High Representative of the Union for Foreign Affairs and Security Policy has proposed the appointment of Mr Karl Åke ROGHE as Head of Mission from 1 August 2012,

HAS ADOPTED THIS DECISION:

Article 1

Mr Karl Åke ROGHE is hereby appointed Head of the European Union Police Mission in Afghanistan as from 1 August 2012 until 31 May 2013.

Article 2

This Decision shall enter into force on the date of its adoption.

Done at Brussels, 10 July 2012.

For the Political and Security Committee

The Chairperson

O. Skoog

As CSDP is mainly intended to establish missions outside the EU, many Decisions have the purpose of adopting international agreements. For the agreements the usual procedures apply (see Chapter 2), which implies that not only does Article 37 TEU serve as the general legal basis, but also that the procedure in Article 218 TFEU applies to the negotiation and conclusion of the agreements. In the case of CSDP agreements, the general rule is to be followed:

Article 218(3) TFEU

The Commission, or the High Representative of the Union for Foreign Affairs and Security Policy where the agreement envisaged relates exclusively or principally to the common foreign and security policy, shall submit recommendations to the Council, which shall adopt a decision authorising the opening of negotiations and, depending on the subject of the agreement envisaged, nominating the Union negotiator or the head of the Union's negotiating team.

Although it may not always be easy to establish whether an agreement 'relates exclusively or principally to the common foreign and security policy' (see also Chapters 5 and 11 on the *ECOWAS* case), most CSDP agreements fall in this category, which implies that they are to be negotiated by the HR.

CSDP agreements are concluded for different purposes. Most agreements concern the *participation of third states in CSDP operations*. These agreements not only regulate the legal issues surrounding the participation of non-EU members, but at the same time ensure the autonomy of the Union's decision-making. Thus, irrespective of the participation of third states (ranging from Switzerland to New Zealand and the USA) the operation remains a true EU mission which is covered by the EU legal order and follows the specific CSDP procedures. With a limited number of third states (currently Ukraine, Canada, Bulgaria, Iceland, Norway, Romania, Turkey, Montenegro, the USA, Serbia, New Zealand and Albania), so-called Framework Participation Agreements have been concluded. These agreements facilitate the participation of those states in operations to which they are invited.

A second category concerns the Status of Forces Agreements (SOFAs) and Status of Missions Agreements (SOMAs). The Agreements regulate the legal rights and duties of the forces/missions and their personnel in the third country where the operation is established. On the basis of these Agreements the CSDP mission enjoys the status of a diplomatic mission under the 1961 Vienna Convention on Diplomatic Relations, and privileges and immunities of personnel are usually regulated in detail.

A. Sari, 'Status of Forces and Status of Mission Agreements under the ESDP: The EU's Evolving Practice' (2008) 19 *European Journal of International Law* 67–100

Even though no single legal regime governing the status of visiting forces and missions has developed in international law, several distinct regimes can nevertheless be identified. For instance, SOFAs concluded in the context of structured military cooperation between politically equal partners are frequently based on the NATO SOFA of 1951. The Member States of the EU have thus modelled the EU SOFA of 2003, which governs the legal position of their military and civilian staff deployed within the territory of the EU for the purposes of the CSDP, on the relevant provisions of the NATO SOFA. The UN and other international actors have also developed distinct arrangements regulating the immunities and privileges of peace support operations. Generally speaking, these legal regimes offer different answers to the same basic question: how to reconcile the divergent interests of the sending State or organization on the one hand and those of the host State on the other hand, in particular as regards the exercise of jurisdiction in the territory of the host State over the visiting force or mission and its members. . . .

The EU's practice in negotiating status agreements with third parties has evolved along two main lines over the past fifteen years. First, the status agreements concluded by the EU have become increasingly more sophisticated. The most recent agreements regulate a broader range of matters and do so in greater detail than most of their predecessors, including the first CSDP status agreement, the EUPM SOMA, did. Second, the process of concluding status agreements under the CSDP has been simplified. The experiences gained during the first few CSDP missions have clearly demonstrated that the procedures governing the conclusion of international agreements under [the former] Article 24 TEU were unwieldy and therefore unsuited for keeping up with the fast pace of international crisis management operations. In response, the Council adopted the EU Model SOFA and SOMA to eliminate the need to issue a fresh negotiating mandate to the Presidency in the course of future EU crisis management operations.

*ESDP has been replaced by CSDP.

Agreement between the European Union and the Republic of Mali on the status in the Republic of Mali of the European Union military mission to contribute to the training of the Malian Armed Forces (EUTM Mali), OJ 2013 No. 106/2

THE EUROPEAN UNION, hereinafter referred to as 'the EU',
of the one part, and
THE REPUBLIC OF MALI, hereinafter referred to as 'the Host State',
of the other part,
hereinafter referred to as 'the Parties', . . .
HAVE AGREED AS FOLLOWS: . . .

Article 2 General provisions

1. EUTM Mali and EUTM Mali personnel shall respect the laws and regulations of the Host State and shall refrain from any action or activity incompatible with the objectives of the mission.
2. EUTM Mali shall regularly inform the Government of the Host State of the number of members of EUTM Mali personnel stationed within the Host State's territory.

Article 3 Identification

1. EUTM Mali personnel present in the territory of the Host State shall carry passports or military identity cards with them at all times.
2. EUTM Mali vehicles and other means of transport shall carry distinctive EUTM Mali identification markings and/or registration plates, of which the relevant Host State authorities shall be notified.
3. EUTM Mali shall have the right to display the flag of the European Union and markings such as military insignia, titles and official symbols on its facilities and means of transport. The uniforms of EUTM Mali personnel shall carry a distinctive EUTM Mali emblem. National flags or insignia of the constituent national contingents of the mission may be displayed on EUTM Mali facilities and means of transport, and uniforms, as decided by the Mission Commander.

Article 4 Border crossing and movement within the Host State's territory

1. EUTM Mali personnel shall enter the Host State's territory only on presentation of a passport accompanied by an individual or collective movement order issued by EUTM Mali. They shall be exempt from visa regulations, immigration inspections and customs control on entering, leaving or within the Host State's territory.
2. EUTM Mali personnel shall be exempt from the Host State's regulations on the registration and control of aliens, but shall not acquire any right to permanent residence or domicile in the territory of the Host State.
3. EUTM Mali assets and means of transport entering or leaving the territory of the Host State in support of the mission shall be exempt from any requirement to produce any customs documentation and from any inspection.
4. EUTM Mali personnel may drive motor vehicles provided they hold a valid national, international or military driving licence issued by a Sending State.
5. For the purposes of the mission, the Host State shall grant EUTM Mali and EUTM Mali personnel freedom of movement and freedom to travel within its territory, including its air space.
6. The Host State shall permit the entry of EUTM Mali assets and means of transport and grant them exemption from all custom duties, fees, tolls, taxes and similar charges other than charges for storage, cartage and other services rendered.
7. For the purposes of the mission, EUTM Mali may use public roads, bridges, ferries and airports without the payment of duties, fees, tolls, taxes and similar charges. EUTM Mali shall not be exempt from charges for services requested and received, under the conditions that apply to those provided to the Host State's armed forces.

Article 5 Privileges and immunities of EUTM Mali granted by the Host State

1. EUTM Mali's facilities shall be inviolable. The Host State's agents shall not enter them without the consent of the commander of the mission.
2. EUTM Mali, wherever located and by whomsoever its assets, means of transport and facilities are held or occupied, shall enjoy immunity from every form of legal process.
3. EUTM Mali personnel, assets, facilities and means of transport shall be immune from search, requisition, attachment or execution.
4. EUTM Mali's archives and documents shall be inviolable at any time, wherever they may be.
5. EUTM Mali's official correspondence shall be inviolable.
6. EUTM Mali shall be exempt from all national, regional and communal dues, taxes and charges of similar nature in respect of purchased and imported EUTM Mali assets and means of transport, EUTM Mali facilities, and services provided for the purposes of EUTM Mali. The application of this exemption may not be made subject to any authorisation or prior notification by EUTM Mali of the competent authorities of the Host State. However, EUTM Mali shall not be exempt from fees or other charges that represent payment for services rendered.

Article 6 Privileges and immunities of EUTM Mali personnel granted by the Host State

1. EUTM Mali personnel shall not be liable to any form of arrest or detention.
2. The papers, correspondence and property of EUTM Mali personnel shall be inviolable, except in case of measures of execution which are permitted pursuant to paragraph 6.
3. EUTM Mali personnel shall enjoy immunity from criminal proceedings in the Host State under all circumstances.

The immunity from criminal proceedings of EUTM Mali personnel may be waived by the Sending State or the EU body concerned, as the case may be. Such waiver shall always be in writing.

4. EUTM Mali personnel shall enjoy immunity from the civil and administrative proceedings in the Host State in respect of words spoken or written and all acts performed by them in the exercise of their official functions.

   If any civil proceedings are instituted against EUTM Mali personnel before any Host State court, the Mission Commander and the competent authority of the Sending State or the EU body concerned shall be notified immediately. Prior to initiation of proceedings before the competent court, the Mission Commander and the competent authority of the Sending State or the EU institution concerned shall certify to the court whether the act in question was performed by EUTM Mali personnel in the exercise of their official functions.

   If the act was performed in the exercise of official functions, proceedings shall not be initiated and the provisions of Article 15 shall apply. If the act was not committed in the exercise of official functions, proceedings may continue. The certification issued by the commander of the mission and the competent authority of the Sending State or the EU body concerned shall be binding upon the court of the Host State, which may not contest it.

   However, the competent authorities of the Host State may challenge the merits of that certification within a period of two months from its date of issue. In such a case, each of the Parties shall commit to resolving the dispute exclusively by diplomatic means.

   The initiation of civil proceedings by EUTM Mali personnel shall preclude them from invoking immunity from jurisdiction in respect of any counter-claim directly connected with the principal claim.

5. EUTM Mali personnel shall not be obliged to give evidence as witnesses.

6. No measures of execution may be taken in respect of EUTM Mali personnel, except in cases where civil proceedings not related to their official functions are instituted against them. The property of EUTM Mali personnel, certified by the Mission Commander to be necessary for the fulfilment of their official functions, shall be free from seizure for the satisfaction of a judgment, decision or order. In civil proceedings, EUTM Mali personnel shall not be subject to any restrictions on their personal liberty or to any other measures of constraint.

7. The immunity of EUTM Mali personnel from jurisdiction in the Host State does not exempt them from jurisdiction in the respective Sending States.

8. EUTM Mali personnel shall be exempt from any form of taxation in the Host State on the salary and emoluments paid to them by EUTM Mali or the Sending States, as well as on any income received from outside the Host State.

9. The Host State shall, in accordance with such laws and regulations as it may adopt, authorise entry of articles for the personal use of EUTM Mali personnel and grant exemption on such articles from all customs duties, taxes and related charges other than charges for storage, cartage and similar services.

The personal baggage of EUTM Mali personnel shall be exempt from inspection, unless there are serious grounds for presuming that it contains articles that are not for the personal use of EUTM Mali personnel, or articles the import or export of which is prohibited by the law or controlled by the quarantine regulations of the Host State. Such inspection shall be conducted only in the presence of the EUTM Mali personnel concerned or of an authorised representative of EUTM Mali. . . .

Done at Bamako on the fourth day of April in the year two thousand and thirteen, in two originals in the French language.

For the European Union

For the Republic of Mali

A specific set of agreements deals with *security procedures for the exchange of information*. Obviously, EU operations depend on classified information which needs to be secured once it is shared with third states.

Finally, in the context of Operation Atalanta in the Somalian waters, a new category of CSDP international agreements emerged: *transfer agreements*. Currently, transfer agreements have been concluded with Kenya, the Seychelles and Mauritius (negotiations with Tanzania being in progress). The agreements are meant to lay down the conditions of transfer of suspected pirates and associated seized property from the EU force to the partner country as well as the treatment of the suspects.

L. McGivern, 'Has Operation Atalanta Changed Global Perceptions of the EU as a Military Force?' (Unpublished paper, 2010)

Despite critical voices that can be heard to claim that Atalanta plays only a 'limited deterrence role', as the number of actually attempted acts of piracy rose from 2009 to 2010, the EUNAVFOR operation on the Gulf of Aden and the Indian Ocean has been generally acknowledged as a successful contribution. The requests from independent state navies to work alongside Operation Atalanta show that they now consider the EU, acting as a unitary force, as an equal partner and a significant power in the region. Using EUNAVFOR as an example, Commander Lintern of the (British) Royal Navy described the 'surprising and welcome change in emphasis on how the EU uses military force.' This successful example of ESDP/CSDP cooperation sends a message to the world that Europe's conception of its own military force and power has changed. As Daniel Korski notes, the rapid development of cooperation between EU states, most recently as part of Operation Atalanta, show that 'the EU now has a key role in European security', and consequently in the European use of military force.

---

4 THE SUDDEN EMERGENCE OF CSDP

The above analysis reflects a strong and key policy area in the Union's external relations. Given the extensive institutionalization it is hardly imaginable that CSDP is one of the youngest policy areas of the EU. Before we turn to the establishment of CSDP missions and operations, we take a short step back in explaining the development of CSDP (see the history of CFSP in Chapter 11).

M. Trybus, 'The Vision of the European Defence Community and a Common Defence for the European Union', in M. Trybus and N. D. White (eds.), *European Security Law* (Oxford: Oxford University Press, 2007), pp. 13–42

European integration is a reaction to World War II. The war had resulted in more than 40 million dead Europeans, a largely destroyed infrastructure in many countries, and a political landscape dominated by the Soviet threat. This experience taught the European leaders a lesson: a new approach to European relations had to be developed to overcome the traditional antagonisms which had led to so much hardship and destruction.

[After the Schuman Declaration] the next step for integration directly concerned the sensitive defence area: the establishment of a more supranational EDC with the participation of the six ECSC

Member States. The EDC envisaged nothing less than the merger of the armed forces of the Member States into European Defence Forces (EDF), including newly-created German divisions. These forces were to be organized and supervised by a supranational EDC administration answerable to a European Assembly. . . .

There are arguments for a more supranational European defence organization. The preamble of the EDC Treaty calls this 'speed and efficiency' to attain the objectives of the Community. A supranational organization with its independent institutions which can take binding decisions, if necessary against the will of individual Member States, can achieve cohesion between the combined military efforts of its Member States. It is this cohesion which represents the added value of such an organization. Instead of six small or medium-size military efforts there is one combined organization and army. . . .

This general approach followed the example of the ECSC. Supranationality also featuring prominently in the preamble to the Treaty, was the most controversial aspect of the EDC and ultimately the reason for the failure of the project. At a conference in Brussels in August 1954, as few weeks before the French Parliament rejected ratification, the French Government under Prime Minister Pierre Mendès-France put forward proposals that essentially undermined the supranational character of the EDC.

After fifty years of regular attempts by some Member States to extend the scope of the European Community/Union to issues of military security and defence, we were witnessing a final breakthrough at the turning of the millennium. Since the end of 1998 the EU has been actively developing a European Security and Defence Policy (ESDP). The 1992 TEU was an important first phase in this ongoing quest to consolidate Western European defence cooperation. A closer defence cooperation was planned in the original version of this Treaty, albeit that its Article J.4 clearly reflected the compromise, as it referred extremely carefully to 'the eventual framing of a common defence policy, which might in time lead to a common defence'. Another international organization, the WEU, would be requested to 'elaborate and implement decisions and actions of the Union which have defence implications'. Indeed, in realizing that it is increasingly difficult to exclude completely decisions on defence issues from the decision-making in the EU, their transfer to the WEU, which was said to form 'an integral part of the development of the Union' (Article J.4(2) of the TEU-Maastricht), seemed to be a workable compromise.[9] A procedure concerning defence issues found its basis in the same article: '[t]he Union requests the Western European Union (WEU) . . . to elaborate and implement decisions and actions of the Union which have defence implications'.[10] Thus a compromise was reached between Member States pointing to the link between a 'security policy' and 'defence issues' and those who would not accept the EU itself being involved in defence issues.

---

[9] The complex formula in Article J.4, para 1 was proposed by the Belgian delegation in order to reconcile the opinions of those who were in favour of a common defence (France in particular) and those who considered a common defence policy already a step too far (the United Kingdom in particular); see E. Remacle, 'La Politique Étrangère et de Sécurité Commune de l'Union Européenne après Maastricht', in M. Telò (ed.), *Vers une Nouvelle Europe?* (Brussels: Editions de l'Université de Bruxelles, 1992), pp. 239–252 at 242.

[10] The Luxembourg Draft Treaty of 18 June 1991 provided in Article L of the CFSP provisions that 'Decisions of the Union on security matters which have defence implications may be wholly or partly implemented in the framework of the Western European Union, insofar as they also fall within that organisation's sphere of competence'. Although this provision boils down to the same idea, the final choice in the 1992 Union Treaty for a formal 'request' to the WEU was certainly more correct from a legal point of view. After all, the decision to implement decisions of the EU is up to the WEU and not to the EU.

The Treaty of Amsterdam of 2 October 1997 (entry into force on 1 May 1999) purported to modify both the Community Treaties and the 1992 TEU. The CFSP provisions were renumbered from Articles J–J.11 to Articles 11–28. Article J.4 was replaced by Article 17, which almost entirely repeated the original provision, but modified the possibility of a request. The Union would no longer merely *request* the WEU to implement its defence decisions; instead Article 17 provided that '[t]he Union *will avail itself of WEU* to elaborate and implement decisions and actions of the Union which have defence implications'.[11] This change was made possible due to a positive reaction by WEU on the provision in the 1992 Treaty. The Treaty revealed no obligation for the WEU to react positively to a request by the Union, but in a Declaration attached to the TEU, the WEU Member States declared: 'The objective is to build up WEU in stages as the defence component of the European Union. To this end, WEU is prepared, at the request of the European Union, to elaborate and implement decisions and actions of the Union which have defence implications.'[12]

On the basis of this provision, one could easily be led to believe that we would never witness the creation of a European Security and Defence Policy. Nevertheless, even this carefully phrased compromise obviously helped recalcitrant Member States (the UK in particular) to get used to the idea of a future role for the EU in this area. The 1997 Amsterdam Treaty took another subtle step forward by formulating a common defence policy as an *objective* of the EU, rather than a mere *possibility*. Thus, the question was not how long this situation would last, but rather how the triangular relationship between the EU, the WEU and NATO could be shaped in such a way as to allow for the Union to put some flesh on the bones of the still rather skinny CFSP, which indeed had remained largely rhetoric in nature. The breakthrough at the end of 1998 therefore came as a surprise to many observers and completely changed the institutional agenda in the years that followed. It also paved the way to yet another modification of Article 17 of the EU Treaty, which became effective on 1 February 2003, with the entry into force of the Treaty of Nice. On the basis of that Treaty, Article 17 TEU was modified with the effect that all references to the WEU were deleted. This implied that the Union had been given the competence to operate within the full range of the so-called 'Petersberg tasks', that were originally in the hand of the WEU: 'humanitarian and rescue tasks, peacekeeping tasks and tasks of combat forces in crisis management, including peacemaking' (Article 17(2) TEU-Lisbon). Yet, Article 17 still referred to the 'progressive framing of a common defence policy' after that same policy had entered into force on the basis of the same article. Provisions like these reveal the fact that, although a final consensus was reached on a 'European Security and Defence Policy', some Member States are more eager to lay everything down in treaty arrangements than others. Nevertheless one cannot overlook the gradual development from the first provision in the Maastricht Treaty ('the *eventual* framing of a common defence policy, which *might in time* lead to a common defence'), to the Amsterdam Treaty ('the *progressive* framing of a common defence policy, which *might* lead to a common defence'),[13] and finally to Nice where all references to the WEU were deleted, thereby making the EU itself responsible for the elaboration and implementation of decisions and actions which have defence implications.

---

[11] Emphasis added.

[12] A. Bloed and R. A. Wessel (eds.), *The Changing Functions of the Western European Union (WEU): Introduction and Basic Documents* (Dordrecht: Martinus Nijhoff Publishers, 1994), document no. 28.

[13] Emphasis added.

Taking this struggle into account, the current developments are truly historic. Indeed, for the development of a common security and defence policy, the first decade of the new millennium meant more than the fifty years that preceded it. In a political sense, the most important development was the change in the traditional British attitude concerning an intensification of European defence cooperation. While military units of the ten WEU Member States, all also EU Member States, conducted operations in the Adriatic and on the Danube, they did not do so in support of the EU. The only official request of the EU in the first half of the 1990s to make use of WEU capabilities concerned the support for the EU administration of the Bosnian town of Mostar (1994). Unfortunately, this operation was generally perceived a failure, especially by the parties to the conflict.[14] With the crises in Albania (1997) and Kosovo (1999), the EU was further embarrassed at how little it could contribute to the 'management' of crises at its doorstep.

At the end of 1998 the British and French governments met in Saint-Malo (Bretagne, France) and issued a statement that heralded the birth of CSDP.

Franco–British Summit, Joint Declaration on European Defence, Saint-Malo, 4 December 1998

The Heads of State and Government of France and the United Kingdom agreed that:

1. The European Union needs to be in a position to play its full role on the international stage. This means making a reality of the Treaty of Amsterdam, which will provide the essential basis for action by the Union. It will be important to achieve full and rapid implementation of the Amsterdam provisions on CFSP. This includes the responsibility of the European Council to decide on the progressive framing of a common defence policy in the framework of CFSP. The Council must be able to take decisions on an intergovernmental basis, covering the whole range of activity set out in Title V of the Treaty of European Union.

2. To this end, the Union must have the capacity for autonomous action, backed up by credible military forces, the means to decide to use them and a readiness to do so, in order to respond to international crises.

   In pursuing our objective, the collective defence commitments to which member states subscribe (set out in Article 5 of the Washington Treaty, Article V of the Brussels Treaty) must be maintained. In strengthening the solidarity between the member states of the European Union, in order that Europe can make its voice heard in world affairs, while acting in conformity with our respective obligations in NATO, we are contributing to the vitality of a modernised Atlantic Alliance which is the foundation of the collective defence of its members.

   Europeans will operate within the institutional framework of the European Union (European Council, General Affairs Council and meetings of Defence Ministers).

   The reinforcement of European solidarity must take into account the various positions of European states. The different situations of countries in relation to NATO must be respected.

3. In order for the European Union to take decisions and approve military action where the Alliance as a whole is not engaged, the Union must be given appropriate structures and a capacity for analysis of situations, sources of intelligence and a capability for relevant strategic planning, without unnecessary duplication, taking account of the existing assets of the WEU and the evolution of its relations with the EU.

---

[14] W. van Eekelen and S. Blockmans, 'European Crisis Management *avant la lettre*', in Blockmans (ed.), *The European Union and Crisis Management: Policy and Legal Aspects* (The Hague: T.M.C. Asser Press, 2008), pp. 37–52 at 45.

In this regard, the European Union will also need to have recourse to suitable military means (European capabilities pre-designated within NATO's European pillar or national or multinational European means outside the NATO framework).

4. Europe needs strengthened armed forces that can react rapidly to the new risks, and which are supported by a strong and competitive European defence industry and technology.

5. We are determined to unite in our efforts to enable the European Union to give concrete expression to these objectives.

'The capacity for autonomous action, backed up by credible military forces, the means to decide to use them and a readiness to do so, in order to respond to international crises.' This simple sentence – which according to political commentators inter alia finds its basis in Britain's wish to take the lead in a major European development as well as in the possibility to 'sell' Europe back home – triggered a number of subsequent decisions by the EU. The Saint-Malo Declaration was followed by a number of decisions of the European Council in Cologne on 3 and 4 June 1999 concerning the strengthening of the common European policy regarding security and defence. The European Council decided to establish an autonomous operational capacity supported by credible means and decision-making institutions. It was furthermore decided that the Council would be given the competence to use military instruments alongside the already existing political and economic ones. The Declaration further referred to a number of WEU institutions that would also be needed in the EU (a Military Committee, a Military Staff, a Satellite Centre and an ISS). This Declaration set in motion a new development during which the EU gradually established new institutions at the expense of the WEU, which was stripped of almost its entire institutional infrastructure.

In November 1999 the WEU Council demonstrated that it would accept its fate and decided to 'prepare the WEU legacy and the inclusion of those functions of the WEU, which will be deemed necessary by the EU to fulfil its new responsibilities in the area of crisis management tasks'.[15] On 15 November 1999, for the first time in its history, the Council of the European Union met informally in the composition of Ministers for Foreign Affairs and Ministers of Defence.[16] While this may seem a logical step in the current developments, it highlights the revolution that has taken place within the EU. Previously, meetings of defence ministers were unthinkable within the EU framework. During this meeting France and the UK launched their plan for a rapid reaction force, an idea that was adopted by the European Council in Helsinki in December 1999 when it decided to develop an autonomous military capacity.[17] Probably to reassure (the parliaments of) certain Member States, the somewhat ambiguous sentence was added that this does not imply the creation of a European army. Nevertheless, all developments pointed in the direction of a sincere attempt on the part of the EU to create a military force. The European Council formulated a 'headline goal' and decided that by 2003, Member States must be able to develop rapidly and then sustain forces 'capable of the full range of Petersberg tasks, including the most demanding, in operations up to corps level; up to 15 brigades, or 50,000–60,000 persons'. These forces should be self-sustaining with the necessary

---

[15] WEU Ministerial Council, Luxembourg Declaration, 23 November 1999, para 4.

[16] Conclusions of the General Affairs Council of 15 November 1999, Council Press Release No. 12642/99 (*Presse* 344). The first formal meeting of the Defence Ministers took place in May 2002; see Conclusions of the General Affairs Council, 13–14 May 2002.

[17] European Council, Conclusions of the Presidency, Helsinki, 10–11 December 1999.

command and control and intelligence capabilities, logistics, and other combat support services and, additionally, appropriate naval and air elements. The readiness requirement is sixty days, with some units at very high readiness, capable of deployment within days or weeks.

The Nice IGC did reach an agreement on 'the progressive framing of a common defence policy', but Article 17 continued to refer to a 'common defence' as a future possibility. At the same time, all references to the WEU as the 'defence arm' of the EU were deleted. This meant that the WEU essentially returned to the organization that was originally set up to deal with collective defence matters between the Benelux countries and the United Kingdom and France in 1948: the Brussels Treaty Organization. The states party to the Modified Treaty of Brussels decided to terminate that Treaty on 31 March 2010, and the WEU finally ceased to exist as a treaty-based international organization on 30 June 2011.

As far as the EU is concerned, the story has not ended. The EU has worked hard to close the infamous 'capabilities–expectations gap' in the field of the CSDP.[18] In subsequent steps, the European Council agreed to the institution of new political and military bodies, structures and procedures to ensure political guidance and strategic direction; the principles for consultation and cooperation with non-European allies and the UN, NATO and other international organizations; measures to enhance the Union's military and civilian capabilities and timetables for carrying forward work in both domains; and the adoption of an *acquis sécuritaire*,[19] including an ESS, the EU's first comprehensive approach to security issues. Thus, in a very short time frame, the EU has developed what was needed to create an ability of its own to undertake the full range of the so-called 'Petersberg tasks', as incorporated in Article 43(1) TEU (see also above).

Article 43(1) TEU

The tasks . . . in the course of which the Union may use civilian and military means, shall include joint disarmament operations, humanitarian and rescue tasks, military advice and assistance tasks, conflict prevention and peace-keeping tasks, tasks of combat forces in crisis management, including peace-making and post-conflict stabilisation. All these tasks may contribute to the fight against terrorism, including by supporting third countries in combating terrorism in their territories.

A secure Europe in a better world, European Security Strategy, Brussels, 12 December 2003

Europe has never been so prosperous, so secure nor so free. The violence of the first half of the 20th Century has given way to a period of peace and stability unprecedented in European history.

The creation of the European Union has been central to this development. It has transformed the relations between our states, and the lives of our citizens. European countries are committed to dealing peacefully with disputes and to co-operating through common institutions. Over this period, the progressive spread of the rule of law and democracy has seen authoritarian regimes change into secure, stable and dynamic democracies. Successive enlargements are making a reality of the vision of a united and peaceful continent.

---

[18] See C. Hill, 'The Capability–Expectations Gap, or Conceptualising Europe's International Role' (1993) 31 *Journal of Common Market Studies* 305–328; and Hill, 'Closing the Capabilities–Expectations Gap?', in J. Peterson and H. Sjursen (eds.), *A Common Foreign Policy for Europe: Competing Visions of the CFSP* (London: Routledge, 1998), pp. 18–38.

[19] See C. Glière, *EU Security and Defence: Core Documents 2007 (Vol. VIII)* (Paris: EUISS, Chaillot Paper No. 112, 2008).

The United States has played a critical role in European integration and European security, in particular through NATO. The end of the Cold War has left the United States in a dominant position as a military actor. However, no single country is able to tackle today's complex problems on its own.

Europe still faces security threats and challenges. The outbreak of conflict in the Balkans was a reminder that war has not disappeared from our continent. Over the last decade, no region of the world has been untouched by armed conflict. Most of these conflicts have been within rather than between states, and most of the victims have been civilians.

As a union of 25 states with over 450 million people producing a quarter of the world's Gross National Product (GNP), and with a wide range of instruments at its disposal, the European Union is inevitably a global player. In the last decade European forces have been deployed abroad to places as distant as Afghanistan, East Timor and the DRC. The increasing convergence of European interests and the strengthening of mutual solidarity of the EU makes us a more credible and effective actor. Europe should be ready to share in the responsibility for global security and in building a better world.

5 CSDP MISSIONS AND OPERATIONS

(i) The coming of age of CSDP operations

Both military and civilian missions may be established on the basis of the CSDP provisions. On 1 January 2003, the EU launched the European Union Police Mission in Bosnia and Herzegovina (EUPOL) as its first civilian crisis management operation within the framework of the CSDP.[20] On 31 March 2003, the EU deployed Operation Concordia, its inaugural military mission, to follow up on NATO's efforts to contribute to a stable and secure environment in the Former Yugoslav Republic of Macedonia (FYROM).[21] Since 2003, the EU has affirmed its operational capability through the launching of more than twenty ESDP operations,[22] mainly in Africa and in the Western Balkans, but also in the EU's eastern neighbourhood, the Middle East and Asia. The EU has acted as a crisis manager in several guises:[23]

- as an honest broker of peace between the parties to a conflict (e.g. Aceh);
- as an assistant to border management (e.g. Moldova/Ukraine);
- as an adviser in justice reform (e.g. Georgia);
- as a trainer of police and prison staff (e.g. Iraq);
- as a security sector reformer (e.g. Guinea-Bissau);
- as a security guarantor during elections (e.g. Democratic Republic of Congo);
- as a peacekeeper on the invitation of a host country (e.g. FYROM);

---

[20] See Council Decision 2002/968/CFSP of 10 December 2002 concerning the implementation of Joint Action 2002/210/ CFSP on the European Union Police Mission, OJ 2002 No. L335/1.

[21] See Council Decision 2003/202/CFSP of 18 March 2003 relating to the launch of the EU military operation in the Former Yugoslav Republic of Macedonia, OJ 2003 No. L76/43.

[22] For an up-to-date list, see the website of the Council of the EU, ESDP operations, at www.consilium.europa.eu/ cms3_fo/showPage.asp?id=268&lang=en&mode=g.

[23] This section is partly based on Blockmans and Wessel, 'The European Union and Peaceful Settlement of Disputes in its Neighbourhood: The Emergence of a New Regional Security Actor?', in A. Antoniadis, R. Schütze and E. Spaventa (eds.), *The European Union and Global Emergencies: A Law and Policy Analysis* (Oxford: Hart Publishing, 2011), pp. 73–103.

- as a regional arrangement operating under a mandate by the United Nations Security Council, to counter the threat to international peace and security (posed by, e.g., piracy and armed robberies against vulnerable vessels off the Somali coast), and to assist peacekeeping operations carried out by other international organizations (e.g. Chad and, indirectly, Darfur); and
- as a component of an international transitional administration (e.g. Pillar IV in United Nations Interim Administration Mission in Kosovo (UNMIK)).

The EU has never acted in the capacity of enforcer of the peace (like NATO in Kosovo in 1999) nor in defence against an armed attack on its territory.

While most of the early operations were fairly successful, largely thanks to the fact that they were usually short term and limited in both scope and size, they have also revealed shortfalls, bottlenecks as well as broader issues in crisis management. They range from 'growing pains', as well as the planning and drawing up of appropriate mandates for CSDP missions, to more enduring challenges such as coherence among EU policies, institutions and instruments, coordination with other international organizations, notably NATO and the UN, and consistency of 'output'. As we have seen, CSDP has developed quickly over a relatively short period of time, and the EU is now facing its 'maturity test' as an international crisis manager.

In spite of the growing pains in the development of CSDP, the EU has made significant strides in deploying crisis management operations. However, the issue of defining success of the CSDP is no longer measured in terms of merely launching missions, ensuring mission output and gathering operational experience. Not only is greater intra- and inter-institutional coordination and cross-pillar coherence required by EU law and policy, the Union is also expected to conduct several operations at the same time,[24] to carry them out in line with both human rights law and international humanitarian law (IHL, see below), to live up to its promises by accomplishing its tasks, to effect positive change on the ground, and to show that it can take the lead among other international and institutional actors. These issues have become more pressing since the EU embarked on bigger and more difficult CSDP operations, for instance in the high-risk theatres of Kosovo, Afghanistan and Chad. If such crises are managed badly, then the EU risks losing its recently found confidence and acquired image as a regional and global actor serving the interest of international peace and security, especially if an ill-prepared and/or under-equipped CSDP operation stumbles into another 'Srebrenica'. In short, the EU is facing a big maturity test in CSDP. At the same time, a move towards 'hard security' may not always be in the interest of the Union's overall objectives.

---

[24] In its Declaration on Strengthening Capabilities of 11 December 2008, the Council mentioned the following ambitions: 'two major stabilisation and reconstruction operations, with a suitable civilian component, supported by up to 10,000 troops for at least two years; two rapid-response operations of limited duration using inter alia EU battle groups; an emergency operation for the evacuation of European nationals (in less than ten days), bearing in mind the primary role of each Member State as regards its nationals and making use of the consular lead State concept; a maritime or air surveillance/interdiction mission; a civilian–military humanitarian assistance operation lasting up to 90 days; around a dozen ESDP civilian missions (inter alia police, rule-of-law, civilian administration, civil protection, security sector reform, and observation missions) of varying formats, including in rapid-response situations, together with a major mission (possibly up to 3000 experts) which could last several years'. The Declaration is available on the website of the Council of the EU, among the reference documents about civilian crisis management, at http://ue.eu.int/showPage. aspx?id=1378&lang=En.

N. Tsagourias, 'EU Peacekeeping Operations: Legal and Theoretical Issues', in M. Trybus and N. D. White (eds.), *European Security Law* (Oxford: Oxford University Press, 2007), pp. 102–133.

Peacekeeping combined with the other – political, economic, social – instruments used by the Union in its external relations is an instrument of soft security that eventually attains hard security. The Union should continue to develop its professional expertise in this area while at the same time establishing mechanisms to facilitate security and defence cooperation with other organizations. At this point we should express a note of caution as to whether the Union should develop hard security policy and dogma. The EU represents a policy of multilevel governance with multiple clusters of legitimacy. People who primarily identify themselves with the State unit because of the deeper sense of sharing and solidarity that exists at the national level, and the tangible sense of security that it offers, may be reluctant to transfer their loyalties to the EU. At the Union level no amalgamated security and defence policy exists because it is practically impossible for the Union to absorb each and every security interest. The 'civilian' character of the CSDP is also supported by a number of other factors. In the first instance, soft security and civilian identity is exactly how the Union has understood and experienced security since its creation. The aim behind integration is to attain peace and security through political, economic, and social interaction and communication, and through de-securitization of threats. The Union's policies, particularly towards CEEC or the Balkans, show how this security paradigm is projected to the outside world. Indeed, the European Security Strategy's motto of 'a secure Europe in a better world' implies affirmative structural action. Secondly, the adoption of full military capabilities for hard security will inexorably transform the way the Union is perceived internally and externally. It may jeopardize the internal consensus if states start antagonising each other. A military mentality may also affect or compromise other areas of EU action such as humanitarian aid and assistance or reintroduce intergovernmentalism in current federal areas. There is also the possibility that third States may change the way they view the EU.

(ii) CSDP operations and international humanitarian law

As discussed in Chapter 7 the EU's external dimension by definition involves a discussion on the relevant rules of international law. With the coming of age of the CSDP operations, the question of the relevance of international law has become more important. While human rights law (as for instance laid down in the ECHR) may be applicable to EU operations as well,[25] the question of the application of IHL in CSDP operation has in particular become more prominent.

F. Naert, 'The Application of International Humanitarian Law and Human Rights Law in CSDP Operations', in E. Cannizzaro, P. Palchetti and R. A. Wessel (eds.), *International Law as Law of the European Union* (Boston/Leiden: Martinus Nijhoff Publishers, 2011), pp. 189–212

In line with the scope of application of IHL, the EU and its Member States accept that if EU-led forces become a party to an armed conflict, IHL will apply to them. For example, the Salamanca Presidency

---

[25] F. Naert, 'The Application of International Humanitarian Law and Human Rights Law in CSDP Operations', in E. Cannizzaro, P. Palchetti and Wessel (eds.), *International Law as Law of the European Union* (Boston/Leiden: Martinus Nijhoff Publishers, 2011), pp. 189–212.

Declaration provided that "Respect for [IHL] is relevant in EU-led operations when the situation they are operating in constitutes an armed conflict to which the forces are party". However, this situation will not often arise. EU policy is, therefore, that IHL does not necessarily apply in all CSDP operations. However, even when it does not apply to EU forces, it may be relevant for the parties to the conflict, and EU forces are aware of their potential obligations under IHL if a situation escalates.

So far EU forces have not become engaged in combat as a party to an armed conflict. While IHL could have become applicable if the situation would have escalated in some of the operations, especially ARTEMIS and EUFOR Tchad/RCA, this did not happen. . . .

Irrespective of possible Member State responsibility on the basis of the establishment of an international organization or for voting in its framework, it is general State practice that forces put at the disposal of international organizations are always to comply with the IHL obligations of their sending State, even when they are under the effective command and/or control of an international organization. This mainly stems from the obligation under Article 1 common to the Geneva Conventions to "respect and to ensure respect for the [Conventions] in all circumstances". This obligation, reaffirmed in Article 1(1) AP I, is also widely considered to be part of customary international law and probably also applies in non-international armed conflicts. It also requires efforts by States to ensure that third parties comply with their own IHL obligations. In practice, this rule is also supported by the fact that in most States, personnel of the armed forces are subject to national criminal law of the sending State even when deployed abroad. Moreover, Article 91 AP I states that "a Party to the conflict which violates the provisions of the Conventions or of this Protocol shall . . . be responsible for all acts committed by persons forming part of its armed forces".

State practice, both within NATO and within the EU, indicates that IHL obligations are primarily conceived as a Member State responsibility. Concerning the EU, the Salamanca Presidency Declaration states that "The responsibility for complying with [IHL], in cases where it applies, in [an EU] led-operation, rests primarily with the State to which the troops belong", but adds that "The political and military structures of the Union . . . should ensure that in exercising the strategic direction and political control, relevant rules of . . . [IHL] are duly taken into account". It goes on to say that "in exercising the strategic direction and political control, the [EU] will ensure that all relevant rules of international law, including [IHL] as appropriate are duly taken into account". Similarly, the Presidency Conclusion of the 19–20 June 2003 European Council stated that "The European Council stresses the importance of national armed forces observing applicable humanitarian law".

(iii) The responsibilities of the EU as a global security actor

In Chapter 7 we discussed the international responsibility of the EU in general. Obviously, questions on responsibility may emerge in relation to the CSDP operations. Although most missions launched by the Union so far have been relatively modest in their size and objectives, even small-scale operations may give rise to a breach of international law or cause damage and injury to private parties. Yet holding EU missions accountable for their activities is hampered by a range of legal and practical difficulties. One particularly thorny issue concerns the attribution of the wrongful acts committed by EU military operations: since they are composed of personnel made available to the Union by its Member States and third states, it is not immediately obvious which party – the EU, the contributing states or both – should bear responsibility for their conduct. This question is of great practical significance, for accountability cannot be discharged effectively if it is unclear where responsibility lies.

As we have seen, as an international legal person, the EU bears responsibility under international law for any violations of its international obligations. The applicability of this principle is reinforced by Article 3(5) TEU, which provides that in its relations with the wider world, the Union shall contribute to 'the strict observance and the development of international law'.

The conduct of military operations by the EU raises an important question: taking account of the EU's ambitions laid down in the current Treaties to contribute to global security governance, do the rules of attribution laid down in the ARIO (see Chapter 8) provide an adequate system for allocating responsibility between the EU and contributing states? Whereas the European Commission played a visible role in the debate on the ARIO by pointing to the special nature of the Community, its contribution did not extend to the complex questions emerging from the role of the EU as a global security actor. One could argue that the way in which the ARIO purports to apply the rules on the allocation of responsibility to peace operations is too narrow. The rules on international responsibility as laid down in the ARIO focus exclusively on *factual control* as a ground for attribution, and the Commentary to the ARIO disregards the institutional and legal ties which may exist between national contingents and international organizations. This approach is inappropriate in cases where an international organization incorporates national contingents into its own institutional structure, since such an act of incorporation gives rise to a rebuttable presumption that the conduct of national contingents is attributable to the international organization rather than to the contributing states.

Whether or not such a presumption of attribution exists in the case of EU military operations depends on their status within the institutional and legal order of the EU. One may argue that the picture is a mixed one. The EU certainly enjoys the competence to incorporate military assets into its institutional structure, and the Council is competent to establish military operations as its subsidiary organs. However, none of the legal acts adopted in relation to EU military operations provides clear evidence of the Council's intention to confer the status of a subsidiary organ on them. Since this intention cannot be presumed, we may be led to conclude that EU military operations are not *de iure* organs of the EU. However, they may still be classified as de facto organs, provided that the Union exercises the necessary degree of control over them. Although EU operations do not satisfy the high threshold of complete dependence demanded by the ICJ in its case law, a strong argument can be made that they are subject to a particularly high degree of normative control by the EU and may be considered as its de facto organs on this basis. Accordingly, if our analysis is correct, a presumption exists in favour of attributing the conduct of EU military operations to the EU on the grounds that they constitute de facto organs of the Union.

A formal recognition by the Council that the conduct of EU military operations is attributable to the EU would signal to the international community that the EU is ready to accept that its growing global engagement as an international security actor brings with it a duty to act in an accountable manner. The EU cannot entrust the implementation of its security and defence policy to its Member States and other parties and disavow responsibility for its adverse effects or hide behind the effective control test set down in Article 7 ARIO. Accepting that the wrongful conduct of its crisis management missions engages the Union's international responsibility would not only better reflect the spirit of the principles laid down in Article 21 TEU, but it could also serve as an example for other international organizations, including NATO, and thereby make a broader contribution to the development of the law of international responsibility in this particular field.

With the coming of age of the CSDP missions, the question of their relation to the human rights objectives of the Union is more frequently raised.[26] The founding Treaties thus suggest that the EU is subject to its own legal obligations to respect human rights and fundamental freedoms in addition to the obligations binding its Member States. The Treaties also signal a broader political or moral commitment on the part of the Union to conduct its external activities in a manner that upholds the highest human rights standards. On the other hand, the promotion of human rights at the international level is one of the principal foreign policy objectives of the EU's external action as a whole.[27] European crisis management missions can make a significant contribution to this objective. For example, the EU may deploy military forces in order to contribute to the establishment of a secure environment in which the humanitarian needs of local populations can be addressed.[28]

However, in practice the implementation of this dual commitment to ensure respect for and to promote human rights encounters certain difficulties. First, the protection of human rights in EU crisis management missions is not governed by a single legal regime. Rather, EU-led operations involve action by a multitude of entities – including the EU, its Member States and any contributing third states and international organizations – subject to diverse instruments and obligations (international, regional and domestic). This not only raises questions about the consistency of human rights protection in EU missions, but it also means that it may be unclear where responsibility for violations of individual rights lies in specific cases. Second, the legal effect and applicability of the relevant human rights instruments is uncertain in important respects. For example, while the extra-territorial applicability of the ECHR is well established in principle, significant doubts remain about the Convention's reach in crisis management missions, especially in the light of the decision of the European Court of Human Rights in the *Behrami* and *Saramati* cases. Third, the entry into force of the Lisbon Treaty has significantly altered the regulatory framework of EU external action. In particular, the Treaty calls for the accession of the EU to the ECHR and provides that the EU Charter of Fundamental Rights has the same legal value as the founding Treaties. These are major developments with potentially far-reaching implications that need to be investigated as a matter of urgency. Fourth, the fact that EU missions are deployed in operationally challenging environments may lead to certain tensions between human rights and operational effectiveness. For instance, EU personnel normally benefit from certain immunities from local jurisdiction. Such derogations raise questions about their compatibility with the Union's obligations and commitments to uphold human

---

[26] Partly based on A. Sari and Wessel (eds.), *Human Rights in EU Crisis Management Operations: A Duty to Respect and to Protect?* (The Hague: CLEER Working Paper series 2012/6).

[27] This is evident from Article 3(5) TEU, which provides that 'In its relations with the wider world, the Union shall uphold and promote its values and interests and contribute to the protection of its citizens. It shall contribute to peace, security, the sustainable development of the Earth, solidarity and mutual respect among peoples, free and fair trade, eradication of poverty and the protection of human rights, in particular the rights of the child, as well as to the strict observance and the development of international law, including respect for the principles of the United Nations Charter.' This basic principle is once again applied to the area of foreign and security policy by Article 21(2), which states that 'The Union shall define and pursue common policies and actions, and shall work for a high degree of cooperation in all fields of international relations, in order to: ... (b) consolidate and support democracy, the rule of law, human rights and the principles of international law.'

[28] E.g. Council Joint Action 2007/677/CFSP of 15 October 2007 on the European Union military operation in the Republic of Chad and in the Central African Republic, OJ 2007 No. L279/21.

rights, in particular as regards their necessity and proportionality. Fifth, the EU's long-standing commitment to human rights, its relatively high level of political homogeneity and the robustness of its decision-making processes suggests that it should be an ideal framework for the development of best practices and standards in crisis management. It is unclear, however, to what extent the EU has succeeded in setting an example for other organizations or indeed what lessons it should learn in areas where it has not fully lived up to its commitments and potential.

H. Hazelzet, 'Common Security and Defence Policy: What Nexus between Human Rights and Security?', in A. Sari and R. A. Wessel (eds.), *Human Rights in EU Crisis Management Operations: A Duty to Respect and to Protect?* (The Hague: CLEER Working Paper series 2012/6)

What contribution has the EU's Common Security and Defence Policy (CSDP) made to the protection and promotion of human rights? I would argue that based on an analysis of ten years of CSDP, the EU has made a very important indirect contribution to human rights protection by helping to build the rule of law and stability in many post-crisis situations around the world. An analysis of a decade of mainstreaming human rights policy into CSDP, however, shows that efforts to explicitly integrate human rights concerns into the missions' mandates and conduct have some way to go. In order to assure lasting results on the ground, more political pressure could be brought to bear on host-governments to adhere to human rights standards in the context of deploying an EU mission or operation. Using hard power responsibly and pursuing a truly comprehensive approach means acknowledging the triangular nexus between human rights, security and development. . . .

Let us first look at a decade of crisis management. The first EU interventions – in Bosnia and Herzegovina, the former Republic of Macedonia and in Bunia, Eastern Congo in 2003 – certainly aimed, albeit not explicitly, to contribute to the promotion and protection of human rights in a crisis situation. That is still the case for I would say all missions and operations today. During and following crisis situations, human rights are typically violated in the absence of any rule of law. Indeed, had these places been shiny examples of human rights protection, the EU would most likely not have intervened. In that crude sense, human rights are at the heart of CSDP. That said, the EU is usually not at the forefront during violent conflict when human rights violations are at their worst – here we sometimes rather see a multilateral response by the UN. With a number of exceptions, the EU has mainly intervened in post-crisis situations. . . .

The EU should no longer be willing to pay the price for neglect. Actually, we cannot afford it – not principally and not financially. In this time of financial austerity, the EU needs to focus on what it does best, show results from its actions and, by doing so, continue to attract scarce civilian and military capabilities from Member States and generate public support for its foreign and security policy. Results, and thus exit strategies, are most promising when working with willing partners. . . .

A recent EU policy shift following the Arab Spring was labeled 'more for more' and 'less for less' in our neighborhood: those governments committed to democracy and the rule of law get more support, those less committed, get less. Could the same go for CSDP engagement? Lady Ashton already said in a speech to the European Parliament in May last year that 'human rights are the silver thread across our actions'. The paradox and thus dilemma is of course that – if this advice would be taken to the extreme – the EU could end up training and reforming those that need it least and stay clear from those that most need it. We may thus well need to find some middle way, which is, luckily, one of the great strengths of the EU.

In sum, the message to get across to the CSDP establishment is that the nexus between human rights and security is as fundamental as the one between security and development. Kofi Annan's famous statement in his 2005 report on UN reform is a reminder: 'we will not enjoy development without security, we will not enjoy security without development, and we will not enjoy either without respect for human rights'. Indeed, the last part of that sentence is too often forgotten.

(iv) The EU as a regional agency in the sense of the UN Charter

The (partly) new CSDP provisions raise the question of the formal status of the EU in the global legal framework governing the peaceful settlement of disputes. In that respect the question has been raised to what extent the EU can be seen (and hence *used*) as a regional arrangement or agency in the sense of the UN Charter and the Declaration on Friendly Relations. According to Akehurst, 'the difference between an agency and an arrangement would appear to be that an *agency* possesses an institutional superstructure . . . whereas an *arrangement* does not . . . In other words, an agency is simply a more highly developed form of an arrangement'.[29] With regard to the EU, the existence of an 'institutional superstructure' is beyond any doubt. The question, however, to what extent the institutional structure may also be used to fulfil a role as 'regional agency', is less easy to answer.

In any case, regarding the EU as a regional agency would explain the way in which the Union intends to attain its objective to 'preserve peace, *prevent conflicts* and strengthen international security, in accordance with the purposes and principles of the United Nations Charter' (Article 21(2) TEU).[30] The Union's ambitions in this area are formulated in the so-called 'Petersberg tasks' (see *supra*). However, the TEU at this moment does not provide any additional clues for the Union to function as a regional agency. Neither did the Treaty expressly claim to fall within the ambit of Chapter VIII United Nations Charter (UNC). On the other hand, the concept of 'regional arrangements and agencies' is not defined by the Charter, and according to the (former) UN Secretary-General this was intentional:

The Charter deliberately provides no precise definition of regional arrangements and agencies, thus allowing useful flexibility for undertakings by a group of states to deal with a matter appropriate for regional action which also could contribute to the maintenance of international peace and security. Such associations or entities could include treaty-based organizations, whether created before or after the founding of the UN, regional organizations for mutual security and defence, organizations for general regional development or for cooperation on a particular economic topic or function, and groups created to deal with a specific political, economic or social issue of concern.[31]

The UN Secretary-General at the time even explicitly hinted at the possible 'emergence' of new regional arrangements in Europe:

---

[29] M. Akehurst, 'Enforcement Actions by Regional Organizations with Special Reference to the Organization of American States' (1967) 42 *British Yearbook of International Law* 177. Emphasis added.

[30] Emphasis added. The prevention of conflicts was added to the objectives by the Lisbon Treaty.

[31] Report of the Secretary-General, *Agenda for Peace*, UN Doc. A/47/277–S/24111.

Report of the Secretary-General on the Work of the Organizations, United Nations, 16 September 1990, Doc. A/45/1, p. 8

... dealing with new kinds of security challenges, regional arrangements or agencies can render assistance of great value. ... This presupposes the existence of the relationship between the United Nations and regional arrangements envisaged in Chapter VIII of the Charter. The diffusion of tensions between States and the pacific settlement of local disputes are, in many cases, matters appropriate for regional action. The proviso, however, is that efforts of regional agencies should be in harmony with those of the United Nations and in accordance with the Charter. This applies equally to regional arrangements in all areas of the globe, including those which might emerge in Europe.

In its *Agenda for Peace*, the UN stressed the need for flexibility in the post-Cold War era, and the purpose of establishing closer links with regional organizations was not to set forth 'any formal pattern of relationship between regional organisations and the United Nations, or to call for any specific division of labour'.[32]

The many references to the UN in the EU Treaties, including the implicit competence in Protocol 10 to act in response to a request of the UN to participate in the peaceful settlement of disputes ('the United Nations Organization may request the Union's assistance for the urgent implementation of missions undertaken under Chapters VI'), indeed point to new characteristics of this organization.[33] In fact, the EU has already been active in assisting the UN in a number of operations. Based on this, as well as on the above-mentioned objectives in the EU Treaties, it would be difficult for the EU to deny that it is subject to Chapter VIII UNC, even in the absence of internal conflict management mechanisms.[34] The implications of the acceptance of a new role for the EU as a 'Chapter VIII organisation' are not to be disposed of too easily. According to Article 52 UNC, the activities of regional arrangements or agencies are to be consistent with the purposes and principles of the UN. Moreover, regional arrangements and agencies have a *primary* function in the pacific settlement of local disputes;[35] they shall make every effort in that respect before referring the dispute to the Security Council, but they 'have autonomy in diplomacy, in peaceful settlement, and implicitly in the case of consensual peacekeeping, subject to a reporting requirement'.[36] Currently, nothing in the EU Treaties seems sufficient to enable the EU to fulfil this task internally. The Union's policies in this area are primarily (if not exclusively) related to threats to or breaches of the peace within or by states that are *not* members of the EU. This clearly distinguishes the EU from

---

[32] *Ibid.*, p. 10.

[33] A similar competence to act 'in response to requests from the United Nations Organization' may be found in relation to the permanent structured cooperation ex Article 42(6) TEU.

[34] See also N. D. White, 'The EU as Regional Security Actor within the International Legal Order', in M. Trybus and White (eds.), *European Security Law* (Oxford: Oxford University Press, 2007), pp. 329–349.

[35] Local disputes are commonly understood as disputes exclusively involving states which are parties to the regional arrangement or agency. Compare in that respect also Articles 34 and 35 UNC.

[36] White, 'The EU as Regional Security Actor within the International Legal Order'. Article 54 UNC provides that the Security Council shall at all times be kept fully informed of activities which are undertaken or are being contemplated under regional arrangements by regional agencies for the maintenance of international peace and security. This would include all activities by the EU related to the peaceful settlement of disputes.

other regional arrangements and agencies, which see as their primary task the settling of disputes among their Member States.

Apart from possibilities for the peaceful resolution of conflicts, the Petersberg tasks foresee the possibility of the EU engaging in peace-*making* operations. As is well known, the UNC is quite clear on the prohibition on using force (Article 2(4)). Exceptions can be found in the provisions on (collective) self-defence (Article 51) and in actions by the Security Council on the basis of Article 42. In addition, Chapter VIII (Article 53) UNC allows the Security Council to 'utilize . . . regional arrangements or agencies for enforcement action *under its authority*'.[37] Even for regional arrangements and agencies, an authorization of the Security Council to take enforcement action is necessary.

Council Joint Action 2008/749/CFSP of 19 September 2008 on the European Union military coordination action in support of UN Security Council resolution 1816 (2008) (EU NAVCO), OJ 2008 No. L252/39

THE COUNCIL OF THE EUROPEAN UNION . . .
  Whereas:

(1) In resolution 1816 (2008) on the situation in Somalia, adopted on 2 June 2008, the UN Security Council expressed its concern at the threat that acts of piracy and armed robbery against vessels pose to the prompt, safe and effective delivery of humanitarian aid to Somalia, the safety of commercial maritime routes and international navigation. The UN Security Council encouraged, in particular, States interested in the use of commercial maritime routes off the coast of Somalia to increase and coordinate their efforts to deter acts of piracy and armed robbery at sea in cooperation with the Transitional Federal Government of Somalia (TFG).

It authorised, for a period of six months from the date of the resolution, States cooperating with the TFG for which advance notification had been provided by the TFG to the UN Secretary-General to enter the territorial waters of Somalia and to use, in a manner consistent with relevant international law, all necessary means to repress acts of piracy and armed robbery at sea. The UN Security Council further called upon States to coordinate with other participating States their actions taken pursuant to the above provisions.

(2) In its conclusions of 26 May 2008 the Council expressed its concern at the upsurge of piracy attacks off the Somali coast, which affect humanitarian efforts and international maritime traffic in the region and contribute to continued violations of the UN arms embargo. The Council also commended the sequenced initiatives of some EU Member States to provide protection to World Food Programme vessels. It stressed the need for wider participation by the international community in these escorts in order to secure the delivery of humanitarian aid to Somali populations.

(3) On 16 June 2008 the Council requested the Council General Secretariat and the Commission to study possible options for implementing all the commitments contained in its conclusions of 26 May 2008, as well as for how best to contribute to the implementation of UN Security Council resolution 1816 (2008).

(4) On 5 August 2008 the Council approved a crisis management concept for EU action to contribute to the implementation of UN Security Council resolution 1816 (2008).

---

[37] Emphasis added. Article 53 mentions one exception: measures against renewal of aggressive policy on the part of an enemy state (that is, any state which during World War II was an enemy of any signatory of the present Charter). The definition of 'enemy state' highlights the outmoded nature of this provision.

6 THE BROADER PICTURE OF EU EXTERNAL RELATIONS LAW

This chapter revealed the impressive emergence and further development of the Union's security and defence policy. In a relatively short period, the EU has developed into a global security actor. While the number and size of civilian and military missions may not yet be so impressive, CSDP has become an important policy area and a key element of the Union's foreign and security policy.

The importance of CSDP is reflected in the institutional set-up that was created over the past decade. As in the area of CFSP, the familiar institutions play different roles from other areas of the EU's external action. Yet, legal issues are omnipresent and inter alia relate to the CSDP decisions, the agreements concluded with third states and the application of rules of international law.

The coming of age of CSDP missions has triggered debates on the application of IHL and other relevant international rules. These debates also point to the relationship between CSDP and other external policies, including – obviously – CFSP and Development Cooperation. While CSDP is one of the youngest policy areas of the EU, its importance and impact (both internally and externally) can no longer be neglected.

SOURCES AND FURTHER READING

Akehurst, M., 'Enforcement Actions by Regional Organizations with Special Reference to the Organization of American States' (1967) 42 *British Yearbook of International Law* 175–227.

Biscop, S., 'Permanent Structured Cooperation and the Future of the ESDP: Transformation and Integration' (2008) 13 *European Foreign Affairs Review*, 431–448.

Biscop, S., *The European Security Strategy – A Global Agenda for Positive Power* (Aldershot: Ashgate Publishing, 2005).

Blockmans, S., Wouters, J. and Ruys, T. (eds.), *The European Union and Peacebuilding: Policy and Legal Aspects* (The Hague: T.M.C. Asser Press, 2010).

Blockmans, S. and Wessel, R. A., 'The European Union and Peaceful Settlement of Disputes in its Neighbourhood: The Emergence of a New Regional Security Actor?', in A. Antoniadis, R. Schütze and E. Spaventa (eds.), *The European Union and Global Emergencies: A Law and Policy Analysis* (Oxford: Hart Publishing, 2011), pp. 73–103.

Bloed, A. and Wessel, R. A. (eds.), *The Changing Functions of the Western European Union (WEU): Introduction and Basic Documents* (Dordrecht: Martinus Nijhoff Publishers, 1994), document no. 28.

De Wijk, R., 'Convergence Criteria: Measuring Input or Output' (2000) 5 *European Foreign Affairs Review* 397–417.

Duke, S., 'Peculiarities in the Institutionalisation of CFSP and ESDP', in S. Blockmans (ed.), *The European Union and Crisis Management: Policy and Legal Aspects* (The Hague: T.M.C. Asser Press, 2008), pp. 75–105.

Glière, C., *EU Security and Defence: Core Documents 2007 (Vol. VIII)* (Paris: EUISS, Chaillot Paper No. 112, 2008).

Hazelzet, H., 'Common Security and Defence Policy: What Nexus between Human Rights and Security?', in A. Sari and R. A. Wessel (eds.), *Human Rights in EU Crisis Management Operations: A Duty to Respect and to Protect?* (The Hague: CLEER Working Paper series 2012/6).

Hill, C., 'Closing the Capabilities-Expectations Gap?', in J. Peterson and H. Sjursen (eds.), *A Common Foreign Policy for Europe: Competing Visions of the CFSP* (London: Routledge, 1998), pp. 18–38.

Hill, C., 'The Capability–Expectations Gap, or Conceptualising Europe's International Role' (1993) 31 *Journal of Common Market Studies* 305–328.

Hoffmeister, F., 'Inter-Pillar Coherence in the EU's Civilian Crisis Management', in S. Blockmans (ed.), *The European Union and Crisis Management: Policy and Legal Aspects* (The Hague: T.M.C. Asser Press, 2008), pp. 157–180.

Juncos, A. E. and Reynolds, C., 'The Political and Security Committee: Governing in the Shadow' (2007) 12 *European Foreign Affairs Review* 127–147.

Koutrakos, P., 'International Agreements in the Area of the EU's Common Security and Defence Policy', in E. Cannizzaro, P. Palchetti and R. A. Wessel (eds.), *International Law as Law of the European Union* (Boston/Leiden: Martinus Nijhoff Publishers, 2011), pp. 157–187.

Koutrakos, P., 'Security and Defence Policy within the Context of EU External Relations: Issues of Coherence, Consistency and Effectiveness', in M. Trybus and N. D. White (eds.), *European Security Law* (Oxford: Oxford University Press, 2007), pp. 249–269.

Koutrakos, P., *The EU Common Security and Defence Policy* (Oxford: Oxford University Press, 2013).

Laursen, F. and Vanhoonacker, S. (eds.), *The Intergovernmental Conference on Political Union: Institutional Reforms, New Policies and International Identity of the European Community* (Maastricht: EIPA, 1992).

McGivern, L., 'Has Operation Atalanta Changed Global Perceptions of the EU as a Military Force?' (Unpublished paper, 2010).

Naert, F. 'ESDP in Practice: Increasingly Varied and Ambitious EU Security and Defence Operations', in M. Trybus and N. D. White (eds.), *European Security Law* (Oxford: Oxford University Press, 2007), pp. 61–101.

Naert, F., 'The Application of International Humanitarian Law and Human Rights Law in CSDP Operations', in E. Cannizzaro, P. Palchetti and R. A. Wessel (eds.), *International Law as Law of the European Union* (Boston/Leiden: Martinus Nijhoff Publishers, 2011), pp. 189–212.

Remacle, E., 'La Politique Étrangère et de Sécurité Commune de l'Union Européenne après Maastricht', in M. Telò (ed.), *Vers une Nouvelle Europe?* (Brussels: Editions de l'Université de Bruxelles, 1992), pp. 239–252.

Sari, A., 'Status of Forces and Status of Mission Agreements under the ESDP: The EU's Evolving Practice' (2008) 19 *European Journal of International Law* 67–100.

Sari, A. and Wessel, R. A. (eds.), *Human Rights in EU Crisis Management Operations: A Duty to Respect and to Protect?* (The Hague: CLEER Working Paper series 2012/6).

Trybus, M., 'The Vision of the European Defence Community and a Common Defence for the European Union', in M. Trybus and N. D. White (eds.), *European Security Law* (Oxford: Oxford University Press, 2007), pp. 13–42.

Tsagourias, N., 'EU Peacekeeping Operations: Legal and Theoretical Issues', in M. Trybus and N. D. White (eds.), *European Security Law* (Oxford: Oxford University Press, 2007), pp. 102–133.

Van Eekelen, W. and Blockmans, S., 'European Crisis Management *avant la lettre*', in S. Blockmans (ed.), *The European Union and Crisis Management: Policy and Legal Aspects* (The Hague: T.M.C. Asser Press, 2008), pp. 37–52.

Wessel, R. A., 'The EU as Black Widow: Devouring the WEU to Give Birth to a European Security and Defence Policy', in V. Kronenberger (ed.), *The European Union and the International Legal Order – Discord or Harmony?* (The Hague: T.M.C. Asser Press, 2001), pp. 405–434.

Wessel, R. A., 'The State of Affairs in European Security and Defence Policy: The Breakthrough in the Treaty of Nice' (2003) 8 *Journal of Conflict and Security Law* 265–288.

White, N. D., 'The EU as Regional Security Actor within the International Legal Order', in M. Trybus and N. D. White (eds.), *European Security Law* (Oxford: Oxford University Press, 2007), pp. 329–349.

Wouters, J. and Ruys, T., 'UN–EU Cooperation in Crisis Management: Partnership or Rhetoric?', in S. Blockmans (ed.), *The European Union and Crisis Management: Policy and Legal Aspects* (The Hague: T.M.C. Asser Press, 2008), pp. 215–232.

13

The external dimension of the internal energy market

1 CENTRAL ISSUES

- Collaboration in the energy sector goes back to the ECSC, yet to this day no full-blown EU external energy policy exists. In this chapter we first examine the development of the EU internal energy market, focusing on how an external dimension has recently started to develop to serve EU internal needs.
- *Substantive dimension*: the Lisbon Treaty had the purpose of strengthening coherence in EU external relations, and expressly conferred an energy competence onto the EU (Article 194 TFEU). This chapter examines policy coherence in EU external energy policy from the substantive, institutional and vertical dimensions. Here the focus lies on the relationship between energy diplomacy, security of supply and the law-based market-orientated approach. The chapter queries whether the new competence will permit a more integrated approach between different objectives of EU energy policy.
- In the current setting, there is disagreement on the respective roles of the HR and the EEAS; and the Commission and the Energy Commissioner. These bodies have different perspectives on what EU external energy policy is about, with significant impact on the external dimension of the internal energy market. The strengthened role of the EP in EU external energy policy is also to be taken into account.
- The progressive advancement of the internal energy market has suffered from a limited political recognition by the Member States that there was the need for a fully fledged external dimension. This is due to the continued priority of Member State national interests over the common EU interest, leading to a significant lack of Member State compliance with Union law on the path to completing the internal market. Similar processes can be observed in the external dimension of the internal energy market, and this chapter therefore pays significant attention to the duty of cooperation as it has been formalized in a legally binding instrument at the end of 2012.

2 INTRODUCTION

Chapter 9 indicated that the CCP is an indispensable corollary to the internal market: without an external dimension, the internal market could not fully function. Similarly, in areas of the internal market such as telecommunications, aviation or energy, free movement within the

Union is partially dependent on whether a certain degree of commonality can be attained in external relations. This chapter analyses the internal energy market since it is an area which embodies important political, security, economic and environmental concerns; and in fact pooling sovereignty in the field of energy goes back to the origin of European integration itself. The EU internal energy market is focused on gas and electricity specifically, and work towards completing the internal energy market has been ongoing since the end of the 1980s. A common EU external energy policy lagged behind, and only moved up the EU's political agenda from 2005 onwards. Attaining a coherent and effective EU external energy policy has been mired with problems, and is an ongoing process: disagreement over the means to achieve the common EU interest; inter-institutional turf battles; and disagreement on whether the EU should act at all in the face of Member States' national interests. In December 2009 the Lisbon Treaty explicitly conferred a shared competence in the sphere of energy to the EU (Article 194 TFEU). This provides fertile legal ground for the development of a full-blown EU external energy policy. The Energy 2020 strategy of November 2010 was the first initiative to build on the new competence, and opens with an ominous warning: 'The price of failure is too high. Energy is the life blood of our society ... the energy challenge is one of the greatest tests which Europe has to face.'[1] On the external dimension the strategy notes that 'despite serious gas supply crises that have acted as a wake-up call exposing Europe's vulnerability, there is still no common approach towards partner, supply or transit countries.'[2]

3 EXPRESS CONFERRAL OF A SHARED INTERNAL COMPETENCE

(i) Developments in the EU internal energy market

With the ECSC (1952) and EAEC (1958), two of the three foundational Treaties to European integration concerned energy products. Coal rapidly waned in importance, and nuclear energy did not deliver on the promises of the 1950s. As oil (mid 1960s) and later natural gas (early 1970s) became the dominant energy sources for most Member States, Community institutions did not gain similar powers over oil, gas or electricity generation as they had over coal a decade earlier. It is not for lack of trying,[3] but initiatives resulted solely in general agreement on common priorities of Member States' energy policies, and (nevertheless important) Community legislation requiring that Member States maintain oil stocks for at least sixty-five and later ninety days.[4] Riding on the wave of political momentum towards the 1992 internal market objective, in 1988 the Commission proposed the application of the principles of the 1985 White Book to the energy sector,[5] covering coal, oil, natural gas, electricity and atomic energy. Lengthy negotiations resulted in the 1996 Electricity and 1998 Gas Directives known as the 'first

---

[1] Commission Communication, *Energy 2020, A strategy for competitive, sustainable and secure energy*, Brussels, 10 November 2010, COM(2010) 639 final, p. 4.

[2] *Ibid.*, p. 5.

[3] Communication Memorandum, *First Guidelines for a Community Energy Policy*, 18 December 1968 COM(68) 1040 final.

[4] Current version: Council Directive 2009/119/EC of 14 September 2009 imposing an obligation on Member States to maintain minimum stocks of crude oil and/or petroleum products, OJ 2009 No. L265/9.

[5] Commission Communication, *The internal market for energy*, 2 May 1988 COM 88 (238) final.

package'.[6] Results were lacklustre, failing to truly liberalize the sector which was characterized by vertically integrated companies dominating national electricity production and/or gas imports, often with *de iure* or de facto monopolies over delivery infrastructure (gas pipelines or transmission networks). The second package was adopted in June 2003, consisting of two Electricity and Gas Directives which required full electricity and gas market opening for professional and private consumers by 2004 and 2007 respectively.[7] It also sought to counter vertical integration by requiring legal unbundling of entities operating transmission activities and those operating production activities. By 2007 the Commission acknowledged that real choice for all EU consumers and fair and free cross-border trade had not yet been achieved, which led to the negotiation and adoption of the third legislative package by 2009.[8] Throughout these developments, there has been a persistent tension between EU regulatory activity required to create a competitive internal energy market, and Member State activism in defence of the national interest and those of national energy champions. Such action of Member States is often at odds with EU law because it entails price-fixing, market-sharing, abuse of dominant position, illegal state aid, and so on.[9] It is then rather unsurprising that problems of compliance with EU law within the Union translate into difficulties in achieving an effective and coherent EU external energy policy.

(ii) The energy legal basis: Article 194 TFEU

All the above legal developments in the energy sector occurred without the existence of an explicitly conferred energy competence. An express competence in the energy domain was only conferred with the Treaty of Lisbon in December 2009. In competition the Commission thus used the relevant legal bases (Articles 101 TFEU onwards), whereas most legislative instruments were adopted on the basis of the internal market competence (former Article 95 TEC (current 114 TFEU)), in combination with other legal bases where necessary (for example, environment (Article 191 TFEU)). The express competence in energy can now be found in Article 194 TFEU,[10] a power which is shared between the Union and its Member States (Article 4 TFEU).

---

[6] 'First legislative package': Directive 98/30/EC of the European Parliament and of the Council of 22 June 1998 concerning common rules for the internal market in natural gas, OJ 1998 No. L204/1 (now repealed); Directive 96/92/EC of the European Parliament and of the Council of 19 December 1996 concerning common rules for the internal market in electricity, OJ 1997 No. L27/20 (now repealed).

[7] 'Second legislative package': Directive 2003/55/EC of the European Parliament and of the Council of 26 June 2003 concerning common rules for the internal market in natural gas and repealing Directive 98/30/EC, OJ 2003 No. L176/57 (now repealed); Directive 2003/54/EC of the European Parliament and of the Council of 26 June 2003 concerning common rules for the internal market in electricity and repealing Directive 96/92/EC, OJ 2003 No. L176/37 (now repealed).

[8] Commission Communication, *An Energy Policy for Europe*, 10 January 2007, Brussels COM(2007) 1 final; 'Third legislative package': Directive 2009/73/EC of the European Parliament and of the Council of 13 July 2009 concerning common rules for the internal market in natural gas and repealing Directive 2003/55/EC (Text with EEA relevance), OJ 2009 No. L211/94; Directive 2009/72/EC of the European Parliament and of the Council of 13 July 2009 concerning common rules for the internal market in electricity and repealing Directive 2003/54/EC (Text with EEA relevance), OJ 2009 No. L211/55.

[9] Commission Communication, *Inquiry Pursuant to Article 17 of Regulation (EC) No. 1/2003 into the European Gas and Electricity Sectors*, Brussels, 10 January 2006 COM(851) final.

[10] Energy is also mentioned in specific provisions: Article 122 TFEU (measures in case of supply disruption), Article 170 TFEU (developing trans-European energy networks), and Article 192 TFEU (environmental measures which might affect Member States' energy mixes).

Article 194 TFEU – Energy

1. In the context of the establishment and functioning of the internal market and with regard for the need to preserve and improve the environment, Union policy on energy shall aim, in a spirit of solidarity between Member States, to:
    (a) ensure the functioning of the energy market;
    (b) ensure security of energy supply in the Union;
    (c) promote energy efficiency and energy saving and the development of new and renewable forms of energy; and
    (d) promote the interconnection of energy networks.
2. Without prejudice to the application of other provisions of the Treaties, the European Parliament and the Council, acting in accordance with the ordinary legislative procedure, shall establish the measures necessary to achieve the objectives in paragraph 1. Such measures shall be adopted after consultation of the Economic and Social Committee and the Committee of the Regions.
    Such measures shall not affect a Member State's right to determine the conditions for exploiting its energy resources, its choice between different energy sources and the general structure of its energy supply, without prejudice to Article 192(2)(c).
3. By way of derogation from paragraph 2, the Council, acting in accordance with a special legislative procedure, shall unanimously and after consulting the European Parliament, establish the measures referred to therein when they are primarily of a fiscal nature.

From this provision it is clear that no express external competence is conferred on the Union in the energy sector. Hence, any external action of the EU will have to be implied from internal rules adopted by the Union, and Member States will be pre-empted from acting in accordance with the *ERTA* doctrine. The body of common rules which the EU has adopted in the gas and energy markets through the three legislative packages is here of most significance. Notice however the second indent of paragraph 2 of Article 194 TFEU. This has the important consequence that Member States remain competent to conclude international agreements that relate to the composition of their energy mix, and that they could not be pre-empted by any EU internal action from doing so. See section 7 below for the kinds of agreements Member States continue to conclude in this area, subject to Article 4(3) TFEU.

As regards the objectives of this EU competence, Article 194 TFEU focuses on ensuring the well-functioning internal market, security of supplies and environmentally friendly energy policies. Before the inclusion of these objectives in Article 194 TFEU, they were already referred to as the three main dimensions of EU energy policy. As a consequence this provision is not a sea change for EU action in this domain, but rather a codification of the policy process that preceded it. The Energy 2020 programme adopted in 2010 explicitly recognized this:

Commission Communication, *Energy 2020, A Strategy for Competitive, Sustainable and Secure Energy*, Brussels, 10 November 2010, COM(2010) 639 final, p. 2

A common EU energy policy has evolved around the common objective to ensure the uninterrupted physical availability of energy products and services on the market, at a price which is affordable for all consumers (private and industrial), while contributing to the EU's wider social and climate goals. The central goals for energy policy (security of supply, competitiveness, and sustainability) are now laid down in the Lisbon Treaty.

Nonetheless, the importance of such an express legal basis must not be underestimated. It permits the EU to develop a fully fledged energy policy in its own right, rather than an (admittedly coherent) string of initiatives which are based on other legal bases such as the internal market or environment. While the functioning of the EU energy market is still placed front-and-centre, secure energy supplies are now elevated to an objective in EU primary law. This widens the scope of an energy policy that is purely market-orientated, to one that also incorporates the politics and diplomacy of energy security. In the EU's Energy 2020 programme, the Commission made a number of strong claims underlining its wish to grasp the momentum of this new legal basis to develop a true EU energy policy, both as regards the subsidiarity of EU action (Article 5(3) TEU) and the need for loyalty between the EU and its Member States (Article 4 (3) TEU). On *subsidiarity*: 'The EU is the level at which energy policy should be developed. Decisions on energy policy taken by one Member State inevitably have an impact on other Member States. . . . The time has come for energy policy to become truly European.'[11] On *loyalty*, the Commission is equally ambitious: 'The EU must now formalise the principle whereby Member States act in the benefit of the EU as a whole in bilateral energy relations with key partners and in global discussions.'[12] The Council endorsed the Energy 2020 Strategy in February 2011, though with the caveat of 'keeping in line with respective competences of Member States and the Union'.[13] In its conclusions, Council requested the Commission to draw up 'one comprehensive policy document' on EU energy policy, which the Commission delivered on 7 September 2011. The title of this Commission Communication captures the new direction of EU external energy policy: 'On security of energy supply and international cooperation – "The EU Energy Policy: Engaging with Partners beyond our Borders".'[14] These proposals were followed by extensive Council Conclusions in November 2011, endorsed by the European Council in December 2011. A number of initiatives followed, and the most notable for external relations is the Decision organizing the duty of cooperation between the EU and the Member States of October 2012. This is an instrument which sets up a legal binding framework governing EU–Member State obligations of information and coordination with certain aspects of external energy policy. In May 2013, another European Council meeting took place with extensive conclusions further boosting this policy domain. The consistent involvement of this top EU institution illustrates how important (external) energy policy has become for the Union, and underlines the realization that EU-level over national action is expected to bear most fruit for the future.

4 EU EXTERNAL ENERGY POLICY: INTERNAL CHALLENGES 'EXTERNALIZED'

In section (i) below we examine the key objectives of the EU internal market, and the central challenges the EU has faced in developing this policy domain. In section (ii) we then examine how these challenges translate in the domain of EU external relations.

---

[11] *Ibid.*, p. 4.
[12] *Ibid.*, p. 17.
[13] Council Conclusions, *Energy 2020: A strategy for competitive, sustainable and secure energy*, Brussels, 28 February 2011, p. 6.
[14] Commission Communication, *On security of energy supply and international cooperation – 'The EU Energy Policy: Engaging with Partners beyond our Borders'*, Brussels, 7 September 2011, COM(2011) 539 final.

(i) Objectives of EU internal energy policy

Between the adoption of the second and third legislative packages, the European Commission published the ambitious 2007 'First Strategic Energy Review' which was subsequently endorsed by the Council. That document opens with a quote from the 1955 Messina Declaration: 'to these ends, the ministers have agreed on the following objectives: ... putting more abundant energy at a cheaper price at the disposal of the European economies'.[15] Aware of the historical calling of a common EU energy policy, it signals that concerns over security of supply and free and fair market competition have been at its heart from the early days. Since then, environmental sustainability has been added to the mix, and together they form the three objectives the EU aims to tackle with its energy policy. Respectively, they entail 'combating climate change, limiting the EU's external vulnerability to imported hydrocarbons, and promoting growth and jobs, thereby providing secure and affordable energy to consumers';[16] in short: environment, security and competitiveness now embedded in Article 194 TFEU.

- The objective of environmental sustainability revolves around the 20–20–20 targets which serve as a focal point for many different initiatives:[17] a reduction in EU greenhouse gas emissions of at least 20 per cent below 1990 levels; 20 per cent of EU energy consumption should come from renewable sources; and a 20 per cent reduction in primary energy use compared to business-as-usual levels achieved through increased energy efficiency.
- Security of supply concerns stem from the EU's import dependence from 50 per cent in 2007 with a projected increase to 65 per cent by 2030. Reliance on gas imports would increase from 57 per cent to 84 per cent by 2030, and for oil these figures stand at an increase from 82 per cent to 93 per cent.[18] Such dependence creates economic and political risks, requiring action in terms of demand-side and supply-side security of supply.
- Competitiveness entails reducing EU exposure to unfair competition, high prices and price volatility on international energy markets which affects the economic situation of EU companies and citizens. A well-functioning energy market is expected to alleviate these problems, while simultaneously benefiting the EU economy more generally by freeing up wealth for job creation, innovation through R&D and new technologies, and the knowledge-based economy of the EU.[19]

The thread running through these three dimensions is that the Union seeks to realize its secure and affordable energy through a *market-based methodology* which draws heavily on a regulatory approach. Legal frameworks (Regulations, Directives, bilateral or multilateral agreements) then provide dividends on all fronts: they provide a safe investment climate through long-term stability of the regulatory environment and allow for emissions trading to the benefit of the environment, and a well-functioning market can more smoothly cope with sudden shifts in energy imports. Thus, the law-based approach characterizes EU *internal and external* energy

---

[15] Commission Communication, *An Energy Policy for Europe*, 10 January 2007, Brussels, COM(2007) 1 final, p. 3.; see also Green Paper, *A European Strategy for Sustainable, Competitive and Secure Energy*, Brussels, 8 March 2006 COM (2006) 105 final.

[16] Commission Communication, *An Energy Policy for Europe*, 10 January 2007, Brussels, COM(2007) 1 final, p. 5.

[17] For an overview of all EU climate-related *acquis* see: http://ec.europa.eu/dgs/clima/acquis/index_en.htm (last accessed 20 June 2013).

[18] Commission Communication, *An Energy Policy for Europe*, 10 January 2007, Brussels, COM(2007) 1 final, p. 3.

[19] *Ibid.*, p. 4.

policy, and security, competitiveness and sustainability are simultaneously instrument and objective: a well-functioning market increases energy security, lack of secure supplies destabilizes the market, energy efficiency decreases imports and thus increases security – law is the instrument for attaining these desirable objectives.

While there is general agreement on the importance of these elements, there are three sets of challenges in attaining them: vertical, arising from tension between the EU and the Member States; institutional, arising from tension between the organs of the EU; and horizontal, arising from tension between the different policy areas of the EU. This is illustrated in Table 13.1 below.

(ii) Challenges to EU internal energy policy

Table 13.1 – EU internal energy policy: challenges and policy dimensions

		Three main challenges		
		Institutional	*Substantive*	*Vertical*
Three dimensions	*Security of supply*	Member State national interests uploaded through the Council, presence of HR/VP and the EEAS	Interconnecting infrastructure, reliable flow of energy into EU, concern over strategic acquisitions, decreasing EU demand	Inter-Member State solidarity; protection of energy champions' interest as national interest
	Environmental sustainability	DG Clima, DG Env or DG ENER: diversity of views on priorities and vision	Reduced emissions, energy efficiency, 20–20–20, ETS	Member State shift in energy mixes towards renewable sources
	Market/law– based approach	Inter- and intra-institutional diversity and possible disagreement over whether market approach should dominate	Recruitment of market principles as a means for all other ends, and an end in itself	Member States' and energy companies' compliance and enforcement of EU law

(a) Vertical challenges

The energy sources from which a Member State fuels its economy are called the 'energy mix'. According to Article 194(2) 2nd indent TFEU, Member States retain the 'right to determine the conditions for exploiting its energy resources, its choice between different energy sources, and the general structure of its energy supply'.[20] Concretely this means that the Netherlands is free to decide to exploit its natural gas resources in the North Sea, Germany is free to decide to phase out

---

[20] This without prejudice to Article 192(2)(c) TFEU which allows for the adoption of environmental policy provisions through the special legislative procedure and the Council acting by unanimity.

nuclear energy, and Denmark is free to rely on wind farms as much as it wants. This retained competence has important policy and legal consequences. Legally, we have pointed to the fact that it means they can continue to conclude international agreements that relate to their energy mix. On the policy side, it means that one will find hugely diverse energy mixes across different EU Member States. Since each Member State will have their national priorities, they may also diverge. This in turn means that the Member States may seek to upload their interests to EU internal and external energy policy; or that they may pursue their national interest with disregard for the common EU interest. By way of illustration, Germany may be more interested in good relations with Russia because of gas imports, which offends Poland for historical and political reasons. Spain may be mostly concerned with the impact of EU energy policy on Algerian imports.

E. Van der Meulen, 'EU Energy Policy: The Conflict between an Internal Liberalisation Agenda and External Security of Supply', in C. Stolte, T. Buruma, R. Runhardt and F. Smits (eds.), *The Future of the European Union* (Leiden: Sidestone Press, 2008), p. 47

First, the energy mix per country can differ significantly (e.g. France greatly relies on nuclear power, whereas the UK energy mix is more dominated by gas). Secondly, some member states have national gas supplies, significantly decreasing their import dependence. . . . Additionally, some member states are totally dependent on one single gas exporting country, whereas others have [a] more diverse mix of imports – Eastern Europe is almost completely dependent on Russian gas, but Western Europe has a more diverse gas mix. Finally, there is the problem of market power. Policy responses to import dependency can differ greatly between larger and smaller member states. . . . under EU law, every member state can determine its own energy mix. The result is a situation where individual [member states] will have very diverse policies towards the major exporting countries.

(b) Substantive challenges

From a substantive perspective, the presence of competing commercial and political interests expresses itself in disagreement as to whether the emphasis should lie on security, sustainability or competitiveness. Although embedded in Article 194 TFEU, EU energy initiatives have over the past six decades been characterized by a continuing search for a balance between security of supply, environmental goals and market liberalization goals. Whereas the energy crises of the 1970s saw emphasis on security of supply, in the 1980s to 90s the focus was on market liberalization as prices were low and supplies abundant.[21] With prices having skyrocketed from 2000 onwards, and easily accessible and stable sources under pressure, security of supply has again taken a front row seat. In balancing these interests, a Member State that is significantly dependent on a third country for its energy imports may feel pressured to prioritize individual energy security over the principles of a well-functioning EU internal energy market. Similarly, the EU institutions will have to juggle the plethora of national interests and substantive policy considerations in attaining a common EU policy. They will often do so in line with their own competence description.

---

[21] F. McGowan, 'Can the European Union's Market Liberalism Ensure Energy Security in a Time of "Economic Nationalism"?' (2008) 4 *Journal of Contemporary European Research* 90–106 at 93.

(c) Institutional challenges

In institutional terms, when navigating the tangle of commercial, national, political and legal interests in energy policy, 'the Commission', 'the Council', 'the European Parliament' or 'the Member States' do not always represent monoliths or unified fronts. Member States such as the UK and the Netherlands have held prominent positions supporting EU energy market liberalization due to pre-existing perceptions of how the sector should be regulated. Similarly, the EP has transformed itself from being a sceptic of liberalization in the 1990s, to a strong ally of the Commission in its efforts towards market liberalization in the 2000s. Within the Commission too, this institution's action during much of the 2000s has stemmed from an intense cooperation between DG COMP (competition) and DG TREN (transport and energy).[22] The former Commission Directorate General for external relations (RELEX) possessed a separate unit for external energy policy, but has now been integrated in the EEAS. It is thereby possible that its 'foreign policy' orientation does not always match the priorities of DG ENER or DG COMP. These kinds of (shifting) alliances between groups of Member States, institutions and even specific services within institutions are integral to a good understanding of the development of EU internal and external energy policy.[23] This is because even certain services within the institutions may disagree on where the emphasis should be in EU external energy policy: depending on the specific issue, DG competition, energy or internal market may be more favourable to approaches in line with their respective competence descriptions, with DG climate change or environment proposing different emphases. The EEAS and the EP may equally have different points of view, further stirring up the institutional balance.

In the following section, we examine how the internal challenges of EU energy policy translate into an external dimension.

(iii) Internal objectives and challenges externalized

(a) Recent developments in EU external energy policy

The development of an EU external energy policy has only very recently taken place. In the 2003 ESS, energy security was mentioned only in passing.[24] Since then, much has changed under pressure of rising energy prices and uncertainty about energy deliveries from Russia. At the Hampton Court informal European Council of October 2005, leaders agreed that the Union would need to define a common European energy policy. In response the Commission published a Green Paper in March 2006, which was endorsed by the European Council the same month.[25] Numerous policy documents followed, notably the October 2006 Communication entitled 'External energy relations – from principles to action',[26] the January 2007 Communication 'An energy policy for Europe' (e.g. the First Strategic Energy Review),[27] the 2007–2009 Action Plan of the

---

[22] DG Transport and Energy has since the Lisbon Treaty been split into two parts, with a single DG ENER responsible for energy.

[23] J. F. Braun, *EU Energy Policy under the Treaty of Lisbon Rules – Between a New Policy and Business as Usual* (CEPS Working Paper No. 31, 2011), pp. 4–5.

[24] ESS, *A Secure Europe in a Better World*, Brussels, 12 December 2003, p. 4.

[25] Conclusions of the European Council, 23–24 March 2006, DOC 7775/1/06 REV 1.

[26] Commission Communication, *External energy relations – from principles to action*, Brussels, 12 October 2006, COM (2006) 590 final.

[27] Commission Communication, *An Energy Policy for Europe*, Brussels, 10 January 2007, COM(2007) 1 final.

European Council,[28] and the Second Strategic Energy Review of November 2008.[29] By the time of the 2008 review of the ESS, energy was mentioned as the 'artery of the European economy' facing a wide array of security challenges, and 'our response must be an EU energy policy which combines external and internal dimensions'.[30]

After the entry into force of the Lisbon Treaty on December 2009, the new legal basis was supposed to create momentum for a grand launch of a revamped EU energy policy. Initial momentum was lost due to the Arab Spring and the Sovereign Debt Crisis pushing energy policy down on the priority list of EU leadership. In November 2010 the Commission published a Communication setting out the EU's 'Energy Strategy for 2020', which was to be endorsed at an 'energy summit' on 4 February 2011, e.g. a European Council meeting organized solely for the purpose of discussing EU energy policy. While that summit did take place, and the Conclusions did contain a number of guidelines for energy policy, much of the discussions and final outcome concerned the EU's response to the aforementioned crises. As a consequence, weight shifted to the ministerial level, namely the 28 February 2011 Energy Council which adopted a set of formal conclusions endorsing the Energy 2020 programme.[31] The February 2011 'energy summit' did request that the Commission submit 'a communication on security of supply and international cooperation aimed at further improving the consistency and coherence of the EU's external action in the field of energy'.[32] The Communication finally arrived on 7 September 2011, together with a proposal for a new binding instrument organizing the relationship between the EU and its Member States in external energy relations. On 24 November 2011 the Energy Council adopted meticulously drafted and extensive Conclusions on 'strengthening the external dimension of the EU energy policy',[33] finally endorsed by the European Council on 9 December 2011. The proposed Decision on the EU–Member State relationship was adopted by the Council on 4 October 2012. In the following paragraphs we shall briefly elaborate on the three main obstacles to EU energy policy in their application to EU external relations.

The March 2006 Green Paper recognized that 'a coherent external policy is essential to deliver sustainable, competitive and secure energy', adding that 'it would be a break from the past, and show Member States' commitment to common solutions to shared problems'.[34] The European Council of June 2006 endorsed its content, and in preparation of this June meeting, the Commission and the Secretary-General/High Representative jointly wrote a paper for the European Council entitled 'An external policy to serve Europe's energy interests'.[35] The paper wished to show 'how EU external relations, including CFSP' could be used effectively towards securing the three objectives of energy policy. The five-page paper was divided in a fashion reminiscent of

---

[28] Annex 1 attached to the Brussels European Council, Presidency Conclusions, *Action Plan 2007–2009, An Energy Policy for Europe*, 8–9 March 2007.

[29] Commission Communication, *Second Strategic Energy Review, An EU Energy Security and Solidarity Action Plan*, Brussels, 13 November 2008, COM(2008) 781 final.

[30] Conclusions of the European Council, 23–24 March 2006, DOC 7775/1/06 REV 1, pp. 1 and 8.

[31] Commission Communication, *Energy 2020, A strategy for competitive, sustainable and secure energy*, Brussels, 10 November 2010, COM(2010) 639 final.

[32] Conclusions of the European Council, Brussels, 4 February 2011, DOC EUCO 2/1/11, p. 4.

[33] Council Conclusions, *On strengthening the external dimension of the EU energy policy*, Brussels, 24 November 2011.

[34] Green Paper, *A European Strategy for Sustainable, Competitive and Secure Energy*, 8 March 2006, Brussels, COM(2006) 105 final, p. 14.

[35] Report from the Commission and the Secretary-General/High Representative to the European Council, Joint Paper *'An external policy to serve Europe's energy interests'*, Brussels, 30 May 2006, DOC 9971/06.

a CFSP-type strategic approach: a risk assessment, a statement on guiding principles, and a statement on how to 'get results' at bilateral, regional and multilateral level.

Report from the Commission and the Secretary-General/High Representative to the European Council, Joint Paper *'An external policy to serve Europe's energy interests'*, Brussels, 30 May 2006, DOC 9971/06

[An EU external energy policy] must be *coherent* (backed up by all Union policies, the Member States and industry), *strategic* (fully recognizing the geo-political dimensions of energy-related security issues) and *focused* (geared towards initiatives where Union-level action can have a clear impact in furthering its interests). It must also be *consistent with the EU's broader foreign policy objectives* such as conflict prevention and resolution, non-proliferation and promoting human rights. An external energy policy has to be based on a clear prior identification of EU interests, and reliable risk assessments.[36]

In light of this, we can transpose the internal challenges identified to the external context, with added complexity given that they play out in the international arena as opposed to the EU legal order.

(b) Substantive challenges

In substantive terms, the core challenge lies in disagreement on whether it is in the Union's best interest to pursue a dominantly market-based approach, or whether exigencies of international energy relations require an approach which focuses on the geopolitical and strategic dimension of relations with producer and transit countries. The latter implies an energy policy based on political or strategic rationales. It means that decisions are not made purely on the basis of an economic reality, but that they reflect political or strategic considerations: low prices for friendly nations or companies, market delineation to guarantee strategic pricing policies, investment decisions and even unilateral action in relation to production, transit or supply of energy products largely informed by strategic considerations. In the market-based approach, the same energy actors are expected to make those decisions based on economic and commercial considerations. They do so within a regulatory environment which is characterized by the rule of law and long-term, stable regulatory conditions in a protected climate which stimulates (foreign) investment. The latter is what the internal energy market aims to ensure, and in EU external energy policy it translates into efforts to create international legal frameworks within which market principles can secure energy supplies at low prices.[37] The Energy Charter[38] of the mid 1990s and the Energy Community in south east Europe in the early 2000s are the prime examples of this. However, the law-based market-orientated approach cannot be a one-size-fits-all

---

[36] Emphasis added.

[37] Commission Communication, *External energy relations – from principles to action*, Brussels, 12 October 2006, COM (2006) 590 final.

[38] The Energy Charter was as an expression of the EU's market-based approach in relations with the wider world first proposed in the early 1990s. The idea was to replicate the ECSC to bring together Eastern and Western Europe on the basis of open markets, non-discrimination and access for FDI in the energy sector. The Treaty was signed in 1994 and entered into force in April 1998. See further www.encharter.org (last accessed 10 September 2012).

solution: countries such as Russia or Azerbaijan may not be interested in applying the EU internal market *acquis* to their energy relations with the Union, and the geopolitical approach may be more appropriate. It could then be problematic for the EU common external energy policy if EU institutions and (groups of) Member States disagree on which approach is preferable.

(c) Institutional challenges

This substantive disagreement can be the consequence of – and be reinforced by – intra- and inter-institutional fragmentation. Within the Commission the thematic DGs may have different priorities: DGs responsible for competition, internal market, energy, environment or climate change. Intra-institutional diversity may also flow from the fact that the Council General Secretariat holds opinions different from those within (certain DGs of) the Commission; and notably since the Lisbon Treaty, the EEAS which is largely organized along geographic lines (Eastern Partnership, Russia, Southern Mediterranean). The latter, with its CFSP-orientation, may equally emphasize different aspects of external energy policy. Thus, the emphasis on extending 'the benefits of the internal market' beyond EU borders can potentially clash with those Member States and parts of the EU institutions more inclined towards the 'geopolitical' route in external energy policy. In a pre-Lisbon book based on extensive interviews, Youngs captured this issue as follows.

> **R. Youngs, *Energy Security – Europe's New Foreign Policy Challenge* (New York: Routledge, 2009), pp. 40–41**
>
> ... the principal division was described by officials as being between the Commission's Energy and Transport directorate, on the one hand, and Relex and the Council on the other hand. The latter berated the former's influence as an 'energy technocracy' whose market-based recipes were blind to geopolitical realities. The 'energy technocrats' complained that too much alliance-oriented foreign policy had already infected the coherence of EU strategies. ... In sum, officials acknowledged that the situation was not one of the 'markets and institutions' storyline having triumphed, but rather of sharply contrasting policy preferences persisting within different institutions and forums.

(d) Vertical challenges

As with the progressive completion of the internal market, in external relations too, national energy champions' interests may be uploaded to the Member State level, and Member States may seek to prioritize their national interest over that of the Union. Alternatively, Member States may seek to shape the Union interest so that it equates to their national interest, potentially disregarding considerations which are valid for the Union as a whole. Pre-Lisbon, this can be illustrated by the February 2009 Council meeting which took place a few weeks after the Russian–Ukrainian gas dispute had left many of the Eastern EU countries in the cold and dark. The Council said that 'Solidarity between Member States has to be strengthened and balanced with Member States' responsibility over their energy security, fully respecting Member States' choice of energy mix and sovereignty over energy sources.'[39] Even with several EU Member

---

[39] Council Conclusions, Brussels, 19 February 2009, DOC 6692/09, p. 2.

States having suffered severely, the emphasis on sovereignty stood front-and-centre. A post-crisis evaluation report of the Commission illustrates this further. On the positive side, solidarity between the Member States was certainly present when for example Czech gas storage was made available to Slovakia, Austrian gas storage to Slovenia.[40] However, a well-functioning internal market would have significantly eased the crisis. For example, 'additional supplies from the Netherlands could not reach Bulgaria because the interconnections and same gas standards were not there. Lacking infrastructure also meant that available LNG supplies could not be supplied to where they were most needed, particularly from Spain and Greece'.[41] Most notable for EU external relations as such, the national fall-back logic of the Member States failed to safeguard them from supply deficiencies. In the carefully chosen words of the Commission report: 'Political bilateral agreements (e.g. Bulgaria and Serbia with Russia) proved to be less effective than market arrangements between gas undertakings within the EU internal market framework in helping to keep supplies flowing.'[42] Hence, on the one hand there is the 'EU interest', the recognition that acting together will be to the benefit of the Union as a whole; on the other hand, there is the pursuit of national interests and possibly breaking ranks by individual Member States.

5 INSTRUMENTS OF EU EXTERNAL ENERGY POLICY

In the following three sections we briefly examine three dominant instruments of EU external energy policy. First, there is EU internal market legislation which can have a significant external legal and policy dimension. Second, there are the multilateral legally binding instruments, e.g. the Energy Charter and Energy Community Treaty. Third is the plethora of binding and non-binding instruments adopted by the Union to further its energy interests on a bilateral third-country basis.

(i) External dimension of the internal market: ownership unbundling

In seeking to complete the integrated EU energy market in the context of the third legislative package, the Commission persistently pursued the separation of producers and suppliers.[43] This is called 'unbundling' and entails the legal and functional separation of companies producing energy and those that supply that energy to avoid conflicts of interests. This was considered necessary because such vertically integrated companies possess potentially anti-competitive characteristics which can negatively impact EU market liberalization efforts. It applies to both the electricity and gas internal markets.

---

[40] Commission Staff Working Document, *The January 2009 Gas Supply Disruption to the EU: An Assessment*, Brussels, 16 July 2009 COM(2009) 363 final, p. 9.

[41] *Ibid.*, pp. 10–11.

[42] *Ibid.*, p. 9.

[43] Draft explanatory memorandum to the proposal for the third package of energy market liberalization, pp. 4–5. Available at: http://ec.europa.eu/energy/electricity/package_2007/doc/2007_09_19_explanatory_memorandum_en.pdf (last accessed 20 June 2013).

Proposal for a Directive of the European Parliament and of the Council, amending Directive 2003/54/EC concerning common rules for the internal market in electricity, COM(2007) 528 final Brussels, 2007/0195 (COD)

[E]xperience has shown that where the transmission system operator is a legal entity within an integrated company, three types of problems arise. First, the transmission system operator may treat its affiliated companies better than competing third parties. In fact, integrated companies may use network assets to make entry more difficult for competitors. Second, under the current unbundling rules, non-discriminatory access to information cannot be guaranteed as there is no effective means of preventing transmission system operators releasing market sensitive information to the generation or supply branch of the integrated company. Third, investment incentives within an integrated company are distorted.

Directive 2009/73/EC of 13 July 2009 concerning common rules for the internal market in natural gas and repealing Directive 2003/55/EC, OJ 2009 No. L211/94, Recital 8

8. Only the removal of the incentive for vertically integrated undertakings to discriminate against competitors as regards network access and investment can ensure effective unbundling. Ownership unbundling, which implies the appointment of the network owner as the system operator and its independence from any supply and production interests, is clearly an effective and stable way to solve the inherent conflict of interests and to ensure security of supply.

From the external perspective, the application of unbundling also to non-EU companies active in the EU energy market has been particularly politically sensitive in the gas sector because several Member States are highly dependent on Russian imports. The law-based approach seeking to utilize market principles as the basis for international energy trade is somewhat at odds with that country's strategic divide-and-rule approach to foreign (energy) policy. During the negotiations on the third legislative package, unbundling acquired an external dimension since the Commission proposal stated that non-EU companies are equally required to respect the effective unbundling of transmission from supply and production activities. The aim is to guarantee that companies from third countries respect the same rules that apply to EU based undertakings, e.g. not to discriminate against them. The obligation for third countries to unbundle became known under the name of the company that was mainly targeted for its strategic purchasing of EU liberalized assets, e.g. the 'Gazprom' clause. Specifically, the Commission proposed to introduce a requirement that third-country individuals and countries could not acquire control over an EU transmission system or transmission system operator unless this is permitted by an agreement between the EU and the third country. The aim was to guarantee that companies from third countries respect the same rules that apply to EU based undertakings in both letter and spirit – not to discriminate against them.

Directive 2009/73/EC of 13 July 2009 concerning common rules for the internal market in natural gas and repealing Directive 2003/55/EC, OJ 2009 No. L211/94, Recital 22

22. The security of energy supply is an essential element of public security and is therefore inherently connected to the efficient functioning of the internal market in gas and the integration of the isolated gas

markets of Member States. Gas can reach the citizens of the Union only through the network. Functioning open gas markets and, in particular, the networks and other assets associated with gas supply are essential for public security, for the competitiveness of the economy and for the well-being of the citizens of the Union. Persons from third countries should therefore only be allowed to control a transmission system or a transmission system operator if they comply with the requirements of effective separation that apply inside the Community. Without prejudice to the international obligations of the Community, the Community considers that the gas transmission system sector is of high importance to the Community and therefore additional safeguards are necessary regarding the preservation of the security of supply of energy to the Community to avoid any threats to public order and public security in the Community and the welfare of the citizens of the Union. The security of supply of energy to the Community requires, in particular, an assessment of the independence of network operation, the level of the Community's and individual Member States' dependence on energy supply from third countries, and the treatment of both domestic and foreign trade and investment in energy in a particular third country. Security of supply should therefore be assessed in the light of the factual circumstances of each case as well as the rights and obligations arising under international law, in particular the international agreements between the Community and the third country concerned. Where appropriate the Commission is encouraged to submit recommendations to negotiate relevant agreements with third countries addressing the security of supply of energy to the Community or to include the necessary issues in other negotiations with those third countries.

The final version of the 'Gazprom clause' was weakened from what the Commission had originally intended. Initially it would have acted as an EU-wide veto towards companies in third countries acquiring European transmission assets, unless European investors were given the same legal certainty and market access rights in the third-country market (so not just unbundling). The Russian Federation was not pleased, as it considered that the EU should not impose on their foreign partners the idea of how these partners should be organized in order to have a possibility of investing in the European Union's energy sector.[44] In spite of the Commission's strong push joined by a group of Member States, the third Gas Directive has not maintained the initial clause, mainly under heavy pressure from Germany who did not want to upset Gazprom. Under current Article 11 of the IEM Gas Directive, if a transmission system operator or owner is controlled by a person from a third country, a special notification procedure to the Commission applies. The decision as to certification remains with the national regulatory authority. In this decision, it needs to take account of the EU internal market *acquis*, but also of the impact on the security of supply to the Member State and the EU as a whole.

Directive 2009/73/EC of 13 July 2009 concerning common rules for the internal market in natural gas and repealing Directive 2003/55/EC, OJ 2009 No. L211/94

Article 11 Certification in relation to third countries

1. Where certification is requested by a transmission system owner or a transmission system operator which is controlled by a person or persons from a third country or third countries, the regulatory authority shall notify the Commission.

---

[44] Agence Europe, *Russia refuses to be compelled to apply EU-envisaged reforms to its energy sector*, Brussels, 29 April 2008.

The regulatory authority shall also notify to the Commission without delay any circumstances that would result in a person or persons from a third country or third countries acquiring control of a transmission system or a transmission system operator.

2. The transmission system operator shall notify to the regulatory authority any circumstances that would result in a person or persons from a third country or third countries acquiring control of the transmission system or the transmission system operator.

3. The regulatory authority shall adopt a draft decision on the certification of a transmission system operator within four months from the date of notification by the transmission system operator. It shall refuse the certification if it has not been demonstrated:

   (a) that the entity concerned complies with the requirements of Article 9; and

   (b) to the regulatory authority or to another competent authority designated by the Member State that granting certification will not put at risk the security of energy supply of the Member State and the Community. In considering that question the regulatory authority or other competent authority so designated shall take into account:

       (i) the rights and obligations of the Community with respect to that third country arising under international law, including any agreement concluded with one or more third countries to which the Community is a party and which addresses the issues of security of energy supply;

       (ii) the rights and obligations of the Member State with respect to that third country arising under agreements concluded with it, insofar as they are in compliance with Community law; and

       (iii) other specific facts and circumstances of the case and the third country concerned.

This final compromise provision was much to the disappointment of the Baltic States and Poland, who due to historical grievances and past energy cuts from Russia have actively sought to shape a more critical line towards that country on the part of the EU.[45] Germany's opposition to such a forceful stance by the Union has been ascribed to the fact that almost all of its gas imports come directly from the Russian Federation. In EU external energy policy, a balance has always to be found between competing national interests.

P. Van Elsuwege, *Towards a Modernisation of EU–Russia Legal Relations?* (CEURUS EU–Russia Papers, No. 5, 2012), pp. 13–14

[I]t is no secret that Russia is not very happy with the EU's Third Energy Package, which requires [effective unbundling]. Significantly, undertakings from third countries, which intend to acquire control over an electricity or gas network, need to comply with the same unbundling requirements as EU undertakings. If they do not comply with these requirements, they [will be refused certification]. This, of course, has significant implications for Gazprom, which faces a legal obligation to 'unbundle' the ownership and operation of its gas pipelines on EU territory and to allow access to these pipelines to other energy companies. Vladimir Putin described this requirement as 'robbery' and 'confiscation of Russian property' and announced that Russia would take the necessary steps to challenge the validity of ... EU energy legislation. In Russia's view, the Third Energy Package is contrary to Article 34 (1) [EU–Russia partnership

---

[45] M. Leonard and N. Popescu, *A Power Audit of EU–Russia Relations* (European Council on Foreign Relations, November 2007), p. 48.

and Cooperation Agreement], which spells out that the parties shall use their best endeavours to prevent a deterioration of the market conditions under which their respective companies operate. In addition, Moscow announced to raise the issue in the WTO after its accession to this organisation. The 'Gazprom clause' raises questions of compatibility with different provisions of the General Agreement on Trade in Services (GATS) such as the Most Favourite Nation Principle (Art. II GATS), the prohibition of market access barriers (Art. XVI GATS) and the national treatment obligation (Article XVII of GATS). Finally, Russia may invoke investment protection clauses included in bilateral investment treaties (BITs) concluded with certain EU Member States.

(ii) Externalizing the *acquis*: Energy Community Treaty

The example of unbundling concerned the application of EU law to market participants from outside the EU. A second aspect of the external dimension of the internal market concerns the EU's proactive efforts to export EU rules, and effectively extend the internal market to third-country legal orders. The Treaty creating an Energy Community (ECT) between the EC entered into force on 1 July 2006 for a period of ten years, and was concluded between the EU on the one hand, and Albania, Bulgaria, Bosnia and Herzegovina, Croatia, FYROM, Montenegro, Romania, Serbia and the United Nations Mission in Kosovo (on behalf of the entity pursuant to the UN Security Council Resolution 1244 (1999)),[46] on the other. It is a regional, multilateral agreement which aims to create an integrated market in natural gas and electricity between the aforementioned countries and the EU.

Commission Communication, *On security of energy supply and international cooperation – 'The EU Energy Policy: Engaging with Partners beyond our Borders'*, COM(2011) 539 final, 7 September 2011, pp. 6–7

The Energy Community Treaty is the reference point for the majority of the EU's neighbours willing to be a part of the European energy system. With the recent accession of the Republic of Moldova and of Ukraine, the Energy Community has the potential to link the EU market with nine neighbouring countries. Its regulatory scope should be progressively extended and combined with more effective implementation and enforcement, as well as concrete assistance to reform these markets.

The ECT is a highly developed international treaty system equipped with a secretariat and autonomous decision-making bodies, an (albeit limited) dispute settlement system and legal instruments to attain the objective of export and extend the EU's energy *acquis* and related legislation in the areas of environment, competition and renewables.[47] As such, the ECT aims to create a stable regulatory and market framework capable of attracting investment so that all parties have access to the continuous gas and electricity supply that is essential for economic

---

[46] See Council Decision 2006/500/EC of 29 May 2006 on the conclusion by the European Community of the Energy Community Treaty, OJ 2006 No. L198/16.
[47] See Title II ECT.

development and social stability. When this multilateral sectoral agreement was signed on 25 October 2005 in Athens, the Commission's accompanying memorandum stated explicitly that this instrument 'was consciously modelled on the European Coal and Steel Community that is the basis of the European Union'.[48] Through legally binding sectoral multilateralism,[49] the ECT seeks to incentivize the partners of post-war south east Europe to agree on one area of policy and then to develop a shared outlook and integrate accordingly. The parallel with the ECSC is self-evident, though the effective export of the EU *acquis* to third countries with less mature legal systems is by no means self-evident.

S. Blockmans and B. Van Vooren, 'Revitalizing the European Neighbourhood Economic Community, The Case for Legally Binding Sectoral Multilateralism' (2012) 17 *European Foreign Affairs Review* 577–604 at 603

By examining the cases of energy and transport, we have argued that binding sectoral multilateralism can provide clear policy benefits while the legal counterarguments are not insurmountable. The policy argument for sectoral multilateralism was a rather pragmatic one, in that it applies a neo-functional reasoning to EU external relations: ensuring that concrete incentives exist against attaining concrete policy objectives which are laid down in a binding framework which ensures appropriate and sufficient enforcement. . . . On the legal side, there are no doubt challenges both at macroscopic and implementation level. The problem of interpretive uniformity, as well as the static model of adaptation certainly highlights some of the perils associated with binding sectoral multilateralism. However, these hurdles are by no means unknown to the Union through its enlargement policy and Stabilization and Association Process, and we have argued that dismissing binding sectoral multilateralism solely because of this reason would be throwing away the baby with the bathwater.

(iii) Bilateral energy instruments: international agreements and soft law

In the bilateral sphere, the EU utilizes two sets of external instruments. First, it will include provisions on energy cooperation in its bilateral agreements with third countries. We have seen one example of this when examining ownership unbundling: namely Article 34(1) PCA with Russia contains a best endeavour clause to prevent the deterioration of the market conditions under which their respective companies operate. However, such provisions have limited effects. In bilateral relations with third countries, of far greater importance are the many non-legally binding MoU or Joint Declarations which the EU has concluded in the energy sector. Indeed, in contrast to the legal developments in the internal energy market, the fledgling EU external energy policy has been very much 'executive-driven'. This is illustrated by the fact that aside from important instruments such as the ECT which has a limited regional focus, the Union has conducted its external energy relations through bilateral soft law through non-legally binding

---

[48] *An integrated market for electricity and gas across 34 European Countries*, MEMO/05/397, Brussels, 25 October 2005.
[49] S. Blockmans and B. Van Vooren, 'Revitalizing the European Neighbourhood Economic Community, The Case for Legally Binding Sectoral Multilateralism' (2012) 17 *European Foreign Affairs Review* 577–604.

Table 13.2 – MoUs and Joint Declarations in the field of energy

Date	Country	Nature of document	Signatories for EU	Signatories for third country
1 December 2005	Ukraine	MoU on cooperation in the field of energy between the EU and Ukraine	President of the European Council; President of the Commission	President of Ukraine
7 November 2006	Azerbaijan	MoU on a Strategic Partnership between the EU and Azerbaijan in the field of energy	President of the European Council; President of the Commission	President of Azerbaijan
4 December 2006	Kazakhstan	MoU on cooperation in the field of energy between the EU and Kazakhstan	Commissioner for RELEX and ENP and Council Presidency	Not named
24 July 2007	Morocco	Joint Declaration on the priorities for cooperation between the Commission and Morocco in the energy sector	DG RELEX	Director at Energy and Mining Ministry
31 October 2007	Jordan	Joint Declaration on the priorities for cooperation between the Commission and Jordan in the energy sector	Commissioner for RELEX and ENP	Minister for Energy and Mineral Resources
26 May 2008	Turkmenistan	MoU and cooperation in the field of energy between the EU and Turkmenistan	Energy Commissioner Piebalgs and Council Presidency	Not named
2 December 2008	Egypt	MoU on Strategic Partnership on energy between the EU and Egypt	Commissioner for RELEX and ENP and Commissioner for Energy	Minister for Foreign Affairs
16 November 2009	Russia	MoU on Energy Dialogue	Energy Commissioner	Minister of Energy of the Russian Federation
18 January 2010	Iraq	MoU between the government of Iraq and the EU on Strategic Partnership in Energy	Energy Commissioner, 'HR for Foreign Affairs and Security Policy/VP of the Commission', Spanish Presidency	Minister of Oil

Table 13.2 (*cont.*)

Date	Country	Nature of document	Signatories for EU	Signatories for third country
13 January 2011	Azerbaijan	Joint Declaration on the Southern Gas Corridor	President of the European Commission	President of Azerbaijan
24 January 2011	Uzbekistan	MoU on cooperation in the field of energy between the EU and Uzbekistan	Energy Commissioner and Hungarian Ambassador	First Deputy Prime Minister and Minister for Finance
10 February 2012	India	Joint Declaration for Enhanced Cooperation on Energy between the EU and Government of India	Not signed, adopted in margins of EU–India Summit	First Deputy Prime Minister and Minister for Finance
3 May 2012	China	EU–China Joint Declaration on Energy Security	Commissioner for Energy	Administrator of the National Energy Administration

instruments (see also Chapter 15).[50] Table 13.2 provides an overview of the non-binding documents 'concluded' between the EU and third countries for the period 2005 to end 2012.

The express objective of the EU is that these non-legally binding instruments would over time lead to a binding legal framework through which to organize energy trade with a given third country. In that sense, these bilateral soft law documents are considered a temporary, second-best solution (see also Chapter 15 on soft law in the neighbourhood policy).

Commission Communication, *Second Strategic Energy Review*, COM(2008) 781 final, Brussels, 13 November 2008, p. 8

Today the EU has Memoranda of Understanding on energy with a large number of third countries. Europe should develop a new generation of "energy interdependence" provisions in broad-based agreements with producer countries outside Europe. Energy interdependence provisions should aim at a balance between security of demand and security of supply. The focus should be on encouraging upstream investments, facilitating the development of the necessary infrastructures, clear conditions of access to markets (within energy and across economic sectors), dialogue on market and policy developments, and dispute settlement provisions. Transit arrangements must be agreed to guarantee normal flows even in periods of political tension, possibly through innovative approaches such as joint management and even ownership of pipelines by companies of supplier, transit and consumer countries. The provisions should be based on the

---

[50] Van Vooren, *EU External Relations Law and the European Neighbourhood Policy: A Paradigm for Coherence* (Abingdon/New York: Routledge, 2012), pp. 203–205 (on the MoUs and their legal effect).

EU's energy acquis where appropriate, and the principles of the Energy Charter Treaty. The provisions should contribute to a long term political framework, reducing political risks and encouraging commitments by private companies on supply and transit.

The best and most recent example is the EU–Ukraine Deep and Comprehensive Free Trade Agreement (DCFTA), which places bilateral energy trade with a third country on a firm legal footing. At the time this book went to press this agreement was not yet signed or ratified, and this may take a while given the political climate in the country.

Chapter 11 of the EU–Ukraine DCFTA is entitled 'trade related energy' and is structured as follows: Article 268 which contains definitions expressly referring to the internal energy *acquis*; Article 269 on domestic regulated prices; Article 270 on prohibition of dual pricing; Article 271 on the prohibition of customs duties and quantitative restrictions; Article 272 on facilitating transit in accordance with the GATT and the ECT; Article 273 on conditions for transport across the parties' territory; Article 274 on cooperation pertaining to energy infrastructure; Article 275 on measures to prohibit the unauthorized taking of energy goods; Article 276 on measures to ensure that no interruptions occur in the operation of transit or transport of energy goods; Article 277 requiring the setting up of a regulatory authority for electricity and gas (in accordance with EU *acquis*); Article 278 on the relationship with the ECT in which Ukraine participates, where the ECT is given preference; Article 279 on prospecting activities pertaining to hydrocarbons; and finally Article 280 on licensing relating to the previous article. It remains to be seen whether the agreement will enter into force given the tempestuous EU–Ukraine relationship, but it is certain that Chapter 11 of the draft agreement very much reflects the objectives set forth in the Second Strategic Energy Review in 2008, and the EU will thus surely aim to replicate its content in other bilateral relationships and negotiations on a legal framework.

6 THE ROLE OF THE INSTITUTIONS IN EXTERNAL ENERGY POLICY

(i) The Commission, Member States, HR/VP and EEAS

EU external energy policy has undergone a deep shift with the Lisbon Treaty in terms of institutions and personalities responsible in this area: first, within the Commission DG TREN has been split up into two, and now there is a DG (ENER) responsible only for energy. Second, DG RELEX has ceased to exist within the Commission, and was subsumed into the EEAS in January 2011. Third, the former HR/SG Javier Solana has been succeeded by Catherine Ashton who has visibly influenced energy priorities in CFSP. Fourth, while the HR chairs the FAC, the Energy and General Affairs Council formats are still chaired by the rotating Presidency. Finally, through Article 194 *iuncto* 218 TFEU, the EP now has a potentially significant role in EU external energy policy. The two most notable changes examined in this chapter are the division of tasks between the Commission and HR/VP with the EEAS, and the new role for the European Parliament.

One of the central changes post-Lisbon is of course the presence of an EU diplomatic service under the guidance of the HR for CFSP who also holds the post of Vice-President of the Commission. The mandate of the HR/VP is not only to conduct the CFSP, but also to ensure consistency between all aspects of EU external relations (Article 18 TFEU). From Table 13.2, we can make a number of observations on the current institutional balance, but also the continuing presence of the Member States, in EU external energy relations. Four of these documents postdate the Lisbon Treaty: the MoUs with Iraq (2010) and Uzbekistan (2011), and the Joint Declarations with India and China (2012). The signatories on the EU side provide much insight into the vertical division of competence between the EU and Member States, and the horizontal division between the institutions. As regards the horizontal perspective, the Commission is always one of the signatories, be this the head of former DG RELEX, the Energy Commissioner or the Commission President himself. Only in one instance did the HR co-sign, namely the MoU with Iraq. This was six weeks after the entry into force of the Treaty of Lisbon. However, in successive documents the HR's signature was again absent. Vertically then, we see that out of thirteen documents, six were co-signed by a representative of the rotating Presidency, three pre-Lisbon and three post-Lisbon. This overview of signatories on the EU side shows us that in EU external energy the Commission remains the central actor, the Member States through the Presidency assume an important role alongside that institution, and only once was the HR included, but that seems to be an *accident de parcours*.

B. Van Vooren, *Europe Unplugged: Progress, Potential and Limitations of EU External Energy Policy three years post-Lisbon* (SIEPS Working Paper 2012:5), pp. 41–42

In terms of division of competence, we can thus infer the following: the Commission signs for the aspects of the MoU's/Joint Declarations which concern the external dimension of the internal market, which pre-empts Member State action since the competence is shared with the Member States (Articles 194 TFEU iuncto 2 (2) & 4 (2) (i) TFEU).The Member States then, represent those areas of external policy which have not been covered yet by the Union, as well as the foreign and security policy aspects of external energy policy (24 TFEU). How do we explain the fact that the High Representative once co-signed the MoU with Iraq, alongside the Spanish Presidency? Six weeks after the entry into force of the Lisbon Treaty, the institutions and the newly appointed leadership were still finding their bearings on the novel lines of competence between them. In terms of content, the MoU with Iraq was certainly nothing different from other MoU's, basically proposing the development of Iraqi energy policy along the lines of a shared, mutual interest with the EU. Immediately post-Lisbon, it must therefore have been thought that energy security fell within the mandate of the new High Representative, to be exercised jointly with the Energy Commissioner. The fact that four subsequent documents were not signed by the High Representative is then telling, some of which clearly have a significant energy security aspect to them – and are similar to the MoU with Iraq. In conclusion then, the HR's signature under the 2010 Iraqi MoU was due to the "transitionary tug-of-war" which was ongoing in the wake of the Lisbon Treaty's entry into force, with the dust having now firmly settled in the hands of the Commission.

Javier Solana, the predecessor of the current HR was most active in the sphere of EU external energy policy. He viewed security of energy supply as an integral part of the Union's CFSP, but strongly pursued overall coherence with the more market-orientated elements of EU external energy policy. Speaking in 2008, Solana said:

There is no single solution. We will have to work on multiple fronts: savings and efficiency, renewables and biofuels; carbon capture, interconnections and storage. . . . [T]here is not just an internal solution. We also need a credible European external energy policy. . . . I sometimes wonder if we are keeping up with the speed and scope of the changes in the international energy landscape. Big deals are being made every day. In the Middle East, the Caucasus, the Balkans and Asia. From decisions on pipelines, to exploration deals to strategic partnerships among producers. Our future options seem to be narrowing while others move in a determined manner.[51]

It is for that reason that when EU energy policy was being drawn up during the first half of 2006, he ensured that his services drafted jointly with the Commission a non-paper for the attention of the European Council to support a coherent and overarching approach to its external dimension. Furthermore, Solana made regular appearances and speeches at prominent events where he emphasized the importance of energy in his work: 'Hardly a day goes by that I am not confronted in my role as High Representative with the impact that energy has: from Sudan to Venezuela, from Iran to the Caucasus and beyond.' [52] However, whereas in May 2006 the services of the then HR and the RELEX Commissioner wrote a joint paper at the request of the European Council 'to harness the EU's collective resources' towards a coherent, strategic and focused external energy policy, the HR post-Lisbon plays almost no role in energy policy. Notably then, the September 2011 Communication on security of energy supply and international cooperation is a publication of the Commission only. Such an exclusion of the EEAS is not merely coincidental, as indeed the Commission has proactively 'sought to protect the house' in drawing up post-Lisbon EU external energy policy.

(ii) The European Parliament

Article 194(2) TFEU prescribes that the ordinary legislative procedure (Article 294 TFEU) shall apply to establish the measures necessary to achieve the objectives of EU energy policy in paragraph 1 of that article. In the external field, the consequence is that in accordance with Article 218(6)(a)(v) TFEU, international agreements within the scope of Article 194 require the consent of the EP (Article 218 TFEU).

Looking again at Table 13.2, an observation directly pertinent to the role of the EP in EU external energy policy is that because all of these documents are considered 'non legal', this entails the complete exclusion of the normal treaty-making procedure of Article 218 TFEU. For example, the EU–Russia MoU setting up the Energy Dialogue states in 'section 13' (purposively not called 'Article' 13 to avoid legal language) that 'This Memorandum does not constitute an international agreement or other legally binding document and does not establish rights and obligations governed by international law.'[53] From the perspective of the EP, the message is evident: if the MoUs are negotiated, concluded and implemented entirely in the 'executive' sphere of EU external relations, and since all memoranda are considered merely 'non-legally binding' instruments, the EP will be excluded from giving its consent on these agreements, with commensurate lack of parliamentary influence on the negotiated outcome of such documents. However, in EU external energy policy, as in other external policy fields, there is a consistent

---

[51] Speech by Javier Solana, former EU HR, *The External Energy Policy of the European Union*, delivered at the Annual Conference of the French Institute of International Relations (IFRI), Brussels, 1 February 2008. www.consilium.europa. eu/ueDocs/cms_Data/docs/pressdata/EN/discours/98532.pdf (last accessed 19 October 2012).

[52] J. Solana, *Address to the External Energy Policy Conference*, Brussels, 20 November 2006, DOC S324/06.

[53] Section 13 EU-Russia MoU setting up an early warning system, on file with author.

tendency of the Union to initiate relations through non-legally binding soft law first, and then move to legally binding commitments (see further Chapter 15). As we have discussed in relation to the EU–Ukraine DCFTA, this trend is certainly present in EU external energy policy. As this dynamic progresses, consent of the EP will be required. If we may then draw lessons from other areas of EU external relations post-Lisbon – for example the EU–South Korea FTA or the SWIFT Agreement with the USA,[54] this implies that the EP will keep a close eye on these negotiations and assert its perceived interests where necessary. In this respect, the role of the EP could be crucial in ensuring coherence between EU energy interests and EU values (Articles 3(5) and 21 TEU). With its 2007 report entitled 'Towards common European foreign policy in energy', Parliament has clearly indicated an ambition in that direction.[55]

7 THE EU–MEMBER STATES' DUTY OF COOPERATION IN ENERGY

(i) Origin and rationale of the decision

In the Energy 2020 Strategy published in 2010, the Commission said that it would propose mechanisms to ensure that the Member States act for the benefit of the EU supply security in their bilateral relations, and to ensure that the agreements which they conclude are in line with the internal market rules. In response to the request for more formalized solidarity mechanisms, the European Council of 4 February 2011 made the following statement:

> **Conclusions of the European Council, Brussels, 4 February 2011, DOC EUCO 2/1/11**
>
> The Member States are invited to inform from 1 January 2012 the Commission on all their new and existing bilateral energy agreements with third countries; the Commission will make this information available to all other Member States in an appropriate form, having regard to the need for protection of commercially sensitive information.

Previous experience from other policy areas shows that such an open-ended invitation without a formalized legal structure does not suffice to ensure that the common EU interest prevails over national policy priorities.[56] The background to incorporating this 'invitation' in the European Council Conclusions supports that lesson learnt: the Hungarian Presidency had sought a far stronger commitment from leaders to inform each other about energy agreements, but this met with the resistance of Italy and the UK, resulting in the open-ended 'invitation' to do so.[57] With this in mind, on 7 September 2011, the European Commission published alongside its Communication also the proposal for a 'Decision of the European Parliament and of the Council setting up

---

[54] J. Monar, 'The Rejection of the EU–US SWIFT Interim Agreement by the European Parliament: A Historic Vote and its Implications' (2010) 15 *European Foreign Affairs Review* 143.

[55] Report of the European Parliament, Committee on Foreign Affairs, *Towards a common European foreign policy on energy*, Committee on Foreign Affairs, 11 September 2007, p. 5.

[56] Council Decision 80/50/EEC of 20 December 1979 setting up a consultation procedure on relations between Member States and third countries in the field of air transport and on action relating to such matters within international organizations, OJ 1980 No. L 18/24.

[57] S. Taylor, 'Safety-First Approach to European Energy Policy', *European Voice*, 23–29 June 2011.

an information exchange mechanism with regard to intergovernmental agreements between Member States and third countries in the field of energy' (hereafter the 'Energy Decision').[58] This proposal is meant to transform the European Council invitation into a mechanism with detailed procedures information exchange and EU-level coordination on intergovernmental agreements which 'are likely to have an impact on the operation or the functioning of the internal market for energy or on the security of energy supply in the Union'.[59] The positive vote in Parliament took place on 13 September 2012, and the Council approved the Decision on 4 October 2012.[60]

Instruments such as the Energy Decision are a relative novelty in EU external relations law. Two other such mechanisms are currently in place, though not as Decisions but as Regulations: Regulation 847/2004 in the field of external aviation, and Regulation 664/2009 in external dimension of matrimonial matters.[61] These are instruments which organize the vertical EU–Member State relationship, and are formal expressions of the duty of cooperation embedded in Article 4(3) TEU. They entail binding obligations of information and consultation, and may even require *ex ante* or *ex post* authorization for the Member States to conclude binding instruments. Often, the line between information, consultation and authorization can be rather thin, making these instruments politically contentious and their obligations the result of complex negotiations. This was no different in the energy field.

In the following subsection we first briefly explain the nature of Member State international agreements targeted by the Energy Decision. This will allow for a better assessment of whether it will be able to command Member State loyalty in the pursuit of an effective and coherent EU external energy policy. Thereafter, we examine the final text of the information mechanism in light of 'the Union interest' in energy policy, both from a legal and policy perspective.

(ii) Article 194(2) TFEU: Member State intergovernmental agreements

We have seen that Article 194(2) TFEU, second indent safeguards Member States' competence to decide 'the general structure of their energy supply'. Hence, even with a shared pre-emptive competence in external energy policy, Member States remain competent to conclude agreements in this domain to the extent that they are considered integral to deciding the national energy mix stated in Article 194(2) TFEU.

Intergovernmental agreements between Member States and third countries can have as their object both gas and oil, though the Commission estimates that there are more agreements on

---

[58] Proposal from the Commission, *Decision of the European Parliament and of the Council setting up an information exchange mechanism with regard to intergovernmental agreements between Member States and third countries in the field of energy*, 7 September 2011, COM(2011) 540.

[59] Council Conclusions, *Energy 2020: A Strategy for competitive, sustainable and secure energy*, Brussels, 28 February 2011, p. 1.

[60] Decision 994/2012/EU of the European Parliament and of the Council of 25 October 2012 establishing an information exchange mechanism with regard to intergovernmental agreements between Member States and third countries in the field of energy (Text with EEA relevance), OJ 2012 No. L299/13.

[61] Regulation 847/2004/EC of the European Parliament and of the Council of 29 April 2004 on the negotiation and implementation of air service agreements between Member States and third countries, OJ 2004 No. L157/7; Council Regulation 664/2009/EC of 7 July 2009 establishing a procedure for the negotiation and conclusion of agreements between Member States and third countries concerning jurisdiction, recognition and enforcement of judgments and decisions in matrimonial matters, matters of parental responsibility and matters relating to maintenance obligations, and the law applicable to matters relating to maintenance obligations, OJ 2009 No. L200/46.

gas.[62] This is because gas trade is more infrastructure-dependent than oil, though with the latter hydrocarbon is sometimes also transported through pipelines (rather than oil tankers, which makes the oil market more liquid and global). In either case, such international agreements can have as their subject the construction of new infrastructure, such as a new gas pipeline to be constructed between the parties; or they can relate to agreements on actual supply and delivery of the relevant hydrocarbon. Often there is then an intimate relationship between the energy companies based in the Member State, with the intergovernmental agreement providing (long-term) political and regulatory backing to the commercial relationship of the energy companies (national champions) involved. All these agreements have the potential of being at odds with EU internal market laws.

Gas deliveries are commonly agreed as take-or-pay contracts between energy giants and/or the governments of the countries in which they are based. These are contracts whereby the contracted supplies have to be paid ('pay') for regardless of whether they have been used ('take') because demand in the consumer country has been lower than agreed in the agreement. They generally have a long duration up to twenty-five years to counterbalance the substantial investment connected to infrastructure, and provide a guaranteed income to the producer country/company. Additionally, these agreements have persistently contained clauses which prohibit European companies from reselling gas outside their home country: 'destination clauses'. These clauses protect gas deliveries against having to compete with themselves, and guarantee the effectiveness of bilateral price negotiations between the third country and the various EU Member States. Such carving up of the market is obviously a concern from the perspective of EU law: on the one hand, territorial restrictions are clearly prohibited by Article 101 TFEU, and on the other hand the decade-long length of the agreements with preferential national pricing is equally incompatible with an EU-wide liberalized market. Taking the example of Russia, this country has fiercely defended such take-or-pay contracts with their destination clauses. The Commission has already from 2000 onwards threatened legal action against European companies,[63] and while it was unable to have any impact on the length of the Member States' agreements with these countries, between 2000 and 2004 destination clauses were being dismantled and removed from bilateral agreements with Russia.[64]

Infrastructure agreements can also be problematic. Namely, Member States are regularly under pressure to accept clauses violating EU energy *acquis*, notably when there are clauses that reserve the right of a particular company to contract the full capacity or part of the capacity of the pipeline subject to the intergovernmental agreement. For example, in the case of the South Stream project, several EU Member States have concluded bilateral agreements with Russia which, if they are applied upon completion of the pipeline, will contravene EU law. Agreements on pipelines should allow non-discriminatory access to booking capacity for transit and non-discriminatory tariffs, as well as allowing for bi-directional flows in line with the Gas Security Regulation.

The key point to take home is that these bilateral agreements are legally not always in line with the internal market rules, but also that they may be hampering the policy objectives of

---

[62] Proposal from the Commission, *Decision of the European Parliament and of the Council setting up an information exchange mechanism with regard to intergovernmental agreements between Member States and third countries in the field of energy*, 7 September 2011, COM(2011) 540, p. 2.

[63] P. Aalto, *The EU–Russian Energy Dialogue* (Aldershot: Ashgate, 2008), p. 68.

[64] See the list of cases provided by the Commission in MEMO/03/159, *Application of competition rules to the gas sector*, Brussels, 29 July 2003.

Article 194 TFEU, EU supply security in particular: secretive, individual deals by Member States and third countries make the EU very much susceptible to geostrategic divide-and-rule approaches on the part of third countries. The case of Nord Stream is a recent well-known example. Economically, the project which runs through the Baltic Sea was questioned by some as not the most cost-effective, safe or environmentally friendly route for gas deliveries from Russia to Germany. However, the project went ahead and it avoids traditional routes for Russian gas deliveries: Belarus and Poland in the north, and Ukraine in the south. From an EU perspective, Poland was certainly displeased at what its Foreign Minister in 2010 termed the 'Molotov–Ribbentrop pipeline'.

(iii) Formalizing the duty of cooperation towards the 'EU interest'

As we have seen in Chapter 6, Article 4(3) TEU requires that the 'Union and the Member State shall, in full mutual respect, assist each other in carrying out the tasks which flow from the Treaties'. The Energy Decision is a legally binding instrument which seeks to compel Member States to act for the benefit of the EU legal and political interest, in the context of their intergovernmental energy agreements. As a formal instrument implementing that obligation of primary law, this instrument must be unequivocal on what are the 'tasks which flow from the treaties', and which obligations are entailed by the duty of cooperation in pursuit of 'the Union interest'.

There are two distinct aspects of the EU–Member State relationship which the Decision addresses to different degrees. First, there is the legal dimension which requires that Member State bilateral agreements do not violate principles essential to the proper functioning of the internal market. Second, there is the political dimension that Member States' agreements substantively take into account the 'Union interest' to ensure security of supply for all twenty-eight Members as one, and proactively work with the institutions towards that objective. In what follows we examine the legal and policy obligations of the duty of cooperation as they are laid down in the Energy Decision.[65] An overview of the structure of the instrument is necessary:

- A lengthy preamble with a number of important qualifications and clarifications.
- Article 1 defining the subject matter and scope of the mechanism.
- Article 2 containing a definition of 'intergovernmental agreements'
- Article 3 on exchange of information between the Commission and the Member States; and Article 3a on confidentiality in this regard.
- Article 4 concerns 'assistance from the Commission' following from the previous article.
- Article 5 which was entitled 'ex ante compatibility control' in the original Commission version, but which has been renamed as 'Compatibility Assessment' in the final compromise text.
- Article 6 entitled 'coordination with the Member States'.
- Article 7 on confidentiality and Article 8 planning for a review of the mechanism four years after its entry into force.

[65] Decision 994/2012/EU of the European Parliament and of the Council of 25 October 2012 establishing an information exchange mechanism with regard to intergovernmental agreements between Member States and third countries in the field of energy (Text with EEA relevance), OJ 2012 No. L299/13 (Referred to as 'Energy Decision').

(iv) Scope of application of the Energy Decision

Article 2 of the Energy Decision defines an intergovernmental agreement which falls within its scope as follows.

Energy Decision, Article 2: Definitions

For the purposes of this Decision the following definitions apply:

1. "intergovernmental agreement" means any legally binding agreement between one or more Member States and one or more third countries having an impact on the operation or the functioning of the internal energy market or on the security of energy supply in the Union; however, where such a legally binding agreement also covers other issues, only those provisions that relate to energy, including general provisions applicable to those energy-related provisions, shall constitute an "intergovernmental agreement";
2. "existing intergovernmental agreement" means an intergovernmental agreement which entered into force or is applied provisionally prior to the entry into force of this Decision.

This definition of international agreements has two important elements: first, it encompasses legally binding agreements only, and thus does not capture non-binding MoU. We have seen previously in this chapter that such instruments do play an important role in (EU) energy policy. Second, it leaves open the question as to when the agreement impacts the internal market and/or EU security of supply, and who gets to decide. We look at these two elements in turn.

(a) Legally binding agreements only

Article 2(1) of the Decision defines an international agreement as 'any legally binding agreement'. Previously in this chapter we have indicated that it is commonplace for the Union to use non-legal binding documents (MoUs) to give political backing to future energy relations. Transposing that reality to the Member State level, the Decision then explicitly states that it will solely apply to intergovernmental agreements of Member States *with legal binding force*. The question is thus whether such limitation will create the temptation for Member States to venture further into the soft law sphere to avoid this EU-level information exchange mechanism. Indeed, as the EU itself has done in its MoUs, one could conclude a very meticulously drafted international agreement, but simply add a final provision saying that 'this document does not constitute a legally binding document' thereby avoiding the information obligation. What is more, an informal (and secret) gentlemen's agreement between Member State and third-country leadership may sometimes suffice as political backing for commercial entities to continue or set up a business relationship. A pertinent example – though obviously public and certainly with Commission knowledge – is the political agreement between Italy, Albania and Greece on the Trans Adriatic Pipeline (TAP).[66] The TAP is one of the proposals which would complete the EU's Southern Corridor, to transport gas from Azerbaijan and some of its neighbours to European markets. This 'political agreement' on TAP paved the way for a formal intergovernmental

---

[66] Press Release, *Commissioner Oettinger welcomes the signature of the political agreement on TAP*, 28 September 2012, IP/712/1041.

agreement setting out the legal framework for the pipeline, which in turn will be implemented by participating commercial actors in the TAP consortium (E.ON, Statoil and Axpo). If we apply the information exchange mechanism in the Energy Decision to these events, the first political agreement on TAP would not have to be notified, the commercial agreements between the aforementioned companies are a priori excluded, and only the legally binding agreement at Member State level is captured by the regime.

(b) 'Optionally' organizing the EU–MS duty of cooperation

The Energy Decision contains a duty to inform the Commission in case the Member State intergovernmental agreements have an impact on the functioning or operation of the internal energy market, or on the security of energy supply in the Union. Importantly, it is initially up to the Member States to decide whether this is the case.

Energy Decision, Preamble, paragraph 4

The initial assessment as to whether an intergovernmental agreement, or another text to which an intergovernmental agreement refers to explicitly, has an impact on the internal market for energy or the security of energy supply in the Union should be the responsibility of Member States; in case of doubt, a Member State should consult the Commission. In principle, agreements that are no longer in force or are no longer applied, do not have an impact on the internal market for energy or on the security of energy supply in the Union and are thus not covered by this information exchange mechanism.

This is mirrored in paragraph 9 of the preamble, which states that more transparency on future agreements will be beneficial for compliance and EU supply security, and that 'therefore, Member States should have *the option* to inform the Commission' (emphasis added)[67] of new negotiations. This renders the mechanism 'non-automatic' through giving the Member States initial control over the information that feeds into the EU mechanism. The question is then: to what extent does this allow for (continued) secrecy on the part of the Member States in certain international negotiations? The definition of intergovernmental agreements allows little leeway in this regard, since it is difficult to envisage Member State agreements that would not 'impact' the internal energy market or EU supply security. However, this depends entirely on the narrow or wide definition of the notion 'impact', and no definition or clarification can be found in the Energy Decision. For example, as regards impact on the internal market, the most obvious example is that of EU competition law. Article 101(1) TFEU states that 'the following shall be prohibited as incompatible with the internal market: all agreements . . . which may affect trade between Member States . . . and which have as their object or effect the prevention, restriction or distortion of competition within the internal market'. The meaning of the scope and interpretation of this phrase has generated a large body of literature, but even so, the notion of 'impact' in the Energy Decision is certainly broader: the Decision does not say what kind of impact (positive

---

[67] Decision 994/2012/EU of the European Parliament and of the Council of 25 October 2012 establishing an information exchange mechanism with regard to intergovernmental agreements between Member States and third countries in the field of energy (Text with EEA relevance), OJ 2012 No. L299/13, para 9 of the preamble.

or negative) the agreement should have, and since impact relates to any form of EU internal market law, all eventualities fall within the scope of the information mechanism: e.g. not just competition but also all pertinent internal market secondary legislation. Add to that, that even if the agreement does not impact the internal market, if it impacts EU security of supply it is subject to the discipline of the Decision. Security of supply is broad, in that it can be a positive or negative effect, and includes demand-side and supply-side security. Arguably, any intergovernmental agreement pertaining to planned new infrastructure from a third country into an EU Member State, or a long-term agreement on terms for delivery of hydrocarbons into a Member State, would impact 'EU' security of supply.

Thus, if we accept that the notion of 'impact' is rather broad, the safeguard function of this initial assessment is merely a political palliative to ease the pain of Member States 'giving up powers' to the supranational institutions. However, by inserting this preliminary assessment, the Energy Decision creates new uncertainties through opening a clear avenue for litigation before the CJEU. Paragraph 2 of the preamble of the Decision paraphrases the text from Article 4(3) TEU, thereby confirming that the instrument is essentially an expression of the EU–Member State duty of loyal cooperation. Suppose that indeed a Member State decides that certain negotiations will not affect EU security of supply or the internal market, and it goes ahead without consulting and/or notifying the Commission. When word of the agreement gets out (at the moment of ratification or earlier), the Commission asks for information, which the Member State either refuses, or more likely, provides but in a limited fashion. Subsequently, the Member State goes ahead and ratifies the agreement. The Commission has been most proactive and successful in having the Member States convicted for violations of the duty of cooperation, and situations such as the one described here would exactly be captured by that case law (see Chapter 6). Thus, this instrument which seeks to organize the duty of cooperation, might still give rise to litigation due to the 'initial assessment' by a Member State which may be at odds with later assessments on the part of the Commission. Thus, legal certainty and effectiveness of the regime have been partially sacrificed on the altar of continuing Member State sensitivities over the national interest in face of the common EU interest in transparency, information-sharing and cooperation.

(v) The obligation to provide information on existing agreements

Article 3(1) requires that existing intergovernmental agreements of the Member States with third countries are communicated to the Commission within three months of the entry into force of the Decision. The proposed decision is in that sense a broadened version of Article 13(6) of the Gas Security Regulation.[68] That article requires that intergovernmental agreements which have 'an impact on the development of gas infrastructure and gas supplies' be communicated. Agreements submitted under the Gas Security Regulation are considered to have been submitted for the purposes of this Decision. Following this communication, the Commission checks the agreement, and informs the Member State if there may be a problem.

---

[68] Regulation 994/2010/EU of the European Parliament and of the Council of 20 October 2010 concerning measures to safeguard security of gas supply and repealing Council Directive 2004/67/EC, OJ 2010 No. L295/1.

> **Energy Decision, Article 3(2)**
>
> Where following its first assessment, the Commission has doubts as to the compatibility with Union law of agreements submitted to it under paragraph 1, in particular with Union competition law and internal energy market legislation, the Commission shall inform the Member States concerned accordingly within 9 months following the submission of those agreements.

The scope of this assessment is not defined further, and neither are its legal consequences. The quoted passage states that the compatibility check 'in particular' will look at competition and internal market rules, which means that beyond a legality assessment, there may also be a policy-orientated assessment focusing on 'EU security of supply', which would be in line with Article 194(1) TFEU. The consequences of the Commission informing the Member State of its assessment are then left open. In legal terms, this compatibility check with the *acquis* does not take on the form of a 'reasoned opinion' under Article 258 TFEU. The potential impact or role of this check by the Commission in relation to future infringement proceedings is left open by the Decision. Similarly, what happens if the Commission finds incompatibility with EU security of supply? For example, it could trigger discussions under Article 7 of the Decision: paragraph (d) of that article states that the Commission shall facilitate coordination among Member States with a view to supporting the development of multilateral intergovernmental agreements involving several Member States or the Union as a whole. In other words, if current intergovernmental agreements are found to violate EU energy policy objectives in legal and/or political terms, will this mechanism be used to trigger their replacement by EU (–Member State mixed) energy agreements with the relevant third country? It is undoubtedly the case that Commission DG ENER sees the Energy Decision as an instrument potentially leading to such international agreements concluded by the Union.

(vi) Obligations relating to negotiating new agreements

> **Energy Decision, Article 3(3)**
>
> Before or during negotiations with a third country on an intergovernmental agreement or on the amendment of an existing intergovernmental agreement, a Member State may inform the Commission in writing of the objectives of, and the provisions to be addressed in, the negotiations and may communicate any other relevant information to the Commission. Where the Member State gives the Commission such notice of negotiations, the Member State concerned shall keep the Commission regularly informed of the progress of the negotiations.

Article 3(3) applies the same duty of information when Member States wish to open negotiations on a new agreement, and while they are ongoing. In the original proposal on the Energy Decision, the text required that a Member State 'shall' notify the Commission 'when it intends' to enter into negotiations. The final version has been watered down, since a Member State 'may'[69] inform the Commission 'before or during' the negotiations rather than at the moment of 'intention' to that effect. The original version then also stated that such a notification would include 'the relevant documentation, and indication of the provisions to be addressed', and this level of specificity has been dropped in favour of a more general duty of information 'on the objectives of the negotiations'. Thus, the information obligation as it stands is a possibility, the substance of the notification is limited to what the Member State hopes to achieve without further detail on what it intends to negotiate, and information no longer needs to arrive before negotiations are opened. When negotiations are ongoing, the Commission shall be kept 'regularly informed of the progress of negotiations'. It of course depends on the goodwill of the Member State to decide the depth of the information provided in fulfilling that obligation. During the negotiations, there is a role for the Commission which is focused purely on legal compatibility with EU energy policy, but not political compatibility as in relation to agreements already in existence. Namely, Article 3(4) states that when the Member State 'gives notice of negotiations' the Commission 'may provide the negotiating Member State with advice on how to avoid incompatibility [of the agreement] with Union law'.

In all cases, this information will be shared with other Member States in a secure electronic form. However, there are limitations to the notion of full, reciprocal information-sharing integral to the mechanism. As stated, there is the possibility for exceptions where the Member States can instruct the Commission not to communicate the intergovernmental agreement to other Member States, but only a summary of the information submitted (Article 3, paragraphs 6 and 7, and Article 4). This is possible when Member States indicate that any part of the information could harm the activities of the parties involved. The Commission gets access to the information in full, but the Decision does not foresee a role for that institution to assess the arguments of the Member States as valid or not. Finally, note that paragraphs 1 and 5 of this article explicitly exclude the applicability of these obligations 'in respect of agreements between commercial entities'.

(vii) The consequences of Member State compliance with the information duty

In the explanatory memorandum to the proposed Energy Decision, the Commission stated that fulfilling the notification obligation of Article 3 does not prevent it from starting infringement procedures if necessary, i.e. when an agreement still infringes internal market rules. Indeed, throughout the Energy Decision there is no clarity on the legal consequences of compatibility or compliance by the Member States with the information obligations imposed by this legal instrument. This is underlined by a Commission statement which it communicated at the moment of adoption of the decision in the Council.

---

[69] Decision 994/2012/EU of the European Parliament and of the Council of 25 October 2012 establishing an information exchange mechanism with regard to intergovernmental agreements between Member States and third countries in the field of energy (Text with EEA relevance), OJ 2012 No. L299/13, at 13. Further quotations from the text in this subsection are from this instrument, and not referenced in further detail.

Council of the European Union, *Addendum to the 'I/A' Item Note, Commission Statement,* Brussels, 21 September 2012, DOC 13790/12

The Commission considers that the adoption of the Decision of the European Parliament and of the Council setting up an information exchange mechanism with regard to intergovernmental agreements between Member States and third countries in the field of energy represents a first step towards more transparency, solidarity and consistency with internal market rules. The Commission will continue to encourage – as outlined in the original proposal – a more ambitious approach that would reflect and be more consistent with the EU's challenges and far-reaching objectives in the area of energy policy.

In particular as provisions proposed as mandatory by the Commission have been made voluntary by the legislator, notably as regards an ex ante compatibility assessment mechanism to ensure that new intergovernmental agreements which have an impact on the operation or the functioning of the internal market are in compliance with Union law, the Commission will closely monitor the effectiveness of the adopted legislation, reserving its Treaty rights, and make use of its review clause as appropriate.

With this statement the Commission clearly expresses its disappointment at the extent to which mandatory language has been watered down, emphasizing that the Decision is but a starting point. As to the consequences of this watering down, it warns that it intends to use the review clause which foresees assessing the effectiveness of the Decision by 2016 (Article 8). More importantly, it warns the Member States that it 'reserves its Treaty rights'. In other words, the shadow of the infringement procedure looms in the background. Thus, compliance with the obligations under this information exchange mechanism does not provide conclusive legal certainty to the Member States that their agreements will be compatible, and therefore remain in force. This 'shadow of litigation' is not without its policy consequences, as it creates a 'chain of legal uncertainty' which is at odds with the objectives of the Decision. Specifically, the Commission's intention with this Decision was to ensure the creation of a long-term stable investment climate to the benefit of EU energy policy objectives, through creating legal certainty that intergovernmental agreements comply with EU law. Indeed, the commercial agreements which are often negotiated in parallel or following the intergovernmental agreements would be guaranteed that the legal framework on which they depend will not need to be reneged if a violation is found.

(viii) Commission assistance during negotiations

For reasons of commercial interest or national considerations on security of supply, Member States are under increased pressure to accept concessions in their international agreements with third countries which are incompatible with Union energy law. The section on intergovernmental agreements has illustrated how that may be the case, such as pre-assigning the usage of pipeline infrastructure. In order to avoid such non-conformity, Article 5 of the Energy Decision states that if a Member State gives notice of negotiations pursuant to Article 3(3) on the (re-)negotiation of an international agreement, that Member State may 'request the assistance' of the Commission in its negotiations with that third country. The Decision does not specify the nature of such assistance. The next indent of that Article 5 then continues that the Commission may participate as an observer in the negotiations on request of the Member State or on request of the

Commission with the Member State's approval. If the Commission 'participates in the negotiations as an observer', it 'may provide advice' on how to avoid incompatibility with Union law.

From a legal perspective, the consequences for the Member States asking and/or receiving such assistance and/or advice on legal compatibility must be examined. In the explanatory memorandum we find how the Commission envisages its own role in negotiations: continuous contacts, exchange of information and the possibility of a compatibility check are expected to aid compliance where the current (threat of) infringement procedures does not seem to suffice. Furthermore, the Commission has argued that the experience gained through these exchange mechanisms should enable the joint development of voluntary standard clauses that Member States can use in future intergovernmental agreements. The assumption is that the use of such standard clauses would help prevent conflicts of intergovernmental agreements with Union law. From a policy perspective, past experience has shown that the presence of Commission personnel in the negotiating room has indeed helped Member States (Poland) effectively refute pressure from third countries (Russia) to accept EU incompliant terms, and even negotiate more beneficial prices for hydrocarbon imports.

The connection with the development of voluntary clauses to be inserted in Member State agreements implies that the Energy Decision is not a 'fixed mechanism', but rather an 'organic process' which is expected to create an increasingly close relationship between the EU and the Member States.

(ix) The use of optional standard clauses

One of the techniques mechanisms which the Energy Decision wished to utilize to ensure compliance with EU law and thus guarantee legal certainty for commercial actors benefiting from the intergovernmental agreement, is the insertion of standard clauses into the Member State agreements. The use of such standard clauses is not new. Namely, in 2004 the EU adopted a Regulation on relations between the EU and the Member States on the negotiation and conclusion of Member State civil aviation agreements. Just like in the field of energy, the objective was to ensure compliance with Union law. In the Aviation Regulation, standard clauses were developed during the negotiations in the Co-Decision procedure, and were actually *integrated* into the notification procedure itself. Member States should indeed communicate whether or not these standard clauses have been used.[70] If so, then the Aviation Regulation builds in a presumption of compliance, and the Member States shall be authorized to conclude the agreement thus providing commercial airlines operating under the relevant international agreement with the benefit of legal certainty.[71] If these clauses have not been used, then the Comitology procedure would commence to examine whether or not the Member State aviation agreement 'does not harm the object and purpose of the Community common transport policy'.[72] This system has not been emulated in the context of the Energy Decision. Indeed, the standard clauses are not integrated into the information exchange mechanism itself, but in Article 7 on 'coordination among Member States'. In paragraph 3 of that article we find that: 'on the basis of best

---

[70] Regulation 847/2004/EC of the European Parliament and of the Council of 29 April 2004 on the negotiation and implementation of air service agreements between Member States and third countries, OJ 2004 No. L157/7, Article 1(1).
[71] *Ibid.*, Article 4(2).
[72] *Ibid.*, Article 4(3).

practice and in consultation with the Member States, developing optional model clauses . . . if applied, would significantly improve compliance of future intergovernmental agreements with Union law'.

(x) An 'EU' energy policy and coordination 'among' the Member States

The heading of Article 7 reads 'coordination among Member States'. The original of the proposed decision read 'with' Member States. This is not a minor change, since it negates the idea of the Commission as a central actor coordinating energy policy. It thus denies that the Member States could be subjects of Commission policy direction, and they as individual actors remain firmly in control. Article 7 of the Energy Decision is the only provision with a clear policy-orientated objective, as opposed to other articles which are aimed at ensuring legal conformity with Union law.

Article 7 – Coordination among Member States

The Commission shall facilitate and encourage the coordination among Member States with a view to:

(a) review developments in relation to intergovernmental agreements and strive for consistency and coherence in the Union's external energy relations with producer, transit, and consumer countries;

(b) identify common problems in relation to intergovernmental agreements and to consider appropriate action to address these problems, and, where appropriate, propose solutions;

(c) on the basis of best practice and in consultation with the Member States, develop optional, model clauses that if applied would significantly improve compliance of future intergovernmental agreements with Union energy legislation;

(d) support where appropriate the development of multilateral intergovernmental agreements involving several Member States or the Union as a whole.

The formalization of a consultation procedure in this Decision is an important development for EU external energy relations. In particular paragraphs (a), (b) and (d) contain language which clearly and irreversibly allows the Commission to undertake action to pursue EU external energy relations in a legal and political sense. Notably, paragraphs (b) and (d) should be read as opening the door to the Commission to submit requests to open negotiations for future EU agreements such as that being negotiated with Azerbaijan and Turkmenistan on a legal framework for a Trans-Caspian natural gas pipeline system.[73] Furthermore, paragraph (b) allows for 'the identification or problems and proposing solutions' which can be connected to the fact that the Commission shall encourage Member States to strive for consistency in 'the Union's' external energy relations.

A final point pertains to the EEAS in relation to the Energy Decision. Namely, paragraph 15 of the preamble reads:

A permanent exchange of information on intergovernmental agreements at Union level should enable best practices to be developed. On the basis of those best practices, the Commission, where appropriate in

---

[73] Council of the European Union, *The Council gives go-ahead for negotiations on Trans-Caspian Pipeline System*, Brussels, 12 September 2011, DOC 14095/11.

cooperation with the European External Action Service (EEAS) as regards the Union's external policies, should develop optional model clauses to be used in intergovernmental agreements between Member States and third countries.

The EEAS was originally not mentioned in the proposal of the Commission. While it is certainly commendable that the EEAS be involved in the formulation of EU external energy policy, the specific connection to the model clauses is rather beside the point. The model clauses would focus specifically on compliance with Union law (non-discrimination in pricing and access to infrastructure, etc.), and would have little to do with EU security of supply or the 'foreign policy mandate' of the EEAS. Thus, the cooperation of the EEAS is not particularly necessary in relation to paragraph (c) of Article 7 (standard clauses), but rather in relation to paragraphs (a), (b) and (d).

8 THE BROADER PICTURE OF EU EXTERNAL RELATIONS LAW

EU external energy policy is an area which has developed very rapidly in the past decade, and illustrates the importance of law in EU external relations in different ways: on the one hand, legal frameworks are the bread and butter of external energy policy itself. It is at the heart of EU policy, given the belief that stable, regulated energy markets are the best way to guarantee secure energy supplies, environmentally friendly policies and competitive energy prices. On the other hand, we also see the piecemeal fashion in which EU external energy policy has developed, and the progressive way in which primary and secondary law was utilized to cement these developments. Article 194 TFEU came only with the Lisbon Treaty, and the Energy Decision is a legal halfway house to enable the Member States to get along with EU external energy policy.

Looking specifically at the various challenges of EU external energy policy, we have seen a number of dynamics emerge. In the institutional dimension, this chapter has shown that the EEAS finds itself broadly excluded from the policy-making process of EU external energy relations. Symptomatic was the fact that the Commission Communication of autumn 2011 was not even drawn up jointly with the Service. Furthermore, the examination of the soft legal documents signed in EU external energy policy has shown that the Commission remains firmly in the driver's seat, and that the Member States' role through the rotating presidency remains as it was prior to the Lisbon Treaty. As regards the role of the EP, the Lisbon Treaty could have a significant impact. A number of legally binding agreements are planned or under negotiation, and under Article 194 TFEU these require the consent of Parliament. Taking a cue from CCP or the external dimension of the AFSJ, Parliament is sure to use its new powers to effect. As regards the relationship between the EU and the Member States the newly adopted instrument is an interesting illustration of a formalized implementation of Article 4(3) TEU. However, thorough scrutiny reveals a number of deficiencies which show that the instrument is only an intermediate step towards a fully fledged energy policy. In sum, at present, EU external energy policy is very much under construction.

SOURCES AND FURTHER READING

Aalto, P., *The EU–Russian Energy Dialogue* (Aldershot: Ashgate, 2008).

Andoura, S., Hancher, L. and Van der Woude, M., *Towards a European Energy Community: A Policy Proposal* [Policy Proposal by Jacques Delors] (Brussels: Notre Europe, 2010, No. 76).

Birchfield, V. L. and Duffield, J. S. (eds.), *Toward a Common European Union Energy Policy: Problems, Progress, and Prospects* (New York: Palgrave Macmillan, 2011).

Blockmans, S. and Van Vooren, B., 'Revitalizing the European Neighbourhood Economic Community, The Case for Legally Binding Sectoral Multilateralism' (2012) 17 *European Foreign Affairs Review* 577–604.

Braun, J. F., *EU Energy Policy under the Treaty of Lisbon Rules – Between a New Policy and Business as Usual* (CEPS Working Paper No. 31, 2011).

Eikeland, P., 'EU Internal Energy Market Policy: Achievements and Hurdles', in V. L. Birchfield and J. S. Duffield (eds.), *Toward a Common European Union Energy Policy: Problems, Progress, and Prospects* (New York: Palgrave Macmillan, 2011), pp. 13–40.

Haghighi, S., *Energy Security: The External Legal Relations of the European Union with Major Oil and Gas Supplying Countries* (Oxford: Hart Publishing, 2007).

Karova, R., *Energy Community for South East Europe: Rationale and Implementation to Date* (EUI-RSCAS Working Papers 2009/12).

Leonard, M. and Popescu, N., *A Power Audit of EU-Russia Relations* (European Council on Foreign Relations, November 2007).

McGowan, F., 'Can the European Union's Market Liberalism Ensure Energy Security in a Time of "Economic Nationalism"?' (2008) 4 *Journal of Contemporary European Research* 90–106.

Monar, J., 'The Rejection of the EU–US SWIFT Interim Agreement by the European Parliament: A Historic Vote and its Implications' (2010) 15 *European Foreign Affairs Review* 143–151.

Riley, A., 'Editorial – EU Energy Liberalisation: Coming to a Member State Near You!' (2008) 4 *Competition Law Review*, 2, 73–75.

Taylor, S. 'Safety-First Approach to European Energy Policy', *European Voice*, 23–29 June 2011.

Van der Meulen, E., 'EU Energy Policy: The Conflict between an Internal Liberalisation Agenda and External Security of Supply', in C. Stolte, T. Buruma, R. Runhardt and F. Smits (eds.), *The Future of the European Union* (Leiden: Sidestone Press, 2008).

Van Elsuwege, P., *Towards a Modernisation of EU-Russia Legal Relations?* (CEURUS EU-Russia Papers, No. 5, 2012).

Van Vooren, B., 'EU Energy Policy and the European Neighbourhood Policy: Added-Value or Emulating its Deficiencies?', in A. Delgado Casteleiro and M. Spernbauer (eds.), *Security in EU External Relations* (EUI Law Working Paper 2009/1).

Van Vooren, B., *EU External Relations Law and the European Neighbourhood Policy: A Paradigm for Coherence* (Abingdon/New York: Routledge, 2012).

Van Vooren, B., *Europe Unplugged: Progress, Potential and Limitations of EU External Energy Policy Three Years post-Lisbon* (SIEPS Working Paper 2012:5).

Wouters, J., Sterckx, S. and De Jong, S., 'The 2009 Russian–Ukrainian Gas Dispute: Lessons for European Energy Crisis Management after Lisbon' (2010) 15 *European Foreign Affairs Review* 511–538.

Youngs, R., *Energy Security – Europe's New Foreign Policy Challenge* (New York: Routledge, 2009).

Youngs, R., *Europe's External Energy Policy: Between Geopolitics and the Market* (CEPS Working Document 2007/278).

14

The external dimension of freedom, security and justice

1 CENTRAL ISSUES

- The AFSJ is a relatively new policy area that was mainly designed to facilitate cooperation between the EU Member States.[1] The further development of the AFSJ followed a traditional pattern: as it started to function well internally, it soon required an external dimension and the Union soon found itself concluding international agreements and formulating policies on the wide range of issues covered by the AFSJ. Like many aspects of EU external relations law, the relatively fast coming of age of AFSJ was triggered by a number of external events and developments, including crime, drug-trafficking and terrorist attacks.
- In all main areas of the AFSJ (immigration, judicial cooperation in civil and criminal matters, approximation of criminal law, police cooperation and fundamental rights protection) the EU has enacted legislation and concluded international agreements revealing the strong link between internal and external policies. One of the elements that distinguish AFSJ external relations from other areas is that the issues almost always relate to what are perceived as fundamental and sometimes constitutional dimensions or prerogatives of statehood.

2 THE EXTERNAL DIMENSION OF AN INTERNAL CONCEPT

(i) The AFSJ as an internal, organizational concept

The AFSJ was primarily created as an internal concept, and therefore its position in EU external relations may not be self-evident. The core Treaty provisions in the TEU and the TFEU underline the inward-focused nature of the AFSJ.

---

[1] Many thanks to Dr Claudio Matera and to Dr Luisa Marin for their textual contributions and suggestions throughout this chapter. The usual disclaimer applies.

Article 3(2) TEU

The Union shall offer its citizens an area of freedom, security and justice without internal frontiers, in which the free movement of persons is ensured in conjunction with appropriate measures with respect to external border controls, asylum, immigration and the prevention and combating of crime.

Article 67 TFEU

1. The Union shall constitute an area of freedom, security and justice with respect for fundamental rights and the different legal systems and traditions of the Member States.
2. It shall ensure the absence of internal border controls for persons and shall frame a common policy on asylum, immigration and external border control, based on solidarity between Member States, which is fair towards third-country nationals. For the purpose of this Title, stateless persons shall be treated as third-country nationals.
3. The Union shall endeavour to ensure a high level of security through measures to prevent and combat crime, racism and xenophobia, and through measures for coordination and cooperation between police and judicial authorities and other competent authorities, as well as through the mutual recognition of judgments in criminal matters and, if necessary, through the approximation of criminal laws.
4. The Union shall facilitate access to justice, in particular through the principle of mutual recognition of judicial and extrajudicial decisions in civil matters.

These provisions confirm that the AFSJ is offered to the *citizens of the Union* and aims to provide, within the context of free movement within the Union, a common approach to securing the external borders, as well as instruments and cooperation mechanisms to fight crime and guarantee access to justice for those who benefit from the free movement provisions. The image that emerges is one of an inward-looking area rather than an area with an open attitude towards the rest of the world. The AFSJ has therefore been characterized as contributing to a 'fortress Europe' in a globalizing world.

Given our findings in the chapters on CCP (9) and EU Energy Policy (13), and through the operation of the seminal implied powers doctrine, it is unsurprising that the intense internal cooperation has lead to an increase in rules on external relations. Furthermore, the AFSJ's external dimension is not an external policy in its own right, but rather a product of its internal development, existing purely for the function of internal needs. With a view to the specific nature of the AFSJ and the sensitive issue areas it covers (public order, security, judicial cooperation, migration), the legal questions go beyond the classical institutional or competence questions, but are often directly related to the constitutional dimension of the Union. One key issue is indeed 'the balance between protection of human rights and civil liberties on the one hand and the States' interest in public order, security, and migration control on the other',[2] projected externally.

---

[2] S. Peers, *EU Justice and Home Affairs Law*, 3rd edn (Oxford: Oxford University Press, 2011), p. 1.

The AFSJ was introduced by the Treaty of Amsterdam in 1999, replacing the earlier reference to 'Justice and Home Affairs' introduced by the Maastricht Treaty. Following the entry into force of the Lisbon Treaty, the AFSJ concept appears as the second Treaty objective in Article 3 TEU. In the light of the existing *acquis* in this field and of the wording of Article 67 TFEU (above), the AFSJ encompasses the following EU policies: immigration, judicial cooperation in civil and criminal matters, approximation of criminal law, police cooperation and fundamental rights protection. The AFSJ domain thus covers fields 'at the heart of State sovereignty', and 'unlike many major domains [of] European law, whether core domains such as the internal market, competition, agriculture or fisheries, or flanking domains such as employment or social policy, the subject matters assembled under AFSJ do not form a "natural" unity in terms of a clearly defined overall project'.[3] The AFSJ is thus a new concept or construction, tailored to the specific nature of the subject area. The policies are highly sensitive and may indeed have national constitutional implications since they touch on issues such as the monopoly of force that are closely related to state sovereignty. The AFSJ does not form 'a "natural" unity in terms of a clearly defined overall project'. At first sight, the AFSJ as such rather appears as a mere constitutional *fictio iuris* that serves two organizational purposes: first, it provides a framework for a plurality of specific policies and, second, it indicates that the different policies do not form a common policy in the sense of other EU policies such as the CCP or the CAP.

(ii) Scope of the AFSJ, and position of the Member States

As regards the scope of AFSJ, there are two important constraining elements.

First of all, the Treaties suggest that the Union will have to develop comprehensive policies in order to offer more justice, freedom and security to its citizens. In that sense the AFSJ is much broader than the JHA cooperation that was introduced by the Maastricht Treaty. At the same time, the ambiguity of the AFSJ is reflected in the fact that, irrespective of the new competences of the EU in this area, they 'shall not affect the exercise of the responsibilities incumbent upon Member States with regard to the maintenance of law and order and the safeguarding of internal security' (Article 72 TFEU). As we will see, however, it is questionable whether Member States' responsibilities will not be affected at all.

Second, the broad and ambiguous objective enshrined in Article 3(2) TEU must be read in the light of Article 67 TFEU and subsequent policy-specific provisions. Irrespective of the widely defined objectives in Article 3(2) TEU (inter alia related to the maintenance of public order and public security), the Union's competences are limited by the specific provisions. In fact, the mandate of the EU to offer its citizens an area in which public order is guaranteed has three main characteristics:

(a) it is limited to certain specific aspects of public order, i.e. the ones identified by Article 67 TFEU;
(b) it relates to cross-border issues only. There is no doubt that this includes immigration policy issues related to the free movement of persons, but it becomes a defining element in relation to criminal justice matters, judicial cooperation in civil law and police cooperation. The reference to the free movement of persons codified in Article 3(2) TEU clearly represents the

---

[3] N. Walker, 'In Search of the Area of Freedom, Security and Justice: A Constitutional Odyssey', in Walker (ed.), *Europe's Area of Freedom Security and Justice* (Oxford: Academy of European Law–European University Institute, 2004), p. 5.

causal nexus, the spillover effect between the four freedoms of the internal market and the development of the AFSJ;

(c) the mandate does not cover enforcement.

Article 72 TFEU

This Title shall not affect the exercise of the responsibilities incumbent upon Member States with regard to the maintenance of law and order and the safeguarding of internal security.

Article 4(2) TEU

The Union shall respect the equality of Member States before the Treaties as well as their national identities, inherent in their fundamental structures, political and constitutional, inclusive of regional and local self-government. It shall respect their essential State functions, including ensuring the territorial integrity of the State, maintaining law and order and safeguarding national security. In particular, national security remains the sole responsibility of each Member State.

Since the adoption of the Maastricht Treaty, this limitation to the mandate of the EU has been a constant feature in the domains that make up the AFSJ.[4] This clause obviously intends to avoid any ambiguity in respect of the possibility of establishing a European police force or something similar. The Member States maintain the monopoly in the area of law enforcement, but allow the EU to approximate and link the different systems in order to enhance cooperation and avoid loopholes that could jeopardize the security of EU territory, a territory without internal borders.

Notwithstanding the formal difficulties of streamlining and unifying a field of EU action which maintains a high degree of fragmentation, an analysis of the AFSJ cannot ignore the reactive nature of public order as a policy. Contrary to areas such as the CAP, the internal market and the common currency, the AFSJ introduced an objective that did not need to be established from scratch. Indeed, the AFSJ led to the introduction of an objective that calls for the preservation of something familiar, namely public order and internal security. The predominant reactive nature of the policies of the AFSJ is probably best reflected in the very wording of the Treaty when it calls upon the Union's institutions to build measures to combat crime and build a common policy on asylum and immigration. In both cases the EU is called upon to react to societal phenomena which relate to public order and security. However, 'the reactive, security-centred approach may have an in-built tendency to marginalize familiar constitutional constraints, such as the proper balancing of fundamental values, the primacy of democratic decision, due process in individual cases, and a robust system of separation and diversification of powers and of institutional checks and balances'.[5] And indeed one of the main criticisms of the developments concerning the AFSJ over the past years has been that it has disregarded fundamental rights concerns.

---

[4] Article 33 TEU pre-Lisbon and Article 64 TEC.
[5] Walker, 'In Search of the Area of Freedom, Security and Justice', p. 13.

In line with the reactive character of the AFSJ, it must be borne in mind that the EU is also called upon to foster civil rights and freedoms. Indeed, it is under this dimension of the AFSJ that the Union has adopted instruments to promote fundamental rights and civil liberties, notably with the institution of an ad hoc agency and the adoption of a number of legislative measures such as the citizenship directive, framework decision on the standing of victims in criminal proceedings, and other instruments to fight against hate crimes, racism and xenophobia.

(iii) The relation between the internal and external dimension

J. Monar, *The External Dimension of the EU's Area of Freedom, Security and Justice: Progress, Potential and Limitations after the Treaty of Lisbon* (Stockholm: SIEPS Report 2012/1)

The European Union's "area of freedom, security and justice" (AFSJ) has developed into a much more dynamic and substantial European policymaking domain than its modest origins might have suggested. What was still referred to as mere "cooperation" in the fields of justice and home affairs (JHA) at the time of the Maastricht Treaty has turned into a major political project of the EU which the Treaty of Lisbon has placed even before the Internal Market and Economic and Monetary Union in the list of fundamental treaty objectives of Article 3 of the Treaty on European Union (TEU). More than 1400 texts dealing with AFSJ matters adopted by the JHA Council since the extensive Treaty of Amsterdam reforms of 1999 and the creation of a range of special offices and agencies (starting with the formation of the Europol Drugs Unit in 1994) testify to the enormous growth of this policymaking domain.

The main rationale of the AFSJ as a political project is clearly an internal one. Article 3(2) TEU expresses this in clear terms by providing that the Union "shall offer to its citizens" an AFSJ "without internal frontiers, in which the free movement of persons is ensured in conjunction with appropriate measures with respect to external border controls, asylum, immigration and the prevention and combating of crime". While the objective is to offer citizens the fundamental public goods of "freedom, security and justice" in an internal area, this objective can never be achieved by purely internal EU measures because of the essentially transnational nature of the primary challenges of asylum, migration and crime on which the Treaty provides for "appropriate measures" of the EU. These cross not only borders inside the EU but also – and this is the often the bigger challenge – the EU's external borders, so that external action in relations with third-countries is not an option but a necessity.

The development of an external dimension can thus be regarded as intrinsically linked to the project of an internal AFSJ. Starting with the Tampere European Council of October 1999, all EU five-year programmes for the development of the AFSJ have therefore provided for external action to help achieve the AFSJ internal objectives. In the latest of these programmes, the 2010–2014 Stockholm Programme, an entire section is dedicated to the "external dimension" of the AFSJ on top of a whole range of external measures provided for in the individual policy fields.

Unsurprisingly this external dimension has been growing with the rapid extension of internal action since the Amsterdam Treaty reforms, and by 2011 26 out of a total of 136 texts adopted by the JHA Council, i.e., 19.1%, dealt primarily with the conclusion of agreements with third-countries and other external dimension issues. As a result the EU has also increasingly emerged as an international actor in its own right on AFSJ matters and has been recognised as such by third-countries. This is demonstrated, for instance, by the obvious interest of the US in counterterrorism cooperation with the EU since the 9/11 attacks.

The demand to strengthen the internal security of the EU territory in order to enhance the freedom achieved through the consolidation of the internal market has also been influenced by the emergence of external threats. The objective of the EU to offer to its citizens an AFSJ was confronted with phenomena such as illegal immigration, international terrorism and organized crime. Thus, the emergence of external security threats has played a major role in the development of the EU in relation to the AFSJ. For example, the political agreement to adopt the European Arrest Warrant was reached only after the events of 9/11. Therefore external security threats have played a considerable role in the development of the EU's AFSJ. In reaction to such externalities, the EU and the Member States agreed that the establishment of the AFSJ could not be achieved without allowing the EU to become a global actor that could respond to an uncontrolled flow of migrants and to the threats posed by terrorism and crime. Consequently the EU has engaged in concluding agreements falling squarely within the scope of one or more of the policies of the AFSJ, or by concluding agreements with AFSJ clauses, but falling within other external policies such as development policy and the neighbouring policy. Often, the external dimension of the AFSJ is also linked to the Union's CFSP, as is the case with the fight against international terrorism. Moreover, the agencies of the EU in the domains of the AFSJ – such as Europol, Eurojust and FRONTEX (see *infra*) – also conclude agreements with third countries.

W. Rys, 'The External Face of Internal Security', in C. Hill and N. Smith (eds.), *International Relations and the European Union*, 2nd edn (Oxford: Oxford University Press, 2011), pp. 226–245 at 227

Two factors have driven the external dimension of the EU's internal security policy. First, changing perceptions of security among the member states and how these translate into internal security challenges. As the EU has assumed new responsibilities, it has needed to respond to its members' insecurities. The traditional preoccupation with interstate, military security issues has diminished, as has the division between internal and external security. State borders have become more porous in the face of sub-state threats, such as crime and drug trafficking. Terrorism has become de-territorialized and global in nature, as exemplified by groups espousing the ideology of al-Qaeda conducting mass-casualty attacks across Europe, North Africa, and Turkey. The environment of post-Cold War Europe has amplified the risks arising from these new threats. The collapse of former socialist states; the economic turbulence and corresponding social dislocation surrounding the transition to market economies in the east; the opening up of borders and the emergence of inter-ethnic conflicts all served to increase the sense of vulnerability in Western Europe. The dark side of globalization has meant that illegal activities are increasingly being conducted across borders rather than just in the territories of vulnerable states. . . .

The second factor has been the exigencies of the EU enlargement process. As the EU has expanded its membership, and as its borders have come up against new neighbours, the Union has recognized the need to externalize its security policy to these other countries. The EU has sought to export its internal security *acquis communautaire* as a cost-effective way of enhancing its own safety. It has sought to achieve this through employing a range of its own instruments and seeking to influence the domestic priorities of states in close proximity to its borders. The extent to which it has been successful has been influenced by 'power' and reputation within its region.

3 EXTERNAL COMPETENCES IN THE AFSJ

(i) AFSJ external competences in the Treaties

The objective of ensuring 'a high level of security' within the AFSJ provided for by Article 67(3) TFEU must be understood as incorporating external threats to the AFSJ. Europol reports have assessed the most serious challenges, and have inter alia pointed to a serious increase in criminal activities originating from many countries in the EU's neighbourhood or further away. Apart from crime, threats relate to terrorism, mass migration flows, and refugees from third countries seeking political asylum or temporary protection from war or violent strife affecting their home countries.[6] 'All these external challenges for the AFSJ have in common that the EU's capacity to respond effectively to them depends crucially on cooperation with third-countries.'[7]

In order to cope with the new challenges, the Treaty combines the former provisions from Title IV EC Treaty (first pillar) on 'visas, asylum, immigration, and other policies related to free movement of persons' with the provisions in former Title VI TEU (third pillar) on 'police and judicial cooperation in criminal matters'. The result is the current Title V in the TFEU, which is now labelled 'Area of freedom, security and justice'. In Article 4(2) TFEU the AFSJ is listed as a *shared* competence between the Union and its Member States. The competences conferred upon the EU in the field of AFSJ are almost all internal competences, and only in relation to immigration policy is there an express external competence.

Article 79(3) TFEU

The Union may conclude agreements with third countries for the readmission to their countries of origin or provenance of third-country nationals who do not or who no longer fulfil the conditions for entry, presence or residence in the territory of one of the Member States.

In relation to the other AFSJ policies, the EU can only act externally through the application of the implied powers doctrine. The possibility for the EU to conclude international agreements in the domain of AFSJ is confirmed in a special Declaration on Article 218 TFEU, the procedure pertaining to the conclusion of international agreements by the EU.

---

36. Declaration on Article 218 of the Treaty on the Functioning of the European Union concerning the negotiation and conclusion of international agreements by Member States relating to the area of freedom, security and justice, OJ 2010 No. C83/349

The Conference confirms that Member States may negotiate and conclude agreements with third countries or international organisations in the areas covered by Chapters 3, 4 and 5 of Title V of Part Three in so far as such agreements comply with Union law.

---

[6] Respectively: Europol, *EU Organised Crime Assessment. OCTA 2011* (The Hague: Europol, 2011), pp. 6–7, 16 and 18; Europol, *EU TE-STAT 2011. Terrorism Situation and Trend Report* (The Hague: Europol, 2011), p. 26; Frontex, *Annual Risk Analysis 2011* (Warsaw: Frontex, 2011), p. 13; UNHCR, *Asylum Levels and Trends in Industrialized Countries* (Geneva: UNHCR, 2011), p. 15.

[7] J. Monar, *The External Dimension of the EU's Area of Freedom, Security and Justice: Progress, Potential and Limitations after the Treaty of Lisbon* (Stockholm: SIEPS Report 2012/1), p. 16.

Chapter 3 concerns 'judicial cooperation in civil matters', Chapter 4 'judicial cooperation in criminal matters' and Chapter 5 deals with 'police cooperation'. Apart from the express competence to conclude readmission agreements, the other parts of Chapter 2 (border checks and asylum) have not been mentioned expressly. The question arises whether, in light of the Declaration, international agreements may be concluded. Declaration 36 can only be seen as a positive re-affirmation of the general application of the implied powers doctrine as described in Chapters 3 and 4 of this book. The fact that Chapter 2 of Title V TFEU is not mentioned in Declaration 36 does not cause the non-application of the general rules of EU external competence.

(ii) The role of the institutions

(a) The European Council

As in other EU policy areas, the leading strategic role is laid in the hands of the European Council.

Article 68 TFEU

The European Council defines the strategic guidelines for legislative and operational planning within the area of freedom, security and justice.

Over the years the European Council made use of this competence also to strengthen further the external relations of the AFSJ. This is partly based on the general competence of the European Council to take strategic decisions covering the wide field of external relations, including the 'foreign affairs' dimension.

Article 22(1) TEU

... Decisions of the European Council on the strategic interests and objectives of the Union shall relate to the common foreign and security policy and to other areas of the external action of the Union.

European Council conclusions have indeed placed an emphasis on linking different external policy measures (including financial and development policy instruments) for achieving EU migration management objectives in the context of a reinforced cooperation with third countries.[8] The extract below is from the Tampere European Council conclusions, and underlines the crucial top-down political role the European Council has played in driving forward the very young policy domain that is the AFSJ.

---

[8] See for instance European Council: Presidency Conclusions Santa Maria da Feira European Council, 19–20 June 2002, Council document 200/1/00, para 51; European Council: Presidency Conclusions European Council, 14–15 December 2005, Council document 15914/1/05 REV 1, paras 8–10; and European Council: Presidency Conclusions European Council 24–25 June 2011, Council document EUCO 23/11, pp. 1 and 10–11. The latter, for instance, pointed to new migration challenges following the Arab Spring.

Tampere European Council (15 and 16 October 1999)

The European Council held a special meeting on 15 and 16 October 1999 in Tampere on the creation of an area of freedom, security and justice in the European Union. . . .

The European Council is determined to develop the Union as an area of freedom, security and justice by making full use of the possibilities offered by the Treaty of Amsterdam. The European Council sends a strong political message to reaffirm the importance of this objective and has agreed on a number of policy orientations and priorities which will speedily make this area a reality.

The European Council will place and maintain this objective at the very top of the political agenda. It will keep under constant review progress made towards implementing the necessary measures and meeting the deadlines set by the Treaty of Amsterdam, the Vienna Action Plan and the present conclusions. The Commission is invited to make a proposal for an appropriate scoreboard to that end. The European Council underlines the importance of ensuring the necessary transparency and of keeping the European Parliament regularly informed. It will hold a full debate assessing progress at its December meeting in 2001. . . .

Given that one of the focal points of the Union's work in the years ahead will be to strengthen the common foreign and security policy, including developing a European security and defence policy, the European Council expects the new Secretary-General of the Council and High Representative for the CFSP, Mr. Javier Solana, to make a key contribution to this objective. Mr. Solana will be able to rely on the full backing of the European Council in exercising his powers according to Article 18(3) of the Treaty so he can do full justice to his tasks. His responsibilities will include cooperating with the Presidency to ensure that deliberations and action in foreign and security policy matters are efficiently conducted with the aim of fostering continuity and consistency of policy on the basis of the common interests of the Union.

From this extract, it also becomes clear that the security dimension of the AFSJ, and in particular in its external dimension, is closely intertwined with that of the EU's CFSP (see also Chapter 11).

C. Matera, 'The European Union Area of Freedom, Security and Justice and the Fight against New Security Threats. New Trends and Old Constitutional Challenges', in M. Arcari and L. Balmond (eds.), *La Gouvernance Globale Face aux Défis de la Securité Collective – Global Governance and the Challenges of Collective Security* (Naples: Editoriale Scientifica, 2012), pp. 69–88

The two tasks assigned to the Union appear, prima facie, distinct. Firstly, the tasks referred to in Article 21(c) are related to Title V TEU on the Common Foreign and Security Policy (CFSP), whereas the AFSJ objective is disciplined in Title V Part Three of the Treaty on the Functioning of the European Union (TFEU); therefore, the two policies must be considered formally separate and belonging to two different methods of integration: one based on "intergovernmentalism" and the other belonging to "supranationalism". Secondly, tasks such as preserving peace, preventing conflicts and strengthening international security clearly fall within the context of collective security and, consequentially, create a nexus between action of the Union and action by the United Nations (UN) and NATO, whereas the tasks assigned to the EU in relation to its AFSJ such as judicial cooperation in criminal matters, police cooperation and external borders control seem to exclusively fall within a municipal (regional) discourse aiming at the maintenance and development of a European Public Order. However, recent developments at EU and UN level suggest that the aforementioned distinction is losing its relevance and the two separate policies should be understood as possessing common objectives.

From the perspective of the EU, this was firstly established in the European Security Strategy of 2003 where it was held that the collective (regional) security was facing new threats such as organised crime and terrorism. Therefore, in order to face these new threats the Council called for a better coordination between external action based on the AFSJ pillar and external action based on other external policies, including the CFSP. This new 'multi-policy' and 'multi-pillar' approach was then reiterated also in the 2008 report on the implementation of the Security Strategy where for the first time, internal and external security matters were deemed to be inseparable. Moreover, and conversely, the strategy documents on the development of the EU qua Area of Freedom, Security and Justice have also emphasised the importance of the external projection of this field of EU competence. Thus, not only the so-called "external dimension of the AFSJ" is presented as a projection of internal powers necessary to attain the overall AFSJ objectives; but the external dimension of the AFSJ is also presented as a piece of a broader strategy that aims at integrating the different fields of EU external action in a coherent manner. . . .

It follows that internal and external action on (regional) security issues must be developed on the basis of a systematic approach that should lead to a coherent implementation of the different policy texts in the light of the treaties' objectives. However, while from a policy perspective the practice of using various external channels to promote the AFSJ agenda has grown into a characterising feature of EU action, the legal implications of this phenomenon have not yet been fully clarified. Thus, for instance, the hasty reaction to international terrorism aiming at securing Europe and the world in cooperation with the UN has led to a strand of case-law on the relationship between the rule of law and effectiveness that has not yet found a balance. Parallel to the externalisation of AFSJ objectives through the different channels of EU external action, the EU has also developed the external dimension of the AFSJ by means of network governance where the legislative dimension of a goal is replaced by institutionalised interactions among administrative agencies. In the context of the AFSJ this is the case of executive agreements concluded by agencies such as Europol, Eurojust and Frontex with their foreign counter parts. Often, the externalisation of the AFSJ through different channels of external action and the expansion of the AFSJ external activities through the agencies of the Union merge for the purpose of developing and consolidating a specific geostrategic objective: this is the case, for instance, of the European Neighbourhood Policy where multi-policy factors of external relations coexist and actually typify this type of external action.

(b) The Council

Key decisions are taken by the Council in its configuration as JHA Council. The JHA Council approves all programming documents for the JHA external dimension, whether these are submitted to the European Council for formal adoption or not; adopts all relevant legislative acts; takes the decisions on the opening, signing and conclusion of international agreements in the AFSJ domain; approves the Commission's negotiation mandates; decides on external risk assessments and defines action priorities regarding specific third countries or regions. Given the original internal focus of the AFSJ, policy preparation in the Working Groups often needs input from a special Group on External JHA Issues (JAIEX), which gathers experts on international AFSJ issues from the national ministries, and the respective regional CFSP working groups.

An EU Counter-Terrorism Coordinator (CTC) works under the authority of the HR but takes his instructions from and reports primarily to the JHA Council. The CTC coordinates counter-terrorism activities within the Council and monitors the implementation of EU counter-terrorism measures; he can also be described as the Union's 'chief counter-terrorism diplomat',[9] as he has the task of ensuring the effective communication of EU objectives and cooperation offers to third countries.

Decisions are taken on the basis of the 'ordinary legislative procedure' (Article 294 TFEU) with QMV in the Council and co-decision by the EP. In relation to the external dimension, exceptions are measures in the domain of family law (Article 81(3) TFEU: unanimity and consultation only of the European Parliament); measures in the field of criminal procedural law not already foreseen by the Treaty (Article 82(2)(d) TFEU: unanimity and consent only by the European Parliament); minimum rules in the domain of substantive criminal law in other areas than already defined by the Treaty (Article 83(1) TFEU: unanimity and consent by the European Parliament) and establishment of the European Public Prosecutor's Office and extension of its powers (Article 86(1) and (4): unanimity and consent of the European Parliament).

(c) The Commission, the HR and the EEAS

Given the application of the ordinary legislative procedure, the role of the Commission follows the general rules of that procedure. The composition of the JHA Council (Ministers for Justice and Ministers for Home Affairs) is mirrored in the involvement of the Commission, with two responsible DGs: 'Home Affairs' (HOME) and 'Justice' (JUST). The still somewhat hybrid nature of the AFSJ is reflected in the non-exclusive right of initiative of the Commission in the fields of judicial cooperation in criminal matters (AFSJ Chapter 4) and police cooperation (AFSJ Chapter 5).

Article 76 TFEU

The acts referred to in Chapters 4 and 5, together with the measures referred to in Article 74 which ensure administrative cooperation in the areas covered by these Chapters, shall be adopted:

(a) on a proposal from the Commission, or

(b) on the initiative of a quarter of the Member States.

In the external domain, the negotiation and conclusion of AFSJ agreements follows the general rules laid down in Article 218. This implies that the Commission is normally responsible for submitting the negotiation recommendation to the Council (Article 218(3) TFEU), except where the agreement relates exclusively or principally to the CFSP (see further Chapters 2 and 11).

Recommendation from the Commission to the Council for an Authorisation to Open Negotiations for an Agreement with the United States of America on the Use of Passenger Name Records (PNR) Data to Prevent and Combat Terrorism and Transnational Crime, including Organised Crime, Brussels, 16 June 2006, SEC(2006) 812 final

EXPLANATORY MEMORANDUM

1. In the aftermath of the terrorist attacks of 11 September 2001, the Congress of the United States passed a series of laws aiming to enhance domestic security against terrorist threats. The European Union fully

---

[9] Monar, *The External Dimension of the EU's Area of Freedom, Security and Justice*, p. 38.

supports the United States in the fight against terrorism and transnational crime, including organised crime.

2. The US Aviation and Transportation Security Act (ATSA) of 19 November 2001 provides that air carriers operating passenger flights to or from the United States must make Passenger Name Record (PNR) information available to the Bureau of Customs and Border Protection (CBP) Department of Homeland Security.

3. The 'Passenger Name Record' (PNR) is a record of each passenger's travel requirements which contains all information necessary to enable reservations to be processed and controlled by the booking and participating airlines.

4. Since February 2003, CBP requires each carrier operating passenger flights in foreign air transportation to or from the United States to provide CBP with electronic access to PNR to the extent it is collected and contained in the air carrier's automated reservation system.

5. Airlines face sanctions in the United States for non-compliance with U.S. requirements.

6. On 17 May 2004 the Council adopted Decision 2004/496/EC ("the Council Decision"), authorising the President of the Council to sign the Agreement with the United States of America on PNR on behalf of the Community. The Agreement was signed on 28 May 2004 and entered into force on the same day. This decision was taken on the basis of Article 95 of the EC Treaty. On the same day the Adequacy Decision adopted by the Commission on 14 May 2004 ("the Commission Adequacy Decision") was notified to Member States.

7. The European Parliament sought the annulment of the Council decision. The Parliament argued, inter alia, that the choice of Article 95 EC as legal basis for the decision was incorrect.

8. On 30 May 2006 the Court of Justice ruled in Joined Cases C-317/04 and 318/04 and annulled both Decisions. The Court stated that the Council Decision could not be validly adopted on the basis of Article 95 of the EC Treaty, since the transfer to and the use of PNR data by CBP relates to data processing operations concerning public security and activities of the State in areas of criminal law, which fall outside the scope of Directive 95/46/EC. The Court also annulled the Commission Adequacy Decision for the same reason. The Court noted that the current agreement provides that termination will take place 90 days after its notification to the other party and therefore left the Commission Adequacy Decision in force until 30th of September 2006 pending the adoption of the necessary measures.

9. Following the ruling of the Court of Justice, the Union should open negotiations with the US in order to replace the current agreement by a new agreement to be concluded on a correct legal basis; these negotiations will need to take place in conjunction with the denunciation procedure for the current agreement which has been annulled by the Court. In view of the ruling of the Court, the current agreement should be terminated by 30th September 2006.

10. The negotiations should take into account that the processing by CBP of personal data contained in the PNR of air passengers travelling to or from the United States is governed by the conditions set out in the Undertakings of the Department of Homeland Security Bureau of Customs and Border Protection of 11 May 2004 (hereinafter referred to as the Undertakings) and in United States domestic legislation to the extent indicated in the Undertakings.

11. The Commission therefore recommends to the Council to authorise the opening of negotiations with the United States of America to conclude an Agreement on the use of PNR data to prevent and combat terrorism and transnational crime, including organised crime.

. . . Taking into account the aforementioned, the Commission recommends:

 – that the Council authorise its Presidency, assisted by the Commission, to negotiate an Agreement on the use of Passenger Name Records (PNR) data to prevent and combat terrorism and transnational crime, including organised crime;
 – that the Council adopt the enclosed negotiating directives

ANNEX

NEGOTIATING DIRECTIVES

– The Agreement is to be negotiated and concluded on the basis of articles 24 and 38 of the Treaty on European Union.

– The Agreement must replace with effect from 1 October 2006 the terminated agreement concluded by Council Decision 2004/496/EC.

– To ensure continuity, to provide legal certainty to economic operators and to ensure respect for fundamental rights and freedoms, the content of the Agreement should be the same, in the sense that it should offer same level of legal certainty and protection of the persons concerned, as the Agreement concluded by Decision 2004/496/EC and the Adequacy Decision adopted by the Commission on 14 May 2004; reference should therefore be made to the US CBP Undertakings of 11 May 2004 in the new Agreement. With regard to police and judicial cooperation it should in particular ensure the possibility of transfer of PNR by CBP data to police and judicial authorities of the Member States.

– To ensure continuity and legal certainty the Agreement should provide a valid basis for air carriers to process PNR data contained in their automated reservation systems as required by CBP.

As we have seen in Chapter 1, the scope of the EEAS covers all areas of the EU's external action. Indeed, it has been argued that the EEAS can play a significant role in the external dimension of the AFSJ, through contributions to the coherence of the EU's external action law-making, and through its integration within the Council and the Commission.[10] And, given the strong link between a number of AFSJ and CFSP issues, a similar role can be foreseen for the HR.

Yet, and in spite of the comprehensive mandate, it has been argued that it is unlikely that the EEAS will have any major impact on policy formulation in the external dimension of the AFSJ.

J. Monar, *The External Dimension of the EU's Area of Freedom, Security and Justice: Progress, Potential and Limitations after the Treaty of Lisbon* (Stockholm: SIEPS Report 2012/1), p. 41

Not only have the Commission's DG "Home Affairs" and "Justice" and the Council's DG H (JHA) retained their respective external relations responsibilities, but the EEAS – which has its main focus CFSP and the external diplomatic representation of the EU – also lacks any unit in its "Global and Multilateral Issues" Department specifically tasked to cover external AFSJ matters.

Perhaps more importantly, the HRVP (currently Baroness Catherine Ashton) has also so far stayed largely clear of major external AFSJ matters such as illegal immigration and the fight against international organised crime. During her high profile visit to Tunisia in February 2011, for instance, the HRVP avoided answering questions about migration challenges although thousands of Tunisian illegal immigrants had by that time already reached Italian shores. While CFSP issues (and the internal battles over the EEAS) have no doubt kept her busy enough, her abstention on the external AFSJ side is likely to be motivated also by the wish to avoid a potential turf war with the JHA Council and especially the ministers

[10] M. Gatti, 'The Role of the European External Action Service in the External Dimension of the Area of Freedom Security and Justice', in C. Flaesch-Mougin and L. S. Rossi (eds.), *La Dimension Extérieure de l'Espace de Liberté, Sécurité et de Justice* (Brussels: Bruylant, 2012), pp. 171–193.

of interior, who have been accustomed during the last decade to handle "their" external JHA issues largely amongst themselves. Yet the EEAS itself could – as the Commission noted in its November 2010 Communication on the implementation of the EU Internal Security Strategy – bring to the AFSJ external dimension additional "skills and expertise" from the Member States and help with the deployment of expertise in the field to EU delegations abroad. The EEAS only started to function during 2011, so time will tell whether this potential is going to be realised.

(d) The European Parliament

Again through the general application of the ordinary legislative procedure, the position of the EP is comparable to what it can do in most other areas of Union action: co-decision (decisions are finally taken together by the Council and the EP) and consent for the conclusion of international agreements have by now turned the EP into a serious player in this area. The EP has been given a role that is more in line with the potential effects of the AFSJ decisions on EU citizens. In the field of external relations a first example was provided when the EP voted on 11 February 2010 not to give its consent to the interim agreement between the EU and the USA on bank data transfers via the SWIFT network. This vote prevented the agreement coming into force and was based on the EP's right of consent laid down in Article 218(6)(a) TFEU. In the extract below, we can further see that Parliament is proactively safeguarding its role in EU external relations under the Article 218 TFEU procedure on the conclusion of international agreements.

Action brought on 21 December 2011 – *European Parliament* v. *Council of the European Union* (Case C-658/11) (Case in progress)

Parties
Applicant: European Parliament
Defendant: Council of the European Union
The applicant claims that the Court should:
  annul Council Decision 2011/640/CFSP of 12 July 2011on the signing and conclusion of the agreement between the European Union and the Republic of Mauritius on the conditions of transfer of suspected pirates and associated seized property from the European Union-led naval force to the Republic of Mauritius and on the conditions of suspected pirates after transfer; order that the effects of Council Decision 2011/640/CFSP of 12 July 2011 be maintained until it is replaced; order the Council of the European Union to pay the costs.

Pleas in law and main arguments
The European Parliament considers that Council Decision 2011/640/CFSP of 12 July 2011 on the signing and conclusion of the Agreement between the European Union and the Republic of Mauritius on the conditions of transfer of suspected pirates and associated seized property from the European Union-led naval force to the Republic of Mauritius and on the conditions of suspected pirates after transfer is invalid because it does not relate exclusively to the common foreign and security policy, as expressly provided for in Article 218(6), second paragraph, TFEU.

The European Parliament considers that the Agreement between the European Union and the Republic of Mauritius also relates to judicial cooperation in criminal matters, police cooperation, and development cooperation, covering fields to which the ordinary legislative procedure applies.

Therefore, this Agreement should have been concluded after obtaining the consent of the European Parliament in accordance with Article 218(6)(a)(v) TFEU.

For this reason the Council has violated the Treaties by failing to choose the appropriate legal basis for the conclusion of the Agreement.

Furthermore, the European Parliament considers that the Council has violated Article 218(10) TFEU, because it did not inform Parliament fully and immediately at the stages of negotiation and conclusion of the Agreement.

Should the Court of Justice annul the contested Decision, the European Parliament nonetheless proposes that the Court exercise its discretion to maintain the effects of the contested Decision, in accordance with Article 264, second paragraph, TFEU, until such time as it is replaced.

(e) AFSJ-related agencies

In order to support and enhance the Union's activities to pursue the establishment and development of the AFSJ, a number of specialized European 'agencies' were created:[11] Europol, Eurojust, FRONTEX, CEPOL, and EASO.[12] The bodies cover respectively main domains of the AFSJ: police cooperation (Europol and CEPOL), judicial cooperation in criminal matters (Eurojust), the management of the external border of the Union (FRONTEX) and support to national authorities in the application of the common asylum system (EASO).

In each case these agencies have been given legal personality and have been conferred with express treaty-making power. Use of these competences is for instance reflected in the agreements concluded between Europol and a large number of third countries on the sharing of strategic data (fight against organized crime and terrorism, in particular) and on the sharing of personal data (so-called 'operational agreements'). Eurojust, for instance, has agreements with the US, Norway and Switzerland on the posting of liaison magistrates, whereas legal cooperation agreements have also been concluded with a number of other countries.

While the actual wording of the different founding instruments of the agencies differs, it is possible to affirm, in principle, that the agencies of the AFSJ have been conferred a limited external competence with a specific purpose: that is to say that these agencies have the power to conclude agreements with external partners 'in so far as is required for the performance of their

---

[11] It is however disputed that all of these bodies are EU agencies. According to Chiti, Europol and Eurojust cannot be seen as agencies. E. Chiti, 'An Important Part of the EU's Institutional Machinery: Features, Problems and Perspectives of European Agencies' (2009) 46 *Common Market Law Review* 1395–1442 at 1398.

[12] Respectively: Council Decision 2009/371/JHA Establishing the European Police Office (Europol), OJ 2009 No. L121/37; Council Decision 2009/426/JHA on the strengthening of Eurojust and amending Decision 2002/187/JHA setting up Eurojust with a view to reinforcing the fight against serious crime, OJ 2009 No. L138/14; Council Regulation 2007/2004/EC Establishing a European Agency for the Management of Operational Cooperation at the External Borders of the Member States of the European Union, OJ 2004 No. L349/1, as amended by Regulation 863/2007/EC, OJ 2007 No. L199/30, and as amended by Regulation 1168/2011/EU, OJ 2011 No. L304/1; Council Decision 2005/681/JHA establishing the European Police College (CEPOL), OJ 2005 No. L256/63; Regulation 439/2010 establishing a European Asylum Support Office, OJ 2010 No. L132/11.

tasks'.[13] The teleological nature of external powers for AFSJ agencies serves two purposes. First, it identifies the objectives that the agencies must pursue when negotiating agreements with their external partners and, second, it serves as a limiting tool to prevent abuses of powers.

In the light of the current legal framework it is possible to classify the agreements that the AFSJ agencies can conclude into two categories: cooperation agreements and operational agreements. Under the first type of agreement, AFSJ agencies are given the power to establish stable mechanisms in order to work together with external partners. For instance, the Europol–Russia Agreement of 2003 creates a platform for cooperation in order to allow the parties to:

1) exchange technical and strategic information such as crime situations and development reports, threat assessments; 2) exchange of law enforcement experience including the organization of scientific and practice-oriented conferences, internships, consultations and seminars; 3) exchange of legislation, manuals, technical literature and other law enforcement materials; and 4) training.[14]

In order to give effect to the agreement, a cooperation agreement usually identifies contact points for each party so as to facilitate direct contact, cooperation and coordination.

Operational agreements are distinguished from cooperation agreements for two, related, reasons. Substantially, operational agreements are those agreements concluded by one of the AFSJ agencies that include mechanisms to share personal data between the parties and/or that foresee concrete operational mechanisms such as joint patrolling of borders or the coordination of investigations. Procedurally, in order to conclude an agreement that envisages the exchange of personal data, the EU agency will have to go through a number of authorizations. Thus for instance Article 23 of the Europol Regulation affirms that the agency can conclude an agreement containing provisions on the exchange of personal data 'after the approval by the Council, which shall previously have consulted the Management Board and, as far as it concerns the exchange of personal data, obtained the opinion of the Joint Supervisory Body (an independent body that monitors the use of personal data by the Agency) via the Management Board' for the purpose of assessing the existence of an adequate level of data protection by that entity.[15] Because of their material scope, operational agreements require a thorough scrutiny of the envisaged agreements and an assessment of the international partner with which the agency wants to conclude it so as to make sure that EU standards on rights protection and rule of law are respected.[16] Other than the possibility of exchanging personal data, operational agreements concluded by the agencies may even go as far as establishing the position of liaison desks (Eurojust and FRONTEX),[17] and foresee participation of third countries' officials in border control operations (FRONTEX).[18] Thus, depending on the agency's mandate, an operational agreement concluded by an AFSJ agency is

---

[13] Article 23(1) of the Europol Decision and Article 26a para 1 of the Eurojust Decision.

[14] Article 5 Europol–Russia Agreement of 6 November 2003, available at www.europol.eu.

[15] The rules are similar for Eurojust. Eurojust makes the exchange of personal data dependent on either an ad hoc assessment of data protection standards or the question of whether the third country in question is a party to the Council of Europe Convention of 28 January 1981 on data protection.

[16] V. Mitsilegas, *EU Criminal Law* (Oxford/Portland: Hart Publishing, 2009); and Matera, 'The Influence of International Organisations on the EU's Area of Freedom, Security and Justice: A First Inquiry', in R. A. Wessel and S. Blockmans (eds.), *Between Autonomy and Dependence: The EU Legal Order under the Influence of International Organisations* (The Hague: T.M.C. Asser Press/Springer, 2013), pp. 269–296.

[17] Articles 26 and 26a Eurojust Regulation and 14(3) and (4) Frontex Regulation.

[18] Article 14(6) Frontex Regulation.

an agreement that goes beyond the establishment of cooperative tools and that establishes means of cooperation at the enforcement moment.

Because of the sensitivity in relation to the rule of law and human rights in relation to the fields of the AFSJ, the activities carried out by the agencies should also be subject to a thorough scrutiny. While the legal framework for internal and external activities by the agencies is constantly developing,[19] instruments of administrative accountability and democratic checks and balances have not been developed consistently and coherently. Thus, while the Europol Regulation conditions the exercise of the agency's external powers to a Decision containing the list of third countries with whom to enter agreements adopted by the Council in consultation with the EP,[20] the FRONTEX Regulation not only lacks a provision on the preliminary identification of international partners, but merely affirms that the EP 'shall be fully informed *as soon as possible*'.[21] Moreover, while Europol and Eurojust publish their agreements on their website, FRONTEX does not do so, with the result that binding instruments of international relations are not directly accessible to the public. However, as the law stands today individuals could challenge these agreements through the European Ombudsman and the ECJ, provided that the requirements of Article 263 TFEU are met.

Therefore, while the different tasks assigned to the different agencies should be taken into due account, the lack of coherence and consistency in relation to the respect of the rule of law, human rights and international law have, in the past, raised serious concerns.

E. Papastravridis, '"Fortress Europe" and FRONTEX: Within or without International Law?' (2010) 79 *Nordic Journal of International Law* 75–111 at 110–111

FRONTEX was established in 2004 to help Member States in implementing community legislation on the surveillance of EU borders and to coordinate their operational cooperation in order to strengthen security at external borders. No matter how efficient it has been in the attainment of these objectives, there appear to be sound reasons for concluding that many of its operations, especially in the maritime domain, are not in full consistency with international law. Moreover, as was recognized by the European Commission, there is "disunity within the EU over which obligations arise from EU fundamental rights and international human rights and refugee law, and how these obligations relate to the law of the sea". This ambiguity over the relevant legal obligations of the Member States is significantly enhanced by the secrecy and non-transparency governing the Agency's operations. . . .

Of specific interest is the application of the principle of *non-refoulement* in the present context, which appears to be especially problematic in the majority of these operations since it is very likely that the persons onboard the intercepted vessels would be forced to return to their countries of origin where they may face prosecution or be subjected to torture or inhuman or degrading treatment. This has been very recently acknowledged by the European Commission with regard to Member States, in particular when engaged in joint operations or in operations taking place within the territorial waters of another State or in the high seas.

---

[19] With the exception of Europol (fully operational since 1999, and its forerunner, the 1994 Europol Drugs Unit), all the AFSJ agencies were established in the current millennium (starting with Eurojust in 2002) and have all (including Europol) undergone important amendments in the past years.

[20] Article 26 Europol Regulation.

[21] Emphasis added; Article 14 Frontex Regulation.

However, the recent conclusion of a working arrangement between FRONTEX and UNHCR shows the way forward, and if coupled with other relevant initiatives would not only "strengthen the security and freedom of the citizens of the EU", but also the security and freedom of all human beings in need of protections. It is apt to conclude by recalling Article 1 of the European Convention on Human Rights: "The High Contracting Parties shall secure to everyone within their jurisdiction the rights and freedoms defined in Section I of the Convention." It is for FRONTEX and EU member States, which are all parties to the latter Convention, to assume that responsibility and bring it to fruition.

The issue concerning the respect for rule of law and human rights standards is also linked to the different partners of the agencies, i.e. the countries with whom AFSJ bodies conclude the agreements. The founding instruments of the agencies do not a priori fix the third countries with which agencies have to conclude agreements. As we have seen, only the Europol Regulation regulates the procedure that leads to the identification of 'targeted countries' at the political level. Thus, the choice of international partners will depend on a set of considerations that can be summarized as follows: (1) geostrategic importance, (2) policy context, (3) existence of special relations or specific importance of a third country in relation to a specific policy. In the first category we find leading partners of the EU in AFSJ matters such as the US and Canada. Thus the three leading AFSJ agencies, Europol, Eurojust and FRONTEX, have signed agreements with the USA. The second and largest category refers to agreements signed with countries that are connected to the EU as a result of a specific policy context. The ENP countries constitute the most important group of states falling within this category; while the importance of the ENP has been reinforced by the introduction of Article 8 TEU, the security dimension of this policy has played a central role since its inception in 2004 (see Chapter 15). However, it should be noted that agreements have been successfully concluded mostly with Eastern neighbours of the Union and not with the southern neighbours of the EU. Furthermore, special attention has been naturally given to candidate countries and pre-candidate countries, with the exception of Turkey. Lastly, because of their participation to the Schengen area and because of their connection to the internal market, Iceland, Norway and Switzerland also have concluded agreements with the agencies.

At the same time, the founding instruments of AFSJ agencies expressly regulate and foresee the conclusion of agreements with international organizations.[22] Again, while some founding instruments expressly refer to an international organization with which an AFSJ agency should conclude agreements,[23] all founding instruments leave the choice to the discretion of the agencies, albeit under the general condition that an agreement with an international organization must also be 'necessary for the performance of the tasks' of an agency. To date, all the main AFSJ agencies have made use of this possibility. Thus, Europol has concluded cooperation agreements with the World Customs Organization and the United Nations Office on Drugs and Crime (UNODC) as well as an operational agreement with Interpol; whereas Eurojust has

---

[22] For example Article 52 of Regulation 439/2010/EU establishing the EASO, OJ 2010 No. L132/11.

[23] For example Article 50 of Regulation 439/2010/EU establishing EASO provides for cooperation mechanisms with the UNHCR and Article 23(b)(iii) of the Europol Regulation provides the legal basis for the conclusion of an agreement with Interpol.

concluded an agreement with UNODC, and FRONTEX has concluded agreements with the International Organization for Migration (IOM) and the UNHCR.

The role of the agencies for the development of the EU qua AFSJ is growing both internally and externally. Although their action may appear uncoordinated, careful scrutiny reveals that the external projection of the agencies follows a certain pattern. Thus, privileged partners such as the USA and candidate countries have concluded mostly operational agreements, whereas with other third countries the scope of the agreements will depend on the data protection standards present in the third country and on the political will to conclude an agreement by the EU authorities. At the same time, the concerns raised by the EP, the Ombudsman and academics in relation to the applicability rule of law standards, accountability and transparency in the actions of the agencies have lead to a series of recasts of the founding Regulations that, although not decisive, have brought some improvements.

(f) The Court of Justice

Given the subject area, the CJEU's contribution to the AFSJ is facilitated by certain special procedures which allow particular cases to be dealt with more rapidly when required. Article 267 TFEU thus allows for the usually lengthy preliminary procedure to be applied more swiftly whenever it concerns a person in custody.

Article 267 TFEU

If such a question is raised in a case pending before a court or tribunal of a Member State with regard to a person in custody, the Court of Justice of the European Union shall act with the minimum of delay.

Such questions may also be raised in relation to international agreements concluded in the AFSJ area. In general, however, most AFSJ cases before the Court concern internal issues; albeit that the 'external dimension' is almost always visible in the background (e.g. international treaties on asylum, migration or fundamental rights).

Yet, the Court is fully competent to scrutinize all AFSJ legal action by the Council and the EP. Unlike CFSP (see Chapter 11), no exceptions have been made for preliminary references or direct actions, although a number of quite complicated transitional rules were formulated at the time of the move of the AFSJ from the EC Treaty to the TFEU. This distinction between pre-existing acts and acts adopted after the entry into force of the Lisbon Treaty is also relevant for the current external AFSJ actions.

K. Lenaerts, 'The Contribution of the European Court of Justice to the Area of Freedom, Security and Justice' (2010) 59 *International and Comparative Law Quarterly* 255–301

As to [EU acts in the field of police cooperation and judicial cooperation in criminal matters which had been adopted before the entry into force of the Treaty of Lisbon], article 10 provides that for a period of five years after the entry into force of the Treaty of Lisbon, the Commission may not bring infringement actions in respect of them. Article 10 also states that for the same period of time, the jurisdiction of the ECJ 'in the field of police and judicial cooperation in criminal matters, in the version in force prior to entry into force of the Treaty of Lisbon, shall remain the same'. Stated differently, in relation to pre-existing EU acts, the jurisdiction of the ECJ continues to be governed by ex article 35 EU until 30 November 2014. Upon expiration of the transitional period, pre-existing EU acts are subject to the regime described below.

As to EU acts adopted after 1 December 2009 (which include pre-existing EU acts amended after that date), the ECJ enjoys jurisdiction to review the legality of acts adopted in the Area of Freedom, Security and Justice by way of actions for annulment or on the occasion of actions for damages. Hence, if today the Council adopts an EU act containing a list of terrorist organizations in relation to which the EU aims to reinforce police and judicial cooperation, such organizations may bring an action for annulment as well as an action for damages against the Council. In other words, regarding EU acts adopted after the entry into force of the Treaty of Lisbon, there would be a different outcome to a case like *Gestoras Pro-Amnistía* and *Segi*. Likewise, the Commission (or a Member State) may bring proceedings against a Member State which fails to fulfil its obligations under Title V of Part Three of the FEU Treaty. This means that the *exceptio non adimpleti contractus* ceases to be a valid justification. In addition, the jurisdiction of the ECJ to issue preliminary rulings is no longer conditioned upon a declaration of a Member State to this effect. Nor is the preliminary reference procedure limited to national courts of last instance. However, when the EU exercises its powers regarding Treaty provisions on police cooperation and judicial cooperation in criminal matters, article 276 TFEU ... provides that the ECJ lacks jurisdiction to 'review the validity or proportionality of operations carried out by the police or other law-enforcement services of a Member State or the exercise of the responsibilities incumbent upon Member States with regard to the maintenance of law and order and the safeguarding of internal security'.

Moreover, in order to assess the legal effects of EU acts in the field of police and judicial cooperation in criminal matters, the distinction between pre-existing EU acts and acts adopted after the entry into force of the Treaty of Lisbon is also relevant. In this regard, article 9 of Protocol (No 36) states that the legal effects of pre-existing EU acts should be preserved until those acts are repealed, annulled or amended. In accordance with ex article 34(2)(b) EU, this means that pre-existing EU acts (Framework Decisions) may not have direct effect unless the EU legislator decides to amend them. Thus, the *Pupino* jurisprudence is still of paramount importance, requiring national courts to interpret national law in the light of the wording and the purpose of pre-existing EU acts. For acts adopted after 1 December 2009, the classic case-law on direct effect applies.

(iii) Opt-outs

The opt-outs negotiated by certain Member States in relation to the AFSJ affect the external competences of the Union in this area. With the adoption of Protocol 21 on the position of the UK and Ireland in respect of the AFSJ annexed to the Treaty of Lisbon, the two Member States claimed far-reaching exceptions relating to all matters falling under Title V, Part III TFEU. This means that, for example, the UK and Ireland may henceforth opt out of Directives harmonizing criminal offences.

Protocol (No. 21) On the Position of the United Kingdom and Ireland in Respect of the Area of Freedom, Security and Justice, OJ 2010 No. C83/295

Article 1
Subject to Article 3, the United Kingdom and Ireland shall not take part in the adoption by the Council of proposed measures pursuant to Title V of Part Three of the Treaty on the Functioning of the European

Union. The unanimity of the members of the Council, with the exception of the representatives of the governments of the United Kingdom and Ireland, shall be necessary for decisions of the Council which must be adopted unanimously.

For the purposes of this Article, a qualified majority shall be defined in accordance with Article 238(3) of the Treaty on the Functioning of the European Union.

Article 2

In consequence of Article 1 and subject to Articles 3, 4 and 6, none of the provisions of Title V of Part Three of the Treaty on the Functioning of the European Union, no measure adopted pursuant to that Title, no provision of any international agreement concluded by the Union pursuant to that Title, and no decision of the Court of Justice interpreting any such provision or measure shall be binding upon or applicable in the United Kingdom or Ireland; and no such provision, measure or decision shall in any way affect the competences, rights and obligations of those States; and no such provision, measure or decision shall in any way affect the Community or Union *acquis* nor form part of Union law as they apply to the United Kingdom or Ireland.

The remaining part of Protocol 21 lays down a complex regime with regard to the obligations (and in particular freedoms) enjoyed by the two Member States. While external relations are not mentioned explicitly, Protocol 21 refers to 'measures pursuant to Title V of Part Three of the Treaty on the Functioning of the European Union' in general, including the Title on AFSJ. This implies that the UK and Ireland have also opted out of acts adopting international agreements in this area. Article 2 explicitly refers to the fact that 'no provision of any international agreement concluded by the Union ... shall be binding upon or applicable' in those Member States. In fact, it would be difficult to see the two countries bound by international agreements in an area in which they do not participate, although time will tell to what extent the principles of sincere cooperation and consistency will affect their freedom.

A similar regime relates to Denmark (see Protocol 22), although differences occur because of the participation of this Member State in the Schengen rules on the free movement of persons. This further complicates the position of Denmark, for instance in relation to visa facilitation agreements, which will have to be concluded separately by Denmark with third states alongside the EU agreements.

Agreement between the European Community and the Russian Federation on the facilitation of the issuance of visas to the citizens of the European Union and the Russian Federation, OJ 2007 No. L129/27

... Article 3

For the purpose of this Agreement:

(a) 'Member State' shall mean any Member State of the European Union, with the exception of the Kingdom of Denmark, Ireland and the United Kingdom of Great Britain and Northern Ireland.

Similar constructions have to be found with regard to the participation of the EU in multilateral conventions or whenever the AFSJ agencies engage in the negotiation and conclusion of international agreements. When the EU border management agency FRONTEX negotiates and concludes working arrangements with third-country authorities, Ireland and the UK are not part of these arrangements as they do not participate in FRONTEX. It goes without saying that this complicated system of opt-outs (and possible opt-ins) is far from beneficial to the EU's ambition to speak with one voice.

4 THE EMERGENCE OF THE EXTERNAL DIMENSION OF THE AFSJ

The above analyses of the current provisions guiding the functioning of the AFSJ reveal the compromises that have been reached over the years by the Member States. We expand on these developments in the following paragraphs.

(i) Pre-Lisbon external competences: fragmentation across pillars

(a) Differences between Title IV EC and Title VI EU

The EU, which was established on the basis of the 1992 Maastricht Treaty, dealt with JHA in its third pillar only. The newly established JHA competences were meant to lead to 'Common Positions' in areas that were listed as 'matters of common interest': asylum policy, control of external borders, migration by nationals of non-Member States, judicial cooperation in civil and criminal matters, customs and police cooperation (see the former Article K.1 TEU). Although many of these 'matters' had a clear external dimension, the focus was on internal cooperation between the Member States, and a formal external relations reference was limited to the obligation to defend the Common Positions within international organizations and at international conferences (Article K.5).

The transfer by the 1997 Amsterdam Treaty of immigration, asylum and civil law matters to the EC Treaty also implied a 'communitarization' of the external competences in those areas. From that moment on, the regular Community external relations competences applied to these areas as well. In the absence of expressly established competences, external relations in new Title IV EC (on 'visas, asylum, immigration, and other policies related to free movement of persons') were established on the basis of implied powers in the line with the *ERTA* doctrine (see Chapter 3) as explicit external competences were absent.[24]

However, the legal regime covering the external action of the Community under Title IV has always been somewhat different from the one that emerged from the case law of the ECJ on the general law of external relations. The reason was that the Amsterdam Treaty contained a number of Declarations and Protocols that had the clear objective of preserving the pre-existing national competences in respect of certain external aspects of immigration policy. Thus, Declaration 18 attached to the Treaty of Amsterdam guaranteed Member States' competences to conclude agreements concerning 'conditions of entry and residence, and standards on procedures for the issue by Member States of long term visas and residence permits, including those for the purpose of family reunion', and a similar provision was contained in Protocol 31 on external relations in respect of external borders.[25] Moreover, the exclusivity of the Union's competences

---

[24] Case 22/70 *Commission* v. *Council (ERTA)* [1971] ECR 263.

[25] Protocol 31: 'The provisions on the measures on the crossing of external borders included in Article 62(2)(a) of Title IV of the Treaty shall be without prejudice to the competence of Member States to negotiate or conclude agreements with third countries as long as they respect Community law and other relevant international agreements.' This clause has been preserved and is now Protocol (23) of the Treaties.

on these matters was also put into perspective by the Danish, Irish and UK opt-outs in this field; a situation that was maintained by the Lisbon Treaty.

Taking into consideration these peculiarities of the external dimension of Title IV EC, it seems that policies such as the European visa policy did not constitute an exclusive external competence. In fact, it has been observed[26] that the visa policy as a whole did not meet any of the requirements and conditions set up by the ECJ in other fields of EC competence to become exclusive. Thus, the EU visa policy could not be considered an exclusive competence *in re ipsa* as is the case of the CCP as established in Opinion 1/75[27] and in *Donckerwolke*.[28] Similarly, the developments concerning visa policy do not seem to point to an exclusive competence of the Union *by necessity*, a scenario first described in Opinion 1/76[29] and now codified in Article 3(2) TFEU. Possibly, the only room for an exclusive competence of the Union in the visa policy is left in respect of the short-term visa if one considers the development of internal harmonization in this respect, but this could be impeded by Declaration 18 and Protocol 31 mentioned above.

A similar conclusion may be drawn in respect of readmission agreements. Even here, although this subject matter could potentially fall within the exclusive competence of the EU, the practice until the entry into force of the Lisbon Treaty has been that both the Member States and the EU have concluded readmission agreements. Although the acquiescence of the Commission in this respect does not allow drawing legal conclusions as to a concurrent competence of the EU and its Member States, it is politically meaningful that the Commission avoided any conflict on the matter. In this respect it is interesting to note that, just like at the EU level, Member States attain internal AFSJ objectives by concluding agreements which do not solely cover matters in that area and reveal a link between trade policy, CFSP and AFSJ matters.

Fragmentation was above all caused by the fact that the legal framework regulating the external competences of the EU in respect of the third pillar was very different from the Community's competences in Title IV EC. This, for instance resulted in the conclusion of separate agreements concluded by either the EC or the EU. As mentioned before, 9/11 influenced a large amount of legislation within the EU and simultaneously pushed for a new series of cooperation agreements with the US.

(b) The conclusion of international agreements

The conclusion of agreements related to PJCC (as the JHA pillar was called after the Amsterdam Treaty) was possible because of the introduction of an explicit legal basis for the EU to conclude agreements with third states and other international organizations. The new formal legal basis in Article 24 TEU was first used in the second pillar (CFSP) for the conclusion of the Agreement between the European Union and the Federal Republic of Yugoslavia on the activities of the European Union Monitoring Mission (EUMM) in 2001.[30] Since then, the Union has made full use of

---

[26] B. Martenczuk, 'Visa Policy and EU External Relations', in Martenczuk and S. van Thiel (eds.), *Justice, Liberty and Security. New Challenges for EU External Relations* (Brussels: VUB, 2008), note 1, pp. 36–42.

[27] Opinion 1/75, *Re Understanding on a Local Costs Standard* [1975] ECR 1355.

[28] Case 41/76 *Donckerwolke* v. *Procureur de la République* [1976] ECR 1921.

[29] Opinion 1/76, *Draft Agreement establishing a European laying-up fund for inland waterway vessels* [1977] ECR 741.

[30] Agreement between the European Union and the Federal Republic of Yugoslavia on the activities of the European Union Monitoring Mission (EUMM) in the Federal Republic of Yugoslavia, OJ 2001 No. L125/2. The reference to Article 24 can be found in Council Decision 2001/352/CFSP of 9 April 2001 concerning the conclusion of the Agreement between the European Union and the Federal Republic of Yugoslavia (FRY) on the activities of the European Union Monitoring Mission (EUMM) in the FRY, OJ 2001 No. L125/1.

this competence, also in conjunction with former Article 38 TEU in the case of agreements in the area of PJCC. Introduced by the Treaty of Amsterdam, Article 38 was part of Title VI TEU (PJCC). It served as a bridge to allow the Union to use its treaty-making competence in the area of the third pillar: 'Agreements referred to in Article 24 may cover matters falling under this title.' This turned the combination of Articles 24 and 38 into the general legal basis for the Union's treaty-making activities in the third pillar whenever agreements could not be based on the Community Treaty.

Because of the link between PJCC policies and other EU/EC policies, cross-pillar measures to create a coherent external policy were already explicitly promoted by the European Council at Feira in 2000 when, in relation to third pillar policy, it said that it:

should be incorporated into the Union's external policy on the basis of a 'cross-pillar' approach and 'cross-pillar' measures. Once the objectives have been defined, they should be implemented by making joint use of the Community provisions, those available under the CFSP and those on cooperation laid down in Title VI of the TEU.[31]

However, this was easier said than done. Where second/third pillar combinations – when limited to true cross-pillar agreements – were already scarce, this was even more the case in relation to EU/EC combinations. The classic example is formed by the Agreement between the European Union, the EC and the Swiss Confederation, concerning the Swiss Confederation's association with the implementation, application and development of the Schengen *acquis*.[32] Because this agreement concerned both Community and other Union issues, and a combination of an EC and an EU legal basis was not considered to be possible, the Council adopted two Decisions, one 'on behalf of the European Union' (with a reference to Articles 24 and 38 TEU) and one 'on behalf of the European Community' (with a reference to Articles 62, point 3, 63, 66 and 95 in conjunction with Article 200(2) EC).[33]

Indeed, the delimitation of competences over the pillars was already a major issue in the pre-Lisbon period (see also the *ECOWAS* judgment referred to in Chapters 10 and 11). Also in relation to the 'third pillar', the Court decided that situations could be envisaged in which the Community encroaches upon competences of the Union in other pillars. In the *PNR* case (referred to above), the Court held that the EU–US Agreement on PNR should not have been based on the Community Treaty (Article 95 EC, internal market) but on the Union Treaty.[34] Hence, in determining the centre of gravity of a Community instrument, the Court was no longer restricted to the legal bases offered by the Community Treaty itself, but – even before Lisbon – it was compelled to use the overall Union legal order as the interpretative framework.[35]

---

[31] See *A Strategy for the External Dimension of JHA*, doc 14366/3/05, REV 3, at para 6.

[32] Council Decision 2004/860/EC of 25 October 2004 on the signing, on behalf of the European Community, and on the provisional application of certain provisions of the Agreement between the European Union, the European Community and the Swiss Confederation, concerning the Swiss Confederation's association with the implementation, application and development of the Schengen *acquis*, OJ 2004 No. L370/78.

[33] Council Decision 2004/849/EC of 25 October 2004, OJ 2004 No. L368/26, and Council Decision 2004/860/EC of 25 October 2004, OJ 2004 No. L370/78.

[34] Joined Cases C-317/04 & C-318/04 *Parliament v. Commission (European Network and Information Security Agency)* [2006] ECR I-3771.

[35] In this respect, see also Case C-301/06 *Ireland v. Council and European Parliament* [2009] ECR I-593, in which Ireland unsuccessfully argued that the Data Retention Directive (2006/24/EC) should not have been based on Article 95 EC but on Article 34 TEU.

In fact, it was the development of this 'interpretative framework' that paved the way to a consolidation of the different AFSJ policies in the Lisbon Treaty. The convergence of the 'bits and pieces' that were originally said to make up the Union's structure created a new institutional and normative situation. In that view, the very fact that both the CFSP and the PJCC were not based on regular cooperation treaties, but together with the EC formed part of a European Union, had an impact on their development. Thus, the years before the entry into force of the Lisbon Treaty not only already revealed a clear interplay between the different Union policies, but also showed that the nature of the pillars could best be understood when their mutual relation is taken into account.

(ii) Milestones in the development of the external dimension of the AFSJ

The following section will provide an overview of some milestones in the emergence and further development of the external dimension of the AFSJ, highlighting only the significant moments in the development or the (re-)orientation of the external dimension of the AFSJ. In the period from the entry into force of the Amsterdam Treaty to the adoption of the Lisbon Treaty, the agenda of the AFSJ was characterized by programmatic documents. These programmes always had a specific feature, allowing for AFSJ objectives to be attained by making full use of the different external competences of the Union. In other words, while the EU could conclude international instruments specifically to AFSJ, EU external relations instruments from other policy areas would be recruited to attain AFSJ-related objectives. This reflects the fact that the external dimension of the AFSJ was never meant to be an independent external policy with specific objectives; rather, the external dimension of the AFSJ emerged either as a tool for the attainment of the overall AFSJ objectives, or as a dimension of other external competences of the EU.

(a) The development of the external dimension of the AFSJ: the Tampere mandate

The external dimension of the AFSJ gained momentum as a result of three events. The first is represented by the Tampere European Council of 1999 and initiatives/actions taken thereafter. The second is the terrorist attacks of 9/11 in New York and Washington, which had an impact on the overall strategy of the AFSJ, namely in respect of external relations and the fight against terrorism. Third, we may point to 'The Hague Programme' of December 2004, resulting in a new strategic and programmatic plan for the external AFSJ which was presented to and endorsed by the Council in December 2005.

As we have seen while discussing the role of the European Council, the seminal meeting at Tampere in 1999[36] launched the AFSJ following the entry into force of the Amsterdam Treaty, and for the first time the external dimension of the AFSJ received the political attention of the highest political forum of the EU.

Tampere Conclusions of the European Council, 1999, paragraph 59

The European Council underlines that all competences and instruments at the disposal of the Union, and in particular, in external relations must be used in an integrated and consistent way to build the area of freedom, security and justice. Justice and Home Affairs concerns must be integrated in the definition and implementation of other Union policies and activities.

---

[36] See the Presidency Conclusions of the Tampere European Council (15–16 October 1999).

The European Council made a general call for attention to JHA issues, affirming the need to integrate JHA concerns into the definition and implementation of other Union policies and activities. Through its conclusions, the European Council invited the Council to draw up – in close cooperation with the Commission – a proposal to define policy priorities, objectives and measures in order to feed the newly formulated external action of AFSJ.[37] Although the European Council refers to 'policy objectives', in the first preparatory documents the external dimension of the AFSJ is not labelled as an independent *policy*, but as an *action* complementing the establishment of the AFSJ.[38] It stated that '[d]eveloping the JHA external dimension is not an objective in itself. Its primary purpose is to contribute to the establishment of an area of freedom, security and justice. The aim is certainly not to develop a "foreign policy" specific to JHA. Quite the contrary'.

In the run-up to the Feira European Council of June 2000,[39] the European Council approved a strategic document[40] adopted by the Council in close cooperation with the Commission upon a proposal by COREPER, and in line with the Tampere mandate, on the EU's priorities and policy objectives for external relations in the field of JHA. This document may be seen as a first blueprint towards the definition of the external action in the domain of JHA. Any and all JHA external action was considered to complement the internal dimension, while also being aligned with the Union's broader external policy. Regarding the fields of action, the European Council of Santa Maria da Feira decided to give priority to a number of ('horizontal') policy areas:[41] external migration policy, the fight against organized crime and terrorism, against specific forms of crime, drug-trafficking, and the development and consolidation of the rule of law in countries on the road to democracy.[42] We should stress the fundamental role played by COREPER, the Council and the European Council: everything began within these political arenas, leaving the Commission to perform a 'supporting' role.

(b) The Hague Programme and its implications

A further step was taken by the Hague Programme,[43] which called for the development of a coherent external dimension of the JHA cooperation. The programme itself, dealing with external issues in many fields, including security, asylum and migration, and counter-terrorism,[44] invited the Commission and the Secretary-General/HR to present an overall strategy on the external dimension of the AFSJ, prioritizing some countries or groups of countries or regions, as well as on the specific need for the EU to establish JHA cooperation with these groups of countries. Interestingly enough, the European Council guidelines for the development of this new plan had already been proposed by COREPER to the Council in order to fulfil the Tampere mandate.[45]

---

[37] This is the mandate of the Tampere European Council: see para 61 of the Conclusions of the Presidency, and more generally paras 59–62.

[38] Quotation from the document, *European Union priorities and policy objectives for external relations in the field of justice and home affairs*, Doc. No. 7653/00 of 6 June 2000.

[39] M. Cremona, Monar and S. Poli (eds.), *The External Dimension of the European Union's Area of Freedom, Security and Justice* (Brussels: P.I.E. Peter Lang, 2011).

[40] *European Union priorities and policy objectives for external relations in the field of justice and home affairs*, Doc. No. 7653/00 of 6 June 2000.

[41] *Ibid.*

[42] *Ibid.*, pp. 7–8.

[43] The Hague Programme: strengthening freedom, security and justice in the European Union, OJ 2005 No. C53/1.

[44] The Hague Programme, points 1, 1.6 and 2.2.

[45] The reference is to Council Document 7653/00 quoted and discussed above. For comparison see the Hague Programme at para 4, where the European Council proposes as a guideline that the existence of internal policies is required to

The political impulse given by the European Council became visible in a number of subsequent policy documents, both from the Commission and from the Council, on the basis of the mandate received in the Hague Programme. In its Communication on the Hague Programme,[46] the Commission focused on identifying and elaborating policy projects in order to fulfil the political targets put forward by the European Council. The Commission identified ten priorities for the new multi-annual plan for the AFSJ. Second, the Commission elaborated its strategy on the external dimension of the AFSJ, fulfilling the mandate received in the Hague Programme, in a specific policy document,[47] as did the Council.[48] In its programmatic document for the development of the external dimension of the AFSJ, the Commission distinguishes between two perspectives, one related to the AFSJ as such and the other more generally within the broader framework of EU external relations. However, the external dimension continues to be conceived as a 'projection' of the internal AFSJ, since it is 'linked' to the ultimate goal of EU's internal security. Thus, the rationale of the external dimension was underlined: to complement the realization of the internal AFSJ and to support the EU's external relations in general.

Commission Communication, *A Strategy on the External Dimension of the Area of Freedom, Security and Justice*, Brussels, 12 October 2005, COM(2005) 491, p. 3

The purpose of this Communication is to demonstrate how the external dimension of justice and home affairs contributes to the establishment of the internal area of freedom, security and justice and at the same time supports the political objectives of the European Union's external relations, including sharing and promoting the values of freedom, security and justice in third countries. Although the instruments covering the external aspects of the EU's policies on freedom, justice and security are in place, the EU is for the first time organizing them around defined principles and guidelines into a strategy. This strategy must form an integral part of the EU's external relations policy but within it, the justice, freedom and security aspects should be reinforced. ... Freedom, security and justice issues lie at the heart of maintaining international stability and security both outside and inside the European Union. ...

The projection of the values underpinning the area of freedom, security and justice is essential in order to safeguard the internal security of the EU. Menaces such as terrorism, organized crime and drug trafficking also originate outside the EU. It is thus crucial that the EU develop a strategy to engage with third countries worldwide.

It could be argued that, irrespective of the external developments, which certainly played a role in the agenda-setting, the development of the external dimension of the AFSJ is above all triggered by the prior internal development of this area. As in many other EU policy areas, the realization of values and projects characterizing the AFSJ inside Europe both legitimizes and forces the EU to look outside as well.

---

justify external action; that there should be an added value in comparison to projects carried out by the Member States; and that the action contributes to the political objectives of the EU's foreign policies.

[46] Communication from the Commission to the Council and the European Parliament: *The Hague Programme: Ten priorities for the next five years. The Partnership for European renewal in the field of Freedom, Security and Justice.* Document COM(2005) 184 final of 10 May 2005.

[47] Communication from the Commission: *A Strategy on the External Dimension of the Area of Freedom, Security and Justice.* Document COM(2005) 491 final of 12 October 2005.

[48] Council Document No. 14366/3/05 on strategy for the external dimension of JHA affairs: global FSJ.

(c) The external dimension in the Stockholm Programme

Subsequently, the multi-annual programme (2010–2014) for the AFSJ was adopted: the Stockholm Programme.[49] The programme is ambitious and aims to exploit the new arrangements and possibilities offered by the Lisbon Treaty, called 'An open and secure Europe serving and protecting the citizens'. Openness and security are the two conflicting paradigms which have inspired the programme. The reference to openness and security postulates also freedoms and controls, and the exercise of sovereign powers on individuals. In the programme there is also an indication of a specific group of individuals, the citizens, which are the beneficiaries of it. At the same time there are clear indications that non-citizens are excluded.

The programme foresees several actions with an external dimension, but the external dimension of AFSJ is also addressed in a specific chapter on Europe in the globalized world. In terms of thematic priorities, two main issues are relevant: (1) controlling *migration* flows, strengthening cooperation with countries of origin and transit, and working on some convergence in asylum policies across Member States; and (2) improving *security* in Europe, by controlling the serious criminal phenomena threatening it, both inside and outside.[50]

In spite of a clear continuity with regard to the ultimate goal of achieving the internal targets of the AFSJ, the Stockholm Programme displayed stronger attention to the protection of rights and the dissemination of the Union's values. The programme reveals the ambition of a comprehensive plan for a system of structured actions, not reactive but planned and coordinated, implemented and assessed, to address the needs of the Union. This is also a consequence of the Union's increased activity in these policies, and of the higher number of institutional actors, namely the plethora of agencies with external competences. The ambition laid down in the Stockholm Programme is that the external dimension of the AFSJ becomes an *organized* framework policy, ever more integrated in the main policies of the AFSJ, keeping in mind the strong complementarity between the internal and external aspects of this policy field. The obvious question here is to what extent the EU is competent to become more active in combining internal and external AFSJ actions. The next section aims to provide an answer to this question.

European Council, *The Stockholm Programme – An Open and Secure Europe serving and protecting Citizens*, OJ 2010 No. C 115/1

7. Europe in a globalised world – the external dimension of freedom, security and justice

   The European Council emphasises the importance of the external dimension of the Union's policy in the area of freedom, security and justice and underlines the need for the increased integration of these policies into the general policies of the Union. The external dimension is crucial to the successful implementation of the objectives of this programme and should in particular be fully coherent with all other aspects of Union foreign policy.

   The Union must continue to ensure effective implementation, and to conduct evaluations also in this area. All action should be based on transparency and accountability, in particular, with regard to the financial instruments.

---

[49] Council Document No. 17024/09: *The Stockholm Programme – An open and secure Europe serving and protecting the citizen.*

[50] Communication from the Commission to the European Parliament and the Council: *An Area of Freedom, Security and Justice Serving the Citizen.* Document COM(2009) 262 final, 10 June 2009.

As reiterated by the 2008 European Security Strategy report, internal and external security are inseparable. Addressing threats, even far away from our continent, is essential to protecting Europe and its citizens.

The European Council invites the Council and the Commission to ensure that coherence and complementarity are guaranteed between the political and the operational level of activities in the area of freedom, security and justice. Priorities in external relations should inform and guide the prioritisation of the work of relevant Union agencies (Europol, Eurojust, Frontex, CEPOL, EMCDDA and EASO).

Member States' Liaison officers should be encouraged to further strengthen their cooperation, sharing of information and best practices.

The European Council underscores the need for complementarity between the Union and Member States' action. To that end, increased commitment from the Union and the Member States is required.

7.1. A reinforced external dimension

The European Council has decided that the following principles will continue to guide the Union action in the external dimension of the area of freedom, security and justice in the future:

- the Union has a single external relations policy,
- the Union and the Member States must work in partnership with third countries,
- the Union and the Member States will actively develop and promote European and international standards,
- the Union and the Member States will cooperate closely with their neighbours,
- the Member States will increase further the exchange of information between themselves and within the Union on multilateral and bilateral activities,
- the Union and the Member States must act with solidarity, coherence and complementarity,
- the Union will make full use of all ranges of instruments available to it,
- the Member States should coordinate with the Union so as to optimise the effective use of resources,
- the Union will engage in information, monitoring and evaluation, inter alia, with the involvement of the European Parliament,
- the Union will work with a proactive approach in its external relations.

The European Council considers that the policies in the area of freedom, security and justice should be well integrated into the general policies of the Union. The adoption of the Lisbon Treaty offers new possibilities for the Union to act more efficiently in the external relations. The High Representative of the Union for foreign affairs and security policy, who is also a Vice President of the Commission, the European External Action Service and the Commission will ensure better coherence between traditional external policy instruments and internal policy instruments with significant external dimensions, such as freedom, security and justice. Consideration should be given to the added value that could be achieved by including specific competence in the area of freedom, security and justice in Union delegations in strategic partner countries. Furthermore, the legal personality of the Union should enable the Union to act with increased strength in international organisations.

The Council recognises that CSDP and many external actions in the area of freedom, security and justice have shared or complementary objectives. CSDP missions also make an important contribution to the Union's internal security in their efforts to support the fight against serious transnational crime in their host countries and to build respect for the rule of law. The European Council encourages greater cooperation and coherence between the policies in the area of freedom, security and justice and CSDP to further these shared objectives.

The new basis under the Treaty for concluding international agreements will ensure that the Union can negotiate more effectively with key partners. The European Council intends to capitalise on all these new instruments to the fullest extent.

> The European Council underscores the need for complementary between the Union and Member States' action. This will require a further commitment from the Union and the Member States. The European Council therefore asks the Commission to report on ways to ensure complementarity by December 2011 at the latest.

5 THE EXTERNAL DIMENSION OF THE MAIN AFSJ POLICY AREAS

(i) Policies on border checks, asylum and immigration

Chapter 2 of Title V TFEU contains primary law provisions on border checks (Article 77 TFEU), asylum (Article 78 TFEU) and immigration (Article 79 TFEU). Thus, Article 77(2) TFEU is dedicated to internal and external borders and mandates the EU to adopt measures relating to: (1) a common policy on visas and other short-stay permits, (2) the checks at the external borders of the EU, (3) the establishment of the conditions upon which third-country nationals can move freely within the EU, (4) the establishment of an integrated management system of the external borders and, finally (5) the absence of controls at the crossing of the internal borders of the EU. Secondly, Article 78 TFEU on asylum, subsidiary protection and temporary protection mandates the Union to develop a common policy in these domains in paragraph 1 and identifies the different specific legal basis in paragraph 2.

Article 78(2) TFEU

For the purposes of paragraph 1, the European Parliament and the Council, acting in accordance with the ordinary legislative procedure, shall adopt measures for a common European asylum system comprising:

(a) a uniform status of asylum for nationals of third countries, valid throughout the Union;

(b) a uniform status of subsidiary protection for nationals of third countries who, without obtaining European asylum, are in need of international protection;

(c) a common system of temporary protection for displaced persons in the event of a massive inflow;

(d) common procedures for the granting and withdrawing of uniform asylum or subsidiary protection status;

(e) criteria and mechanisms for determining which Member State is responsible for considering an application for asylum or subsidiary protection;

(f) standards concerning the conditions for the reception of applicants for asylum or subsidiary protection;

(g) partnership and cooperation with third countries for the purpose of managing inflows of people applying for asylum or subsidiary or temporary protection.

Article 79 in relation to the development of a common immigration policy further confers on the EU the necessary powers to (1) determine the conditions of entry and residence for third-country nationals, (2) define the rights conferred to third-country nationals residing within the EU, (3) adopt measures to fight illegal migrations and unauthorized residence, including removal and repatriation and, (4) combatting human trafficking.

In relation to the external dimension of this policy, this section looks at three issues possessing a particular importance: border controls, short-stay visa policy and readmission agreements. A number of international agreements have been signed by the EU pertaining to these policies.

A first aspect in which the EU has been active concerns the management – *sensu stricto* – of the external borders; an external projection of the enforcement and application of the Schengen Border Code.[51] In this perspective the salient feature is constituted by the agreements that FRONTEX has been concluding with neighbouring countries with a view to cooperating on the surveillance of borders. This type of external action has been developed principally with third countries that physically share a frontier with the EU (e.g., Ukraine, Belarus and Moldova), but not exclusively (Georgia). Moreover, every candidate country (except for Turkey) has also signed an agreement with FRONTEX. The agreements signed by the agency with neighbouring countries and candidate countries envisage direct means of communication and the establishment of contact points. Furthermore, agreements contain clauses on training, exchange of best practices and information. Lastly, agreements with candidate countries and countries in preparation for becoming candidate countries usually contain clauses on enforcement cooperation and data exchange (FYROM, Bosnia and Herzegovina, Albania).

Parallel to agreements directly pertaining to the management and surveillance of external borders, the EU has made use of its powers to conclude visa-related agreements and readmission agreements. Concerning visa policy, it must be borne in mind that, because the EU is an area without internal borders, it plays a key role in establishing the rules concerning the documents necessary to enter the EU as well as conditioning the time frame in which third-country nationals are allowed to enter and move within the EU. The latter issue must be read in connection with the three month time frame in which EU citizens and third-country nationals settled within the EU can move freely without having to obtain papers of register within a certain city. As a result, short-term visa policy (i.e. visas valid for three months within the Schengen area) is a domain that can be considered as falling within the exclusive competence of the EU. This central bargaining power of the institutions in Brussels provides the necessary leverage for the EU institutions to negotiate documents relevant for important groups of travellers such as tourists and business people; and this power has been used to develop two main types of external action in relation to visas. First, the EU has concluded 'short-stay visa waiver treaties' whereby the EU and the third country in question decide reciprocally to stop requiring short-term visas; the EU has concluded this type of agreements with, for instance, Brazil, the Bahamas and the Seychelles. Should, however, the waiver of visa requirement appear too risky in relation to the potential migratory pressure of a certain country, the EU has developed the practice of concluding visa facilitation agreements whereby the two parties agree on easing the procedural and administrative steps for short-term visas, such as decreasing the price of an EU or third-country visa. Agreements of this type have been concluded with Russia and Georgia. The latter type of agreement, however, is usually conditioned to the acceptance, by the third country in question, of concluding also a readmission agreement.

Readmission agreements constitute the fourth type of agreement linked to border management. The EU and its Member States have placed an increasing importance on the conclusion of this type of bilateral agreement, given the important role of 'managing migration'.

---

[51] Regulation 562/2006/EC, OJ 2006 No. L105/1. This Regulation contains the rules on patrolling the external borders of the Member States and thus the EU.

This particular field is also at the centre of tensions between states and the EU in relation to the question of competence. Indeed, while the EU has sought to use its negotiating powers to include readmission clauses with several ENP countries, the EU itself has only concluded a rather disparate set of agreements with countries in – and beyond – the neighbourhood. Thus, while agreements falling under the ENP and other PCAs will always contain clauses on readmission, these clauses are never self-executing and require the conclusion of a separate ad hoc agreement. So far the EU has concluded a number of readmission agreements: first with eastern ENP countries such as Ukraine and Moldova, and with countries in the pre-candidate phase such as Albania, and Bosnia and Herzegovina. On the other side, readmission clauses with Mediterranean countries such as Algeria have not gone beyond the general clause contained in the partnership agreement. Outside the European continent, the EU has concluded readmission agreements with Pakistan, Macao and Hong Kong.

A question that pertains specifically to this dimension of the external AFSJ is the nature of this EU competence. Because this is the most developed field of the AFSJ in terms of legislation, the division of competences between Member States and the EU cannot be considered abstractly, but must take into consideration the practical elements of a certain policy. Thus, precisely in the field of readmission, and in spite of the numerous clauses on readmission agreements that the EU has inserted in its partnership and AAs, Member States have been allowed to negotiate their own specific bilateral agreements;[52] for instance, Spain has concluded an agreement with Mauritania, France with Algeria, and Italy concluded an agreement with Libya.

(ii) Judicial cooperation in civil matters

Article 81 TFEU on judicial cooperation in civil law is structured in a familiar way: a first paragraph on objectives and a second one on substantive measures. The latter part of the provision contains eight fields of competence for the EU, ranging from cross-border service of judicial and extrajudicial documents to the training of the judiciary of the Member States and their staff. Moreover, paragraph 3 of Article 81 TFEU contains a mandate for action in the field of family law, but in this case the institutions will have to follow the special legislative procedure and the Council will act unanimously. However, the core of this provision is related to the conferral of legislative powers to the EU in relation to 'mutual recognition of and enforcement between member States of judgements and of decisions in extrajudicial cases' and in relation to 'the compatibility of the rules applicable in the member states concerning conflict of laws and jurisdiction'.

Article 81 TFEU

1. The Union shall develop judicial cooperation in civil matters having cross-border implications, based on the principle of mutual recognition of judgments and of decisions in extrajudicial cases. Such cooperation may include the adoption of measures for the approximation of the laws and regulations of the Member States.

---

[52] For an overview of the readmission agreements concluded by Member States with neighbouring countries, see the website managed by a research group of the EUI: www.mirem.eu.

2. For the purposes of paragraph 1, the European Parliament and the Council, acting in accordance with the ordinary legislative procedure, shall adopt measures, particularly when necessary for the proper functioning of the internal market, aimed at ensuring:
   (a) the mutual recognition and enforcement between Member States of judgments and of decisions in extrajudicial cases;
   (b) the cross-border service of judicial and extrajudicial documents;
   (c) the compatibility of the rules applicable in the Member States concerning conflict of laws and of jurisdiction;
   (d) cooperation in the taking of evidence;
   (e) effective access to justice;
   (f) the elimination of obstacles to the proper functioning of civil proceedings, if necessary by promoting the compatibility of the rules on civil procedure applicable in the Member States;
   (g) the development of alternative methods of dispute settlement;
   (h) support for the training of the judiciary and judicial staff.

Judicial cooperation in civil matters, together with judicial cooperation in criminal matters and police cooperation, distinguishes itself from the role the EU is called upon to exercise. Contrary to areas in which the EU is called to substitute, lead or support Member States in the decision-making process, in these cases the Union is called upon to create the instruments necessary for national judicial authorities of the Member States to enter in a direct discourse without requiring technical and administrative support of the (national or EU-based) central administrations.

The history of judicial cooperation in civil law, however, does not solely rely on the principle of mutual recognition and the impact of the Amsterdam Treaty and the Tampere decision; rather, this dimension of the AFSJ is built upon the successful history of negative integration that can be traced back to the Brussels Convention of 1968, a sort of external AFSJ 'avant la lettre'. And while the scope of the Brussels Convention of 1968[53] has been absorbed by the emergence of proper competences within the EU and the adoption of internal measures through what has now become the 'ordinary legislative procedure', the external projection of this policy has developed into an exclusive external competence of the EU, as prominently affirmed by the ECJ in its Opinion 1/2003 concerning the Lugano Convention.

Opinion 1/03, *Lugano Convention* [2006] ECR I-1145

134. The request for an opinion does not concern the actual existence of competence of the Community to conclude the agreement envisaged, but whether that competence is exclusive or shared. Suffice it to note in this regard that the Community has already adopted internal rules relating to jurisdiction and the recognition and enforcement of judgments in civil and commercial matters, whether in the form of Regulation No 44/2001, adopted on the basis of Articles 61(c) EC and 67(1) EC, or the specific provisions which appear in sectoral regulations, such as Title X of Regulation No 40/94 or Article 6 of Directive 96/71.

135. Regulation No 44/2001 was adopted to replace, as between the Member States apart from the Kingdom of Denmark, the Brussels Convention. It applies in civil and commercial matters, within the limits

---

[53] OJ 1998 No. C27/1, for the consolidated version after the accession to the EU of Austria, Finland and Sweden.

laid down by its scope as defined by Article 1 of that regulation. Since the purpose and the provisions of the regulation are largely reproduced in that Convention, reference will be made, so far as may be necessary, to the Court's interpretation of that Convention.

136. The purpose of the agreement envisaged is to replace the Lugano Convention, described as 'a parallel Convention to the ... Brussels Convention' in the fifth recital to Regulation No 44/2001. . . .

139. The purpose of a rule of jurisdiction is to determine, in a given situation, which is the competent court to hear a dispute. In order to do so, the rule contains a test enabling the dispute to be 'linked' to the court which will be recognised as having jurisdiction. The linking factors vary, usually according to the subject-matter of the dispute. But they may also take account of the date when the action was brought, the particular characteristics of the claimant or defendant, or any other factor.

140. The variety of linking factors used by different legal systems generates conflicts between the rules of jurisdiction. These may be resolved by express provisions of the *lex fori* or by the application of general principles common to several legal systems. It may also happen that a law leaves to the applicant the choice between several courts whose jurisdiction is determined by several separate linking factors.

141. It follows from those factors that international provisions containing rules to resolve conflicts between different rules of jurisdiction drawn up by various legal systems using different linking factors may be a particularly complex system which, to be consistent, must be as comprehensive as possible. The smallest lacuna in those rules could give rise to the concurrent jurisdiction of several courts to resolve the same dispute, but also to a complete lack of judicial protection, since no court may have jurisdiction to decide such a dispute. . . .

152. The purpose of the new Lugano Convention is the same as that of Regulation No 44/2001, but it has a wider territorial scope. Its provisions implement the same system as that of Regulation No 44/2001, in particular by using the same rules of jurisdiction, which, according to most of the governments which have submitted observations to the Court, ensures consistency between the two legal instruments and thus ensures that the Convention does not affect the Community rules.

161. It follows from the analysis of the provisions of the new Lugano Convention relating to the rules on jurisdiction that those provisions affect the uniform and consistent application of the Community rules on jurisdiction and the proper functioning of the system established by those rules.

The Opinion of the ECJ in relation to the Lugano Convention and the resulting exclusive external competence of the EU to negotiate and conclude the Convention is only one aspect of the type of external action in the field of private internal law. Both Opinion 1/2003 and Article 3(2) TEU confirm that the jurisdiction and the enforcement of judgments in civil and commercial matters fall under the exclusive competence of the EU.

In the light of the *Lugano* Opinion, the EU has concluded or has acceded to a number of agreements and covenants in this field; yet, because the scope of the agreements was broader than distribution of jurisdiction and enforcement issues, the majority of the agreements concluded in this domain are mixed agreements (see Chapter 2). Thus the EU has only *signed* the Hague Convention on choice of courts agreements,[54] but *concluded* the Protocol on the Hague convention on maintenance obligations concerning the choice of law.[55]

---

[54] Council Decision 2009/397/EC of 26 February 2009 on the signing on behalf of the European Community of the Convention on Choice of Courts Agreements, OJ 2009 No. L333/1.

[55] Council Decision 2009/941/EC of 30 November 2009 on the conclusion by the European Community of the Hague Protocol of 23 November 2007 on the Law Applicable to Maintenance Obligations, OJ 2009 No. L331/17.

Parallel to these developments, the EU has developed an intense cooperation relationship with the Hague Conference on Private International Law. The EU did in fact join the Conference in 2007[56] and since then has consolidated its role as a proactive member in the field of private international law. In this respect, having participated in the negotiations of covenants within the framework of activities of the Conference since the 1960s, and having proactively worked for the adoption of a number of conventions in that context, EU membership of this international organization came as a natural development of the EU's role in the field of private international law. EU participation in this forum should be read as a means for the EU to coordinate with the Member States the rules on conflicts of law and jurisdiction adopted at EU level with the '*acquis de la Haye*'.

A third phenomenon in this area is the adoption, by the EU, of authorizations of Member States to conclude international conventions falling within this AFSJ domain as 'trustees' of EU law. The Council has thus far adopted a number of these decisions on matters such as parental responsibility for children. Fourthly, it must be emphasized that in the aftermath of the *Lugano* Opinion, the Council has adopted two separate Regulations where the EU disciplines the conditions under which, in spite of *Lugano*, Member States are conferred powers to conclude their own treaties in civil and commercial matters linked to Article 81 TEFU.[57]

(iii) Judicial cooperation in criminal matters

The provisions on judicial cooperation in criminal matters (JCCM) present more nuances than those concerned with civil justice cooperation, and they best portray the ambivalent role that 'judicial cooperation' is really called to play within the European integration process. Chapter 3 of Title V on the AFSJ contains both bridging norms, aiming to create direct dialogue between national legal systems; and provisions reflecting the general interest of the EU, thus allowing the EU to develop a genuine European policy on criminal law and on criminal procedural law. In this perspective it is possible to refer to the objectives and measures envisaged in Article 82(1) TFEU as bridging measures aiming to establish cooperation based on mutual recognition; whereas in paragraph 2 of the same article, the EU has been granted powers to introduce some degree of (instrumental) approximation in order to supersede the shortcomings of the application of mutual recognition. Thus, the EU as a polity will inevitably engage in a discourse concerned with the general principles of criminal law.

Article 82 TFEU

1. Judicial cooperation in criminal matters in the Union shall be based on the principle of mutual recognition of judgments and judicial decisions and shall include the approximation of the laws and regulations of the Member States in the areas referred to in paragraph 2 and in Article 83.

   The European Parliament and the Council, acting in accordance with the ordinary legislative procedure, shall adopt measures to:

---

[56] Council Decision 2006/719/EC of 5 October 2006 on the accession of the Community to the Hague Conference on Private International Law, OJ 2006 No. L297/1.

[57] Regulation 662/2009/EC, OJ 2009 No. L200/25, applicable to treaties falling within the scope of the Rome I regulation.

(a) lay down rules and procedures for ensuring recognition throughout the Union of all forms of judgments and judicial decisions;

(b) prevent and settle conflicts of jurisdiction between Member States;

(c) support the training of the judiciary and judicial staff;

(d) facilitate cooperation between judicial or equivalent authorities of the Member States in relation to proceedings in criminal matters and the enforcement of decisions.

2. To the extent necessary to facilitate mutual recognition of judgments and judicial decisions and police and judicial cooperation in criminal matters having a cross-border dimension, the European Parliament and the Council may, by means of directives adopted in accordance with the ordinary legislative procedure, establish minimum rules. Such rules shall take into account the differences between the legal traditions and systems of the Member States.

They shall concern:

(a) mutual admissibility of evidence between Member States;

(b) the rights of individuals in criminal procedure;

(c) the rights of victims of crime;

(d) any other specific aspects of criminal procedure which the Council has identified in advance by a decision; for the adoption of such a decision, the Council shall act unanimously after obtaining the consent of the European Parliament.

Adoption of the minimum rules referred to in this paragraph shall not prevent Member States from maintaining or introducing a higher level of protection for individuals.

This leads to the notion that the immediate scope of the powers conferred on the Union in this domain is internal; yet, on the basis of the implied powers theory now codified in Article 216 TFEU, the EU has acted as an external actor also in the field of criminal law, both bilaterally and multilaterally.

From the multilateral perspective, the EU has ratified instruments such as the UN Convention against Transnational Organized Crime[58] and its two protocols: the Protocol against the Smuggling of Migrants by Land, Sea and Air[59] on the basis of Articles 179 and 181 TEC (now: 209 and 211 TFEU), and the Protocol to Prevent, Suppress and Punish Trafficking in Persons, Especially Women and Children on the same legal basis.[60] Therefore, while the EU Treaties at the time contained a specific legal basis to ratify the above-mentioned instruments, the EU chose to use the Development Cooperation ones to do so. In general, the biggest interlocutor and reference in relation to criminal law and criminal law standards remain the Council of Europe and the ECHR, which are used by the Union not only as benchmarks for the adoption of EU legislation in criminal matters, but also to grant legitimacy to internal EU measures.

From a bilateral perspective, the EU has concluded two main sets of agreements that directly fall within the scope of the JCCM provisions of the TFEU: the Mutual Legal Assistance (MLA) and

---

[58] Council Decision 2004/579/EC of 29 April 2004 on the conclusion, on behalf of the European Community, of the United Nations Convention against Transnational Organized Crime, OJ 2004 No. L261/69.

[59] Council Decision 2006/617/EC of 24 July 2006 on the conclusion, on behalf of the European Community, of the Protocol against the Smuggling of Migrants by Land, Sea and Air, supplementing the United Nations Convention against Transnational Organized Crime concerning the provisions of the Protocol, in so far as the provisions of the Protocol fall within the scope of Part III, Title IV of the Treaty establishing the European Community, OJ 2006 No. L262/34.

[60] Council Decision 2006/618/EC, OJ 2006 No. L 262/44.

extradition agreements with the USA and Japan. Moreover, it has also concluded MLA agreements with Norway, Iceland, Switzerland and Lichtenstein as a result of the special association position these countries have with the EU.

MLA and extradition agreements are instruments that aim to discipline cooperation in criminal affairs. MLA agreements discipline judicial and administrative cooperation in a number of fields such as transmission and collection of evidence between two different states and establishment of joint investigation teams; extradition agreements discipline the conditions concerning the surrendering of individuals suspected of having committed a crime with a view to making the suspect stand trial or the surrendering of convicted individuals for the purpose of executing the sentence.

The USA–EU MLA and extradition agreements[61] are the first examples of criminal law-based international treaties concluded by the EU. The agreements work as a 'framework agreement' or 'umbrella agreement' (Articles 14 MLA and 18 Extradition Agreement), providing a common framework and content for MLA and extradition rules in relation to the individual agreements existing between individual Member States and the USA. In other words, the EU–USA agreement sets minimum and common rules that must be respected by the USA and the Member States when negotiating their respective bilateral instruments. This type of agreement is a clear expression of the division of tasks between Member States and the EU in respect of many AFSJ fields: the EU as a norm-setting authority, with enforcement-related rules carried out by Member States. In contrast, the MLA agreement with Japan[62] contains no clause on bilateral agreements and must therefore be understood as a self-standing agreement that nonetheless authorizes Japan and Member States to 'request and provide assistance on the basis of other applicable international conventions' and even to conclude agreements 'confirming, supplementing, extending or amplifying' the provisions of the EU–Japan agreement.[63]

(iv) Data protection in international agreements

The external dimension of the AFSJ raises complex questions from a legal-constitutional perspective, and specifically the capacity of the EU to maintain in its external relations the constitutional standards that have been agreed upon within the EU. These constitutional concerns do not relate solely to the relation between EU competences and Member States competences, but also to the impact that these agreements may have on the life of individuals and on the relations between the international community and the EU. In the CFSP area we have seen a clear example of this in the *Kadi* cases (see Chapter 7); an example directly related to the AFSJ is formed by the *PNR* cases, which concern the transfer of personal data by airlines to the United States. The *PNR* case forms a good example of AFSJ decisions concerning public security, and the Court quite clearly relates the transfer of the PNR data to the US to 'activities of the State in areas of criminal law'. It also shows that agreements with third states in this area may directly affect individuals in ways that would traditionally be covered (and protected) by domestic law.

---

[61] Agreement on extradition between the European Union and the United States of America, OJ 2003 No. L 181/27, and Agreement on mutual legal assistance between the European Union and the United States of America, OJ 2003 No. L 181/34.

[62] Agreement between the European Union and Japan on mutual legal assistance in criminal matters, OJ 2010 No. L39/20.

[63] Article 27 of the EU–Japan agreement, OJ 2010 No. L39/20.

Joined Cases C-317/04 & C-318/04 *Parliament* v. *Commission (European Network and Information Security Agency)* [2006] ECR I-3771, 30 May 2006 (PNR)

33. Following the terrorist attacks of 11 September 2001, the United States passed legislation in November 2001 providing that air carriers operating flights to or from the United States or across United States territory had to provide the United States customs authorities with electronic access to the data contained in their automated reservation and departure control systems, referred to as 'Passenger Name Records' ('PNR data'). While acknowledging the legitimacy of the security interests at stake, the Commission informed the United States authorities, in June 2002, that those provisions could come into conflict with Community and Member State legislation on data protection . . . The United States authorities postponed the entry into force of the new provisions but, ultimately, refused to waive the right to impose penalties on airlines failing to comply with the legislation on electronic access to PNR data after 5 March 2003. Since then, a number of large airlines in the European Union have granted the United States authorities access to their PNR data. . . .

50. The Parliament advances four pleas for annulment, alleging, respectively, ultra vires action, breach of the fundamental principles of the Directive, breach of fundamental rights and breach of the principle of proportionality. . . .

55. The decision on adequacy concerns only PNR data transferred to CBP [the US Bureau of Customs and Border Protection]. It is apparent from the sixth recital in the preamble to the decision that the requirements for that transfer are based on a statute enacted by the United States in November 2001 and on implementing regulations adopted by CBP under that statute. According to the seventh recital in the preamble, the United States legislation in question concerns the enhancement of security and the conditions under which persons may enter and leave the country. The eighth recital states that the Community is fully committed to supporting the United States in the fight against terrorism within the limits imposed by Community law. The 15th recital states that PNR data will be used strictly for purposes of preventing and combating terrorism and related crimes, other serious crimes, including organised crime, that are transnational in nature, and flight from warrants or custody for those crimes.

56. It follows that the transfer of PNR data to CBP constitutes processing operations concerning public security and the activities of the State in areas of criminal law.

57. While the view may rightly be taken that PNR data are initially collected by airlines in the course of an activity which falls within the scope of Community law, namely sale of an aeroplane ticket which provides entitlement to a supply of services, the data processing which is taken into account in the decision on adequacy is, however, quite different in nature. As pointed out in paragraph 55 of the present judgment, that decision concerns not data processing necessary for a supply of services, but data processing regarded as necessary for safeguarding public security and for law-enforcement purposes.

58. The Court held in paragraph 43 of *Lindqvist*, which was relied upon by the Commission in its defence, that the activities mentioned by way of example in the first indent of Article 3(2) of the Directive are, in any event, activities of the State or of State authorities and unrelated to the fields of activity of individuals. However, this does not mean that, because the PNR data have been collected by private operators for commercial purposes and it is they who arrange for their transfer to a third country, the transfer in question is not covered by that provision. The transfer falls within a framework established by the public authorities that relates to public security.

59. It follows from the foregoing considerations that the decision on adequacy concerns processing of personal data as referred to in the first indent of Article 3(2) of the Directive. That decision therefore does not fall within the scope of the Directive.

6 THE BROADER PICTURE OF EU EXTERNAL RELATIONS LAW

The internal dimension of the EU's objectives in AFSJ revealed the need for the EU to become active in the external dimension of this area as well, and the analysis revealed the impact of external developments on the progression towards EU international action in the domain. In that sense it can be concluded that the internal and external developments mutually reinforced one another.

The external dimension added more complexity to an already highly sensitive area. While 'respect for fundamental rights' is referred to in the first AFSJ provision (Article 67(1)), this principle is even more difficult to respect once norms are not merely decided on within the EU legal order, but are found in international agreements or decisions by other international organizations, such as the UN. Balancing security and fundamental rights may very well become one of the biggest constitutional challenges facing the EU, with the further development of the AFSJ and its external dimension.

The Stockholm Programme states that '[t]he external dimension is crucial to the successful implementation of the objectives of this programme'.[64] Indeed, this chapter showed a direct link between the internal and the external dimension of the AFSJ. This link is certainly strengthened now that the Lisbon Treaty allows for an active role of the EP and the Court. The coming years will have to clarify to what extent these institutions in particular are capable not only of striking the right balance between the different elements of the AFSJ (free movement, security and justice), but also of upholding this balance in a world in which both territorial borders and borders between legal orders are increasingly more fuzzy.

Despite their separate places, AFSJ (TFEU) and CFSP (TEU) are quite connected, and it may become increasingly difficult to draw clear separating lines between the external policies in these areas. In that respect the further development of the scope of the EEAS and the role of the HR will define the ways in which the Union succeeds in improving consistency in its external action.

SOURCES AND FURTHER READING

Balzacq, T., *The External Dimension of EU Justice and Home Affairs: Tools, Processes, Outcomes* (Brussels: CEPS Working Document 2008/303).

Chiti, E., 'An Important Part of the EU's Institutional Machinery: Features, Problems and Perspectives of European Agencies' (2009) 46 *Common Market Law Review* 1395–1442.

Cremona, M., *EU External Action in the JHA Domain: A Legal Perspective* (EUI Law Working Paper 2008/24).

Cremona, M., Monar, J. and Poli, S. (eds.), *The External Dimension of the European Union's Area of Freedom, Security and Justice* (Brussels: P.I.E. Peter Lang, 2011).

Eckes, C., 'The Legal Framework of the European Union's Counter-Terrorist Policies: Full of Good Intentions?', in C. Eckes and Th. Konstadinides (eds.), *Crime within the Area of Freedom, Security and Justice: A European Public Order* (Cambridge: Cambridge University Press, 2011).

Fletcher, M., Lööf, R. and Gilmore, B., *EU Criminal Law and Justice* (Cheltenham/Northampton: Edward Elgar Publishing, 2008).

---

[64] Council Document No. 17024/09: *The Stockholm Programme – An open and secure Europe serving and protecting the citizen*, p. 73.

Gatti, M., 'The Role of the European External Action Service in the External Dimension of the Area of Freedom, Security and Justice', in C. Flaesch-Mougin and L. S. Rossi (eds.), *La Dimension Extérieure de l'Espace de Liberté, Sécurité et de Justice* (Brussels: Bruylant, 2012), pp. 171–193.

Gilmore, B., *The Twin Towers and the Third Pillar: Some Security Agenda Developments* (EUI Law Working Paper 2003/7).

Guild, E. and Marin, L. (eds.), *Still not Resolved? Constitutional Challenges to the European Arrest Warrant* (Nijmegen: Wolf Legal Publishers, 2009).

Lenaerts, K., 'The Contribution of the European Court of Justice to the Area of Freedom, Security and Justice' (2010) 59 *International and Comparative Law Quarterly* 255–301.

Martenczuk, B., 'Variable Geometry and the External Relations of the EU: The Experience of Justice and Home Affairs', in B. Martenczuk and S. van Thiel (eds.), *Justice, Liberty, Security. New Challenges for EU External Relations* (Brussels: VUB, 2008), pp. 493–523.

Martenczuk, B., 'Visa Policy and EU External Relations', in B. Martenczuk and S. van Thiel (eds.), *Justice, Liberty, Security. New Challenges for EU External Relations* (Brussels: VUB, 2008), pp. 21–52.

Matera, C., 'La Coopération Frontalière avec les Etats Tiers Voisins', in J. C. Martin (ed.), *La Gestion des Frontières Extérieures de l'Union Européenne: Défis et Perspectives en Matière de Sécurité et de Sûreté* (Paris: Pedone, 2011), pp. 209–229.

Matera, C., 'The European Union Area of Freedom, Security and Justice and the Fight against New Security Threats. New Trends and Old Constitutional Challenges', in M. Arcari and L. Balmond (eds.), *La Gouvernance Globale Face aux Défis de la Securité Collective – Global Governance and the Challenges of Collective Security* (Naples: Editoriale Scientifica, 2012), pp. 69–88.

Matera, C., 'The Influence of International Organisations on the EU's Area of Freedom, Security and Justice: A First Inquiry', in R. A. Wessel and S. Blockmans (eds.), *Between Autonomy and Dependence: The EU Legal Order under the Influence of International Organisations* (The Hague: T.M.C. Asser Press/Springer, 2013), pp. 269–296.

Mitsilegas, V., *EU Criminal Law* (Oxford/Portland: Hart Publishing, 2009).

Monar, J., 'The Area of Freedom, Security and Justice', in A. von Bogdandy and J. Bast (eds.), *Principles of European Constitutional Law*, 2nd edn (Oxford/Munich: Hart Publishing/Verlag CH Beck, 2009), pp. 551–585.

Monar, J., *The External Dimension of the EU's Area of Freedom, Security and Justice: Progress, Potential and Limitations after the Treaty of Lisbon* (Stockholm: SIEPS Report 2012/1).

Papastravridis, E., '"Fortress Europe" and FRONTEX: Within or without International Law?' (2010) 79 *Nordic Journal of International Law* 75–111.

Pawlak, P., 'The External Dimension of the Area of Freedom, Security and Justice: Hijacker or Hostage of Cross-Pillarization?' (2009) 31 *Journal of European Integration* 25–44.

Peers, S., *EU Justice and Home Affairs Law*, 3rd edn (Oxford: Oxford University Press, 2011).

Rys, W., 'The External Face of Internal Security', in C. Hill and N. Smith (eds.), *International Relations and the European Union*, 2nd edn (Oxford: Oxford University Press, 2011), pp. 226–245.

Schieffer, M., 'Readmission and Repatriation of Illegal Residents', in B. Martenczuk and S. van Thiel (eds.), *Justice, Liberty, Security. New Challenges for EU External Relations* (Brussels: VUB, 2008), pp. 89–110.

Trauner, F. and Kruse, I., 'EC Visa Facilitation and Readmission Agreements: A New Standard EU Foreign Policy Tool?' (2008) 10 *European Journal of Migration and Law* 411–438.

Walker, N., 'In search of the Area of Freedom, Security and Justice: A Constitutional Odyssey', in N. Walker (ed.), *Europe's Area of Freedom Security and Justice* (Oxford: Academy of European Law–European University Institute, 2004).

Wessel, R. A., 'Cross-Pillar Mixity: Combining Competences in the Conclusion of EU International Agreements', in C. Hillion and P. Koutrakos (eds.), *Mixed Agreements in EU Law Revisited* (Oxford: Hart Publishing, 2010).

Wessel, R. A., 'The Dynamics of the European Union Legal Order: An Increasingly Coherent Framework of Action and Interpretation' (2009) 5 *European Constitutional Law Review* 117–142.

Wessel, R. A., Marin, L. and Matera, C., 'The External Dimension of the EU's Area of Freedom, Security and Justice', in C. Eckes and Th. Konstadinides (eds.), *Crime within the Area of Freedom, Security and Justice: A European Public Order* (Cambridge: Cambridge University Press, 2011), pp. 272–300.

15

The EU and its neighbours

1 CENTRAL ISSUES

- This chapter examines the wide ranges of policies and means through which the EU engages with the countries in its neighbourhood: first, EU enlargement policy, which is sometimes considered the most successful of all EU external policies; second, the EU has developed the ENP for those countries that are not eligible for membership either permanently or in the short to medium term; third, the Stability and Association Process (SAP) with the Western Balkan countries; fourth, EU relations with the EEA/EFTA countries; fifth and finally, EU relations with the Russian Federation.

- The EU has gone through seven rounds of enlargement. At present, we can speak of a true EU enlargement 'policy' with its own legal basis, rationale, objectives, instruments and decision-making dynamic. This chapter explains the key criteria and soft and hard legal instruments that make up this policy. It utilizes the 2004 'big bang enlargement' to explain how this policy has grown in a piecemeal fashion. Looking to the future, the chapter indicates how future enlargements may raise novel questions, and how the EU's response will almost certainly be influenced by individual Member State interests.

- The ENP originated from the fifth enlargement in 2004, and aims to create a special relationship with those third countries to the south and east that were not included in that process. From an instrumental perspective, this policy provides an excellent case study of the use of soft law in EU external relations law. From a methodological perspective, it illustrates how the EU has drawn on objectives and processes from EU enlargement policy, and applied them in a non-accession context, with commensurate difficulties. As regards instruments, it builds on binding bilateral frameworks, and then utilizes a plethora of soft legal documents to reorientate them towards new neighbourhood objectives.

- The SAP applies to the Western Balkans countries, and has an express EU accession perspective: Serbia, FYROM, Albania, Kosovo, Montenegro, and Bosnia and Herzegovina. Croatia emancipated from this policy upon its accession in July 2013. The policy is based on Stabilisation and Association Agreements (SAA) which have been concluded specifically to stabilize the region, utilizing conditionality and legal approximation to attain their accession objective.

- The Russian Federation was initially going to be included in the neighbourhood policy, but refused to be incorporated in this framework, and instead the EU has erected a 'Strategic

Partnership' with that country. Relations with the Russian Federation are frigid, and negotiations on a new bilateral agreement are not particularly promising.

- With the EEA/EFTA countries the EU has attained a depth of integration that is so extensive that should these countries wish, they could accede to the EU rather rapidly. However, for most of these countries there is no such desire, and alternative legal structures are presently in place: the so-called 'bilaterals' with Switzerland, and the EEA with Iceland, Liechtenstein and Norway. These legal relationships present the Union with a specific challenge of 'legal homogeneity' in the application of the EU *acquis* across the EU legal space.

2 EU ENLARGEMENT POLICY: PROCEDURE AND CRITERIA

(i) Treaty basis and procedure of EU enlargement

(a) Legal basis: Article 49 TEU

Since the High Contracting Parties to the Treaty of Rome came together in 1957, the original Community of six Members has gone through seven rounds of enlargement, the last time in July 2013:

- First enlargement – 1 January 1973: Denmark, Ireland and the United Kingdom;
- Second enlargement – 1 January 1981: Greece;
- Third enlargement – 1 January 1986: Spain and Portugal;
- Fourth enlargement – 1 January 1995: Austria, Finland and Sweden;
- Fifth enlargement – 1 May 2004: Czech Republic, Estonia, Cyprus, Latvia, Lithuania, Hungary, Malta, Poland, Slovakia and Slovenia;
- Sixth enlargement – 1 January 2007: Bulgaria and Romania;
- Seventh enlargement – 1 July 2013: Croatia.

The procedure for acceding to the EU is laid down in Article 49 TEU, an article which predominantly prescribes the steps to be followed, with few indications of substantive requirements to be fulfilled by applicant countries.

Article 49 TEU

Any European State which respects the values referred to in Article 2 and is committed to promoting them may apply to become a member of the Union. The European Parliament and national Parliaments shall be notified of this application. The applicant State shall address its application to the Council, which shall act unanimously after consulting the Commission and after receiving the consent of the European Parliament, which shall act by a majority of its component members. The conditions of eligibility agreed upon by the European Council shall be taken into account.

The conditions of admission and the adjustments to the Treaties on which the Union is founded, which such admission entails, shall be the subject of an agreement between the Member States and the applicant State. This agreement shall be submitted for ratification by all the contracting States in accordance with their respective constitutional requirements.

The procedure in this article can be described as predominantly intergovernmental with significant supranational aspects. First, there is the unanimity requirement in the Council at the outset to decide whether a third country can indeed receive applicant status. At the end of the procedure, it is the 'contracting' parties (to the EU Treaties) which must all ratify the Treaty of Accession with the new Member State. Upon ratification, this Treaty then becomes part of EU primary law. This article has changed through successive treaty changes: notably, consent of the EP is now required, and the provision speaks of 'consulting' the Commission. Additionally, the article now also includes a few substantive requirements. In the Treaty of Rome the only substantive accession condition was that a *European state* can apply to become a member, but in the post-Lisbon version we find the explicit need for a commitment to the values stated in Article 2 TEU, as well as respect for the 'conditions of eligibility agreed upon by the European Council'. The latter sentence is important, as it opens the door to the application of an extensive 'EU accession *acquis*' which has been elaborated in a piecemeal fashion through successive enlargements. This occurred predominantly during the 1990s, where successive European Council meetings laid the bricks of a pre-accession policy in preparation for the fifth enlargement in 2004. This also explains why the Commission is now 'to be consulted': it indicates that over time enlargement has become a *policy* in its own right, whereby the Commission plays a crucial policy function in ensuring convergence and compliance with the criteria set out by the Member States qua European Council. Thus, Article 49 TEU does not provide a complete picture of the steps a third country must take to become a member of the EU.

(b) Procedure for accession to the EU: a rough sketch

In what follows we provide an overview of the path towards EU accession for a third country. The description that follows is at a relative level of abstraction, since the path towards accession of any third country will be specific to the political, socio-economic, historical and cultural background of the applicant country.

- A third country first presents its application to the Council of Ministers. This is a highly political act, and usually such an application will already have been preceded by (extensive) political discussions. This formal request is not unlike a proposal for marriage: it will usually not occur until it is relatively certain that a positive reply will follow, and this within a reasonable time period. For example: Ukraine has clearly expressed a wish to join the EU in the medium term, but there remains significant reluctance on the part of the Union. Thus, Ukraine is yet to submit its formal request under Article 49 TEU.
- Once the third country has submitted its application, the Council requests the opinion of the Commission. A response of the Council may then come rather swiftly, or it may not. In the case of Morocco the rejection came soon after its application in 1987, but Turkey received its formal candidate status only in 1997, ten years after its application. In any case, when the third country has presented its application, the Council will request the Commission to submit its opinion on this application in line with Article 49 TEU.
- The Commission's opinion is published rather quickly after the request by the Council. For example, Serbia presented its application on 22 December 2009, the Council requested the Commission's opinion on 25 October 2010, and the Commission delivered this opinion one year later in October 2011.[1] In this opinion, one will find a macroscopic overview of the extent to

---

[1] Communication from the Commission to the European Parliament and the Council, *Commission Opinion on Serbia's application for membership to the European Union*, COM(2011) 668 final, Brussels, 12 October 2011.

which the applicant lives up to the accession criteria at that moment in time (see further below on the accession criteria). The granting of the status of 'candidate country' on the basis of this report is then not automatic, and is an important hurdle to overcome. Granting such status may be conditional upon continued efforts in certain problematic areas. In the case of Serbia, the Commission's positive recommendation was predicated 'on the understanding that Serbia re-engages in the dialogue with Kosovo'.[2]

- Contrary to Article 49 TEU, the practice is such that the final decision on granting candidate status is made by the European Council, rather than the Council. Thus, in the case of Serbia, on 28 February 2012 the General Affairs Council stated that it 'recommends to grant Serbia candidate status and looks forward to the confirmation of this decision by the European Council'.[3] This confirmation followed in March that year.[4]

- The fact that the applicant is granted candidate status does not mean that formal accession negotiations are immediately opened with that country. That decision is again taken by the Council and European Council on the basis of strict conditionality. For Serbia, the 11 December 2012 Council outlined the need for further progress on Kosovo – among others – as precondition for opening accession negotiations. In these conclusions the Council invited the Commission to report on progress in 2013, stating that a positive recommendation from that institution would lead to opening formal negotiations during the following rotating Presidency.

- Once the Council – again as confirmed by the European Council – agrees, negotiations are opened on the basis of a negotiation framework proposed by the Commission. For Serbia, this step at European Council level occurred on 28 June 2013, with the first round of negotiations expected to take place no later than January 2014. Such negotiations concern the adoption, implementation and enforcement of the EU *acquis* which is composed of thirty-five chapters divided according to policy field.[5] One should not understand these 'negotiations' in the traditional sense of negotiating an international agreement between equal sovereign nations. In fact, it concerns a lengthy process of agreeing on how and when to adopt and implement EU rules, without flexibility on defining the substance of the rules themselves. In these negotiations, chapters are then also not taken all at once, imposing further hurdles of conditionality in the pre-accession process: the Council may politically prioritize which to open first, before it is possible to move to other areas of the *acquis*. During these negotiations – which can and do take many years – the EU then provides extensive support to the candidate country for the effective incorporation

---

[2] *Ibid.*, p. 12.

[3] General Affairs Council, *Conclusions on Enlargement and the Stabilisation and Association Process*, Brussels, 28 February 2012.

[4] Conclusions of the European Council, 1–2 March 2012, EUCO 4/3/12 REV 3.

[5] (1) free movement of goods, (2) free movement of workers, (3) right of establishment and freedom to provide services, (4) free movement of capital, (5) public procurement, (6) company law, (7) intellectual property law, (8) competition policy, (9) financial services, (10) information society and media, (11) agriculture and rural development, (12) food safety, veterinary and phytosanitary policy, (13) fisheries, (14) transport policy, (15) energy, (16) taxation, (17) economic and monetary policy, (18) statistics, (19) social policy and employment, (20) enterprise and industrial policy, (21) trans-European networks, (22) regional policy and coordination of structural instruments, (23) judiciary and fundamental rights, (24) justice, freedom and security, (25) science and research, (26) education and culture, (27) environment, (28) consumer and health protection, (29) customs union, (30) external relations, (31) foreign, security and defence policy, (32) financial control, (33) financial and budgetary provisions, (34) institutions, and (35) other issues.

of the *acquis*. Overall, this 'negotiation' is a constant 'back and forth' between the third country, the Commission and the Council consisting of regular progress reports, strategy papers, etc., in order to 'close' the chapters progressively and prepare the applicant for membership.

Conclusions of the General Affairs Council, 25 June 2013

The Council recommends to the June European Council [held three days later], with a view to holding the first intergovernmental conference with Serbia in January 2014 at the very latest, to invite the Commission to submit without delay a proposal for a framework for negotiations in line with the European Council's December 2006 conclusions and established practice, also incorporating the new approach to the chapters on the judiciary and fundamental rights and justice, freedom and security. The steps leading to the normalisation of relations between Belgrade and Pristina will also be addressed in the framework. Prior to the first intergovernmental conference, this negotiating framework will be adopted by the Council and confirmed by the European Council. The Council also recommends to the June European Council to invite the Commission to carry out the process of analytical examination of the acquis communautaire with Serbia, starting with the above-mentioned chapters, in order to facilitate rapid early progress in these negotiations.

- Once the negotiations and accompanying reforms have been completed, the country can join the Union. This will be signalled by a 'Commission Opinion on the application for accession to the EU' by the third country. For Croatia, this 'favourable opinion' addressed to the Council of Ministers was given on 12 October 2011.[6]
- A candidate country accedes to the Union once all the Member States have ratified the accession treaty between them and that country. This treaty is specific in that the EU itself is not a party, and the agreement is ratified by all EU Member States as contracting parties. The accession Treaties are therefore part of the primary law of the EU, although their content is rather technical: they will usually make adjustments to TEU and TFEU which are mostly of an institutional nature (weighing of votes in QMV, etc.) so as to prepare the Union (institutions) to welcome the new Member State. However, it is not impossible that more substantive changes to primary law are made through an accession treaty, such as in the case of fisheries policy and the UK accession.

(ii) The 'conditions of eligibility': the Copenhagen criteria

Article 49 TEU states that any *European* state may apply to become a member, a criterion which is open to many interpretations. In the run-up to the June 1993 Copenhagen European Council, the Commission captured the difficulty of defining what it means to fulfil this condition for eligibility.

---

[6] Commission Opinion on the application for accession to the European Union by the Republic of Croatia, COM(2011) 667 final, Brussels, 12 October 2011.

European Commission, *Europe and the Challenge of Enlargement*, 24 June 1992, Bulletin of the EC, supplement 3/92, para 7

The term 'European' has not been officially defined. It combines geographical, historical and cultural elements which all contribute to the European identity. The shared experience of proximity, ideas, values, and historical interaction cannot be condensed into a simple formula, and is subject to review each succeeding generation. The Commission believes that it is neither possible nor opportune to establish now the frontiers of the European Union whose contours will be shaped over many years to come.

In 1987 Morocco submitted an application to become a member of the European Communities, but was rejected by the Council on the grounds that it was not a European state.[7] Turkey also applied in 1987, and it received candidate status a decade later. However, its accession negotiations have been significantly hampered by the political debate in Member States over whether this criterion is indeed fulfilled. The EU institutions and Member States have never explicitly defined what it means to 'be European', and further attempts to do so would have been futile. At the 1993 Copenhagen European Council which authoritatively codified the conditions for accession, the focus was entirely political and economic in nature. These 'Copenhagen criteria' have been incorporated into the Article 49 TEU procedure, through the statement that 'the conditions of eligibility agreed upon by the European Council shall be taken into account'.

Presidency Conclusions, Copenhagen European Council, 21–22 June 1993 at 13[8]

Membership requires that the candidate country has (1) achieved stability of institutions guaranteeing democracy, the rule of law, human rights and respect for and protection of minorities, (2) the existence of a functioning market economy as well as the capacity to cope with competitive pressure and market forces within the Union. Membership presupposes (3) the candidate's ability to take on the obligations of membership including adherence to the aims of political, economic and monetary union.

(4) The Union's capacity to absorb new members, while maintaining the momentum of European integration, is also an important consideration in the general interest of both the Union and the candidate countries.

The first criterion is one of political conditionality, the second is an economic criterion, the third entails the need to fully adopt the *acquis*, and the fourth criterion pertains to the Union's own 'absorption capacity' and the debate over widening versus deepening the EU. We will discuss these Copenhagen criteria in turn.

(a) First criterion: political conditionality and stability of institutions
Article 49 TEU refers to the need for applicant countries to respect and show commitment to the values listed in Article 2 TEU. These include human dignity, freedom, democracy, equality,

---

[7] European Parliament Legal Service, *Briefing No. 23 Legal Questions of Enlargement*, Luxembourg 19 May 1998, PE 167.617, p. 5.
[8] Numbering added.

the rule of law and respect for human rights, including the rights of persons belonging to minorities. This reference was not present in the pre-Amsterdam version of the accession procedure, and hence this inclusion represents the constitutionalization of the political conditionality embedded in the first Copenhagen criterion.[9] The notion of a European Community based on free and democratic European states was already stated in the Treaty of Rome itself, and was explicitly taken up as a criterion during the second and third enlargements of 1981 and 1986 to countries transitioning from non-democratic regimes.

> ### C. Hillion, 'The Copenhagen Criteria and their Progeny', in C. Hillion (ed.), *EU Enlargement: A Legal Approach* (Oxford: Hart Publishing, 2004), pp. 4–5
>
> [T]he political conditionality first materialised in the context of the EEC relations with Greece, Portugal and Spain. Discussions on their potential membership were made conditional to their acceptance and establishment of democracy. Indeed, the development of Greece's relations with the EEC was frozen following the coup of the 'Colonels', while Spain and Portugal had to free themselves of their dictatorships before they could eventually be regarded as admissible states. ... the Preamble of the Commission's opinions on the applications of the three southern candidates ... underlined that: the principles of pluralist democracy and respect for human rights form part of the common heritage of the peoples of the States brought together in the European communities and are therefore essential elements of membership of the said Communities.

The concrete implementation of the political conditionality criterion means that the Commission carries out a systematic examination of the main ways in which the applicant country's public authorities are organized and operate, as well as the mechanisms for the protection of fundamental rights.[10] Therefore, it aims to assess the extent to which democracy and the rule of law operate *in practice*, and indeed this is not merely a formal or abstract requirement. This examination therefore includes a substantive assessment of the structure, powers and functioning of the legislative, executive and judicial branches; and a concrete look at the actual exercise of civil and political rights and the protection of minorities.

During later European Councils, political conditionality was fleshed out further due to specific geopolitical requirements. For example, at the Helsinki European Council, the HoSG required that candidates settle their bilateral disputes, through involvement of the International Court of Justice if need be, before entering the EU.[11] However, the consistent and firm application of accession criteria is not always a given, as was illustrated by the accession of a still divided Cyprus to the Union on May 2004.

(b) Second criterion: functioning market economy

Membership of the Union requires a functioning and competitive market economy. If an applicant would accede without it, membership would be more likely to harm than benefit the

---

[9] C. Hillion, 'The Copenhagen Criteria and their Progeny', in Hillion (ed.), *EU Enlargement: A Legal Approach* (Oxford: Hart Publishing, 2004), p. 3.

[10] Commission Opinion on Hungary's Application for Membership of the European Union, Doc. 97/13, 15 July 1997 (no page numbering, see title 1).

[11] Presidency Conclusions, Helsinki European Council, 10/11 December 1999, pt 4.

economy of such a country, but it would also disrupt the good functioning of the internal market.[12] The reasoning goes that in the absence of flexibility in the economy, and without a sufficient level of human and physical capital and infrastructure, competitive pressures upon entering could soon be considered too intense by some sections of society. The consequence could be calls for protective measures and a national reflex, which if implemented, would undermine the single market.[13]

Commission Opinion on Hungary's Application for Membership of the European Union, Doc. 97/13, 15 July 1997, title 2.2

The existence of a market economy requires that equilibrium between supply and demand is established by the free interplay of market forces. A market economy is functioning when the legal system, including the regulation of property rights, is in place and can be enforced. The performance of a market economy is facilitated and improved by macroeconomic stability and a degree of consensus about the essentials of economic policy. A well-developed financial sector and an absence of significant barriers to market entry and exit help to improve the efficiency with which an economy works.

(c) Third criterion: taking on the obligations of membership

Membership equally implies the acceptance of the EU *acquis* – e.g. the rights and obligations, actual and potential, of the Union legal and political system, and its institutional framework.[14] The *acquis* is a broad notion which includes (1) the contents principles and political objectives of the Treaties, (2) the secondary legislation adopted to implement the Treaties as well as the jurisprudence of EU Courts, (3) soft legal documents such as Declarations and Resolutions adopted in the Union framework, (4) as well as international agreements concluded by the Union and its Member States in relation to Union policies.[15] The criterion that an applicant must take on the obligations of membership then has two predominant implications, which essentially means that if a country wishes to accede, the *acquis* is very much a take-it-or-leave-it affair.

First, the applicant must *accept the entire acquis*. This obligation of full legal approximation means that any difficulties on the side of the applicant should be resolved through transitional measures in the third country rather than by adapting EU rules.[16] During the Maastricht Treaty negotiations, Denmark and the UK had negotiated opt-outs to the third stage of EMU, and the UK of the Social Chapter also. In relation to the subsequent fifth enlargement, the Commission thus strongly expressed the fact that the *acquis* must be accepted as a whole in order to safeguard the achievements of European integration.[17] Thus, the possibility of past opt-outs becoming the rule

---

[12] European Commission, *Europe and the Challenge of Enlargement*, 24 June 1992, Bulletin of the EC, supplement 3/92, 9.

[13] Commission Opinion on Hungary's Application for Membership of the European Union, Doc. 97/13, 15 July 1997 (no page numbering, see title 2.2).

[14] European Commission, *Europe and the Challenge of Enlargement*, 24 June 1992, Bulletin of the EC, supplement 3/92, p. 11.

[15] *Ibid.*

[16] Hillion, 'The Copenhagen Criteria and their Progeny', in Hillion (ed.), *EU Enlargement: A Legal Approach*, p. 9.

[17] European Commission, *Europe and the Challenge of Enlargement*, 24 June 1992, Bulletin of the EC, supplement 3/92, p. 12.

rather than the exception was to be severely limited. This implies that new entrants are expected to work towards joining the euro, or that they must accept and implement the CFSP as it stands upon accession and its subsequent evolution. If an applicant country's stance in international affairs does not permit such, it could not be satisfactorily integrated into the Union. For CFSP, this was particularly relevant for the accession of Austria, Finland and Sweden in 1995, due to their long-standing neutrality. This was resolved with the phrase in the TEU that the ESDP (now CSDP) 'shall not prejudice the specific character of the security and defence policy of certain member States'[18] (current Article 42(2) TEU; see Chapter 12).

Second, taking on the obligations of membership also means that the applicant state needs to *apply and implement the acquis effectively*. In this sense, it means that the applicant state should have the legal and administrative framework in the public and private sectors to implement and enforce all aspects of the *acquis* (and thus also the first two Copenhagen criteria).[19] This consideration was particularly acute in relation to the CEECs during the fifth enlargement. It is for that reason that the 1995 Madrid European Council expanded on this third Copenhagen criterion by stating that EU pre-accession strategy should also include the 'adjustment of their administrative structures'. Below we shall expand how EU enlargement *policy* has been devised exactly to guarantee that countries fulfil what is essentially a horizontal accession requirement: the institutional capacity to *in concreto* apply, support and implement the legal, political and economic obligations of membership.

(d) Fourth criterion: absorption capacity

The Copenhagen European Council added a fourth accession criterion which applies to the Union itself. Namely, it is important to take into consideration the general interest of the Union in terms of 'absorption capacity' so as to ensure the momentum of European integration.

B. de Witte, 'The Impact of Enlargement on the Constitution of the European Union', in M. Cremona (ed.), *The Enlargement of the European Union* (Oxford: Oxford University Press, 2003), pp. 213–214

The most important EU institutions ... were conceived in the 1950s for a European Community of six Member States. The division of powers between these institutions has been changed several times since. However, their composition and internal organization have not been radically modified since those early days. The ineluctable question is whether this institutional framework, conceived for a small international organization of six members, and already coping uneasily with the increased membership and growing agenda of the EU, will be able to function as the EU expands eastwards and southwards to include, eventually, 27 or more states. ... From 1989 onwards, with the immediate prospect of the accession of Austria, Finland and Sweden ... and the long-term prospect of the accession of a host of other countries further east, it became fashionable to put the future of the EU in terms of a dilemma between 'deepening' and 'widening'. ...

---

[18] K. E. Smith, 'The Evolution and Application of EU Membership Conditionality', in M. Cremona (ed.), *The Enlargement of the European Union* (Oxford: Oxford University Press, 2003), p. 112.

[19] European Commission, *Europe and the Challenge of Enlargement*, 24 June 1992, Bulletin of the EC, supplement 3/92, p. 9.

> [W]hen looking at these two decades of widening and deepening in combination, it appears that the threat to the EU's institutional capacity that could prima facie result from increasing numbers of Member States was addressed in some areas of European policy-making by easing the conditions for making decisions, but this did not happen in other areas. Institutional reform continued to be a constant preoccupation for the states and for the EU institutions themselves, and new urgency was lent to this preoccupation when a new process of enlargement, of an unprecedented scale, was set in motion in the mid-1990s. Internal institutional reform of the European Union became so closely wedded to its new eastward enlargement that the two successive intergovernmental conferences leading to the Treaty of Amsterdam (1997) and the Treaty of Nice (2000) were expressly mandated to grapple with this problem.

There is broad consensus that the Amsterdam and Nice Treaties did not sufficiently address the question of efficient decision-making and working of the institutions for a Union of twenty-eight Member States. For example, at present the European Commission is still composed of twenty-eight Commissioners, one for each Member State. Article 244 TFEU allows the European Council to adopt a different composition on the basis of a system or rotation adequately reflecting the geographic diversity of the Member States. However, among other concerns, fear of losing a Commissioner caused difficulties in the ratification of the Lisbon Treaty in Ireland, and this national logic continues to stifle an evolution towards a leaner Commission.

3 EU ENLARGEMENT POLICY IN PRACTICE: THE FIFTH ENLARGEMENT

(i) Prelude: the first four rounds of enlargement

In this section, we examine the development of a fully fledged EU enlargement *policy* in preparation for the 2004, 2007 and 2013 enlargements. As a starting point it is notable that there is a world of difference between the latest three rounds and the preceding rounds of enlargement, because in the preceding rounds one could not speak of a strategy or 'policy of pre-accession'. We have seen that acceding to the Union requires the aspiring Member State to make numerous legislative, institutional, economic and political adaptations. During the first four enlargements, difficulties for the applicant in adapting to the *acquis* were commonly resolved during transitional measures included in the accession treaty, therefore taking place *after* accession. However, in the lead-up to the 2004 enlargement of the CEECs, a true strategic pre-accession process unfolded on the basis of the 1993 Copenhagen criteria. This was a consequence of the fact that the complexity and volume of the *acquis* had significantly grown between the 1970s and the 1990s, but more importantly because greater convergence between the EU and the aspiring CEECs was required to ensure a successful enlargement for both parties.

M. Maresceau, 'Pre-Accession', in M. Cremona (ed.), *The Enlargement of the European Union* (Oxford: Oxford University Press, 2003), pp. 10–11

... one of the most difficult adjustments to the acquis communautaire when the UK joined the EC concerned agriculture. In the early 1960s application for membership by the UK led to an unrealistic demand for derogations from the fundamental principles of the common agricultural policy, and it was only in the accession negotiations at the beginning of the 1970s that a compromise could be reached allowing for an orderly adjustment of the UK's national agriculture policy during a transitional period after accession. That being said in past enlargements it was sometimes also the case that important legislative activity in candidate states appeared to be indispensable before accession to the EC. This was usually achieved in the, sometimes long, accession negotiations phase and it was not part of a preconceived strategy of the EC. A striking example ... is again that of the UK where existing domestic constitutional law practice required fundamental adjustments. This was done through the 1972 European Communities Act creating an extremely subtle legal construction allowing existing and future EC law to be applied in the UK at the moment of entry to the EC ... Basically it had as consequence that British constitutional law concepts, at first sight irreconcilable with basic EC law principles such as supremacy and direct effect ... could be smoothly integrated into the British legal order.

In the following paragraphs we offer a case study of the nearly twenty years leading up to the 1 May 2004 'big bang' enlargement in a chronological fashion. It illustrates the deep connection between European integration, external political events and the (legal) development of a fully fledged EU enlargement policy. By approaching the subject chronologically, we can observe how Article 49 TEU, through a blend of internal and external political and socio-economic needs and pressures, has become the legal basis for a fully fledged EU enlargement policy with its distinct roles for EU institutions and the Member States, and with its distinctive logic, objectives, toolbox, and mix of legal and non-legal instruments.

(ii) Trade and Cooperation Agreements and PHARE (end 1980s)

From 1986 onwards, USSR President Mikhail Gorbachev instituted the policies of 'restructuring' and 'openness' in the USSR. This led to a number of declarations of independence in 1988 (the Baltic States), the crumbling of the Iron Curtain from the summer of 1989 (Hungary) onwards, and eventually the collapse of the USSR itself in 1991. EU Member States acting through EPC (see Chapter 11) adopted a 'wait and see' attitude.[20] Thus, on 13 June 1988, the Foreign Ministers of the Twelve merely declared that they were 'paying close attention to the developments currently taking place in the Soviet Union and Eastern Europe'.[21] However, on the Community side more action was undertaken. In June 1988, the 'Joint Declaration on the Establishment of Official Relations between the European Economic Community and the Council for Mutual Economic Assistance' (CMEA, or COMECON) was signed.[22] The CMEA had given up its long-standing position of only accepting an agreement between them as a group and the Community, which paved the way for the conclusion of individual agreements with Member States of the

---

[20] R. Rummel (ed.), *Toward Political Union – Planning a Common Foreign and Security Policy in the European Community* (Baden-Baden: Nomos, 1992), p. 362.

[21] Bulletin EC, June 1988, 2.4.2.

[22] Council Decision 88/345/EEC of 22 June 1988 on the conclusion of the Joint Declaration on the establishment of official relations between the European Economic Community and the Council for Mutual Economic Assistance, OJ 1988 No. L157/34.

CMEA. Thus, in September 1988, the first Trade and Cooperation Agreement (TCA) was signed between the Community and Hungary.[23] Following the Hungarian example, the Community went on to conclude TCAs with Poland, the Soviet Union, and in 1990 with Bulgaria and Romania. Czechoslovakia initially only had a 'trade' agreement, later replaced by a Trade *and* Cooperation Agreement.[24]

In parallel with the development of important contractual relations with the CEECs and the Newly Independent States (NIS), a new aid instrument saw the light of day. At a G-7 Paris summit in July 1989, the leaders requested with regard to 'concerted support for reform in Poland and Hungary' that 'the Commission of the European Communities [would] take the necessary initiatives in agreement with the other Member States of the Community, and to associate, besides the Summit participants, all interested countries'.[25] Taking up this task, the Commission chaired the first coordination meeting of all twenty-four members of the OECD. This aid operation, as the Community's own aid initiative set up a few months later, was dubbed PHARE: '*Pologne, Hongrie – Assistance à la Restructuration des Economies.*'

(iii) Contractual relations with the CEECs and the NIS (1989–1993)

The ink was not dry on the TCAs, with some of them not even having been concluded yet, and already the pressure grew to replace them with a strengthened commitment more in keeping with the evolving situation.[26] The idea of offering Association with the Community to the CEECs was initially floated by Giscard d'Estaing, MEP and finally decided at the Strasbourg European Council in December 1989, which said that 'The Community ... will encourage the necessary economic reforms by all the means at its disposal, and will continue its examination of the appropriate forms of association with the countries which are pursuing the path of economic and political reform.'[27] Although these AAs initially did not have an accession objective, it was notable that these conclusions already established a link between European integration and ongoing external events: 'the building of European Union will permit the further development of effective and harmonious relations with the other countries of Europe'.[28]

The first so-called 'Europe Agreements' (EAs) were negotiated with Poland, Hungary and what was then still the Czech and Slovak Federal Republic, and were signed on 16 December 1991.[29] When the Czech and Slovak Republic dissolved, a new agreement had to be negotiated leading to

---

[23] Council Decision 88/595/EEC of 21 November 1988 concerning the conclusion of an Agreement between the European Economic Community and the Hungarian People's Republic on trade and commercial and economic cooperation, OJ 1988 No. L327/1.

[24] Agreement between the European Economic Community and the Polish People's Republic on trade and commercial and economic cooperation, OJ 1989 No. L339/2; Agreement between the European Economic Community and the European Atomic Energy Community and the Union of Soviet Socialist Republics on trade and commercial and economic cooperation, OJ 1990 No. L68/3.

[25] G-7 Summit Paris, 14–16 July 1989, Declaration on East–West Relations of July 15, 1989.

[26] A. Mayhew, *Recreating Europe: The European Union's Policy Towards Central and Eastern Europe* (Cambridge: Cambridge University Press, 1998), pp. 19–21.

[27] European Council Conclusions, Strasbourg 8–9 December 1989, in *European Parliament Activities, Special Edition*, 2/S-89, p. 11.

[28] *Ibid.*, p. 16.

[29] Europe Agreement Hungary, OJ 1993 No. L347/1, in force since 1 February 1994, and Europe Agreement Poland, OJ 1993 No. L348/1, in force since 1 February 1994.

individual agreements on 4 October 1993.[30] In the years that followed, Romania,[31] Bulgaria,[32] Lithuania,[33] Latvia,[34] Estonia[35] and Slovenia[36] also concluded EAs.

K. Inglis, 'The Europe Agreements Compared in the Light of their Pre-Accession Reorientation' (2000) 37 *Common Market Law Review* 1173–1210 at 1179

Originally, the main objectives that guided the EC/CEEC relations under the EAs were: to establish political dialogue where it had previously been absent; to bring about bilateral free trade areas with each of the CEEC countries within ten years, in order to achieve a liberalization of trade in industrial products; and to provide for broad ranging economic cooperation in a number of key areas as well as cultural cooperation and financial cooperation. Provisions on movement of persons, establishment, supply of services, payments, capital, competition and approximation of laws apply to the association, and a variety of bodies were established under the EAs through which the European Community and the EA countries would cooperate to strengthen and widen their relations. The Union contributed to the reconstruction and then the market reform of its eastern neighbours through the PHARE instrument dating back to 1989, an autonomous instrument of the European Community quite distinct from the EAs.

During and after the dissolution of the USSR, the EC and its Member States differentiated between the CEECs in their 'return to Europe', and the NIS. Notably, for historical, socio-economic and political reasons relations with the NIS were placed on a weaker footing compared to the CEECs, and the EC did not conclude EAs with them: Armenia, Azerbaijan, Belarus, Georgia, Kazakhstan, Kyrgyzstan, Moldova, the Russian Federation, Tajikistan, Turkmenistan, Ukraine and Uzbekistan. These countries (except for the Baltic States which were treated as CEECs) were not offered Association, but instead were proposed PCAs.

C. Hillion, 'Partnership and Cooperation Agreements between the European Union and the New Independent States of the Ex-Soviet Union' (1998) 3 *European Foreign Affairs Review* 399–420

[PCAs] were designed to establish the new framework for developing bilateral relations between the EC and each of the NIS that were to replace the outdated 1989 TCA. Moreover, they actually constituted an alternative to the Europe Agreements signed with certain CEECs. Relying on its weakened but superpower [heritage], the Russian Federation, further followed by other NIS, strongly tried to obtain an agreement close and comparable to those Europe Agreements. Nevertheless, the EC upheld a much looser approach in economic, political and legal terms both because of the geopolitical situation of Russia and the other NIS, and the uncertainties of the transformation process in the region. . . .

---

[30] Czech Republic: OJ 1994 No. L360/2 *et seq.* In force since 1 February 1995; Slovak Republic: OJ 1994 No. L359/2 *et seq.* In force since 1 February 1995.
[31] OJ 1994 No. L357/2 *et seq.* In force since 1 February 1995.
[32] OJ 1994 No. L358/3 *et seq.* In force since 1 February 1995.
[33] OJ 1998 No. L51/3 *et seq.* In force since 1 February 1998.
[34] OJ 1998 No. L26/3 *et seq.* In force since 1 February 1998.
[35] OJ 1998 No. L68/3 *et seq.* In force since 1 February 1998.
[36] OJ 1999 No. L51/3 *et seq.* In force since 1 February 1999.

The nature of the PCAs also differs from that of Europe Agreements based on Article 238 EC in that it does not create a 'privileged link' between the parties. Associated countries are called upon 'to participate', at least to a certain extent to the EC legal system. The distinction between the two legal bases thus implies differentiation in substance and particularly in terms of objectives. Indeed, following the Copenhagen European Council in 1993, the Europe Agreements are deemed to establish an Association of which the final aim is the accession of the associated countries to the Union.

(iv) From Europe Agreement to enhanced pre-accession policy (1993–1997)

At the 1993 Copenhagen European Council the HoSG decided that the CEECs that so desired would become members of the EU. The CEECs' formal applications of membership would follow between 1994 and 1996.[37] In same time, it was necessary that they prepare to fulfil the conditions for membership. In December 1994 the Essen European Council formally launched the 'pre-accession strategy' to attain that objective,[38] which implied a novel dual bilateral and multilateral strategy.[39] Note that at this point in time the CEECs had not yet been recognized as applicant countries (see timeline above in this chapter).

On the bilateral end, it meant a substantive reorientation of the EAs from association to pre-accession instruments, without actually renegotiating the texts of these and future EAs. It was rather through a pragmatic policy process that the EAs and the institutions became the bilateral conduit for intensified, tailor-made pre-accession collaboration. On the multilateral side, there was the creation of the 'Structured Dialogue' as part of the pre-accession strategy.[40] This structured relationship covered all areas of the *acquis* and was meant to familiarize the candidate countries with the various activities of the Union by allowing CEECs' representatives to meet with their EU counterparts, commonly in the margins of formal Council of Ministers meetings.[41] As part of the pre-accession strategy, the aid instrument PHARE was also reorientated in line with the Copenhagen criteria,[42] and subsequently in 1995 the Technical Assistance and Information Exchange Office (TAIEX) was created. The purpose of TAIEX was to support the associated countries in adopting and implementing the internal market *acquis* on the basis of a multi-country approach reflective of future obligations as an EU Member State.[43] Finally, it is important to recall that the launch of the pre-accession strategy was also meant to prepare the EU itself in line with the fourth Copenhagen criterion. Thus, the European Council as part of the strategy announced that the institutional conditions for ensuring the proper functioning of the Union must be created at the 1996 IGC, in what became known as the Amsterdam Treaty.

Meanwhile, Malta and Cyprus had also submitted applications for EU membership, and they were also included in the pre-accession process. In December 1995, the Madrid European

---

[37] M. Maresceau, 'Pre-Accession', in Cremona (ed.), *The Enlargement of the European Union*, p. 25.

[38] European Council Conclusions, Essen, 9–10 December 1994, Annex IV.

[39] European Commission, *White Paper – Preparation of the Associated Countries of Central and Eastern Europe for Integration into the Internal Market of the Union*, Brussels, 3 May 1995, COM(95) 163 final.

[40] K. Inglis, 'The Europe Agreements Compared in the Light of their Pre-Accession Reorientation' (2000) 37 *Common Market Law Review* 1173–1210 at 1182.

[41] Maresceau, 'Pre-Accession', p. 20.

[42] Inglis, 'The Europe Agreements Compared', 1179.

[43] Inglis, 'The Europe Agreements Compared', 1181.

Council decided that accession negotiations could start six months after the end of the 1996 IGC. In June 1997, the European Council reached the following conclusions:

European Council Conclusions, Amsterdam, 16–17 June 1997

The European Council notes that, with the successful conclusion of the Intergovernmental Conference, the way is now open for launching the enlargement process in accordance with the conclusions of the Madrid European Council.

It welcomes the Commission's intention to present by mid-July its opinions on the accession applications as well as a comprehensive communication ("Agenda 2000") covering the development of Union policies including the agricultural and structural policies, the horizontal questions related to enlargement and finally the future financial framework beyond 1999.

The European Council notes that the Commission in its Agenda 2000 communication will draw the main conclusions and recommendations from the opinions and give its views on the launching of the accession process including proposals on reinforcing pre-accession strategy and further developing pre-accession assistance building on ongoing reforms of PHARE.

The Commission Communication entitled 'Agenda 2000: For a stronger and wider union', was published in July 1997,[44] and contained Commission opinions on each application for membership. The individual country opinions were contentious, as the Commission stated that only five CEECs were ready to open accession negotiations: Poland, Hungary, the Czech Republic, Slovenia, and Estonia.[45] The Commission opinion on Cyprus was positive, whereas Malta had excluded itself by freezing its application for membership. The December 1997 Luxembourg European Council confirmed the choice for the five CEECs made by the Commission, and agreed upon Agenda 2000's *enhanced* pre-accession strategy which – sensitive to negative political responses from excluded applicants – was applied to all CEEC countries.[46] Enhanced pre-accession was applied to Cyprus and Malta[47] from 2000 onwards.

The purpose of the reinforced/enhanced pre-accession strategy was to give the EU and third countries the guarantee of a well-prepared accession, and was aimed at ensuring that applicant countries adapt their laws and institutions *prior* to entering the Union. In this fashion, systematic recourse to long transition periods in the accession treaty would be avoided, as that could jeopardize the *acquis* and the cohesion of the Union.[48] Agenda 2000 thus set out an improved legal framework through which the Union and each applicant country could further clarify their individual accession preparation programmes and implement them on a bilateral basis: to that end a new instrument was created, namely the 'Accession Partnerships', and the Commission also foresaw a further reorientation of the EAs.

---

[44] European Commission, *Agenda 2000: For a stronger and wider Union*, 15 July 1997, COM(97) 2000 final.

[45] Maresceau, 'Pre-Accession', p. 25.

[46] Maresceau, 'Pre-Accession', p. 27.

[47] Between 1996–1998 the Maltese government froze its application for membership, until new elections in 1998 restarted that process.

[48] Commission Communication, *Agenda 2000: For a stronger and wider Union*, COM(97) 2000 final, 15 July 1997, p. 89.

European Commission, *Agenda 2000: For a stronger and wider Union*, 15 July 1997, COM(97) 2000 final, pp. 87–88[49]

The Accession Partnership will be a key feature of the reinforced strategy and will mobilize all forms of assistance to the applicant countries within a single framework for the implementation of national programmes to prepare them for membership of the European Union.

Accession Partnerships would involve: precise commitments on the part of the applicant country, relating in particular to democracy, macroeconomic stabilization, industrial restructuring, nuclear safety and a national programme for adopting the *acquis* within a precise timetable, focusing on the priority areas identified in each opinion; mobilization of all the resources available to the Community for preparing the applicant countries for accession. . . .

A programme for adopting the *acquis* would be worked out by the Commission in partnership with each applicant country. The priorities set should initially correspond to the sectors identified as deficient in the opinions. Work towards the objectives would be covered by an indicative timetable. The granting of assistance – on the basis of annual financing agreements – will be conditional on achieving these objectives and on progress made. Implementation of the programme would thus depend on strict 'accession conditionality' based on suitable evaluation machinery, and on ongoing dialogue with the Commission.

The Commission will report regularly to the European Council on progress (and the prospects for opening negotiations with those countries with which such negotiations have not yet begun). . . .

Preparation of the Accession Partnerships will start in the second half of 1997.

The Europe Agreements introduced bilateral cooperation with the Union, which will lead to advanced integration in a large number of fields (trade agreements, competition, approximation of laws, standardization, etc.). The bodies set up under these agreements (councils, association committees and subcommittees, parliamentary committees) are the preferred bodies for consulting the applicant countries. The work carried out under the agreements will help to implement the reinforced pre-accession strategy through the cooperation achieved in particular in the association subcommittees for monitoring progress on the approximation of laws and the exchange of information on the evolution of the *acquis*. Since the agreements cover most of the fields associated with the *acquis*, they will be used to help the applicant countries establish their national programme for adopting the *acquis*.

(v) The 2004 'big bang' enlargement

With characteristically grand language, the December 2002 European Council in Copenhagen confirmed the conclusion of accession negotiations with the CEECs (minus Romania and Bulgaria), Cyprus and Malta.[50] The HoSG stated that:

[this] achievement testifies to the common determination of the peoples of Europe to come together in a Union that has become the driving force for peace, democracy, stability and prosperity on our continent. As fully fledged members of a Union based on solidarity, these States will play a full role in shaping the further development of the European project.[51]

---

[49] Emphasis added.
[50] OJ 2003 No. L236/1.
[51] European Council Conclusions, Copenhagen, 13–14 December 2002.

The Accession Treaty between the candidates and the (then) fifteen Member States was signed in April 2003, and entered into force on 1 May 2004. However, the fifth accession (and the 2007 accession of Romania and Bulgaria) did not come without its caveats. Namely, significant transitional arrangements were included in the Accession Treaty, including post-accession conditionality.

K. Inglis, 'The Union's Fifth Accession Treaty: New Means to Make Enlargement Possible' (2004) 41 *Common Market Law Review* 937–973 at 971–972

The current Accession Treaty distinguishes itself from previous accession treaty practice for a number of reasons. While this is the first enlargement where the in-comers are not acceding to the entirety of the Union's activities, the new Member States are given no option to permanently derogate from the *acquis* nor to opt out from those chapters where certain of the Fifteen have opted out – Schengen and EMU. Also, the trust of the Fifteen Member States in the new Member States' capacity and willingness to meet the obligations of membership has arisen in the current enlargement. Trust arises as an issue because of the lack of proven performance of the ex-communist countries. In the context of an enlarged Union, expectations with respect to the incoming Member States' future behaviour is put under further strain due to the dramatic increase in the number of Member States combined with the deepening and widening of EU integration, and the consequent intensification of monitoring and enforcement efforts to ensure the integrity of the *acquis* in a Union of twenty-five. . . .

Perhaps the single most controversial topic in the months that preceded enlargement was that of the movement of workers. Public fears of mass migration to the Fifteen led most of them to make use of the transitional arrangements for workers in respect of workers from the eight CEEC Member States. . . .

The conditionality that characterized the pre-accession period can also be seen in the Accession Treaty. . . . The very fact that the safeguard clauses have been included in the Accession Treaty rings of doubts as to the readiness of the Ten to accede, as does the introduction of the new Transition and Schengen Facilities to support capacity building and compliance. This question mark is emphasized by the lack of time frames established for entry into Schengen and EMU.

---

4 THE FUTURE OF EU ENLARGEMENT POLICY?

In legal, political and socio-economic terms, the EU during the second decade of the twenty-first century is no longer that to which the CEECs acceded in 2004. European integration as a project has indubitably been affected by the wake of the failed Draft Constitutional Treaty and the sovereign debt crisis, and is facing a new global landscape. In the following two extracts, we illustrate the highly complex interaction between the EU's accession criteria, the aspiration of EU integration, the impact of domestic (Member State and third country) and international politics. The extract from the 2012 Commission Communication setting out an enlargement strategy emphasizes the central calling of European integration as expressed through EU enlargement policy: the European Union as a project of stabilization and peace. However, it does recognize the core challenges facing the EU today: first of all, and this is true for all external policies of the Union, the EU has been significantly weakened by the Eurozone crisis. Second, whereas consensus on enlargement towards the CEECs was perhaps not complete in the 1990s, recognition of the historical significance of European reunification did exist. Such a high level of agreement on EU enlargement, notably on the accession of Turkey, is certainly not there at present. This is then but one expression of what the author of the second extract below calls the 'creeping nationalisation' of EU enlargement policy. EU enlargement is less than before the result of a consensus on the common EU interest and transformative power of accession. It is now more strongly influenced by the domestic political agendas of EU Member States, which affects its efficacy and the EU's credibility writ large.

Commission Communication, *Enlargement Strategy and Main Challenges 2012–2013*, COM(2012) 600 final, Brussels, 10 October 2012, pp. 22–29[52]

1. Through its enlargement policy, the EU has, since its inception, responded to the legitimate aspiration of the peoples of our continent to be *united in a common European endeavour*. From an original six, the EU is due to welcome Croatia as its 28th member on 1 July 2013.

2. At a time when the EU faces major challenges and significant global uncertainty and gains new momentum for economic, financial and political integration, enlargement policy continues to contribute to *peace, security and prosperity* on our continent. The imminent accession of Croatia, the start of accession negotiations with Montenegro and candidate status for Serbia send a strong signal of the *transformative power* of enlargement and what is possible in an area ridden by war just half a generation ago. Enlargement to southeast Europe helps avoid the far higher costs of dealing with the consequences of instability. It is an investment in sustainable democracy and demonstrates the EU's continued capacity as a global actor.

3. The challenges facing the Eurozone together with the recent global financial crisis have highlighted the interdependence of national economies both within and beyond the EU. They underline the importance of further *consolidating economic and financial stability* and fostering reforms and growth, also in the enlargement countries. The enlargement process is a powerful tool to that end. . . .

5. *The credibility* of the enlargement process is crucial to its success. Maintaining the momentum for enlargement as well as for reforms are two sides of the same coin. The renewed consensus on enlargement, agreed by the European Council, remains the basis for the EU's enlargement policy. Enlargement is by definition a gradual process, based on solid and sustainable implementation of reforms by the countries concerned. Enlargement policy has been adjusted based on the lessons learned from successive accessions to ensure the smooth integration of new Member States and to better address the needs of countries in transformation, particularly in the rule of law area. . . .

15. Enlargement policy needs public understanding and support in order to be successful and sustainable. Member States and enlargement countries have the main role in the *information and communication* efforts towards their citizens. It is essential to foster understanding and informed debate on the impact of enlargement policy, particularly at a time when the EU is facing major challenges. The Commission for its part will continue to provide information about the enlargement process, contributing to an informed public debate on enlargement. . . .

24. *Turkey:* Turkey is a key country for the EU, considering its dynamic economy, its strategic location and its important regional role. The Commission underlines the importance of the on-going cooperation and dialogue on foreign policy issues of common interest to the EU and Turkey, such as North Africa, and the Middle East.

   The potential of the EU–Turkey relationship can be fully tapped only within the framework of an active and credible accession process which respects the EU's commitments and the established conditionality. It is in the interest of both the EU and Turkey that accession negotiations regain their

---

[52] Emphasis in original.

momentum, not least to ensure the EU remains the benchmark for reforms in Turkey. The Commission therefore believes it is important that, in line with established procedures and relevant Council conclusions, work resumes on negotiating chapters interrupted over a number of years due to the lack of consensus amongst Member States.

To revive the accession process and bring fresh dynamism to EU–Turkey relations, the Commission will continue to implement the positive agenda in the relations with Turkey launched in May 2012 and which is already delivering its first results.

Turkey's active support to the positive agenda and its European perspective remains essential. Concerns are growing regarding Turkey's lack of substantial progress towards fully meeting the political criteria. The situation regarding the respect for fundamental rights on the ground, including freedom of expression, continues to be a source of serious preoccupation – despite recent legislative improvements. It is important that Turkey addresses all issues regarding the independence, impartiality and efficiency of the judiciary. The Commission welcomes the commitment of the Turkish government to present swiftly the fourth judicial reform package and calls for it to address all the core issues which are presently affecting the exercise of freedom of expression in practice.

Turkey has frozen its relations with the rotating *Presidency* of the Council of the EU during the second half of 2012 [Cyprus]. The Commission reiterates its serious concerns with regard to Turkish statements and threats and calls for full respect of the role of the Presidency of the Council.

The EU has also stressed all the sovereign rights of EU Member States which include entering into bilateral agreements, and exploring and exploiting their natural resources, in accordance with the EU *acquis* and international law, including the UN Convention on the Law of the Sea. In line with the repeated Council and Commission positions from previous years, the Commission reiterates that it is urgent that Turkey fulfils its obligation of fully implementing the Additional Protocol and makes progress towards normalisation of bilateral relations with the Republic of Cyprus. This could provide new momentum to the accession process. In the absence of progress in these areas, the Commission recommends that the EU maintains its measures from 2006. It also urges the avoidance of any kind of threat, source of friction or action that could damage good neighbourly relations and the peaceful settlement of disputes. Turkey is encouraged to increase in concrete terms its commitment and contribution to the talks under the good offices of the UN Secretary General to find a comprehensive settlement to the Cyprus issue.

C. Hillion, *The Creeping Nationalisation of the EU Enlargement Policy* (Stockholm: SIEPS Report 2010/6)

Originally conceived as an intergovernmental procedure to allow third states to become contracting parties to the EU treaties, enlargement has become a policy through which the Union's institutions transform third states into Member States. This EU Member State-building policy has allowed the Union to exercise its normative power, and to organise the continent in its own image.

Hailed as 'the most successful EU foreign policy', enlargement has nonetheless been marked by shortcomings that have weakened the credibility, effectiveness and legitimacy of the policy. Motivated by past experiences of some candidates' lack of preparedness for admission, mounting doubts about the systemic sustainability of further expansion and increased demands for democratic accountability, adjustments have been made in recent years. On the whole, these changes have entailed the strengthening of Member States' control over the conduct of the policy.

Beyond their craving for control, Member States have also been showing less scruple in instrumentalising enlargement for domestic political gains. The EU Member State-building policy is thus increasingly dominated, if not held hostage, by national agendas. The result of this creeping nationalisation has been a process congested with (sometimes unpredictable) legal and political hurdles, raising new questions as to the credibility of the EU commitments towards aspirant states, and consequently the effectiveness of the enlargement policy's acclaimed transformative power. It may also compromise the integrity of the Treaty provisions and conflict with fundamental principles of EU law, not least the very goal of European (re)unification reaffirmed by the Treaty of Lisbon.

The following extract from European Council conclusions starkly illustrates the point made by Hillion. This meeting took place only six months after the fifth enlargement, and in it the HoSG agreed a revised framework for future accession negotiations. With these revisions, the European Council strengthened the role for the Member States – which is not necessarily purely negative. However, it also aimed to soothe worries mainly with regard to the opening of accession talks with Turkey. Thus, long transition periods, derogations and specific arrangements could now be taken, and these could even take on the form of permanent safeguard clauses such as those which would permanently limit free movement of persons with regard to certain countries. These are highly problematic for a legal order such as that of the EU, since it would introduce discrimination on the ground of nationality and touch upon the core that is the EU.[53]

European Council Conclusions, Brussels, 16–17 December 2004

The European Council agreed that accession negotiations with individual candidate States will be based on a framework for negotiations. Each framework, which will be established by the Council on a proposal by the Commission, taking account of the experience of the fifth enlargement process and of the evolving acquis, will address the following elements according to their own merits and the specific situations and characteristics of each candidate State:

- As in previous negotiations, the substance of the negotiations, which will be conducted in an Intergovernmental Conference with the participation of all Member States on the one hand and the candidate State concerned on the other, where decisions require unanimity, will be broken down into a number of chapters, each covering a specific policy area. The Council, acting by unanimity on a proposal by the Commission, will lay down benchmarks for the provisional closure and, where appropriate, for the opening of each chapter; depending on the chapter concerned, these benchmarks will refer to legislative alignment and a satisfactory track record of implementation of the acquis as well as obligations deriving from contractual relations with the European Union.

- Long transitional periods, derogations, specific arrangements or permanent safeguard clauses, i.e. clauses which are permanently available as a basis for safeguard measures, may be considered. The Commission will include these, as appropriate, in its proposals for each framework, for areas such as freedom of movement of persons, structural policies or agriculture. Furthermore, the decision-taking process regarding the eventual establishment of freedom of movement of persons should allow for a maximum role of

---

[53] Hillion, 'The European Union Is Dead. Long Live the European Union . . . A Commentary on the Accession Treaty 2003' (2004) 29 *European Law Review* 583–612 at 593.

individual Member States. Transitional arrangements or safeguards should be reviewed regarding their impact on competition or the functioning of the internal market. . . .

- The shared objective of the negotiations is accession. These negotiations are an open-ended process, the outcome of which cannot be guaranteed beforehand. While taking account of all Copenhagen criteria, if the candidate State is not in a position to assume in full all the obligations of membership it must be ensured that the candidate State concerned is fully anchored in the European structures through the strongest possible bond.
- In the case of a serious and persistent breach in a candidate State of the principles of liberty, democracy, respect for human rights and fundamental freedoms and the rule of law on which the Union is founded, the Commission will, on its own initiative or on the request of one third of the Member States, recommend the suspension of negotiations and propose the conditions for eventual resumption. The Council will decide by qualified majority on such a recommendation, after having heard the candidate State, whether to suspend the negotiations and on the conditions for their resumption. The Member States will act in the IGC in accordance with the Council decision, without prejudice to the general requirement for unanimity in the IGC. The European Parliament will be informed.
- Parallel to accession negotiations, the Union will engage with every candidate State in an intensive political and cultural dialogue. With the aim of enhancing mutual understanding by bringing people together, this inclusive dialogue also will involve civil society.

5 THE EUROPEAN NEIGHBOURHOOD POLICY

(i) The ENP legal basis: EU competence or objective?

Those countries which are not eligible for accession to the EU, or which are at present not viewed as potential candidates by the Union, may develop their cooperation with the EU through the so-called ENP. With the Treaty of Lisbon, the ENP has received an explicit legal grounding in EU primary law. The origin and location of this article in the common provisions of the TEU lies in the original structure of the failed Draft Treaty establishing a Constitution. The reason for the existence of Article 8 TEU is that the European Convention viewed it as important to embed the EU's special relations constitutionally with the neighbourhood. In this way, the Treaty would constitutionalize the special relationship with the neighbourhood that was considered politically expedient so as to not create new dividing lines between those nations that were part of the fifth enlargement in 2004, and those that were not.[54]

Article 8 TEU

1. The Union shall develop a special relationship with neighbouring countries, aiming to establish an area of prosperity and good neighbourliness, founded on the values of the Union and characterised by close and peaceful relations based on cooperation.

---

[54] European Convention, *Title IX: The Union and its immediate environment*, Brussels, 2 April 2003, CONV 649/03.

2. For the purposes of paragraph 1, the Union may conclude specific agreements with the countries concerned. These agreements may contain reciprocal rights and obligations as well as the possibility of undertaking activities jointly. Their implementation shall be the subject of periodic consultation.

The text of paragraph 1 was described by the Treaty drafters as 'a loose but coherent framework for relations with its neighbours', 'setting out the intention' to establish a neighbourhood policy.[55] The first paragraph of Article 8 could thus be associated with Article 21 TEU in that it sets out an objective for the Union, specific to its neighbourhood. Importantly however, the provision is strongly worded. First of all, the Union 'shall' develop special relations with the neighbours, meaning that the EU cannot therefore choose not to have a neighbourhood policy. Second, the policy creates an 'area' of prosperity, pointing to a multilateral dimension to the ENP.[56] Third, the relationship must be based on the values of the Union, thereby referring back to Article 3(5) TEU and injecting the latter provision into the relationship with the neighbours.

The second paragraph of this provision pertains to the instrument through which to attain the objective set out in relation to the neighbourhood: 'specific' agreements with the neighbours. The Treaty drafters recognized that the point of departure is the existing provision on AAs, and explicitly repeats the language of Article 217 on association by referring to reciprocal rights and obligations. The question is thus whether Article 8(2) TEU can be considered a legal basis for a distinct type of EU international agreements, subject to specific political and geographic criteria which are distinct from AAs concluded on the basis of Article 217 TFEU. Overall, this treaty provision should be viewed in a similar vein to Articles 3(5) and 21 TEU: stating an objective, but not providing a substantive legal basis. Article 8 TEU indicates the key features and objectives of EU engagement with its neighbours, but does not confer new or distinct powers upon the Union. This is supported by the fact that the Commission proposal for the ENP funding Regulation from 2014 onwards views Article 8 TEU as 'providing the general thrust and basis for the ENP', but that the actual legal basis for the financing instrument would be Articles 209(1) and 212(2) TFEU.[57] Similarly, the draft agreement between the EU, its Member States and Ukraine which would replace the PCA with that country is the first which would be concluded upon entry into force of Article 8 TEU. It is entitled 'Association Agreement', thus implying Article 217 TEU as the most likely legal basis (see Chapter 2).

P. Van Elsuwege and R. Petrov, 'Article 8 TEU: Towards a New Generation of Agreements with the Neighbouring Countries of the European Union?' (2011) 36 *European Law Review* 688–703

The introduction of a special Treaty provision for the development of the European Union's relations with its neighbouring countries . . . serves a number of political objectives. First, article 8 TEU underlines

---

[55] *Ibid.*, p. 2.

[56] S. Blockmans and B. Van Vooren, 'Revitalizing the European Neighbourhood Economic Community: The Case for Legally Binding Sectoral Multilateralism' (2012) 17 *European Foreign Affairs Review* 577–604.

[57] European Commission, *Proposal for a Regulation of the European Parliament and of the Council establishing a European Neighbourhood Instrument*, Brussels, 7 December 2011, COM(2011) 839 final, p. 7.

that the Union is interested in privileged relations with its neighbouring countries and lays down the constitutional foundations for the development of the ENP. Secondly, this article clarifies that the European Union's neighbourhood relations are based upon a policy of conditionality and respect for the European Union's values and norms. Thirdly, article 8(2) TEU provides an opportunity to conclude a new generation of agreements with the neighbouring countries of the Union. In contrast to article 217 TFEU, which remains silent on the concrete content and objectives of the established privileged relationship, agreements under article 8(2) TEU aim to establish "an area of prosperity and good neighbourliness".

… the added value of having a specific legal basis for the development of a "special relationship with neighbouring countries" is not very clear because this type of privileged relations can perfectly be established under article 217 TFEU. Moreover, the codification of the European Union's conditionality approach in its neighbourhood relations does not make a difference either, mainly because article 3(5) TEU already lays down that the Union shall uphold and promote its values and interests in its relations with the wider world. Hence article 8 TEU is essentially a political provision the significance of which for the practical development of the European Union's neighbourhood relations is questionable.

(ii) Predecessors to the ENP

The ENP did not mushroom out of nowhere, and the EEC has indeed previously pursued policies tailored specifically to the neighbours. To the south there was the 'Global Mediterranean Policy'[58] launched at the 1972 Paris Summit. This policy was deployed against a tumultuous political background in the Middle East and the energy crisis in Europe. There is a significant parallel between this policy and today's ENP as regards the relationship with EU enlargement. This is because 'the fall of the dictatorships in Portugal and Greece and the death of Franco opened up the prospect of a further enlargement of the Community towards the south and therefore turned the EEC's Mediterranean policy into a policy addressed mainly to the Arab countries of the area'.[59] During the same time period, relations with the Soviet Union were dominated by the Cold War, but with the Eastern European countries, the Community had proposed individual trade agreements with all 'state trading' countries in 1974. Although this was not put into practice initially, this did not mean that no trade relations existed between EEC Member States and the CEECs. In the years that followed specific agreements were concluded on textiles with Bulgaria, Czechoslovakia, Hungary, Poland and Romania, as well as voluntary restraint arrangements on steel products and a few trade agreements on industrial and agricultural products. For the conclusion of a broader trade agreement, COMECON insisted on an agreement between itself and the EEC, which the latter rejected for lack of competence in CCP on the part of COMECON. Thus, at the regional level no relations existed until their 'normalization' through the Joint Declaration of 1988.[60]

---

[58] European Commission, *Relations between the Community and the Countries of the Mediterranean Basin*, SEC(72) 3111 final, Brussels, September 1972.

[59] L. Tsoukalis, 'The EEC and the Mediterranean: Is 'Global' Policy a Misnomer?' (1977) 53 *International Affairs* 422–438 at 422.

[60] Memorandum, *Signing of the EC/Comecon Joint Declaration*, MEMO/88/97, 24 June 1988.

During the 1990s two separate policy processes continued towards the east and south. Above, we have seen that during the dissolution of the Soviet Union a process unfolded whereby relations with the CEECs were conducted through the conclusion of EAs which were soon upgraded to pre-accession agreements from the 1993 Copenhagen European Council onwards. In parallel, during the 1990s the NIS were offered PCAs, a weaker relationship than the association established with the EAs.

To the south, the EU engaged the Mediterranean basin through the 'Euro–Mediterranean Partnership' (EMP or Euromed). This initiative was launched in 1995, and was the result of significant efforts on the part of the southern Member States (notably Spain) who viewed the priority accorded by the EC to Eastern Europe as problematic for their national interests.[61] The November 1995 Barcelona Ministerial Meeting which launched what became known as the Barcelona Process was a high-profile event. It was considered a significant diplomatic victory for the Union post-Maastricht because it managed to bring together the then President of the Palestinian Authority and the Israeli Minister for Foreign Affairs. In the Barcelona Declaration proclaimed at that meeting, the participants agreed to establish a common area of peace and stability in accordance with the UN Charter,[62] to establish an economic 'area of shared prosperity', and to promote cultural exchanges and understanding between their societies. The area of shared prosperity concretely entailed an ambitious EU–Mediterranean free trade area, which would be gradually established by 2010 through the adoption of FTAs between the EU and third countries, and between the partner countries themselves. While the 'South–South' free trade area was not achieved by the planned deadline, a key achievement of the Barcelona Process has been the conclusion of AAs with all partners involved except Syria:[63] Palestinian Authority,[64] Tunisia,[65] Morocco,[66] Israel,[67] Egypt,[68] Algeria[69] and Lebanon[70].

European Commission, *The Barcelona Process, five years on: 1995–2000* (introduction by former RELEX Commissioner C. Patten)

The Euro-Mediterranean Partnership has led to remarkable achievements. It has brought together all the countries of the region at ministerial level, even in very difficult political circumstances; substantial progress in the negotiation and signature of association agreements has been achieved; and significant funding has been mobilised for the region under the MEDA programme.

However, despite these achievements, it would be pointless to deny that problems exist. The Middle East peace process has run into difficulties and affected the general Barcelona process; progress with the association agreements has been slower than expected; trade among the partners themselves is very low;

---

[61] E. Philippart and G. Edwards, 'The Euro–Mediterranean Partnership: Fragmentation and Reconstruction' (1997) 2 *European Foreign Affairs Review* 465–489 at 469.

[62] Barcelona Declaration, adopted at the Euro–Mediterranean Conference, 27–28 November 1995.

[63] AAs were already in place with Cyprus, Malta and Turkey.

[64] Specifically, it concerned an 'interim association agreement between EU and the PLO on behalf of the Palestinian Authority', entry into force on 1 July 1997, OJ 1997 No. L187/3.

[65] EU–Tunisia Association Agreement, entry into force on 1 March 1998, OJ 1998 No. L97/2, OJ 2005 No. L278/9.

[66] EU–Morocco Association Agreement, entry into force on 1 March 2000, OJ 2000 No. L70/2.

[67] EU–Israel Association Agreement, entry into force on 1 June 2000, OJ 2000 No. L147/1.

[68] EU–Egypt Association Agreement, entry into force on 1 June 2004, OJ 2004 No. L304/39.

[69] EU–Algeria Association Agreement, entry into force on 1 September 2005, OJ 2005 No. L265/1.

[70] EU–Lebanon Association Agreement, entry into force on 1 June 2006, OJ 2006 No. L143/2.

disagreements between us persist on some sensitive trade issues like agriculture; . . . finally there is the need to raise awareness among the general public of the Barcelona process and to improve the sense of ownership of the southern partners of the process.

History repeats itself, as do EU policy approaches. The emergence of a 'European Neighbourhood Policy' in 2002–2003 is intimately linked to the fifth enlargement of May 2004. The famous Agenda 2000 Communication published in 1997 pointed to the fact that accession of ten countries would significantly redraw the borders of the EU (see above). At a highly general level, and without making concrete proposals, it signalled that stability through cooperation with this region would be important for the enlarged EU. At that point in time, the Commission only mentions an 'Eastern dimension' to its proposal and contains little if any substance on what a 'wider Europe' policy should look like.

European Commission, *Agenda 2000 – Volume I: For a Stronger and Wider Europe,* COM(97) 2000, 15 July 1997

An enlarged Union will have more direct frontiers with Russia as well as frontiers with Ukraine, Belarus and Moldova. It will enjoy direct access to the Black Sea which will lead to intensified contacts with the countries of the Caucasus and Central Asia. An enlarged Union will also surround the Kaliningrad oblast, which is part of Russia, and will contain several hundred thousand ethnic Russians, living mainly in Estonia and Latvia. It will be important for the enlarged Union to deepen its relationship with Russia, Ukraine and the other NIS on the basis of the Partnership and Cooperation Agreements (PCAs). Among the Union's new neighbouring countries will be those of the Balkan region. Stability through cooperation in this region will be all the more important for the enlarged Union.

Following the remarks made in Agenda 2000, it took the Union almost five years to inject life into the policy process that would lead to the ENP. At the request of the GAER Council in April 2002, former HR Javier Solana and former Commissioner for External Relations Chris Patten drafted a 'Joint Letter' addressed to the Council of Ministers. In this somewhat peculiar policy instrument, they formulated ideas on the EU's relations with its neighbours under the heading 'Wider Europe'.[71] This Joint Letter provides an excellent basis from which to examine the key design features of the ENP, and the key challenges the EU has to consider in its southern and eastern relations up to the present day.

6 KEY FEATURES OF THE ENP

The 2002 Solana–Patten Joint Letter sketched four key issues the Union would have to consider in designing the ENP, and outlined tentative answers:

- The geographic scope of policy: which neighbours to include and not to include?
- What the EU would hope to achieve with the new initiative: what are its interests, values and objectives?

[71] Javier Solana and Chris Patten, *Joint Letter, Wider Europe*, 7 August 2002, on file with authors.

- How to ensure there is no ambiguity on the (absence of) link with further enlargement?
- What would be the method and instruments through which to carry out the policy: full application of conditionality?

J. Solana and C. Patten, *Joint Letter, Wider Europe*, 7 August 2002[72]

1. What should be the geographical coverage of this exercise? The enlarged Union's neighbours fall into three main regional groupings: the Mediterranean (Barcelona Process); the Western Balkans (Stabilisation and Association Process); and Russia and the other eastern neighbours (Partnership and Co-operation Agreements). . . . The imminent enlargement presents an opportunity to develop a more coherent and durable basis for relations with our immediate neighbours. The pace and scope of this process will have to be flexible – there can be no one-size-fits-all approach. . . . Looking to the medium and longer term, we could foresee a gradually evolving framework surrounding the Union, which would nevertheless stop short of full membership or creating shared institutions.

2. How do we want to develop our relations with present and future neighbours? The three main geographical groupings above can be distinguished by what we say about their prospect of accession to the EU. For the Balkans it is an explicit goal, . . . in the Mediterranean (apart from current candidates) membership is explicitly excluded, . . . [while] our future eastern neighbours fall somewhat uncomfortably in between. Making their situation less ambivalent . . . particularly for Ukraine which is most actively seeking more concrete recognition of her European aspirations is probably the most immediate challenge for our neighbourhood policy. This requires the delineation of an ambitious but workable policy framework for the next ten years or so, without closing any options for the more distant future.

3. What are our interests and what do we want to achieve? There are a number of overriding objectives for our neighbourhood policy: Stability, prosperity, shared values and rule of law . . . failure in any of these will lead to increased risks of negative spill-over on the Union. . . .

5. Do we need to create new contractual arrangements such as Neighbourhood or Proximity Agreements? There is already scope to upgrade relations within the existing agreements with the countries concerned and we must guard against cosmetic changes . . . becoming a substitute for substantive measures. The debate needs careful handling to avoid unrealistic expectations over the prospects of future enlargement. On the other hand, if we decide to set out specific and qualitatively enhanced objectives for our policy, this could justify a relabeling of our relations. Moreover, the strong symbolism of a new label that marks a strengthened commitment of the Union could help to raise the profile of relations with the EU and thus unlock additional political will and administrative capacity.

On the basis of the Joint Letter, we can examine the key choices which were subsequently made in designing the ENP.

- Geographic comprehensiveness: eastern and southern countries drawn together in one single policy.
- The final objective of security, stability and prosperity through conditionally offering a stake in the internal market, disconnected from potential EU enlargement.
- Drawing together the whole range of EU policies under the single EU umbrella, through a methodology highly reminiscent of EU pre-accession approaches.

---

[72] Emphasis in original.

(i) Geographic scope: confluence of geopolitics and Member State interests

The Solana–Patten Joint Letter questioned the scope of the ENP: east, or south, or both at the same time? Article 8 TEU simply speaks of 'neighbours', thus implying that special relations ought to be developed with all countries in the EU's neighbourhood (see however below on the EEA/EFTA and SAP countries). There has never been a single, principled decision on the geographic scope of the ENP. Instead, individual Member State foreign policy priorities, as well as third-country demands and external geopolitical events, have progressively shaped the geographic outlook of this policy. Anno 2014, the ENP is de facto split into a southern and eastern dimension. However, the term 'ENP' remains in existence as a political umbrella: it encompasses all initiatives which share the neighbourhood as their geographic focus, and which have certain methodological and financial approaches in common.

State of play ENP 2014	South	East
Regional/multilateral dimension	Union for the Mediterranean	Eastern Partnership
Bilateral dimension	Maghreb and Mashreq countries	Ukraine and Moldova, Southern Caucasus

In line with Agenda 2000 and the later Solana–Patten Joint Letter, the 'New Neighbours Initiative' discussed in the Council in October 2002 focused on the eastern neighbours only, and was bilateral in nature: an upgrade in relations with Ukraine, Moldova and Belarus, as well as Russia.[73] However, in 2003 the Russian Federation refused to be treated on an equal basis with the other three countries, so that the Union instead decided to create a bilateral 'Strategic Partnership' with that country. Subsequently, under pressure from Member States such as France and Spain who did not want to see the southern nations receive less attention in EU external policy, similar to the emergence of the Barcelona Process in 1995, the Mediterranean rim was also included in the ENP.[74] As the 'Rose Revolution' unfolded in Georgia in 2003, by 2005 the ENP also came to encompass the Southern Caucasus: the EU wished to reward that country for its turn to democracy, but to include Georgia is to include Azerbaijan, and to include the latter is to include Armenia. Thus the policy came to include Armenia, Azerbaijan, Egypt, Georgia, Israel, Jordan, Lebanon, Moldova, Morocco, Occupied Palestinian Territory, Tunisia and Ukraine. Four other neighbouring countries were not actively involved because political reasons stood in the way of developing 'standard' ENP relations: Algeria did not have an AA in force with the EU, and Belarus, Libya and Syria were not included predominantly for absence of compliance with EU values on rule of law and democracy (as later codified in Article 8 TEU).

The single geographic scope was rather artificial, which was all the more clear when the French EU Presidency in 2008 strongly pushed for the launch of a 'Union for the Mediterranean' (UMED). Former President Sarkozy saw it as a distinct regional component separate from the ENP, but other Member States and the Commission strongly objected to France moving ahead with this proposal.[75] Thus, as a compromise this southern dimension was 'latched on' to the ENP

---

[73] Conclusions of the GAER Council, *New Neighbours Initiative*, 30 September 2002.

[74] Conclusions of the GAER Council, *European Neighbourhood Policy*, 14 June 2004.

[75] *Déclaration commune du sommet de Paris pour la Méditerranée*, Paris, 13 July 2008. Available from: www.eeas.europa.eu/euromed/index_en.htm (last accessed 30 November 2012).

as a regional dimension to the ENP, named 'Barcelona Process – Union for the Mediterranean'. However, because of lack of enthusiasm in the institutions and Member States, and due to events in the Middle East in early 2009, the UMED broadly failed to deliver. Subsequently, the idea of carving out a more clear eastern dimension to the ENP was floated in a Polish–Swedish non-paper of May 2008, partially in response to the French UMED proposal.[76] This 'Eastern Partnership' (EaP) was also regional in focus, and wished to reinvigorate the ENP through a number of flagship projects. Like the UMED, the EaP is a remarkable example of Member States' national interests and priorities continuously shaping 'EU' external relations with its neighbours. The Polish Foreign Ministry has been most vocal about its role in pushing the EaP onto the Union agenda: 'The Eastern Partnership is the first Polish initiative incorporated into the system of the European Union's external relations. ... The Eastern Partnership is designed to facilitate the achievement of one of the key goals of Polish foreign policy, the approximation and integration of East European countries with the European Union.'[77]

The European Council of 19–20 June 2008 had already invited the Commission to prepare a proposal on the Eastern Partnership, but the Extraordinary European Council of 1 September 2008 asked for this work to be accelerated, according to the Commission 'responding to the need for a clearer signal of EU commitment following the conflict in Georgia and its broader repercussions'.[78] The growing confidence of the Russian Federation to project its weight in the neighbourhood, through military force if need be, thus resulted in strong high-level political support for the EU upgrade relations with the eastern neighbours. Also during 2009, relations between the EU, Libya and Belarus began to improve. The Commission proposed to conclude an FTA with Libya, and Belarus was included in the Eastern Partnership launched in May 2009. The violent post-election crackdown in Belarus in 2010, and the conflict in Libya with NATO intervention during 2011, soon reversed that evolution. A review for the ENP was already scheduled for the early months of 2011, but the Arab Spring caught the Union by surprise and led to another round of purportedly strengthening the ENP in May 2011, this time to the south.

(ii) Objectives: a stable and prosperous neighbourhood for a secure union

The Council of Ministers has described the objectives of the neighbourhood policy as sharing 'the benefits of an enlarged EU with neighbouring countries in order to contribute to increased stability, security and prosperity of the European Union and its neighbours'.[79] This mirrored the Commission's formulation which was 'to avoid drawing new dividing lines in Europe and to promote stability and prosperity within and beyond the new borders of the Union'.[80] These formulations indicated the logic on which the ENP was constructed. In essence, the ENP was to be considered a security policy because following the 2004 enlargement, the EU would have very different countries and challenges right outside its borders. Thus, with this policy the EU wished

---

[76] Swedish–Polish Non-Paper, Eastern partnership, on file with authors.

[77] Ministry of Foreign Affairs of the Republic of Poland, *Eastern Partnership*, on file with authors.

[78] Communication from the Commission to the European Parliament and the Council, *Eastern Partnership*, COM(2008) 823/4, Brussels, 8 December 2008, p. 2.

[79] Conclusion of the GAER Council, 14 June 2004, pp. 11–14.

[80] Communication from the Commission, *Wider Europe – Neighbourhood: A New Framework for Relations with our Eastern and Southern Neighbours*, Brussels, 11 March 2003, COM(2003) 104 final, p. 4 (hereafter: Wider Europe Communication).

to create stable and prosperous neighbours so as to ensure its own security upon enlargement. The December 2003 ESS was drafted and published in parallel to the process of devising the ENP in preparation for the fifth enlargement, and unequivocally confirmed the security underpinning of the ENP.

European Security Strategy, *A Secure Europe in a Better World*, December 2003

Even in an era of globalisation, geography is still important. It is in the European interest that countries on our borders are well-governed. Neighbours who are engaged in violent conflict, weak states where organised crime flourishes, dysfunctional societies or exploding population growth on its borders all pose problems for Europe.

The integration of acceding states increases our security but also brings the EU closer to troubled areas. Our task is to promote a ring of well governed countries to the East of the European Union and on the borders of the Mediterranean with whom we can enjoy close and cooperative relations.

It is not in our interest that enlargement should create new dividing lines in Europe. We need to extend the benefits of economic and political cooperation to our neighbours in the East while tackling political problems there. . . .

The Mediterranean area generally continues to undergo serious problems of economic stagnation, social unrest and unresolved conflicts. The European Union's interests require a continued engagement with Mediterranean partners, through more effective economic, security and cultural cooperation in the framework of the Barcelona Process.

The fact that the ENP is a security policy should not be understood as meaning that this policy falls squarely within the remit of the Union's CFSP competence. Rather, the ENP and the ESS reflect a broad consensus that security in the twenty-first century is 'comprehensive', and must bring together all the instruments, capabilities and policies of the EU and its Member States.[81] This means that the ENP is very much an 'umbrella policy' which aims to coalesce all aspects of EU external relations in a coherent whole: CFSP, but also trade, migration, environment, energy and so on, encompassing both EU and Member State external policies. This explains why Article 8 TEU was not inserted by the Lisbon Treaty as a distinct legal basis in Part V TFEU. Rather than a specific policy competence, the ENP is more a specific policy method, with a distinct rationale and set of instruments and objectives tailored towards the neighbourhood; drawing on policy-specific competences of the EU *and* Member States. Thus, because of the geographic proximity, all policies of the EU and its Member States 'shall' be placed on a privileged footing in line with Article 8 TEU.

M. Cremona and C. Hillion, *L'Union fait la force? Potential and Limitations of the European Neighbourhood Policy as an Integrated EU Foreign and Security Policy* (EUI Law Working Paper 2006/49), p. 5

. . . the idea of security as underpinning EU policy towards the region more generally . . . is linked to the terrorist attacks on the US on 11 September 2001, leading to a greater concern with terrorism and its links

---

[81] ESS, pp. 11–12.

to organised crime and the regulation of cross-border movement. It is also related to the impact of EU enlargement, the moving eastwards of the EU's borders, which runs parallel to the efforts to remove internal border controls within the EU, thus placing increased emphasis on the security of external borders. Indeed, enlargement entails the creation of new 'dividing lines' within Europe, and the ensuing risk of economic and political instability at the EU's doorstep. Further, for the eastern dimension of the ENP, the concern for security may be traced to the size, strategic importance and economic potential of Ukraine, and its potential as a regional leader. . . .

[S]ecurity is taken to imply security within the neighbouring States, security within the region, security at the external borders of the EU, and security within the EU itself, each of these impacting on the others. Also, and as [former] High Representative Javier Solana has argued, security extends beyond the purely military to include broader political, economic, social and even environmental aspects: 'It is a long time since security was thought of only in terms of military force. We all know that security is far broader today, that it includes economic, environmental, and social issues. Indeed, non-military threats to security loom much larger in the mind of most people . . . These non-military security threats are not adequately dealt with by any of our international institutions. . . . This is where the European Union must take up the challenge.' . . .

No longer is security just one aspect of the Common Foreign and Security Policy. Rather, it has become a cross-pillar policy in its own right, creating a potentially more coherent EU external action which integrates the three poles of decision-making: the Member States, the Community pillar and the EU pillars.

As can be seen from the ESS, there was a good level of consensus on what a secure neighbourhood meant for the Union. However, the notion of 'well-governed' countries from the ESS, and thus the meaning of 'stability' and 'prosperity' in the ENP mantra, have been far more contentious. What does the EU offer to its neighbouring partner countries in order to reform in line with EU requirements? Who defines stability and prosperity: the EU and/or the third country? Finally, if these nations share the EU's values and are well-governed and prosperous, how is the ENP any different from (pre-)accession policy? The first strategy paper published on the ENP was the Wider Europe Communication of March 2003 and aimed to give some content to these questions and the notions of stability and prosperity.

Commission Communication, *Wider Europe – Neighbourhood: A New Framework for Relations with our Eastern and Southern Neighbours*, Brussels, 11 March 2003, COM(2003) 104 final

On 1 May 2004, the European Union will enter a new and historic phase. An enlarged Union of 25 countries, with a combined population of more than 450 million and GDP of almost €10000 billion, will fundamentally increase the political, geographic and economic weight of the EU on the European continent. . . . Beyond the EU's borders, enlargement will change the shape of the EU's political and economic relations with other parts of the world. . . .

For the EU's part, the whole range of the Union's policies (foreign, security, trade, development, environment and others) will need to rise to meet this challenge. . . . The December 2002 Copenhagen European Council confirmed that the Union should take the opportunity offered by enlargement to enhance relations with its neighbours on the basis of shared values. It repeated the Union's determination to avoid drawing new dividing lines in Europe and to promote stability and prosperity within and beyond the new borders of the Union. It reaffirmed that enlargement will serve to strengthen relations with Russia, and called for enhanced relations with Ukraine, Moldova, Belarus and the Southern Mediterranean countries to be based on a long term approach. . . .

This Communication considers how to strengthen the framework for the Union's relations with those neighbouring countries that do not currently have the perspective of membership of the EU. . . . The Communication argues that enhanced interdependence – both political and economic – can itself be a means to promote stability, security and sustainable development both within and without the EU. The communication proposes that the EU should aim to develop a zone of prosperity and a friendly neighbourhood – a 'ring of friends' – with whom the EU enjoys close, peaceful and co-operative relations.

In return for concrete progress demonstrating shared values and effective implementation of political, economic and institutional reforms, including in aligning legislation with the acquis, the EU's neighbourhood should benefit from the prospect of closer economic integration with the EU. To this end, Russia, the countries of the Western NIS and the Southern Mediterranean should be offered the prospect of a stake in the EU's Internal Market and further integration and liberalisation to promote the free movement of – persons, goods, services and capital (four freedoms). . . .

A new EU approach cannot be a one-size-fits-all policy. Different stages of reform and economic development also means that different rates of progress can be expected from the neighbouring countries over the coming decade. On the other hand, it is increasingly clear that the EU shares an important set of mutual interests with each of its neighbours.

The Wider Europe Communication outlines a logic whereby the promise of EU accession is not deemed necessary by the Union to generate the desired reforms in the EU's neighbourhood. Instead, enhanced political and economic interdependence is asserted to function simultaneously as the means and end of the policy. Stability then refers to democratization, political reform and good governance; and it is no coincidence that this mirrors the first Copenhagen criterion. 'This implies that stability is a pre-condition for democracy, but there is also a sense in which both internal and regional stability and security are seen as the fruit of political modernization and democratization.'[82] Prosperity is then connected with economic reforms reminiscent of the second Copenhagen criterion: a functioning market economy as a path to economic integration. Together, political and economic reform are encapsulated in the promise of a 'stake in the internal market', and progressive reforms towards extending the four freedoms to the neighbourhood would attain stability, prosperity and security in a mutually beneficial arrangement for the EU and neighbouring countries. There is then an inherent tension which remains in the ENP to this day. Certain countries such as Ukraine still aspire to become EU Member States, but this policy is clearly an alternative possibility which does not exclude or make any promise of the possibility of some day becoming EU Member States.[83] It does not help that much of the methodology and language is de facto borrowed from the EU's pre-accession policy.

---

[82] Cremona, 'The European Neighbourhood Policy: More than a Partnership?', in Cremona (ed.) *Developments in EU External Relations Law* (Oxford: Oxford University Press, 2008), p. 258.

[83] Romano Prodi, *A Wider Europe – A Proximity Policy as the Key to Stability*, Sixth ECSA World Conference Brussels, 5–6 December 2002, Speech/02/619 (2002).

> **G. Meloni, 'Is the Same Toolkit Used During Enlargement Still Applicable to the Countries of the New Neighbourhood? A Problem of Mismatching between Objectives and Instruments',** in M. Cremona and G. Meloni, *The European Neighbourhood Policy: A Framework for Modernisation?* (EUI Law Working Paper 2007/21), p. 96
>
> The whole system of the ENP hinges on the provision of an economic incentive – a "stake into the internal market" – which is supposed not only to increase the prosperity of partner countries, but also to give them a proper motivation to engage in an expensive process of legislative approximation. However, yet not enough efforts have been dedicated to the definition of what a "stake into the internal market" might mean. The [ENP Action Plans] are designed so as to provide a series of rewards to neighbours essentially in terms of a preferential access to the single market. However, the offer from an economic point of view does not go further than an FTA+ (Free Trade Area plus) or, as it has been in the Communication of December 2006 on "Strengthening the ENP", a "deep and comprehensive Free Trade Area". . . . In a nutshell, the economic incentive thus far offered by the Union is not enough in order to justify *per se* the engagement in a far-reaching process of legislative approximation.

(iii) Methodology: inspiration from enlargement

The objectives of stability and prosperity are clearly inspired by EU pre-accession policy, but the parallel of the ENP with enlargement does not stop there. The incentives and objectives of the ENP have been defined as being separate from enlargement. While enlargement is clearly stated not to be the final objective, ENP and enlargement do share the same formulation of objectives (except the very final one – e.g. 'everything but institutions'),[84] but also share methodologies and instruments to bring the objectives to fruition. When examining the fifth enlargement in this chapter, we have seen that pre-accession was based on a number of central methodological considerations implemented through two main instruments. First, (enhanced) pre-accession was conducted on a tailor-made basis specific to the needs of each country. Second, the EU applied conditionality, implying that rewards would be given or withheld depending on whether certain benchmarks were reached or conditions fulfilled. Third, these policies were pursued on the basis of bilateral AAs which were transformed into pre-accession instruments, notably in terms of utilizing the institutions they set up. Fourth and finally, alongside these bilateral agreements, the enlargement policy used a large array of soft legal documents: notably, accession partnerships agreed with each country alongside the bilateral agreement, and yearly progress reports to assess the work of the past year in implementing reforms towards the accession goal. In a similar vein, it is a precondition for a third country to be included in the ENP that the EU and the third country have a contractual agreement which is in force: an AA or a PCA. As with pre-accession policy, the ENP then utilizes this legal instrument to deepen the relationship progressively through a structured process of conditionality and bilaterally agreed non-binding documents alongside the legally binding agreement.

[84] *Ibid.*

Wider Europe Communication, March 2003, pp. 17–18

I. Dialogue in the existing frameworks (Association and Partnership and Cooperation Agreements) jointly analysing the achievements and failures of reform hitherto. The Association and Cooperation Committees should be mandated to prepare this work.

II. A document would then be drawn up by the Commission and the Member States, to be agreed in association with each country, setting out common objectives and benchmarks and a timetable for their achievement. This action plan should be given a political endorsement by the EU and the partner(s) involved, if appropriate at the level of the Association and Cooperation Councils.

III. An annual review of progress in implementing the Action Plan, integrated into the existing institutional cooperation framework with the partner countries, would be a concrete demonstration of enhanced EU political interest and provide governments with the opportunity to receive credit from the EU for their political and economic reform efforts.

This parallel in methodologies makes the separation between ENP and enlargement even more ambiguous: pre-accession policies essentially export EU *acquis* to the third country, and build government institutions so that the third country can cope with the obligations of membership. Similarly, the ENP creates closer economic integration by doing exactly that: exporting the *acquis* and stimulating political, institutional and economic reforms in the partner country. That is then also one of the core tensions of the neighbourhood policy: deep similarity with the methods and instruments of accession, with similar convergence objectives, yet with significant ambiguity on the membership prize as incentive for cooperation and reform.

7 INSTRUMENTS: HYBRID LEGAL NATURE OF THE ENP

(i) Soft law in the ENP

In the preceding sections we have already pointed to several legal peculiarities of the ENP. First, it does not have a legal basis in the Treaties comparable to the CCP, development policy or energy policy; but rather Article 8 TEU is a statement of intent on special relations implemented through all other EU external policies. Second, the significant milestone in the policy process that led to the ENP was a so-called Joint Letter to the Council of Ministers by the former HR for CFSP and the former Commissioner for external relations (in their pre-Lisbon form) (see Chapter 2).

B. Van Vooren, *EU External Relations Law and the European Neighbourhood Policy: A Paradigm for Coherence* (Abingdon/New York: Routledge, 2012), p. 178

The ENP was constructed in a focused effort to provide synergies between different policies towards the Southern and Eastern neighbourhood, and sought to upgrade Union action across the board in light of the security, stability and prosperity objectives. In constructing the ENP towards these ends, we can observe a skeleton of hard legal instruments co-existing with a plethora of soft (legal) instruments which are not specifically connected to competences or policy areas. . . . the true innovation of the ENP's policy framework [is] its legal and political construction in comparison to other policies such as trade or development [i.e.,] its use of 'soft law' to attain a coherent external policy for the European Union as a whole.

During the fifth enlargement, accession partnerships were used to complete the reorientation of the EAs to pre-accession instruments. These accession partnerships were concluded as 'policy documents' complementary to the legally binding AAs between the EU and the CEECs. The ENP further builds on enlargement by emulating this methodology: the AAs with the Mediterranean countries and the PCAs with the NIS are reorientated towards objectives of the ENP through negotiation of an 'ENP Action Plan' complementary to those bilateral agreements. But the ENP goes further than that: because the policy does not have a distinct legal basis, the policy is effectively constructed – within the EU legal order and outside it – through a large amount of policy documents together constituting the policy as required by Article 8 TEU. The ENP Action Plans are an example of external soft law, whereas the Solana–Patten Joint Letter, as well as the Wider Europe Communication are examples of such documents internal to the EU policy-making process. In the ENP context, the financing Regulation of 2006 and the proposed instrument for the 2014–2020 MFF elevate this 'hybrid legal framework' to a defining feature of the ENP.

European Commission, *Proposal for a Regulation of the European Parliament and of the Council establishing a European Neighbourhood Instrument*, Brussels, 7 December 2011, COM(2011) 839 final

Article 3 – Policy framework

1. The partnership and cooperation agreements, the association agreements and other existing or future agreements that establish a relationship with partner countries, corresponding Communications, Council conclusions and European Parliament Resolutions as well as relevant conclusions of ministerial meetings with the partner countries shall constitute the overall policy framework for programming and implementing Union support under this Regulation.

2. Jointly agreed action plans or other equivalent documents between the partner countries and the Union shall provide the key point of reference for setting the priorities for Union support.

This provision in the proposed ENI had its full equivalent in the preceding ENPI Regulation, and from the outset ENP relations were based on a bilateral mixed agreement. Indeed, its conclusion is a prerequisite to developing a 'privileged relationship' between the EU and the partner country. In Eastern Europe and the Southern Caucasus they are the PCAs, and in the Mediterranean the AAs. The provision also points to future agreements. At present the prime candidate is the AA between the EU and Ukraine, which also includes a DCFTA. The AA was initialled in March 2012 and the DCFTA portion in July 2012, but final conclusion of the agreement is contentious and pending at the time this book went to press, due to the worsened political climate in Ukraine. Aside from substantive content, the importance of these international agreements for the ENP lies in their institutions: the Association Council or Partnership and Cooperation Councils. These are bodies which meet once or twice a year at ministerial level, but which also consist of a number of thematic working groups which meet more regularly at the technical, civil servant level. These institutionalized contacts are the forum through which EU–third-country initiatives in the ENP context are discussed, deployed and monitored. Recall in this context the excerpt from the 1997 Commission Communication entitled 'Agenda 2000', which described the importance of the EAs in exactly the same fashion as EU pre-accession policy.

The above Article 3 further points to the important role of non-legally binding instruments of the Commission, Council and the EP. The inclusion of the latter institution is new compared to the ENPI, which reflects the greater role for the Parliament in EU external relations post-Lisbon. Aside from those documents which are adopted unilaterally by the Union, this Article 3 also mentions conclusions of the ministerial meetings and the Action Plans. Both are documents which are adopted by the institutions of the AAs or PCAs, each with their own function: ministerial meetings are more topical, political and time-bound, whereas the Action Plans are more long-term documents looking how EU–third-country relations will evolve across a three-to-five-year time span. Table 15.1 provides an overview of all the legal instruments which are used in the implementation of the ENP. The table is organized in a 'progressive fashion' from the perspective of conducting ENP relations: starting with the basic legal instruments from an EU perspective, to the instruments through which the ENP over time can be implemented. It includes instruments which are legally binding, as well as 'soft law' instruments.

Table 15.1 – Policy framework of the ENP

	Nature of instrument	Actor/procedure	Description of policy function
Article 8 TEU	EU Primary Law	Article 48 TEU	Fundamental choices on conditionality and EU values
Financing Regulation	EU Secondary Law	Ordinary legislative procedure	Provision of financial assistance
Association Agreements/ Partnership and Cooperation Agreements	International agreement	Article 218 TFEU	Legal and institutional framework with basic provisions on political dialogue, free trade, etc.
Commission Communication	Soft legal instrument	Commission	Non-binding policy initiative, preparatory or informative document
Council Conclusion	Soft legal instrument	Council	Non-legally binding document, but political indication of future direction for EU policy
EP Resolution	Soft legal instrument	European Parliament	Non-binding political statement of Parliament
Ministerial Declaration	Soft legal instrument	AA/PCA Council	Stocktaking and political decisions on future of relations at the moment of the high-level EU–third-country meeting

Table 15.1 (*cont.*)

	Nature of instrument	Actor/procedure	Description of policy function
Decision of the Association Council	Binding instrument of international institution	AA Council	Decision implementing the underlying bilateral agreement (PCAs have this option only in a non-binding version)
ENP Country Report	Commission Communication (soft legal instrument)	Commission	EU assessment of political, economic, environmental situation in a partner country preceding the action plan
Action Plan/ Association Agenda	Adopted as non-binding recommendation of the relevant AA/PCA Council	Jointly negotiated between EU and third country	Bilateral instrument
Progress Report	Commission Communication (soft legal instrument)	Commission in consultation with civil society, Member States, local stakeholders	EU assessment of progress in implementation of the Action Plan
Country Strategy Paper	Undefined, soft legal instrument linked to financing instrument	Commission in consultation with civil society, Member States, local stakeholders and the partner country	Sets out overall EU assistance priorities for the duration of the financing instrument
National Indicative Programme	Undefined, soft legal instrument linked to financing instrument	Commission	Specific financing priorities and indicators for success in a shorter time frame
Deep and Comprehensive Free Trade Agreement	International agreement	Article 218 TFEU	An FTA which is further reaching by also covering issues such as non-tariff barriers and alignment with the *acquis*

(ii) Soft law in EU external relations

The use of non-legally binding documents or 'soft law' is a widespread practice in EU external relations, and it is important to familiarize oneself with the intimate connection between law and non-law in EU external policy-making (see Chapter 2). Table 15.1 shows that the ENP significantly draws on its composite of instruments which have legal binding force, or not. Looking specifically at the ENP Action Plans, it is possible to uncover some of the reasons why the EU would not renegotiate the AAs or PCAs with the southern or eastern countries. These rationales applied equally to the informal reorientation of the EAs, and *mutatis mutandis* apply to soft law in its various forms in EU external policy-making.

B. Van Vooren, *EU External Relations Law and the European Neighbourhood Policy: A Paradigm for Coherence* (Abingdon/New York: Routledge, 2012), pp. 193–194

A first characteristic is that soft instruments such as the action plans can be speedily adopted since they are not burdened by the procedural requirements of traditional international agreements. This characteristic is all the more important, since soft legal instruments will more easily encompass different Union competences and the Member States. Was the Union to adopt such a cross-pillar mixed instrument as a binding international agreement, complicated legal questions would follow suit: who shall negotiate the agreement, which procedure shall be followed in its adoption, where does responsibility for its breach lie, and so on. A soft instrument avoids all those issues and . . . contributes to policy coherence in that fashion.

Second, the negotiation of new legally binding agreements was considered of insufficient added-value when constructing the ENP given the significant financial and human resources required negotiating a treaty. In an effort to reinforce the idea that the Commission was not negotiating a binding international agreement, the Commission steadily used the term "consultations" between the institutions and the third countries in place of the more loaded term "negotiations". A Commission official would later confirm that this choice in rhetoric was very much conscious since it underlined the "political nature" of the process.

A third rationale for the soft legal action plans is not connected to their adoption but lies at the heart of their steering function, namely flexibility in terms of responding to changing needs as political relations evolve. Originally, most action plans were planned to run for an initial period of three years with the possibility of being amended "to reflect progress in addressing the priorities". At various points in this period, the Action Plans have indeed been elaborated through a range of soft and/or hard legal instruments: for example, in relations with Ukraine the first action plan has been replaced by an 'Association Agenda' – in essence a second generation action plan. . . .

In sum, non-binding action plans are speedily adopted, functionally flexible, easily adapted, and pose few procedural constraints thereby avoiding the pitfalls of competence related struggles.

8 THE FUTURE OF THE ENP?

Today, we can use the benefit of hindsight to evaluate briefly the accomplishments of the ENP over the past decade. During its development from the global Mediterranean policy, the 1990s and the fifth enlargement to the ENP of the present day, we can see that EU policy towards its geographically closest partners is one that keeps re-inventing itself utilizing similar language, methodologies, and instruments. The Communication of May 2011 was the EU's response to the Arab Spring which had unfolded since January that year. Whereas the title of the Communication reflects the new institutional framework post-Lisbon, the substance bears much similarity to the Wider Europe Communication a decade earlier.

Joint Communication from the European Commission and the High Representative, *A new response to a changing Neighbourhood*, COM(2011) 303, Brussels, 25 May 2011

To the East and South of the European Union (EU) lie sixteen countries whose hopes and futures make a direct and significant difference to us. Recent events have brought this into sharper relief, highlighting the challenges we face together. The overthrow of long-standing repressive regimes in Egypt and Tunisia; the ongoing military conflict in Libya, the recent violent crackdown in Syria, continued repression in Belarus and the lingering protracted conflicts in the region, including in the Middle East, require us to look afresh at the EU's relationship with our neighbours. The encouraging progress made by other neighbours, for example by Republic of Moldova in its reform efforts, Ukraine in the negotiations of the Association Agreement or Morocco and Jordan in their announcement of constitutional reform, need also to be supported. The Lisbon Treaty has allowed the EU to strengthen the delivery of its foreign policy: co-operation with neighbouring countries can now be broadened to cover the full range of issues in an integrated and more effective manner. This was a key driver for initiating a review, in consultation with partner countries and other stakeholders, of the European Neighbourhood Policy (ENP) in summer 2010. Recent events throughout the Southern Mediterranean have made the case for this review even more compelling. The EU needs to rise to the historical challenges in our neighbourhood. . . .

A new approach is needed to strengthen the partnership between the EU and the countries and societies of the neighbourhood: to build and consolidate healthy democracies, pursue sustainable economic growth and manage cross-border links. The ENP should be a policy of the Union with the Member States aligning their own bilateral efforts in support of its overall political objectives. . . .

The new approach must be based on mutual accountability and a shared commitment to the universal values of human rights, democracy and the rule of law. It will involve a much higher level of differentiation allowing each partner country to develop its links with the EU as far as its own aspirations, needs and capacities allow. For those southern and eastern neighbours able and willing to take part, this vision includes closer economic integration and stronger political co-operation on governance reforms, security, conflict-resolution matters, including joint initiatives in international fora on issues of common interest. . . .

The new approach, as described above, aims to:

(1) provide greater support to partners engaged in building deep democracy – the kind that lasts because the right to vote is accompanied by rights to exercise free speech, form competing political parties, receive impartial justice from independent judges, security from accountable police and army forces, access to a competent and non-corrupt civil service – and other civil and human rights that many Europeans take for granted, such as the freedom of thought, conscience and religion;

(2) support inclusive economic development – so that EU neighbours can trade, invest and grow in a sustainable way, reducing social and regional inequalities, creating jobs for their workers and higher standards of living for their people;

(3) strengthen the two regional dimensions of the European Neighbourhood Policy, covering respectively the Eastern Partnership and the Southern Mediterranean, so that we can work out consistent regional initiatives in areas such as trade, energy, transport or migration and mobility complementing and strengthening our bilateral co-operation;

(4) provide the mechanisms and instruments fit to deliver these objectives.

9 EU RELATIONS WITH OTHER NEIGHBOURING COUNTRIES

The geographic scope of the ENP does not encompass Russia, Iceland, Liechtenstein, Norway, Switzerland and the countries of the Western Balkans. Because of political expediency, economic differences and diverse accession perspectives, the EU engages these countries through a different set of policies. With Russia, instead of the ENP, the EU has set up Strategic Partnerships with thematic cooperation through four common spaces. With Norway, Iceland and Liechtenstein relations are conducted through the EEA, and with Switzerland through the EFTA and a large number of bilateral agreements. Finally, with the Western Balkan countries the EU has pursued the SAP which has an express pre-accession dimension. In this final section it is difficult to do justice to the full scope of EU legal relations with the aforementioned countries and regions, and exigencies of space permit a limited overview of core legal and policy questions.

(i) EU relations with the Russian Federation

Relations between the EU and Russia are at present still conducted on the basis of a PCA which was concluded in 1994 and entered into force in 1997 for a period of ten years, with automatic renewal every six months.[85] In May 2006 both parties agreed that a new framework agreement would be negotiated to replace the PCA. However, due to political obstacles such as the Russia–Georgia conflict of August 2008, negotiations are still ongoing at the time this book went to press. The agreement is overdue as many of the PCA provisions have become outdated, and more generally, the nature of EU–Russia relations has changed significantly since 1994. The PCAs date back to a post-Cold War era where the Soviet Union had been brought to its knees in political and economic terms, and as a consequence the PCA is 'based upon a unilateral adaptation of Russian legislation to EU values and norms'.[86] The refusal of the Russian Federation to participate in the ENP in 2002 signalled a major turnaround in EU–Russia relations. The May 2003 St Petersburg summit thus announced the start of the 'Strategic Partnership' between them, this time on the basis of common values and reciprocal arrangements between the two partners.[87] As part of this new approach, four common spaces were created within which the EU and Russia would cooperate: a common economic space, a common space of freedom, security and justice, a space of cooperation in the field of external security, as well as a space of research and education, including cultural aspects.

P. Van Elsuwege, *Towards a Modernisation of EU-Russia Legal Relations?* (CEURUS EU–Russia Papers, No. 5. 2012), pp. 23–24

Both within the EU and in Russia there is a consensus that the legal framework of their bilateral relationship needs modernisation. The PCA reflects the spirit of the early 1990s, but does not seem adapted to the new challenges of the 21st century. The weak dispute settlement mechanism, the impossibility to adopt legally binding decisions and the absence of formal legal provisions on issues such as energy and migration are the most obvious examples. Even though this has been partially solved through the conclusion of specific bilateral agreements and Russia's accession to the WTO, an updated bilateral framework agreement remains important for reasons of legal certainty and to ensure that the Strategic

---

[85] Agreement on Partnership and Cooperation establishing a partnership between the European Communities and their Member States, of one part, and the Russian Federation, of the other part, OJ 1997 No. L327/3 (renewed automatically every six months in accordance with Article 106).

[86] *Ibid.*, p. 2.

[87] EU–Russia Summit, Joint Statement, 31 May 2003, available from: www.consilium.europa.eu/uedocs/cms_data/docs/pressdata/en/er/75969.pdf (last accessed 27 October 2013).

Partnership is based on a solid institutional structure. However, several issues complicate the negotiations that started back in 2008.

First, both partners have different perceptions on the interpretation of fundamental values such as respect for the rule of law, democracy and human rights. ... Given the importance attached to the export of EU values in the Treaty of Lisbon, it is impossible to escape this issue in the context of EU–Russia relations. ...

Second, energy is not surprisingly a hot issue in EU–Russia relations. ... Despite the obvious mutual interdependence, both partners have different strategic interests leading to opposing views on the preferred legal framework. ...

Third, Vladimir Putin may be right when he assessed that "a genuine partnership between Russia and the European Union is impossible as long as there are barriers that impede human and economic contacts, first and foremost visa requirements" . ...

Fourth, there is a risk of clashing neighbourhood strategies. Putin's proposals on the establishment of a Eurasian union and the sometimes subtle pressure on countries such as Ukraine and – to a lesser extent – Moldova to join the EurAsEC customs union irritate the European Union policy makers. ...

The connecting factor between all identified problem areas (values, energy, visa, neighbourhood relations) is a lack of trust between the parties. In this context, the negotiation of a new framework agreement is a very difficult exercise.

(ii) EU relations with the EEA/EFTA countries

Several European countries (Austria, Denmark, Norway, Portugal, Switzerland and the UK) had originally refrained from participating in the EEC. Instead, in 1960, they concluded the EFTA with the objective of liberalizing trade in goods among them, without however pursuing the political integration objectives of the EEC. In 1961 Finland joined that project, followed by Iceland in 1970 and Liechtenstein in 1991. However, through the first, second and third enlargements of the EU, today only Iceland, Liechtenstein, Norway and Switzerland remain as EFTA Member States. In January 1994, the Agreement creating the EEA entered into force.[88] The objective of this agreement is to extend the EU internal market to its members, three of the four EFTA States. Switzerland was originally meant to participate in the EEA, but in a 1992 referendum only 49.7 per cent of the Swiss people voted in favour of that country's participation.[89] Instead of the EEA, in subsequent years the EU and Switzerland concluded a large number of bilateral agreements establishing cooperation between the partners in a large number of specific sectors. Following the 2008 financial crisis, Iceland commenced accession negotiations with the EU, but political support rapidly dwindled afterwards and these negotiations are unlikely to be concluded successfully. Norway has in the past also held two referenda on joining the EU, with the 'no' vote prevailing each time.

On a two-yearly basis, the Council reviews the state of EU relations with the EFTA countries. The following extract of the conclusions of December 2012 illustrates the extent and depth of

[88] Agreement on the European Economic Area, entry into force 1 January 1994, OJ 1994 L1/3.
[89] C. Kaddous, 'The Relations between the EU and Switzerland', in A. Dashwood and M. Maresceau (eds.), *Law and Practice of EU External Relations – Salient Features of a Changing Landscape* (Cambridge: Cambridge University Press, 2008), p. 228.

integration that exists between these countries, but also the diversity between EEA countries and Switzerland. In terms of policy areas, cooperation between the EEA countries and the EU is evidently deep and far-reaching on internal market issues, but equally encompasses cooperation in the context of the EU's CFSP. On Switzerland, note in particular the distinction between that country and EEA countries, and how firmly the Council expressed the view that the 'cherry-picking' approach through the bilaterals has reached its limits.

Council Conclusions on EU relations with EFTA countries, 20 December 2012

The Council adopted the following conclusions:

1. In accordance with its conclusions of December 2010, the Council has assessed the development of EU relations with the four Member States of the European Free Trade Association (EFTA), namely the Kingdom of Norway, Iceland, the Principality of Liechtenstein and the Swiss Confederation, in the past two years. During that period, EU relations with the EFTA countries remained stable and close (details on developments are set out below in country-specific paragraphs). The Council is looking forward to further strengthening and deepening relations with the four countries in question in the future. It will reassess the state of relations between the EU and the EFTA countries in two years.

Principality of Liechtenstein

2. The Council recognizes that over the past 17 years, Liechtenstein – though a country of small territorial size – has become a successful EEA member through political determination and significant administrative efforts, and might be a useful reference for further intensifying the relations between the EU and other European countries of small territorial size.
3. The Council strongly welcomes the solidarity shown by the people of Liechtenstein through their contribution to reduce social and economic disparities in the EEA for the period 2009–2014.
4. The Council notes with satisfaction that in the period 2010 to 2012, relations between the EU and Liechtenstein were further extended and strengthened in a number of areas. In particular, the Council welcomes the entry of Liechtenstein into the Schengen area and its association to the Dublin acquis in December 2011.
5. The Council welcomes in general efforts made by Liechtenstein in order to adapt its tax legislation and practices to EEA rules and international standards, in particular the comprehensive tax reform, which entered into force on 1 January 2011.
6. Regarding cooperation and information exchange in tax matters and the fight against fraud and tax evasion, the Council takes note of the efforts of the Principality to live up to its commitment to implement OECD standards on transparency and on tax information exchange and to fight against fraud, and notes that it has concluded a number of bilateral agreements including provisions on tax information exchange. The Council expects Liechtenstein to continue the implementation of its commitment to combat tax fraud and tax evasion in its relationship with the EU and all its Member States.
7. Concerning the taxation of savings, the Council welcomes the openness of Liechtenstein to enter into negotiations on the revision of the savings taxation agreement to reflect the evolution of the corresponding EU acquis, once the Council has adopted a decision authorising the opening of negotiations, including negotiating directives. Regarding the latter, the European Council stated in its conclusions of 28/29 June 2012 that rapid agreement must be reached by the Council on the negotiating directives for saving taxation agreements with third countries. This was reaffirmed in the conclusions of the Council on tax evasion and fraud, adopted on 13 November 2012. . . .

Kingdom of Norway

10. The Council notes with satisfaction that over the past two years, relations with Norway have continued to be marked by a high level of cooperation and stability. In the difficult period of the sovereign debt crisis in the Eurozone, Norway has demonstrated its solidarity, inter alia with a contribution of 6 billion SDRs (over 7 billion EUR) to the IMF. The close relationship between the EU and Norway has further evolved both through the EEA Agreement and bilaterally, in particular in the areas of Justice and Home Affairs, Common Foreign and Security Policy and Agriculture.

11. Concerning Justice and Home Affairs, including Schengen, the Council notes that relations have further strengthened in a number of sectors. In the aftermath of the tragic attacks in Oslo and Utøya in July 2011, cooperation on counter-terrorism, anti-radicalisation and police cooperation in the framework of Europol has also been stepped up. The Council acknowledges the benefits of increased cooperation. With regard to judicial cooperation in civil matters, the Council is ready to examine proposals for further extending the cooperation.

12. The Council welcomes Norway's cooperation in the area of Common Foreign and Security Policy, which has further intensified since 2010. The Council highly appreciates the participation of Norway in numerous Common Security and Defence Policy (CSDP) operations and missions, in the Nordic Battle Group, as well as in the activities of the European Defence Agency. The Council also welcomes the frequent alignment of Norway to EU statements, the regular political dialogues held at all levels, as well as the cooperation in the framework of the Ad-hoc Liaison Committee on Palestine (AHLC), chaired by Norway. The Council is committed to further deepening this partnership, in particular through the continuous participation of Norway in CSDP operations.

13. Norway is the fifth largest trade partner of the EU, while the EU remains the main trade partner of Norway for both imports and exports. Overall, trade relations are strong and intense. In this context and in the spirit of the EEA, the Council expects Norway to closely coordinate with the EU its positions for matters that fall under the EEA Agreement, including matters related to trade. The Council therefore regrets that Norway has decided to proceed with the WTO dispute settlement proceeding against the EU measures on trade in seal products. ...

16. The Council is well aware of the high priority attached by Norway to the Arctic and shares its interest in developments regarding this region. The EU is ready to step up its cooperation on Arctic matters in a number of sectors of common interest, inter alia through its bilateral dialogues with Norway and through regional cooperation. Regarding the latter, the Council welcomes cooperation in the framework of the Council of the Baltic Sea States. The Council also commends the Norwegian chairmanship of the Barents Euro-Arctic Council, whose 20th anniversary will be celebrated next year. It also welcomes the continued support of Norway with regard to the Commission's application on behalf of the EU for an observer status in the Arctic Council. Furthermore, the Council acknowledges the important role of Norway in the Northern Dimension. The EU continues to be committed to regional cooperation in the framework of the Northern Dimension partnerships in the field of the environment, transport and logistics, public health and social well-being and culture. ...

Iceland

19. The Council welcomes the continued progress made in the negotiations on the EU accession process of Iceland since 2010, takes note of the findings presented by the Commission on 10 October 2012 to the Council and the European Parliament in the Progress Report on Iceland and refers to its conclusions on

enlargement of 11 December 2012. The Council encourages Iceland to continue to make progress in the alignment with and the implementation of the EU acquis.

20. The Council strongly welcomes the solidarity shown by Iceland in continuing its contribution to the reduction of social and economic disparities in the EEA for the period 2009–2014.

21. The Council notes with satisfaction that besides the evolution of the relationship in the framework of the accession process, relations have also further developed in the past two years in the traditional framework of cooperation under the EEA Agreement, as well as in the Schengen area. The Council appreciates the ever closer cooperation with Iceland in a wide range of policy areas, including the Common Foreign and Security Policy. It looks forward to further deepening cooperation, in particular in key areas of common interest such as the global promotion of human rights, renewable energy, climate change, fisheries, the Northern Dimension and Arctic policy.

22. The Council acknowledges the high priority given by Iceland to Arctic Policy and confirms the EU's strategic interest in developments regarding this region. It appreciates the support of Iceland with regard to the Commission's application on behalf of the EU for an observer status in the Arctic Council. The Council stands ready to further intensify the cooperation on Arctic issues. . . .

25. The Council welcomes the recent positive development of the Icelandic economy following a long and severe recession, as well as Iceland's continued commitment to move towards economic stabilization and to address all issues deriving from the 2008 banking collapse. However, the Council notes that certain economic issues, including capital controls, still need to be addressed. Furthermore, it recalls the need for Iceland to address existing obligations under the EEA Agreement as well as remaining weaknesses in the area of financial services.

European Economic Area

26. In the past two years, the EU, Norway and Liechtenstein have undertaken or launched reviews of the Agreement on the European Economic Area ("EEA Agreement"). The EU welcomes the Report of the Norwegian Review Committee and the ensuing White Paper of the Norwegian Government on the EEA Agreement and Norway's other agreements with the EU. Moreover, the Council welcomes the EEA Review commissioned by Liechtenstein, and will consider its content with interest. . . .

28. The Council notes that overall, the EEA Agreement has continued to function in a satisfactory manner. The Council welcomes the substantial efforts made by the three EEA EFTA countries (Iceland, Liechtenstein and Norway) in the course of the past year to reduce the number of outstanding legal acts still to be incorporated into the EEA Agreement. The Council draws the attention to the importance of addressing, as a matter of priority, the remaining large number of legal acts, for which the compliance date in the EU has passed, but which have not entered into force in the EEA EFTA countries as their incorporation into the EEA Agreement has been delayed. In this regard, the Council underlines that the principles of homogeneity and legal certainty guarantee the efficiency, sustainability and ultimately the credibility of the single market and must therefore continue to guide the action of all parties in relation to the functioning of the EEA Agreement.

Swiss Confederation

29. The Council underlines the importance of close relations between the EU and Switzerland. Both are faced with the same global challenges, to which Europe needs to respond in a responsible and coordinated manner. Over the past decades, Switzerland has come ever closer to the EU, becoming inter alia its fourth biggest trading partner and a reliable partner in the Schengen area.

30. The Council notes that in the last years, negotiations as regards Switzerland's further participation in parts of the Internal Market have been marked by a stalemate, partly due to unresolved institutional issues. While the Council welcomes the continuation of intensive and close cooperation with Switzerland in many areas, it is of the view that the conclusion of any negotiation regarding the participation of Switzerland in the Internal Market is, in particular, dependent on solving the institutional issues outlined in the Council conclusions of 2008 and 2010.

31. Recalling its conclusions of 2010, the Council reaffirms that the approach taken by Switzerland to participate in EU policies and programmes through sectoral agreements in more and more areas in the absence of any horizontal institutional framework, has reached its limits and needs to be reconsidered. Any further development of the complex system of agreements would put at stake the homogeneity of the Internal Market and increase legal insecurity as well as make it more difficult to manage such an extensive and heterogeneous system of agreements. In the light of the high level of integration of Switzerland with the EU, any further extension of this system would in addition bear the risk of undermining the EU's relations with the EEA EFTA partners.

32. The Council welcomes the efforts made by Switzerland to formalize proposals on these institutional issues, as submitted in June 2012. In particular, the Council notes with satisfaction that Switzerland recognizes that the principle of homogeneity, a principle requiring in particular a dynamic adaptation to the evolving EU acquis, should be at the core of the EU–Switzerland relationship.

33. However, the Council considers that further steps are necessary in order to ensure the homogeneous interpretation and application of the Internal Market rules. In particular, the Council deems it necessary to establish a suitable framework applicable to all existing and future agreements. This framework should, inter alia, provide for a legally binding mechanism as regards the adaptation of the agreements to the evolving EU acquis. Furthermore, it should include international mechanisms for surveillance and judicial control. In this context, the Council notes that by participating in parts of the EU internal market and policies, Switzerland is not only engaging in a bilateral relation but becomes a participant in a multilateral project. All in all, this institutional framework should present a level of legal certainty and independence equivalent to the mechanisms created under the EEA Agreement.

34. The Council underlines that it attaches great importance to the continuation of a dialogue with Switzerland on possible solutions to the institutional issues as set out in previous paragraphs. The Council invites the Commission to report on the progress in the exploratory discussions and, in the light of such progress, to consider the possibility of presenting a recommendation for the opening of negotiations with Switzerland.

35. The Council welcomes the mobility of citizens between the EU and Switzerland, based on the Agreement on the Free Movement of Persons and enhanced by other Agreements, such as those on the participation of Switzerland in the Life Long Learning and Youth in Action Programmes and on Switzerland's association to the Research Framework Programme of the EU. However, the Council notes with regret that Switzerland has taken a number of measures, which are not compatible with the provisions and the spirit of the Agreement on the Free Movement of Persons and undermine its implementation. In particular, the Council deeply regrets that Switzerland has unilaterally re-introduced quotas for certain categories of residence permits for citizens of 8 EU Member States. The Council considers this step to be discriminatory and clearly in breach of the Agreement, and strongly urges Switzerland to reverse its decision and to respect the agreed provisions. Furthermore, the Council regrets that Switzerland has not yet abolished certain unilaterally introduced flanking measures to the Agreement (such as the obligation to provide prior notification with an 8-day waiting period), which restrict the provision of services under the Agreement and are particularly burdensome for SMEs wishing to provide

services in Switzerland. The Council reiterates its call on Switzerland to abrogate these measures as soon as possible and to refrain from adopting any new measure incompatible with the Agreement.

A distinct legal problem of EU relations with EEA/EFTA countries is highlighted several times in these Conclusions. Specifically in relation to measures adopted by the Swiss on free movement of persons, the Council deplores measures which are not in accordance with what was previously agreed in the relevant EU–Switzerland bilateral instrument. Such clear contravention is perhaps rather exceptional, but it illustrates the more general concern these Conclusions also raise in relation to the overall functioning of the EEA. Namely, the extension of the internal market to third countries raises the concern of 'legal homogeneity', i.e. ensuring that a level playing field is created in the existence, application and enforcement of the *acquis* that is being 'exported' by the EU through multilateral arrangements such as the EEA, or bilateral agreements such as those with Switzerland. Specifically, the Council draws attention to the fact that there are a large number of legal acts for which the compliance date in the EU has passed, but which have not entered into force in the EEA/EFTA countries. Pointing to the importance of homogeneity and legal certainty, the credibility of the internal market is ultimately at stake.

A. Lazowski, 'Enhanced Multilateralism and Enhanced Bilateralism: Integration without Membership in the European Union' (2008) 45 *Common Market Law Review* 1433–1458 at 1445

The legislative methods of securing homogeneity have one particular purpose – the adjustment of the EEA, Energy Community and EC/EU–Swiss framework to changes of the ever developing *acquis communautaire*. To start with, one has to acknowledge the limited participation of these third countries in the EU's decision making. The participation of EFTA–EEA members as well as Swiss representatives is primarily limited to the early stages of legislative procedures; therefore it is often referred to as decision-shaping. . . . The EEA Joint Committee plays a central role in securing the homogeneity of the EEA framework. In this regard one of its main tasks is to adjust the EEA agreement and its annexes to developments in EC law. Practice provides that this remains one of its core activities. For example, in 2005 it adopted 156 decisions incorporating 314 EC acts . . . [T]he annexes to the EEA Agreement contain lists of EC legislation with EEA relevance and may be amended by decisions of the EEA Joint Committee. The relevant procedure is set forth in Articles 102–104 EEA. Following the adoption of the EC legislation, the relevant EU decision-making bodies have an obligation to transfer new legislation to the relevant authorities of EFTA States. It is the task of the EEA Joint Committee to secure the homogeneity of the EEA legal space and amend the annexes as fast as possible in order to allow simultaneous entry into force of the legislation in the entire EEA. . . . Once a piece of EC legislation is brought within the ambit of EEA framework the EEA–EFTA countries have the obligation to transpose the measures in national legal orders. . . . Unlike in the EC legal order, regulations are not directly applicable and should be transposed to domestic legal orders. In case of delays in the transposition or any shortcomings in this respect, the EFTA Surveillance authority has the power to initiate an infringement procedure, and submit infringement actions to the EFTA Court.

(iii) The SAP in the Western Balkans

At the outset of this chapter, we pointed to the accession of Croatia on 1 July 2013. Two days before that date, the European Council also endorsed the Council recommendation to open accession negotiations with Serbia. At the same time, that institution decided that negotiations could commence between the EU and Kosovo on an SAA.[90] The President of the European Council hailed these events as 'historic', and indeed, as a sign of the transformative power of EU (accession), these decisions were taken just two decades after the violent dissolution of the Yugoslav Republic. They are the result of the SAP that the EU launched in 1999.

A. Elbasani, *The Stabilisation and Association Process in the Balkans: Overloaded Agenda and Weak Incentives?* (EUI Working Paper, SPS 2008/03), pp. 3–4

The explosion of successive conflicts in Slovenia, Croatia, and Bosnia (1991–1995), Kosovo (1999), Macedonia (2001), as well as the violent collapse of the economic system in Bulgaria (1997) and wholesale collapse of state institutions in Albania (1997), brought the Balkans to the fore of international concerns and security issues. The nearby EU countries became especially vulnerable and interested to solve the security risks spilling over their borders. . . .

Initially, the EU was seen as a leading international mediator, which promised to smooth the emerging crisis in the region. It managed to negotiate a cease-fire between Slovenia and the Yugoslav federation and soon in July 1991 recognised Slovenia's right of independence. The Luxembourg presidency at the time voiced the great expectations to the Union when declaring that "the hour of Europe" [is now]. Yet, that proved to be illusionary as the EU could not prevent the subsequent explosion of conflicts in Croatia and Bosnia. Moreover, the EU seemingly experienced total humiliation when implementing a UN mandate to safeguard one of the cities of Bosnia in 1994. The war in Bosnia became one of the bleak chapters of the European Common Foreign Policy, showing rather clearly that the Europeans lacked "the cohesiveness, the determination and the instruments to bring the crisis under control". . . .

The US had been quite reluctant to engage in the Balkans as no important security interests were at stake. Yet, the US diplomacy was to send the main impetus to the end of the Bosnian war when it became clear that the EU failed to deal with the crisis despite increasing bloodshed and urgent humanitarian emergency. The US government proceeded to take the decisive measures to end the war, employing NATO in support of the other diplomatic efforts to mediate the conflict. Its more active engagement in the second half of 1995 finally produced the Dayton Accords agreed in November 1995. The US special envoy, Holbrooke [would . . .] complain on Europeans' passivity to deal with the Balkans when admitting: "You have to wonder why Europe does not seem capable of taking decisive action in its own theatre . . . Unless the US is willing to put its political and military muscle behind the quest for solutions to European stability nothing really gets done." . . .

The overall division of roles between Europe and US did not change much in the post-Dayton period. Europe still contributed the lion's share of financial assistance, expertise and troops but its political influence was not commensurate to the strong turn of US foreign policy in determinate moments of crisis. The crisis in Albania once again showed the incapacity of the EU to take collective action against the collapse of central authorities in 1997 and left Italy to lead a "coalition of the willing". The Kosovo crisis between 1998–1999 also put in clear light the lack of EU capability to prevent the escalation of conflict.

---

[90] European Council, Conclusions of 27–28 June 2013, EUCO 104/2/13.

At every point of the crisis the impetus and the conditions for ending the conflict came from the US. As a recent study of the EU influence in the Balkans puts it "by the end of the decade and in light of Kosovo, the EU's ability to manage conflict in its own backyard had been exposed as a myth and Europe's continued reliance upon a US military presence was clear for all to see".

Under the German presidency, the EU worked to make amends for earlier failures through the 'Stability Pact' (SP) launched in Cologne on 10 June 1999. Initiated in the context of the EU's CFSP,[91] it was not an EU foreign policy instrument but rather a multilateral political declaration and framework agreement including, alongside the EU and its Member States, also the G-8 countries and a wide range of international organizations including the international financial institutions, as well as the UN, OSCE, OECD, NATO and others. A crucial aspect of that initiative was that the Union provided an express accession perspective to the Western Balkan countries, applying the methodology which had been developed earlier in relation to the CEECs: the conclusion of bilateral agreements with a strong element of conditionality and exporting of the EU *acquis* to third countries (the SAA), as a means of preparing those countries for EU accession. This became known as the SAP covering: Bosnia and Herzegovina,[92] Croatia,[93] FYROM,[94] Albania[95] and the Federal Republic of Yugoslavia (which later became Montenegro[96] and Serbia,[97] including Kosovo according to Resolution 1244 of the United Nations Security Council.[98]

Stability Pact for South Eastern Europe, Cologne, 10 June 1999

18. We welcome the European Union's initiative in launching the Stability Pact and the leading role the EU is playing, in cooperation with other participating and facilitating States, international Organisations and Institutions. The launching of the Pact will give a firm European anchorage to the region. The ultimate success of the Pact will depend largely on the efforts of the States concerned to fulfil the objectives of the Pact and to develop regional cooperation through multilateral and bilateral agreements. . . .

20. The EU will draw the region closer to the perspective of full integration of these countries into its structures. In case of countries which have not yet concluded association agreements with the EU, this will

---

[91] Common Position 1999/345/CFSP of 17 May 1999, OJ 1999 No. L133/1; Blockmans, *Tough Love: The European Union's Relations with the Western Balkans* (The Hague: T.M.C. Asser Press, 2007), p. 248.

[92] Interim agreement on trade and trade-related matters between the European Community, of the one part, and Bosnia and Herzegovina, of the other part, OJ 2008 No. L169/10.

[93] Stabilisation and Association Agreement between the European Communities and their Member States, of the one part, and the Republic of Croatia, of the other part, OJ 2005 No. L26/3.

[94] Stabilisation and Association Agreement between the European Communities and their Member States, of the one part, and the former Yugoslav Republic of Macedonia, of the other part, OJ 2004 No. L84/1.

[95] Stabilisation and Association Agreement between the European Communities and their Member States, of the one part, and the Republic of Albania, of the other part, OJ 2009 No. L107/166.

[96] Stabilisation and Association Agreement between the European Communities and their Member States, of the one part, and the Republic of Montenegro, of the other part, OJ 2010 No. L108/3.

[97] Stabilisation and Association Agreement between the European Communities and their Member States, of the one part, and the Republic of Serbia, of the other part, signature 29 April 2008, pending ratification Lithuania and EU.

[98] Commission Communication, *On a Feasibility Study for a Stabilisation and Association Agreement between the European Union and Kosovo* [sic], Brussels, 10 October 2012, COM(2012) 602 final.

be done through a new kind of contractual relationship taking fully into account the individual situations of each country with the perspective of EU membership, on the basis of the Amsterdam Treaty and once the Copenhagen criteria have been met. We note the European Union's willingness that, while deciding autonomously, it will consider the achievement of the objectives of the Stability Pact, in particular progress in developing regional cooperation, among the important elements in evaluating the merits of such a perspective.

Commission Communication, *On the Stabilisation and Association Process for Countries of South-Eastern Europe*, Brussels, 26 May 1999, COM(99) 235

Despite major efforts to stabilise individual countries and the region as a whole, the progress made has been fragile. This is clear from the degree to which it has been jeopardised by the current conflict in Kosovo. The region is now at a turning point. ... At this time of tremendous upheaval and uncertainty in the region, the EU has a responsibility to contribute to the resolution both of the immediate instability and, in the longer term, to the general stabilisation and development of the region. ... Fulfilling this responsibility will necessitate decisions on considerable amounts of further assistance, as well as on appropriate implementation mechanisms and legal bases. ...

The proposals in the present Communication for the development of a Stabilisation and Association process will also help the development of the EU Common Strategy towards the Western Balkans which will constitute the framework for EU relations with the region in the coming years ... As at two other key stages in recent history – the emergence of independent states in Central and Eastern Europe in 1989–90 and the dissolution of the former Soviet Union in 1991 – the European Union is confronted with geopolitical challenges requiring the development of new policies, and instruments, towards a group of countries. On this occasion, it must respond by offering a perspective of integration; based on a progressive approach adapted to the situation of the specific countries. ...

To respond to the present, changed, circumstances in the region ... and the proposed wording of the Stability Pact, the commission considers it appropriate that a new Stabilisation and Association process should be launched, an element of which would be the new category of agreements – Stabilisation and Association Agreements ... [T]hese agreements would be tailor-made, differentiated to take account of the specific situation of the country concerned. The main objectives would be:

- To draw the region closer to the perspective of full integration into EU structures,
- To support the consolidation of democracy, rule of law, economic development and reform, adequate administrative structures, and regional cooperation,
- To establish a formalized framework for political dialogue; both at bilateral and regional level,
- To promote economic relations, trade, investment, enterprise policy, transport and development, and cooperation in the customs area, with the perspective of closer integration into the world trading system, including the possibility of establishing a free area or areas, when sufficient progress has been made in economic reform,
- To provide a basis for cooperation in the field of justice and home affairs,
- To provide a basis for economic, social, civil, educational, scientific, technological, energy, environmental and cultural cooperation ... underpinned by "association-oriented" assistance programmes which would also be designed to facilitate approximation of legislation in accordance with relevant EC *acquis*.

The accession perspective for SAP countries was confirmed at the European Council Summit at Santa Maria da Feira held in June 2000. In 2003, an EU–Western Balkans Summit in Thessaloniki took place, and launched the 'Thessaloniki Agenda for the Western Balkans: Moving Towards European Integration'.[99]

S. Blockmans, *Tough Love: The European Union's Relations with the Western Balkans* (The Hague: T.M.C. Asser Press, 2007), pp. 253 and 335–336

As such, the European Union and the Western Balkans agreed on an 'agenda' for the pre-accession process of the countries of the region, very much like Agenda 2000 set the tune for the countries that joined the European Union in its fifth wave of enlargement. In addition, the Thessaloniki Agenda was meant to further strengthen and enhance the political visibility of the SAP, inter alia, by launching the high-level multilateral EU–Western Balkans Forum and 'European Partnerships' (reminiscent of the Accession Partnerships for the CEECs) as well as by promoting the decisions for enhanced cooperation in the areas of political dialogue and the Common Foreign and Security Policy, parliamentary cooperation, support for institution-building, the opening of Community programmes and regional economic development. ...

Concluding Remarks

The European Union has come a long way in the Western Balkans in just a few years. During the 1990s, while it stood by and watched the Balkans burn, it was the United States, in the framework of NATO, that acted decisively to stop the war in Bosnia–Herzegovina and the crisis in Kosovo. ... the Union's Stabilisation and Association Process has made a critical contribution to progress achieved throughout the region, but the returns on its investment are dwindling. In contrast to the CEECs, the Western Balkans still contain the possibility of a genuine security threat. Therefore, there is currently a real imperative to move the region as a whole from the stage of international protectorates and weak states to the stage of accession to the European Union and NATO. This scenario not only presupposes a reinvigorated drive for reform by the countries concerned but also presumes a continued, albeit reconfigured engagement by the Euro-Atlantic security organisations under the leadership of the European Union. Such a strategy would be significant not just practically but symbolically as well: if the Western Balkans were to be successfully integrated into the European Union, it would finally banish the possibility of a revival of the type of armed conflict that so plagued the continent's nineteenth and twentieth century history. Incidentally, defusing the 'powder keg' would also be a landmark achievement for the European Union in its quest for a more prominent role internationally. By opening accession negotiations with Croatia and granting candidate country status to Macedonia, the European Union has finally shown its commitment to the countries of this troubled region. ... By transcending the 'potential members' mindset and showing its commitment to Albania, Bosnia–Herzegovina, Montenegro, Serbia and Kosovo, the Union will render the Stabilisation and Association Process a much more credible framework. But it will have to do more than that to prevent these least stable parts of the Western Balkans from turning into a new ghetto. The Union will have to address the remaining constitutional and status issues and put its money where its mouth is. While nation-building in the Western Balkans has entered its final stages with the functional separation of Serbia and Montenegro, the search for the end of international governance in Bosnia–Herzegovina and a final status for Kosovo, the EU Member States seem unwilling to release the necessary funds to see these defining processes through. Only a bigger effort based on a fair but firm

---

[99] Council Conclusions of 16 June 2003, Annex A 'Thessaloniki Agenda'.

application of the conditionality principle will lead to the integration of the Western Balkans into the European mainstream. This means that countries should gain substantial rewards if they meet tough political, economic and legal conditions and that rewards will be denied or withdrawn if they lapse back into bad habits. Today, probably more than ever, tough love is required.

As stated at the outset of this section, the SAP has now led to Croatia joining the EU on 1 July 2013, the opening of accession negotiations with Serbia, the opening of negotiations on an SAA with Kosovo, and the conclusion of such agreements with FYROM, Albania and Montenegro; though not yet with Bosnia and Herzegovina.

10 THE BROADER PICTURE OF EU EXTERNAL RELATIONS LAW

In the introduction to this textbook, we pointed to the deep interconnection between EU external relations law, the politics of European integration and the issue of effective and coherent EU external policies. This trinity of law–policy–coherence is most evident in this concluding chapter on the means and policies through which the EU engages its neighbours.

First and foremost, notice the diverse roles of law in EU enlargement policy, the ENP and the SAP, and the differentiated approaches between EEA/EFTA countries and Switzerland. In all these policies, a similar legal toolbox is used by the EU, tailor-made to the specific situation at issue. In all of these legal relationships, an international agreement is the core framework to establish relations with the EU: an EA, an SAA, a PCA, a set of bilateral agreements, a multilateral legal framework such as the EEA or the Energy Community Treaty. Surrounding this legal core, there is then a whole set of instruments and methodologies which the EU employs in diverse ways: soft legal accession partnerships, Action Plans, progress reports, communications, MoUs. A constant methodological choice in all of these policies is the idea of law as an EU export product, in pursuit of certain objectives. The EU will work with third countries for them to adopt the EU *acquis*, in order for them to prepare for EU membership, or to create a stable and secure neighbourhood to the east or south, or to create an extended internal market with advanced European nations that have no desire to join the European integration project. In this sense, law has a dual function: it organizes EU external relations with its entire neighbourhood, and it is also the substance itself of EU policies. Thus, the EU certainly lives up to the *chapeau* of Article 21 TEU (mirrored in Article 8 TEU) that its 'action on the international scene shall be guided by the principles which have inspired its own creation, development and enlargement, and which it seeks to advance in the wider world'.

Second, there is the issue of coherence between all these policies. At their core, they follow a similar methodology and toolbox consisting of soft and hard legal instruments. However, their objectives are different, and this raises questions as to the efficacy and applicability of certain methodologies with certain countries or regions. Exporting the EU *acquis* may be the method of choice with Ukraine given its European aspirations, but as Chapter 13 on energy has also shown, it may be less applicable in relations with the Russian Federation. Thus, the fact that the ENP is inspired by EU enlargement may lend a certain degree of coherence to EU methodologies and instruments in its external relations, but this is not necessarily entirely positive.

Third, the shadow of European integration is quite self-evident throughout this chapter. Not with the Russian Federation, but in all other policies examined in this chapter, the accession perspective, lack thereof, and willingness or unwillingness to join the EU, constitute the essence of that policy: the question as to whether the ENP can function without the accession perspective; the question in certain EU Member States as to whether EU enlargement with certain third countries is desirable, and the impact on the efficacy of EU enlargement policy. The relationship with law was then also present: namely, if indeed certain Member States wish to create permanent safeguards in future enlargements, what then is the impact on the EU legal order writ large? Would permanent exceptions built into the eighth or ninth enlargement not effectively question the essence of European integration?

The challenges for the EU in its neighbourhood are many, and here lies the greatest potential for the EU to be vindicated as an international actor. Coherence between the different policies of the EU and those of its Member States remains as great as challenge as ever, as does the limited scope of certain EU competences. The financial crisis that has gripped Europe has not helped to increase the attractiveness of the EU and Member States' external policies. Alternative means of cooperation which are far less 'on EU terms' have presented themselves, and lead to new challenges: important third countries that used to aspire to become EU members have reorientated their foreign policies (Turkey, Ukraine), the Arab Spring has created an entirely new political, economic and security environment to the south, and new actors with strengthened regional or global aspirations have stood up (Russia). In all this, law is but an instrument at the service of politics and policies working to render the EU a successful international actor.

Joint Communication of the European Commission and the High Representative of the EU for Foreign Affairs and Security Policy, *European Neighbourhood Policy: Working Towards a Stronger Partnership*, Brussels, 20 March 2013, JOIN(2013) 4 final, pp. 20–22

The ENP is a prime example of a comprehensive approach to external policy. Cooperation with our neighbours uses all instruments and policies at the EU's disposal. It combines long-term political association, trade policy, sector policies and financial cooperation with shorter-term policies and measures of CFSP/CSDP instruments. It shows how a comprehensive approach can be used to generate coherent action involving all relevant EU actors. . . .

EU Institutions and individual Member States must strive towards maximizing coherence, which is essential to bring EU added value. The Delegations of the EU in partner countries have an important role to play in bringing all actors together, ensuring coherence and synergies on the ground. They will also need to take on a bigger role as hubs for partner countries' authorities, civil society, or businesses to obtain information about policy and the opportunities for seeking support. . . .

The universal values on which the EU is built – freedom, democracy, respect for human rights and fundamental freedoms, and the rule of law – also underpin the ENP. For partners who want to become as close to the EU as possible, it is the main reference point for their domestic reforms. This reform process must be inclusive. Only if the whole societies, not just the political elites or certain parts of the political spectrum, makes this choice and adheres to the universal values referred to above, will the process be sustainable and ultimately successful. . . .

Shifts in the foreign policy orientation of partner countries and the increasing involvement of other actors in the region may also make the EU less attractive as a model and partner. This will require the EU to reflect on how to have a more multilateral policy approach, involving and working with, more systematically than it does now, the other actors working in the neighbourhood in addressing, together with partner countries themselves, issues of shared interest. In the Southern Mediterranean, Turkey, countries of the Gulf and organisations such as the Arab League are playing a more prominent role in attempts to resolve conflicts and are promoting their economic and political interests more. The emergence of alternative regional integration schemes in the Eastern neighbourhood presents a new challenge. The emergence of the Eurasian Union between the Russian Federation, Belarus and Kazakhstan has changed the landscape. This is perceived as offering an alternative model of political and economic development to integration with the EU. However, there is a choice to be made. For example, joining the Customs Union that is part of the Eurasian Union would preclude economic integration with the EU through a DCFTA.

While the underlying principles and objectives of the ENP continue to apply to all partners and all parts of the policy, the EU's relationship with each one of its partners is unique, and the instruments of the ENP are tailored to serve each of those relationships. The ENP provides the EU with a toolbox of instruments that allows it to adapt its policy approach and response to the individual context of its partners and their aspirations for their relationship with the EU. It will increasingly need to differentiate its policy response, in line with the different developments, ambitions and needs of its partners.

Partners should not lower their ambition and commitment to reform their societies and their political and economic systems. This remains essential to fulfil the aspirations and meet the needs of their populations. A renewed political commitment to actually implementing often difficult reforms is crucial. For its part, the EU needs to continue to live up to its commitments of stronger political association, greater economic integration and support for reforms.

SOURCES AND FURTHER READING

Blockmans, S., *Tough Love: The European Union's Relations with the Western Balkans* (The Hague: T.M.C. Asser Press, 2007).

Blockmans, S. and Lazowski, A. (eds.), *The European Union and its Neighbours – A Legal Appraisal of the EU's Policies of Stabilisation, Partnership and Integration* (The Hague: T.M.C. Asser Press, 2006).

Blockmans, S. and Van Vooren, B., 'Revitalizing the European Neighbourhood Economic Community, The Case for Legally Binding Sectoral Multilateralism' (2012) 17 *European Foreign Affairs Review* 577–604.

Cremona, M. (ed.), *The Enlargement of the European Union* (Oxford: Oxford University Press, 2003).

Cremona, M., 'EU Enlargement: Solidarity and Conditionality' (2005) 30 *European Law Review* 3–22.

Cremona, M., *The European Neighbourhood Policy: Legal and Institutional Issues* (CDDRL Working Paper No. 2004/25).

Cremona, M., 'The European Neighbourhood Policy: More than a Partnership?', in M. Cremona (ed.) *Developments in EU External Relations Law* (Oxford: Oxford University Press, 2008).

Cremona, M. and Hillion, C., *L'Union fait la force? Potential and Limitations of the European Neighbourhood Policy as an Integrated EU Foreign and Security Policy* (EUI Law Working Paper 2006/49).

Cremona, M. and Meloni, G., *The European Neighbourhood Policy: A Framework for Modernisation?* (EUI Law Working Paper 2007/21).

Dannreuther, R., 'Developing the Alternative to Enlargement: The European Neighbourhood Policy' (2006) 11 *European Foreign Affairs Review* 183–201.

De Witte, B., 'The Impact of Enlargement on the Constitution of the European Union', in M. Cremona (ed.), *The Enlargement of the European Union* (Oxford: Oxford University Press, 2003).

Elbasani, A., *The European Integration and Transformation in the Western Balkans: Europeanization or Business as Usual?* (Abingdon/New York: Routledge, 2013).

Elbasani, A., *The Stabilisation and Association Process in the Balkans: Overloaded Agenda and Weak Incentives?* (EUI Working Paper, SPS 2008/03).

Hillion, C. (ed.), *EU Enlargement: A Legal Approach* (Oxford: Hart Publishing, 2004).

Hillion, C., 'Mapping-Out the New Contractual Relations between the European Union and its Neighbours: Learning from the EU–Ukraine "Enhanced Agreement"' (2007) 12 *European Foreign Affairs Review* 169–182.

Hillion, C., 'Partnership and Cooperation Agreements between the European Union and the New Independent States of the Ex-Soviet Union' (1998) 3 *European Foreign Affairs Review* 399–420.

Hillion, C., 'The Copenhagen Criteria and their Progeny', in C. Hillion (ed.), *EU Enlargement: A Legal Approach* (Oxford: Hart Publishing, 2004), pp. 1–23.

Hillion, C., *The Creeping Nationalisation of the EU Enlargement Policy* (Stockholm: SIEPS Report 2010/6).

Hillion, C., 'The European Union Is dead. Long Live the European Union . . . A Commentary on the Accession Treaty 2003' (2004) 29 *European Law Review* 583–612.

Inglis, K., 'The Europe Agreements Compared in the Light of their Pre-Accession Reorientation' (2000) 37 *Common Market Law Review* 1173–1210.

Inglis, K., 'The Union's Fifth Accession Treaty: New Means to Make Enlargement Possible' (2004) 41 *Common Market Law Review* 937–973.

Kaddous, C., 'The Relations between the EU and Switzerland', in A. Dashwood and M. Maresceau (eds.), *Law and Practice of EU External Relations – Salient Features of a Changing Landscape* (Cambridge: Cambridge University Press, 2008), pp. 227–269.

Lazowski, A., 'Enhanced Multilateralism and Enhanced Bilateralism: Integration without Membership in the European Union' (2008) 45 *Common Market Law Review* 1433–1458.

Leino, P. and Petrov, R., 'Between 'Common Values' and Competing Universals – The Promotion of the EU's Common Values through the European Neighbourhood Policy' (2009) 15 *European Law Journal* 654–671.

Maresceau, M., 'Pre-Accession', in M. Cremona (ed.), *The Enlargement of the European Union* (Oxford: Oxford University Press, 2003).

Mayhew, A., *Recreating Europe: The European Union's Policy Towards Central and Eastern Europe* (Cambridge: Cambridge University Press, 1998).

Meloni, G. 'Is the Same Toolkit Used During Enlargement Still Applicable to the Countries of the New Neighbourhood? A Problem of Mismatching between Objectives and Instruments', in M. Cremona and G. Meloni, *The European Neighbourhood Policy: A Framework for Modernisation?* (EUI Law Working Paper 2007/21).

Ott, A. and Inglis, K. (eds.), *Handbook on European Enlargement – A Commentary on the Enlargement Process* (The Hague: T.M.C. Asser Press, 2002).

Philippart, E. and Edwards, G., 'The Euro–Mediterranean Partnership: Fragmentation and Reconstruction' (1997) 2 *European Foreign Affairs Review* 465–489.

Rhein, E., 'European and the Mediterranean: A Newly Emerging Geopolitical Area?' (1996) 1 *European Foreign Affairs Review* 79–86.

Rummel, R. (ed.), *Toward Political Union – Planning a Common Foreign and Security Policy in the European Community* (Baden-Baden: Nomos, 1992).

Skoutaris, N., *The Cyprus Issue: The Four Freedoms in a Member State under Siege* (Oxford: Hart Publishing, 2011).

Smith, K. E., 'The Evolution and Application of EU Membership Conditionality', in M. Cremona (ed.), *The Enlargement of the European Union* (Oxford: Oxford University Press, 2003).

Tsoukalis, L., 'The EEC and the Mediterranean: Is "Global" Policy a Misnomer?' (1977) 53 *International Affairs* 422–438.

Tulmets, E., 'The European Neighbourhood Policy: A Flavour of Coherence in the EU's External Relations?' (2008) 3 *Hamburg Review of Social Sciences* 107–141.

Van Elsuwege, P. 'The Four Common Spaces: New Impetus to the EU-Russia Strategic Partnership?', in A. Dashwood and M. Maresceau (eds.), *Law and Practice of EU External Relations – Salient Features of a Changing Landscape* (Cambridge: Cambridge University Press, 2008), pp. 334–359.

Van Elsuwege, P., *Towards a Modernisation of EU-Russia Legal Relations?* (CEURUS EU-Russia Papers, No. 5, 2012).

Van Elsuwege, P. and Petrov, R., 'Article 8 TEU: Towards a New Generation of Agreements with the Neighbouring Countries of the European Union?' (2011) 36 *European Law Review* 688–703.

Van Vooren, B., 'A Case Study of "Soft Law" in EU External Relations: The European Neighbourhood Policy' (2009) 34 *European Law Review* 696–719.

Van Vooren, B., *EU External Relations Law and the European Neighbourhood Policy: A Paradigm for Coherence* (Abingdon/New York: Routledge, 2012).

Index